Iterative Learning Control over Random Fading Channels

Random fading communication is a type of attenuation damage of data over certain propagation media. Establishing a systematic framework for the design and analysis of learning control schemes, the book studies in depth the iterative learning control for stochastic systems with random fading communication.

The authors introduce both cases where the statistics of the random fading channels are known in advance and unknown. They then extend the framework to other systems, including multi-agent systems, point-to-point tracking systems, and multi-sensor systems. More importantly, a learning control scheme is established to solve the multi-objective tracking problem with faded measurements, which can help practical applications of learning control for high-precision tracking of networked systems.

The book will be of interest to researchers and engineers interested in learning control, data-driven control, and networked control systems.

Dong Shen is a Professor at the School of Mathematics, Renmin University of China, Beijing, China. His research interests include iterative learning control, stochastic optimization, and distributed artificial intelligence.

Xinghuo Yu is a Distinguished Professor, a Vice-Chancellor's Professorial Fellow, and an Associate Deputy Vice-Chancellor at the Royal Melbourne Institute of Technology (RMIT University), Melbourne, Australia. He is a Fellow of the Australian Academy of Science, an Honorary Fellow of Engineers Australia, and a Fellow of the IEEE and several other professional associations.

Iterative Learning Control over Random Fading Channels

Dong Shen and Xinghuo Yu

CRC Press
Taylor & Francis Group
Boca Raton London New York

CRC Press is an imprint of the
Taylor & Francis Group, an **informa** business

Designed cover image: © Dong Shen and Xinghuo Yu

First edition published 2024
by CRC Press
2385 NW Executive Center Drive, Suite 320, Boca Raton FL 33431

and by CRC Press
4 Park Square, Milton Park, Abingdon, Oxon, OX14 4RN

CRC Press is an imprint of Taylor & Francis Group, LLC

ISBN: 978-1-032-64637-4 (hbk)
ISBN: 978-1-032-64643-5 (pbk)
ISBN: 978-1-032-64640-4 (ebk)

DOI: 10.1201/9781032646404

Typeset in Nimbus font
by KnowledgeWorks Global Ltd.

Publisher's note: This book has been prepared from camera-ready copy provided by the authors.

Contents

Preface

We usually learn a skill such as bicycling, swimming, and writing by trial and error. That is, we practice a given task and correct our operation according to the performance error repetitively. Through repetition, one can continuously improve performance as the experience from the previous trials is merged into the practice. Such an understanding motivates the proposal of iterative learning control (ILC), a typical type of intelligent control for industrial production systems. ILC requires the systems to complete a tracking objective in a finite time interval and repeat the same process again and again. During the repetition, the input for the current iteration is generated by combining the input and tracking performance of the previous iterations in a certain formulation such as a linear function. It is expected that the gradual correction of the input as per the tracking performance can improve the tracking performance iteration by iteration. After its development for four decades, ILC has attracted significant attention from both scholars and engineering and created fruitful theoretical achievements. In addition, due to its simple control structure and excellent performance for complex systems, ILC has been applied to numerous industrial and mechanical fields.

With the fast development of communication techniques, more and more control systems have adopted the networked control structure to enhance the robustness and flexibility of the whole control system. However, an unavoidable problem existing in the networked control structure is communication-induced data incompleteness such as data dropouts, communication delay, and random noise. Among various issues, this monograph concentrates on the fading communication issue, which is generated by reflection, refraction, and diffraction of signals during propagation. The fading gain is usually modeled by a random variable multiplied by the original signals subject to a certain probability distribution. This model can take the data dropout and additive noise as its special cases. Few monographs have been found on the topic of control over fading channels.

There are several studies on the control design and analysis meeting the data dropout problem. However, those techniques cannot be applied to the fading problem due to the essential difference between data dropout and random fading. Particularly, in the data dropout problem, the data is either dropped or successfully transmitted; therefore, the received signal is always accurate. In contrast, after fading transmission, the received signals are probably inaccurate subject to unknown distributions. Thus, the received signal is statistically biased compared with the original signal, and an additional correction mechanism should be established.

This monograph contributes to the first systematic design and analysis framework for ILC over random fading channels. Three aspects are elaborated on in detail: The learning control design, convergence analysis, and performance evaluation in the presence of fading randomness. The materials are organized into three parts. The first part is devoted to the case of known fading statistics, where the mean of the random fading gain is assumed known for correcting the received signals. The effect of fading communication is carefully investigated and addressed. The second part contributes to the case of unknown fading statistics, where the mean of the random fading gain should be estimated during the learning process. The coupling effect of fading and estimation is explored. The third part consists of several extensions to multi-agent systems, point-to-point tracking problems, and multi-sensor systems.

This monograph is self-contained and written for researchers, engineers, and students in the field of ILC.

The authors would like to express their sincere appreciation to all their collaborators and students supervised, as several chapters in this monograph originate from the joint articles with them. The authors would like to thank all ILC experts worldwide, as they benefited a lot from the previous foundational works when preparing this book.

Beijing, P.R. China, *Dong Shen*
Melbourne, Australia, *Xinghuo Yu*
June 2023

Acknowledgments

We are pleased to thank the support of the National Natural Science Foundation of China under grants 61673045 and 62173333, Beijing Natural Science Foundation under grant 4152040, and Australian Research Council Discovery Program under grant DP200101199. We sincerely appreciate IEEE for granting us the permission to reuse materials in the copyrighted papers.

Author Bios

Professor **Dong Shen** received the BS and PhD degrees in mathematics from Shandong University, Jinan, China, and the Academy of Mathematics and Systems Science, Chinese Academy of Sciences (CAS), Beijing, China in 2005 and 2010, respectively. From 2010 to 2012, he was a Post-Doctoral Fellow with the Institute of Automation, CAS. From 2012 to 2019, he was with the Beijing University of Chemical Technology, Beijing, China. From 2016.02 to 2017.02, he was a Visiting Scholar at National University of Singapore, Singapore. From 2019.07 to 2019.08, he was a Visiting Research Fellow at RMIT University, Australia. Since 2020, he has been a Professor with the School of Mathematics, Renmin University of China, Beijing, China. His research interests include iterative learning control, stochastic optimization, and distributed artificial intelligence.

Distinguished Professor **Xinghuo Yu** is a Vice-Chancellor's Professorial Fellow and an Associate Deputy Vice-Chancellor at the Royal Melbourne Institute of Technology (RMIT University), Melbourne, Australia. He was the President of IEEE Industrial Electronics Society for 2018 and 2019. He received his BEng and MEng degrees in electrical and electronic engineering from the University of Science and Technology of China, Hefei, China, in 1982 and 1984, and his PhD degree in control science and engineering from Southeast University, Nanjing, China in 1988, respectively. His research interests are in control systems, intelligent and complex systems, and power and energy systems. He received a number of awards and honours for his contributions, including the 2018 MA Sargent Medal from Engineers Australia, 2018 Australasian AI Distinguished Research Contribution Award from the Australian Computer Society, and the 2013 Dr.-Ing. Eugene Mittelmann Achievement Award from the IEEE Industrial Electronics Society. He was a Clarivate's Highly Cited Researcher from 2015 to 2022. He is a Fellow of the Australian Academy of Science, an Honorary Fellow of Engineers Australia, and a Fellow of the IEEE and several other professional associations.

CHAPTER 1

Introduction

THIS chapter provides a background of iterative learning control and fading channel.

1.1 ESSENCE OF LEARNING CONTROL

Learning is the fundamental characteristic of learning control. It is of significance to first elaborate the essence of learning in system control before presenting the specific concepts related to learning control. A person masters various skills, such as swimming and biking, essentially by learning. Taking a basketball shooting as an example, one may fail to hit the basket on his first try at a fixed point; however, he can make a goal after a series of exercises, during which the one should adjust his actions according to the exercise outcomes. This process is a simplified description of the learning process, but it reveals a pivotal principle of learning: practice makes perfect. In fact, we learn almost every skill through a similar process.

By reviewing the learning principle in our daily lives, we notice that the essence of learning control can be understood as a simple mechanism: trial and error. In particular, an action, such as control input, is imposed and a corresponding outcome, such as tracking error, is observed; then, a new action is generated by a combination of the action and its corresponding outcome. In system and control theory, the latter combination is generally formulated as a linear or nonlinear function of the available information and data. We should emphasize that this mechanism has covered a significantly large range of specific presentations even for the linear combination case. For the linear combination case, it is generally formulated as follows:

$$\text{Next action} = \text{Current action} + g(\text{Corresponding outcome}) \tag{1.1}$$

DOI: 10.1201/9781032646404-1

where $g(\cdot)$ denotes a function of the involved quantities. In this equation, $g(\cdot)$ is called the innovation term, which is regarded as a correction of the current action. It is expected that the innovation term contributes zero ideally if the outcome has achieved the desired objective. For example, considering a trajectory tracking problem for a deterministic system, where the desired objective is a given trajectory and the outcome is the output, the innovation term is expected to be zero if the actual output coincides with the desired trajectory completely. Therefore, the innovation term is generally formulated as a function of the outcome with the desired objective being its root.

We have observed the successful applications of the above formula in various fields such as system identification, parameter estimation, Kalman filtering, and algorithms design. In recursive system identification and parameter estimation, a kernel step is to calculate unknown parameters based on input and output data under a predefined system structure. In this example, the current and next actions correspond to the current and next estimates of unknown parameters, and the innovation term $g(\cdot)$ is a product of an update gain and the error between the actual output and the estimated output generated by the current parameter estimation. In Kalman filtering for linear time-invariant systems, the state is estimated by two phases: prediction and update. The prediction step provides a rough guess of the state and the update step makes a correction to generate a posteriori estimation. In the update step, the current and next actions correspond to the priori and posteriori state estimates, and the innovation term is a product of the optimal Kalman gain and a residual between the actual output and the one predicted by the priori state estimate. In algorithm design, the common recursive algorithms such as recursive least-square algorithm and gradient descent algorithm certainly fit the fundamental structure of (1.1). Generally, it is an essential mechanism in (1.1) that the unknowns are learned gradually by continuous trials and corrections using available information and data. This mechanism accords with the basic learning ability of humans, which can be regarded as a primary argument why the above-mentioned methods have achieved excellent performance in various applications.

1.2 ITERATIVE LEARNING CONTROL

Following the fundamental principle of learning, one is interested in whether the principle can be introduced to the design of automatic control so that the machine can own certain ability of learning. The answer is yes. This basic cognition motivates the introduction and developments of a novel learning control method, iterative learning control (ILC). The idea of ILC was first proposed by Uchiyama [64] in 1978. It should be noted that the stability analysis was restricted to classical control concepts and did not explicitly cover the ILC approach. However, this paper is written in Japanese and thus fails to attract widespread attention in the academic community. In 1984, three papers were published independently [2,9,15], which is regarded as the opening of the research on ILC. In most papers, it is widely agreed that the paper written by Arimoto [2] is the first proposal of ILC.

ILC adopts this structure in constructing its essential learning procedure in the iteration domain, differing from the time-domain-based learning processes mentioned above. In particular, ILC focuses on the batch-mode systems, such as chemical production processes and pick-and-place robotics, which complete a given task in a finite time interval and repeat the process continuously. For these systems, the operation dynamics in an individual iteration may contain nothing invariant during the whole time interval. Meanwhile, the dynamics are expected to be repetitive in the iteration domain, which is a necessary requirement to learn from experience. The repetitiveness over a finite-time interval constitutes an essential difference between ILC and the conventional control methodologies involved with the concept of learning such as adaptive control. In particular, the conventional control methodologies work in an infinite time interval that they learn the invariant factors by continuous trials and corrections in the time domain, while ILC conducts the learning process in the iteration domain. Consequently, the current action and its corresponding outcome in (1.1) correspond to the input and output at the current iteration, respectively, while the next action is the computed input for the subsequent iteration. Furthermore, the innovation term in ILC is generally formulated as a function of the tracking error which is equal to zero if the actual output has achieved the desired trajectory.

The operation procedure of ILC is illustrated in Fig. 1.1. In this figure, a subplot displays the profile of the input, output, and error for a specified iteration in blue, orange, and red, respectively. The black curves in the middle row denote the desired trajectory. From Fig. 1.1, we can observe the fundamental mechanism of ILC as follows. In particular, at the initial iteration (i.e., the 0th iteration), we provide an arbitrary input signal. Since no priori knowledge is assumed, we can set the input signal to zero over the whole time interval and then get the corresponding output. With certain knowledge of the system and desired trajectory, we may provide a good initial input candidate. However, the asymptotical convergence property of ILC is generally independent of the selection of initial input signals. After the operation of each iteration, say the kth iteration, the tracking error can be calculated by subtracting the actual output from the desired trajectory. Then, the input signal for the next

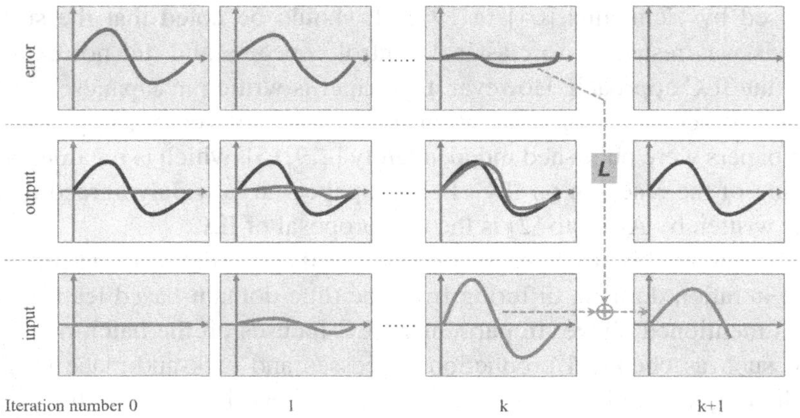

Figure 1.1 Illustration of ILC.

iteration, i.e., the $(k+1)$th iteration, is generated by correcting the input of the current iteration (i.e., the kth iteration) with a function of the corresponding tracking error information. A common formulation of this correction is the well-known proportional type (P-type) update law, in which the tracking error is linearly added to the input. With this learning mechanism, it is expected that the tracking performance can be gradually improved as the iteration number increases.

Thus, ILC has the following features: (1) the system can finish a task in a finite time interval, (2) the system can be reset to the same initial value, and (3) the tracking objective is iteration-invariant. We give a brief explanation to such features. First of all, the feature that the operation length is finite is a specified character for ILC, which is satisfied in many practical applications such as the production line automation and pick-and-place robots. From the generic requirement of repetition, the resetting condition, i.e., the second feature, is a natural but specific formulation of ILC. Meanwhile, it is also a major criticizing point on ILC. In past decades, this condition has attracted much attention and many literature are published to relax it. Last, the invariance of tracking objective is a specific formulation of repetition. Noticing that the human being could apply the knowledge learned from other targets to a new target but with similarities, we expect such a feature to be relaxed to the iteration-varying case.

The block diagram of ILC is shown in Fig. 1.2, where z^{-1} denotes iteration-based shift operator to coordinate the notation index, u_k and y_k denote the input and output for the kth iteration, and y_d denotes the desired

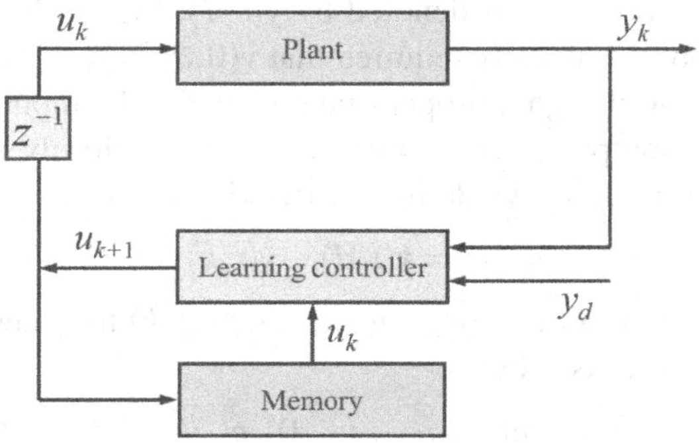

Figure 1.2 Block diagram of ILC.

trajectory. The input u_{k+1} for the $(k+1)$th iteration is generated by the learning controller based on all available information of input, output, and the desired trajectory. In other words, the entire input signal is generated prior to the actual operation process. For example, the input for the $(k+1)$th iteration is generated before the operation of the $(k+1)$th iteration using the information up to the kth iteration. From this point of view, ILC is a typical kind of feedforward control. Meanwhile, concentrating on the iteration domain, we can observe that the learning process actually constitutes a feedback control structure in the iteration domain.

1.3 BRIEF FORMULATION OF DISCRETE-TIME ILC

As an illustration, we provide a brief formulation of the discrete-time ILC. Consider the following discrete-time linear time-invariant system

$$\begin{aligned} x(t+1,k) &= Ax(t,k) + Bu(t,k), \\ y(t,k) &= Cx(t,k), \end{aligned} \tag{1.2}$$

where $k = 0, 1, 2, \cdots$ denotes different iterations and t denotes an arbitrary time instant in an operation iteration, $t = 0, 1, \cdots, N$, with N being the length of the operation iteration. Vectors $x \in \mathbf{R}^n$, $u \in \mathbf{R}^p$, and $y \in \mathbf{R}^q$ denote the system state, input, and output, respectively. Matrices A, B, and C are system matrices with appropriate dimensions.

Because it is required that a given tracking task should be repeated, the initial state needs to be reset at each iteration. The following is a basic reset condition, which has been used in many publications.

$$x(0,k) = x_0, \quad \forall k. \tag{1.3}$$

The reference trajectory is denoted by $y(t,d)$, $t \in [0,N]$. With regard to the reset condition, it is usually required that $y(0,d) = y_0 \triangleq Cx_0$. The control purpose of ILC is to design a proper update law for the input $u(t,k)$, so that the corresponding output $y(t,k)$ can track $y(t,d)$ as closely as possible. To this end, for any t in $[0,N]$, we define the tracking error as

$$e(t,k) = y(t,d) - y(t,k). \tag{1.4}$$

Then the update law is a function of $u(t,k)$ and $e(t,k)$ to generate $u(t,k+1)$, whose general form is as follows:

$$u(t,k+1) = h(u(\cdot,k),\cdots,u(\cdot,0),e(\cdot,k),\cdots,e(\cdot,0)). \tag{1.5}$$

If the above relationship depends only on the last iteration, it is called a first-order ILC update law; otherwise, it is called a high-order ILC update law. Generally, considering the simplicity of the algorithm, most update laws are first-order laws, i.e.,

$$u(t,k+1) = h(u(\cdot,k),e(\cdot,k)). \tag{1.6}$$

Additionally, the update law is usually linear. The simplest update law is as follows:

$$u(t,k+1) = u(t,k) + Ke(t+1,k), \tag{1.7}$$

where K is the learning gain matrix, which is the designed parameter. In (1.7), $u(t,k)$ is the input of the current iteration, while $Ke(t+1,k)$ is the innovation term. The update law (1.7) is called a P-type ILC update law. If the innovation term is replaced by $K(e(t+1,k) - e(t,k))$, the update law is a D-type one.

For system (1.2) and update law (1.7), a basic convergence result is that K satisfies

$$\|I - CBK\| < 1. \tag{1.8}$$

Then, one has $\|e(t,k)\| \xrightarrow[k\to\infty]{} 0$, where $\|\cdot\|$ denotes the operator norm.

From this result, one can deduce that the design of K needs no information regarding the system matrix A, but for the coupling matrix CB. This illustrates the advantage of ILC from the perspective that ILC has little dependence on the system information. Thus, ILC can handle tracking problems that have more uncertainties.

We should point out that although in most ILC papers we employ the simplest P-type law (1.7), which in essence is a linear control law, it does not mean that such control law is the best, not even in the class of linear control laws. Indeed, when we design some nonlinear type control laws from the general formulation (1.6), additional advantages may arise. However, it is still open in this direction. Only a few papers designed the nonlinear-type control laws dispersedly for different objectives.

1.4 FADING CHANNELS AND RELATED CONTROL ISSUES

Networked control structures have been extensively studied in the existing literature due to their distinct advantages such as robustness, ease of use, and flexibility [29, 44, 76, 78, 82]. In particular, a controlled plant and controller are usually located in different sites and communicate with the other one via wired or wireless networks. Moreover, with this configuration, operators can avoid dangerous environments, as they monitor control conditions and adjust control signals in a location separate from the plant. Such network implementations are benefited by rapid developments in internet and communication technologies. However, networked structures suffer from various communication problems, such as data dropouts, communication delays, sampling and quantization, and channel noise [44, 78, 79]. Many efforts have been devoted to addressing these problems. However, the fading communication has not been thoroughly investigated by the control community.

The fading problem is generally caused by reflection, refraction, and diffraction during propagation; this is a type of attenuation damage of data over certain propagation media [78]. In other words, fading is a kind of multiplicative randomness associated with transmitted packets. It is similar to the randomness of data dropouts in form but is fundamentally different. Data dropouts consist of two cases: data is either successfully transmitted or dropped. The received information is accurate if it is successfully transmitted. In contrast, fading refers to an attenuated gain subject to a specified probability distribution; that is, information can always be received, but it may be inaccurate. Thus, studies on the data dropout issue seek for a compensation of the lost data such as leveraging redundant channel scheme [79], whereas the fading problem focuses on the inherent influence of imprecise information [21]. Compared with other channel-induced randomness such as data dropouts and communication delays, fading has attracted less attention from the control community. The existing literature can be categorized into three areas of focus: stabilization, filtering, and stochastic control.

An early study on fading channels is outlined in [21], in which the stabilization problem is examined for a multi-input-multi-output (MIMO) system with independent fading channels dedicated to the actuator and sensor. A transformation method is developed to establish the mean square stability subject to bounded variance uncertainty caused by random fading channels. Furthermore, a minimal channel capacity for mean square stability is calculated for the single-input-single-output (SISO) case. Several extensions of this topic can be found in [59, 70, 73]. The result was extended to MIMO plants with multiple fading channels at the input side in [70], using linear control policies. Additional extensions were provided in [59] for the robust stability of polytopic uncertain systems as well as [73] for linear systems with input power constraints. With a prescribed channel capacity, an interesting challenge involves optimizing resource allocation among multiple fading channels from the perspective of information theory [27, 48, 67], which is an important branch of networked control systems. For example, an efficient approximate projection approach is presented in [48] to maximize a general concave utility function of the average transmission rates of multiple-access fading channels.

Another large area of research on fading channels involves filtering [16, 28, 39]. This topic has been extensively investigated in the presence of data dropouts [29, 44, 78]; however, few studies address the fading problem. In this area of research, the primary focus is the design and analysis of Kalman filtering with faded measurements. A detailed calculation of the upper bound of the error covariance matrix is provided for the conventional Kalman filtering with respect to the fading process in [16]. In addition, a relay mechanism is proposed to improve the performance of Kalman filtering in [39]. In the study, packet reception probabilities are determined by fading channel gains and relay transmit powers. Both optimal and suboptimal methods for selecting the best relay configuration were addressed. The Tobit Kalman filtering problem was presented in [28] for discrete-time systems with both censored and fading measurements. These early results demonstrate that the specific formulation of Kalman filtering using faded measurements is an extension of the case with data dropouts.

Compared with the above contributions, the control problem in the presence of fading channels has been studied less. For example, [17, 18] present attempts of $\mathcal{H}_\infty$ control with faded measurements using recursive Riccati difference equations and matrix inequalities. Fuzzy control and output-feedback control for similar problems were provided in [80]. In the studies, fading randomness is treated as structured uncertainties, and the main objective is to derive certain conditions such that degraded performance is guaranteed. Additional efforts to control performance evaluation and improvement with faded signals are required.

In reviewing the recent progress regarding the stabilization, filtering, and control over fading channels, we have observed that most of the literature focuses on the amount of channel capacity that should be allocated to achieve a designated performance index. In other words, the necessary and/or sufficient conditions for fading variables are derived according to the performance indices in the existing literature. This observation has motivated us to consider the means of improving performance over specified fading channels. In this book, we focus on the influence of fading on control system performance and investigate possible mechanisms for further enhancing performance without imposing fading restrictions.

1.5 STRUCTURE OF THIS MONOGRAPH

In this monograph, we concentrate on ILC for systems with fading channels. Our primary objective is to establish a systematic framework of the synthesis and analysis of ILC schemes to achieve perfect tracking performance in the presence of fading randomness. To this end, we will clarify the following aspects in detail: the scheme design, the convergence and performance analysis, and the effects of fading communication. The investigation of this monograph would greatly help to understand ILC over fading channels.

The following materials are arranged into three parts: known channel statistics, unknown channel statistics, and extensions of systems and problems. In the first part, we assume the channel statistics, i.e., the mean of the channel randomness, is known a priori. In this case, the received signals can be directly corrected for the scheme design and analysis. In the second part, the channel statistics is unknown. Therefore, additional estimation mechanisms are necessary to establish an appropriate correction of the received signals. In the third part, the synthesis and analysis framework established in the first two parts is extended to other systems and problems, such as multi-agent systems and point-to-point tracking problems.

Chapter 2 proposes the basic framework of learning control via fading channels. In particular, the output and input data are transmitted through multiple independent fading channels. The traditional P-type learning control scheme is revised according to the specific fading positions, where the constant learning gain is replaced by a variable one to suppress the effect of various uncertainties. Strong convergence of the proposed scheme is established under random fading phenomena and system noise. The input error is shown convergent to zero as the cycle number increases.

Chapter 3 continues to address the input fading issue because the faded input would destroy the time-domain dynamics. To this end, a moving-average operator is introduced at the input side to reduce the fading effect and improve control system performance. Accordingly, the generic learning control algorithm is modified and analyzed. Both multiplicative and additive randomness of the fading channel are addressed, and the effects of fading communication on the data are carefully analyzed.

Chapter 4 investigates learning control over fading channels to gradually improve learning and tracking performance. It is observed that the effect of fading on input transmission greatly compromises tracking ability in practical implementations. Three average techniques are examined: moving average, general average with all historical information, and forgetting-based average. The results reveal a trade-off between learning ability and tracking ability for learning control algorithms, where learning ability refers to the convergence rate of a proposed learning algorithm, and tracking ability refers to the final tracking precision of the output to the desired reference. The convergence results for the three schemes with these averaging techniques are strictly proved.

Chapter 5 proposes a novel data-driven learning control scheme for unknown systems with unknown fading sensor channels. The fading randomness is modeled by multiplicative and additive random variables subject to certain unknown distributions. In this scheme, we propose an error transmission mode and an iterative gradient estimation method. Unlike the conventional transmission mode where the output is directly transmitted back to the controller, in the error transmission mode, we send the desired reference to the plant such that tracking errors can be calculated locally and then transmitted back through the fading channel. Using the faded tracking error data only, the gradient for updating input is iteratively estimated by a random difference technique along the iteration axis. This gradient acts as the updating term of the control signal; therefore, information on the system and the fading channel is no longer required.

Chapter 6 investigates how to guarantee superior control performance in the presence of unknown fading channels. This chapter presents a learning strategy for gradually improving the tracking performance. To this end, an iterative estimation mechanism is first introduced to provide necessary statistical information such that the biased signals after transmission can be corrected before being utilized. Then, learning control algorithms incorporating with a decreasing step-size sequence are designed for both output and input fading cases respectively. The convergence in both mean-square and almost-sure senses of the proposed schemes are strictly proved.

Chapter 7 considers the learning-tracking problem for stochastic systems through unreliable communication channels. The channels suffer from both multiplicative and additive randomness subject to unknown probability distributions. The statistics of this randomness, such as mean and covariance, are nonrepetitive in the iteration domain. This nonrepetitive randomness introduces non stationary contamination and drifts to the actual signals, yielding essential challenges in signal processing and learning control. Therefore, a practical framework constituted by an unbiased estimator of the mean inverse, a signal correction mechanism, and learning control schemes is proposed. The convergence and tracking performance are strictly established for both constant and decreasing step-lengths. If the statistics satisfy asymptotic repetitiveness in the iteration domain, a consistent estimator applies to the framework while retaining the framework's asymptotic properties.

Chapter 8 addresses the batch-based learning consensus for linear and nonlinear multi-agent systems (MAS) with faded neighborhood information. The motivation comes from the observation that agents exchange information via wireless networks, which inevitably introduces random fading effect and channel additive noise to the transmitted signals. It is therefore of great significance to investigate how to ensure the precise consensus tracking to a given reference leader using heavily contaminated information. To this end, a novel distributed learning consensus scheme is proposed, which consists of a classic distributed control structure, a preliminary correction mechanism, and a separated design of learning gain and regulation matrix. The influences of biased and unbiased randomness are discussed in detail according to the convergence rate and consensus performance. The iteration-wise asymptotic consensus tracking is strictly established for linear MAS first to demonstrate the inherent principles for the effectiveness of the proposed scheme. Then, the results are extended to nonlinear systems with nonidentical initialization condition and diverse gain design.

Chapter 9 studies the point-to-point learning and tracking problem for networked stochastic systems with fading communications by iterative learning control. The point-to-point tracking problem indicates that only partial positions rather than the whole reference are required to achieve high tracking precision. An auxiliary matrix is introduced to connect the entire reference and the required tracking targets. The fading communication introduces multiplicative randomness to the transmitted signals, which leads to the biased available information. A direct correction mechanism is employed using statistics of the communication channel. A learning control scheme is then proposed with a decreasing gain sequence to ensure steady convergence in the presence of various types of randomness. Two scenarios of varying initial states are considered.

Chapter 10 concentrates on the point-to-point tracking problem via fading communications by proposing a reference update strategy. Using this strategy, the tracking performance is continuously improved even with faded information as the number of iterations increases. A learning control scheme is established and proved convergent in both mean square and almost sure senses under mild conditions. The convergence rate is accelerated by introducing the virtual reference compared with the traditional update approach.

Chapter 11 studies the multi-objective tracking problem with faded measurements by a learning control scheme. A discrete-time linear multi-sensor system is considered, where the output of each sensor is required to track an individual trajectory. These reference trajectories are not consistent in the sense that improving the tracking precision of one sensor can worsen the tracking performance of another sensor. A weighted performance index is presented to balance the overall tracking performance of all the involved sensors. Based on this weighted index, the group of the best achievable references and their corresponding desired input are explicitly defined. In addition, all outputs are transmitted back to the controller via random fading channels, where the fading randomness is described by both multiplicative and additive random variables. A learning control scheme is proposed to resolve the multi-objective tracking problem in the presence of fading communication.

I

Known Channel Statistics

CHAPTER 2

Learning Control over Random Fading Channel

THIS chapter studies the learning control strategy for networked stochastic systems, where the output and input data are transmitted through multiple independent fading channels. The traditional P-type learning control scheme is revised according to the specific fading positions, where the constant learning gain is replaced by a variable one to suppress the effect of various uncertainties. Strong convergence of the proposed scheme is established under random fading phenomena and system noise. The input error is shown convergent to zero as the iteration number increases.

2.1 INTRODUCTION

The random fading, coming from wireless or shared links, is one of the most common network-induced phenomena. Because the propagation suffers refraction, reflection, and diffraction, the transmitted signals are likely to be affected as a random deviation rather than lost. However, this phenomenon has not received sufficient investigation in the control community in contrast to other networked-induced problems such as data dropout. The control issue with fading channels is to suppress the random influence, which is much challenging. In learning control, such randomness damages the precision of the original signals, which should be carefully considered and treated in the design and analysis. Meanwhile, the learning control strategy concerns more on the performance enhancement in the iteration domain, in contrast to other control strategies that focus on time-domain-based performance; thus it is a challenging issue.

DOI: 10.1201/9781032646404-2

In this chapter, we establish a basic synthesis and analysis framework of learning control over multi-dimensional fading channels, where the generated output and input signals will be transmitted through multiple independent channels. Here, the fading phenomenon for each dimension acts as a random variable subject to a continuous probability distribution, while additive channel noises are omitted because they can be treated as part of the system noises. First, the optimal learning control problem over fading channels is formulated according to an asymptotical tracking index due to the existence of various uncertainties in the plant and communication channels. Then, we proceed to present a learning control scheme for the output fading case and establish strong convergence of the input sequence to the one driving the reference. We introduce iteration-varying gains to suppress the influence of unknown randomness. A potential convergence speed evaluation is presented. Moreover, the input fading would yield a novel issue of the system dynamics; we revise the learning scheme accordingly, demonstrate the differences between the two scenarios, and conduct the convergence analysis. To show the influence of different uncertainties and parameters for practical applications, two examples are comprehensively discussed.

2.2 PROBLEM FORMULATION

Consider the following multi-input-multi-output (MIMO) time-varying system

$$\begin{aligned} x_k(t+1) =& A_t x_k(t) + B_t u_k(t) + w_k(t) \\ y_k(t) =& C_t x_k(t) + v_k(t). \end{aligned} \tag{2.1}$$

where $k = 1, 2, \ldots$ is the iteration index and $t = 0, 1, \ldots, T$ is the time index. T is the iteration length. The variable vectors $x_k(t) \in \mathbf{R}^n$, $u_k(t) \in \mathbf{R}^p$, and $y_k(t) \in \mathbf{R}^q$ are the system state, input, and output, respectively, where n, p, and q are the dimensions. System matrices A_t, B_t, and C_t are time varying. System and measurement noises are denoted by $w_k(t)$ and $v_k(t)$. Moreover, without loss of generality, the coupling matrix $C_{t+1}B_t$ is of full column rank for all t. Thus, the system relative degree is one in this study.

The desired reference is given by $y_d(t)$, $0 \le t \le T$. We employ the assumptions as follows.

Assumption 2.1 *For the desired reference $y_d(t)$, suitable initial state $x_d(0)$ and input $u_d(t)$ exist to satisfy the following equation:*

$$\begin{aligned} x_d(t+1) =& A_t x_d(t) + B_t u_d(t) \\ y_d(t) =& C_t x_d(t). \end{aligned} \tag{2.2}$$

Assumption 2.2 *The initial state $x_k(0)$ is independent and identically distributed for all iterations. Meanwhile, $\mathbb{E}x_k(0) = x_d(0)$, where $x_d(0)$ is given in Assumption 2.1, and $\mathbb{E}\|x_k(0)\|^2 < \infty$.*

Assumption 2.3 *Both $w_k(t)$ and $v_k(t)$ are assumed to be independent and identically distributed along the iteration axis, for all t. Meanwhile, $\mathbb{E}w_k(t) = 0$, $\mathbb{E}v_k(t) = 0$, $\mathbb{E}\|w_k(t)\|^2 < \infty$, and $\mathbb{E}\|v_k(t)\|^2 < \infty$, $\forall t$.*

We denote $\Delta x_k(0) = x_k(0) - x_d(0)$. Because the initial state error $\Delta x_k(0)$, system noise $w_k(t)$, and measurement noise $v_k(t)$ cannot be eliminated from the output, it is impossible to achieve the precise tracking of $y_k(t)$ to $y_d(t)$. Then, the best achievable tracking performance is that the difference between $y_k(t)$ and $y_d(t)$ is constituted by the above mentioned noise factors. In other words, perfect tracking performance can be achieved if all additive random variables in the current iteration are excluded. To express this tracking target, we introduce an asymptotical tracking index as follows:

$$J_t = \limsup_{n \to \infty} \frac{1}{n} \sum_{k=1}^{n} \|y_d(t) - y_k(t)\|^2, \quad \forall t. \tag{2.3}$$

This index can be minimized whenever the input sequence $\{u_k(t)\}$ converges to $u_d(t)$ as the iteration number goes to infinity. The limitation of (2.3) exists if the initial state error and system/measurement noise are with bounded second moment. The derivations are as follows.

By (2.1) and (2.2), we have

$$\begin{aligned}\Delta x_k(t+1) &= A_t \Delta x_k(t) + B_t \Delta u_k(t) - w_k(t)\\ &= \sum_{i=1}^{t+1} \Phi_{t,i} B_{i-1} \Delta u_k(i-1) + \Phi_{t,0} \Delta x_k(0) - \sum_{i=1}^{t} \Phi_{t,i} w_k(i-1),\end{aligned}$$

where $\Delta x_k(t) = x_d(t) - x_k(t)$ and $\Delta u_k(t) = u_d(t) - u_k(t)$, $\Phi_{i,j} = A_i \cdots A_j$, $i \geq j$, and $\Phi_{i,i+1} = I$.

Therefore, the tracking error

$$\begin{aligned}y_d(t+1) - y_k(t+1) &= C_{t+1} \Delta x_k(t+1) - v_k(t+1)\\ &= \phi_k(t+1) + \varphi_k(t+1) - v_k(t+1)\end{aligned}$$

where

$$\phi_k(t+1) = C_{t+1} \sum_{i=1}^{t+1} \Phi_{t,i} B_{i-1} \Delta u_k(i-1),$$

$$\varphi_k(t+1) = C_{t+1}[\Phi_{t,0}\Delta x_k(0) - \sum_{i=1}^{t}\Phi_{t,i}w_k(i-1)].$$

According to the statistical assumptions of noises and initial state errors as well as the definition of $u_k(t)$, we are evident that $\phi_k(t+1)$, $\varphi_k(t+1)$, and $v_k(t+1)$ are mutually independent.

By the estimation of weighted sums of martingale difference sequence [11, Theorem 2.8], the following estimates hold almost surely, $\forall\eta > 0$,

$$\sum_{k=1}^{n}\phi_k^T(t+1)[\varphi_k(t+1) - v_k(t+1)] = O\left(\left(\sum_{k=1}^{n}\|\phi_k(t+1)\|^2\right)^{\frac{1}{2}+\eta}\right),$$

$$\sum_{k=1}^{n}\varphi_k^T(t+1)v_k(t+1) = O\left(\left(\sum_{k=1}^{n}\|v_k(t+1)\|^2\right)^{\frac{1}{2}+\eta}\right).$$

Consequently, we have

$$\begin{aligned}
&\limsup_{n\to\infty}\frac{1}{n}\sum_{k=1}^{n}\|y_d(t+1) - y_k(t+1)\|^2 \\
&= \limsup_{n\to\infty}\frac{1}{n}\sum_{k=1}^{n}(\|\phi_k(t^+)\|^2 + \|\varphi_k(t^+)\|^2 + \|v_k(t^+)\|^2) \\
&\quad + \limsup_{n\to\infty}\frac{1}{n}\sum_{k=1}^{n}2\phi_k^T(t^+)[\varphi_k(t^+) - v_k(t^+)] - \limsup_{n\to\infty}\frac{1}{n}\sum_{k=1}^{n}2\varphi_k^T(t^+)v_k(t^+) \\
&= \limsup_{n\to\infty}\frac{1}{n}\sum_{k=1}^{n}\|\phi_k(t^+)\|^2(1+o(1)) + \limsup_{n\to\infty}\frac{1}{n}\sum_{k=1}^{n}\|\varphi_k(t^+)\|^2 \\
&\quad + \limsup_{n\to\infty}\frac{1}{n}\sum_{k=1}^{n}\|v_k(t^+)\|^2(1+o(1)) \\
&= \limsup_{n\to\infty}\frac{1}{n}\sum_{k=1}^{n}\|\phi_k(t^+)\|^2 + \mathrm{tr}\left[C_{t+1}\left(\sum_{i=1}^{t}\Phi_{t,i}R_t^w\Phi_{t,i}^T + \Phi_{t,0}R_0^{\Delta x}\Phi_{t,0}^T\right)C_{t+1}^T\right] \\
&\quad + \mathrm{tr}\left[R_{t+1}^v\right],
\end{aligned}$$

where $R_t^\bullet$ denotes the covariance matrix of associated quantities with $\bullet$ being w, Δx, or v. The little-o denotes the infinitesimal of higher order; that is, $o(1)\to 0$. It is observed that the last term of the above equation is independent of the specific control sequence. Thus, the minimum is achieved if andonly

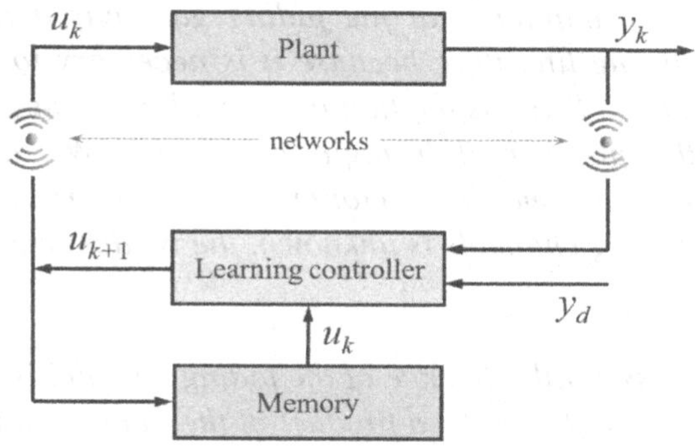

Figure 2.1 System setup of learning control over fading networks.

if the first term on the right-hand side of the last equation is zero. This corresponds to a sufficient condition that $\Delta u_k(i) \to 0$ for $0 \le i \le t$. Therefore, our objective in this chapter is to establish the convergence property of the proposed learning control scheme, i.e., $\lim_{k\to\infty} u_k(t) \to u_d(t)$.

Fig. 2.1 presents the overall system setup for learning control over fading channels. Here, the plant and the controller exchange data and information through unreliable networks, where random fading phenomena occur. The fading phenomena introduce random deviations depending on the transmitted signals, which can be regarded as a multiplicative random variable. We call this multiplicative variable a fading gain. In this chapter, the fading gain has a known mean because most wireless channels undergo slow fading and then, the received signals can be corrected. Moreover, we consider the case of multiple fading channels; that is, different entries of the output and input are sent separately through different channels. To this end, we characterize the channel by a random vector $\theta_k(t) = (\theta_{k,i}(t), \dots, \theta_{k,m}(t))^T$, where m is equal to p or q corresponding to the input or output side, respectively. That is, the fading gain $\theta_{k,i}(t)$ is multiplied to the corresponding entry separately. To simplify the notation, $\theta_{k,i}(t)$ is independent and identically distributed with respect to all indices, and its probability distribution $f(\theta)$ is continuous over the probability space with $\mathbb{P}(\theta_{k,i}(t) > 0) = 1$, $\forall k,i,t$. Extensions to the general fading condition are straightforward.

We assume that $\theta_{k,i}(t)$ satisfies

$$\mu = \mathbb{E}[\theta_{k,i}(t)], \quad \sigma = \mathbb{E}[(\theta_{k,i}(t) - \mu)^2]. \tag{2.4}$$

Remark 2.1 *The assumption that the fading gain has a known mean is widely accepted in the literature because it is necessary to correct the received imprecise data. This assumption is rational as communication conditions are normally unconverted during a long period. We can have a fairly comprehension of these conditions before the operation process. If the statistical property of fading channels is unknown, the readers can refer to Chapters 5–7.*

Remark 2.2 *The essential influence of the fading channel is as follows. The signal deviations are reflected by a product of the fading gain and the original signal; that is, the randomness in a multiplicative form. A transformation of the multiplicative randomness to the additive type can be made. However, the newly generated additive randomness is state dependent, which requires careful calculations to derive the convergence analysis. The state-dependent randomness introduces one of the major challenges of this chapter. The details are given in Sections 2.3 and 2.4.*

Remark 2.3 *In this chapter, we omit the additive channel noise to save notation. In fact, if the channel noise is added to the channel, we can treat it similarly to $w_k(t)$ and $v_k(t)$. In other words, the channel noise can be regarded as part of these noise terms. From this viewpoint, the scenario with additive channel noise is straightforward and trivial.*

Since the received output or input has been contaminated by the fading channel, these imprecise signals introduce biased derivations to learning algorithms. In the following, we propose a learning control scheme to ensure that the performance index (2.3) is still minimized. Meanwhile, we establish the asymptotical convergence under random noise and fading gains.

2.3 OUTPUT FADING CHANNEL CASE

In this section, we assume that fading occurs at the output side while the communication at the input side works well (cf. Fig. 2.1). Then, the actual input employed by the actuator is identical to the one generated by the controller.

The system output is $y_k(t)$. This signal is not available to the controller. We denote the received signal by $z_k(t)$, which is deviated from $y_k(t)$ randomly:

$$z_k(t) = \Theta_k(t) y_k(t), \tag{2.5}$$

where $\Theta_k(t) = \text{diag}\{\theta_{k,1}(t), \ldots, \theta_{k,q}(t)\}$. Evidently, $z_k(t)$ is biased and thus cannot be applied for updating. In other words, certain corrections to the received signals are necessary. An intuitive idea to provide an unbiased estimate is to divide the fading mean defined in (2.4). We define the modified tracking error $\varepsilon_k(t) \triangleq y_d(t) - \mu^{-1} z_k(t)$. The following learning control scheme is applied:

$$u_{k+1}(t) = u_k(t) + a_k L_t \varepsilon_k(t+1), \tag{2.6}$$

where L_t is the control direction regulation matrix and $\{a_k\}$ is the learning gain sequence. The sequence $\{a_k\}$ should satisfy that $a_k > 0$, $\sum_{k=1}^{\infty} a_k = \infty$, and $\sum_{k=1}^{\infty} a_k^2 < \infty$. For example, we can let $a_k = \alpha / k^{\beta}$ with $\frac{1}{2} < \beta < 1$ and $\alpha > 0$.

Before presenting the main result, we first establish the lifted model to simplify the expressions. In particular, define the lifted vectors of input and output as follows:

$$\begin{aligned} \boldsymbol{u}_\star &= [u_\star(0)^T, u_\star(1)^T, \ldots, u_\star(T-1)^T]^T, \\ \boldsymbol{y}_\star &= [y_\star(1)^T, y_\star(2)^T, \ldots, y_\star(T)^T]^T, \end{aligned}$$

where the subscript "$\star$" denotes "k" or "d". Then, from (2.1) and (2.2), we have

$$\boldsymbol{y}_d = \mathbf{H}\boldsymbol{u}_d + \mathbf{M}x_d(0), \tag{2.7}$$

$$\boldsymbol{y}_k = \mathbf{H}\boldsymbol{u}_k + \mathbf{M}x_k(0) + \xi_k, \tag{2.8}$$

where

$$\mathbf{H} = \begin{bmatrix} C_1 B_0 & 0 & 0 & 0 \\ C_2 A_1 B_0 & C_2 B_1 & 0 & 0 \\ \vdots & \vdots & \ddots & \vdots \\ C_T A_{T-1,1} B_0 & C_T A_{T-1,2} B_1 & \cdots & C_T B_{T-1} \end{bmatrix}$$

is block lower triangular. Moreover, we denote $A_{j,i} \triangleq A_j A_{j-1} \cdots A_i$, $j \geq i$, and $\mathbf{M} = [(C_1 A_0)^T, \ldots, (C_T A_{T-1,0})^T]^T$. Furthermore, ξ_k denotes the combination of various noises, given by

$$\xi_k = \begin{bmatrix} v_k(1) + C_1 w_k(0) \\ v_k(2) + C_2 w_k(1) + C_2 A_1 w_k(0) \\ \vdots \\ v_k(T) + \sum_{j=1}^{T} C_T A_{T-1,j} w_k(j-1) \end{bmatrix}.$$

Clearly, ξ_k is a random vector satisfying that $\mathbb{E}[\xi_k] = 0$ and $\mathbb{E}[\|\xi_k\|^2]$ is bounded.

Now, we present the mean-square convergence result.

Theorem 2.1 *Consider system* (2.1) *with fading at the output side and assume Assumptions 2.1–2.3 hold. Apply the learning control scheme* (2.6) *with the modified tracking error* $\varepsilon_k(t)$. *Select a regulation matrix* L_t *such that all eigenvalues of* $L_t C_{t+1} B_t$ *have positive real parts. Then, the input sequence generated by* (2.6) *will converge to the desired value* $u_d(t)$ *in the mean-square sense, i.e.,* $\mathbb{E}[\|\boldsymbol{u}_d - \boldsymbol{u}_k\|^2] \to 0$. *Meanwhile, the mean square of tracking errors* $\mathbb{E}[\|\boldsymbol{y}_d - \boldsymbol{y}_k\|^2]$ *converges to a finite limitation independent of the control sequence.*

Proof: Let $\Delta x_k(t) = x_d(t) - x_k(t)$ and $\Delta u_k(t) = u_d(t) - u_k(t)$ be the state and input errors. For concise notation, we use $t^+ \triangleq t+1$ and $t^- \triangleq t-1$.

Then, from (2.6) we have

$$\begin{aligned}
\Delta u_{k+1}(t) =& \Delta u_k(t) - a_k L_t[y_d(t^+) - \mu^{-1}\Theta_k(t) y_k(t^+)] \\
=& \Delta u_k(t) - a_k L_t \mu^{-1}\Theta_k(t)[y_d(t^+) - y_k(t^+)] \\
& - a_k L_t[I - \mu^{-1}\Theta_k(t)] y_d(t^+) \\
=& \Delta u_k(t) - a_k L_t C_{t+1} B_t \Delta u_k(t) \\
& + a_k L_t[I - \mu^{-1}\Theta_k(t)] C_{t+1} B_t \Delta u_k(t) \\
& - a_k L_t \mu^{-1}\Theta_k(t) C_{t+1} A_t \Delta x_k(t) \\
& + a_k L_t \mu^{-1}\Theta_k(t)[v_k(t^+) + C_{t+1} w_k(t)] \\
& - a_k L_t[I - \mu^{-1}\Theta_k(t)] y_d(t^+).
\end{aligned}$$

By (2.1) and (2.2) we have

$$\begin{aligned}
\Delta x_k(t) =& A_{t-1}\Delta x_k(t^-) + B_{t-1}\Delta u_k(t^-) - w_k(t^-) \\
=& A_{t-1}A_{t-2}\Delta x_k(t-2) + A_{t-1}B_{t-2}\Delta u_k(t-2) \\
& + B_{t-1}\Delta u_k(t-1) - w_k(t^-) - A_{t-1} w_k(t-2) \\
=& \sum_{j=0}^{t-1} A_{t-1,j+1} B_j \Delta u_k(j) - \sum_{j=1}^{t} A_{t-1,j} w_k(j^-) \\
& - A_{t-1,0}\Delta x_k(0),
\end{aligned}$$

where $A_{j,i} = I$ if $j < i$.

Combining these two equations into the lifted form, we have

$$\Delta \boldsymbol{u}_{k+1} = \Delta \boldsymbol{u}_k - a_k \mathbf{L}\mathbf{H}\Delta \boldsymbol{u}_k + a_k \mathbf{L}(I - \mu^{-1}\boldsymbol{\Theta}_k)\mathbf{H}\Delta \boldsymbol{u}_k + a_k \mathbf{L}\mu^{-1}\boldsymbol{\Theta}_k \zeta_k - a_k \mathbf{L}(I - \mu^{-1}\boldsymbol{\Theta}_k)\boldsymbol{y}_d, \tag{2.9}$$

where $\Delta \boldsymbol{u}_k = \boldsymbol{u}_d - \boldsymbol{u}_k$, $\mathbf{L} = \text{diag}\{L_0, L_1, \ldots, L_{T-1}\}$, $\boldsymbol{\Theta}_k = \text{diag}\{\Theta_k(1), \Theta_k(2), \ldots, \Theta_k(T)\}$, and $\zeta_k = \xi_k + \mathbf{M}\Delta x_k(0)$. Clearly, $\mathbb{E}[\zeta_k] = 0$ and $\sup_k \mathbb{E}[\|\zeta_k\|^2] < \infty$ by Assumptions 2.2 and 2.3.

By the definition, $\mathbf{H}$ and $\mathbf{L}$ are block lower triangular and diagonal. Then, $\mathbf{LH}$ is block lower triangular with $L_t C_{t+1} B_t$ being its diagonal blocks. By the condition of L_t, we conclude that eigenvalues of $\mathbf{LH}$ have positive real parts. Then, the following Lyapunov equality

$$(\mathbf{LH})^T \mathbf{Q} + \mathbf{Q}(\mathbf{LH}) = I \tag{2.10}$$

has a unique solution $\mathbf{Q} = \int_0^\infty e^{-[(\mathbf{LH})^T + (\mathbf{LH})]t} dt$, which is positive definite.

Using this matrix $\mathbf{Q}$, construct a Lyapunov function $V_k = (\Delta \boldsymbol{u}_k)^T \mathbf{Q} \Delta \boldsymbol{u}_k$. It is evident that

$$\begin{aligned}
& V_{k+1} \\
=& (\Delta \boldsymbol{u}_{k+1})^T \mathbf{Q} \Delta \boldsymbol{u}_{k+1} \\
=& (\Delta \boldsymbol{u}_k)^T \mathbf{Q} \Delta \boldsymbol{u}_k + a_k^2 (\mathbf{LH}\Delta \boldsymbol{u}_k)^T \mathbf{Q}(\mathbf{LH}\Delta \boldsymbol{u}_k) \\
& + a_k^2 [\mathbf{L}(I - \mu^{-1}\boldsymbol{\Theta}_k)\mathbf{H}\Delta \boldsymbol{u}_k]^T \mathbf{Q}[\mathbf{L}(I - \mu^{-1}\boldsymbol{\Theta}_k)\mathbf{H}\Delta \boldsymbol{u}_k] \\
& + a_k^2 (\mathbf{L}\mu^{-1}\boldsymbol{\Theta}_k \zeta_k)^T \mathbf{Q}(\mathbf{L}\mu^{-1}\boldsymbol{\Theta}_k \zeta_k) \\
& + a_k^2 [\mathbf{L}(I - \mu^{-1}\boldsymbol{\Theta}_k)\boldsymbol{y}_d]^T \mathbf{Q}[\mathbf{L}(I - \mu^{-1}\boldsymbol{\Theta}_k)\boldsymbol{y}_d] \\
& - a_k (\Delta \boldsymbol{u}_k)^T [(\mathbf{LH})^T \mathbf{Q} + \mathbf{QLH}]\Delta \boldsymbol{u}_k \\
& + 2a_k (\Delta \boldsymbol{u}_k)^T \mathbf{Q}[\mathbf{L}(I - \mu^{-1}\boldsymbol{\Theta}_k)\mathbf{H}]\Delta \boldsymbol{u}_k \\
& + 2a_k (\Delta \boldsymbol{u}_k)^T \mathbf{Q}[\mathbf{L}\mu^{-1}\boldsymbol{\Theta}_k \zeta_k - \mathbf{L}(I - \mu^{-1}\boldsymbol{\Theta}_k)\boldsymbol{y}_d] \\
& - 2a_k^2 (\Delta \boldsymbol{u}_k)^T (\mathbf{LH})^T \mathbf{Q}[\mathbf{L}(I - \mu^{-1}\boldsymbol{\Theta}_k)\mathbf{H}\Delta \boldsymbol{u}_k] \\
& - 2a_k^2 (\Delta \boldsymbol{u}_k)^T (\mathbf{LH})^T \mathbf{Q}[\mathbf{L}\mu^{-1}\boldsymbol{\Theta}_k \zeta_k - \mathbf{L}(I - \mu^{-1}\boldsymbol{\Theta}_k)\boldsymbol{y}_d] \\
& + 2a_k^2 (\Delta \boldsymbol{u}_k)^T [\mathbf{L}(I - \mu^{-1}\boldsymbol{\Theta}_k)\mathbf{H}]^T \mathbf{QL}\mu^{-1}\boldsymbol{\Theta}_k \zeta_k \\
& - 2a_k^2 (\Delta \boldsymbol{u}_k)^T [\mathbf{L}(I - \mu^{-1}\boldsymbol{\Theta}_k)\mathbf{H}]^T \mathbf{Q}[\mathbf{L}(I - \mu^{-1}\boldsymbol{\Theta}_k)\boldsymbol{y}_d] \\
& - 2a_k^2 \boldsymbol{y}_d^T [\mathbf{L}(I - \mu^{-1}\boldsymbol{\Theta}_k)]^T \mathbf{QL}\mu^{-1}\boldsymbol{\Theta}_k \zeta_k.
\end{aligned} \tag{2.11}$$

We introduce an increasing σ-algebra $\mathcal{F}_k = \sigma\{u_1(t), x_i(0), w_i(t), v_i(t), \Theta_i(t), 1 \le i \le k, 0 \le t \le T\}$. By (2.6), it is clear that $u_k(t) \in \mathcal{F}_{k-1}$ because the computation of $u_k(t)$ merely depends on the σ-algebra $\mathcal{F}_{k-1}$. Moreover,

$\Theta_k(t)$ consists of random fading gains at the kth iteration, which are independent of $\mathcal{F}_{k-1}$. Meanwhile, $w_k(t)$ and $v_k(t)$ are independent of $\mathcal{F}_{k-1}$ and $\Theta_k(t)$. Noting that $\mathbb{E}[\Theta_k(t)] = \mu I$, we have:

$$\mathbb{E}\{2a_k(\Delta \boldsymbol{u}_k)^T \mathbf{Q}[\mathbf{L}\boldsymbol{\Xi}_k\mathbf{H}]\Delta \boldsymbol{u}_k \mid \mathcal{F}_{k-1}\} = 0, \tag{2.12}$$

$$\mathbb{E}\{2a_k(\Delta \boldsymbol{u}_k)^T \mathbf{QL}\mu^{-1}\boldsymbol{\Theta}_k\zeta_k \mid \mathcal{F}_{k-1}\} = 0 \tag{2.13}$$

$$\mathbb{E}\{2a_k(\Delta \boldsymbol{u}_k)^T \mathbf{QL}\boldsymbol{\Xi}_k\boldsymbol{y}_d \mid \mathcal{F}_{k-1}\} = 0, \tag{2.14}$$

$$\mathbb{E}\{2a_k^2(\Delta \boldsymbol{u}_k)^T (\mathbf{LH})^T \mathbf{Q}[\mathbf{L}\boldsymbol{\Xi}_k\mathbf{H}\Delta \boldsymbol{u}_k] \mid \mathcal{F}_{k-1}\} = 0, \tag{2.15}$$

$$\mathbb{E}\{2a_k^2(\Delta \boldsymbol{u}_k)^T (\mathbf{LH})^T \mathbf{QL}\mu^{-1}\boldsymbol{\Theta}_k\zeta_k \mid \mathcal{F}_{k-1}\} = 0, \tag{2.16}$$

$$\mathbb{E}\{2a_k^2(\Delta \boldsymbol{u}_k)^T (\mathbf{LH})^T \mathbf{QL}\boldsymbol{\Xi}_k\boldsymbol{y}_d \mid \mathcal{F}_{k-1}\} = 0, \tag{2.17}$$

$$\mathbb{E}\{2a_k^2(\Delta \boldsymbol{u}_k)^T [\mathbf{L}\boldsymbol{\Xi}_k\mathbf{H}]^T \mathbf{QL}\mu^{-1}\boldsymbol{\Theta}_k\zeta_k \mid \mathcal{F}_{k-1}\} = 0, \tag{2.18}$$

$$\mathbb{E}\{2a_k^2\mathbf{y}_d^T [\mathbf{L}\boldsymbol{\Xi}_k]^T \mathbf{QL}\mu^{-1}\boldsymbol{\Theta}_k\zeta_k \mid \mathcal{F}_{k-1}\} = 0, \tag{2.19}$$

where $\boldsymbol{\Xi}_k \triangleq I - \mu^{-1}\boldsymbol{\Theta}_k$.

Moreover, by Assumptions 2.2 and 2.3, and the conditions on the random fading variables, we can obtain the following estimates:

$$\mathbb{E}\{(\mathbf{L}\mu^{-1}\boldsymbol{\Theta}_k\zeta_k)^T \mathbf{Q}(\mathbf{L}\mu^{-1}\boldsymbol{\Theta}_k\zeta_k) \mid \mathcal{F}_{k-1}\} \leq c_1, \tag{2.20}$$

$$\mathbb{E}\{(\mathbf{L}\boldsymbol{\Xi}_k\boldsymbol{y}_d)^T \mathbf{Q}(\mathbf{L}\boldsymbol{\Xi}_k\boldsymbol{y}_d) \mid \mathcal{F}_{k-1}\} \leq c_2, \tag{2.21}$$

where $c_1 > 0$ and $c_2 > 0$ are suitable constants.

Furthermore, there are $c_3 > 0$ and $c_4 > 0$ satisfying that

$$\begin{aligned}
&\mathbb{E}\{(\mathbf{LH}\Delta \boldsymbol{u}_k)^T \mathbf{Q}(\mathbf{LH}\Delta \boldsymbol{u}_k) \mid \mathcal{F}_{k-1}\} \\
&\quad = (\mathbf{LH}\Delta \boldsymbol{u}_k)^T \mathbf{Q}(\mathbf{LH}\Delta \boldsymbol{u}_k) \\
&\quad \leq c_3(\Delta \boldsymbol{u}_k)^T \mathbf{Q}(\Delta \boldsymbol{u}_k),
\end{aligned} \tag{2.22}$$

$$\begin{aligned}
&\mathbb{E}\{(\mathbf{L}\boldsymbol{\Xi}_k\mathbf{H}\Delta \boldsymbol{u}_k)^T \mathbf{Q}(\mathbf{L}\boldsymbol{\Xi}_k\mathbf{H}\Delta \boldsymbol{u}_k]) \mid \mathcal{F}_{k-1}\} \\
&\quad = (\Delta \boldsymbol{u}_k)^T \mathbb{E}\{[\mathbf{L}\boldsymbol{\Xi}_k\mathbf{H}]^T \mathbf{Q}[\mathbf{L}\boldsymbol{\Xi}_k\mathbf{H}] \mid \mathcal{F}_{k-1}\}(\Delta \boldsymbol{u}_k) \\
&\quad = (\Delta \boldsymbol{u}_k)^T \mathbb{E}\{[\mathbf{L}\boldsymbol{\Xi}_k\mathbf{H}]^T \mathbf{Q}[\mathbf{L}\boldsymbol{\Xi}_k\mathbf{H}]\}(\Delta \boldsymbol{u}_k) \\
&\quad \leq c_4(\Delta \boldsymbol{u}_k)^T \mathbf{Q}(\Delta \boldsymbol{u}_k).
\end{aligned} \tag{2.23}$$

Consequently,

$$\begin{aligned}
&\mathbb{E}\{2(\Delta \boldsymbol{u}_k)^T (\mathbf{L}\boldsymbol{\Xi}_k\mathbf{H})^T \mathbf{Q}(\mathbf{L}\boldsymbol{\Xi}_k\boldsymbol{y}_d) \mid \mathcal{F}_{k-1}\} \\
&\quad \leq \mathbb{E}\{(\Delta \boldsymbol{u}_k)^T (\mathbf{L}\boldsymbol{\Xi}_k\mathbf{H})^T \mathbf{QL}\boldsymbol{\Xi}_k\mathbf{H}(\Delta \boldsymbol{u}_k) \mid \mathcal{F}_{k-1}\} \\
&\qquad + \mathbb{E}\{(\mathbf{L}\boldsymbol{\Xi}_k\boldsymbol{y}_d)^T \mathbf{Q}(\mathbf{L}\boldsymbol{\Xi}_k\boldsymbol{y}_d) \mid \mathcal{F}_{k-1}\} \\
&\quad \leq c_4(\Delta \boldsymbol{u}_k)^T \mathbf{Q}(\Delta \boldsymbol{u}_k) + c_2.
\end{aligned} \tag{2.24}$$

In addition, there must exist constant $c_5 > 0$ such that $I \geq c_5\mathbf{Q}$. This facts leads to

$$\begin{aligned}
&\mathbb{E}\{(\Delta\boldsymbol{u}_k)^T[(\mathbf{LH})^T\mathbf{Q}+\mathbf{QLH}]\Delta\boldsymbol{u}_k \mid \mathcal{F}_{k-1}\} \\
&= (\Delta\boldsymbol{u}_k)^T\Delta\boldsymbol{u}_k \\
&\geq c_5(\Delta\boldsymbol{u}_k)^T\mathbf{Q}(\Delta\boldsymbol{u}_k). \qquad (2.25)
\end{aligned}$$

Now, we take the conditional expectation to (2.11) with respect to the σ-algebra $\mathcal{F}_{k-1}$ and then substitute (2.12)–(2.25). It follows that

$$\begin{aligned}
&\mathbb{E}\{V_{k+1} \mid \mathcal{F}_{k-1}\} \\
&\leq V_k - c_5 a_k V_k + a_k^2(c_3+2c_4)V_k + a_k^2(c_1+2c_2) \\
&= (1-d_1 a_k)V_k + d_2 a_k^2(d_3+V_k), \qquad (2.26)
\end{aligned}$$

where $d_1 = c_5$, $d_2 = c_3+2c_4$, and $d_3 = (c_1+2c_2)/d_2$. Taking expectation to the above inequality again, we have

$$\mathbb{E}V_{k+1} \leq (1-d_1 a_k)\mathbb{E}[V_k] + d_2 a_k^2(d_3+\mathbb{E}[V_k]). \qquad (2.27)$$

Therefore, using Lemma A.1, we obtain that $\mathbb{E}[V_k] \to 0$ as $k \to \infty$. Moreover, because $\mathbf{Q}$ is positive definite, we conclude that $\mathbb{E}[\|\boldsymbol{u}_d - \boldsymbol{u}_k\|^2] \leq \lambda_{\min}^{-1}(\mathbf{Q})\mathbb{E}[V_k]$ and then $\mathbb{E}[\|\Delta\boldsymbol{u}_k\|^2] \to 0$.

By (2.7) and (2.8), we have

$$\begin{aligned}
\mathbb{E}[\|\boldsymbol{y}_d - \boldsymbol{y}_k\|^2] &= \mathbb{E}[\|\mathbf{H}\Delta\boldsymbol{u}_k - \mathbf{M}\Delta\boldsymbol{x}_k(0) - \xi_k\|^2] \\
&= \mathbb{E}[\|\mathbf{H}\Delta\boldsymbol{u}_k\|^2] + \mathbb{E}[\|\zeta_k\|^2] \\
&= \mathbb{E}[\|\zeta_k\|^2],
\end{aligned}$$

where the second inequality holds because of the independence of involved quantities and the zero-mean property from Assumptions 2.2 and 2.3, and the last equality holds because $\mathbb{E}[\|\Delta\boldsymbol{u}_k\|^2] \to 0$. Clearly, $\mathbb{E}[\|\zeta_k\|^2]$ is a finite value independent of any control sequence. The proof is completed. □

Theorem 2.1 demonstrates the robustness of the inherent learning mechanism of (2.6) against random output deviations caused by the fading channel. The fading effect has been corrected with the channel statistics (cf. the definition of $\varepsilon_k(t)$ where μ^{-1} is involved); however, it still yields argument-dependent and -independent random disturbance terms to the learning algorithms (see (2.9)). To ensure the asymptotical convergence and eliminate the random disturbances, a decreasing gain is introduced in the scheme (2.6), which suppresses effect of the random fading channel by diminishing the randomness and regulates the output to the desired one by accumulating the main correction forces. This is the inherent mechanism why the proposed algorithm works well with fading channels.

The eigenvalue requirement of $L_tC_{t+1}B_t$ in the theorem indicates a well regulation of the control direction. This requirement is satisfied by solving the linear matrix inequality $L_tC_{t+1}B_t > 0$, for which $L_t = (C_{t+1}B_t)^T$ acts as an apparent selection provided that the system matrices are available.

Theorem 2.1 establishes the bounded convergence of tracking errors in the mean-square sense. One may wonder what the expectation of the tracking error would be. The following corollary provides an answer.

Corollary 2.1 *Consider system* (2.1) *with fading at the output side and assume Assumptions 2.1–2.3 hold. Apply the learning control scheme* (2.6) *with the modified tracking error* $\varepsilon_k(t)$. *Under the same condition of Theorem 2.1, the expectation of both input error and tracking error will converge to zero, i.e.,* $\lim_{k\to\infty}\mathbb{E}[\Delta \boldsymbol{u}_k] = 0$ *and* $\lim_{k\to\infty}\mathbb{E}[\boldsymbol{y}_d - \boldsymbol{y}_k] = 0$.

Proof: By probability theory, the mean square convergence implies convergence in probability. We can obtain $\mathbb{E}[\Delta \boldsymbol{u}_k] \to 0$ by the conclusion $\mathbb{E}[\|\Delta \boldsymbol{u}_k\|^2] \to 0$ in Theorem 2.1. Here, we can derive this conclusion from the regression equation (2.9). By $\mathbb{E}[\zeta_k] = 0$ and $\mathbb{E}[I - \mu^{-1}\boldsymbol{\Theta}_k] = 0$, taking expectation of (2.9) yields $\mathbb{E}[\Delta \boldsymbol{u}_{k+1}] = (I - a_k\mathbf{LH})\mathbb{E}[\Delta \boldsymbol{u}_k]$. This leads to $\mathbb{E}[\Delta \boldsymbol{u}_{k+1}] = \boldsymbol{\Gamma}_{k,1}\mathbb{E}[\Delta \boldsymbol{u}_1]$, where $\boldsymbol{\Gamma}_{j,i} = (I - a_j\mathbf{LH})(I - a_{j-1}\mathbf{LH})\cdots(I - a_i\mathbf{LH})$, $\forall j \geq i$.

Under the conditions of Theorem 2.1, we can obtain that there exist $c_0 > 0$ and $c_1 > 0$ such that $\|\boldsymbol{\Gamma}_{j,i}\| \leq c_0 \exp(-c_1\sum_{k=i}^{j} a_k)$. The details are as follows. We use the positive-definite matrix $\mathbf{Q}$ defined in (2.10). Then, we have

$$\begin{aligned}
\boldsymbol{\Gamma}_{j,i}^T\mathbf{Q}\boldsymbol{\Gamma}_{j,i} &= \boldsymbol{\Gamma}_{j-1,i}^T(I - a_j\mathbf{LH})^T\mathbf{Q}(I - a_j\mathbf{LH})\boldsymbol{\Gamma}_{j-1,i}\\
&= \boldsymbol{\Gamma}_{j-1,i}^T\left(\mathbf{Q} + a_j^2(\mathbf{LH})^T\mathbf{QLH} - a_jI\right)\boldsymbol{\Gamma}_{j-1,i}\\
&= \boldsymbol{\Gamma}_{j-1,i}^T\mathbf{Q}^{\frac{1}{2}}\big(I - a_j\mathbf{Q}^{-1}\\
&\quad + a_j^2\mathbf{Q}^{-\frac{1}{2}}(\mathbf{LH})^T\mathbf{QLHQ}^{-\frac{1}{2}}\big)\mathbf{Q}^{\frac{1}{2}}\boldsymbol{\Gamma}_{j-1,i},
\end{aligned}$$

where the Lyapunov equality (2.10) is applied to derive the second equality. Without loss of generality, we may assume that k_0 is sufficiently large such that $\forall i \geq k_0$,

$$\|I - a_j\mathbf{Q}^{-1} + a_j^2\mathbf{Q}^{-\frac{1}{2}}(\mathbf{LH})^T\mathbf{QLHQ}^{-\frac{1}{2}}\| \leq 1 - 2c_1a_j,$$

for some suitable constant $c_1 > 0$. This inequality holds because $a_j \to 0$ as $j \to \infty$ and $\mathbf{Q}^{-1}$ is positive definite. Therefore,

$$\begin{aligned}\mathbf{\Gamma}_{j,i}^T \mathbf{Q} \mathbf{\Gamma}_{j,i} &\leq (1-2c_1 a_j) \mathbf{\Gamma}_{j-1,i}^T \mathbf{Q} \mathbf{\Gamma}_{j-1,i} \\ &\leq \exp(-2c_1 a_j) \mathbf{\Gamma}_{j-1,i}^T \mathbf{Q} \mathbf{\Gamma}_{j-1,i} \\ &\leq \left(\exp(-2c_1 \sum_{k=i}^{j} a_k) \right) I,\end{aligned}$$

and hence $\|\mathbf{\Gamma}_{j,i}\| \leq \lambda_{\min}^{-\frac{1}{2}}(\mathbf{Q}) \exp(-c_1 \sum_{k=i}^{j} a_k)$. Note that k_0 is a finite number, thus the estimate holds for all integers by selecting suitable constant $c_0 > 0$.

Therefore, $\mathbf{\Gamma}_{k,1} \to 0$ as $k \to \infty$, which leads to $\lim_{k\to\infty} \mathbb{E}[\Delta \boldsymbol{u}_k] = 0$. For the tracking errors, it is clear that $\mathbb{E}[\boldsymbol{y}_d - \boldsymbol{y}_k] = \mathbf{H}\mathbb{E}[\Delta \boldsymbol{u}_k] - \mathbf{M}\mathbb{E}[\Delta \boldsymbol{x}_k(0)] - \mathbb{E}[\xi_k] = \mathbf{H}\mathbb{E}[\Delta \boldsymbol{u}_k] \to 0$.The proof is completed. □

Remark 2.4 *In the algorithm* (2.6)*, a prior defined decreasing gain sequence* $\{a_k\}$ *is employed to guarantee the convergence. However, the selection of* $\{a_k\}$ *may be independent of the specific problem and environments; that is, none system and channel information is required for selection of* $\{a_k\}$*. Instead of the decreasing gain, we can employ a small constant gain* ρ*, which can accelerate the convergence rate. However, with a constant gain, we can just ensure* $\mathbb{E}[\|u_d(t) - u_k(t)\|^2]$ *to be convergent to a zone, where the zone's range depends on the learning gain* ρ *as well as fading variance* σ *and mean* μ*. Moreover, taking the learning process data into account, we can define a self-regulation or event-triggered mechanism of the learning gain to further improve the transient performance. It is left as a future issue.*

Theorem 2.2 *Consider system* (2.1) *with fading at the output side and assume Assumptions 2.1–2.3 hold. Apply the learning control scheme* (2.6) *with the modified tracking error* $\varepsilon_k(t)$*. Select a regulation matrix* L_t *such that all eigenvalues of* $L_t C_{t+1} B_t$ *have positive real parts. Then, the input sequence generated by* (2.6) *will converge to the desired value* $u_d(t)$ *in the almost-sure sense, i.e.,* $\mathbb{P}(\lim_{k\to\infty} \boldsymbol{u}_k = \boldsymbol{u}_d) = 1$*. Moreover, the averaged tracking error index defined in* (2.3) *achieves its minimum almost surely.*

Proof: We employ Lemma A.2 to prove this theorem. To this end, we start from (2.26),

$$\mathbb{E}\{V_{k+1} \mid \mathcal{F}_{k-1}\} \leq (1-d_1 a_k) V_k + d_2 a_k^2 (d_3 + V_k). \tag{2.28}$$

Noticing that V_k is positive, we have

$$\mathbb{E}\{V_{k+1} \mid \mathcal{F}_{k-1}\} \leq V_k + d_2 a_k^2 (d_3 + V_k). \tag{2.29}$$

Comparing with Lemma A.2, it is clear that $\mathcal{D}_k$ in the lemma corresponds to $d_2 a_k^2 (d_3 + V_k)$ in the above inequality, which is clearly positive. Thus, it is sufficient to prove that

$$\sum_{k=1}^{\infty} \mathbb{E}[d_2 a_k^2 (d_3 + V_k)] < \infty. \tag{2.30}$$

To this end, we note that $\mathbb{E}[V_k]$ has been proved convergent to zero as k approaches infinity. Therefore, $\mathbb{E}[V_k]$ is bounded for all k, say $\mathbb{E}[V_k] < m$ with m being a suitable constant. Then,

$$\begin{aligned}\sum_{k=1}^{\infty} \mathbb{E}[d_2 a_k^2 (d_3 + V_k)] =& d_2 d_3 \sum_{k=1}^{\infty} a_k^2 + d_2 \sum_{k=1}^{\infty} a_k^2 \mathbb{E}[V_k] \\ \leq& d_2 (d_3 + m) \sum_{k=1}^{\infty} a_k^2 < \infty.\end{aligned} \tag{2.31}$$

That is, (2.30) is valid. Thus, V_k converges almost surely.

In addition, we have proved in Theorem 2.1 that $\mathbb{E}[V_k]$ converges to zero. The limitation of V_k under different senses should coincide with each other from probability theory. Thus, V_k must converge to zero almost surely. The index (2.3) achieves its minimum almost surely. The proof is completed. □

As a companion of Theorem 2.1, Theorem 2.2 elaborates the almost sure convergence for the proposed scheme. Generally, Theorems 2.1 and 2.2 offer the strongest convergence meanings in probability theory. However, the mean-square convergence cannot imply the almost-sure convergence, and vice versa. Thus, the results are established separately based on different analysis techniques. In addition, we can conclude Corollary 2.1 from Theorem 2.2 because the almost-sure convergence means convergence in probability.

Remark 2.5 *At the end of this section, we provide a rough estimate of the convergence speed. Taking sum of* (2.27), *we have* $\sum_{k=1}^{\infty} a_k \mathbb{E}[V_k] < \infty$. *If the gain sequence satisfies* $a_k \downarrow 0$, *one can obtain* $\lim_{k\to\infty} a_k \sum_{i=1}^{k} \mathbb{E}[V_k] = 0$ *by the Kronecker lemma. Then, applying the Cauchy's inequality leads to*

$$\frac{1}{k}\sum_{i=1}^{k} \sqrt{\mathbb{E}[V_i]} \leq \frac{1}{\sqrt{k a_k}} \left(a_k \sum_{i=1}^{k} \mathbb{E}[V_i] \right)^{1/2} = o\left(\frac{1}{\sqrt{k a_k}}\right),$$

where $o(\cdot)$ denotes a high-order infinitesimal. This estimate of convergence rate provides us with novel understandings of the proposed scheme. In particular, the averaged input error along the iteration axis converges to zero faster than the inverse of $\sqrt{ka_k}$. Meanwhile, this estimate presents a guideline for the gain selection in applications.

Remark 2.6 *The necessity of the decreasing gain a_k is to eliminate the effect of random noise and uncertainties asymptotically; therefore, the input sequence has a steady limit. Slight relaxations can be made for mean-square convergence that the finite requirement of infinite-square-sum of a_k can be removed. That is, $\sum_{k=1}^{\infty} a_k^2 < \infty$ is not necessary for the mean-square convergence but for the almost-sure convergence. In addition, it is strict to depict the relationship between the selection of decreasing gains and convergence performance. Generally speaking, the faster-decreasing speed of the gain sequence $\{a_k\}$ would slow down the convergence speed because the innovation process is not sufficient within earlier iterations. If a_k is selected as $a_k = \alpha/k^\beta$ with $1/2 < \beta < 1$ and $\alpha > 0$, we usually let β be suitably small and tune the parameter α.*

2.4 INPUT FADING CHANNEL CASE

Now, we address the case of fading at the input side, where the communication at the output side works well. It is not a simple repetition of Section 2.3 but establishes a foundation for the general case. Unlike the output fading case, the input fading phenomenon would significantly alter the input signal; thus, the tracking performance would be greatly influenced by the contaminated input. Indeed, it is difficult to expect the actual input to converge to desired values. The objective turns to a verification of the input sequence converging to a limit.

Differing from $u_k(t)$, we define $u_k'(t)$ to indicate the actual input that is fed to the plant:

$$u_k'(t) = \Theta_k(t) u_k(t), \tag{2.32}$$

where $\Theta_k(t) = \text{diag}\{\theta_{k,1}(t), \theta_{k,2}(t), \ldots, \theta_{k,p}(t)\}$ corresponds to the dimensionality of the input vector. Here, we use the same symbol for saving notations.

Clearly, $u_k'(t)$ is randomly deviated from $u_k(t)$. Using this control signal without correction would worsen the tracking and learning performance because it will yield the biased output and in turn destroy the iterative learning process. Similar to Section 2.3, we make an intuitive correction:

$$u_k^\circ(t) = \mu^{-1}u_k'(t) = \mu^{-1}\Theta_k(t)u_k(t). \tag{2.33}$$

The system dynamics is given by:

$$\begin{aligned} x_k(t+1) =& A_t x_k(t) + B_t u_k^\circ(t) + w_k(t) \\ =& A_t x_k(t) + \mu^{-1}B_t\Theta_k(t)u_k(t) + w_k(t). \end{aligned} \tag{2.34}$$

The learning algorithm still adopts the conventional P-type scheme

$$u_{k+1}(t) = u_k(t) + a_k L_t e_k(t+1), \tag{2.35}$$

where $e_k(t) = y_d(t) - y_k(t)$ is the tracking error.

We lift the system dynamics and learning algorithm into the supervector form for analysis. By (2.34), we have

$$\begin{aligned} x_k(t+1) =& A_t x_k(t) + \mu^{-1}B_t\Theta_k(t)u_k(t) + w_k(t) \\ =& A_t A_{t-1}x_k(t-1) + \mu^{-1}B_t\Theta_k(t)u_k(t) \\ &+ A_t B_{t-1}\mu^{-1}\Theta_k(t-1)u_k(t-1) \\ &+ w_k(t) + A_t w_k(t-1) \\ =& A_{t,0}x_k(0) + \sum_{j=0}^{t} A_{t,j+1}B_j\mu^{-1}\Theta_k(j)u_k(j) \\ &+ \sum_{j=0}^{t} A_{t,j+1}w_k(j). \end{aligned}$$

In consideration of $y_k(t) = C_t x_k(t) + v_k(t)$, we have that

$$\boldsymbol{y}_k = \mathbf{H}\mu^{-1}\boldsymbol{\Theta}_k\boldsymbol{u}_k + \mathbf{M}x_k(0) + \xi_k, \tag{2.36}$$

where $\boldsymbol{\Theta}_k = \mathrm{diag}\{\Theta_k(0), \ldots, \Theta_k(T-1)\}$ according to the time index of inputs. In other words, the relationship between the input and the output involves fading randomness. Lifting the tracking errors, we have

$$\boldsymbol{e}_k \triangleq \boldsymbol{y}_d - \boldsymbol{y}_k = \mathbf{H}(\boldsymbol{u}_d - \mu^{-1}\boldsymbol{\Theta}_k\boldsymbol{u}_k) - \zeta_k. \tag{2.37}$$

Now, we present the mean-square convergence result.

Theorem 2.3 *Consider system* (2.1) *with fading at the input side and assume Assumptions 2.1–2.3 hold. Apply the learning control scheme* (2.35) *with the* *tracking error $e_k(t)$. Select a regulation matrix L_t such that all eigenvalues of $L_tC_{t+1}B_t$ have positive real parts, $\forall t$. Then, the input sequence generated by* (2.35) *will converge to the desired value $u_d(t)$ in the mean-square sense, i.e., $\mathbb{E}[\|\boldsymbol{u}_d - \boldsymbol{u}_k\|^2] \to 0$. Meanwhile, the mean square of tracking errors $\mathbb{E}[\|\boldsymbol{y}_d - \boldsymbol{y}_k\|^2]$ converges to a finite limitation independent of the control sequence.*

Proof: Considering the learning algorithm (2.35), we are evident to have

$$\begin{aligned}\boldsymbol{u}_{k+1} =&\boldsymbol{u}_k + a_k\mathbf{L}\boldsymbol{e}_k\\ =&\boldsymbol{u}_k + a_k\mathbf{LH}(\boldsymbol{u}_d - \mu^{-1}\boldsymbol{\Theta}_k\boldsymbol{u}_k) - a_k\mathbf{L}\zeta_k.\end{aligned} \tag{2.38}$$

By subtracting (2.38) from $\boldsymbol{u}_d$, we have

$$\begin{aligned}\Delta\boldsymbol{u}_{k+1} =&\Delta\boldsymbol{u}_k - a_k\mathbf{LH}(\boldsymbol{u}_d - \mu^{-1}\boldsymbol{\Theta}_k\boldsymbol{u}_k) + a_k\mathbf{L}\zeta_k\\ =&\Delta\boldsymbol{u}_k - a_k\mathbf{LH}\Delta\boldsymbol{u}_k + a_k\mathbf{LH}(I - \mu^{-1}\boldsymbol{\Theta}_k)\Delta\boldsymbol{u}_k\\ &- a_k\mathbf{LH}(I - \mu^{-1}\boldsymbol{\Theta}_k)\boldsymbol{u}_d + a_k\mathbf{L}\zeta_k.\end{aligned} \tag{2.39}$$

Clearly, this derivation is similar to (2.9). The major differences include the location of random matrix $\boldsymbol{\Theta}_k$ and random disturbance terms.

Similar to the proof of Theorem 2.1, we employ the positive-definite matrix $\mathbf{Q}$ satisfying (2.10) and apply Lyapunov function $V_k = (\Delta\boldsymbol{u}_k)^T\mathbf{Q}\Delta\boldsymbol{u}_k$.

Then, (2.39) leads to

$$\begin{aligned}&V_{k+1}\\ =&V_k + a_k^2(\Delta\boldsymbol{u}_k)^T(\mathbf{LH})^T\mathbf{QLH}\Delta\boldsymbol{u}_k + a_k^2\zeta_k^T\mathbf{L}^T\mathbf{QL}\zeta_k\\ &+ a_k^2(\Delta\boldsymbol{u}_k)^T(I - \mu^{-1}\boldsymbol{\Theta}_k)^T(\mathbf{LH})^T\mathbf{QLH}(I - \mu^{-1}\boldsymbol{\Theta}_k)\Delta\boldsymbol{u}_k\\ &+ a_k^2\boldsymbol{u}_d^T(I - \mu^{-1}\boldsymbol{\Theta}_k)^T(\mathbf{LH})^T\mathbf{QLH}(I - \mu^{-1}\boldsymbol{\Theta}_k)\boldsymbol{u}_d\\ &- a_k(\Delta\boldsymbol{u}_k)^T[(\mathbf{LH})^T\mathbf{Q} + \mathbf{Q}(\mathbf{LH})]\Delta\boldsymbol{u}_k\\ &+ 2a_k(\Delta\boldsymbol{u}_k)^T\mathbf{QLH}(I - \mu^{-1}\boldsymbol{\Theta}_k)\Delta\boldsymbol{u}_k\\ &- 2a_k(\Delta\boldsymbol{u}_k)^T\mathbf{QLH}(I - \mu^{-1}\boldsymbol{\Theta}_k)\boldsymbol{u}_d + 2a_k(\Delta\boldsymbol{u}_k)^T\mathbf{QL}\zeta_k\\ &- 2a_k^2(\Delta\boldsymbol{u}_k)^T(\mathbf{LH})^T\mathbf{QLH}(I - \mu^{-1}\boldsymbol{\Theta}_k)\Delta\boldsymbol{u}_k\\ &+ 2a_k^2(\Delta\boldsymbol{u}_k)^T(\mathbf{LH})^T\mathbf{QL}[\mathbf{H}(I - \mu^{-1}\boldsymbol{\Theta}_k)\boldsymbol{u}_d - \zeta_k]\\ &- 2a_k^2(\Delta\boldsymbol{u}_k)^T(I - \mu^{-1}\boldsymbol{\Theta}_k)^T(\mathbf{LH})^T\mathbf{QLH}(I - \mu^{-1}\boldsymbol{\Theta}_k)\boldsymbol{u}_d\\ &+ 2a_k^2(\Delta\boldsymbol{u}_k)^T(I - \mu^{-1}\boldsymbol{\Theta}_k)^T(\mathbf{LH})^T\mathbf{QL}\zeta_k\\ &- 2a_k^2\boldsymbol{u}_d^T(I - \mu^{-1}\boldsymbol{\Theta}_k)^T(\mathbf{LH})^T\mathbf{QL}\zeta_k.\end{aligned}$$

Employing the σ-algebra defined in Section 2.3, we are evident to have

$$\mathbb{E}\{V_{k+1} \mid \mathcal{F}_{k-1}\}$$

$$
\begin{aligned}
=&V_k + a_k^2(\Delta \boldsymbol{u}_k)^T(\mathbf{LH})^T\mathbf{QLH}\Delta \boldsymbol{u}_k + a_k^2\mathbb{E}\left[\zeta_k^T\mathbf{L}^T\mathbf{QL}\zeta_k\right] \\
&+ a_k^2(\Delta \boldsymbol{u}_k)^T\mathbb{E}\left[\Xi_k^T(\mathbf{LH})^T\mathbf{QLH}\Xi_k\right](\Delta \boldsymbol{u}_k) \\
&+ a_k^2\boldsymbol{u}_d^T\mathbb{E}\left[\Xi_k^T(\mathbf{LH})^T\mathbf{QLH}\Xi_k\right]\boldsymbol{u}_d - a_k(\Delta \boldsymbol{u}_k)^T\Delta \boldsymbol{u}_k \\
&- 2a_k^2\mathbb{E}\{(\Delta \boldsymbol{u}_k)^T\Xi_k^T(\mathbf{LH})^T\mathbf{QLH}\Xi_k\boldsymbol{u}_d \mid \mathcal{F}_{k-1}\},
\end{aligned}
$$

where $\Xi_k = I - \mu^{-1}\boldsymbol{\Theta}_k$.

Regarding the expanded terms in the equation, we first notice that

$$
\begin{aligned}
&\mathbb{E}\left[\zeta_k^T\mathbf{L}^T\mathbf{QL}\zeta_k\right] \le c_6, \\
&\boldsymbol{u}_d^T\mathbb{E}\left[\Xi_k^T(\mathbf{LH})^T\mathbf{QLH}\Xi_k\right]\boldsymbol{u}_d \le c_7.
\end{aligned}
$$

Moreover, it is clear that

$$
\begin{aligned}
&(\Delta \boldsymbol{u}_k)^T(\mathbf{LH})^T\mathbf{QLH}\Delta \boldsymbol{u}_k \le c_8V_k, \\
&(\Delta \boldsymbol{u}_k)^T\mathbb{E}\left[\Xi_k^T(\mathbf{LH})^T\mathbf{QLH}\Xi_k\right](\Delta \boldsymbol{u}_k) \le c_9V_k, \\
&-2\mathbb{E}\{(\Delta \boldsymbol{u}_k)^T\Xi_k^T(\mathbf{LH})^T\mathbf{QLH}\Xi_k\boldsymbol{u}_d \mid \mathcal{F}_{k-1}\} \le c_9V_k + c_7.
\end{aligned}
$$

Therefore, we obtain

$$
\begin{aligned}
\mathbb{E}\{V_{k+1} \mid \mathcal{F}_{k-1}\} \le &[1 - c_5a_k + a_k^2(c_8 + 2c_9)]V_k \\
&+ a_k^2(c_6 + 2c_7). \qquad (2.40)
\end{aligned}
$$

In other words, a contraction of the Lyapunov function is established similar to that of Theorem 2.1. Therefore, by the detailed analysis given in Theorem 2.1, it is valid that $\mathbb{E}[\|\Delta \boldsymbol{u}_k\|^2] \to 0$.

Moreover, by (2.37) we have

$$
\begin{aligned}
\mathbb{E}[\|\boldsymbol{e}_k\|^2] &= \mathbb{E}[\|\mathbf{H}(\boldsymbol{u}_d - \mu^{-1}\boldsymbol{\Theta}_k\boldsymbol{u}_k) - \zeta_k\|^2] \\
&= \mathbb{E}[\|\mathbf{H}(I - \mu^{-1}\boldsymbol{\Theta}_k)\boldsymbol{u}_d + \mathbf{H}\mu^{-1}\boldsymbol{\Theta}_k\Delta \boldsymbol{u}_k - \zeta_k\|^2] \\
&= \mathbb{E}[\|\mathbf{H}(I - \mu^{-1}\boldsymbol{\Theta}_k)\boldsymbol{u}_d\|^2] + \mathbb{E}[\|\zeta_k\|^2] \\
&\quad + \mathbb{E}[\|\mathbf{H}\mu^{-1}\boldsymbol{\Theta}_k\Delta \boldsymbol{u}_k\|^2] \\
&\quad + \mu^{-1}\mathbb{E}[\boldsymbol{u}_d^T(I - \mu^{-1}\boldsymbol{\Theta}_k)^T\mathbf{H}^T\mathbf{H}\boldsymbol{\Theta}_k\Delta \boldsymbol{u}_k] \\
&= \mathbb{E}[\|\mathbf{H}(I - \mu^{-1}\boldsymbol{\Theta}_k)\boldsymbol{u}_d\|^2] + \mathbb{E}[\|\zeta_k\|^2],
\end{aligned}
$$

where the right-hand side is independent of specific control sequences. This completes the proof. □

Next, we proceed to give the following almost-sure convergence result, where the proof is similar to that of Theorem 2.2 and thus omitted to avoid repetition.

Theorem 2.4 *Consider system* (2.1) *with fading at the input side and assume Assumptions 2.1–2.3 hold. Apply the learning control scheme* (2.35) *with the tracking error* $e_k(t)$. *Select a regulation matrix* L_t *such that all eigenvalues of* $L_t C_{t+1} B_t$ *have positive real parts. Then, the input sequence generated by* (2.35) *will converge to the desired value* $u_d(t)$ *in the almost-sure sense, i.e.,* $\mathbb{P}(\lim_{k\to\infty} \boldsymbol{u}_k = \boldsymbol{u}_d) = 1$. *Moreover, the averaged tracking error index defined in* (2.3) *achieves its minimum almost surely.*

Remark 2.7 *We make some clarifications of fading effect between the input and output cases. First of all, the inherent convergence principle is the same for both cases; that is, the random disturbances generated by fading channels is asymptotically suppressed by the decreasing gain sequence, which guarantees the asymptotical convergence. The differences between the two cases in the convergence is the location of random variable* $\Theta_k(t)$ *as can be seen from the lifted input error recursions* (2.9) *and* (2.39). *However, because of the separation techniques in* (2.9) *and* (2.39), *the effect of random fading problem can be well handled by the proposed algorithms.*

Remark 2.8 *In this chapter, we separately consider the output fading and input fading such that the essential effect of fading randomness can be well revealed. In practical applications, the data communication usually employs the same channel resulting in that both sides would suffer random fading problem independently. This case can be solved by combining the schemes in Sections 2.3 and 2.4. In particular, due to the input fading, the output is given by (cf.* (2.36)*)*

$$\boldsymbol{y}_k = \mathbf{H}\mu^{-1}\boldsymbol{\Theta}_k^{\text{input}}\boldsymbol{u}_k + \mathbf{M}x_k(0) + \xi_k,$$

while the received signal at the controller is denoted by $\boldsymbol{\Theta}_k^{\text{output}}\boldsymbol{y}_k$ *(cf.* (2.5)*) and the associated update algorithm is*

$$\boldsymbol{u}_{k+1} = \boldsymbol{u}_k + a_k\mathbf{L}\left(\boldsymbol{y}_d - \mu^{-1}\boldsymbol{\Theta}_k^{\text{output}}\boldsymbol{y}_k\right).$$

Note that the input fading $\boldsymbol{\Theta}_k^{\text{input}}$ *is independent of the output fading* $\boldsymbol{\Theta}_k^{\text{output}}$. *The convergence of this overall scheme is similar to that present in the above theorems, which is omitted here for saving space.*

Remark 2.9 *The channel fading evidently affects the controller design and system performance. The impact on the controller design is twofold. On the one hand, the expectation of the received signal is biased compared with its original signal and thus an additional correction mechanism is necessary. On* *the other hand, the random bias error caused by the channel fading is signal dependent and unpredictable; thus, the learning gain should be selected appropriately to ensure a steady convergence of the proposed algorithms. The system performance is worsened mainly for the input channel fading case because more uncertainties are involved in the input and the overall tracking index* (2.3) *is enlarged.*

2.5 ILLUSTRATIVE SIMULATIONS

We first present a numerical simulation on an MIMO time-varying system, where the influences of various factors are carefully analyzed. Then, we present the simulation on a permanent magnet linear motor (PMLM) as an example of practical systems.

2.5.1 MIMO System

Consider the MIMO system (A_t, B_t, C_t) with

$$A_t = \begin{bmatrix} 0.05\sin 0.2t & -0.2 & 0.02t \\ 0.1 & -0.01t & -0.02\cos 0.5t \\ 0.1 & 0.1 & 0.2+0.05\cos 0.2t \end{bmatrix},$$

$$B_t = \begin{bmatrix} 1-0.2\sin^2(0.5\pi t) & 0 \\ 0.01t & 0.01t \\ 0 & 1+0.1\sin(0.5\pi t) \end{bmatrix},$$

$$C_t = \begin{bmatrix} 0.2+0.1\sin^2(0.5\pi t) & 0.1 & -0.1 \\ 0 & 0.1 & 0.2-0.1\sin(0.5\pi t) \end{bmatrix}.$$

The initial state $x_k(0)$, system noise $w_k(t)$, and measurement noise $v_k(t)$ are all set to Gaussian random variables subject to $N(0, 0.1^2)$. All fading variables $\theta_{k,i}(t)$ satisfy Gaussian distribution $N(\mu_0, \sigma_0)$, where $\mu_0 = 0.95$ and $\sigma_0 = 0.1^2$. The reference is $y_d(t) = 0.9\sin(\frac{t}{3}) - 0.5\cos(\frac{t}{4}) + 0.5$. The iteration length takes $T = 50$. All of the following simulations are executed for 50 trials.

The learning gain sequence chooses $1/k^{0.55}$ and the regulation matrix L_t is set to

$$L_t = \begin{bmatrix} 9.1632-0.2\sin(0.5\pi t) & 2.6493 \\ -0.5297 & 2.87-0.1\sin(0.5\pi t) \end{bmatrix}.$$

Figs. 2.2 and 2.3 demonstrate the tracking performance of the 4th and 40th iterations and the continuously decreasing trend of the input error as

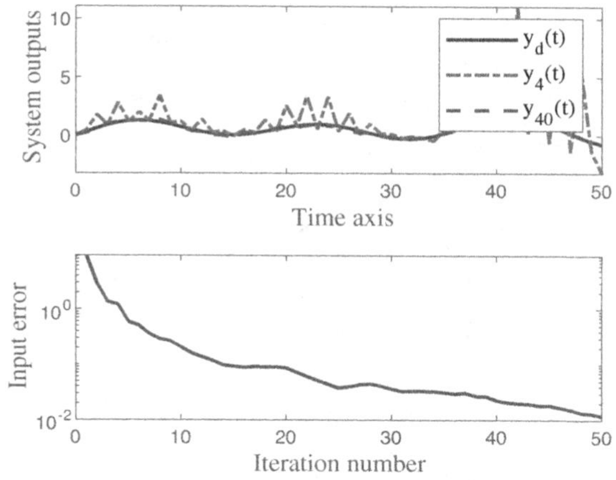

Figure 2.2 Output fading: (upper) tracking performance of the selected iterations; (bottom) input error profile in the iteration domain.

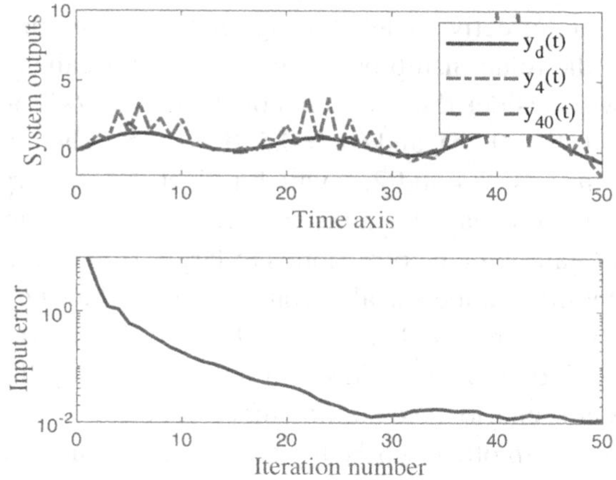

Figure 2.3 Input fading: (upper) tracking performance of the selected iterations; (bottom) input error profile in the iteration domain.

iteration number increases, all for the first dimension for illustration. In particular, the upper plots show the tracking performance for different learning stages. The results show that the actual output is significantly improved by the proposed scheme for a few iterations. The lower plots present the iteration profile of input errors in the averaged Euclidean-norm, which is defined

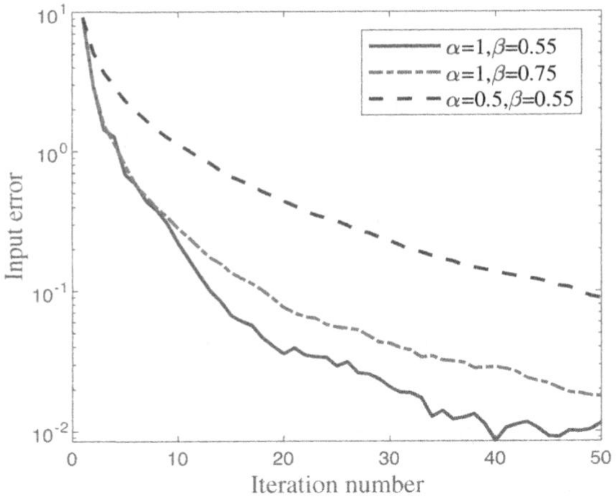

Figure 2.4 Relation of decreasing gain sequence and convergence rate for the output fading case.

by $\|\Delta \boldsymbol{u}_k\|^2/T$. We can see that the input error decreases fast. In short, the proposed schemes are effective in addressing the fading randomness.

To understand the relationship between the learning gain $\{a_k\}$ and convergence speed, we consider three variants of the $a_k = \alpha/k^\beta$, namely, ($\alpha = 1, \beta = 0.55$), ($\alpha = 1, \beta = 0.75$), and ($\alpha = 0.5, \beta = 0.55$). The input error profiles are provided in Figs. 2.4 and 2.7, which reflect the convergence rate of the proposed scheme. It reveals that a faster convergence rate can be achieved by a suitable larger gain, which corresponds to larger α and smaller β.

The effect of fading channels is also considered. To this end, we simulate three variants of the fading model: ($\mu = 0.95, \sigma = 0.1^2$), ($\mu = 0.85, \sigma = 0.1^2$), and ($\mu = 0.85, \sigma = 0.05^2$). Figs. 2.5 and 2.6 display the input error profiles for different scenarios. No significant effect has been observed from the input error profiles. In other words, the proposed schemes are effective to deal with the channel uncertainty.

2.5.2 PMLM System

Consider the discrete PMLM system as follows

$$\begin{aligned} x(t+1) &= x(t) + v(t)\Delta, \\ v(t+1) &= v(t) - \Delta\frac{k_1 k_2 \Psi_f^2}{Rm} v(t) + \Delta\frac{k_2 \Psi_f}{Rm} u(t), \\ y(t) &= v(t), \end{aligned}$$

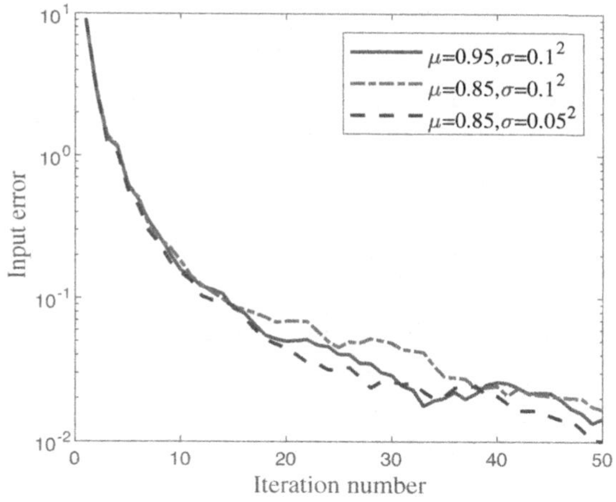

Figure 2.5 Effect of fading settings for the output fading case.

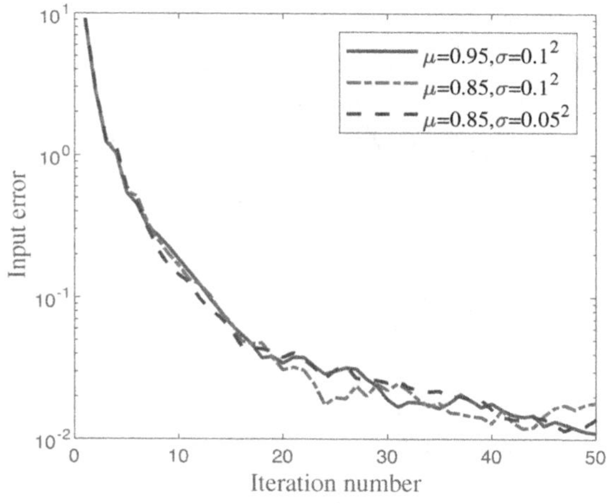

Figure 2.6 Effect of fading settings for the input fading case.

where $\Delta = 0.01$ s is the sampling time interval. The other notations are given in Table 2.1. The operation period is set to $T = 0.5$ s. The reference is $y_d(t) = 0.3\sin(\frac{\pi t}{10}) + 0.25\sin(\frac{\pi t}{6})$.

The learning gain L_t is set to $L_t = 13$, $\forall t$. The decreasing gain sequence adopts $a_k = 1/k^{0.6}$. The learning control schemes are run for 50 iterations for each case. Figs. 2.8 and 2.9 demonstrate tracking performance for the 2nd

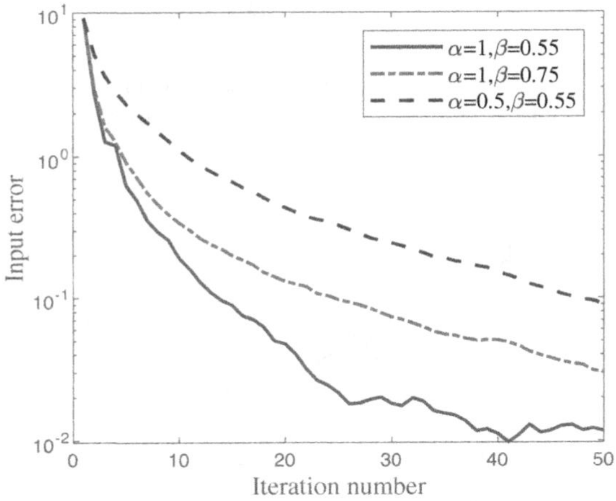

Figure 2.7 Relation of decreasing gain sequence and convergence rate for the input fading case.

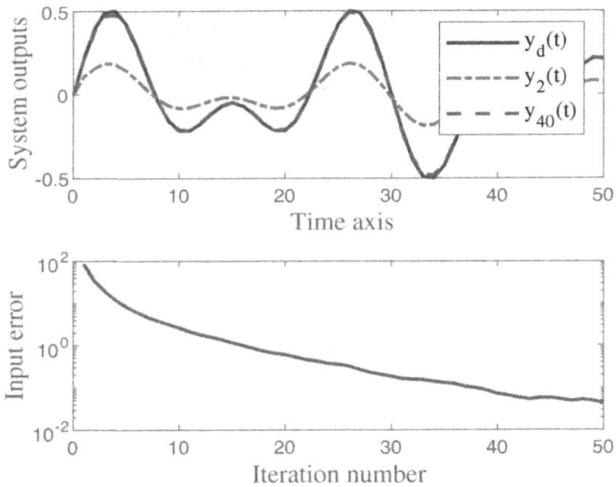

Figure 2.8 Output fading for PMLM: (upper) tracking performance of the selected iterations; (bottom) input error profile in the iteration domain.

and 40th iterations (upper plot) and iteration profiles of input errors in the averaged Euclidean-norm (lower plot). It is observed that similar performance is accessible compared to Subsection 2.5.1. In addition, removing the effect of random noises, we notice that the tracking performance at the 40th iteration for input fading (cf. upper plot of Fig. 2.9) is a little worse than that for

TABLE 2.1 Parameters in PMLM model

Notation	Meaning
x	motor position
v	rotor velocity
R	resistance of stator, $R = 8.6\,\Omega$
m	rotor mass, $m = 1.635\,\text{kg}$
ψ_f	flux linkage, $\psi_f = 0.35\,\text{Wb}$
τ	pole pitch, $\tau = 0.031\,\text{m}$
k_1	π/τ
k_2	$1.5\pi/\tau$

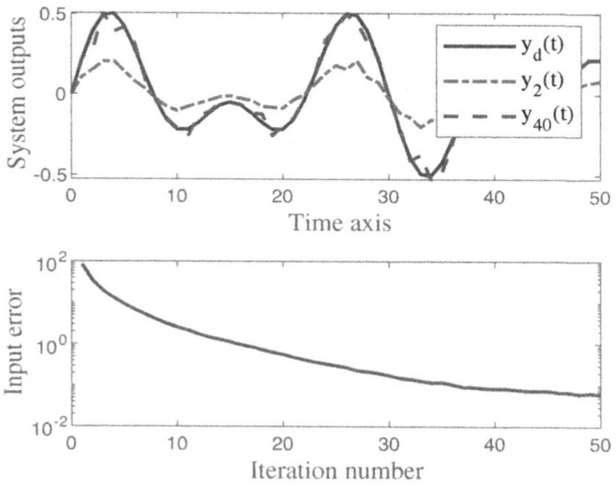

Figure 2.9 Input fading for PMLM: (upper) tracking performance of the selected iterations; (bottom) input error profile in the iteration domain.

output fading (cf. upper plot of Fig. 2.8) because the former case introduces unavoidable deviations. Consequently, the actually employed input signal is not correct in the presence of input fading. This observation verifies the discussions at the beginning of Section 2.4. In addition, the effect of different decreasing gain sequences and fading channel models is similar to that of the previous subsection. We omit the detailed figures and discussions to avoid repetition.

2.6 SUMMARY

This chapter provides a first investigation on the learning control strategies with random fading communications. The output and input fading cases are explored subsequently. First, the entire structure consisting of the controlled plant, learning unit, and fading channels is elaborated with a formal formulation of the control objective. Then, two learning control schemes are proposed to achieve the objective under random fading and system noises. We employ a decreasing sequence to eliminate the randomness asymptotically and therefore, guarantee the asymptotical convergence in the iteration domain. In brief, we have established a stochastic synthesis and analysis framework of learning control with fading communications.

CHAPTER 3

Tracking Performance Enhancement by Input Averaging

THIS chapter applies learning control to repetitive systems over fading channels at both output and input sides to improve tracking performance without applying restrictive fading conditions. Both multiplicative and additive randomness of the fading channel are addressed, and the effects of fading communication on the data are carefully analyzed. A decreasing gain sequence and moving-average operator are introduced to modify the generic learning control algorithm to reduce the fading effect and improve control system performance. Results reveal that the tracking error converges to zero in the mean-square sense as the iteration number increases.

3.1 INTRODUCTION

In Chapter 2, we have established a basic learning control scheme for stochastic systems with random fading communications, where the fading randomness is described by a multiplicative random variable. Two observations arise to be further improved. First, additive communication noise is not considered. Second, the corrected input fed to the plant involves additional uncertainties that may destroy the transient dynamics. Indeed, the imprecise input cannot only lead to unacceptable tracking performance but also negatively impact the learning process.

In this chapter, we present a general formulation of fading channels in which both multiplicative and additive forms of randomness are accounted

DOI: 10.1201/9781032646404-3

for, as they represent the typical uncertainties during transmission over wireless or shared links. We discuss output fading and input fading separately, as they affect the algorithm design uniquely. For each type of fading, a fading effect analysis, algorithm design, and convergence analysis are provided. In particular, in output fading, fading measurements may introduce random deviations in both the multiplicative and additive sense, and these cannot be predicted in advance. Thus, the algorithm uses a decreasing gain sequence to reduce this effect asymptotically as the iteration number increases. Strict convergence of the tracking error to zero is presented in the mean-square sense. In input fading, in addition to the random deviations similar to output fading, fading input may lead to unacceptable transient performance and worsen the learning process even after sufficient learning trials. To solve this problem, a moving-average operator is applied to the received input signals such that the transient performance can be improved. A detailed convergence and performance analysis is also performed. A P-type learning algorithm is used as it is easily implemented and widely employed in learning control. The results can be extended to other control schemes with slight modifications.

3.2 PROBLEM FORMULATION

Consider the following MIMO linear system

$$\begin{aligned} x_k(t+1) &= Ax_k(t) + Bu_k(t), \\ y_k(t) &= Cx_k(t) \end{aligned} \tag{3.1}$$

where subscript k denotes the iteration index ($k = 1, 2, \ldots$) and argument t is the time label ($t = 0, 1, \ldots, N$, where N is the operation length of each iteration). Variables $x_k(t) \in \mathbf{R}^n$, $u_k(t) \in \mathbf{R}^p$, and $y_k(t) \in \mathbf{R}^q$ are the system state, input, and output, respectively, where n, p, and q are the corresponding dimensions. The system matrices A, B, and C have appropriate dimensions. Although time-invariant matrices are used here, an extension to time-varying systems (A_t, B_t, C_t) can be easily achieved using steps similar to those below. Without loss of generality, we assume the input/output coupling matrix CB to be of full-column rank for all t, which indicates that the system relative degree is 1 and the dimension of the input is not greater than that of the output.

We denote the desired tracking reference $y_d(t), t = 0, 1, \ldots, N$ and assume that it is achievable. In other words, the following assumption holds:

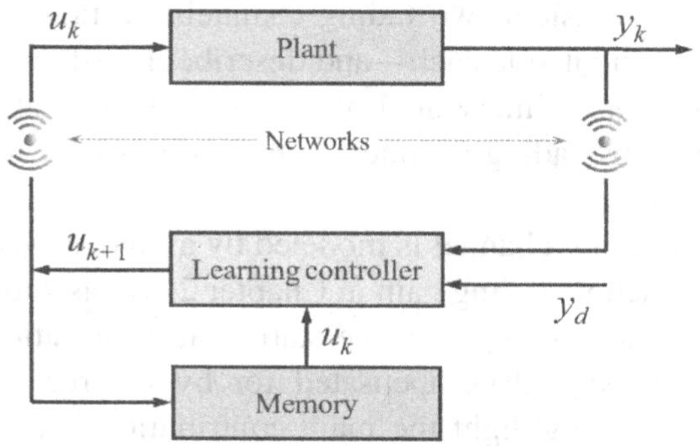

Figure 3.1 Block diagram of learning systems over fading channels.

Assumption 3.1 *There exist a unique input $u_d(t)$ and suitable initial state $x_d(0)$ such that the following relationship holds:*

$$\begin{aligned} x_d(t+1) &= Ax_d(t) + Bu_d(t), \\ y_d(t) &= Cx_d(t). \end{aligned} \tag{3.2}$$

If the above assumption is invalid, then the desired reference is not achievable, indicating that the given reference cannot be precisely tracked by any input sequence. In this case, the best attainable option is to track the trajectory closest to the given reference.

For repetitive systems, the following initialization condition is required:

Assumption 3.2 *The initial state of each iteration $x_k(0)$ is identical to the desired state $x_d(0)$; i.e., $x_k(0) = x_d(0)$.*

The above assumption is the widely used identical initialization condition (i.i.c.) in the field of learning control. If this condition is invalid, then precise tracking performance is no longer achievable. Several studies have been devoted to relaxing this condition by introducing additional learning mechanisms.

A conventional objective of a learning system is to derive a learning algorithm such that the generated input sequence can drive the system to precisely track the given reference as the iteration number increases, i.e., $y_k(t) \to y_d(t)$, $\forall t$, as $k \to \infty$. Based on Assumption 3.1 and the assumption that CB is of full-column rank, it is evident that the objective can be achieved as long as $u_k(t) \to u_d(t)$, $\forall t$, as $k \to \infty$, where $u_d(t)$ is given in Assumption 3.1.

The learning system setup is illustrated in Fig. 3.1, in which the plant and controller are located at different sites and transmit signals over fading channels. Here, we consider two fading channels—a fading channel at the output side and the input side each—and describe the effects of these fading channels in detail. The primary goal of this study is to deal with additional randomness caused by fading channels, which are usually modeled by random variables.

Specifically, a fading channel is modeled by a random variable in a multiplicative form to denote fading gain in Chapter 2. We assume that the channels undergo slow fading such that the statistical information of the fading gain can be estimated and compensated for by the receiver before it is used for updating. To highlight the main contribution, we assume a scalar fading gain for each transmitted signal; i.e., for input and output vectors at arbitrary time instant t, a scalar random variable $\mu_k(t)$ is multiplied to illustrate the fading effect. It should be noted that the extension to multiple fading channels wherein each dimension of the output and input is transmitted through individual channels does not require additional efforts and uses steps identical to those below but with tedious notation. In addition, we consider random variable $\mu_k(t)$ to be independent and identically distributed with respect to k and t according to a continuous fading distribution $f(\mu)$ such that $\mathbb{P}(\mu_k(t) > 0) = 1$. We assume that $\mu_k(t)$ has the following statistics

$$\mu = \mathbb{E}[\mu_k(t)], \quad \sigma^2 = \mathbb{E}[(\mu_k(t) - \mu)^2]. \tag{3.3}$$

However, because transmission through wireless networks is considered, introducing additive random noise during signal transmission is generally unavoidable. The received signal is not only driven by the fading gain but also by unpredictable noise that can be modeled by a random vector with dimension $\nu_k(t) \in \mathbf{R}^m$, where m can be p or q depending on an input or output signal. The additive noise is independent and identically distributed in different iterations and time instants satisfying the following statistics:

$$\mathbb{E}[\nu_k(t)] = 0, \quad \mathbb{E}[\nu_k(t)\nu_k^T(t)] = R_t, \tag{3.4}$$

where R_t is a semi-positive matrix.

In short, assuming that the transmitted signal is $m_k(t) \in \mathbf{R}^m$, the fading channel model can be described as follows:

$$m_k^\circ(t) = \mu_k(t)m_k(t) + \nu_k(t), \tag{3.5}$$

where $m_k^\circ(t)$ denotes the received signal, and $\mu_k(t)$ and $\nu_k(t)$ are given in (3.3) and (3.4).

We note that a time-invariant deterministic system is considered in the formulation; however, we consider additive random noise in communication networks. Therefore, a stochastic system can be successfully addressed using the same techniques that are proposed in the following sections because system noise can be transformed as a part of the network noise. In addition, it should be emphasized that random deviations remain even when additive noise is absent. The primary reason for this is that the multiplicative fading gain in fact leads to a signal-dependent transmission error.

With respect to learning systems, this chapter performs an in-depth investigation of the effects of fading channels and presents corresponding solutions for suppressing these effects. In particular, the following tasks are addressed:

1) performing intuitive analysis of the effects of fading channels at the output and input sides;

2) designing suitable learning mechanisms to suppress the fading effect; and

3) providing convergence analysis of the proposed algorithms under random fading phenomena.

To present a clear explanation of fading channels, we discuss the output case and input case separately.

3.3 OUTPUT FADING CASE

In this section, we consider the case of output fading, in which the network suffers from random fading from the plant to the controller and involves additive noise. However, the network works well from the controller to the plant; i.e., there is no fading or noise. In other words, the output received by the controller contains multiple types of randomness, while the generated input signal is effectively transmitted to the plant for running operations.

3.3.1 Fading Effect Analysis

The actual output is $y_k(t)$, and the signal received by the controller is $y_k^\circ(t)$. According to the fading channel setting, we have

$$y_k^\circ(t) = \mu_k(t)y_k(t) + \nu_k(t). \tag{3.6}$$

This received signal, $y_k^\circ(t)$, cannot be used in the learning algorithm because it differs from the original output $y_k(t)$. Consequently, a correction should be applied to the received output to establish the learning algorithm. An intuitive strategy is to multiply the received output by the mean inverse of the fading gain as follows:

$$y'_k(t) = \mu^{-1} y^{\circ}_k(t), \tag{3.7}$$

where $y'_k(t)$ denotes the corrected signal. By a direct calculation, we have

$$\begin{aligned} y'_k(t) &= \mu^{-1}\mu_k(t)y_k(t) + \mu^{-1}v_k(t) \\ &= y_k(t) - \left(1 - \frac{\mu_k(t)}{\mu}\right) y_k(t) + \mu^{-1}v_k(t). \end{aligned} \tag{3.8}$$

It can be seen from (3.8) that the effect of the fading channel on the output data is in two parts.

1) The first part is $\left(1 - \frac{\mu_k(t)}{\mu}\right) y_k(t)$, an information-dependent error. Noting the independence between the fading variable $\mu_k(t)$ and output $y_k(t)$, we observe that the mathematical expectation of this term is zero. This observation provides us with a solid baseline for guaranteeing acceptable tracking performance of the learning algorithm. However, the variance of this term is output dependent, which is likely to influence asymptotic convergence analysis.

2) The second part is $\mu^{-1}v_k(t)$, a zero-mean random variable with bounded variance. In other words, this term retains favorable statistics for algorithm design and analysis, and it is evident that its variance is affected by the mean inverse, μ^{-1}. The influence of additive noise thus increases if the mean of the fading channel gain is smaller than 1.

In short, special attention must be paid to two issues in algorithm design and analysis. First, due to the existence of random deviations, a conventional learning algorithm with fixed gain cannot guarantee stable convergence. The first issue thus involves introducing a suitable learning gain sequence to suppress the effect of random deviations. Second, the second term on the right-hand side of (3.8) is output dependent; thus, the boundedness of the proposed algorithm should be handled carefully. This raises the second issue of a strict proof of boundedness and convergence. Details are provided in the following subsections.

3.3.2 Learning Algorithm Design

Because the original output $y_k(t)$ is not available for the learning algorithm, the actual tracking error $e_k(t) \triangleq y_d(t) - y_k(t)$ cannot be applied directly. We express the modified tracking error as $\varepsilon_k(t) \triangleq y_d(t) - y'_k(t)$ for updating. Then, the update law for the system (3.1) with an output fading channel is defined as follows:

$$u_{k+1}(t) = u_k(t) + a_k L \varepsilon_k(t+1), \tag{3.9}$$

where L is a control direction regulation matrix and $\{a_k\}$ is a decreasing sequence such that

$$a_k > 0, \quad \sum_{k=1}^{\infty} a_k = \infty, \quad \sum_{k=1}^{\infty} a_k^2 < \infty. \tag{3.10}$$

It should be noted that policy (3.9) is modified from the most common P-type update law in iterative learning control by introducing a decreasing gain sequence $\{a_k\}$.

Remark 3.1 *A brief explanation of the design idea of policy* (3.9) *should be offered before presenting the main results. The essential structure of* (3.9) *is a P-type update law. Matrix L is employed for regulating the control direction of a MIMO system. In particular, for a single-input-single-output system, the input/output coupling matrix becomes a scalar value whose direction is the sign of this scalar value. In this case, the control direction regulation matrix L can be removed. In addition, the decreasing sequence, $\{a_k\}$, is introduced to suppress the effect of random deviations (see Section 3.3.1) and guarantee a stable convergence (see convergence proof in Section 3.3.3). It is clear that $a_k = \alpha/k^{\beta}$, with $1/2 < \beta < 1$ and $\alpha > 0$, satisfies all conditions (the effect of parameters α and β is discussed in Section 3.5.1). In general, a decreasing gain is necessary for addressing the control problem for stochastic systems.*

3.3.3 Convergence Analysis

To simplify the expressions in the proof, we first lift the variables within an iteration into a supervector. In particular, the lifted input and output are defined as follows:

$$\begin{aligned}
\boldsymbol{u}_* &= [u_*(0)^T, u_*(1)^T, \ldots, u_*(N-1)^T]^T \in \mathbf{R}^{Np}, \\
\boldsymbol{y}_* &= [y_*(1)^T, y_*(2)^T, \ldots, y_*(N)^T]^T \in \mathbf{R}^{Nq},
\end{aligned}$$

where subscript "$*$" indicates k and d for the kth iteration and desired values, respectively. Then, from (3.1) and (3.2), we have

$$\boldsymbol{y}_d = \mathbf{H}\boldsymbol{u}_d + \mathbf{M}x_d(0), \tag{3.11}$$

$$\boldsymbol{y}_k = \mathbf{H}\boldsymbol{u}_k + \mathbf{M}x_k(0), \tag{3.12}$$

where

$$\mathbf{H} = \begin{bmatrix} CB & 0 & 0 & 0 \\ CAB & CB & 0 & 0 \\ \vdots & \vdots & \ddots & \vdots \\ CA^{N-1}B & CA^{N-2}B & \cdots & CB \end{bmatrix} \in \mathbf{R}^{Nq\times Np}$$

is a block lower-triangular matrix in which diagonal element is the coupling matrix, CB, and $\mathbf{M} = [(CA)^T, \ldots, (CA^N)^T]^T$. According to Assumption 3.2, we have

$$\boldsymbol{e}_k \triangleq \boldsymbol{y}_d - \boldsymbol{y}_k = \mathbf{H}(\boldsymbol{u}_d - \boldsymbol{u}_k). \tag{3.13}$$

Let $\boldsymbol{v}_k = [v_k^T(1), \ldots, v_k^T(N)]^T$ and $\theta_k(t) \triangleq 1 - \frac{\mu_k(t)}{\mu}$. It is clear that $\mathbb{E}[\theta_k(t)] = 0$ and $\sup_{k,t} \mathbb{E}[\theta_k^2(t)] < \infty$, $\forall k,t$, according to (3.3). With (3.8), we can derive the lifted form of policy (3.9) as follows:

$$\boldsymbol{u}_{k+1} = \boldsymbol{u}_k + a_k(I_N \otimes L)\left(\boldsymbol{e}_k + (\Theta_k \otimes I_q)\boldsymbol{y}_k - \mu^{-1}\boldsymbol{v}_k\right), \tag{3.14}$$

where $\Theta_k \triangleq \text{diag}\{\theta_k(1), \ldots, \theta_k(N)\}$ and $\otimes$ denotes the Kronecker product. In the rest of this chapter, we denote $\mathbf{L} \triangleq I_N \otimes L$ and $\boldsymbol{\Theta}_k \triangleq \Theta_k \otimes I_q$ for concise notation.

The first result of this chapter is presented in the following theorem.

Theorem 3.1 *Consider system* (3.1) *with output fading channels and assume that Assumptions 3.1 and 3.2 hold. Apply policy* (3.9) *with a decreasing gain sequence satisfying* (3.10)*. If the control direction regulation matrix L is designed such that all eigenvalues of LCB have positive real parts, then the input sequence generated by* (3.9) *converges asymptotically in the mean-square sense to the desired value $u_d(t)$. That is, $\mathbb{E}[\|\boldsymbol{u}_d - \boldsymbol{u}_k\|^2] \to 0$ as $k \to \infty$. Consequently, the tracking error converges to zero in the mean-square sense; i.e., $\mathbb{E}[\|\boldsymbol{e}_k\|^2] \to 0$.*

Proof: Note that the term $(\Theta_k \otimes I_N)\boldsymbol{y}_k$ in (3.14) is output dependent and is therefore input dependent. This term may involve a boundedness issue in the convergence proof. Thus, (3.14) is modified as follows:

$$\begin{aligned} \boldsymbol{u}_{k+1} &= \boldsymbol{u}_k + a_k\mathbf{L}\left[\boldsymbol{e}_k - \boldsymbol{\Theta}_k\boldsymbol{e}_k + \boldsymbol{\Theta}_k\boldsymbol{y}_d - \mu^{-1}\boldsymbol{v}_k\right] \\ &= \boldsymbol{u}_k + a_k\mathbf{L}\mathbf{H}\Delta\boldsymbol{u}_k - a_k\mathbf{L}\boldsymbol{\Theta}_k\mathbf{H}\Delta\boldsymbol{u}_k \end{aligned}$$

$$\begin{aligned}
&+a_k\mathbf{L}[\boldsymbol{\Theta}_k\boldsymbol{y}_d-\mu^{-1}\boldsymbol{v}_k]\\
&=\boldsymbol{u}_k+a_k\mathbf{LH}\Delta\boldsymbol{u}_k-a_k(\Theta_k\otimes L)\mathbf{H}\Delta\boldsymbol{u}_k\\
&+a_k(\Theta_k\otimes L)\boldsymbol{y}_d-a_k\mu^{-1}\mathbf{L}\boldsymbol{v}_k,
\end{aligned}$$

where $\Delta\boldsymbol{u}_k \triangleq \boldsymbol{u}_d-\boldsymbol{u}_k$.

Subtracting both sides of the above equation from $\boldsymbol{u}_d$ yields

$$\begin{aligned}
\Delta\boldsymbol{u}_{k+1}=\Delta\boldsymbol{u}_k-a_k\mathbf{LH}\Delta\boldsymbol{u}_k+a_k(\Theta_k\otimes L)\mathbf{H}\Delta\boldsymbol{u}_k\\
-a_k(\Theta_k\otimes L)\boldsymbol{y}_d+a_k\mu^{-1}\mathbf{L}\boldsymbol{v}_k.
\end{aligned}\tag{3.15}$$

Because $\mathbf{L}$ is a block diagonal matrix and $\mathbf{H}$ is a block lower-triangular matrix, it is evident that $\mathbf{LH}$ is a block diagonal matrix with LCB as its diagonal blocks. Because matrix L is designed such that all eigenvalues of LCB have positive real parts, all eigenvalues of matrix $\mathbf{LH}$ have positive real parts as well. According to the Lyapunov stability theory, there exists a positive-definite matrix $\mathbf{S}$ with appropriate dimensions such that the following relationship holds:

$$[\mathbf{LH}]^T\mathbf{S}+\mathbf{S}[\mathbf{LH}]=I_{Np}.\tag{3.16}$$

We define a Lyapunov function based on the newly introduced matrix, $\mathbf{S}$:

$$V_k=(\Delta\boldsymbol{u}_k)^T\mathbf{S}(\Delta\boldsymbol{u}_k).\tag{3.17}$$

We then have

$$\begin{aligned}
V_{k+1}&=(\Delta\boldsymbol{u}_{k+1})^T\mathbf{S}(\Delta\boldsymbol{u}_{k+1})\\
&=(\Delta\boldsymbol{u}_k)^T\mathbf{S}(\Delta\boldsymbol{u}_k)+a_k^2(\Delta\boldsymbol{u}_k)^T[\mathbf{LH}]^T\mathbf{SLH}\Delta\boldsymbol{u}_k\\
&+a_k^2(\Delta\boldsymbol{u}_k)^T[(\Theta_k\otimes L)\mathbf{H}]^T\mathbf{S}(\Theta_k\otimes L)\mathbf{H}\Delta\boldsymbol{u}_k\\
&+a_k^2\boldsymbol{y}_d^T(\Theta_k\otimes L)^T\mathbf{S}(\Theta_k\otimes L)\boldsymbol{y}_d+a_k^2\mu^{-2}\boldsymbol{v}_k^T\mathbf{L}^T\mathbf{SL}\boldsymbol{v}_k\\
&-a_k(\Delta\boldsymbol{u}_k)^T\{[\mathbf{LH}]^T\mathbf{S}+\mathbf{S}[\mathbf{LH}]\}(\Delta\boldsymbol{u}_k)\\
&+a_k(\Delta\boldsymbol{u}_k)^T\{[(\Theta_k\otimes L)\mathbf{H}]^T\mathbf{S}+\mathbf{S}(\Theta_k\otimes L)\mathbf{H}\}(\Delta\boldsymbol{u}_k)\\
&-2a_k(\Delta\boldsymbol{u}_k)^T\mathbf{S}[(\Theta_k\otimes L)\boldsymbol{y}_d-\mu^{-1}\mathbf{L}\boldsymbol{v}_k]\\
&-2a_k^2(\Delta\boldsymbol{u}_k)^T[\mathbf{LH}]^T\mathbf{S}(\Theta_k\otimes L)\mathbf{H}\Delta\boldsymbol{u}_k\\
&+2a_k^2(\Delta\boldsymbol{u}_k)^T[\mathbf{LH}]^T\mathbf{S}(\Theta_k\otimes L)\boldsymbol{y}_d\\
&-2a_k^2\mu^{-1}(\Delta\boldsymbol{u}_k)^T[\mathbf{LH}]^T\mathbf{SL}\boldsymbol{v}_k\\
&-2a_k^2(\Delta\boldsymbol{u}_k)^T[(\Theta_k\otimes L)\mathbf{H}]^T\mathbf{S}(\Theta_k\otimes L)\boldsymbol{y}_d
\end{aligned}$$

$$
\begin{aligned}
&+2a_k^2\mu^{-1}(\Delta \boldsymbol{u}_k)^T[(\Theta_k\otimes L)\mathbf{H}]^T\mathbf{S}\mathbf{L}\boldsymbol{v}_k \\
&-2a_k^2\mu^{-1}\boldsymbol{y}_d^T(\Theta_k\otimes L)^T\mathbf{S}\mathbf{L}\boldsymbol{v}_k. \qquad (3.18)
\end{aligned}
$$

We define $\mathcal{F}_k=\sigma\{u_1(t),\, x_i(0),\, \mu_i(t),\, v_i(t),\, 0\le t\le N,\, 1\le i\le k\}$ as an increasing σ-algebra representing the set of all events induced by random variables up to the kth iteration. Because the input for the kth iteration is generated using information from the previous iteration (i.e., the $(k-1)$th iteration), we have $\boldsymbol{u}_k\in\mathcal{F}_{k-1}$; that is, $\boldsymbol{u}_k$ is adapted to the σ-algebra $\mathcal{F}_{k-1}$. In addition, $\mu_k(t)$ and $v_k(t)$ occur randomly in the kth iteration; thus, they are both independent of $\mathcal{F}_{k-1}$ according to the conditions of fading gain and channel noise. Consequently, we have $\mathbb{E}[\mu_k(t)\mid\mathcal{F}_{k-1}]=\mu$, $\mathbb{E}[\theta_k(t)\mid\mathcal{F}_{k-1}]=0$, and $\mathbb{E}[v_k(t)\mid\mathcal{F}_{k-1}]=0$, which further implies that $\mathbb{E}[\Theta_k\mid\mathcal{F}_{k-1}]=0$ and $\mathbb{E}[\boldsymbol{v}_k\mid\mathcal{F}_{k-1}]=0$. Moreover, Θ_k and $\boldsymbol{v}_k$ are conditionally independent with respect to $\mathcal{F}_{k-1}$. In addition, the conditional variances of both $\theta_k(t)$ and $v_k(t)$ are bounded. These properties produce the following equalities:

$$
\begin{aligned}
&\mathbb{E}[(\Delta \boldsymbol{u}_k)^T\big([(\Theta_k\otimes L)\mathbf{H}]^T\mathbf{S} \\
&\qquad +\mathbf{S}(\Theta_k\otimes L)\mathbf{H}\big)(\Delta \boldsymbol{u}_k)\mid\mathcal{F}_{k-1}]=0, && (3.19)\\
&\mathbb{E}[(\Delta \boldsymbol{u}_k)^T\mathbf{S}(\Theta_k\otimes L)\boldsymbol{y}_d\mid\mathcal{F}_{k-1}]=0, && (3.20)\\
&\mathbb{E}[(\Delta \boldsymbol{u}_k)^T\mathbf{S}\mathbf{L}\boldsymbol{v}_k\mid\mathcal{F}_{k-1}]=0, && (3.21)\\
&\mathbb{E}[(\Delta \boldsymbol{u}_k)^T[\mathbf{L}\mathbf{H}]^T\mathbf{S}(\Theta_k\otimes L)\mathbf{H}\Delta \boldsymbol{u}_k\mid\mathcal{F}_{k-1}]=0, && (3.22)\\
&\mathbb{E}[(\Delta \boldsymbol{u}_k)^T[\mathbf{L}\mathbf{H}]^T\mathbf{S}(\Theta_k\otimes L)\boldsymbol{y}_d\mid\mathcal{F}_{k-1}]=0, && (3.23)\\
&\mathbb{E}[(\Delta \boldsymbol{u}_k)^T[\mathbf{L}\mathbf{H}]^T\mathbf{S}\mathbf{L}\boldsymbol{v}_k\mid\mathcal{F}_{k-1}]=0, && (3.24)\\
&\mathbb{E}[(\Delta \boldsymbol{u}_k)^T[(\Theta_k\otimes L)\mathbf{H}]^T\mathbf{S}\mathbf{L}\boldsymbol{v}_k\mid\mathcal{F}_{k-1}]=0, && (3.25)\\
&\mathbb{E}[\boldsymbol{y}_d^T(\Theta_k\otimes L)^T\mathbf{S}\mathbf{L}\boldsymbol{v}_k\mid\mathcal{F}_{k-1}]=0. && (3.26)
\end{aligned}
$$

Next, we consider the other items on the right-hand side (RHS) of (3.18). There exist $c_1>0$ and $c_2>0$ such that

$$
\begin{aligned}
&\mathbb{E}[(\Delta \boldsymbol{u}_k)^T(\mathbf{L}\mathbf{H})^T\mathbf{S}(\mathbf{L}\mathbf{H})\Delta \boldsymbol{u}_k\mid\mathcal{F}_{k-1}] \\
&\quad=(\Delta \boldsymbol{u}_k)^T(\mathbf{L}\mathbf{H})^T\mathbf{S}(\mathbf{L}\mathbf{H})\Delta \boldsymbol{u}_k \\
&\quad\le c_1(\Delta \boldsymbol{u}_k)^T\mathbf{S}\Delta \boldsymbol{u}_k=c_1V_k, && (3.27)\\
&\mathbb{E}[(\Delta \boldsymbol{u}_k)^T[(\Theta_k\otimes L)\mathbf{H}]^T\mathbf{S}(\Theta_k\otimes L)\mathbf{H}\Delta \boldsymbol{u}_k\mid\mathcal{F}_{k-1}] \\
&\quad\le(\mathbf{H}\Delta \boldsymbol{u}_k)^T\mathbb{E}[(\Theta_k\otimes L)^T\mathbf{S}(\Theta_k\otimes L)\mid\mathcal{F}_{k-1}]\mathbf{H}\Delta \boldsymbol{u}_k \\
&\quad\le c_2(\Delta \boldsymbol{u}_k)^T\mathbf{S}\Delta \boldsymbol{u}_k=c_2V_k. && (3.28)
\end{aligned}
$$

Noticing that the second-order moments of both Θ_k and $\boldsymbol{v}_k$ are bounded, we have

$$\mathbb{E}[\boldsymbol{y}_d^T(\Theta_k \otimes L)^T\mathbf{S}(\Theta_k \otimes L)\boldsymbol{y}_d \mid \mathcal{F}_{k-1}] \leq c_3, \tag{3.29}$$

$$\mathbb{E}[\boldsymbol{v}_k^T\mathbf{L}^T\mathbf{S}\mathbf{L}\boldsymbol{v}_k \mid \mathcal{F}_{k-1}] \leq c_4, \tag{3.30}$$

where $c_3 > 0$ and $c_4 > 0$ are suitable constants.

Using the Lyapunov equation (3.16), we obtain

$$\begin{aligned}&(\Delta\boldsymbol{u}_k)^T[(\mathbf{LH})^T\mathbf{S}+\mathbf{S}(\mathbf{LH})](\Delta\boldsymbol{u}_k)\\&=(\Delta\boldsymbol{u}_k)^T(\Delta\boldsymbol{u}_k) \geq c_5(\Delta\boldsymbol{u}_k)^T\mathbf{S}(\Delta\boldsymbol{u}_k) = c_5V_k,\end{aligned} \tag{3.31}$$

where c_5 is selected such that $I_{Np} \geq c_5\mathbf{S}$.

Because $\mathbf{S}$ is a positive-definite matrix, it can be written as $\mathbf{S} = \mathbf{S}^{\frac{1}{2}}\mathbf{S}^{\frac{1}{2}}$. Then, we have

$$\begin{aligned}&-2(\Delta\boldsymbol{u}_k)^T[(\Theta_k \otimes L)\mathbf{H}]^T\mathbf{S}(\Theta_k \otimes L)\boldsymbol{y}_d\\&\leq 2|\underbrace{(\Delta\boldsymbol{u}_k)^T[(\Theta_k \otimes L)\mathbf{H}]^T\mathbf{S}^{\frac{1}{2}}}_{\mathbf{a}^T}\underbrace{\mathbf{S}^{\frac{1}{2}}(\Theta_k \otimes L)\boldsymbol{y}_d}_{\mathbf{b}}|\\&\leq \underbrace{(\Delta\boldsymbol{u}_k)^T[(\Theta_k \otimes L)\mathbf{H}]^T\mathbf{S}(\Theta_k \otimes L)\mathbf{H}\Delta\boldsymbol{u}_k}_{\mathbf{a}^T\mathbf{a}}\\&\quad+\underbrace{\boldsymbol{y}_d^T(\Theta_k \otimes L)^T\mathbf{S}(\Theta_k \otimes L)\boldsymbol{y}_d}_{\mathbf{b}^T\mathbf{b}},\end{aligned} \tag{3.32}$$

which further leads to

$$\begin{aligned}&\mathbb{E}[-2(\Delta\boldsymbol{u}_k)^T[(\Theta_k \otimes L)\mathbf{H}]^T\mathbf{S}(\Theta_k \otimes L)\boldsymbol{y}_d \mid \mathcal{F}_{k-1}]\\&\leq c_2V_k + c_3.\end{aligned} \tag{3.33}$$

Combining (3.19)–(3.33) and (3.18) results in

$$\begin{aligned}&\mathbb{E}[V_{k+1} \mid \mathcal{F}_{k-1}]\\&= V_k - a_kc_5V_k + a_k^2(c_1+2c_2)V_k + a_k^2(2c_3+\mu^{-2}c_4).\end{aligned} \tag{3.34}$$

Taking the mathematical expectation of both sides of the above equation leads to

$$\begin{aligned}\mathbb{E}[V_{k+1}] \leq &(1-c_5a_k)\mathbb{E}[V_k]\\&+(c_1+2c_2)a_k^2\left(\frac{2c_3+\mu^{-2}c_4}{c_1+2c_2}+\mathbb{E}[V_k]\right).\end{aligned} \tag{3.35}$$

Comparing (3.35) and (A.1) reveals that m_k, α_1, α_2, and α_3 in (A.1) correspond to $\mathbb{E}[V_k]$, c_5, (c_1+2c_2), and $(2c_3+\mu^{-2}c_4)/(c_1+2c_2)$, respectively. Therefore, by Lemma A.1, it is evident that $\lim_{k\to\infty}\mathbb{E}[V_k]=0$. In addition, $\mathbf{S}$ is a positive-definite matrix; thus, $\mathbb{E}[\|\boldsymbol{u}_d-\boldsymbol{u}_k\|^2]\le\lambda_{\min}^{-1}(\mathbf{S})\mathbb{E}[V_k]$. This yields the conclusion that $\mathbb{E}[\|\boldsymbol{u}_d-\boldsymbol{u}_k\|^2]\to 0$ as $k\to\infty$. □

Theorem 3.1 demonstrates the asymptotic convergence of the generated input sequence to the desired control values as the iteration number increases in the mean-square sense. It should be noted that both output-dependent deviations and additive noise are accounted for (see (3.8)). The former is caused by the random fading gain, which is in multiplicative form, while the latter is caused by channel disturbances. Several remarks are provided below to facilitate an intuitive understanding.

Remark 3.2 *To avoid bounded growth analysis of the proposed algorithm, the output-dependent deviation $(\Theta_k\otimes I_q)\boldsymbol{y}_k$ is rewritten as the sum of $(\Theta_k\otimes L)\boldsymbol{y}_d$ and $(\Theta_k\otimes L)\boldsymbol{H}\Delta\boldsymbol{u}_k$ (cf.* (3.15)*). The former summand is output independent and can thus be analyzed similarly to additive noise, while the latter can be analyzed similarly to the original input error.*

Remark 3.3 *Several remarks are provided on the solution of the control direction regulation matrix, L. The mild condition of L involves ensuring all eigenvalues of LCB have positive real parts, which is comparatively more relaxed than the conventional contraction type condition, $\|I-LCB\|\le\gamma<1$. If B and C are available, a direct solution of L can be obtained by solving the linear matrix inequality: $LCB>0$. An intuitive solution is $L=\eta(CB)^T$, where $\eta>0$ is a tunable parameter. If B and C are unavailable, L can still be calculated based on the estimation of B and C, because the algorithm has the ability to tolerate a certain amount of model uncertainty.*

Remark 3.4 *A decreasing gain sequence, $\{a_k\}$, is introduced to suppress the effects of additive noise asymptotically. However, it must not decrease too rapidly, or precise tracking performance cannot be achieved. This observation leads to condition* (3.10)*. It should be noted that two problems arise in this design procedure. First, the convergence speed of the proposed algorithm with gain sequence $\{a_k\}$ may be slow; however, this is a sacrifice for guaranteeing precise tracking under various forms of randomness. If a_k is replaced by a small constant gain, such as ρ, the convergence speed may be increased. However, only bounded convergence of the input error can be ensured, where the upper bound of the final input error depends on the fading conditions μ and σ, additive noise variance R_t, and the constant learning* *gain ρ. The second design concern is that a gain sequence $\{a_k\}$ is defined independently of the actual operation process and is usually not optimal. A promising research idea along this direction can consider a self-regulated or event-triggered gain sequence, in which operation data is involved in design and analysis.*

Remark 3.5 *Because $\mathbb{E}[V_k] \to 0$ from Theorem 3.1, it is apparent that $\mathbb{E}[V_k]$ is bounded and $\sum_{k=1}^{\infty} a_k^2 \mathbb{E}[V_k] < \infty$. Then, taking the sum of (3.35) from $k = 1$ to ∞, we have*

$$\sum_{k=1}^{\infty} a_k \mathbb{E}[V_k] \leq c_5^{-1} \left\{ \mathbb{E}[V_1] + (c_1 + 2c_2) \sum_{k=1}^{\infty} a_k^2 \mathbb{E}[V_k] \right.$$
$$\left. + (2c_3 + \mu^{-2} c_4) \sum_{k=1}^{\infty} a_k^2 \right\} < \infty.$$

If the gain sequence satisfies $a_k \downarrow 0$, by the Kronecker lemma, we have

$$\lim_{k \to \infty} a_k \sum_{i=1}^{k} \mathbb{E}[V_i] = 0.$$

This limitation can provide a rough estimation of the convergence speed for the asymptotically averaging value of $\mathbb{E}[V_k]$ as follows:

$$\frac{1}{k} \sum_{i=1}^{k} \sqrt{\mathbb{E}[V_i]} \leq \frac{1}{\sqrt{k a_k}} \left(a_k \sum_{i=1}^{k} \mathbb{E}[V_i] \right)^{1/2} = o\left(\frac{1}{\sqrt{k a_k}} \right).$$

3.4 INPUT FADING CASE

In this section, we consider the case of input fading, in which the network from the controller to the plant suffers from random fading problem and involves additive noise. The network from the plant to the controller, however, functions well. In other words, the received tracking information for updating is precise; however, the received control signal for driving the system dynamics may heavily deviate from the generated signal. For practical applications, this deviation should be well handled.

3.4.1 Fading Effect Analysis

The generated input signal is denoted by $u_k(t)$, while the signal received by the plant is denoted by $u_k^{\circ}(t)$. According to the fading channel setting, we have

$$u_k^\circ(t) = \mu_k(t)u_k(t) + \nu_k(t). \tag{3.36}$$

As in the case of output fading, the received signal is corrected to reduce the biased gain effect before it is applied to the system dynamics:

$$u_k'(t) = \mu^{-1}u_k^\circ(t), \tag{3.37}$$

where $u_k'(t)$ is the corrected signal. Similarly to the case of output fading, we have

$$\begin{aligned} u_k'(t) &= \mu^{-1}\mu_k(t)u_k(t) + \mu^{-1}\nu_k(t) \\ &= u_k(t) - \left(1 - \frac{\mu_k}{\mu}\right)u_k(t) + \mu^{-1}\nu_k(t). \end{aligned} \tag{3.38}$$

Although the corrected signal, $u_k'(t)$, is unbiased with respect to the original input, it can still differ greatly from the actual value $u_k(t)$ due to two random disturbances. Because this signal is used to drive the dynamics, this fading effect is more significant than output fading. In particular, the effects of the fading channel on input data are as follows:

1) The term $\left(1 - \frac{\mu_k}{\mu}\right)u_k(t)$ is an input-dependent error with zero-mean and bounded second-order moment. As in the case of output fading, this term may lead to a linear growth problem in the convergence analysis of the learning algorithm. This problem should be addressed as it is for the case of output fading.

2) The term $\mu^{-1}\nu_k(t)$ has a similar effect to that in output fading. That is, the effect of additive noise should be asymptotically reduced in the learning algorithm to guarantee a stable convergence. Additionally, the variance of this term is affected by the mean inverse, μ^{-1}.

3) In addition to the above two items, the system dynamics can be greatly influenced by the random input signal, $u_k'(t)$, if no correction is performed. A direct consequence of applying this signal to the system is that the state will diverge, as demonstrated by the following equation:

$$\begin{aligned} x_k(t+1) &= Ax_k(t) + Bu_k'(t) \\ &= Ax_k(t) + \mu^{-1}B\mu_k(t)u_k(t) + \mu^{-1}B\nu_k(t). \end{aligned}$$

Incorrect data cannot only lead to unacceptable tracking performance but also negatively impact the learning process.

In summary, a specific synthesis method should be investigated for achieving improved tracking performance while ensuring stable convergence. Specifically, in addition to suppressing the effect of random noise in the learning algorithm, such as in the case of output fading, we should also provide an effective mechanism for improving the transient tracking performance as the iteration number increases. The details are discussed in the remainder of this section.

3.4.2 Learning Algorithm Design

To suppress the effect caused by random noise, we adopt a learning structure with a decreasing gain sequence,

$$u_{k+1}(t) = u_k(t) + a_k L e_k(t+1), \tag{3.39}$$

where $e_k(t) = y_d(t) - y_k(t)$ is the actual tracking error and $\{a_k\}$ satisfies (3.10). In addition, it is required that $a_j = a_k(1 + O(a_k))$, $\forall j = k-1, \ldots, k-m+1$. Because the actual output can be precisely transmitted in the case of input fading, the tracking error, $e_k(t)$, in (3.39) becomes available.

However, it should be noted that the input signal actually available for the plant is $u'_k(t)$ rather than $u_k(t)$. Using incorrect input $u'_k(t)$ would introduce unpredictable randomness into the system dynamics, leading to unacceptable transient performance. A possible method for resolving this problem involves filtering or smoothing the received signals by the averaging technique. To this end, we introduce a moving-average operator as follows:

$$\mathbb{A}[m_k] = \frac{1}{m} \sum_{i=1}^{m} m_{k+1-i}, \tag{3.40}$$

where m_k is a signal defined in the iteration-domain and m is the width of the moving window. Then, the control signal that is actually applied is defined as follows:

$$u_k^*(t) = \mathbb{A}[u'_k(t)] = \frac{1}{m} \sum_{i=1}^{m} u'_{k+1-i}(t). \tag{3.41}$$

Accordingly, the update law is modified from (3.39) as follows:

$$u_{k+1}(t) = \mathbb{A}[u_k(t)] + a_k L e_k(t+1), \tag{3.42}$$

where $e_k(t) = y_d(t) - y_k(t)$, and $y_k(t)$ is driven by $u_k^*(t)$.

Remark 3.6 *We note that the input signal employed in the learning algorithm* (3.42) *is* $\mathbb{A}[u_k(t)]$ *rather than* $u_k^*(t)$*, although it is the latter that is applied to the system. The reason for this is that* $u_k^*(t)$ *is not available to the controller, whereas* $\mathbb{A}[u_k(t)]$ *can be generated by the data stored in memory. The fundamental principle of* (3.42) *involves introducing a moving-average operator to smooth the input signal so that correspondence with the tracking error can be established; that is, the tracking error* $e_k(t+1)$ *in* (3.42) *is generated by* $u_k^*(t)$*, whose counterpart is* $\mathbb{A}[u_k(t)]$.

3.4.3 Convergence Analysis

This subsection presents the convergence of the proposed algorithm (3.42) with a decreasing gain sequence and a moving-average operator. To this end, the involved quantities are first lifted.

Substituting (3.41) into system (3.1), we have

$$\begin{aligned} x_k(t+1) &= Ax_k(t) + B\mathbb{A}[u_k'(t)] \\ &= Ax_k + \mu^{-1}B\frac{1}{m}\sum_{i=1}^{m}\mu_{k+1-i}(t)u_{k+1-i}(t) \\ &\quad + \mu^{-1}B\frac{1}{m}\sum_{i=1}^{m}v_{k+1-i}(t). \end{aligned} \tag{3.43}$$

Remark 3.7 *The concept of improving transient tracking performance using the average technique can be seen in* (3.43)*. Using additive noise as an example, according to the noise condition, the covariance of* $v_k(t)$ *is* R_t*, while the covariance of the smoothed noise in* (3.43) *is*

$$\begin{aligned} &\mathbb{E}\left[\left(\frac{1}{m}\sum_{i=1}^{m}v_{k+1-i}(t)\right)\left(\frac{1}{m}\sum_{i=1}^{m}v_{k+1-i}(t)\right)^T\right] \\ &= \frac{1}{m^2}\left[\sum_{i=1}^{m}\mathbb{E}v_{k+1-i}(t)v_{k+1-i}^T(t)\right] \\ &= \frac{1}{m^2}mR_t = \frac{1}{m}R_t \xrightarrow[m\to\infty]{} 0, \end{aligned} \tag{3.44}$$

where the iteration-domain-based independence of $v_k(t)$ *is applied. It can be seen that a larger value of m corresponds to an improved smoothing effect of random noise. However, a larger m also involves a greater amount of obsolete information, which reduces the convergence speed. Therefore, there exists a trade-off for the practical selection of window width, m. The smoothing effect on randomness caused by random fading gain can be analyzed similarly. This intuitive calculation illustrates the fundamental principle of the moving-average operator.*

Returning to (3.43), it can be seen that

$$\begin{aligned} \boldsymbol{y}_k = & \frac{1}{\mu m}\mathbf{H}\sum_{i=1}^{m}(\Xi_{k+1-i}\otimes I_p)\boldsymbol{u}_{k+1-i} \\ & +\frac{1}{\mu m}\mathbf{H}\sum_{i=1}^{m}\boldsymbol{v}_{k+1-i}+\mathbf{M}x_k(0), \end{aligned} \tag{3.45}$$

where $\Xi_k = \text{diag}\{\mu_k(0),\dots,\mu_k(N-1)\} \in \mathbf{R}^{N\times N}$. We denote $\boldsymbol{\Xi}_k \triangleq \Xi_{k+1-i}\otimes I_p$ for notation simplicity.

Therefore, the tracking error for the kth iteration is

$$\boldsymbol{e}_k = \mathbf{H}\boldsymbol{u}_d - \frac{1}{\mu m}\mathbf{H}\sum_{i=1}^{m}\boldsymbol{\Xi}_{k+1-i}\boldsymbol{u}_{k+1-i} - \frac{1}{\mu m}\mathbf{H}\sum_{i=1}^{m}\boldsymbol{v}_{k+1-i}. \tag{3.46}$$

The second result of this chapter is presented below.

Theorem 3.2 *Consider system* (3.1) *with input fading channels and assume that Assumptions 3.1 and 3.2 hold. Apply the learning algorithm* (3.42) *with a decreasing gain sequence satisfying* (3.10) *and* $a_j = a_k(1+O(a_k))$, $\forall j = k-1,\dots,k-m+1$. *If control direction regulation matrix L is designed such that all eigenvalues of LCB have positive real parts, then the input sequence generated by* (3.42) *converges asymptotically in the mean-square sense to the desired value* $u_d(t)$. *That is,* $\mathbb{E}[\|\boldsymbol{u}_d - \boldsymbol{u}_k\|^2] \to 0$ *as* $k \to \infty$. *As a consequence, the tracking error converges to bounded zone in the mean-square sense, where the upper bound of the convergent zone can be tuned by the moving window width m.*

Proof: Considering learning algorithm (3.42), we have

$$\boldsymbol{u}_{k+1} = \mathbb{A}[\boldsymbol{u}_k] + a_k\mathbf{L}\boldsymbol{e}_k = \frac{1}{m}\sum_{i=1}^{m}\boldsymbol{u}_{k+1-i} + a_k\mathbf{L}\boldsymbol{e}_k. \tag{3.47}$$

Subtracting both sides of the above equation from $\boldsymbol{u}_d$, we obtain

$$\Delta\boldsymbol{u}_{k+1} = \frac{1}{m}\sum_{i=1}^{m}\Delta\boldsymbol{u}_{k+1-i} - a_k\mathbf{L}\boldsymbol{e}_k$$

$$
\begin{aligned}
&= \underbrace{\frac{1}{m}\sum_{i=1}^{m}\Delta \boldsymbol{u}_{k+1-i}}_{\triangleq \xi_{1,k}} - \underbrace{\frac{a_k}{m}\mathbf{LH}\sum_{i=1}^{m}\Delta \boldsymbol{u}_{k+1-i}}_{\triangleq \xi_{2,k}} \\
&\quad + \underbrace{\frac{a_k}{m}\mathbf{LH}\sum_{i=1}^{m}\boldsymbol{\Xi}_{k+1-i}\Delta \boldsymbol{u}_{k+1-i}}_{\triangleq \xi_{3,k}} \\
&\quad - \underbrace{\frac{a_k}{m}\mathbf{LH}\sum_{i=1}^{m}\boldsymbol{\Xi}_{k+1-i}\boldsymbol{u}_d}_{\triangleq \xi_{4,k}} + \underbrace{\frac{a_k}{\mu m}\mathbf{LH}\sum_{i=1}^{m}\boldsymbol{v}_{k+1-i}}_{\triangleq \xi_{5,k}}.
\end{aligned}
\tag{3.48}
$$

As in the case of output fading, we define $\mathbf{S}$ satisfying (3.16) and employ the following Lyapunov function:

$$
V_k = (\Delta \boldsymbol{u}_k)^T\mathbf{S}(\Delta \boldsymbol{u}_k). \tag{3.49}
$$

Then, we have

$$
\begin{aligned}
V_{k+1} &= (\Delta \boldsymbol{u}_{k+1})^T\mathbf{S}(\Delta \boldsymbol{u}_{k+1}) \\
&= \sum_{i=1}^{5}\xi_{i,k}^T\mathbf{S}\xi_{i,k} + \sum_{i\neq j}\xi_{i,k}^T\mathbf{S}\xi_{j,k}.
\end{aligned}
\tag{3.50}
$$

Next, we provide a detailed estimation of the terms on the RHS of (3.50). First, we have

$$
\begin{aligned}
\xi_{1,k}^T\mathbf{S}\xi_{1,k} &= \frac{1}{m^2}\left(\sum_{i=1}^{m}\Delta \boldsymbol{u}_{k+1-i}\right)^T\mathbf{S}\left(\sum_{i=1}^{m}\Delta \boldsymbol{u}_{k+1-i}\right) \\
&\le \frac{1}{m^2}m\left(\sum_{i=1}^{m}\Delta \boldsymbol{u}_{k+1-i}^T\mathbf{S}\Delta \boldsymbol{u}_{k+1-i}\right) \\
&= \frac{1}{m}\sum_{i=1}^{m}V_{k+1-i}, \\
\xi_{2,k}^T\mathbf{S}\xi_{2,k} &= \frac{a_k^2}{m^2}\left(\mathbf{LH}\sum_{i=1}^{m}\Delta \boldsymbol{u}_{k+1-i}\right)^T\mathbf{S}\left(\mathbf{LH}\sum_{i=1}^{m}\Delta \boldsymbol{u}_{k+1-i}\right) \\
&\le \frac{a_k^2}{m^2}\left(\sum_{i=1}^{m}\Delta \boldsymbol{u}_{k+1-i}\right)^T[\mathbf{LH}]^T\mathbf{SLH}\left(\sum_{i=1}^{m}\Delta \boldsymbol{u}_{k+1-i}\right)
\end{aligned}
$$

$$
\begin{aligned}
&\leq c_1 \frac{a_k^2}{m^2} \left(\sum_{i=1}^{m} \Delta \boldsymbol{u}_{k+1-i} \right)^T \mathbf{S} \left(\sum_{i=1}^{m} \Delta \boldsymbol{u}_{k+1-i} \right) \\
&\leq c_1 a_k^2 \left(\frac{1}{m} \sum_{i=1}^{m} V_{k+1-i} \right), \\
\xi_{3,k}^T \mathbf{S} \xi_{3,k} &= \frac{a_k^2}{m^2} \left(\mathbf{LH} \sum_{i=1}^{m} \boldsymbol{\Xi}_{k+1-i} \Delta \boldsymbol{u}_{k+1-i} \right)^T \mathbf{S} \left(\mathbf{LH} \sum_{i=1}^{m} \boldsymbol{\Xi}_{k+1-i} \Delta \boldsymbol{u}_{k+1-i} \right) \\
&\leq c_1 \frac{a_k^2}{m^2} \left(\sum_{i=1}^{m} \boldsymbol{\Xi}_{k+1-i} \Delta \boldsymbol{u}_{k+1-i} \right)^T \mathbf{S} \left(\sum_{i=1}^{m} \boldsymbol{\Xi}_{k+1-i} \Delta \boldsymbol{u}_{k+1-i} \right) \\
&\leq c_1 \frac{a_k^2}{m^2} m \left(\sum_{i=1}^{m} \Delta \boldsymbol{u}_{k+1-i}^T \boldsymbol{\Xi}_{k+1-i}^T \mathbf{S} \boldsymbol{\Xi}_{k+1-i} \Delta \boldsymbol{u}_{k+1-i} \right) \\
&\leq c_2 a_k^2 \left(\frac{1}{m} \sum_{i=1}^{m} V_{k+1-i} \right), \\
\xi_{4,k}^T \mathbf{S} \xi_{4,k} &= \frac{a_k^2}{m^2} \left(\mathbf{LH} \sum_{i=1}^{m} \boldsymbol{\Xi}_{k+1-i} \boldsymbol{u}_d \right)^T \mathbf{S} \left(\mathbf{LH} \sum_{i=1}^{m} \boldsymbol{\Xi}_{k+1-i} \boldsymbol{u}_d \right) \\
&\leq c_2 \frac{a_k^2}{m} \left(\sum_{i=1}^{m} \boldsymbol{u}_d^T \mathbf{S} \boldsymbol{u}_d \right) \\
&\leq c_3 a_k^2, \\
\xi_{5,k}^T \mathbf{S} \xi_{5,k} &= \frac{a_k^2}{m^2} \left(\mathbf{LH} \sum_{i=1}^{m} \boldsymbol{v}_{k+1-i} \right)^T \mathbf{S} \left(\mathbf{LH} \sum_{i=1}^{m} \boldsymbol{v}_{k+1-i} \right) \\
&\leq c_1 \frac{a_k^2}{m^2} \left(\sum_{i=1}^{m} \boldsymbol{v}_{k+1-i} \right)^T \mathbf{S} \left(\sum_{i=1}^{m} \boldsymbol{v}_{k+1-i} \right) \\
&\leq c_1 \frac{a_k^2}{m} \left(\sum_{i=1}^{m} \boldsymbol{v}_{k+1-i}^T \mathbf{S} \boldsymbol{v}_{k+1-i} \right),
\end{aligned}
$$

where c_1, c_2, and c_3 are suitable constants. In addition,

$$
\mathbb{E}[\xi_{5,k}^T \mathbf{S} \xi_{5,k}] \leq c_1 \frac{a_k^2}{m} \left(\sum_{i=1}^{m} \mathbb{E}[\boldsymbol{v}_{k+1-i}^T \mathbf{S} \boldsymbol{v}_{k+1-i}] \right) \leq c_4 a_k^2.
$$

We then verify the cross terms, first considering the cross term with $\xi_{1,k}$:

$$\begin{aligned}
2\xi_{1,k}^T \mathbf{S}\xi_{2,k} &= \frac{a_k}{m^2}\left(\sum_{i=1}^m \Delta\boldsymbol{u}_{k+1-i}\right)^T \big[\mathbf{S}(\mathbf{LH}) \\
&\quad + (\mathbf{LH})^T\mathbf{S}\big]\left(\sum_{i=1}^m \Delta\boldsymbol{u}_{k+1-i}\right) \\
&= \frac{a_k}{m^2}\left(\sum_{i=1}^m \Delta\boldsymbol{u}_{k+1-i}\right)^T \left(\sum_{i=1}^m \Delta\boldsymbol{u}_{k+1-i}\right) \\
&\geq c_5\frac{a_k}{m^2}\left(\sum_{i=1}^m \Delta\boldsymbol{u}_{k+1-i}\right)^T \mathbf{S}\left(\sum_{i=1}^m \Delta\boldsymbol{u}_{k+1-i}\right) \\
&= c_5 a_k \xi_{1,k}^T \mathbf{S}\xi_{1,k}.
\end{aligned}$$

Then, paying attention to the individual terms in

$$\begin{aligned}
2\xi_{1,k}^T \mathbf{S}\xi_{3,k} &= \frac{2a_k}{m^2}\left(\sum_{i=1}^m \Delta\boldsymbol{u}_{k+1-i}\right)^T \mathbf{S} \\
&\quad \times \left(\mathbf{LH}\sum_{i=1}^m \Xi_{k+1-i}\Delta\boldsymbol{u}_{k+1-i}\right) \\
&= \frac{2a_k}{m^2}\left(\sum_{1\leq i,j\leq m} \Delta\boldsymbol{u}_{k+1-i}^T \mathbf{SLH}\Xi_{k+1-j}\Delta\boldsymbol{u}_{k+1-j}\right),
\end{aligned}$$

we detect two cases to be addressed. If $i \geq j$, then the mathematical expectation of $\Delta\boldsymbol{u}_{k+1-i}\mathbf{SLH}\Xi_{k+1-j}\Delta\boldsymbol{u}_{k+1-j}$ is zero because Ξ_{k+1-j} is independent of all other quantities. Otherwise, $\Delta\boldsymbol{u}_{k+1-i}$ contains information related to Ξ_{k+1-j}, which leads the expectation of the corresponding terms to be bounded by $\sum_{i=1}^m V_{k+1-i}$. Therefore, it can be concluded that for suitable constant c_6,

$$\mathbb{E}[2\xi_{1,k}^T \mathbf{S}\xi_{3,k}] \leq c_6\frac{2a_k^2}{m}\left(\frac{1}{m}\sum_{i=1}^m V_{k+1-i}\right),$$

where a_k in the coefficient results from the expansion of $\Delta\boldsymbol{u}_{k+1-i}$ (we note that m is a finite number while being fixed). A Similar estimation applies to $2\xi_{1,k}^T \mathbf{S}\xi_{4,k}$ and $2\xi_{1,k}^T \mathbf{S}\xi_{5,k}$; the repetition is omitted for the sake of brevity.

For the left cross terms, because $\xi_{2,k}$ is similar to $\xi_{1,k}$ with left-multiplied matrix **LH** and coefficient a_k, the estimation of $\xi_{2,k}^T\mathbf{S}\xi_{i,k}$ $(3 \le i \le 5)$ is similar to that of $\xi_{1,k}^T\mathbf{S}\xi_{i,k}$. That is, there exists $c_7 > 0$ such that

$$\mathbb{E}[2\xi_{2,k}^T\mathbf{S}\xi_{i,k}] \le c_7\frac{2a_k^2}{m}\left(\frac{1}{m}\sum_{i=1}^{m}V_{k+1-i}\right), \quad 3 \le i \le 5.$$

In addition, we have

$$\begin{aligned}
2\xi_{3,k}^T\mathbf{S}\xi_{4,k} &\le \xi_{3,k}^T\mathbf{S}\xi_{3,k} + \xi_{4,k}^T\mathbf{S}\xi_{4,k} \\
&\le c_2a_k^2\left(\frac{1}{m}\sum_{i=1}^{m}V_{k+1-i}\right) + c_3a_k^2, \\
2\xi_{3,k}^T\mathbf{S}\xi_{5,k} &\le \xi_{3,k}^T\mathbf{S}\xi_{3,k} + \xi_{5,k}^T\mathbf{S}\xi_{5,k} \\
&\le c_2a_k^2\left(\frac{1}{m}\sum_{i=1}^{m}V_{k+1-i}\right) \\
&\quad + c_1\frac{a_k^2}{m}\left(\sum_{i=1}^{m}\mathbf{v}_{k+1-i}^T\mathbf{S}\mathbf{v}_{k+1-i}\right), \\
2\xi_{4,k}^T\mathbf{S}\xi_{5,k} &\le \xi_{4,k}^T\mathbf{S}\xi_{4,k} + \xi_{5,k}^T\mathbf{S}\xi_{5,k} \\
&\le c_3a_k^2 + c_1\frac{a_k^2}{m}\left(\sum_{i=1}^{m}\mathbf{v}_{k+1-i}^T\mathbf{S}\mathbf{v}_{k+1-i}\right).
\end{aligned}$$

Taking the mathematical expectation of both sides of (3.50) and substituting all of the inequalities listed below (3.50), we obtain

$$\begin{aligned}
\mathbb{E}[V_{k+1}] &= \sum_{i=1}^{5}\mathbb{E}[\xi_{i,k}^T\mathbf{S}\xi_{i,k}] + \sum_{i\neq j}\mathbb{E}[\xi_{i,k}^T\mathbf{S}\xi_{j,k}] \\
&\le (1 - c_5a_k)\,\mathbb{E}[\xi_{1,k}^T\mathbf{S}\xi_{1,k}] \\
&\quad + r_1a_k^2\left(\frac{1}{m}\sum_{i=1}^{m}\mathbb{E}[V_{k+1-i}]\right) + r_2a_k^2 \\
&\le (1 - c_5a_k + r_1a_k^2)\left(\frac{1}{m}\sum_{i=1}^{m}\mathbb{E}[V_{k+1-i}]\right) \\
&\quad + r_2a_k^2,
\end{aligned} \tag{3.51}$$

where $r_1 = c_1 + 3c_2 + 6(c_6 + c_7)/m$ and $r_2 = 3c_3 + 3c_4$.

It is clear that for a sufficiently large iteration number, it holds that $1 - c_5a_k + r_1a_k^2 < 1$. We denote $\rho_k \triangleq 1 - c_5a_k + r_1a_k^2$. From (3.51), we have

$$\begin{aligned}\mathbb{E}[V_{k+1}] &\leq \rho_k \left(\frac{1}{m} \sum_{i=1}^{m} \mathbb{E}[V_{k+1-i}] \right) + r_2 a_k^2 \\ &\leq \rho_k \max_{1\leq i\leq m} \{\mathbb{E}[V_{k+1-i}]\} + r_2 a_k^2. \end{aligned} \tag{3.52}$$

We then proceed to derive the following inequality,

$$\begin{aligned}\mathbb{E}[V_{k+2}] &\leq \rho_{k+1} \max_{1\leq i\leq m} \{\mathbb{E}[V_{k+2-i}]\} + r_2 a_{k+1}^2 \\ &\leq \rho_{k+1} \max \left\{ \mathbb{E}[V_{k+1}], \max_{1\leq i\leq m} \{\mathbb{E}[V_{k+1-i}]\} \right\} + r_2 a_{k+1}^2 \\ &\leq \rho_{k+1} \max \left\{ \rho_k \max_{1\leq i\leq m} \{\mathbb{E}[V_{k+1-i}]\} + r_2 a_k^2, \right. \\ &\qquad \left. \max_{1\leq i\leq m} \{\mathbb{E}[V_{k+1-i}]\} \right\} + r_2 a_{k+1}^2 \\ &\leq \rho_{k+1} \max_{1\leq i\leq m} \{\mathbb{E}[V_{k+1-i}]\} + r_2 a_k^2 + r_2 a_{k+1}^2. \end{aligned}$$

Similarly, $\forall 3 \leq j \leq m$,

$$\mathbb{E}[V_{k+j}] \leq \rho_{k+j-1} \max_{1\leq i\leq m} \{\mathbb{E}[V_{k+1-i}]\} + r_2 \sum_{i=0}^{j-1} a_{k+i}^2. \tag{3.53}$$

Assuming $a_k \downarrow 0$, we draw the following conclusion:

$$\begin{aligned}&\max_{1\leq i\leq m} \{\mathbb{E}[V_{k+i}]\} \\ &\leq \rho_{k+m-1} \max_{1\leq i\leq m} \{\mathbb{E}[V_{k+1-i}]\} + r_2 \sum_{i=0}^{m-1} a_{k+i}^2 \\ &\leq \rho_{k+m-1} \max_{1\leq i\leq m} \{\mathbb{E}[V_{k+1-i}]\} + m r_2 a_{k+m-1}^2. \end{aligned} \tag{3.54}$$

By Lemma A.1, we obtain $\lim_{k\to\infty} \max_{1\leq i\leq m} \mathbb{E}[V_{k+i}] = 0$ by grouping iterations for every m successive iterations, which further implies that $\lim_{k\to\infty} \mathbb{E}[V_k] = 0$. Because $\mathbf{S}$ is a positive-definite matrix, $\mathbb{E}[\|\boldsymbol{u}_d - \boldsymbol{u}_k\|^2] \to 0$ as $k \to \infty$.

In addition, from (3.46),

$$\boldsymbol{e}_k = \frac{1}{m} \mathbf{H} \sum_{i=1}^{m} \mu^{-1} \boldsymbol{\Xi}_{k+1-i} \Delta \boldsymbol{u}_{k+1-i}$$

$$+\frac{1}{m}\mathbf{H}\sum_{i=1}^{m}\Xi_{k+1-i}\boldsymbol{u}_d-\frac{1}{\mu m}\mathbf{H}\sum_{i=1}^{m}\boldsymbol{v}_{k+1-i}.$$

It can be seen that the upper bound of $\mathbb{E}[\|\boldsymbol{e}_k\|^2]$ depends on the last two terms on the RHS of the above equation, which can be reduced by enlarging the width m. This completes the proof. □

Theorem 3.2 reveals that introducing a moving-average operator does not affect the asymptotic convergence property but greatly reduces fluctuations in transient output signals. The convergence speed is not clearly specified for the algorithm with a moving-average operator; in other words, the operator may decrease or increase the convergence speed. This issue is discussed in the simulation.

Remark 3.8 *The input fading case is significantly more complex than the output fading case, and the reasons for this are as follows. First, an input fading channel introduces randomness at different locations, as can be seen from a comparison between* (3.48) *and* (3.15)*. Moreover, the input fading channel employs a moving-average operator for reducing the disturbances caused by incorrect input signals. This process introduces a great amount of complexity. In addition, the average operator in the learning algorithm* (3.42) *further introduces a correlation effect among different terms, also leading to difficulty in convergence analysis.*

Remark 3.9 *Output and input fading are addressed in Sections 3.3 and 3.4, respectively, to reveal effects of different fading sides. A question that remains is whether the results are applicable to a general two-sided fading scenario. The answer is affirmative, provided that the schemes in Sections 3.3 and 3.4 are combined. We outline an integrated framework as follows. The computed input is $u_k(t)$, while the input that is actually applied is $u_k^*(t)$ (see* (3.41)*). The system output, $y_k(t)$, is driven by $u_k^*(t)$, which cannot be used for updating due to output fading; the modified tracking error, $\varepsilon_k(t)$, defined in Subsection 3.3.2 is thus adopted. As a result, the combined learning algorithm is as follows:*

$$u_{k+1}(t)=\mathbb{A}[u_k(t)]+a_kL\varepsilon_k(t+1).$$

The convergence of this combined scheme can be performed in the same manner as in the above theorems; it is thus omitted for brevity.

3.5 ILLUSTRATIVE SIMULATIONS

In this section, we present two simulations to verify the theoretical results. The first simulation is a numerical example for MIMO systems, and the second is a discretized DC-motor model.

3.5.1 MIMO Numerical Example

We consider a MIMO system (A_t, B_t, C_t) with

$$A_t = \begin{bmatrix} 0.05\sin 0.2t & -0.2 & 0.02t \\ 0.1 & -0.01t & -0.02\cos 0.5t \\ 0.1 & 0.1 & 0.2+0.05\cos 0.2t \end{bmatrix},$$

$$B_t = \begin{bmatrix} 1-0.2\sin^2(0.5\pi t) & 0 \\ 0.01t & 0.01t \\ 0 & 1+0.1\sin(0.5\pi t) \end{bmatrix},$$

$$C_t = \begin{bmatrix} 0.2+0.1\sin^2(0.5\pi t) & 0.1 & -0.1 \\ 0 & 0.1 & 0.2-0.1\sin(0.5\pi t) \end{bmatrix}.$$

The operation length is $N = 50$, and the initial state is assumed to be $x_k(0) = x_d(0) = 0$ according to A3.2. The random fading channel is modeled by Gaussian distribution variables. For multiplicative fading gain $\mu_k(t)$, $\mu_k(t) \sim N(\mu, \sigma^2)$ with $\mu = 0.95$ and $\sigma = 0.1$. The effects of μ and σ are demonstrated later. For additive noise $v_k(t)$, we set $v_{k,i}(t) \sim N(0, 0.1^2)$.

The desired reference is $y_d(t) = 0.7\sin(t/3) + 0.5(1-\cos(t/4)), 0 \le t \le 50$ for both dimensions of the output vector.

The control direction regulation matrix in the algorithm is as follows:

$$L_t = \begin{bmatrix} 9.1632-0.2\sin(0.5\pi t) & 2.6493 \\ -0.5297 & 2.87-0.1\sin(0.5\pi t) \end{bmatrix},$$

and the decreasing gain is set to $1/k^\beta$ with $\beta = 0.55$ (see (3.10) and Remark 3.1). The moving window width for the input fading case is set to $m = 6$. The effects of both β and m will be demonstrated later in this subsection. The algorithm is run for 60 iterations for each case below. Because an MIMO system with two-dimensional input and two-dimensional output is considered, we primarily present the corresponding profiles for the second dimension for clarity; the profiles for the first dimension are similar.

The output tracking performance is demonstrated in Fig. 3.2. In Fig. 3.2(a) and (b), the output profiles at the 6th and 60th iterations and the desired reference are plotted in a dash-dotted line, dashed line, and solid line,

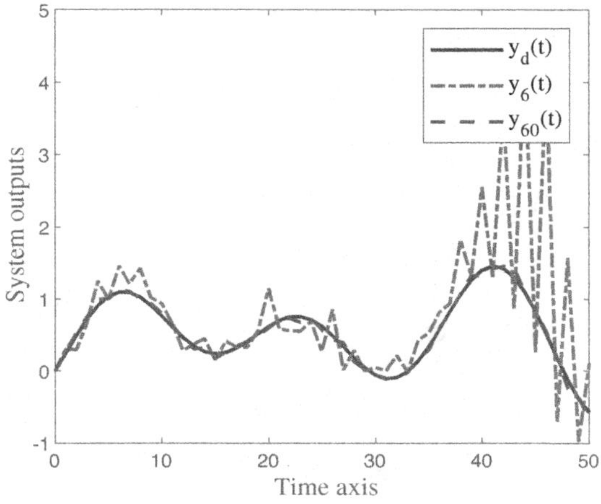

(a) Output case

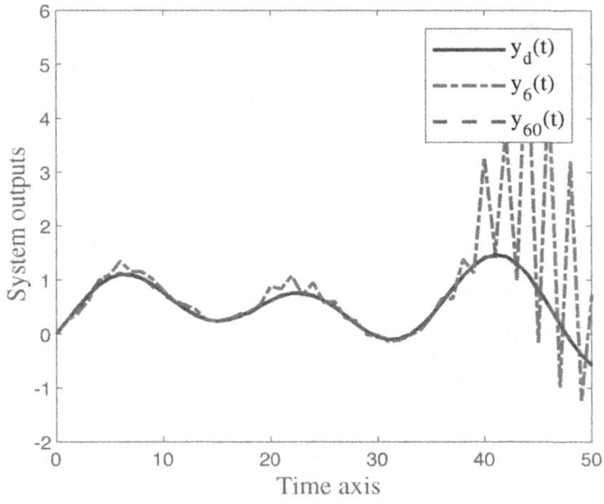

(b) Input case

Figure 3.2 Output profiles at the 6th and 60th iterations, and the desired reference for the second dimension: (a) Output fading case and (b) input fading case.

respectively. It can be seen that the output profiles at the 6th iteration have distinct fluctuations away from the desired reference, implying that the tracking performance is unacceptable. In contrast, the output profiles at the 60th iteration are almost coincident with the desired reference, demonstrating a satisfactory tracking performance following several learning iterations.

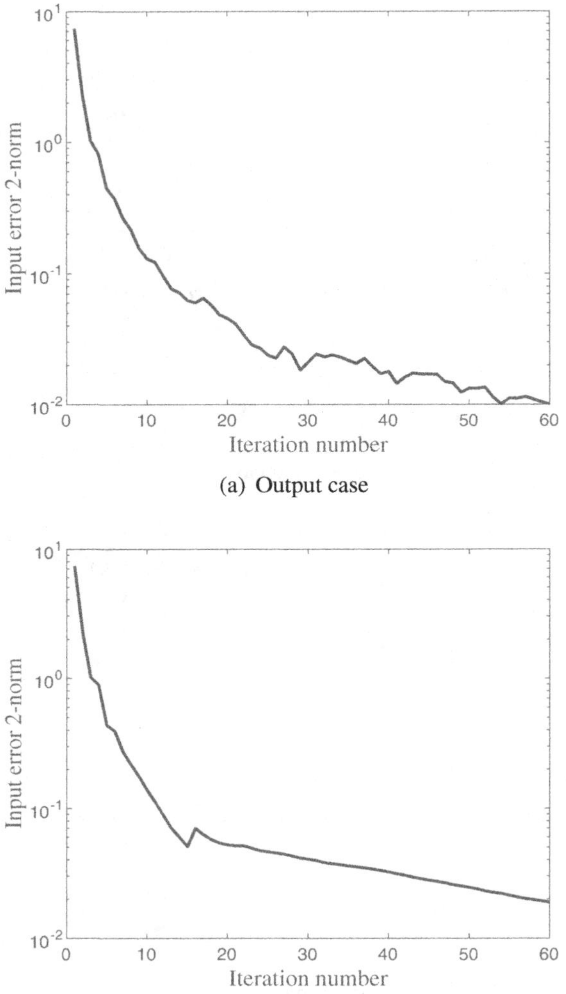

(a) Output case

(b) Input case

Figure 3.3 Accumulative square input error for the second dimension (a) output fading case and (b) input fading case.

The accumulative squared input errors for the second dimension, defined by $\sum_{t=0}^{N-1}(u_d^{(2)}(t) - u_k^{(2)}(t))^2$, are presented in Fig. 3.3(a) and 3.3(b) for the cases of output fading and input fading, respectively. It can be seen that the input error decreases quickly in both cases. These observations illustrate the effectiveness of the proposed algorithms for handling fading signals.

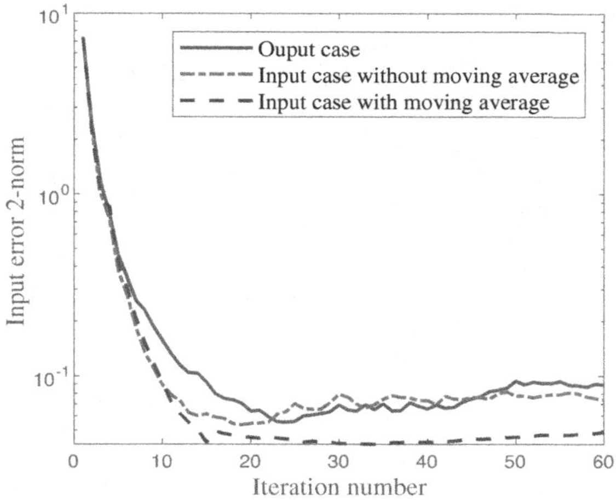

Figure 3.4 Input error profiles without fading correction.

To demonstrate the role of the fading correction and moving-average-operator in the proposed algorithm, we simulate the case of fading-agnostic procedure. Two observations can be noted if the fading channel is neglected. First, the fading correction term, μ^{-1}, should be removed from (3.7) and (3.37). Second, the moving-average operator is no longer required. The results are demonstrated in Fig. 3.4. It can be seen that both the output and input fading cases demonstrate a divergent trend after several iterations. However, retaining a moving-average operator in the algorithm may decrease the divergence speed.

The impact of selecting different decreasing gain sequences on convergence speed is discussed below. The decreasing gain sequence is usually set to $a_k = \alpha/k^\beta$, with $1/2 < \beta < 1$ and $\alpha > 0$. Here, we consider three variations: $\alpha = 1$ and $\beta = 0.55$, $\alpha = 1$ and $\beta = 0.75$, and $\alpha = 0.5$ and $\beta = 0.55$. The corresponding input error profiles along the iteration axis for the second dimension of the input are plotted in Fig. 3.5(a) and (b) for output fading and input fading, respectively. In this figure, the three variants are represented by a solid, dash-dotted, and dashed line. For both output fading and input fading, it can be seen that a larger α and smaller β may lead to a faster convergence speed. The reason for this may lie in the fact that this selection applies a large correction to the update algorithm with new information.

Moreover, we are interested in the effect of different fading distributions on the convergence property. To this end, we consider three distributions of

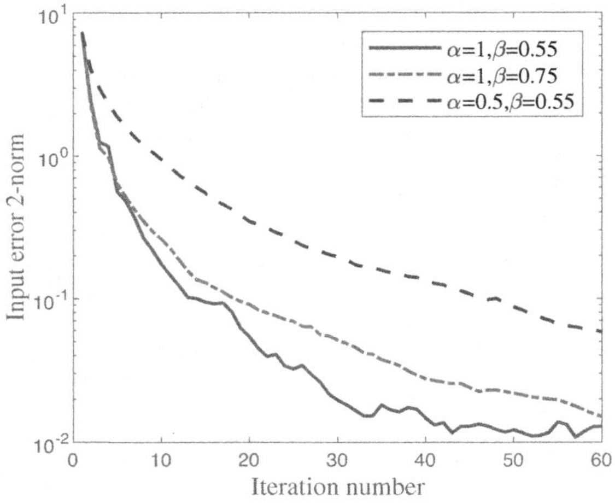

(a) Output case

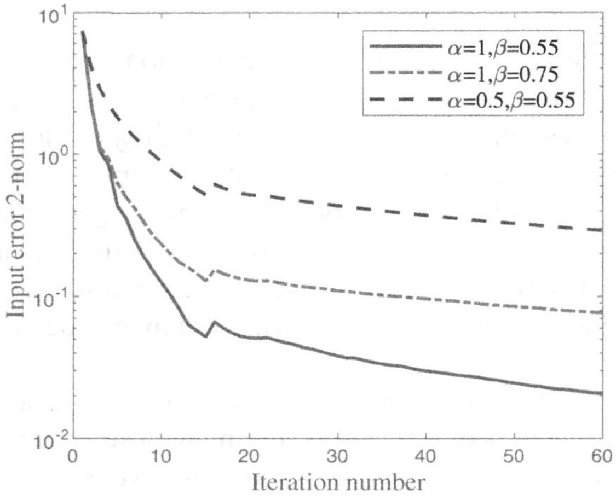

(b) Input case

Figure 3.5 Input error profiles for different decreasing gain sequences: (a) Output fading case and (b) input fading case.

the fading gain, $\mu_k(t)$, as follows: $\mu = 0.95$ and $\sigma = 0.1$, $\mu = 0.85$ and $\sigma = 1$, and $\mu = 0.95$ and $\sigma = 0.05$. The results for both output fading and input fading are presented in Fig. 3.6(a) and (b), respectively. It can be seen that the input error profiles are similar to each other for different distribution settings, implying that the fading distributions may have an effect on convergence

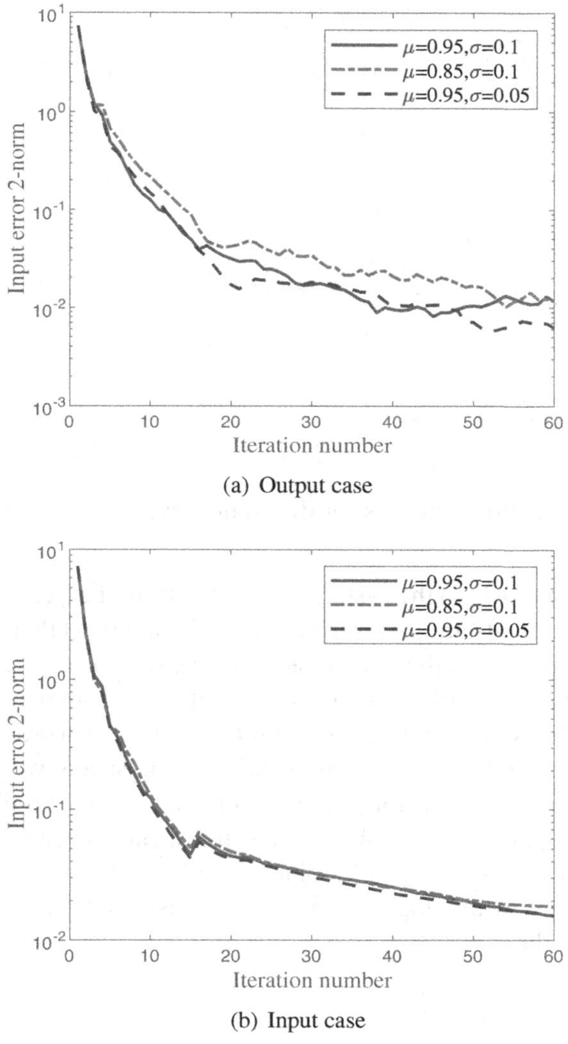

Figure 3.6 Input error profiles for different fading distributions: (a) Output fading case and (b) input fading case.

speed, albeit not a very significant one. This result also implies that the proposed algorithms can effectively handle fading uncertainties.

In addition, we have mentioned in Section 3.4 that the moving window width, m, affects convergence performance; it is unknown whether a trade-off exists for an optimal value. Therefore, we simulate algorithm (3.42) and

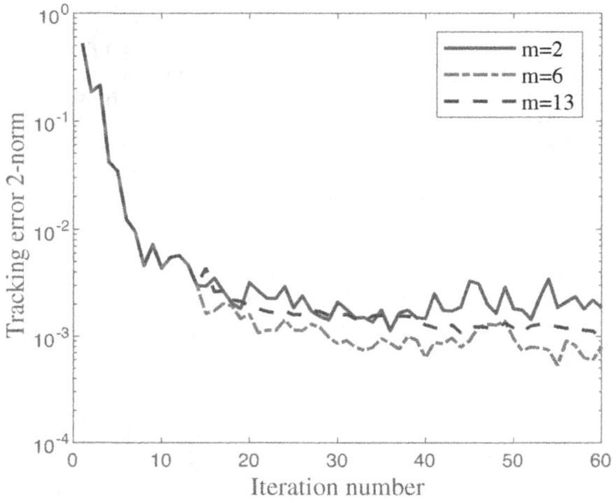

Figure 3.7 Tracking error profiles for different moving window widths.

apply the input in (3.41) to the system for three different cases: $m = 2$, $m = 6$, and $m = 13$. The results are presented in Fig. 3.7 and reveal that the case with $m = 6$ is superior to the other two cases. The reason for this result is that a smaller value of m is unable to reduce the effect of random deviations, while a larger value slows down the learning process. In other words, there exists a trade-off between deviation reduction and learning speed, which motivates us to select a suitable width for practical applications. Generally, the range of width m is suggested to be 4–7 according to our experience. It should be noted that the lines in Fig. 3.7 coincide with each other for the first 15 iterations because no moving-average operator is imposed at this stage to obtain the initial data.

3.5.2 DC-Motor Example

In this subsection, a scenario taken from [66] regarding a DC motor driving a single rigid link through a gear is used as an example. The dynamics are expressed as the following second-order differential equation:

$$(J_m + \frac{J_l}{n^2})\ddot{\theta}_m + (B_m + \frac{B_l}{n^2})\dot{\theta}_m + \frac{Mgl}{n}\sin(\frac{\theta_m}{n}) = u \tag{3.55}$$

where the notations are described as follows: J_m represents motor inertia, B_m represents the motor damping coefficient, θ_m represents the motor angle, J_l represents the link inertia, B_l represents the link damping coefficient, θ_l

represents the link angle with $\theta_l = \theta_m/n$, n represents the gear ratio, u represents the motor torque, M represents the lumped mass, g represents the gravitational acceleration, and l represents the center of mass from the axis of motion.

By Euler's approximation, a discrete-time state-space expression can be obtained, where sate and output are $x = (x_1, x_2)^T = (\theta_m, \dot{\theta}_m)^T$ and $y = \dot{\theta}_l$, respectively. The system function and matrices are

$$f(x,t) = \begin{bmatrix} x_1(t) + \Delta x_2(t) \\ x_2(t) + \frac{\Delta}{J_m + J_l/n^2}\Big[-(B_m + \frac{B_l}{n^2})x_2(t) \\ \qquad -\frac{Mgl}{n}\sin\left(\frac{x_1(t)}{n}\right)\Big] \end{bmatrix}$$

$$B = \begin{bmatrix} 0 \\ \frac{\Delta}{J_m + J_l/n^2} \end{bmatrix}, \quad C = \begin{bmatrix} 0, \frac{1}{n} \end{bmatrix}$$

where Δ is the discrete time interval. In this simulation, we let $\Delta = 50\,\text{ms}$, the operation period be $3s$, and the iteration length be $N = 60$. Other parameters are as follows: $J_m = 0.3$, $J_l = 0.44$, $B_m = 0.3$, $B_l = 0.25$, $M = 0.5$, $g = 9.8$, $n = 1.6$, and $l = 0.15$.

The desired reference is $y_d(t) = \pi t^2/12 - \pi t^3/27$. The fading gain, $\mu_k(t)$, satisfies $\mu_k(t) \sim N(\mu, \sigma^2)$, where $\mu = 0.95$ and $\sigma = 0.1$. The additive channel noise, $v_k(t)$, satisfies $v_{k,i}(t) \sim N(0, 0.1^2)$. The learning gain is set to $L = 1.5$ and the decreasing sequence uses $a_k = 1.2/k^{0.65}$. For the case of input fading, the moving window width is set to $m = 4$. Both algorithms are run for 20 iterations.

The results for output and input fading cases are presented in Figs. 3.8 and 3.9, respectively. The tracking performance at the 2nd, 4th, and 20th iterations is displayed in the upper subplots, which demonstrate that the tracking precision at the 20th iteration is already acceptable for both output and input fading. The accumulative input errors of the whole iteration are displayed in the lower subplots with respect to the iteration axis; here, a fast convergence to zero can be observed. These results reveal the effectiveness of the proposed algorithms in handling random channel uncertainties. In addition, this simulation is also conducted for different decreasing gain sequences and fading distributions. The results lead to similar conclusions as in Section 3.5.1, and for the sake of brevity, the details are omitted.

3.6 SUMMARY

This chapter provides a systematic design and analysis framework for a learning control strategy for repetitive systems over fading channels. In this

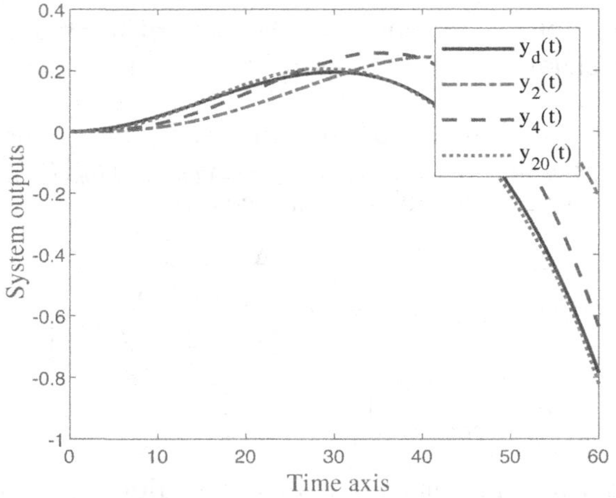

(a) Tracking

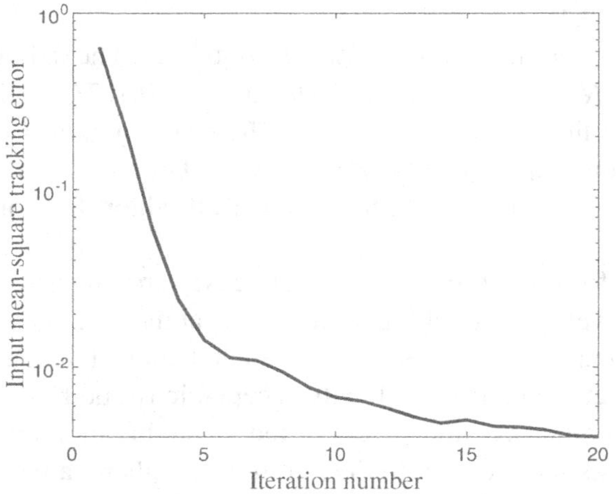

(b) Error

Figure 3.8 Output fading case: (a) Output tracking performance for selected iterations; (b) input error profiles along the iteration axis.

framework, a fundamental learning concept is employed to improve control performance without applying additional restrictions on the fading channel. Both output fading and input fading are addressed, and both multiplicative and additive randomness generated during the transmission are accounted for. A classic P-type learning algorithm is used to generate asymptotically

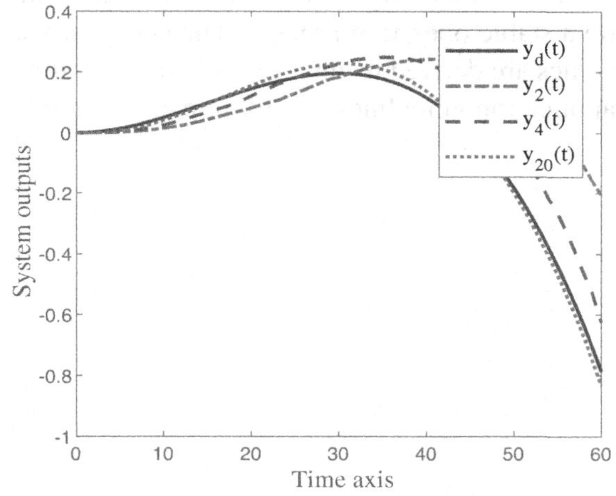

(a) Tracking

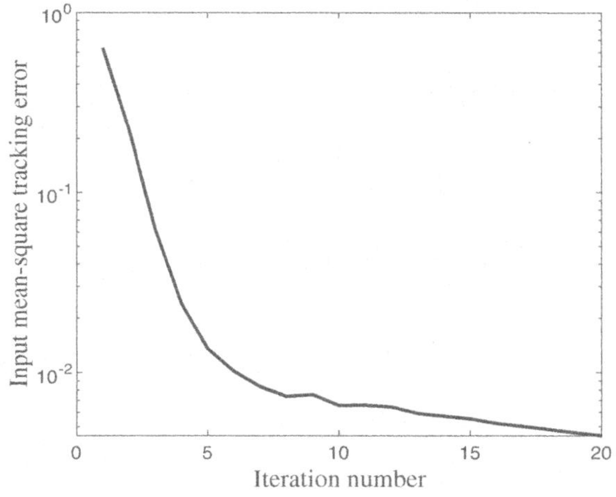

(b) Error

Figure 3.9 Input fading case: (a) Output tracking performance for selected iterations; (b) input error profiles along the iteration axis.

convergent input sequences as the iteration number increases; slight modifications are made to handle various instances of randomness. In particular, a decreasing gain sequence is introduced to both output and input fading for eliminating the fading effect asymptotically and guaranteeing good tracking performance. In addition, a moving-average operator is used in the input fading case to ensure a stable operation process. The convergence properties of the proposed schemes are derived using a careful understanding of the fading effect. General application guidelines regarding parameter selection are also addressed.

CHAPTER 4

Averaging Techniques for Balancing Learning and Tracking Abilities

THIS chapter investigates learning control over fading channels to gradually improve learning and tracking performance. It is observed that the effect of fading on input transmission greatly compromises tracking ability in practical implementations. Three average techniques are examined: Moving average, general average with all historical information, and forgetting-based average. The results reveal a trade-off between learning ability and tracking ability for learning control algorithms, where learning ability refers to the convergence rate of a proposed learning algorithm, and tracking ability refers to the final tracking precision of the output to the desired reference. The convergence results for the three schemes with these averaging techniques are strictly proved. The results demonstrate that the forgetting-based average operator-based scheme can connect the other two schemes by tuning the forgetting factor. Extensions of several general scenarios are provided to expand the application range.

4.1 INTRODUCTION

Preliminary analysis in Chapters 2 and 3 indicates that faded signals can be transformed into a combination of original signals and the corresponding errors (i.e., errors between original and faded signals). Therefore, our primary point in the design and analysis of learning control is to address these quantity-dependent errors. Therefore, effective mechanisms are required to

DOI: 10.1201/9781032646404-4

reduce or eliminate the influence of these errors. In this chapter, we focus on tracking performance evaluation and improvement with faded inputs, which is a practical problem in networked learning control. In particular, if the communication from the controller to the plant experiences random fading, the plant is driven by imperfect commands even if the generated control has been satisfactory. In this case, the actual output always deviates from its reference unless certain effective corrections are performed; this is the specific motivation of this chapter.

Because the faded input affects tracking performance greatly and the random fading gain is difficult to obtain, a heuristic approach to improve tracking performance involves introducing an averaging technique to smooth the faded inputs such that the channel-introduced random deviations can be canceled. However, in general, the average of the generated input signal can lower the convergence rate. The final tracking performance and convergence rate reflect the tracking ability and learning ability, respectively, of any given control scheme. Thus, a challenge is to determine how to balance learning ability and tracking ability. To address this problem, we investigate three representative average scenarios: Moving average (MA), general average (GA) of all historical information, and forgetting-based average (FA) of all historical information. For each scenario, we propose an average-operator-based learning control scheme, introduce the main convergence theorem, and perform a quantitative evaluation of both learning and tracking abilities. Application-related issues, such as parameter tuning, are also explicitly formulated. The obtained results indicate that the MA provides a geometric convergence but only ensures bounded convergence of the corresponding learning algorithm. In contrast, the GA guarantees a perfect tracking performance as the iteration number increases to infinity; however, the convergence rate is rather slow. The FA-based scheme can approach either the MA-based scheme or the GA-based scheme by tuning the forgetting factor. These observations provide guidelines for applications in the presence of fading randomness. Specifically, MA is a common selection but cannot ensure a consistent estimate, while GA is a simple mechanism to achieve a consistent estimate but with a slow convergence speed. By comparison, FA offers a flexible combination of MA and GA by adjusting the forgetting factor.

The major contributions of this chapter are twofold. First, this chapter presents a detailed analysis of a learning control approach using averaging operators to reduce the influence of fading randomness. The results establish the effectiveness of learning control for systems with networked fading channels. Second, the learning and tracking abilities of the proposed schemes are evaluated qualitatively and quantitatively, and the results provide an intuitive understanding of the trade-off between learning ability and tracking ability for practical implementations.

4.2 PROBLEM FORMULATION

4.2.1 System Formulation

Consider the following lifted system formulation:

$$\boldsymbol{y}_k = \mathcal{P}\boldsymbol{u}_k + \boldsymbol{d}_k, \tag{4.1}$$

where subscript k is the iteration index. The variables $\boldsymbol{y}_k$, $\boldsymbol{u}_k$, and $\boldsymbol{d}_k$ are the system output, input, and system response to the initial state, respectively. Both $\boldsymbol{y}_k$ and $\boldsymbol{u}_k$ are lifted vectors of $y_k(t)$ and $u_k(t)$, $0 \leq t \leq n$, where t is the time instant and n is the iteration length; that is, $\boldsymbol{y}_k = [y_k(1), y_k(2), \dots, y_k(n)]^T \in \mathbf{R}^n$ and $\boldsymbol{u}_k = [u_k(0), y_k(1), \dots, u_k(n-1)]^T \in \mathbf{R}^n$. The matrix $\mathcal{P} \in \mathbf{R}^{n\times n}$ is as follows:

$$\mathcal{P} = \begin{bmatrix} p_1 & 0 & \cdots & 0 \\ p_2 & p_1 & \cdots & 0 \\ \vdots & \vdots & \ddots & \vdots \\ p_n & p_{n-1} & \cdots & p_1 \end{bmatrix}, \tag{4.2}$$

where p_1, p_2, ..., p_n are Markov parameters. Without loss of generality, we assume that $p_1 \neq 0$. Thus, $\mathcal{P}$ is nonsingular.

We denote the tracking reference $\boldsymbol{y}_r$. The reference is assumed to be achievable in the sense that there is a unique input $\boldsymbol{u}_r$ such that

$$\boldsymbol{y}_r = \mathcal{P}\boldsymbol{u}_r + \boldsymbol{d}_r, \tag{4.3}$$

where $\boldsymbol{d}_r$ denotes the ideal system response to the initial state. We assume the system can be precisely reset for all iterations, i.e., $\boldsymbol{d}_k = \boldsymbol{d}_r$, $\forall k$. This is a common condition in ILC [8, 55, 57, 71]. Extensions of this condition are given in Section 4.5.2.

Here, we discuss the system formulation. First, we employ the lifted formulation of a SISO plant model for concise derivations. The general state space form of a system can be easily transformed into the lifted form, as the iteration length is finite. Moreover, the initial response $\boldsymbol{d}_k$ is usually determined by the initial state; thus, the condition $\boldsymbol{d}_k = \boldsymbol{d}_r$ is valid as long as the initial state is reset to the desired state at the beginning of each iteration. In addition, the condition of $p_1 \neq 0$ implies that the relative degree is one for the system. If $p_1 = 0$, a high-order relative degree is implied, which can be addressed by reformulating the lifted vectors. However, this is beyond our scope and thus omitted.

For system (4.1) and the reference $\boldsymbol{y}_r$, denoting the tracking error $\boldsymbol{e}_k = \boldsymbol{y}_r - \boldsymbol{y}_d$, the learning algorithm is as follows:

$$\boldsymbol{u}_{k+1} = \boldsymbol{u}_k + \varepsilon \mathcal{L} \boldsymbol{e}_k, \tag{4.4}$$

where ε is a learning step size and $\mathcal{L}$ is a gain matrix. It is evident that the input sequence generated by (4.4) converges to the desired input if the condition $\rho(I - \varepsilon \mathcal{L} \mathcal{P}) < 1$ is fulfilled, where $\rho(\cdot)$ denotes the spectral radius of a matrix.

4.2.2 Fading Channel

In this section, we present the fading channel model. In particular, a random variable is multiplied by the original signals to reflect the fading effect of the channels while transmitting signals. We assume that the channels undergo slow fading such that the statistical information of the fading gain can be estimated a priori. This assumption is generally valid in practical applications because fading is usually determined by physical environments and network devices [62, Chapter 2]. In addition, certain estimation methods can be performed before operating the systems to obtain a relatively precise estimate. Therefore, statistical information is assumed to be known.

In particular, let scalar variable $\theta_k(t)$ denote the fading gain, which is independent and identically distributed for all time instants t and iteration indices k. Moreover, $\theta_k(t)$ is subject to a continuous distribution $\mathbb{F}(\theta)$ such that $\mathbb{P}(\theta_k(t) > 0) = 1$; that is, $\theta_k(t)$ is positive because it indicates signal reflection, refraction, and diffraction. Furthermore, we have the following statistical properties:

$$\theta = \mathbb{E}[\theta_k(t)], \quad \sigma_\theta^2 = \mathbb{E}[(\theta_k(t) - \theta)^2], \quad \forall t \tag{4.5}$$

where θ is known to compensate the received signals in the subsequent algorithm design. Generally, θ is not equal to 1, indicating that the signals have deviated. The variance σ_θ^2 is not always known; however, it should be finite. The iteration-invariant statistics assumption in (4.5) is for concise derivations and can be extended to the iteration-dependent expectation case (i.e., θ is replaced with θ_k) without any difficulty.

Fig. 4.1 displays the setup of the learning control system over fading channels. The plant and controller communicate with each other through fading channels. Such channels at output and input sides introduce fading randomness to the system output signals and generated input signals, of which the effect analysis is given in the next subsection.

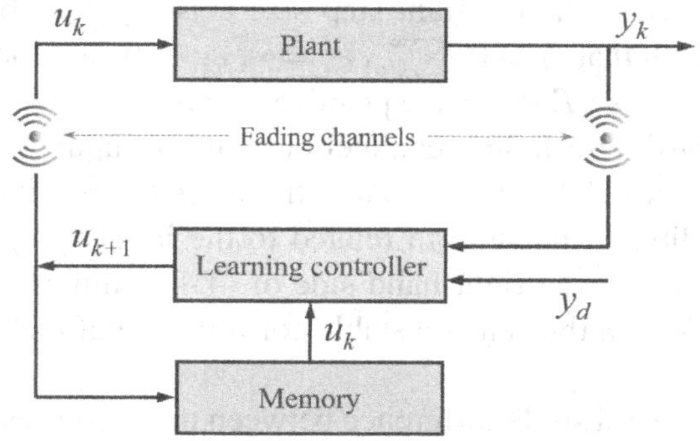

Figure 4.1 Block diagram of learning system over fading channels.

4.2.3 Effect Analysis

Denoting the transmitted signal $s_k(t)$ (output or input), the received signal through a fading channel is given by

$$s_k^*(t) = \theta_k(t)s_k(t). \tag{4.6}$$

It is evident that $s_k^*(t)$ has deviated from its original value. Furthermore, the expectation of $s_k^*(t)$ is not equal to $s_k(t)$, indicating that this signal cannot be employed in the learning algorithms directly. An intuitive correction is to multiply θ^{-1} by the received signal $s_k^*(t)$, leading to an unbiased estimate of the original signal; that is,

$$s_k^c(t) = \theta^{-1}s_k^*(t) = \theta^{-1}\theta_k(t)s_k(t). \tag{4.7}$$

We notice that

$$s_k^c(t) = s_k(t) + \phi_k(t)s_k(t), \tag{4.8}$$

where $\phi_k(t) = \theta^{-1}\theta_k(t) - 1$. It is clear that $\mathbb{E}[\phi_k] = 0$ and $\mathbb{E}[\phi_k^2] = \mathbb{E}[(\theta^{-1}\theta_k(t) - 1)^2] = \sigma_\theta^2/\theta^2$. Thus, compared with the original signal $s_k(t)$, additional noise is added in $s_k^c(t)$, which has zero mean and signal-dependent variance. In the following, we separate the effect analysis of this term on the learning process according to output fading and input fading.

First, we consider a fading channel only at the output side; that is, only the output signal $y_k(t)$ is faded, while the input signal is received precisely. In this case, an additional noise term $\Phi_k \boldsymbol{y}_k$ is added to the right-hand side of (4.4) as part of the tracking error $\boldsymbol{e}_k$, where $\Phi_k = \text{diag}\{\phi_k(1), \phi_k(2), \ldots, \phi_k(n)\}$. Stable convergence of the input sequence generated by the learning algorithm (4.4) can still be ensured if the constant step size ε is replaced by a decreasing sequence $\{\varepsilon_k\}$ such that $\varepsilon_k > 0$, $\sum_{k=1}^{\infty}\varepsilon_k = \infty$, $\varepsilon_k \to 0$, and the gain matrix $\mathcal{L}$ leads all eigenvalues of $\mathcal{LP}$ to have positive real parts.

Then, we consider a fading channel only at the input side; that is, only the generated input $u_k(t)$ is faded, while the output is received precisely. In this case, an additional noise term related to the input $u_k(t)$ and correction error $\phi_k(t)$ is added to the right-hand side of (4.4). Similar treatment of the output fading case can thus ensure stable convergence of the generated input sequence.

However, there is a slight difference between the two cases. For the output fading case, as long as the input sequence $\{\boldsymbol{u}_k\}$ stably converges to the desired input $\boldsymbol{u}_r$, precise tracking performance naturally occurs. However, for input fading, even if an algorithm generates a convergent input sequence, the actual tracking performance can be unsatisfactory because the received input signal may be faded through transmission. In other words, the actual input used for the plant is $\Phi_k\boldsymbol{u}_k$ rather than $\boldsymbol{u}_k$, as randomness is introduced. The previously mentioned correction mechanism (i.e., multiplying by θ^{-1}) cannot eliminate such random disturbances. This observation motivates us to consider how to further improve tracking ability over input fading channels.

4.2.4 Open Problems

In this chapter, we consider effective mechanisms for improving tracking ability over input fading channels. It is evident that tracking performance is influenced mainly by the fading effect in the received input signals. To convey this point, we describe the received input as follows:

$$\begin{aligned}\boldsymbol{u}_k^c &= \theta^{-1}\Theta_k\boldsymbol{u}_k\\ &= \boldsymbol{u}_k - \Phi_k(\boldsymbol{u}_r - \boldsymbol{u}_k) + \Phi_k\boldsymbol{u}_r,\end{aligned} \tag{4.9}$$

where $\Theta_k = \text{diag}\{\theta_k(0), \theta_k(1), \ldots, \theta_k(n-1)\}$ and $\Phi_k = \text{diag}\{\phi_k(0), \phi_k(1), \ldots, \phi_k(n-1)\}$ according to the formulation of $\boldsymbol{u}_k$. Applying this input to system (4.1), the tracking error is as follows:

$$\begin{aligned}\boldsymbol{e}_k &= \mathcal{P}(\boldsymbol{u}_r - \boldsymbol{u}_k^c)\\ &= \mathcal{P}\Delta\boldsymbol{u}_k + \mathcal{P}\Phi_k\Delta\boldsymbol{u}_k - \mathcal{P}\Phi_k\boldsymbol{u}_r,\end{aligned} \tag{4.10}$$

where $\Delta\boldsymbol{u}_k \triangleq \boldsymbol{u}_r - \boldsymbol{u}_k$. In addition to the input error, the tracking error contains another two additional terms: $\alpha_1 \triangleq \mathcal{P}\Phi_k\Delta\boldsymbol{u}_k$ and $\alpha_2 \triangleq \mathcal{P}\Phi_k\boldsymbol{u}_r$, where α_1 denotes the random deviation dependent on the input error and α_2 denotes pure fading deviation related to the desired input. Provided that we can ensure $\Delta\boldsymbol{u}_k$

to converge to zero, α_1 vanishes; however, α_2 remains. To improve tracking performance, an additional mechanism to address α_2 is required.

Since we have only faded inputs at the input side of the plant, an intuitive idea involves introducing an averaging mechanism such that the fading channel-introduced deviations can be eliminated or suppressed. However, by averaging the earlier input, information is retained to drive the system dynamics, which yields new problems such as a low convergence rate. Thus, more elaborate investigations are required. In particular, two open problems are investigated in this chapter.

1) While introducing averaging techniques, we first examine the convergence properties of the proposed algorithms and study the condition under which convergence is ensured. If the algorithms are convergent, the convergence limitation is determined as either zero or a bounded zone around zero.

2) We also examine the effects of averaging techniques on balancing learning and tracking abilities. Here, learning ability refers to the convergence rate of the proposed algorithms, which implies the transient performance in the iteration domain. Tracking ability refers to the actual tracking performance of the system driven by the average input signals, which implies the tracking performance in the time domain.

4.3 MAIN RESULTS

4.3.1 Averaging Techniques and Associated Learning Algorithms

In this section, we introduce three averaging techniques (i.e., MA, GA, and FA) into the ILC scheme to deal with the random fading phenomena for the first time.

The average operators are defined as follows:

1) MA operator $\mathbb{A}^{\mathrm{M}}$:

$$\mathbb{A}^{\mathrm{M}}[\boldsymbol{u}_k] = \frac{1}{m}\sum_{i=1}^{m} \boldsymbol{u}_{k+1-i}, \tag{4.11}$$

where m is the moving width, i.e., the number of successive iterations considered for averaging.

2) GA operator $\mathbb{A}^{\mathrm{G}}$:

$$\mathbb{A}^{\mathrm{G}}[\boldsymbol{u}_k] = \frac{1}{k}\sum_{i=1}^{k} \boldsymbol{u}_i. \tag{4.12}$$

3) FA operator $\mathbb{A}^{\text{F}}$:

$$\mathbb{A}^{\text{F}}[\boldsymbol{u}_k] = \frac{1-\gamma}{1-\gamma^k}\sum_{i=1}^{k}\gamma^{i-1}\boldsymbol{u}_{k+1-i}, \tag{4.13}$$

where $0 < \gamma < 1$ is the forgetting factor. The term $\frac{1-\gamma}{1-\gamma^k}$ makes (4.13) a standard weighted average.

Remark 4.1 *MA uses information from the most recent m iterations, GA considers all historical iterations equally, and FA introduces a decreasing weight to older information. Thus, FA can be regarded as a combination of MA and GA. Letting* $\gamma \to 1$, *we have* $\frac{1-\gamma}{1-\gamma^k} \to \frac{1}{k}$. *Therefore, FA approximates GA as* $\gamma \to 1$. *Moreover, selecting a large m yields* $\gamma^i \approx 0$, $\forall i \geq m$. *We have* $\mathbb{A}^{\text{F}}[\boldsymbol{u}_k] \approx \frac{1-\gamma}{1-\gamma^k}\sum_{i=1}^{m}\gamma^{i-1}\boldsymbol{u}_{k+1-i}$, *which is a weighted MA operator. In short, these three operators can offer us a distinct understanding of the performance improvement using various averaging techniques.*

The generated input for the kth iteration is $\boldsymbol{u}_k$, while the received input is $\Theta_k\boldsymbol{u}_k$. Using the correction mechanism (4.7), we have $\boldsymbol{u}_k^c = \theta^{-1}\Theta_k\boldsymbol{u}_k$, as demonstrated in (4.9). When applying the average operators, system dynamics is driven by the corresponding average signals of the corrected inputs. In other words, for the MA operator, we have

$$\boldsymbol{y}_k^{\text{M}} = \mathcal{P}\mathbb{A}^{\text{M}}[\boldsymbol{u}_k^c] + \boldsymbol{d}_k \tag{4.14}$$

and the associated tracking error using the MA operator is

$$\boldsymbol{e}_k^{\text{M}} = \boldsymbol{y}_r - \boldsymbol{y}_k^{\text{M}} = \mathcal{P}(\boldsymbol{u}_r - \mathbb{A}^{\text{M}}[\boldsymbol{u}_k^c]). \tag{4.15}$$

Similarly, we can define the notations $\boldsymbol{y}_k^{\text{G}}$, $\boldsymbol{y}_k^{\text{F}}$, $\boldsymbol{e}_k^{\text{G}}$, and $\boldsymbol{e}_k^{\text{F}}$ for the GA and FA cases, respectively.

The learning algorithms are defined as follows:

1) MA-based learning algorithm:

$$\boldsymbol{u}_{k+1} = \mathbb{A}^{\text{M}}[\boldsymbol{u}_k] + \varepsilon h\boldsymbol{e}_k^{\text{M}}, \tag{4.16}$$

where $\varepsilon > 0$ is a constant learning step size and h is a value such that $p_1 h > 0$.

2) GA-based learning algorithm:

$$\boldsymbol{u}_{k+1} = \mathbb{A}^{\text{G}}[\boldsymbol{u}_k] + \varepsilon h\boldsymbol{e}_k^{\text{G}}, \tag{4.17}$$

where ε and h are as described above.

3) FA-based learning algorithm:

$$\boldsymbol{u}_{k+1} = \mathbb{A}^{\mathrm{F}}[\boldsymbol{u}_k] + \varepsilon h \boldsymbol{e}_k^{\mathrm{F}}, \tag{4.18}$$

where ε and h are as described above.

In these learning algorithms, the new input $\boldsymbol{u}_{k+1}$ is generated on the basis of the original input $\boldsymbol{u}_i$, $1 \le i \le k$, while the innovation term $\boldsymbol{e}_k^{\star}$ is driven by the corrected input $\boldsymbol{u}_i^c$, $1 \le i \le k$, where "$\star$" represents "M", "G", or "F". This mismatch is addressed by (4.9) and detailed in Section 4.4.

Remark 4.2 *Note that* (4.17) *and* (4.18) *employ all historical information, which may lead to an increasing storage burden. To avoid this problem, a solution is to generate the average recursively. Taking the GA-based case as an example, the recursive calculation of the averaged input is given by*

$$\mathbb{A}^{\mathrm{G}}[\boldsymbol{u}_k] = \frac{1}{k}\sum_{i=1}^{k} \boldsymbol{u}_i = \frac{k-1}{k}\mathbb{A}^{\mathrm{G}}[\boldsymbol{u}_{k-1}] + \frac{1}{k}\theta^{-1}\boldsymbol{u}_k. \tag{4.19}$$

The calculation at the input side can be conducted similarly.

Remark 4.3 *The computational complexity for learning algorithms and averaging operators at the input side is* $k(2mn+3n)$, $2k^2n+3kn$, *and* $4k^2n+3kn$ *for MA, GA, and FA cases, respectively. If the recursive calculation of the average operator is employed, the computational complexity turns into* $11kn$, $9kn$, *and* $9kn$ *in sequence. Moreover, both the averaging processes* (4.11)–(4.13) *and learning algorithms* (4.16)–(4.18) *can be conducted following a time-dependent calculation mode. Thus, a large length* n *would not cause a computation problem.*

In the following subsections, we discuss the convergence properties of all learning algorithms in sequence. The tracking and learning abilities are discussed qualitatively and quantitatively. Technical proofs are provided in Section 4.4. From these results, a general analysis framework of the learning and tracking abilities is provided for all three averaging techniques.

4.3.2 MA-Based Learning Algorithm

In this subsection, we consider the MA-based learning algorithm (4.16) and present the first main result as follows.

Theorem 4.1 *Consider system* (4.1) *and the MA-based learning algorithm* (4.16). *If* ε *is sufficiently small and* h *satisfies* $p_1 h > 0$, *the input error* $\boldsymbol{u}_r - \boldsymbol{u}_k$ *converges to a neighborhood of zero in the mean-square sense:*

$$\lim_{k\to\infty} \mathbb{E}[\|\boldsymbol{u}_r - \boldsymbol{u}_k\|^2] \leq \kappa(\mathcal{O}) \frac{\eta_2 \varepsilon^2 \sigma_\theta^2 \|\boldsymbol{u}_r\|^2}{(1-\rho) m \theta^2}, \tag{4.20}$$

where $\kappa(\mathcal{O})$ *is the condition number of a positive-definite matrix* $\mathcal{O}$, $\mathcal{O}$ *is the solution of the Lyapunov equation* $\mathcal{P}^T \mathcal{O} + \mathcal{O}\mathcal{P} = h^{-1} I$, $\eta_2 > 0$ *is a suitable constant defined in the proof, and* ρ *is a parameter determined by the learning step size* ε.

From this theorem and its proof, we can clarify the open problems described in Subsection 4.2.4 for the MA case.

With the MA operator, we can only ensure that the generated input sequence of (4.16) converges to a neighborhood of the desired input rather than to the desired input itself. In other words, with a constant learning step size, the final input error cannot be zero due to the random fading effect. Furthermore, the upper bound of the neighborhood is determined by the plant ($\mathcal{P}$), the statistics of the fading channel (σ_θ^2 and θ), the desired reference ($\|\boldsymbol{u}_r\|^2$), the learning step size (ε), the regulation parameter (h), and the moving width (m). The explicit function of this dependence is given by (4.20). This result is in agreement with our intuition.

In addition, (4.20) provides guidelines for regulating the limit mean square of the input error. First, the upper bound decreases as the moving width m increases. In other words, when a larger number of iterations are involved in averaging, fading-introduced randomness can be significantly reduced; as a consequence, the input error and the tracking performance is improved. Second, if σ_θ^2 is zero, then zero-error convergence is obtained. In other words, if the fading is deterministic rather than random, a correction mechanism can help achieve perfect tracking performance. Last, the influence of the learning step size is examined. We collect the definition of ρ in the proof: $\rho = 1 - c_3\varepsilon + \varepsilon^2\eta_1$ (see (4.53)), where $c_3 > 0$ and $\eta_1 > 0$ are constants. Then, if $\varepsilon \to 0$, we have

$$\lim_{\varepsilon\to 0} \frac{\varepsilon^2}{1-\rho} = \frac{\varepsilon^2}{c_3\varepsilon - \varepsilon^2\eta_1} \to 0.$$

In other words, by decreasing the learning step size, the final input error can be effectively improved. In fact, if the constant step size ε is replaced by a decreasing sequence $\{\varepsilon_k\}$, zero-error convergence of the input error can be obtained. This result is presented in the following corollary, which can be proved similar to Theorem 4.1.

Corollary 4.1 *Consider system* (4.1) *and the MA-based learning algorithm* (4.16), *where the constant learning step size ε is replaced by a decreasing sequence $\{\varepsilon_k\}$. If ε_k satisfies $\varepsilon_k > 0$, $\varepsilon_k \to 0$, and $\sum_{k=1}^{\infty} \varepsilon_k = \infty$, and h satisfies $p_1 h > 0$, the input error $\boldsymbol{u}_r - \boldsymbol{u}_k$ converges to zero in the mean-square sense as the iteration number increases:*

$$\lim_{k\to\infty} \mathbb{E}[\|\boldsymbol{u}_r - \boldsymbol{u}_k\|^2] = 0. \tag{4.21}$$

However, the sacrifice of improving the input error by reducing the learning step size is slowing the convergence rate down. That is, the convergence rate decreases as ε approaches zero. Therefore, selecting a small learning step size is not definitely preferable to selecting a large learning step size. To determine the convergence rate, we rewrite an estimate in the proof (i.e., (4.54)) as follows:

$$\begin{aligned} &\mathbb{E}\left[(\Delta \boldsymbol{u}_{k+1})^T \mathcal{O}(\Delta \boldsymbol{u}_{k+1})\right] \\ &\quad \le \rho \max_{1\le i\le m} \mathbb{E}\left[(\Delta \boldsymbol{u}_{k+1-i})^T \mathcal{O}(\Delta \boldsymbol{u}_{k+1-i})\right] + \eta_2 \delta, \end{aligned} \tag{4.22}$$

where $\delta = \frac{\varepsilon^2 \lambda_{\max}(\mathcal{O}) \sigma_\theta^2 \|\boldsymbol{u}_r\|^2}{m\theta^2}$. In general, in the worst case, the energy $\mathbb{E}\left[(\Delta \boldsymbol{u}_k)^T \mathcal{O}(\Delta \boldsymbol{u}_k)\right]$ is reduced every m iterations, and it approximately holds that

$$\begin{aligned} &\mathbb{E}\left[(\Delta \boldsymbol{u}_k)^T \mathcal{O}(\Delta \boldsymbol{u}_k)\right] \\ &\le \rho^{\lfloor \frac{k}{m} \rfloor} \max_{1\le i\le m} \left\{\mathbb{E}\left[(\Delta \boldsymbol{u}_i)^T \mathcal{O}(\Delta \boldsymbol{u}_i)\right]\right\} + \frac{1-\rho^{\lfloor \frac{k}{m} \rfloor}}{1-\rho} \eta_2 \delta. \end{aligned} \tag{4.23}$$

Thus, the convergence is geometrical, and ratio ρ is determined by the learning step size ε. Recalling that $\rho = 1 - c_3\varepsilon + \varepsilon^2 \eta_1$, we notice that $\rho \to 1$ as $\varepsilon \to 0$. This observation describes the learning ability of the MA-based scheme. Therefore, a trade-off exists between the final input error and convergence rate.

We now examine the tracking ability. To this end, we recall that the tracking error is driven by the average value of the corrected inputs rather than the generated inputs. From (4.10) and (4.15), we have

$$\begin{aligned} \boldsymbol{e}_k^{\mathrm{M}} &= \mathcal{P}(\boldsymbol{u}_r - \mathbb{A}^{\mathrm{M}}[\boldsymbol{u}_k^c]) \\ &= \mathbb{A}^{\mathrm{M}}\left[\theta^{-1} \mathcal{P} \Theta_k \Delta \boldsymbol{u}_k - \mathcal{P} \Phi_k \boldsymbol{u}_r\right]. \end{aligned} \tag{4.24}$$

Therefore,

$$
\begin{aligned}
\mathbb{E}[\|\boldsymbol{e}_k^{\mathrm{M}}\|^2] &\leq 2\mathbb{E}\left[\|\mathbb{A}^{\mathrm{M}}[\theta^{-1}\mathcal{P}\Theta_k\Delta\boldsymbol{u}_k]\|^2\right] \\
&\quad + 2\mathbb{E}\left[\|\mathbb{A}^{\mathrm{M}}[\mathcal{P}\Phi_k\boldsymbol{u}_r\|^2]\right] \\
&\leq \underbrace{2\frac{1}{m}\sum_{i=1}^{m}\mathbb{E}[\|\theta^{-1}\mathcal{P}\Theta_{k+1-i}\Delta\boldsymbol{u}_{k+1-i}\|^2]}_{\text{by } (\sum_{i=1}^{n} b_i)^2 \leq n\sum_{i=1}^{n} b_i^2} \\
&\quad \underbrace{+2\frac{1}{m^2}\sum_{i=1}^{m}\mathbb{E}[\|\mathcal{P}\Phi_{k+1-i}\boldsymbol{u}_r\|^2]}_{\text{by independence of } \Phi_k} \\
&\leq 2\max_{1\leq i\leq m}\mathbb{E}[\|\theta^{-1}\mathcal{P}\Theta_{k+1-i}\Delta\boldsymbol{u}_{k+1-i}\|^2] \\
&\quad + \frac{2}{m}\mathbb{E}[\|\mathcal{P}\Phi_{k+1-i}\boldsymbol{u}_r\|^2],
\end{aligned} \tag{4.25}
$$

where the former term on the right-hand side is linearly bounded by the input error, while the latter term is independent of the input. Thus, the second term demonstrates the effect of random fading on the tracking performance. The above estimate demonstrates that this term converges to zero as m approaches infinity, which illustrates the effect of the MA operator in improving the tracking performance.

4.3.3 GA-Based Learning Algorithm

In this subsection, we examine the GA-based learning algorithm (4.17) and present the main results as follows.

Theorem 4.2 *Consider system* (4.1) *and the GA-based learning algorithm* (4.17). *If ε is sufficiently small and h satisfies $p_1 h > 0$, then the average input $\mathbb{A}^{\mathrm{G}}[\boldsymbol{u}_r - \boldsymbol{u}_k]$ converges to zero in the mean-square sense:*

$$\lim_{k\to\infty}\mathbb{E}[\|\mathbb{A}^{\mathrm{G}}[\Delta\boldsymbol{u}_k]\|^2] = 0. \tag{4.26}$$

In addition to the detailed proof given in Section 4.4, the above result can be understood from another angle. From Theorem 4.1, it can be determined that increasing the moving width can reduce the limiting input error. Letting m approach infinity, which becomes the GA case, it holds that $\lim_{m\to\infty}\{\lim_{k\to\infty}\mathbb{E}[\|\Delta\boldsymbol{u}_k\|^2]\} = 0$. This indicates that the input error in the mean-square sense converges to zero using the GA scheme. Then, we have

$$\mathbb{E}\left[\|\mathbb{A}^{\mathrm{G}}[\Delta\boldsymbol{u}_k]\|^2\right] \leq \mathbb{A}^{\mathrm{G}}\left[\mathbb{E}[\|\Delta\boldsymbol{u}_k\|^2]\right] \to 0,$$

which is the conclusion of (4.26)

In contrast to Theorem 4.1, we derive the convergence of the average mean square of the input error directly for the GA case. The reason for this is that we can derive a direct recursion of the average input error (see (4.62) for details). However, it is the average input error rather than the input error of a single iteration that is actually fed to the plant. Thus, it is reasonable to verify the asymptotic properties of $\mathbb{A}^{\mathrm{G}}[\Delta \boldsymbol{u}_k]$.

To determine the learning ability, we rewrite the estimate of $\mathbb{E}[(\mathbb{A}^{\mathrm{G}}[\Delta \boldsymbol{u}_k])^T \mathcal{O}(\mathbb{A}^{\mathrm{G}}[\Delta \boldsymbol{u}_k])]$ (i.e., (4.74)) as follows:

$$\begin{aligned}
&\mathbb{E}[(\mathbb{A}^{\mathrm{G}}[\Delta \boldsymbol{u}_{k+1}])^T \mathcal{O}(\mathbb{A}^{\mathrm{G}}[\Delta \boldsymbol{u}_{k+1}])] \\
&\quad \leq (1-\rho_k)\mathbb{E}[(\mathbb{A}^{\mathrm{G}}[\Delta \boldsymbol{u}_k])^T \mathcal{O}(\mathbb{A}^{\mathrm{G}}[\Delta \boldsymbol{u}_k])] \\
&\quad\quad + \delta_k \frac{\varepsilon^2 \lambda_{\max}(\mathcal{O})\sigma_\theta^2 \|\boldsymbol{u}_r\|^2}{\theta(k+1)k},
\end{aligned} \tag{4.27}$$

where $\rho_k = \frac{c_3\varepsilon-(c_4+c_5)\varepsilon^2}{k+1} - \frac{3(c_1+c_2)\varepsilon^2}{(k+1)^2}$ and $\delta_k = \frac{3c_1}{k+1} + c_6$. As $k \to \infty$, $\rho_k \sim \frac{\nu}{k}$ and $\delta_k \approx c_6$, where $\nu = c_3\varepsilon - (c_4+c_5)\varepsilon^2$. In general, if $\nu > 1$, the convergence rate of $\mathbb{E}[(\mathbb{A}^{\mathrm{G}}[\Delta \boldsymbol{u}_k])^T \mathcal{O}(\mathbb{A}^{\mathrm{G}}[\Delta \boldsymbol{u}_k])]$ is $O(k^{-1})$; if $\nu = 1$, the convergence rate is $O(k^{-\nu}\log k)$; and if $\nu < 1$, the convergence rate is $O(k^{-\nu})$ [49]. Thus, the convergence rate of $\mathbb{E}[(\mathbb{A}^{\mathrm{G}}[\Delta \boldsymbol{u}_k])^T \mathcal{O}(\mathbb{A}^{\mathrm{G}}[\Delta \boldsymbol{u}_k])]$ cannot exceed $O(k^{-1})$, slower than that of the MA case, which is geometrical. In short, the GA-based scheme achieves the zero limit of the input error while sacrificing the convergence rate. In addition, the convergence rate is determined by the learning step size ε.

We now examine tracking ability. Clearly, we have

$$\boldsymbol{e}_k^{\mathrm{G}} = \mathbb{A}^{\mathrm{G}}[\theta^{-1}\mathcal{P}\Theta_k \Delta \boldsymbol{u}_k - \mathcal{P}\Phi_k \boldsymbol{u}_r]. \tag{4.28}$$

Then, we have

$$\begin{aligned}
\mathbb{E}\left[\|\boldsymbol{e}_k^{\mathrm{G}}\|^2\right] &\leq 2\mathbb{E}\left[\|\mathbb{A}^{\mathrm{G}}[\theta^{-1}\mathcal{P}\Theta_k \Delta \boldsymbol{u}_k]\|^2\right] \\
&\quad + 2\mathbb{E}\left[\|\mathbb{A}^{\mathrm{G}}[\mathcal{P}\Phi_k \boldsymbol{u}_r]\|^2\right],
\end{aligned} \tag{4.29}$$

where the first term on the right-hand side converges to zero by Theorem 4.2 and the second term is bounded by

$$\mathbb{E}\left[\|\mathbb{A}^{\mathrm{G}}[\mathcal{P}\Phi_k \boldsymbol{u}_r]\|^2\right] \leq \frac{1}{k} \times \omega \mathbb{E}[\Phi_k^2] \to 0, \tag{4.30}$$

where ω is a positive constant depending on $\mathcal{P}$ and $\boldsymbol{u}_r$. In other words, the tracking error converges to zero gradually, which illustrates the tracking ability of the GA-based scheme.

4.3.4 FA-Based Learning Algorithm

The analysis of the FA-based scheme is similar to the GA-based scheme, as both employ all historical information. However, the FA-based scheme assigns more weight to recent information. It is expected that the convergence rate can be improved while retaining the advantages of the tracking ability. The main result is provided in the following theorem.

Theorem 4.3 *Consider system* (4.1) *and the FA-based learning algorithm* (4.18). *If ε is sufficiently small and h satisfies $p_1 h > 0$, then the average input $\mathbb{A}^{\mathrm{F}}[\boldsymbol{u}_r - \boldsymbol{u}_k]$ converges to a neighborhood of zero in the mean-square sense:*

$$\lim_{k\to\infty} \mathbb{E}[\|\mathbb{A}^{\mathrm{F}}[\Delta \boldsymbol{u}_k]\|^2] \leq \kappa(\mathcal{O}) \frac{\varpi \|\boldsymbol{u}_r\|^2 \sigma_\theta^2}{\theta} \tag{4.31}$$

where

$$\varpi = \frac{[3c_1(1-\gamma)^2 + c_6(1-\gamma)]\varepsilon^2}{c_3\varepsilon - [3(c_1+c_2)(1-\gamma) + (c_4+c_5)]\,\varepsilon^2} \tag{4.32}$$

with constants c_i being given in the proof, $i = 1, \ldots, 6$.

It can be seen seen from the theorem that bounded convergence of the input error is established rather than convergence to zero. However, the upper bound of the neighborhood can be tuned by the forgetting factor λ, as illustrated in (4.32). As $\gamma \to 1$, the upper bound $\varpi \to 0$, which approximates the GA-based scheme, while as $\gamma \to 0$, the upper bound ϖ approaches the result of MA-based scheme with $m = 1$. This conclusion is consistent with Remark 4.1.

To determine the learning ability, we collect the estimate given by (4.87) in the proof for $\mathbb{E}[(\mathbb{A}^{\mathrm{G}}[\Delta \boldsymbol{u}_k])^T \mathcal{O}(\mathbb{A}^{\mathrm{G}}[\Delta \boldsymbol{u}_k])]$:

$$\mathbb{E}[L_{k+1}] \leq (1-\rho_k)\mathbb{E}[L_k] + \delta_k \frac{\|\boldsymbol{u}_r\|^2 \lambda_{\max}(\mathcal{O})\sigma_\theta^2}{\theta}, \tag{4.33}$$

where $\rho_k = c_3\varphi_k\varepsilon - 3(c_1 + c_2)\varphi_k^2\varepsilon^2 - (c_4 + c_5)\varphi_k\varepsilon^2$, $\delta_k = (3c_1\varphi_k + c_6)\varepsilon^2\varphi_k\varphi_{k-1}$, and $\varphi_k = \frac{1-\gamma}{1-\gamma^{k+1}}$. It should be noted that φ_k decreases and is lower bounded by $1-\gamma$; that is,

$$1 > \varphi_1 > \cdots > \varphi_k > \varphi_{k+1} > \cdots > 1-\gamma.$$

Therefore, ρ_k is a positive distance away from zero for all iterations k; that is, there is a $\rho_{\min} > 0$ depending on ε such that $\rho_k \geq \rho_{\min}$. As a result, the convergence rate is geometrical with a ratio no larger than $1-\rho_{\min}$. This is consistent with the MA-based scheme. Therefore, introducing the forgetting factor improves the convergence speed compared with the GA-based scheme.

Here, we provide an intuitive explanation of why the FA-based scheme cannot guarantee zero convergence of the input error, which can be achieved by the GA-based scheme. As demonstrated by the proof, the limit of the mean square of input errors is determined by the pure fading effect $\mathcal{P}_0\Phi_k\boldsymbol{u}_r$ in averaged form. For simplicity, we remove the invariant terms $\mathcal{P}_0$ and $\boldsymbol{u}_r$ and focus on Φ_k, which has zero mean and bounded variance. Using the GA operator, we have $\mathbb{E}\left[\mathbb{A}^{\mathrm{G}}[\Phi_k]\right]=0$ and

$$\mathbb{E}\left[(\mathbb{A}^{\mathrm{G}}[\Phi_k])^2\right]=\frac{\sigma_\theta^2}{k\theta}I\to 0, \quad \text{as } k\to\infty.$$

That is, the average variance of Φ_k converges to zero. Using the FA operator, $\mathbb{E}\left[\mathbb{A}^{\mathrm{F}}[\Phi_k]\right]=0$; however, we have

$$\begin{aligned}\mathbb{E}\left[(\mathbb{A}^{\mathrm{F}}[\Phi_k])^2\right]&=\varphi_{k-1}^2\sum_{i=1}^{k}\gamma^{2(i-1)}\mathbb{E}[\Phi_{k+1-i}^2]\\&\to\frac{1-\gamma}{1+\gamma}\times\frac{\sigma_\theta^2}{\theta}I, \quad \text{as } k\to\infty.\end{aligned} \tag{4.34}$$

Therefore, the weighted summation of random fading variables cannot drive the variance to zero. This biased variance yields bounded convergence of the mean square of input errors.

The tracking ability of the FA-based scheme is similar to that of the MA-based scheme. Specifically, similar to (4.25) and (4.29), we have

$$\begin{aligned}\mathbb{E}\left[\|\boldsymbol{e}_k^{\mathrm{F}}\|^2\right]\le{}&2\mathbb{E}\left[\|\mathbb{A}^{\mathrm{F}}[\theta^{-1}\mathcal{P}\Theta_k\Delta\boldsymbol{u}_k]\|^2\right]\\&+2\mathbb{E}\left[\|\mathbb{A}^{\mathrm{F}}[\mathcal{P}\Phi_k\boldsymbol{u}_r]\|^2\right],\end{aligned} \tag{4.35}$$

where the second term on the right-hand side does not converge to zero, as illustrated above, while the first term is also bounded, as given in Theorem 4.3. Collecting the estimates (4.31) and (4.34), we notice that increasing γ can lead to better tracking performance but may reduce the convergence rate.

4.3.5 Discussions

Fig. 4.2 summarizes the performance comparison and connection between the MA-, GA-, and FA-based schemes, where the horizontal and vertical axes

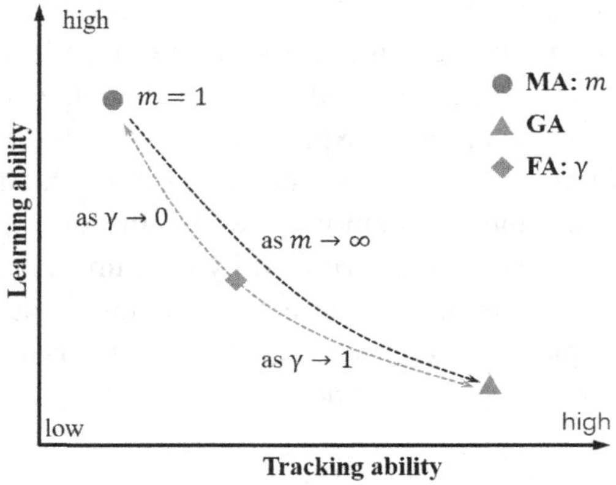

Figure 4.2 Performance of MA-, GA-, and FA-based schemes.

denote tracking ability and learning ability, respectively. Tracking ability represents the limit of tracking precision to a desired reference, while learning ability denotes the convergence rate of the average input signals to their limit. In general, the GA-based scheme has the best tracking ability, as the tracking error converges to zero; however, its convergence rate is rather slow. The MA-based scheme with $m = 1$ (i.e., the classical P-type algorithm) has the best learning ability; however, the learning of its objective is insufficient. Moreover, the performance of the MA-based scheme gradually approximates that of the GA-based scheme as $m \to \infty$. The FA-based scheme can be regarded as a trade-off between the MA-based scheme and the GA-based scheme. In particular, as $\gamma \to 1$, the FA-based scheme gradually turns into the GA-based scheme, while as $\gamma \to 0$, it turns into the MA-based scheme with $m = 1$. These facts provide guidelines for selecting an average operator to balance the learning and tracking abilities in applications. In particular, the MA- and GA-based schemes have distinct advantages and disadvantages in learning and tracking abilities, while the FA-based scheme acts a flexible compromise proposal. We should point out that the step size ε affects the performance: A smaller ε would reduce convergence speed for all schemes but can improve the tracking performance for MA- and FA-based schemes.

4.4 PROOFS OF MAIN THEOREMS

Proof of Theorem 4.1: From (4.15) and (4.9), we have

$$\boldsymbol{e}_k^{\mathrm{M}} = \mathcal{P}(\boldsymbol{u}_r - \mathbb{A}^{\mathrm{M}}[\boldsymbol{u}_k^c])$$

$$= \mathcal{P}\mathbb{A}^{\mathrm{M}}[\Delta \boldsymbol{u}_k] + \mathcal{P}\mathbb{A}^{\mathrm{M}}[\Phi_k \Delta \boldsymbol{u}_k] - \mathcal{P}\mathbb{A}^{\mathrm{M}}[\Phi_k]\boldsymbol{u}_r. \tag{4.36}$$

Subtracting both sides of (4.16) from $\boldsymbol{u}_r$ and substituting the above equation into the resulting equation yields

$$\begin{aligned}\Delta \boldsymbol{u}_{k+1} &= \boldsymbol{u}_r - \mathbb{A}^{\mathrm{M}}[\boldsymbol{u}_k] - \varepsilon h \mathcal{P}\mathbb{A}^{\mathrm{M}}[\Delta \boldsymbol{u}_k] \\ &\quad - \varepsilon h \mathcal{P}\mathbb{A}^{\mathrm{M}}[\Phi_k \Delta \boldsymbol{u}_k] + \varepsilon h \mathcal{P}\mathbb{A}^{\mathrm{M}}[\Phi_k]\boldsymbol{u}_r \\ &= (I - \varepsilon h \mathcal{P})\mathbb{A}^{\mathrm{M}}[\Delta \boldsymbol{u}_k] - \varepsilon h \mathcal{P}\mathbb{A}^{\mathrm{M}}[\Phi_k \Delta \boldsymbol{u}_k] \\ &\quad + \varepsilon h \mathcal{P}\mathbb{A}^{\mathrm{M}}[\Phi_k]\boldsymbol{u}_r. \end{aligned} \tag{4.37}$$

The matrix $\mathcal{P}$ is Toeplitz and lower triangular, and the value h satisfies $p_1 h > 0$; thus, $h\mathcal{P}$ remains Toeplitz and lower triangular. In addition, the diagonal elements of $h\mathcal{P}$ are a positive constant. Thus, by the Lyapunov equation, there is a positive matrix $\mathcal{O}$ that solves the following equation:

$$(h\mathcal{P})^T \mathcal{O} + \mathcal{O}(h\mathcal{P}) = I. \tag{4.38}$$

We define a Lyapunov function

$$L_k = (\Delta \boldsymbol{u}_k)^T \mathcal{O}(\Delta \boldsymbol{u}_k). \tag{4.39}$$

Denote $\Delta \boldsymbol{u}_k^M = \mathbb{A}^{\mathrm{M}}[\Delta \boldsymbol{u}_k]$ and $\mathcal{P}_0 = h\mathcal{P}$. Then, substituting (4.37) into L_{k+1} leads to

$$\begin{aligned} L_{k+1} &= (\Delta \boldsymbol{u}_{k+1})^T \mathcal{O}(\Delta \boldsymbol{u}_{k+1}) \\ &= \sum_{i=1}^{4} \beta_i^T \mathcal{O} \beta_i + \sum_{i \neq j} \beta_i^T \mathcal{O} \beta_j, \end{aligned} \tag{4.40}$$

where β_i, $1 \le i \le 4$, are defined as

$$\begin{aligned} \beta_1 &= \Delta \boldsymbol{u}_k^M, & \beta_2 &= -\varepsilon \mathcal{P}_0 \Delta \boldsymbol{u}_k^M, \\ \beta_3 &= -\varepsilon \mathcal{P}_0 \mathbb{A}^{\mathrm{M}}[\Phi_k \Delta \boldsymbol{u}_k], & \beta_4 &= \varepsilon \mathcal{P}_0 \mathbb{A}^{\mathrm{M}}[\Phi_k]\boldsymbol{u}_r. \end{aligned}$$

We now perform detailed estimates of all terms on the right-hand side of (4.40). First, we have

$$\begin{aligned} \beta_1^T \mathcal{O} \beta_1 &= (\Delta \boldsymbol{u}_k^M)^T \mathcal{O}(\Delta \boldsymbol{u}_k^M) \\ &= \frac{1}{m^2} \left(\sum_{i=1}^{m} \Delta \boldsymbol{u}_{k+1-i} \right)^T \mathcal{O} \left(\sum_{i=1}^{m} \Delta \boldsymbol{u}_{k+1-i} \right) \end{aligned}$$

$$\leq \frac{1}{m}\left(\sum_{i=1}^{m} \Delta \boldsymbol{u}_{k+1-i}^T \mathcal{O} \Delta \boldsymbol{u}_{k+1-i}\right)$$

$$= \frac{1}{m}\sum_{i=1}^{m} L_{k+1-i} = \mathbb{A}^{\mathrm{M}}[L_k], \tag{4.41}$$

$$\begin{aligned}
\beta_2^T \mathcal{O} \beta_2 &= \varepsilon^2 (\Delta \boldsymbol{u}_k^M)^T \mathcal{P}_0^T \mathcal{O} \mathcal{P}_0 (\Delta \boldsymbol{u}_k^M) \\
&= [\text{there exists } c_1 > 0 \text{ such that } \mathcal{P}_0^T \mathcal{O} \mathcal{P}_0 \leq c_1 \mathcal{O}] \\
&\leq c_1 \varepsilon^2 (\Delta \boldsymbol{u}_k^M)^T \mathcal{O} (\Delta \boldsymbol{u}_k^M) \\
&= [\text{substitute (4.41) here}] \\
&\leq c_1 \varepsilon^2 \mathbb{A}^{\mathrm{M}}[L_k],
\end{aligned} \tag{4.42}$$

$$\begin{aligned}
\beta_3^T \mathcal{O} \beta_3 &= \varepsilon^2 (\mathcal{P}_0 \mathbb{A}^{\mathrm{M}}[\Phi_k \Delta \boldsymbol{u}_k])^T \mathcal{O} (\mathcal{P}_0 \mathbb{A}^{\mathrm{M}}[\Phi_k \Delta \boldsymbol{u}_k]) \\
&\leq c_1 \varepsilon^2 (\mathbb{A}^{\mathrm{M}}[\Phi_k \Delta \boldsymbol{u}_k])^T \mathcal{O} (\mathbb{A}^{\mathrm{M}}[\Phi_k \Delta \boldsymbol{u}_k]),
\end{aligned} \tag{4.43}$$

$$\begin{aligned}
\beta_4^T \mathcal{O} \beta_4 &= \varepsilon^2 (\mathcal{P}_0 \mathbb{A}^{\mathrm{M}}[\Phi_k] \boldsymbol{u}_r)^T \mathcal{O} (\mathcal{P}_0 \mathbb{A}^{\mathrm{M}}[\Phi_k] \boldsymbol{u}_r) \\
&\leq c_1 \varepsilon^2 \boldsymbol{u}_r^T (\mathbb{A}^{\mathrm{M}}[\Phi_k])^T \mathcal{O} (\mathbb{A}^{\mathrm{M}}[\Phi_k]) \boldsymbol{u}_r.
\end{aligned} \tag{4.44}$$

Moreover, because $\mathbb{E}[\Phi_k^2]$ is bounded, we have

$$\begin{aligned}
\mathbb{E}[\beta_3^T \mathcal{O} \beta_3] &\leq c_2 \varepsilon^2 \mathbb{E}[(\Delta \boldsymbol{u}_k^M)^T \mathcal{O} (\Delta \boldsymbol{u}_k^M)] \\
&\leq c_2 \varepsilon^2 \mathbb{E}\left[\mathbb{A}^{\mathrm{M}}[L_k]\right],
\end{aligned} \tag{4.45}$$

where $c_2 > 0$ is a suitable constant related to the fading variable and positive-definite matrix $\mathcal{O}$. Similarly, we can derive the following:

$$\begin{aligned}
\mathbb{E}[\beta_4^T \mathcal{O} \beta_4] &\leq c_1 \varepsilon^2 \boldsymbol{u}_r^T \mathbb{E}\left[(\mathbb{A}^{\mathrm{M}}[\Phi_k])^T \mathcal{O} (\mathbb{A}^{\mathrm{M}}[\Phi_k])\right] \boldsymbol{u}_r \\
&\leq c_1 \lambda_{\max}(\mathcal{O}) \varepsilon^2 \frac{1}{m^2} \boldsymbol{u}_r^T \mathbb{E}\left[\sum_{i=1}^{m} \Phi_{k+1-i}^2\right] \boldsymbol{u}_r \\
&= \frac{c_1 \lambda_{\max}(\mathcal{O}) \varepsilon^2 \sigma_\theta^2 \|\boldsymbol{u}_r\|^2}{m \theta^2},
\end{aligned} \tag{4.46}$$

where the independence of fading gain $\phi_k(t)$ with respect to k and t is used.

Next, we consider the crossing terms on the right-hand side of (4.40).

$$\begin{aligned}
\beta_1^T \mathcal{O} \beta_2 + \beta_2^T \mathcal{O} \beta_1 &= -\varepsilon (\Delta \boldsymbol{u}_k^M)^T (\mathcal{O} \mathcal{P}_0 + \mathcal{P}_0^T \mathcal{O}) (\Delta \boldsymbol{u}_k^M) \\
&= [\text{substitute (4.38) here}] \\
&= -\varepsilon (\Delta \boldsymbol{u}_k^M)^T (\Delta \boldsymbol{u}_k^M) \\
&= [\text{there is } c_3 \text{ such that } I \geq c_3 \mathcal{O}]
\end{aligned}$$

$$\leq -c_3\varepsilon(\Delta \boldsymbol{u}_k^M)^T \mathcal{O}(\Delta \boldsymbol{u}_k^M). \tag{4.47}$$

The crossing terms between β_1 and β_3 are estimated as follows:

$$\begin{aligned}
\beta_1^T \mathcal{O}\beta_3 + \beta_3^T \mathcal{O}\beta_1 &= -2\varepsilon(\Delta \boldsymbol{u}_k^M)^T \mathcal{O}(\mathcal{P}_0 \mathbb{A}^{\mathrm{M}}[\Phi_k \Delta \boldsymbol{u}_k]) \\
&= -2\frac{\varepsilon}{m^2}\left(\sum_{1\leq i,j\leq m} (\Delta \boldsymbol{u}_{k+1-i})^T \mathcal{O}\mathcal{P}_0 \Phi_{k+1-j} \Delta \boldsymbol{u}_{k+1-j}\right),
\end{aligned}$$

for which we have two cases to be addressed. If $i \geq j$, then the mathematical expectation of the term $\Delta \boldsymbol{u}_{k+1-i}^T \mathcal{O}\mathcal{P}_0 \Phi_{k+1-j} \Delta \boldsymbol{u}_{k+1-j}$ is zero because Φ_{k+1-j} is independent of all other quantities. Otherwise, $\boldsymbol{u}_{k+1-i}$ contains the information of Φ_{k+1-j}; however, the corresponding terms are bounded by $\frac{\varepsilon}{m}\sum_{i=1}^m L_{k+1-i}$, where ε originates from the expansion of $\Delta \boldsymbol{u}_{k+1-i}$. Therefore, there is a suitable constant $c_4 > 0$ such that

$$\begin{aligned}
&\mathbb{E}[\beta_1^T \mathcal{O}\beta_3 + \beta_3^T \mathcal{O}\beta_1] \\
&\leq -2\frac{\varepsilon}{m^2}\mathbb{E}\left[\sum_{1\leq i<j\leq m} (\Delta \boldsymbol{u}_{k+1-i})^T \mathcal{O}\mathcal{P}_0 \Phi_{k+1-j} \Delta \boldsymbol{u}_{k+1-j}\right] \\
&\leq 2c_4\frac{\varepsilon^2}{m^2} \times \frac{m(m-1)}{2}\mathbb{E}[\mathbb{A}^{\mathrm{M}}[L_k]] \\
&\leq c_4\varepsilon^2 \mathbb{E}\left[\mathbb{A}^{\mathrm{M}}[L_k]\right].
\end{aligned} \tag{4.48}$$

A similar estimate of the crossing terms between β_1 and β_4 is as follows:

$$\begin{aligned}
&\mathbb{E}[\beta_1^T \mathcal{O}\beta_4 + \beta_4^T \mathcal{O}\beta_1] \\
&\leq c_5\varepsilon^2 \mathbb{E}\left[\mathbb{A}^{\mathrm{M}}[L_k]\right] + c_6\varepsilon^2 \frac{\lambda_{\max}(\mathcal{O})\sigma_\theta^2 \|\boldsymbol{u}_r\|^2}{m\theta^2},
\end{aligned} \tag{4.49}$$

where $c_5, c_6 > 0$ are constants.

Additionally, the remaining crossing terms can be estimated using a basic inequality as follows:

$$\begin{aligned}
\mathbb{E}[\beta_2^T \mathcal{O}\beta_3 + \beta_3^T \mathcal{O}\beta_2] &= 2\mathbb{E}[\beta_2^T \mathcal{O}\beta_3] \\
&\leq \mathbb{E}[\beta_2^T \mathcal{O}\beta_2] + \mathbb{E}[\beta_3^T \mathcal{O}\beta_3] \\
&\leq (c_1 + c_2)\varepsilon^2 \mathbb{E}\left[\mathbb{A}^{\mathrm{M}}[L_k]\right], \qquad (4.50) \\
\mathbb{E}[\beta_2^T \mathcal{O}\beta_4 + \beta_4^T \mathcal{O}\beta_2] &= 2\mathbb{E}[\beta_2^T \mathcal{O}\beta_4] \\
&\leq \mathbb{E}[\beta_2^T \mathcal{O}\beta_2] + \mathbb{E}[\beta_4^T \mathcal{O}\beta_4]
\end{aligned}$$

$$\le c_1\varepsilon^2\mathbb{E}\left[\mathbb{A}^{\mathrm{M}}[L_k]\right] + \frac{c_1\lambda_{\max}(\mathcal{O})\varepsilon^2\sigma_\theta^2\|\boldsymbol{u}_r\|^2}{m\theta^2}, \tag{4.51}$$

$$\begin{aligned}\mathbb{E}[\beta_3^T\mathcal{O}\beta_4+\beta_4^T\mathcal{O}\beta_3] &= 2\mathbb{E}[\beta_3^T\mathcal{O}\beta_4]\\ &\le \mathbb{E}[\beta_3^T\mathcal{O}\beta_3]+\mathbb{E}[\beta_4^T\mathcal{O}\beta_4]\\ &\le c_2\varepsilon^2\mathbb{E}\left[\mathbb{A}^{\mathrm{M}}[L_k]\right] + \frac{c_1\lambda_{\max}(\mathcal{O})\varepsilon^2\sigma_\theta^2\|\boldsymbol{u}_r\|^2}{m\theta^2}.\end{aligned} \tag{4.52}$$

Taking mathematical expectations of both sides of (4.40) and substituting estimations (4.41)–(4.52) yields

$$\begin{aligned}\mathbb{E}[L_{k+1}] &= \sum_{i=1}^{4}\mathbb{E}[\beta_i^T\mathcal{O}\beta_i] + \sum_{i\neq j}\mathbb{E}[\beta_i^T\mathcal{O}\beta_j]\\ &= [\text{substitute (4.47) first}]\\ &\le (1-c_3\varepsilon)\mathbb{E}[\beta_1^T\mathcal{O}\beta_1] + \sum_{i=2}^{4}\mathbb{E}[\beta_i^T\mathcal{O}\beta_i] + \sum_{i\neq j}\mathbb{E}[\beta_i^T\mathcal{O}\beta_j]\\ &= [\text{substitute other estimations, } \varepsilon \text{ sufficiently small}]\\ &\le (1-c_3\varepsilon+\eta_1\varepsilon^2)\mathbb{E}\left[\mathbb{A}^{\mathrm{M}}[L_k]\right] + \eta_2\frac{\varepsilon^2\lambda_{\max}(\mathcal{O})\sigma_\theta^2\|\boldsymbol{u}_r\|^2}{m\theta^2},\end{aligned} \tag{4.53}$$

where $\eta_1 = 3(c_1+c_2)+c_4+c_5$ and $\eta_2 = 3c_1+c_6$.

We denote $\rho = 1-c_3\varepsilon+\eta_1\varepsilon^2$ and $\delta = \frac{\varepsilon^2\lambda_{\max}(\mathcal{O})\sigma_\theta^2\|\boldsymbol{u}_r\|^2}{m\theta^2}$. It is evident that if we select $\varepsilon < \min\{\eta_1^{-1}c_3, c_3^{-1}\}$, we can ensure that $0<\rho<1$. In other words, a sufficiently small ε guarantees that $0<\rho<1$. Under this condition, (4.53) becomes

$$\begin{aligned}\mathbb{E}[L_{k+1}] &\le \rho\mathbb{E}\left[\mathbb{A}^{\mathrm{M}}[L_k]\right]+\eta_2\delta\\ &= \rho\mathbb{A}^{\mathrm{M}}\left[\mathbb{E}[L_k]\right]+\eta_2\delta\\ &\le \rho\max_{1\le i\le m}\mathbb{E}[L_{k+1-i}]+\eta_2\delta.\end{aligned} \tag{4.54}$$

We denote $T_k = \mathbb{E}[L_k] - \frac{\eta_2\delta}{1-\rho}$. Then, from (4.54), we have

$$T_{k+1} \le \rho\max_{1\le i\le m} T_{k+1-i}. \tag{4.55}$$

If $T_{k+1}\le 0$, then $\mathbb{E}[L_k]$ has entered the $\frac{\eta_2\delta}{1-\rho}$ neighborhood of zero and will remain in the neighborhood for subsequent iterations. If $T_{k+1}>0$, the proof can be continued by iterating (4.55). Similar to (4.55), we have $T_{k+2} \leq \rho \max_{1\leq i\leq m} T_{k+2-i}$, leading to the following:

$$\begin{aligned}\max_{1\leq i\leq m} T_{k+2-i} &= \max\{\max_{2\leq i\leq m} T_{k+2-i}, T_{k+1}\} \\ &\leq \max\{\max_{1\leq i\leq m} T_{k+1-i}, \rho \max_{1\leq i\leq m} T_{k+1-i}\} \\ &\leq \max_{1\leq i\leq m} T_{k+1-i}. \end{aligned} \tag{4.56}$$

As a consequence, $T_{k+2} \leq \rho \max_{1\leq i\leq m} T_{k+1-i}$. By the mathematical induction method, we can conclude that $T_{k+j} \leq \rho \max_{1\leq i\leq m} T_{k+1-i}$, $\forall j = 1,2,\ldots,m$. Summarizing these estimations, we have

$$\max_{1\leq i\leq m} T_{k+j} \leq \rho \max_{1\leq i\leq m} T_{k+1-i}. \tag{4.57}$$

That is, we group the iterations into groups of m successive iterations, and (4.57) then implies that the maximum value of each group converges to zero as the group number increases. Thus, $T_k \to 0$ as $k \to \infty$. Consequently, we have proved that $\lim_{k\to\infty} \mathbb{E}[L_k] \leq \frac{\eta_2\delta}{1-\rho}$. It should be noted that $\mathcal{O}$ is a positive-definite matrix; thus, $\mathbb{E}[L_k] \geq \lambda_{\min}(\mathcal{O})\mathbb{E}[\|\Delta \boldsymbol{u}_k\|^2]$, which further yields

$$\mathbb{E}[\|\Delta \boldsymbol{u}_k\|^2] \leq \frac{\kappa(\mathcal{O})\eta_2\varepsilon^2\sigma_\theta^2\|\boldsymbol{u}_r\|^2}{(1-\rho)m\theta^2}, \tag{4.58}$$

where $\kappa(\mathcal{O}) = \frac{\lambda_{\max}(\mathcal{O})}{\lambda_{\min}(\mathcal{O})}$ is the condition number of matrix $\mathcal{O}$. The proof is thus completed. □

Proof of Theorem 4.2: The main procedure of this proof is similar to that of Theorem 4.1; however, the recursion differs from that of Theorem 4.1, leading to different formulations of the Lyapunov function and the associated conclusions. Thus, we provide specific derivations but omit repetitive explanations for the sake of brevity.

Similar to (4.15), we have

$$\begin{aligned}\boldsymbol{e}_k^{\mathrm{G}} &= \mathcal{P}(\boldsymbol{u}_r - \mathbb{A}^{\mathrm{G}}[\boldsymbol{u}_k^c]) \\ &= \mathcal{P}\left(\boldsymbol{u}_r - \mathbb{A}^{\mathrm{G}}[\boldsymbol{u}_k - \Phi_k(\boldsymbol{u}_r - \boldsymbol{u}_k) + \Phi_k\boldsymbol{u}_r]\right) \\ &= \mathbb{A}^{\mathrm{G}}[\mathcal{P}\Delta\boldsymbol{u}_k] + \mathbb{A}^{\mathrm{G}}[\mathcal{P}\Phi_k\Delta\boldsymbol{u}_k] - \mathbb{A}^{\mathrm{G}}[\mathcal{P}\Phi_k\boldsymbol{u}_r]. \end{aligned} \tag{4.59}$$

Subtracting both sides of (4.17) from $\boldsymbol{u}_r$ and substituting the above equation into the resulting equation leads to

$$\Delta\boldsymbol{u}_{k+1} = \boldsymbol{u}_r - \mathbb{A}^{\mathrm{G}}[\boldsymbol{u}_k] - \varepsilon h\boldsymbol{e}_k^{\mathrm{G}}$$

$$= \mathbb{A}^{\mathrm{G}}[\Delta \boldsymbol{u}_k] - \varepsilon \mathbb{A}^{\mathrm{G}}[\mathcal{P}_0 \Delta \boldsymbol{u}_k] \\ - \varepsilon \mathbb{A}^{\mathrm{G}}[\mathcal{P}_0 \Phi_k \Delta \boldsymbol{u}_k] + \varepsilon \mathbb{A}^{\mathrm{G}}[\mathcal{P}_0 \Phi_k \boldsymbol{u}_r]. \tag{4.60}$$

Applying the GA operator to $\Delta \boldsymbol{u}_{k+1}$, we have

$$\begin{aligned} \mathbb{A}^{\mathrm{G}}[\Delta \boldsymbol{u}_{k+1}] &= \frac{1}{k+1} \sum_{i=1}^{k+1} \Delta \boldsymbol{u}_i \\ &= \frac{1}{k+1} \Delta \boldsymbol{u}_{k+1} + \frac{k}{k+1} \cdot \frac{1}{k} \sum_{i=1}^{k} \Delta \boldsymbol{u}_i \\ &= \frac{k}{k+1} \mathbb{A}^{\mathrm{G}}[\Delta \boldsymbol{u}_k] + \frac{1}{k+1} \Delta \boldsymbol{u}_{k+1}. \end{aligned} \tag{4.61}$$

Substituting (4.60) into (4.61) yields

$$\begin{aligned} \mathbb{A}^{\mathrm{G}}[\Delta \boldsymbol{u}_{k+1}] = \mathbb{A}^{\mathrm{G}}[\Delta \boldsymbol{u}_k] - \frac{\varepsilon}{k+1} \mathbb{A}^{\mathrm{G}}[\mathcal{P}_0 \Delta \boldsymbol{u}_k] \\ - \frac{\varepsilon}{k+1} \mathbb{A}^{\mathrm{G}}[\mathcal{P}_0 \Phi_k \Delta \boldsymbol{u}_k] + \frac{\varepsilon}{k+1} \mathbb{A}^{\mathrm{G}}[\mathcal{P}_0 \Phi_k \boldsymbol{u}_r]. \end{aligned} \tag{4.62}$$

We define the following Lyapunov function:

$$L_k = (\mathbb{A}^{\mathrm{G}}[\Delta \boldsymbol{u}_k])^T \mathcal{O} (\mathbb{A}^{\mathrm{G}}[\Delta \boldsymbol{u}_k]), \tag{4.63}$$

where $\mathcal{O}$ is the solution of $h(\mathcal{P}^T \mathcal{O} + \mathcal{O}\mathcal{P}) = I$.

Denote $\Delta \boldsymbol{u}_k^{\mathrm{G}} = \mathbb{A}^{\mathrm{G}}[\Delta \boldsymbol{u}_k]$. Then, we have

$$L_{k+1} = \sum_{i=1}^{4} \beta_i^T \mathcal{O} \beta_i + \sum_{i \neq j} \beta_i^T \mathcal{O} \beta_j, \tag{4.64}$$

where β_i, $1 \le i \le 4$, are defined as

$$\beta_1 = \Delta \boldsymbol{u}_k^{\mathrm{G}}, \qquad \beta_2 = -\frac{\varepsilon}{k+1} \mathcal{P}_0 \Delta \boldsymbol{u}_k^{\mathrm{G}},$$

$$\beta_3 = -\frac{\varepsilon}{k+1} \mathbb{A}^{\mathrm{G}}[\mathcal{P}_0 \Phi_k \Delta \boldsymbol{u}_k], \qquad \beta_4 = \frac{\varepsilon}{k+1} \mathbb{A}^{\mathrm{G}}[\mathcal{P}_0 \Phi_k \boldsymbol{u}_r].$$

Similar to the steps of the proof of Theorem 4.1, we have

$$\begin{aligned} \mathbb{E}[\beta_2^T \mathcal{O} \beta_2] &= \frac{\varepsilon^2}{(k+1)^2} \mathbb{E}\left[(\Delta \boldsymbol{u}_k^{\mathrm{G}})^T \mathcal{P}_0 \mathcal{O} \mathcal{P}_0 (\Delta \boldsymbol{u}_k^{\mathrm{G}}) \right] \\ &\le c_1 \frac{\varepsilon^2}{(k+1)^2} \mathbb{E}\left[(\mathbb{A}^{\mathrm{G}}[\Delta \boldsymbol{u}_k])^T \mathcal{O} (\mathbb{A}^{\mathrm{G}}[\Delta \boldsymbol{u}_k]) \right] \end{aligned}$$

$$= c_1 \frac{\varepsilon^2}{(k+1)^2}\mathbb{E}[L_k], \tag{4.65}$$

$$\begin{aligned}
\mathbb{E}[\beta_3^T \mathcal{O} \beta_3] &= \frac{\varepsilon^2}{(k+1)^2}\mathbb{E}\left[(\mathbb{A}^{\mathrm{G}}[\mathcal{P}_0\Phi_k\Delta \boldsymbol{u}_k])^T \mathcal{O}\right. \\
&\qquad \left.\times(\mathbb{A}^{\mathrm{G}}[\mathcal{P}_0\Phi_k\Delta \boldsymbol{u}_k]\right] \\
&\le c_1 \frac{\varepsilon^2}{(k+1)^2}\mathbb{E}\left[(\mathbb{A}^{\mathrm{G}}[\Phi_k\Delta \boldsymbol{u}_k])^T \mathcal{O}(\mathbb{A}^{\mathrm{G}}[\Phi_k\Delta \boldsymbol{u}_k])\right] \\
&\le c_2 \frac{\varepsilon^2}{(k+1)^2}\mathbb{E}[L_k],
\end{aligned} \tag{4.66}$$

$$\begin{aligned}
\mathbb{E}[\beta_4^T \mathcal{O} \beta_4] &= \frac{\varepsilon^2}{(k+1)^2}\mathbb{E}\left[(\mathbb{A}^{\mathrm{G}}[\mathcal{P}_0\Phi_k \boldsymbol{u}_r])^T \mathcal{O}\mathbb{A}^{\mathrm{G}}[\mathcal{P}_0\Phi_k \boldsymbol{u}_r]\right] \\
&\le c_1 \frac{\varepsilon^2}{(k+1)^2}\mathbb{E}\left[\boldsymbol{u}_r^T(\mathbb{A}^{\mathrm{G}}[\Phi_k])^T \mathcal{O}(\mathbb{A}^{\mathrm{G}}[\Phi_k])\boldsymbol{u}_r\right] \\
&= c_1 \frac{\varepsilon^2}{(k+1)^2}\lambda_{\max}(\mathcal{O})\boldsymbol{u}_r^T \frac{\sum_{i=1}^k \mathbb{E}[\Phi_i^2]}{k^2}\boldsymbol{u}_r \\
&= \frac{c_1\varepsilon^2\lambda_{\max}(\mathcal{O})\sigma_\theta^2\|\boldsymbol{u}_r\|^2}{\theta(k+1)^2 k}.
\end{aligned} \tag{4.67}$$

Moreover, for the crossing terms of β_1 and β_2, we have

$$\begin{aligned}
&\mathbb{E}[\beta_1^T \mathcal{O}\beta_2 + \beta_2^T \mathcal{O}\beta_1] \\
&= -\frac{\varepsilon}{k+1}\mathbb{E}\left[(\Delta \boldsymbol{u}_k^{\mathrm{G}})^T[\mathcal{O}\mathcal{P}_0 + \mathcal{P}_0^T\mathcal{O}](\Delta \boldsymbol{u}_k^{\mathrm{G}})\right] \\
&= -\frac{\varepsilon}{k+1}\mathbb{E}[(\Delta \boldsymbol{u}_k^{\mathrm{G}})^T(\Delta \boldsymbol{u}_k^{\mathrm{G}})] \\
&\le -c_3\frac{\varepsilon}{k+1}\mathbb{E}[(\Delta \boldsymbol{u}_k^{\mathrm{G}})^T\mathcal{O}(\Delta \boldsymbol{u}_k^{\mathrm{G}})] \\
&= -c_3\frac{\varepsilon}{k+1}\mathbb{E}[L_k].
\end{aligned} \tag{4.68}$$

For the crossing terms of β_1 and β_3, we have

$$\begin{aligned}
&\mathbb{E}[\beta_1^T \mathcal{O}\beta_3 + \beta_3^T \mathcal{O}\beta_1] \\
&= -\frac{2\varepsilon}{k+1}\mathbb{E}\left[(\Delta \boldsymbol{u}_k^{\mathrm{G}})^T[\mathcal{O}\mathcal{P}_0]\mathbb{A}^{\mathrm{G}}[\Phi_k\Delta \boldsymbol{u}_k]\right] \\
&\le -\frac{2\varepsilon}{(k+1)k^2}\mathbb{E}\left[\sum_{1\le i<j\le k}\Delta \boldsymbol{u}_{k+1-i}^T[\mathcal{O}\mathcal{P}_0]\Phi_{k+1-j}\Delta \boldsymbol{u}_{k+1-j}\right] \\
&\le c_4\frac{2\varepsilon^2}{(k+1)}\times\frac{1}{k^2}\times\frac{k(k-1)}{2}\mathbb{E}[L_k]
\end{aligned}$$

$$\leq c_4 \frac{\varepsilon^2}{k+1} \mathbb{E}[L_k]. \tag{4.69}$$

Similarly, we have the estimate of the crossing terms of β_1 and β_3 as follows:

$$\begin{aligned} &\mathbb{E}[\beta_1^T \mathcal{O} \beta_4 + \beta_4^T \mathcal{O} \beta_1] \\ &\quad \leq c_5 \frac{\varepsilon^2}{k+1} \mathbb{E}[L_k] + c_6 \frac{\varepsilon^2 \lambda_{\max}(\mathcal{O}) \sigma_\theta^2 \|\boldsymbol{u}_r\|^2}{\theta(k+1)k}. \end{aligned} \tag{4.70}$$

For the remaining crossing terms, we have

$$\begin{aligned} &\mathbb{E}[\beta_2^T \mathcal{O} \beta_3 + \beta_3^T \mathcal{O} \beta_2] \leq \mathbb{E}[\beta_2^T \mathcal{O} \beta_2 + \beta_3^T \mathcal{O} \beta_3] \\ &\quad \leq (c_1 + c_2) \frac{\varepsilon^2}{(k+1)^2} \mathbb{E}[L_k], \end{aligned} \tag{4.71}$$

$$\begin{aligned} &\mathbb{E}[\beta_2^T \mathcal{O} \beta_4 + \beta_4^T \mathcal{O} \beta_2] \leq \mathbb{E}[\beta_2^T \mathcal{O} \beta_2 + \beta_4^T \mathcal{O} \beta_4] \\ &\quad \leq c_1 \frac{\varepsilon^2}{(k+1)^2} \mathbb{E}[L_k] + \frac{c_1 \varepsilon^2 \lambda_{\max}(\mathcal{O}) \sigma_\theta^2 \|\boldsymbol{u}_r\|^2}{\theta(k+1)^2 k}, \end{aligned} \tag{4.72}$$

$$\begin{aligned} &\mathbb{E}[\beta_3^T \mathcal{O} \beta_4 + \beta_4^T \mathcal{O} \beta_3] \leq \mathbb{E}[\beta_3^T \mathcal{O} \beta_3 + \beta_4^T \mathcal{O} \beta_4] \\ &\quad \leq c_2 \frac{\varepsilon^2}{(k+1)^2} \mathbb{E}[L_k] + \frac{c_1 \varepsilon^2 \lambda_{\max}(\mathcal{O}) \sigma_\theta^2 \|\boldsymbol{u}_r\|^2}{\theta(k+1)^2 k}. \end{aligned} \tag{4.73}$$

Combining (4.64)–(4.73), we obtain

$$\begin{aligned} &\mathbb{E}[L_{k+1}] \\ &\leq \left(1 - \frac{c_3 \varepsilon - (c_4 + c_5) \varepsilon^2}{k+1} + 3(c_1 + c_2) \frac{\varepsilon^2}{(k+1)^2}\right) \mathbb{E}[L_k] \\ &\quad + \frac{(3c_1 + c_6(k+1)) \varepsilon^2 \lambda_{\max}(\mathcal{O}) \sigma_\theta^2 \|\boldsymbol{u}_r\|^2}{\theta(k+1)^2 k}. \end{aligned} \tag{4.74}$$

Denote $\rho_k = \frac{c_3 \varepsilon - (c_4 + c_5) \varepsilon^2}{k+1} - \frac{3(c_1 + c_2) \varepsilon^2}{(k+1)^2}$ and $\delta_k = \frac{3c_1}{k+1} + c_6$. For a sufficiently small ε, we can ensure that $0 < \rho_k < 1$ and $\rho_k \sim \frac{1}{k}$. In addition, δ_k is bounded.

The terms ρ_k and $\delta_k \frac{\varepsilon^2 \lambda_{\max}(\mathcal{O}) \sigma_\theta^2 \|\boldsymbol{u}_r\|^2}{\theta(k+1)k}$ correspond to τ_k and χ_k in Lemma A.3. It is apparent that all conditions in Lemma A.3 are satisfied; therefore, we can conclude that $\mathbb{E}[L_k] \to 0$ by Lemma A.3. Because $\mathcal{O}$ is a positive-definite matrix, the conclusion is valid. The proof is thus completed. □

Proof of Theorem 4.3: The main steps of this proof are similar to those of Theorem 4.2, with slight modifications to specific recursion derivations.

Thus, the following steps are condensed to clarify the critical steps, and steps similar to those in previous proofs are omitted for the sake of brevity.

Similar to (4.15), we have

$$\begin{aligned}\boldsymbol{e}_k^{\mathrm{F}} &= \mathcal{P}(\boldsymbol{u}_r - \mathbb{A}^{\mathrm{F}}[\boldsymbol{u}_k^c]) \\ &= \mathcal{P}\left(\boldsymbol{u}_r - \mathbb{A}^{\mathrm{F}}[\boldsymbol{u}_k - \Phi_k(\boldsymbol{u}_r - \boldsymbol{u}_k) + \Phi_k \boldsymbol{u}_r]\right) \\ &= \mathbb{A}^{\mathrm{F}}[\mathcal{P}\Delta\boldsymbol{u}_k] + \mathbb{A}^{\mathrm{F}}[\mathcal{P}\Phi_k\Delta\boldsymbol{u}_k] - \mathbb{A}^{\mathrm{F}}[\mathcal{P}\Phi_k\boldsymbol{u}_r]. \end{aligned} \tag{4.75}$$

Subtracting both sides of (4.18) from $\boldsymbol{u}_r$ and substituting the above equation into the resulting equation leads to

$$\begin{aligned}\Delta\boldsymbol{u}_{k+1} &= \boldsymbol{u}_r - \mathbb{A}^{\mathrm{F}}[\boldsymbol{u}_k] - \varepsilon h \boldsymbol{e}_k^{\mathrm{F}} \\ &= \mathbb{A}^{\mathrm{F}}[\Delta\boldsymbol{u}_k] - \varepsilon\mathbb{A}^{\mathrm{F}}[\mathcal{P}_0\Delta\boldsymbol{u}_k] \\ &\quad - \varepsilon\mathbb{A}^{\mathrm{F}}[\mathcal{P}_0\Phi_k\Delta\boldsymbol{u}_k] + \varepsilon\mathbb{A}^{\mathrm{F}}[\mathcal{P}_0\Phi_k\boldsymbol{u}_r]. \end{aligned} \tag{4.76}$$

In addition,

$$\begin{aligned}\mathbb{A}^{\mathrm{F}}[\Delta\boldsymbol{u}_{k+1}] &= \frac{1-\gamma}{1-\gamma^{k+1}}\sum_{i=1}^{k+1}\gamma^{i-1}\Delta\boldsymbol{u}_{k+2-i} \\ &= \frac{1-\gamma}{1-\gamma^{k+1}}\Delta\boldsymbol{u}_{k+1} + \frac{1-\gamma}{1-\gamma^{k+1}}\sum_{i=2}^{k+1}\gamma^{i-1}\Delta\boldsymbol{u}_{k+2-i} \\ &= \frac{1-\gamma}{1-\gamma^{k+1}}\Delta\boldsymbol{u}_{k+1} + \frac{1-\gamma}{1-\gamma^{k+1}}\gamma\sum_{i=1}^{k}\gamma^{i-1}\Delta\boldsymbol{u}_{k+1-i} \\ &= \frac{1-\gamma}{1-\gamma^{k+1}}\Delta\boldsymbol{u}_{k+1} + \frac{1-\gamma}{1-\gamma^{k+1}}\gamma\times\frac{1-\gamma^k}{1-\gamma}\mathbb{A}^{\mathrm{F}}[\Delta\boldsymbol{u}_k] \\ &= \frac{1-\gamma}{1-\gamma^{k+1}}\Delta\boldsymbol{u}_{k+1} + \frac{1-\gamma^k}{1-\gamma^{k+1}}\gamma\mathbb{A}^{\mathrm{F}}[\Delta\boldsymbol{u}_k]. \end{aligned} \tag{4.77}$$

Substituting (4.76) into (4.77) yields

$$\begin{aligned}&\mathbb{A}^{\mathrm{F}}[\Delta\boldsymbol{u}_{k+1}] \\ &= \frac{1-\gamma^k}{1-\gamma^{k+1}}\cdot\gamma\mathbb{A}^{\mathrm{F}}[\Delta\boldsymbol{u}_k] \\ &\quad + \frac{1-\gamma}{1-\gamma^{k+1}}\left(\mathbb{A}^{\mathrm{F}}[\Delta\boldsymbol{u}_k] - \varepsilon\mathbb{A}^{\mathrm{F}}[\mathcal{P}_0\Delta\boldsymbol{u}_k]\right) \\ &\quad + \frac{1-\gamma}{1-\gamma^{k+1}}\left(\varepsilon\mathbb{A}^{\mathrm{F}}[\mathcal{P}_0\Phi_k\boldsymbol{u}_r] - \varepsilon\mathbb{A}^{\mathrm{F}}[\mathcal{P}_0\Phi_k\Delta\boldsymbol{u}_k]\right)\end{aligned}$$

$$= \beta_1 + \beta_2 + \beta_3 + \beta_4, \tag{4.78}$$

where

$$\beta_1 = \mathbb{A}^{\mathrm{F}}[\Delta \boldsymbol{u}_k], \qquad \beta_2 = -\varphi_k \varepsilon \mathbb{A}^{\mathrm{F}}[\mathcal{P}_0 \Delta \boldsymbol{u}_k]$$
$$\beta_3 = -\varphi_k \varepsilon \mathbb{A}^{\mathrm{F}}[\mathcal{P}_0 \Phi_k \Delta \boldsymbol{u}_k], \qquad \beta_4 = \varphi_k \varepsilon \mathbb{A}^{\mathrm{F}}[\mathcal{P}_0 \Phi_k \boldsymbol{u}_r],$$

with $\varphi_k = \frac{1-\gamma}{1-\gamma^{k+1}}$. It is clear that $1-\gamma < \varphi_k < 1$, $\forall k$.

We employ the Lyapunov function $L_k = (\mathbb{A}^{\mathrm{F}}[\Delta \boldsymbol{u}_k])^T \mathcal{O} (\mathbb{A}^{\mathrm{F}}[\Delta \boldsymbol{u}_k])$. Thus,

$$L_{k+1} = \sum_{i=1}^{t} \beta_i^T \mathcal{O} \beta_i + \sum_{i \neq j} \beta_i^T \mathcal{O} \beta_j. \tag{4.79}$$

Following similar derivations for the GA case, we obtain

$$\mathbb{E}[\beta_2^T \mathcal{O} \beta_2] \leq c_1 \varphi_k^2 \varepsilon^2 \mathbb{E}[L_k], \quad \mathbb{E}[\beta_3^T \mathcal{O} \beta_3] \leq c_2 \varphi_k^2 \varepsilon^2 \mathbb{E}[L_k].$$

For the fading deviation term, we have

$$\begin{aligned}
\mathbb{E}[\beta_4^T \mathcal{O} \beta_4] &\leq c_1 \varphi_k^2 \varepsilon^2 \lambda_{\max}(\mathcal{O}) \boldsymbol{u}_r^T \mathbb{E}[(\mathbb{A}^{\mathrm{F}}[\Phi_k])^T \mathbb{A}^{\mathrm{F}}[\Phi_k]] \boldsymbol{u}_r \\
&\leq c_1 \varphi_k^2 \varepsilon^2 \lambda_{\max}(\mathcal{O}) \varphi_{k-1}^2 \boldsymbol{u}_r^T \mathbb{E}\left[\left(\sum_{i=1}^{k} \gamma^{i-1} \Phi_{k+1-i}\right)^2\right] \boldsymbol{u}_r \\
&\leq c_1 \varphi_k^2 \varepsilon^2 \lambda_{\max}(\mathcal{O}) \varphi_{k-1}^2 \boldsymbol{u}_r^T \sum_{i=1}^{k} \gamma^{2(i-1)} \mathbb{E}[\Phi_{k+1-i}^2] \boldsymbol{u}_r \\
&\leq c_1 \varphi_k^2 \varphi_{k-1}^2 \varepsilon^2 \frac{1-\gamma^{2k}}{1-\gamma^2} \times \frac{\|\boldsymbol{u}_r\|^2 \lambda_{\max}(\mathcal{O}) \sigma_\theta^2}{\theta} \\
&\leq c_1 \varphi_k^2 \varphi_{k-1} \varepsilon^2 \times \frac{\|\boldsymbol{u}_r\|^2 \lambda_{\max}(\mathcal{O}) \sigma_\theta^2}{\theta}.
\end{aligned} \tag{4.80}$$

For the crossing terms, we have

$$\mathbb{E}[\beta_1^T \mathcal{O} \beta_2 + \beta_2^T \mathcal{O} \beta_1] \leq -c_3 \varphi_k \varepsilon \mathbb{E}[L_k], \tag{4.81}$$
$$\mathbb{E}[\beta_1^T \mathcal{O} \beta_3 + \beta_3^T \mathcal{O} \beta_1] \leq c_4 \varphi_k \varepsilon^2 \mathbb{E}[L_k], \tag{4.82}$$
$$\begin{aligned}
\mathbb{E}[\beta_1^T \mathcal{O} \beta_4 + \beta_4^T \mathcal{O} \beta_1] \leq{}& c_5 \varphi_k \varepsilon^2 \mathbb{E}[L_k] \\
&+ c_6 \varphi_k \varphi_{k-1} \varepsilon^2 \times \frac{\|\boldsymbol{u}_r\|^2 \lambda_{\max}(\mathcal{O}) \sigma_\theta^2}{\theta},
\end{aligned} \tag{4.83}$$
$$\mathbb{E}[\beta_2^T \mathcal{O} \beta_3 + \beta_3^T \mathcal{O} \beta_2] \leq (c_1 + c_2) \varphi_k^2 \varepsilon^2 \mathbb{E}[L_k], \tag{4.84}$$

$$\mathbb{E}[\beta_2^T \mathcal{O} \beta_4 + \beta_4^T \mathcal{O} \beta_2] \leq c_1 \varphi_k^2 \varepsilon^2 \mathbb{E}[L_k] + c_1 \varphi_k^2 \varphi_{k-1} \varepsilon^2 \times \frac{\|\boldsymbol{u}_r\|^2 \lambda_{\max}(\mathcal{O}) \sigma_\theta^2}{\theta}, \tag{4.85}$$

$$\mathbb{E}[\beta_3^T \mathcal{O} \beta_4 + \beta_4^T \mathcal{O} \beta_3] \leq c_2 \varphi_k^2 \varepsilon^2 \mathbb{E}[L_k] + c_1 \varphi_k^2 \varphi_{k-1} \varepsilon^2 \times \frac{\|\boldsymbol{u}_r\|^2 \lambda_{\max}(\mathcal{O}) \sigma_\theta^2}{\theta}. \tag{4.86}$$

These estimates lead to

$$\mathbb{E}[L_{k+1}] \leq (1 - \rho_k) \mathbb{E}[L_k] + \delta_k \frac{\|\boldsymbol{u}_r\|^2 \lambda_{\max}(\mathcal{O}) \sigma_\theta^2}{\theta}, \tag{4.87}$$

where $\rho_k = c_3 \varphi_k \varepsilon - 3(c_1 + c_2) \varphi_k^2 \varepsilon^2 - (c_4 + c_5) \varphi_k \varepsilon^2$ and $\delta_k = (3c_1 \varphi_k + c_6) \varepsilon^2 \varphi_k \varphi_{k-1}$. Evidently, selecting a sufficiently small ε can ensure that $0 < \rho_k < 1$. Moreover, due to the boundedness of φ_k, ρ_k is a positive distance away from zero for all iterations k as long as ε is fixed. In addition, δ_k is also upper bounded.

It should be noted that

$$\begin{aligned} \lim_{k \to \infty} \frac{\delta_k}{\rho_k} &= \lim_{k \to \infty} \frac{(3c_1 \varphi_k + c_6) \varepsilon^2 \varphi_{k-1}}{c_3 \varepsilon - 3(c_1 + c_2) \varphi_k \varepsilon^2 - (c_4 + c_5) \varepsilon^2} \\ &= \underbrace{\frac{[3c_1(1-\gamma)^2 + c_6(1-\gamma)] \varepsilon^2}{c_3 \varepsilon - [3(c_1 + c_2)(1-\gamma) + (c_4 + c_5)] \varepsilon^2}}_{\triangleq \varpi}. \end{aligned} \tag{4.88}$$

This implies that

$$\lim_{k \to \infty} \mathbb{E}[L_k] = \frac{\varpi \|\boldsymbol{u}_r\|^2 \lambda_{\max}(\mathcal{O}) \sigma_\theta^2}{\theta} \tag{4.89}$$

and

$$\lim_{k \to \infty} \mathbb{E}[\|\mathbb{A}^{\mathrm{F}}[\Delta \boldsymbol{u}_k]\|^2] \leq \kappa(\mathcal{O}) \frac{\varpi \|\boldsymbol{u}_r\|^2 \sigma_\theta^2}{\theta}. \tag{4.90}$$

The proof is thus completed. □

Remark 4.4 *The general analysis frameworks for three cases are similar. However, the proof of the MA case is significantly different from the others. For the MA case, a grouping technique is introduced to overcome the difficulty of the iteration-based moving window issue. For GA and FA cases, a novel Lyapunov function is adopted and for this reason, a recursion of the averaged input is established in the iteration domain.*

4.5 DISCUSSIONS AND EXTENSIONS

4.5.1 Plant Model

In this chapter, we consider the lifted time-invariant system (4.1) to evaluate different averaging techniques. The results can be extended to more general systems without significant effort.

First, the lifted system matrix $\mathcal{P}$ in (4.2) is a Toeplitz matrix, indicating that the system is time-invariant. However, no derivation in Sections 4.3 and 4.4 requires the diagonal elements of $\mathcal{P}$ to be identical. In other words, all results are valid for a time-varying system in which the lifted system matrix $\mathcal{P}$ is formed as follows:

$$\mathcal{P} = \begin{bmatrix} p_{1,1} & 0 & \cdots & 0 \\ p_{2,1} & p_{2,2} & \cdots & 0 \\ \vdots & \vdots & \ddots & \vdots \\ p_{n,1} & p_{n,2} & \cdots & p_{n,n} \end{bmatrix}. \tag{4.91}$$

It should be emphasized that in this case, the scalar gain h in (4.16)–(4.18) should be replaced by $\mathcal{H} = \text{diag}\{h_1, h_2, \ldots, h_n\}$ satisfying the condition $h_i p_{i,i} > 0, \forall i$.

Moreover, both (4.2) and (4.91) correspond to a SISO plant. We address the extension to a MIMO system as follows:

$$\begin{aligned} x_k(t+1) &= A_t x_k(t) + B_t u_k(t), \\ y_k(t) &= C_t x_k(t), \quad 0 \le t \le n, \end{aligned} \tag{4.92}$$

where $u_k(t) \in \mathbb{R}^p$, $y_k(t) \in \mathbb{R}^q$, and $x_k(t) \in \mathbb{R}^o$ are the input, output, and state, respectively. $A_t \in \mathbb{R}^{o\times o}$, $B_t \in \mathbb{R}^{o\times p}$, and $C_t \in \mathbb{R}^{q\times o}$ are matrices with appropriate dimensions. For this system, we can formulate the lifted vectors $\boldsymbol{y}_k = [y_k^T(1), y_k^T(2), \ldots, y_k^T(n)]^T \in \mathbf{R}^{nq}$ and $\boldsymbol{u}_k = [u_k^T(0), y_k^T(1), \ldots, u_k^T(n-1)]^T \in \mathbf{R}^{np}$. We then have

$$\boldsymbol{y}_k = \mathcal{P}^* \boldsymbol{u}_k + \mathcal{M} x_k(0), \tag{4.93}$$

where

$$\mathcal{P}^* = \begin{bmatrix} C_1 B_0 & 0 & \cdots & 0 \\ C_2 A_1 B_0 & C_2 B_1 & \cdots & 0 \\ \vdots & \vdots & \ddots & \vdots \\ C_n A_{n-1} \cdots A_1 B_0 & \cdots & \cdots & C_n B_{n-1} \end{bmatrix}$$

and $\mathcal{M} = [(C_1A_0)^T, \cdots, (C_nA_{n-1}\cdots A_0)^T]^T$. $\mathcal{M}x_k(0)$ corresponds to $\boldsymbol{d}_k$ in (4.1); this explains why we call $\boldsymbol{d}_k$ the system response to the initial state. Accordingly, h in (4.16)–(4.18) is replaced by matrix $\mathcal{H} = \text{diag}\{H_0, H_1, \ldots, H_{n-1}\} \in \mathbb{R}^{np\times nq}$. In addition, the condition $p_1h > 0$ corresponds to an extension that all eigenvalues of $H_tC_{t+1}B_t$ have positive real parts, $\forall t$. Under this condition, all eigenvalues of the block lower triangular matrix $\mathcal{HP}^*$ have positive real parts, and the Lyapunov equation $(\mathcal{HP}^*)^T\mathcal{O} + \mathcal{O}(\mathcal{HP}^*) = I$ is solvable. Then, the previously obtained results hold for (4.92) using similar proofs.

4.5.2 Varying System Responses, Disturbances, and Noise

In the problem formulation, $\boldsymbol{d}_k$ denotes the system response to the initial state. For example, while considering the state space form (4.92), we have $\boldsymbol{d}_k = \mathcal{M}x_k(0)$. In ILC, it is generally assumed that each iteration can start from the same state [8, 55, 57, 71]; that is, $\boldsymbol{d}_k = \boldsymbol{d}_r$. This condition indicates that $\boldsymbol{d}_k$ retains invariant in the iteration domain. Several scholars have proposed relaxations or rectifying methods for varying system responses [60, 72]. Moreover, $\boldsymbol{d}_k$ can be used to model system disturbances and measurement noise, which are random by nature. In addition, channel noise is another critical factor of networked control structure, which can be transformed as a part of $\boldsymbol{d}_k$. In this subsection, we extend results to the variable $\boldsymbol{d}_k$ case to cover varying system responses, disturbances, and measurement/channel noise.

We consider two cases of variable $\boldsymbol{d}_k$. The first is called the asymptotically precise resetting case: $\boldsymbol{d}_k \to \boldsymbol{d}_r$ as $k \to \infty$ indicating that varying uncertainties vanish along the iteration axis. We denote $\boldsymbol{g}_k \triangleq \boldsymbol{d}_r - \boldsymbol{d}_k$. As a result, the tracking error provided in (4.10) contains an additional term:

$$\boldsymbol{e}_k = \mathcal{P}\Delta\boldsymbol{u}_k + \mathcal{P}\Phi_k\Delta\boldsymbol{u}_k - \mathcal{P}\Phi_k\boldsymbol{u}_r + \boldsymbol{g}_k. \tag{4.94}$$

Taking the MA-based scheme for example, an additional term $-\varepsilon h\mathbb{A}^{\mathrm{M}}[\boldsymbol{g}_k]$ should be added to the recursion (4.37) with the property that $\mathbb{A}^{\mathrm{M}}[\boldsymbol{g}_k] \to 0$. It should be noted that this term is independent of other terms. Then, all newly introduced terms in $\mathbb{E}[L_{k+1}]$ converge to zero. Thus, the bounded convergence of the proposed MA-based scheme is retained. By (4.24), the final tracking precision is independent of $\boldsymbol{g}_k$; however, for any k, the tracking performance is degraded by the error $\boldsymbol{g}_k$. Similarly, the results of the GA- and FA-based schemes are also valid.

The second case is called the random resetting case: $\boldsymbol{d}_k$ is random in the iteration domain with expectation $\mathbb{E}[\boldsymbol{d}_k] = \boldsymbol{d}_r$ and bounded covariance.

Additionally, it is independent of all other random variables. This case can effectively describe random system disturbances and measurement/channel noise. It is evident that $\boldsymbol{g}_k = \boldsymbol{d}_r - \boldsymbol{d}_k$ plays a similar role to $\mathcal{P}\Phi_k\boldsymbol{u}_r$ but is independent of all other terms in (4.94). Therefore, $\boldsymbol{g}_k$ does not affect the learning ability, but rather the tracking ability. In particular, the final upper bound of the input error in both the MA- and FA-based schemes is increased.

In summary, the above two cases involving additional randomness do not alter the results established in Section 4.3. Therefore, the main theorems can be extended to systems with nonidentical initial responses and random noise. Strict analysis can be performed similarly to the proofs in Section 4.4.

4.5.3 General Fading Framework

In this chapter, we examine input fading, as the fading of an input signal affects tracking performance even if the generated input sequence has converged to the desired input. In this subsection, we extend to the case involving output and input fading simultaneously.

When output transmission experiences random fading channels, by correcting the received output signals (i.e., by multiplying the inverse of the channel gain mean by the received outputs), we discover that the major concern in this scenario involves adding an output-dependent error with zero mean. This error can be treated similarly to the random $\boldsymbol{g}_k$ discussed in Section 4.5.2. Thus, the convergence of the input sequence is retained even when the outputs experience random fading. Moreover, according to Corollary 4.1, stable convergence to the desired input can be achieved as long as a decreasing learning step size sequence $\{\varepsilon_k\}$ is used such that $\varepsilon_k > 0$, $\varepsilon_k \to 0$, and $\sum_{k=1}^{\infty} \varepsilon_k = \infty$. Thus, if only output fading exists, the average technique is potentially helpful but unnecessary.

For a general two-sided fading scenario in which both input and output channels experience random fading, a general framework can be established by combining the above considerations. In particular, for a given iteration, the system dynamics is driven by the average input signal using one of the average operators, and the corresponding output is obtained and returned to the controller. The received output is then corrected by multiplying the inverse of the fading gain mean. Consequently, the corrected tracking error is obtained on the basis of the corrected output. Next, the learning process is executed using a learning scheme corresponding to the specified average operator. The newly generated input signals are then sent to the plant to drive the process of the following iteration. Thus, the general framework functions iteration by iteration. Similar results to those in Section 4.3 can be obtained following similar proofs to that in Section 4.4.

4.6 ILLUSTRATIVE SIMULATIONS

To demonstrate the properties of the proposed schemes, we consider the following discrete form of a permanent magnet linear motor (PMLM) model:

$$\begin{aligned} x(t+1) &= x(t) + v(t)\Delta, \\ v(t+1) &= v(t) - \Delta\frac{k_1 k_2 \Psi_f^2}{Rm} v(t) + \Delta\frac{k_2 \Psi_f}{Rm} u(t), \\ y(t) &= v(t), \end{aligned}$$

where $\Delta = 0.01$ s is the sampling time interval, x and v denote motor position and rotor velocity, $R = 8.6\,\Omega$ is the resistance of the stator, $m = 1.635$ kg is the rotor mass, $\psi_f = 0.35$ Wb is the flux linkage, $k_1 = \pi/\tau$ and $k_2 = 1.5\pi/\tau$, and $\tau = 0.031$ m is the pole pitch. The entire iteration length is $T = 0.6$ s or $n = 60$. The initial state is set to $x_k(0) = x_d(0) = 0$. The desired reference is given as

$$y_d(t) = 0.45\sin\left(\frac{\pi t}{10}\right) + 0.35\cos\left(\frac{\pi t}{6}\right).$$

Unless otherwise specified, random fading is modeled by a normal distribution, $\theta_k(t) \sim N(\theta, \sigma_\theta^2)$ with $\theta = 0.95$ and $\sigma_\theta = 0.1$. For each scenario and scheme, a repetitive process is run for 100 iterations. In all simulations, the regulation value h is set to 50.

4.6.1 MA-Based Scheme

In this subsection, we examine the performance of the MA-based scheme by determining the effects of the moving width, learning step size, and fading gain.

First, we consider the influence of moving iteration width m. To this end, three scenarios are considered: $m = 3$, $m = 6$, and $m = 10$. The learning step size is set to $\varepsilon = 0.6$. Fig. 4.3 presents the average Euclidean norm of the input errors in the iteration domain, where the average norm is defined as $\frac{1}{n}\|\boldsymbol{u}_r - \boldsymbol{u}_k\|^2$. In addition, the results of the GA-based scheme with $\varepsilon = 0.6$ are included as a reference.

Fig. 4.3 demonstrates that the MA-based scheme only results in bounded convergence of the input errors after several iterations. In addition, the larger

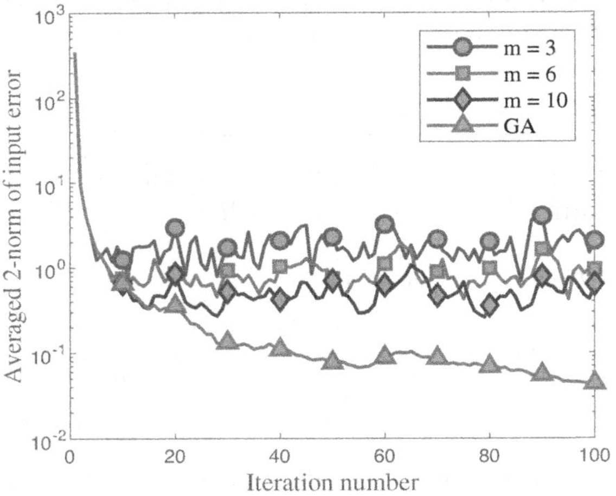

Figure 4.3 Input error norm profiles of the MA-based scheme in the iteration domain: Comparison of different moving widths m.

width m is, the smaller the convergence bound of the input errors is, indicating more accurate learning of the desired input signal. As width m increases, the input error profile approximates that generated by the GA-based scheme.

Next, we fix the moving width to $m = 6$ and consider three scenarios of learning step size ε: $\varepsilon = 0.2$, $\varepsilon = 0.4$, and $\varepsilon = 0.6$. In addition, we include results corresponding to a decreasing step size sequence $\varepsilon_k = k^{-0.7}$. Fig. 4.4 provides the average Euclidean norm of the input errors in the iteration domain.

Fig. 4.4 demonstrates the following observations. First, as the step size decreases from 0.6 to 0.2, the convergence rate of the input error profiles to their convergence bound decreases; that is, the scheme requires a large number of learning iterations to achieve its final convergence range. However, the amplitude of the input error norms decreases as well. Thus, a decrease in the learning step size may lead to more accurate tracking with a large number of learning iterations. In addition, as stated in Corollary 4.1, a decreasing step size sequence can ensure asymptotic zero error learning of the input sequence. This conclusion can be verified by comparing the input error profiles indicated by triangles in Figs. 4.3 and 4.4. It can be seen that a decreasing step size sequence ε_k leads the MA-based scheme to behave similarly to the GA-based scheme.

Lastly, we consider the effects of the fading gain distribution. To this end, we perform a crossing selection of parameters θ and σ_θ. The algorithm

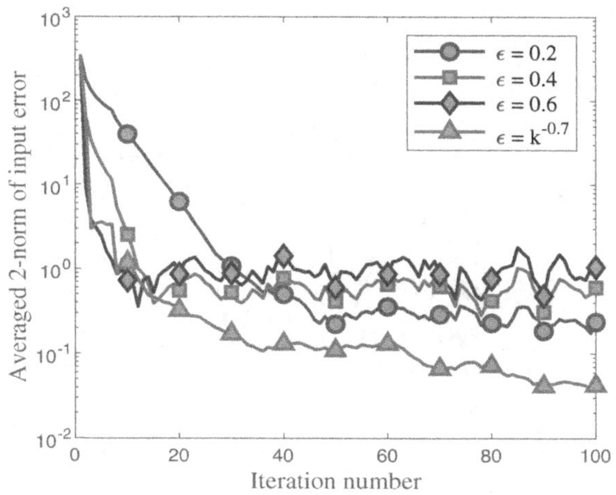

Figure 4.4 Input error norm profiles of the MA-based scheme in the iteration domain: Comparison of different learning step sizes ε and decreasing step size sequences ε_k.

parameters are set to $m = 6$ and $\varepsilon = 0.6$. The input error profiles are displayed in Fig. 4.5, where six combinations are taken into account. From the three solid lines, which have the same variance but different means, it can be seen that a smaller mean of the fading gain leads to a larger upper bound of the convergence range. Furthermore, from the three dashed lines, which have the same mean but different variances, it can be seen that a large variance corresponds to a large upper bound. These results are consistent with the estimation in (4.20). In addition, the variation of fading variance appears to lead to a more significant effect on the change of the convergence bound.

4.6.2 GA-Based Scheme

In this subsection, we examine the performance of the GA-based scheme by determining the effects of the learning step size and fading gain distribution.

From Theorem 4.2, it is known that the limit of the input error is independent of the learning step size because the limit is zero. However, different learning step sizes may affect the convergence rate. This influence is verified by Fig. 4.6, where the fading gain distribution obeys the prespecified distribution $N(0.95, 0.1^2)$. This figure indicates that the learning step size plays a significant role in the convergence rate. Furthermore, a small step size corresponds to a slow convergence rate. Therefore, a suitably large step

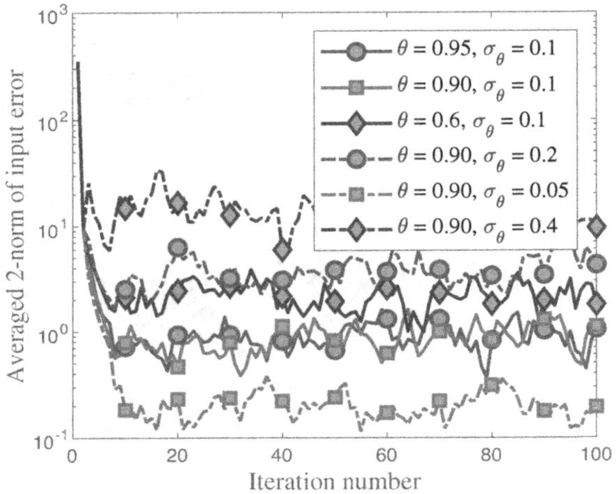

Figure 4.5 Input error norm profiles of the MA-based scheme in the iteration domain: Comparison of different selections of fading gain distributions.

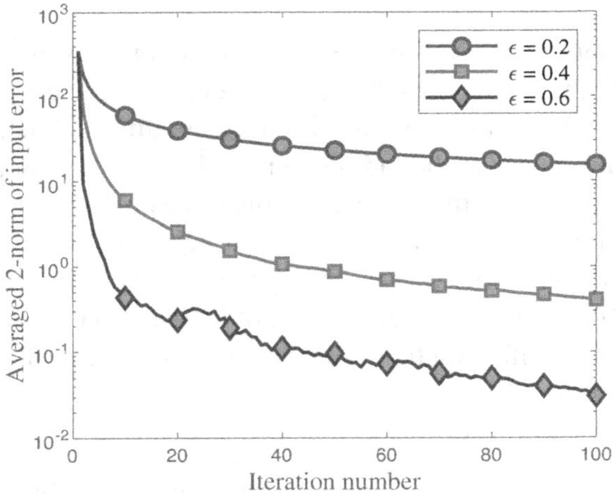

Figure 4.6 Input error norm profiles of the GA-based scheme in the iteration domain: Comparison of different step sizes.

size should be selected while satisfying the requirements in the convergence proof.

Another factor that should be considered in the GA-based scheme is the fading distribution. In particular, we consider the influence of the mean and

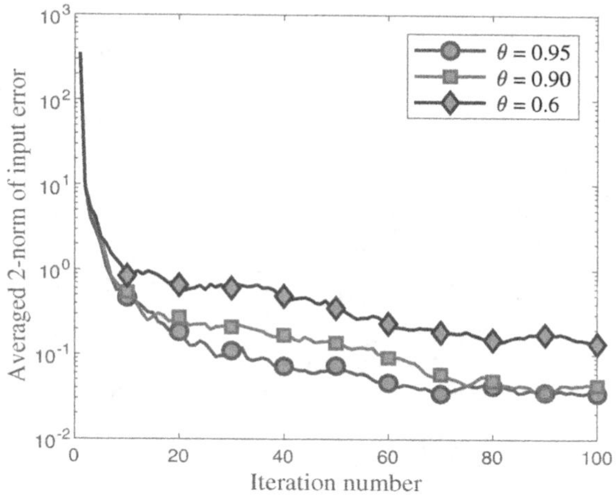

Figure 4.7 Input error norm profiles of the GA-based scheme in the iteration domain: Comparison of different means in fading distribution ($\sigma_\theta = 0.1$).

variance separately. For the mean, we fix the variance $\sigma_\theta = 0.1$, and let θ be 0.6, 0.9, and 0.95. The corresponding input error profiles are provided in Fig. 4.7. The results reveal that different means of the fading gain distribution have a minor impact on the convergence with the GA-based scheme.

For the variance, we fix the mean $\theta = 0.95$, and set the variance σ_θ to $0.1, 0.2$, and 0.4. Fig. 4.8 presents the average norm profiles of the input error in the iteration domain. It is clear that the variance of the fading gain distribution has a significant influence on the convergence rate; in particular, a smaller variance value leads to a faster convergence rate. This observation is consistent with our intuitive understanding that a smaller variance value indicates a relatively deterministic fading effect of the communication channels and can be effectively compensated.

4.6.3 FA-Based Scheme

In this subsection, we examine the performance of the FA-based scheme; here, the investigation focuses more on the influence of the forgetting factor. The step size is set to $\varepsilon = 0.6$, and the fading distribution obeys $N(0.95, 0.1^2)$. We first consider the case in which the forgetting factor approaches 1. In this case, four scenarios of γ are considered: γ =0.8, 0.9, 0.95, and 0.99. The average norm profiles of these four scenarios are presented in Fig. 4.9(a), where the results of the GA-based scheme are included as a reference. As

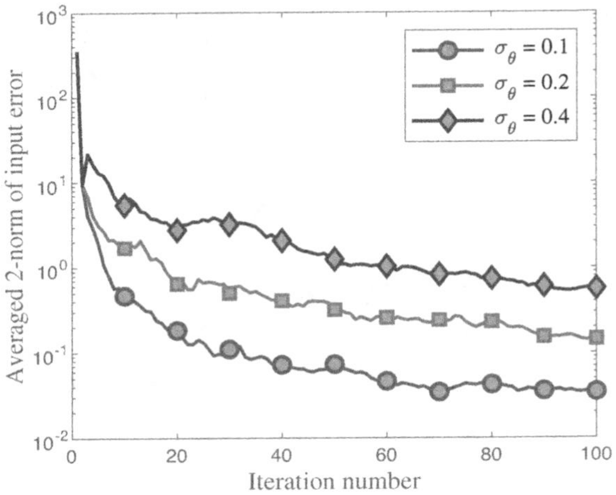

Figure 4.8 Input error norm profiles of the GA-based scheme in the iteration domain: Comparison of different variances in fading distribution ($\theta = 0.95$).

the forgetting factor γ approaches 1, the profiles of the FA-based scheme approximate that of the GA-based scheme. In particular, it can be seen from Fig. 4.9(a) that the profile for the scenario with $\gamma = 0.99$ nearly coincides with that of the GA-based scheme.

Next, we consider the case in which the forgetting factor approaches 0. We present four scenarios of γ: γ=0.6, 0.4, 0.2, and 0.02. The corresponding results are provided in Fig. 4.9(b). Two facts are observed. First, the smaller the forgetting factor is, the larger the upper bound of the convergence range is. Second, with a very small forgetting factor such as $\gamma = 0.02$, the resulting profile nearly coincides with the profile generated by the MA-based scheme with $m = 1$. Therefore, the results in Fig. 4.9 verify the theoretical analysis in Subsection 4.3.4.

The influence of the fading gain distribution on the FA-based scheme is similar to that of the MA-based scheme. The details are omitted.

4.6.4 Comparison between Three Schemes

In the previous subsections, the input error profiles are computed for each iteration independently. However, the tracking performance is determined by the average inputs. In this subsection, we present comparisons between the three schemes. The average Euclidean norm of the average input error, defined as $\frac{1}{n}\|\boldsymbol{u}_d - \mathbb{A}^\star[\boldsymbol{u}_k]\|^2$, is presented in Fig. 4.10. It can be seen that

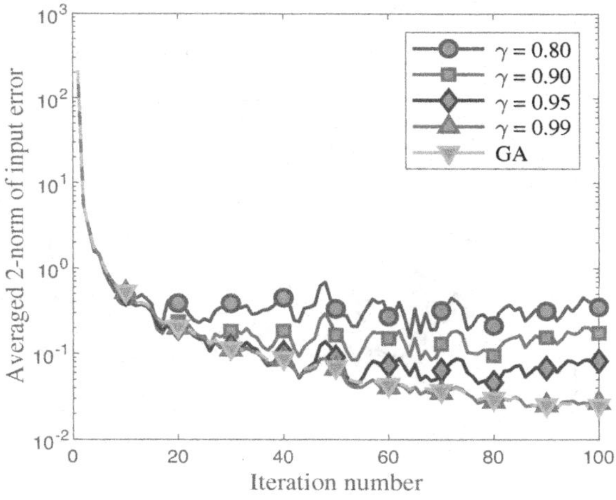

(a) Width

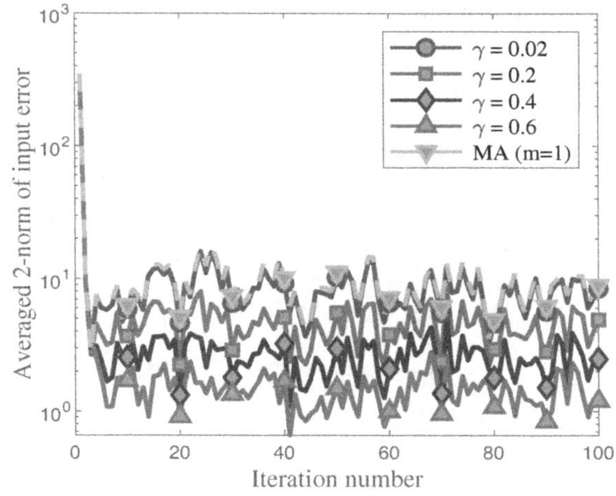

(b) Step size

Figure 4.9 Input error norm profiles of the FA-based scheme in the iteration domain: (a) Comparison of different forgetting factors close to 1; and (b) comparison of different forgetting factors close to 0.

the MA-based scheme converges to its bound rapidly; however, the convergence range is somewhat large. In contrast, the GA-based scheme has a slower convergence rate, but the profile retains a continuously decreasing trend along the iteration axis. As a trade-off, the FA-based scheme provides

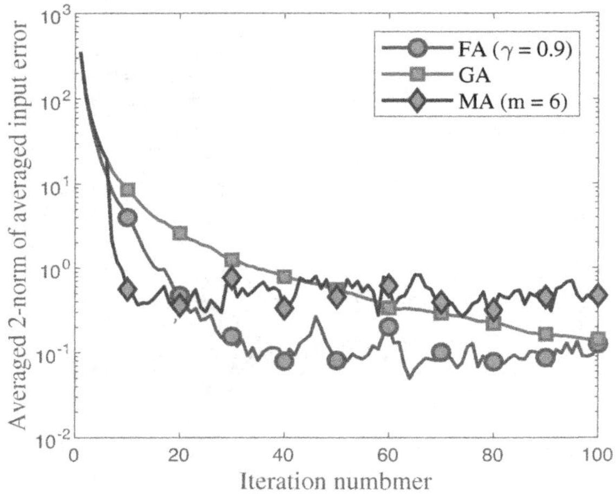

Figure 4.10 Average norm profiles of the average input errors for the three schemes in the iteration domain.

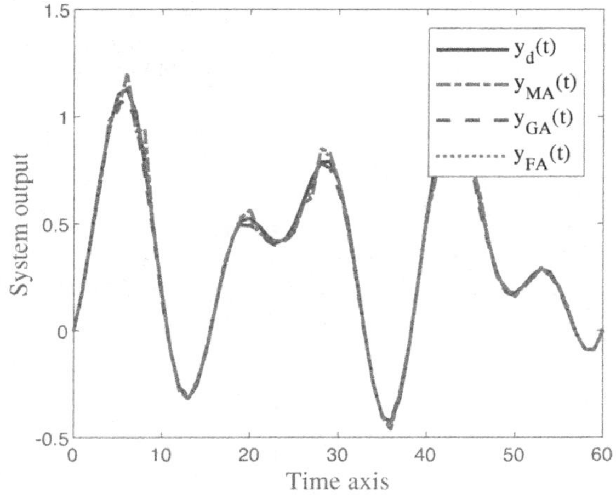

Figure 4.11 Tracking performance of three schemes at the 50th iteration.

tracking precision and a rapid convergence rate, which combines the above two schemes.

To illustrate the tracking performance, Fig. 4.11 presents the outputs for all three schemes at the 50th iteration and the desired reference. The tracking performance is acceptable for all schemes. To demonstrate the slight

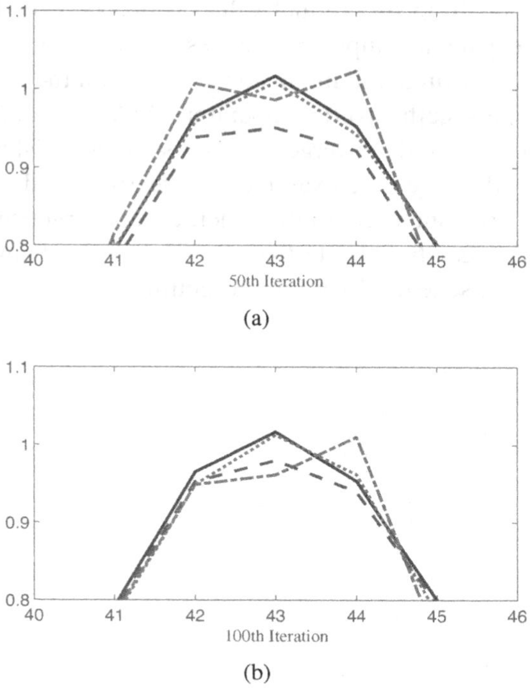

Figure 4.12 Enlarged subplots: (a) 50th Iteration and (b) 100th iteration.

differences between the schemes, Fig. 4.12 presents enlarged subplots over the time interval $40 \leq t \leq 46$ for both the 50th iteration and 100th iteration. At the 50th iteration, the FA-based scheme is superior to the other two schemes; the GA-based scheme does not converge sufficiently, while the MA-based scheme cannot eliminate the fading randomness (see Fig. 4.12(a)). In contrast, at the 100th iteration, the GA-based scheme is superior to the other two schemes, as it continuously improves the tracking performance along the iteration axis. For practical applications, if fast convergence is primary, the MA-based scheme and FA-scheme with small forgetting factor are preferable; if the tracking performance is more important, the GA-based scheme and FA-based scheme with large forgetting factor would be beneficial.

4.7 SUMMARY

In this chapter, we present a detailed analysis of averaging techniques in ILC over fading channels. Multiplicative randomness caused by fading can divert a received input far from its original value, which reduces tracking performance even if the generated input approaches the desired value. We introduce an averaging mechanism at the input side to deal with the fading-introduced randomness. Three specific average operators–MA, GA, and FA operators–are addressed in detail and convergence results are established strictly under mild conditions. Moreover, we examine both learning and tracking abilities for each scheme corresponding to the scheme's convergence rate and tracking precision. The results indicate that the FA-based scheme combines the MA- and GA-based schemes by tuning forgetting factors.

II

Unknown Channel Statistics

CHAPTER 5

Gradient Estimation Method for Unknown Fading Channels

THIS chapter proposes a novel data-driven learning control scheme for unknown systems with unknown fading sensor channels. The fading randomness is modeled by multiplicative and additive random variables subject to certain unknown distributions. In this scheme, we propose an error transmission mode and an iterative gradient estimation method. Unlike the conventional transmission mode where the output is directly transmitted back to the controller, in the error transmission mode, we send the desired reference to the plant such that tracking errors can be calculated locally and then transmitted back through the fading channel. Using the faded tracking error data only, the gradient for updating input is iteratively estimated by a random difference technique along the iteration axis. This gradient acts as the updating term of the control signal; therefore, information on the system and the fading channel is no longer required. The proposed scheme is proved effective in tracking the desired reference under random fading communication environments.

5.1 INTRODUCTION

In Chapters 2, 3, and 4, the learning control for systems with fading channels is studied depending on prior knowledge of communication channels and the system. In those chapters, the effects of fading communication on data are carefully analyzed. A decreasing gain sequence is introduced into the generic

DOI: 10.1201/9781032646404-5

learning control algorithm to reduce the fading effect and improve control system performance along the iteration axis. It should be pointed out that both system information and fading statistics were required a priori to establish the control framework. In particular, the statistics of fading channels are utilized to correct the received signals for providing an unbiased estimation, and the system information is necessary to derive a suitable gain matrix for regulating the control direction for multi-input-multi-output systems. However, it is difficult to acquire this knowledge in many applications; even if possible, the knowledge can be inaccurate. Thus, a completely data-driven framework that does not need any specific information regarding system settings and fading channels is desirable.

The primary contribution of this chapter is an effective learning tracking scheme for unknown systems with unknown fading channels, where two major difficulties are resolved in establishing the learning tracking scheme. The first difficulty is in dealing with the random fading. Particularly, due to fading channels, the received signals are biased after transmission and thus insufficient to drive the learning process. To solve this problem, a novel error transmission mode is proposed. In this mode, the desired reference is transmitted to the plant before operation; then, the tracking error is calculated locally at the plant site and transmitted back through the fading channel. This transmission mode differs from the conventional output transmission mode, where the system output is directly transmitted back to the controller. In this chapter, we reveal that such a mode can provide sufficient information for the learning process. The other difficulty comes from various unknowns in system and communication. To address this difficulty, a random difference technique from stochastic approximation theory is introduced to estimate a gradient for updating input along the iteration axis. In particular, for each odd iteration, a small random perturbation is added to the input signal of the previous iteration. Then, during the subsequent even iteration, a gradient estimation is created only using the faded tracking errors. The learning control scheme is established following the conventional proportional-type of updating structure, where a new input is generated by adding an updating term to the current input, in combination with the above-mentioned techniques. In particular, the updating term in this scheme is produced by the gradient estimation approach, where the involved data is supplied by the error transmission mode. Moreover, we introduce both decreasing and constant gains as learning step size to offer additional freedom in tuning the tracking performance. Detailed convergence analysis is also given. Illustrative simulations are provided to demonstrate the effectiveness of the proposed scheme.

5.2 PROBLEM FORMULATION

Consider the following multi-input-multi-output discrete-time system:

$$\begin{aligned} x_k(t+1) &= A_t x_k(t) + B_t u_k(t) \\ y_k(t) &= C_t x_k(t), \end{aligned} \tag{5.1}$$

where t and k denote the time instant and iteration number, respectively, $t = 0, 1, \ldots, N$ with N being the iteration length and $k = 1, 2, \ldots$. Vectors $x_k(t) \in \mathbf{R}^n$, $u_k(t) \in \mathbf{R}^p$, and $y_k(t) \in \mathbf{R}^q$ are system state, input, and output, respectively. In addition, $A_t \in \mathbf{R}^{n\times n}$, $B_t \in \mathbf{R}^{n\times p}$, and $C_t \in \mathbf{R}^{q\times n}$ are unknown system matrices.

For this system, we make the following assumptions.

Assumption 5.1 *The coupling matrix $C_{t+1}B_t$ is of full column rank, $\forall t$.*

Assumption 5.2 *For the desired tracking reference $y_d(t)$, there exist a unique input $u_d(t)$ and suitable initial state $x_d(0)$ such that*

$$\begin{aligned} x_d(t+1) &= A_t x_d(t) + B_t u_d(t) \\ y_d(t) &= C_t x_d(t). \end{aligned} \tag{5.2}$$

Remark 5.1 *Assumptions 5.1 and 5.2 describe the realizability of the desired reference $y_d(t)$. In particular, Assumption 5.1 indicates the system relative degree is one. The results can be extended to the case of system relative degree higher than one by certain revisions in analysis. Moreover, this assumption implies that the dimension of the input is not larger than that of the output and there is no redundant control quantity. One should keep in mind that Assumption 5.1 cannot guarantee Assumption 5.2 naturally for any desired reference. Indeed, the desired reference defined by Assumption 5.2 should satisfy certain conditions concerning system matrices (see [53] for more details). In addition, if Assumption 5.2 is not valid, it implies that no control input exists to track the given reference precisely. In this case, the best achievable objective is to generate output that approximates the desired reference as closely as possible according to a certain optimal index [53]. In fact, our proposed scheme can well apply to such a case, but the convergence analysis will require more derivations.*

Assumption 5.3 *For each iteration, the initial state $x_k(0)$ is identical to the desired state $x_d(0)$, i.e., $x_k(0) = x_d(0)$.*

Remark 5.2 *Assumption 5.3 is a widely-accepted assumption for ILC as a necessary repeatability requirement. We use this assumption to simplify the following derivations. It can be extended to a random initialization case where the difference between $x_k(0)$ and $x_d(0)$ is a zero-mean random variable and a diminishing case where the difference vanishes to zero asymptotically. The proposed scheme in this chapter is still effective for these extensions by considering them as part of the induced errors of the fading model. Explanations are given in Remark 5.4.*

In this chapter, we consider learning tracking systems over unknown fading channels. In particular, the plant and controller are separated in different locations and communicate through fading channels. To simplify the discussion and notations, we focus on a case where the data at the output side are transmitted to the controller over fading channels, while the communication from the controller to the plant is assumed to work well. In other words, the generated input signal can be transmitted precisely. The results derived in this chapter can be extended to the case where the generated input also suffers random fading while being transmitted back to the plant.

The influence of fading channels on transmitted signals is modeled using two random variables. Here, let $m_k(t)$ denote the signal to be transmitted. Then, the received signal is modeled as follows:

$$m_k^{\circ}(t) = \mu_k(t) m_k(t) + \nu_k(t), \tag{5.3}$$

where $\mu_k(t)$ and $\nu_k(t)$ indicate the multiplicative and additive randomness caused by random fading. The multiplicative variable $\mu_k(t) \in \mathbf{R}$ is assumed to be independent and identically distributed with respect to time instant t and iteration number k, according to a continuous fading distribution function $f(\mu)$ on a closed interval such that $\mathbb{P}(\mu > 0) = 1$. In addition, we have the following statistical property:

$$\mathbb{E}[\mu_k(t)] = \mu, \quad \mathbb{E}[(\mu_k(t) - \mu)^2] = \sigma_\mu^2, \tag{5.4}$$

where both μ and σ_μ^2 are unknown. The additive variable $\nu_k(t) \in \mathbf{R}^m$ denotes the random noise generated by the unreliable communication channel, where m denotes the dimension of $m_k(t)$. This quantity can also represent system disturbances and noise by suitable transformation. Generally, it is independent for different time label and iteration number. We assume the noise to be zero-mean and stationary with finite high-order moments, i.e.,

$$\mathbb{E}[\nu_k(t)] = 0, \quad \mathbb{E}[\nu_k(t)\nu_k^T(t)] = R_\nu^t, \tag{5.5}$$

where R_ν^t is a semi-positive-definite matrix.

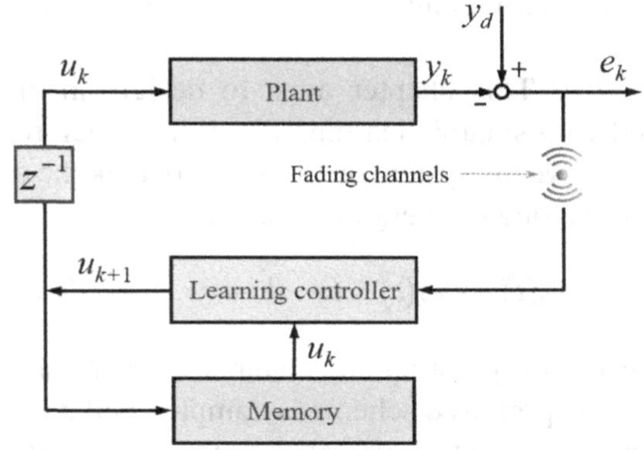

Figure 5.1 Block diagram of learning systems over fading channels.

The statistical properties of the fading channel are determined by the physical environment and devices in the networks. Generally, the expectation of the multiplicative random variable μ is not necessarily equal to one, which indicates that biased information is received. That is,

$$\begin{aligned}\mathbb{E}[m_k^\circ(t)] &= \mathbb{E}[\mu_k(t)m_k(t) + \nu_k(t)] \\ &= \mu m_k(t) \neq m_k(t),\end{aligned}$$

where $m_k(t)$ is considered as a deterministic signal. The received signals are biased and may destroy the learning process. If the mean μ is known, a correction mechanism can be applied to the received signals such that the corrected signals are unbiased in a probability sense. However, in this chapter, the statistical information of the fading channels is unknown. Thus, we have no means to correct those biased signals. In other words, the fundamental fading effect lies in the unknown bias characteristic imposed on all the received signals. Besides, system information is still required in the existing literature.

In this chapter, our primary objective is to design effective schemes to generate the desired input sequence directly based on available input and output data without using system information or estimating fading statistics. To this end, we propose a novel scheme for system implementation. This scheme is shown in Fig. 5.1, where z^{-1} denotes an iteration backward shift operator. In this scheme, the desired reference y_d is first transmitted to the plant before initiating operation. When the system output y_k arrives, the tracking error e_k is computed as $e_k = y_d - y_k$ and then transmitted back to the controller through the fading channel. With this scheme, the proposed learning algorithm can generate an asymptotically convergent input sequence using faded tracking errors.

Control objective: This chapter aims to design an effective learning scheme associated with suitable learning algorithms such that the generated input sequence can drive the system output $y_k(t)$ to track the desired reference $y_d(t)$ asymptotically along the iteration axis, i.e.,

$$y_k(t) \to y_d(t) \quad \text{as} \quad k \to \infty, \quad \forall t.$$

Note that both system information and channel statistics are unknown a priori. Consequently, the proposed scheme is completely data-driven.

Here, the convergence in the control objective is in a deterministic sense, i.e., $y_k(t) \to y_d(t)$ as $k \to \infty$. This is because the plant itself is not subject to any stochastic noise. For expression simplicity, we concentrate on communication randomness as shown in (5.3). The following algorithms are applicable to stochastic systems.

We should emphasize that the essential effect of random fading is to introduce multiplicative and additive randomness to the original measurements. In particular, multiplicative randomness results in state-dependent errors, which is a critical point in convergence analysis. The specific algorithms and their convergence analyses are provided in the next section.

5.3 ILC ALGORITHMS AND CONVERGENCE ANALYSIS

5.3.1 Algorithm Design

To simplify the following derivations, we stack the input and output of the entire iteration into lifting-type vectors separately as follows:

$$\boldsymbol{u}_k = [u_k^T(0), u_k^T(1), \ldots, u_k^T(N-1)]^T \in \mathbf{R}^{Np}, \tag{5.6}$$

$$\boldsymbol{y}_k = [y_k^T(1), y_k^T(2), \ldots, y_k^T(N)]^T \in \mathbf{R}^{Nq}. \tag{5.7}$$

From the system (5.1), we have

$$x_k(t+1) = \sum_{i=0}^{t} A_{t,i+1}B_i u_k(i) + A_{t,0}x_k(0),$$

where $A_{j,i} = A_j A_{j-1} \cdots A_i$, $j > i$, and $A_{t,t+1} = I$. This yields $y_k(t+1) = \sum_{i=0}^{t} C_{t+1}A_{t,i+1}B_i u_k(i) + C_{t+1}A_{t,0}x_k(0)$, $\forall t = 0, \ldots, N-1$. Then, we obtain

$$\boldsymbol{y}_k = \mathcal{H}\boldsymbol{u}_k + \mathcal{J}x_k(0), \tag{5.8}$$

where

$$\mathcal{H} = \begin{bmatrix} C_1B_0 & 0 & \cdots & 0 \\ C_2A_1B_0 & C_2B_1 & \cdots & 0 \\ \vdots & \vdots & \ddots & \vdots \\ C_NA_{N-1,1}B_0 & C_NA_{N-1,2}B_1 & \cdots & C_NB_{N-1} \end{bmatrix}$$

and

$$\mathcal{J} = [(C_1A_0)^T \ (C_2A_{1,0})^T \ \cdots \ (C_NA_{N-1,0})^T]^T.$$

Similarly, we obtain the following:

$$\boldsymbol{y}_d = \mathcal{H}\boldsymbol{u}_d + \mathcal{J}x_d(0), \tag{5.9}$$

where $\boldsymbol{y}_d$ and $\boldsymbol{u}_d$ are defined similarly to $\boldsymbol{y}_k$ and $\boldsymbol{u}_k$ by replacing subscript k with d.

The tracking error is computed as follows:

$$\boldsymbol{e}_k = \boldsymbol{y}_d - \boldsymbol{y}_k = \mathcal{H}\widetilde{\boldsymbol{u}}_k, \tag{5.10}$$

where $\boldsymbol{e}_k \triangleq [e_k^T(1), e_k^T(2), \ldots, e_k^T(N)]^T$, $\widetilde{\boldsymbol{u}}_k \triangleq \boldsymbol{u}_d - \boldsymbol{u}_k$, and Assumption 5.3 is applied.

The fading matrix is defined as follows:

$$\Theta_k = \text{diag}\{\mu_k(1), \mu_k(2), \cdots, \mu_k(N)\}. \tag{5.11}$$

Correspondingly, the received error is given as:

$$\boldsymbol{e}_k^\circ = (\Theta_k \otimes I_q)\boldsymbol{e}_k + \boldsymbol{v}_k, \tag{5.12}$$

where $\boldsymbol{e}_k^\circ$ is the available data to update the input signal, $\otimes$ denotes the Kronecker product, and $\boldsymbol{v}_k = [v_k^T(1), v_k^T(2), \cdots, v_k^T(N)]^T$. Note that $\mathbb{E}[\Theta_k] = \mu I_N$. Generally, $\mu \neq 1$, thus $\boldsymbol{e}_k^\circ$ is a biased version of the tracking error.

The system matrices A_t, B_t, and C_t are unknown; therefore, it is difficult to compute a suitable direction adjustment matrix directly to regulate the input signal with the tracking error information. In the following, we provide a gradient estimation-based and data-driven scheme to regulate control direction automatically using the Kiefer-Wolfowitz stochastic approximation method [10, p. 153]. To this end, we introduce a vector sequence $\{\boldsymbol{\delta}_k, k = 1, 2, \ldots\}$, where $\boldsymbol{\delta}_k \in \mathbf{R}^l$, $\boldsymbol{\delta}_k = [\delta_k^1, \delta_k^2, \ldots, \delta_k^l]^T$ (where $l = Np$). All components $\boldsymbol{\delta}_k^j$ are mutually independent and identically distributed random variables that satisfy the following conditions:

$$|\delta_k^j| < a, \quad \left|\frac{1}{\delta_k^j}\right| < b, \quad \mathbb{E}\left[\frac{1}{\delta_k^j}\right] = 0,$$
$$\forall k = 1,2,\ldots, \quad j = 1,2,\ldots,l, \tag{5.13}$$

where a and b are positive constants. Here, we provide two common selections of δ_k^j. The first is the Bernoulli distribution $\delta_k^j = \pm 1$, where the probability of each case is 0.5. The other is segmented uniform distribution δ_k^j, which is uniformly distributed in the interval $[-d_1, -d_2] \bigcup [d_2, d_1]$, where d_1 and d_2 are positive constants satisfying $0 < d_2 < d_1 \leq a$. In addition, sequence $\{\boldsymbol{\delta}_k\}$ is independent of both $\mu_k(t)$ and $\nu_k(t)$, $\forall t, k$.

We define a vector

$$\overline{\boldsymbol{\delta}}_k = \left[\frac{1}{\delta_k^1}, \frac{1}{\delta_k^2}, \cdots, \frac{1}{\delta_k^l}\right], \quad k = 1,2,\ldots \tag{5.14}$$

and select two sequences $\{a_k\}$ and $\{c_k\}$ of real numbers such that

$$a_k > 0, \quad a_k \to 0, \quad \sum_{k=1}^{\infty} a_k = \infty, \tag{5.15}$$

$$c_k > 0, \quad c_k \to 0, \quad \sum_{k=1}^{\infty} \left(\frac{a_k}{c_k}\right)^2 < \infty. \tag{5.16}$$

The initial input $\boldsymbol{u}_0$ can be arbitrary, which would not affect the asymptotic convergence of the following algorithm. In application, one can estimate a suitable initial input using other techniques to enable a better start of the algorithm such that a safety control can be ensured. In other words, such a relaxation of the initial input provides us with much freedom to address application-related issues.

In particular, the algorithm updates differently at odd and even cycles. For odd cycles, the following perturbation is imposed:

$$\boldsymbol{u}_{2k+1} = \boldsymbol{u}_{2k} + c_k \boldsymbol{\delta}_k. \tag{5.17}$$

For even cycles, the following gradient estimation-based update is established:

$$\boldsymbol{u}_{2k+2} = \boldsymbol{u}_{2k} - \frac{a_k \overline{\boldsymbol{\delta}}_k}{c_k}\left(\|\boldsymbol{e}_{2k+1}^\circ\|^2 - \|\boldsymbol{e}_{2k}^\circ\|^2\right), \tag{5.18}$$

where $\boldsymbol{e}_k^\circ$ is defined in (5.12), $k = 0,1,\ldots$.

Remark 5.3 *In this remark, we provide some intuitions of the algorithm design. To generate a gradient estimation, we need to generate a random perturbation and then calculate the estimation. This is why we separate the algorithms into odd and even iterations.* $\boldsymbol{\delta}$ *is the random perturbation that helps us find the gradient. The sequence* $\{c_k\}$ *is required to converge to zero so that the magnitude of the perturbation gradually reduces to zero. Then, a stable convergence of the input sequence can be guaranteed. Otherwise, we can only prove that the input sequence converges to a bounded zone (see Section 5.3.3). The sequence* $\{a_k\}$ *is decreasing owing to the stochastic approximation theory. The last condition in* (5.16) *implies that* a_k *should decrease faster than* c_k *to dominate the whole scheme. We must emphasize that the controller design does not depend on the knowledge of the desired input* $\boldsymbol{u}_d$. *In other words, we provide an online learning mechanism to generate an input sequence converging to the desired input signal in the iteration domain.*

5.3.2 Convergence Analysis

In this subsection, we discuss the asymptotic convergence analysis for the proposed scheme. The essential mechanism of the scheme, formulated by (5.17) and (5.18), is to calculate the descent gradient (control update direction) for a given reference using the random difference technique. In this mechanism, the random variable $\boldsymbol{\delta}_k$ plays a role of random perturbation to the input signal, as demonstrated by (5.17), whereas the attenuating sequence $\{c_k\}$ eliminates the effect of the perturbation variable (which is distant from zero) as the gradient estimation approaches its actual value such that stable convergence of the input sequence is guaranteed. In (5.18), the control profile is updated, where the updating term is a nonlinear function of the available tracking information. Note that the employed data are the biased tracking error $\boldsymbol{e}_k^\circ$ rather than the original one $\boldsymbol{e}_k$; therefore, the computed gradient contains the information from both the system and the fading channel. In other words, we combine both unknowns in a single step rather than treating the unknown system and unknown fading channel separately.

The main result is given in the following theorem.

Theorem 5.1 *Consider the system* (5.1) *and apply learning algorithms* (5.17) *and* (5.18), *where the involved parameters are defined by* (5.13)–(5.16). *Assume that Assumptions 5.1–5.3 and the fading conditions hold, and the generated input sequence is bounded. Then, the input sequence* $\boldsymbol{u}_k$ *converges to* $\boldsymbol{u}_d$ *asymptotically along the iteration axis. Besides, the output* $y_k(t)$ *will converge to the desired reference* $y_d(t)$ *precisely as the iteration number approaches to infinity.*

Proof: We complete the proof in three steps. In the first step, we transform the update algorithm (5.18) into a linear regression form for the input error at even iterations, where multiple noise terms are involved. Then, in the second step, we prove the asymptotical convergence of the input error sequence to zero by checking the property of all involved noise terms according to a technical lemma. In the last step, we show the precise tracking performance of the output.

Step 1: Algorithm transformation.

Substituting (5.10) into (5.12) yields

$$\boldsymbol{e}_k^\circ = \Xi_k \mathcal{H}\widetilde{\boldsymbol{u}}_k + \boldsymbol{v}_k = \mu\mathcal{H}\widetilde{\boldsymbol{u}}_k + \widehat{\Xi}_k\mathcal{H}\widetilde{\boldsymbol{u}}_k + \boldsymbol{v}_k, \tag{5.19}$$

where $\Xi_k = \Theta_k \otimes I_q$ and $\widehat{\Xi}_k \triangleq \Xi_k - \mu I_{Nq}$. According to (5.4) and (5.11), we obtain $\mathbb{E}[\Xi_k] = \mu I_{Nq}$, $\mathbb{E}[\widehat{\Xi}_k] = 0$, and $\mathbb{E}[\widehat{\Xi}_k^2] = \sigma_\mu^2 I_{Nq}$.

Then, we obtain the following:

$$\begin{aligned}\frac{\overline{\boldsymbol{\delta}}_k}{c_k}\left\|\boldsymbol{e}_{2k}^\circ\right\|^2 &= \frac{\overline{\boldsymbol{\delta}}_k}{c_k}\left\|\mu\mathcal{H}\widetilde{\boldsymbol{u}}_{2k} + \widehat{\Xi}_{2k}\mathcal{H}\widetilde{\boldsymbol{u}}_{2k} + \boldsymbol{v}_{2k}\right\|^2 \\ &= \frac{\overline{\boldsymbol{\delta}}_k}{c_k}\mu^2\left\|\mathcal{H}\widetilde{\boldsymbol{u}}_{2k}\right\|^2 + \frac{\overline{\boldsymbol{\delta}}_k}{c_k}\left\|\widehat{\Xi}_{2k}\mathcal{H}\widetilde{\boldsymbol{u}}_{2k}\right\|^2 \\ &\quad + \frac{\overline{\boldsymbol{\delta}}_k}{c_k}\left\|\boldsymbol{v}_{2k}\right\|^2 + \phi_{2k} + \varphi_{2k} + \psi_{2k},\end{aligned} \tag{5.20}$$

where

$$\begin{aligned}\phi_{2k} &= \frac{2\overline{\boldsymbol{\delta}}_k}{c_k}\mu\widetilde{\boldsymbol{u}}_{2k}^T\mathcal{H}^T\widehat{\Xi}_{2k}\mathcal{H}\widetilde{\boldsymbol{u}}_{2k}, \\ \varphi_{2k} &= \frac{2\overline{\boldsymbol{\delta}}_k}{c_k}\mu\widetilde{\boldsymbol{u}}_{2k}^T\mathcal{H}^T\boldsymbol{v}_{2k}, \\ \psi_{2k} &= \frac{2\overline{\boldsymbol{\delta}}_k}{c_k}\widetilde{\boldsymbol{u}}_{2k}^T\mathcal{H}^T\widehat{\Xi}_{2k}^T\boldsymbol{v}_{2k}.\end{aligned}$$

Similarly, we have

$$\begin{aligned}\frac{\overline{\boldsymbol{\delta}}_k}{c_k}\left\|\boldsymbol{e}_{2k+1}^\circ\right\|^2 &= \frac{\overline{\boldsymbol{\delta}}_k}{c_k}\left\|\mu\mathcal{H}\widetilde{\boldsymbol{u}}_{2k+1} + \widehat{\Xi}_{2k+1}\mathcal{H}\widetilde{\boldsymbol{u}}_{2k+1} + \boldsymbol{v}_{2k+1}\right\|^2 \\ &= \frac{\overline{\boldsymbol{\delta}}_k}{c_k}\mu^2\left\|\mathcal{H}\widetilde{\boldsymbol{u}}_{2k+1}\right\|^2 + \frac{\overline{\boldsymbol{\delta}}_k}{c_k}\left\|\widehat{\Xi}_{2k+1}\mathcal{H}\widetilde{\boldsymbol{u}}_{2k+1}\right\|^2 \\ &\quad + \frac{\overline{\boldsymbol{\delta}}_k}{c_k}\left\|\boldsymbol{v}_{2k+1}\right\|^2 + \phi_{2k+1} + \varphi_{2k+1} + \psi_{2k+1}\end{aligned}$$

$$
\begin{aligned}
&= \frac{\overline{\boldsymbol{\delta}}_k}{c_k}\mu^2 \|\mathcal{H}\widetilde{\boldsymbol{u}}_{2k}\|^2 + \overline{\boldsymbol{\delta}}_k c_k \mu^2 \|\mathcal{H}\boldsymbol{\delta}_k\|^2 \\
&\quad - 2\mu^2 \overline{\boldsymbol{\delta}}_k \boldsymbol{\delta}_k^T \mathcal{H}^T \mathcal{H}\widetilde{\boldsymbol{u}}_{2k} \\
&\quad + \frac{\overline{\boldsymbol{\delta}}_k}{c_k}\left\|\widehat{\Xi}_{2k+1}\mathcal{H}\widetilde{\boldsymbol{u}}_{2k}\right\|^2 + \overline{\boldsymbol{\delta}}_k c_k \left\|\widehat{\Xi}_{2k+1}\mathcal{H}\boldsymbol{\delta}_k\right\|^2 \\
&\quad - 2\overline{\boldsymbol{\delta}}_k \boldsymbol{\delta}_k^T \mathcal{H}^T \widehat{\Xi}_{2k+1}^T \widehat{\Xi}_{2k+1} \mathcal{H}\widetilde{\boldsymbol{u}}_{2k} \\
&\quad + \frac{\overline{\boldsymbol{\delta}}_k}{c_k}\|\boldsymbol{v}_{2k+1}\|^2 + \phi_{2k+1} + \varphi_{2k+1} + \psi_{2k+1},
\end{aligned}
\tag{5.21}
$$

where

$$
\begin{aligned}
\phi_{2k+1} &= \frac{2\overline{\boldsymbol{\delta}}_k}{c_k}\mu \widetilde{\boldsymbol{u}}_{2k+1}^T \mathcal{H}^T \widehat{\Xi}_{2k+1} \mathcal{H}\widetilde{\boldsymbol{u}}_{2k+1}, \\
\varphi_{2k+1} &= \frac{2\overline{\boldsymbol{\delta}}_k}{c_k}\mu \widetilde{\boldsymbol{u}}_{2k+1}^T \mathcal{H}^T \boldsymbol{v}_{2k+1}, \\
\psi_{2k+1} &= \frac{2\overline{\boldsymbol{\delta}}_k}{c_k} \widetilde{\boldsymbol{u}}_{2k+1}^T \mathcal{H}^T \widehat{\Xi}_{2k+1}^T \boldsymbol{v}_{2k+1},
\end{aligned}
$$

and the last equality in (5.21) holds by substituting the relationship $\widetilde{\boldsymbol{u}}_{2k+1} = \widetilde{\boldsymbol{u}}_{2k} - c_k \boldsymbol{\delta}_k$ into the first two items, which is generated by subtracting both sides of (5.17) from $\boldsymbol{u}_d$.

Then, we have

$$
\begin{aligned}
Q_k &\triangleq \frac{\overline{\boldsymbol{\delta}}_k}{c_k}\left(\|\boldsymbol{e}_{2k+1}^{\circ}\|^2 - \|\boldsymbol{e}_{2k}^{\circ}\|^2\right) \\
&= -2(\mu^2 + \sigma_\mu^2)\mathcal{H}^T \mathcal{H}\widetilde{\boldsymbol{u}}_{2k} + \alpha_k + \beta_k + \gamma_k + \eta_k + \lambda_k \\
&\quad + \phi_{2k+1} - \phi_{2k} + \varphi_{2k+1} - \varphi_{2k} + \psi_{2k+1} - \psi_{2k},
\end{aligned}
\tag{5.22}
$$

where

$$
\begin{aligned}
\alpha_k &= 2(I - \overline{\boldsymbol{\delta}}_k \boldsymbol{\delta}_k^T)(\mu^2 + \sigma_\mu^2)\mathcal{H}^T \mathcal{H}\widetilde{\boldsymbol{u}}_{2k}, \\
\beta_k &= 2\overline{\boldsymbol{\delta}}_k \boldsymbol{\delta}_k^T \mathcal{H}^T \left(\sigma_\mu^2 I - \widehat{\Xi}_{2k+1}^T \widehat{\Xi}_{2k+1}\right)\mathcal{H}\widetilde{\boldsymbol{u}}_{2k}, \\
\gamma_k &= \left\|\widehat{\Xi}_{2k+1}\mathcal{H}\widetilde{\boldsymbol{u}}_{2k}\right\|^2 - \left\|\widehat{\Xi}_{2k}\mathcal{H}\widetilde{\boldsymbol{u}}_{2k}\right\|^2, \\
\eta_k &= \|\boldsymbol{v}_{2k+1}\|^2 - \|\boldsymbol{v}_{2k}\|^2, \\
\lambda_k &= c_k \overline{\boldsymbol{\delta}}_k \left(\mu^2 \|\mathcal{H}\boldsymbol{\delta}_k\|^2 + \left\|\widehat{\Xi}_{2k+1}\mathcal{H}\boldsymbol{\delta}_k\right\|^2\right).
\end{aligned}
$$

Now, subtracting both sides of (5.18) from $\boldsymbol{u}_d$ and substituting the above derivations lead to

$$\begin{aligned}\widetilde{\boldsymbol{u}}_{2k+2} &= \widetilde{\boldsymbol{u}}_{2k} + a_k Q_k \\ &= \widetilde{\boldsymbol{u}}_{2k} - 2a_k(\mu^2 + \sigma_\mu^2)\mathcal{H}^T\mathcal{H}\widetilde{\boldsymbol{u}}_{2k} + a_k\boldsymbol{\omega}_k, \end{aligned} \tag{5.23}$$

where $\boldsymbol{\omega}_k \triangleq \alpha_k + \beta_k + \gamma_k + \eta_k + \lambda_k + \phi_{2k+1} - \phi_{2k} + \varphi_{2k+1} - \varphi_{2k} + \psi_{2k+1} - \psi_{2k}$.

Step 2: Convergence of $\{\widetilde{\boldsymbol{u}}_k\}$.

To this end, we use Lemma A.5. Note that the main regression function in (5.23) is a linear function of $\widetilde{\boldsymbol{u}}_{2k}$, i.e., $-2a_k(\mu^2+\sigma_\mu^2)\mathcal{H}^T\mathcal{H}\widetilde{\boldsymbol{u}}_{2k}$. In addition, according to Assumption 5.1, $\mathcal{H}$ is of full-column rank; thus, $\mathcal{H}^T\mathcal{H}$ is a positive-definite matrix. Therefore, $-\mathcal{H}^T\mathcal{H}$ is a stable matrix.

In the following, we evaluate whether noise $\boldsymbol{\omega}_k$ satisfies (A.5). Here, we define σ-algebra $\mathcal{G}_k = \sigma\{\boldsymbol{u}_i, \Theta_i, \boldsymbol{v}_i, i \le 2k+1\}$. It is clear that $\widetilde{\boldsymbol{u}}_{2k} \in \mathcal{G}_{k-1}$ and $\boldsymbol{\omega}_k \in \mathcal{G}_k$ implying that $(\boldsymbol{\omega}_k, \mathcal{G}_k)$ is an adapted process.

First, we check α_k. Note that

$$I - \overline{\boldsymbol{\delta}}_k\boldsymbol{\delta}_k^T = -\begin{bmatrix} 0 & \frac{\delta_k^2}{\delta_k^1} & \frac{\delta_k^3}{\delta_k^1} & \cdots & \frac{\delta_k^l}{\delta_k^1} \\ \frac{\delta_k^1}{\delta_k^2} & 0 & \frac{\delta_k^3}{\delta_k^2} & \cdots & \frac{\delta_k^l}{\delta_k^2} \\ \frac{\delta_k^1}{\delta_k^3} & \frac{\delta_k^2}{\delta_k^3} & 0 & \cdots & \frac{\delta_k^l}{\delta_k^3} \\ \vdots & \vdots & \vdots & \ddots & \vdots \\ \frac{\delta_k^1}{\delta_k^l} & \frac{\delta_k^2}{\delta_k^l} & \frac{\delta_k^3}{\delta_k^l} & \cdots & 0 \end{bmatrix}. \tag{5.24}$$

Because δ_k^i is independent of δ_k^j, $\forall i \neq j$, we have $\mathbb{E}\left[\frac{\delta_k^i}{\delta_k^j}\right] = 0$, $\forall i \neq j$. Therefore, $\mathbb{E}[I - \overline{\boldsymbol{\delta}}_k\boldsymbol{\delta}_k^T] = 0$. Moreover, δ_k^i is independent of $\mathcal{G}_{k-1}$; thus, $\mathbb{E}[\alpha_k \mid \mathcal{G}_{k-1}] = 0$, which implies that $\{\alpha_k, \mathcal{G}_k\}$ is a martingale difference sequence. In addition, both δ_k^i and $\frac{1}{\delta_k^j}$ are bounded. Therefore,

$$\mathbb{E}\left[\|\alpha_k\|^2 \mid \mathcal{G}_{k-1}\right] \le C_0\|\widetilde{\boldsymbol{u}}_{2k}\|^2$$

for some suitable $C_0 > 0$. With the boundedness of $\widetilde{\boldsymbol{u}}_{2k}$, we have $\sum_{k=1}^{\infty} a_k^2\mathbb{E}[\|\alpha_k\|^2] < \infty$. Then, by Chow's convergence theorem for a martingale difference sequence [14], we have $\sum_{k=1}^{\infty} a_k\alpha_k < \infty$ almost surely.

We can verify β_k following the same procedure. Because $\mathbb{E}[\widehat{\Xi}_{2k+1}^T\widehat{\Xi}_{2k+1}] = \sigma_\mu^2 I_{Nq}$ and $\widehat{\Xi}_k$ is independent of all other notations in β_k and $\mathcal{G}_{k-1}$, we have $\mathbb{E}[\beta_k \mid \mathcal{G}_{k-1}] = 0$. In other words, $\{\beta_k, \mathcal{G}_k\}$ is a martingale difference sequence.

Moreover, all involved quantities except $\widetilde{\boldsymbol{u}}_{2k}$ in β_k are bounded; thus, for some suitable C_0, we have

$$\mathbb{E}\left[\|\beta_k\|^2 \mid \mathcal{G}_{k-1}\right] \leq C_0\|\widetilde{\boldsymbol{u}}_{2k}\|^2..$$

Similar to α_k, we have $\sum_{k=1}^{\infty} a_k\beta_k < \infty$ almost surely.

Next, we discuss γ_k. Note that $\widehat{\Xi}_{2k+1}$ is identically distributed with $\widehat{\Xi}_{2k}$; therefore, we have

$$\begin{aligned}&\mathbb{E}[\gamma_k \mid \mathcal{G}_{k-1}]\\&= \mathbb{E}\left[\left\|\widehat{\Xi}_{2k+1}\mathcal{H}\widetilde{\boldsymbol{u}}_{2k}\right\|^2 - \left\|\widehat{\Xi}_{2k}\mathcal{H}\widetilde{\boldsymbol{u}}_{2k}\right\|^2 \mid \mathcal{G}_{k-1}\right] = 0.\end{aligned}$$

In other words, $\{\gamma_k, \mathcal{G}_k\}$ is a martingale difference sequence. By the boundedness of $\widehat{\Xi}_k$ and $\widetilde{\boldsymbol{u}}_{2k}$, we can derive the result of $\sum_{k=1}^{\infty} a_k\gamma_k < \infty$ in almost sure sense similarly to the abovementioned two items.

For item η_k, $\boldsymbol{v}_{2k+1}$ is identically distributed to $\boldsymbol{v}_{2k}$. Consequently, $\mathbb{E}[\eta_k] = 0$ and η_k is independent of $\mathcal{G}_{k-1}$. In addition, for suitable $C_0 > 0$, we have $\mathbb{E}[\|\eta_k\|^2] \leq C_0$. Thus, $\sum_{k=1}^{\infty} a_k^2\mathbb{E}[\|\eta_k\|^2] < \infty$, which leads to $\sum_{k=1}^{\infty} a_k\eta_k < \infty$ almost surely.

We now check λ_k, which differs from the above items. Due to the dependence between $\overline{\boldsymbol{\delta}}_k$ and $\boldsymbol{\delta}_k$, we cannot conclude that $\mathbb{E}[\lambda_k] = 0$. However, by the boundedness of $\boldsymbol{\delta}_k$ and the properties of $\widehat{\Xi}_{2k+1}$, we can conclude that the involved quantities in λ_k are bounded (except c_k, which converges to zero as k approaches infinity). As a result, we have $\lambda_k \to 0$ as $k \to \infty$. This conclusion satisfies the second condition of (A.5).

For item ϕ_{2k}, $\mathbb{E}[\overline{\boldsymbol{\delta}}_k] = 0$ and $\mathbb{E}[\widehat{\Xi}_{2k}] = 0$, and $\overline{\boldsymbol{\delta}}_k$ is independent of $\widehat{\Xi}_{2k}$. Thus, $\{\phi_{2k}, \mathcal{G}_{k-1}\}$ is a martingale difference sequence. In addition, for suitable constant $C_0 > 0$,

$$\begin{aligned}\sum_{k=1}^{\infty} a_k^2\phi_{2k}^2 &= 4\sum_{k=1}^{\infty}\left(\frac{a_k}{c_k}\right)^2 \mathbb{E}\left[\|\overline{\boldsymbol{\delta}}_k\mu\widetilde{\boldsymbol{u}}_{2k}^T\mathcal{H}^T\widehat{\Xi}_{2k}\mathcal{H}\widetilde{\boldsymbol{u}}_{2k}\|^2\right]\\&\leq C_0\sum_{k=1}^{\infty}\left(\frac{a_k}{c_k}\right)^2 \mathbb{E}[\|\widetilde{\boldsymbol{u}}_{2k}\|^4] < \infty.\end{aligned}$$

According to Chow's convergence theorem for a martingale difference sequence [14], we have $\sum_{k=1}^{\infty} a_k\phi_{2k} < \infty$ almost surely. The same conclusion applies to ϕ_{2k+1} as the major difference between ϕ_{2k+1} and ϕ_{2k} is the additional term $c_k\boldsymbol{\delta}_k$ according to (5.17).

In addition, note that $\mathbb{E}[\overline{\boldsymbol{\delta}}_k] = 0$, $\mathbb{E}[\widehat{\Xi}_{2k+1}] = 0$, $\mathbb{E}[\boldsymbol{v}_{2k}] = 0$, and $\mathbb{E}[\boldsymbol{v}_{2k+1}] = 0$, as well as the independence between these terms and $\mathcal{G}_{k-1}$; therefore, the above estimates goes to φ_{2k}, φ_{2k+1}, ψ_{2k}, and ψ_{2k+1}. In other words, noise terms φ_{2k}, φ_{2k+1}, ψ_{2k}, and ψ_{2k+1} satisfy the former condition in (A.5).

Summarizing the above verifications, we conclude that $\boldsymbol{\omega}_k$ in (5.23) satisfies condition (A.5) of Lemma A.5. Then, we have that $\widetilde{\boldsymbol{u}}_{2k} \to 0$ as $k \to \infty$. That is, the inputs of even iterations converge to the desired input. Moreover, the inputs of odd iterations also converge to the same limit according to (5.17) with c_k vanishing to zero. Therefore, we conclude that $\boldsymbol{u}_k \to \boldsymbol{u}_d$ as k goes to infinity.

Step 3: Tracking performance.

Note that the original system is deterministic; therefore, the tracking error depends linearly on the input error, as shown in (5.10). Thus, the convergence of the input sequence $\boldsymbol{u}_k$ to the desired input $\boldsymbol{u}_d$ leads to asymptotically precise tracking performance of the output to the desired reference, i.e., $y_k(t) \to y_d(t)$, $\forall t$. The proof is completed. □

Remark 5.4 *We revisit Assumption 5.3, wherein the initial state at each iteration is set to the desired one. This assumption is primarily imposed to save notations in the derivations. We clarify that the proposed scheme is still effective when Assumption 5.3 is not satisfied. Indeed, the initial state may be difficult to obtain in some practical systems without system information. For this case, uncertainty would arise in the initial state, which further yields an additional term in the error dynamics* (5.10). *In particular, we have* $\boldsymbol{e}_k = \mathcal{H}\widetilde{\boldsymbol{u}}_k + \Delta_k$, *where* $\Delta_k = \mathcal{J}(x_d(0) - x_k(0))$ *indicates the effect of the initial state error. Generally, the uncertainty* Δ_k *can be described by two models: A random vector with zero mean and a diminishing vector that vanishes as iteration number increases. For the former model,* Δ_k *will act in a role similar to the additive noise* $\boldsymbol{v}_k$. *For the latter model, the effect of* Δ_k *is similar to that of* λ_k *in the proof of Theorem 5.1 because of* $\Delta_k \to 0$. *Therefore, the input error will still converge to zero for these extensions of the initial state condition. However, we should point out that for the former model of initial state uncertainty, it is impossible to retain precise output tracking performance. This is because the initial state error will always arise in the actual outputs. In other words, although the relaxation of Assumption 5.3 would not damage the effectiveness of the proposed scheme, it can reduce the actual tracking performance.*

Remark 5.5 *To prove the asymptotical convergence of the proposed scheme, a prior requirement is that the generated input sequence* $\{\boldsymbol{u}_k\}$ *must be bounded. This requirement is rather common when applying the stochastic approximation-based framework, and it is widely satisfied in many practical applications. In fact, given the special linear structure of the final regression* (5.23)*, the boundedness of the generated input sequence is valid according to Theorem 2.1 in [5] and Proposition 1.6 in [3]; however, detailed derivations are extremely complex, technical, and mathematical, and are beyond the scope of this study. We simply assume the boundedness such that readers can quickly grasp the main design idea. In application, if we have certain a priori knowledge about the range of potential input signals, we can introduce a projection mechanism to* (5.17) *and* (5.18) *such that the generated input is always in the desired range. For such a projection-based scheme, the convergence analysis can be performed in a similar manner.*

Remark 5.6 *We provide some intuitive understanding of the influence of random fading on the learning process. First, it is observed from* (5.23) *that both the mean* μ *and variance* σ_μ^2 *of the fading variables appear in the main regression function, i.e.,* $-(\mu^2+\sigma_\mu^2)\mathcal{H}^T\mathcal{H}\tilde{\boldsymbol{u}}_{2k}$*. Thus, different fading distributions certainly affect the learning speed of the proposed algorithm; however, this effect can be tuned by selecting sequences* $\{a_k\}$ *and* $\{c_k\}$*, which is an important topic in the traditional stochastic approximation theory. Besides, we observe that the fading channel affects the possible fluctuation magnitude of* $\boldsymbol{\omega}_k$*, in which* $\widehat{\Xi}_k$ *is often observable. This effect will be reflected by the tracking precision within finite learning iterations. In other words, a larger variance of the fading variable would slow down the convergence speed.*

5.3.3 Variants of the Algorithm with Constant Gains

In (5.17), the decreasing parameter c_k is introduced to asymptotically reduce the effect of random perturbation as the number of iterations increases. In this case, stable convergence can be ensured, which is effective when handling stationary processes. One may wonder about performance if the decreasing sequence is replaced with a constant gain.

Here, we present a variant of the proposed scheme by replacing the decreasing sequence $\{c_k\}$ with a suitable constant τ. In other words, we let $c_k \equiv \tau$. Note that the other decreasing sequence $\{a_k\}$ is retained. As a result, we obtain the following scheme:

$$\boldsymbol{u}_{2k+1} = \boldsymbol{u}_{2k} + \tau\boldsymbol{\delta}_k, \tag{5.25}$$

$$\boldsymbol{u}_{2k+2} = \boldsymbol{u}_{2k} - \frac{a_k \overline{\boldsymbol{\delta}}_k}{\tau}\left(\|\boldsymbol{e}^{\circ}_{2k+1}\|^2 - \|\boldsymbol{e}^{\circ}_{2k}\|^2\right). \tag{5.26}$$

It is clear that the algorithm transform (5.23) in the proof of Theorem 5.1 still holds, with the exception that decreasing parameter c_k should be replaced. In other words, we obtain

$$\widetilde{\boldsymbol{u}}_{2k+2} = \widetilde{\boldsymbol{u}}_{2k} - 2a_k(\mu^2 + \sigma_\mu^2)\mathcal{H}^T\mathcal{H}\widetilde{\boldsymbol{u}}_{2k} + a_k\boldsymbol{\omega}'_k, \tag{5.27}$$

where

$$\begin{aligned}\boldsymbol{\omega}'_k = {} & \alpha_k + \beta_k + \gamma_k + \eta_k + \lambda'_k + \phi'_{2k+1} - \phi'_{2k} \\ & + \varphi'_{2k+1} - \varphi'_{2k} + \psi'_{2k+1} - \psi'_{2k}.\end{aligned}$$

The latter seven terms of $\boldsymbol{\omega}'_k$ are defined similarly to their counterparts $\boldsymbol{\omega}_k$ (except parameter c_k is replaced with τ). Therefore, it is easy to verify that $\{\boldsymbol{\omega}'_k - \lambda'_k, \mathcal{G}_k\}$ is a martingale difference sequence and $\mathbb{E}[\|\boldsymbol{\omega}'_k - \lambda'_k\|^2 \mid \mathcal{G}_{k-1}]$ is bounded by a polynomial of the norm of the input error $\widetilde{\boldsymbol{u}}_{2k}$. In addition, λ'_k no longer vanishes to zero; instead, it is linearly bounded by τ. In other words, $\|\lambda'_k\| \le C_1\tau$, where $C_1 > 0$ is a constant.

We denote $\boldsymbol{\varpi}_k \triangleq \boldsymbol{\omega}'_k - \lambda'_k$ and $\mathcal{Q} = (\mu^2 + \sigma_\mu^2)\mathcal{H}^T\mathcal{H}$. Under the assumption that the input sequence is bounded, we can provide an estimation of the final input error. In particular, from (5.27), we have

$$\begin{aligned}\widetilde{\boldsymbol{u}}_{2k+2} &= (I - 2a_k\mathcal{Q})\widetilde{\boldsymbol{u}}_{2k} + a_k\boldsymbol{\varpi}_k + a_k\lambda'_k \\ &= \Phi(k,0)\widetilde{\boldsymbol{u}}_0 + \sum_{i=0}^{k}\Phi(k,i+1)a_i\boldsymbol{\varpi}_i \\ &\quad + \sum_{i=0}^{k}\Phi(k,i+1)a_i\lambda'_i,\end{aligned} \tag{5.28}$$

where $\Phi(k,i) \triangleq (I - 2a_k\mathcal{Q})\cdots(I - 2a_i\mathcal{Q})$, $\forall k \ge i$, and $\Phi(k,k+1) \triangleq I$.

By direct calculation, we obtain

$$\|\Phi(k,i)\| \le C_2 \exp\left(-h\sum_{j=i}^{k} a_j\right), \quad \forall k \ge i, \forall i \ge 0. \tag{5.29}$$

Using this estimation, it is clear that the first term on the right-hand side (RHS) of (5.28) converges to zero asymptotically. In addition, $\{\boldsymbol{\varpi}_k, \mathcal{G}_k\}$ is a martingale difference sequence satisfying the former condition of (A.5); thus, we conclude that the second term on the RHS of (5.28) also converges to zero as k approaches infinity (using the results of Theorem 5.1 or [10, Lemma 3.3.1]). Because λ_k' does not vanish along the iteration axis, we can no longer ensure zero-error tracking performance. Instead, a bounded convergence of the input error around zero can be obtained, where the upper bound is determined by the last term on the RHS of (5.28). The estimate is given as follows:

$$\begin{aligned}
\left\| \sum_{i=0}^{k} \Phi(k,i+1)a_i\lambda_i' \right\| &= \sum_{i=0}^{k} \|\Phi(k,i+1)\|\|a_i\|\lambda_i'\| \\
&\leq \sum_{i=0}^{k} C_2 \exp\left(-h\sum_{j=i+1}^{k} a_j\right) \cdot a_i \cdot C_1\tau \\
&\leq 2C_1C_2\tau \sum_{i=0}^{k} \exp\left(-h\sum_{j=i+1}^{k} a_j\right)(a_i - \frac{ha_i^2}{2}) \\
&\leq 2C_1C_2\tau \sum_{i=0}^{k} \exp\left(-h\sum_{j=i+1}^{k} a_j\right)(1-\exp(-ha_i)) \\
&\leq 2C_1C_2\tau \sum_{i=0}^{k} \left[\exp\left(-h\sum_{j=i+1}^{k} a_j\right) - \exp\left(-h\sum_{j=i}^{k} a_j\right)\right] \\
&= 2C_1C_2\tau \left[1-\exp\left(-h\sum_{j=0}^{k} a_j\right)\right] \leq 2C_1C_2\tau.
\end{aligned}$$

It is clear that the final input error of $\widetilde{\boldsymbol{u}}_{2k}$ is linearly bounded by τ, where τ can be considered the magnitude of perturbation in (5.17). In addition, in combination with the formulation of (5.17) and (5.13), the input error is bounded as

$$\|\widetilde{\boldsymbol{u}}_k\| \leq (2C_1C_2 + a)\tau. \tag{5.30}$$

In other words, we have obtained an intuitive estimate of the final tracking performance. The tracking performance can be tuned effectively by selecting appropriate values for parameter τ. These results are summarized in the following corollary.

Corollary 5.1 *Consider the system* (5.1) *and apply learning algorithms* (5.25) *and* (5.26), *where the parameters satisfy* (5.13)–(5.15) *and* $\sum_{k=1}^{\infty} a_k^2 < \infty$. *Assume that Assumptions 5.1–5.3 and the fading conditions hold and the* *generated input sequence is bounded. Then, the input error* $\widetilde{\boldsymbol{u}}_k$ *converges to a bounded zone around zero, where the upper bound is linearly dependent on* τ. *As a result, the tracking error is also linearly bounded by the parameter* τ.

From the above derivations, the decreasing sequence $\{a_k\}$ in (5.18) and (5.26) plays an important role in guaranteeing stable convergence of the proposed scheme in the presence of stochastic noise. However, one major drawback of this sequence is slow convergence speed, as discussed in the next section. This is a necessary sacrifice to achieve sufficiently precise tracking performance and stable convergence to a limit without any information about the system and fading channel.

One possible way to accelerate convergence speed is to introduce a constant gain to replace a_k, i.e., let $a_k \equiv \rho$, where $\rho > 0$ is a suitable constant gain. In this case, the regression (5.27) becomes

$$\begin{aligned}\widetilde{\boldsymbol{u}}_{2k+2} &= \widetilde{\boldsymbol{u}}_{2k} - 2\rho(\mu^2+\sigma_\mu^2)\mathcal{H}^T\mathcal{H}\widetilde{\boldsymbol{u}}_{2k} + \rho(\boldsymbol{\varpi}_k + \lambda_k') \\ &= (I-2\rho\mathcal{Q})^k\widetilde{\boldsymbol{u}}_0 + \sum_{i=0}^{k}(I-2\rho\mathcal{Q})^{k-i}\rho\boldsymbol{\varpi}_i \\ &\quad + \sum_{i=0}^{k}(I-2\rho\mathcal{Q})^{k-i}\rho\lambda_i'. \end{aligned} \tag{5.31}$$

Clearly, selecting a sufficiently small ρ can ensure that $\|I-2\rho\mathcal{Q}\| < 1$. In this case, the first term on the RHS of (5.31) approaches zero as k increases. The final input error is bounded by the last two terms on the RHS of (5.31). Provided that the input sequence generated by the scheme with constant gains are bounded, the upper bound of the final input error can be estimated. However, the estimate is fairly complex, which provides little significance relative to practical application. The effects are illustrated by simulations in the next section.

Remark 5.7 *Note that decreasing sequences* $\{a_k\}$ *and* $\{c_k\}$ *are given in advance. Obviously, this cannot represent the optimal and most effective selection for a given system. In other words, arbitrary selection of* $\{a_k\}$ *and* $\{c_k\}$ *satisfying* (5.15) *and* (5.16) *guarantees the asymptotical convergence; however, the transient performance in the iteration domain may be insufficient. It is an interesting issue to consider optimal selection of these sequences relative to some index. In addition, designing an adaptive mechanism for these sequences is also of significance relative to practical applications.*

5.4 ILLUSTRATIVE SIMULATIONS

To illustrate the effectiveness of the proposed scheme for unknown systems with unknown fading channels, we consider the following linear time-varying system (A_t, B_t, C_t):

$$A_t = \begin{bmatrix} 0.4\exp(-t/100) & -0.25 & 0 \\ 0 & 0.8 & \sin(t) \\ 0 & 0 & 0.68 \end{bmatrix},$$
$$B_t = \begin{bmatrix} 0 & 0.48\sin(t) & 1 \end{bmatrix}^T$$
$$C_t = \begin{bmatrix} 0 & 0.1+0.04\cos(t+1) & 0.75 \end{bmatrix}.$$

It is clear that Assumption 5.1 is satisfied because $C_{t+1}B_t > 0, \forall t$. Assumption 5.2 is satisfied by a direct calculation.

We first clarify the system operation information including the iteration length, channel settings, and the desired reference. This information is only used for the simulation and is unknown to the algorithm. The iteration length is $N = 30$. For the channel setting, the multiplicative randomness $\mu_k(t)$ is subject to $N(\mu, \sigma_\mu^2)$ with $\mu = 0.95$ and $\sigma_\mu = 0.1$, and the additive noise $v_k(t)$ is subject to normal distribution $N(0, 0.05^2)$. The desired reference is given as $y_d(t) = 1.5\sin(t/3) + 0.2 - 0.2\cos(t/4)$, and accordingly, the initial state is set to $x_k(0) = x_d(0) = 0$.

Next, we clarify the details of the proposed algorithm in this simulation. The input for the initial iteration is set to $\boldsymbol{u}_0 = \mathbf{0}$. The parameters for (5.17) and (5.18) are summarized as follows. Each dimension of the random perturbation vector $\boldsymbol{\delta}_k$ is generated relative to a standard Bernoulli distribution, i.e., δ_k^i is equal to 1 or -1 with probability 0.5. The decreasing sequences are $a_k = 0.7/(k+700)^{0.96}$ and $c_k = 2.5/(k+100)^{0.45}$. The algorithms are run for 2000 iterations.

The specific procedure of the simulation is given in Algorithm 5.1.

Algorithm 5.1

step 1: Initialize the abovementioned system operation information and algorithm details;

step 2: For the kth iteration, drive the system dynamics to generate system output $\boldsymbol{y}_k$;

step 3: Compute the tracking error according to (5.10) and transmitted through the fading channel;

step 4: Update the input according to (5.17) or (5.18) for odd and even iterations, respectively;

step 5: Check the stopping criterion. If satisfied, end the algorithm; otherwise, let $k := k+1$, go to step **2**, and repeat.

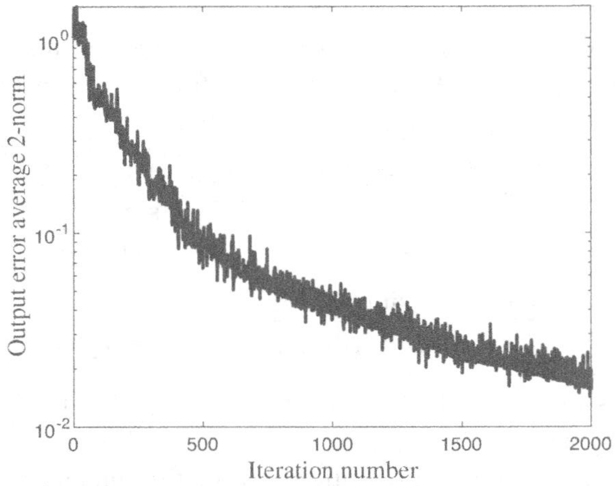

Figure 5.2 Averaged tracking error profile along the iteration axis for the decreasing gain case.

The averaged norm of the tracking error of the kth iteration is defined as $\|\boldsymbol{e}_k\|^2/N = \frac{1}{N}\sum_{t=1}^{N}\|e_k(t)\|^2$. Fig. 5.2 provides the profile of the tracking error norm along the iteration axis. As can be seen, tracking performance is improved continuously as the number of iterations increases. The fluctuations in the profile are caused by the random differences, where both multiplicative and additive randomness are involved. A continuous decreasing trend can be observed for the tracking error; however, the convergence speed is somewhat slow because the scheme must learn the unknown gradient iteration by iteration. This speed can be accelerated if certain a priori information about the system is available. Similarly, we can define the averaged norm of the input error for the kth iteration by $\|\widetilde{\boldsymbol{u}}_k\|^2/N$. The iteration-wise profile of this norm is shown in Fig. 5.3, which shows a decreasing trend of the input error.

To show the statistical significance, we run the simulation for 100 Monte Carlo trials independently and then calculate the average, maximum, and minimum value of the averaged norm of the tracking error for each iteration. The results are shown in Fig. 5.4(a). It is clear that all profiles retain a decreasing trend, which illustrates the effectiveness of the proposed scheme in the iteration domain. To demonstrate the robustness of the proposed scheme against fading randomness, we conduct the simulation for the fading-absence case as a benchmark. Here, the fading-absence case means $\mu_k(t) \equiv 1$ and $\nu_k(t) \equiv 0$; that is, the tracking error can be precisely transmitted always. We

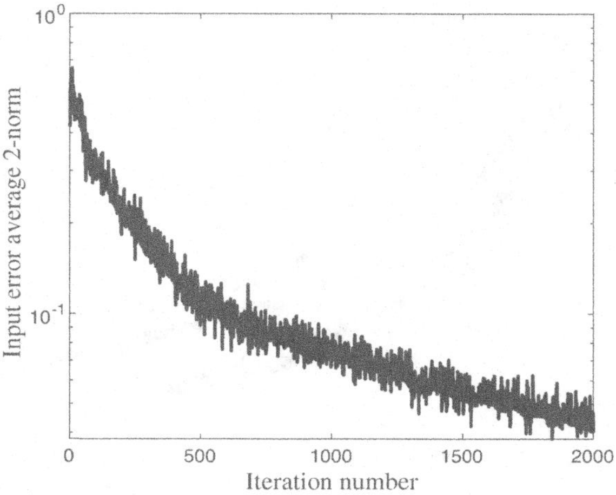

Figure 5.3 Averaged input error profile along the iteration axis for the decreasing gain case.

also run the algorithm for 100 Monte Carlo trials and the results are given in Fig. 5.4(b). Comparing the profiles in Fig. 5.4(a) and (b), one can observe that the performance is considerably similar. This fact demonstrates that the proposed scheme is effective and robust in dealing with fading randomness.

Moreover, to show the effect of the channel-induced randomness, we simulate two variants for different noise distributions. In particular, we consider Case 2 with $\mu_k(t) \sim N(0.95, 0.3^2)$ and $v_k(t) \sim N(0, 0.05^2)$, and Case 3 with $\mu_k(t) \sim N(0.95, 0.1^2)$ and $v_k(t) \sim N(0, 0.2^2)$. Denote the original setting with $\mu_k(t) \sim N(0.95, 0.1^2)$ and $v_k(t) \sim N(0, 0.05^2)$ as Case 1. It is clear that Cases 2 and 3 correspond to the enlarged variance for multiplicative and additive noise, respectively. We conduct 100 Monte Carlo trials for each case and calculate the average value of the averaged tracking error profiles. The results are shown in Fig. 5.5. It is observed that large variance of the channel-induced noise would slow down the convergence speed.

For comparison, we also simulate the constant gain case. First, we set $c_k \equiv 0.1$ and retain $a_k = 0.7/(k+700)^{0.96}$. Note that all other parameters are unchanged. The averaged norm profiles of the tracking and input errors are shown in Figs. 5.6 and 5.7, respectively. The convergent trend is still observed; however, the tracking performance in this case is inferior to that of the decreasing gain case within the same iterations. In addition, the fluctuation

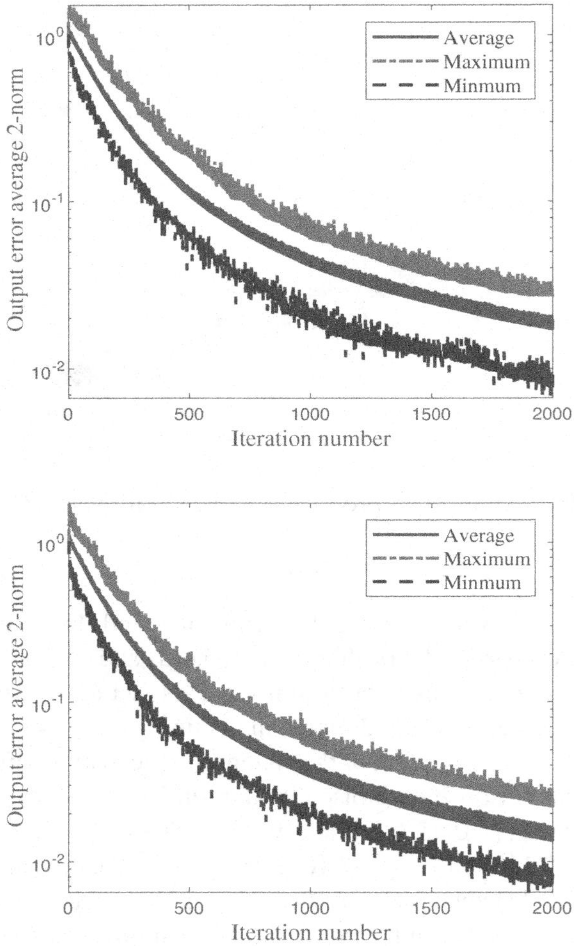

Figure 5.4 Average, maximum, and minimum values for 100 Monte Carlo trials of the averaged tracking error profile along the iteration axis for the decreasing gain case: (a) With fading; (b) without fading.

magnitude of the tracking error expands as the number of iterations increases, which implies instability relative to practical applications.

Furthermore, we keep c_k decreasing as above but let a_k be a constant $a_k \equiv 3 \times 10^{-3}$. The results are shown in Figs. 5.8 and 5.9. As can be seen, the convergence speed is increased slightly because the tracking error enters a specified range with fewer iterations than the decreasing gain case.

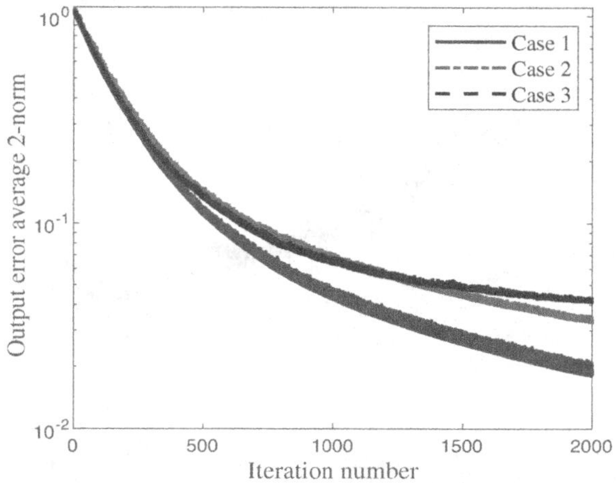

Figure 5.5 Average values for 100 Monte Carlo trials of the averaged tracking error profiles along the iteration axis for different noise distribution cases.

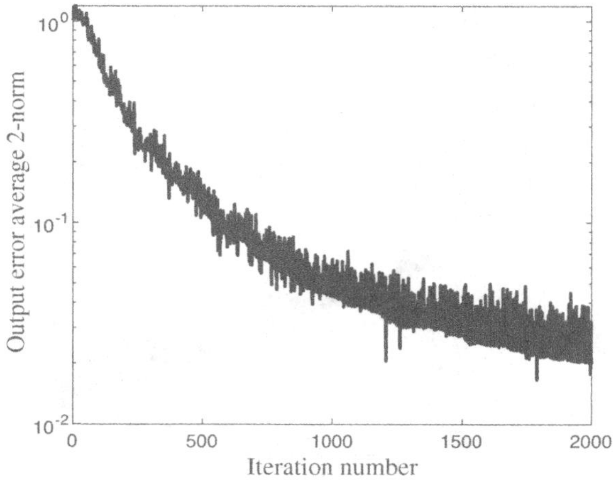

Figure 5.6 Averaged tracking error profile along the iteration axis: Fixed c_k case.

However, by simulating more iterations, we observe that the profile is unstable because constant a_k cannot guarantee stable convergence in the presence of various random factors. The statistical results of simulations are similar to the decreasing gain case; thus, we omit these figures.

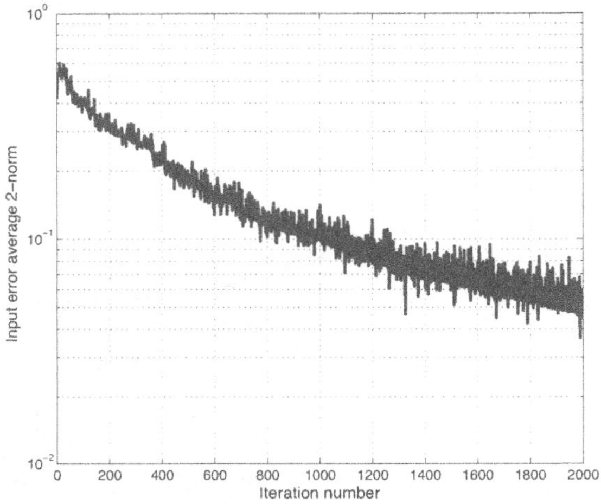

Figure 5.7 Averaged input error profile along the iteration axis: Fixed c_k case.

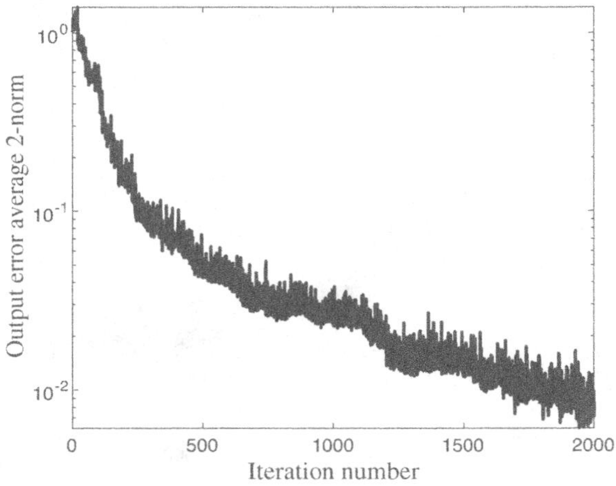

Figure 5.8 Averaged tracking error profile along the iteration axis: Fixed a_k case.

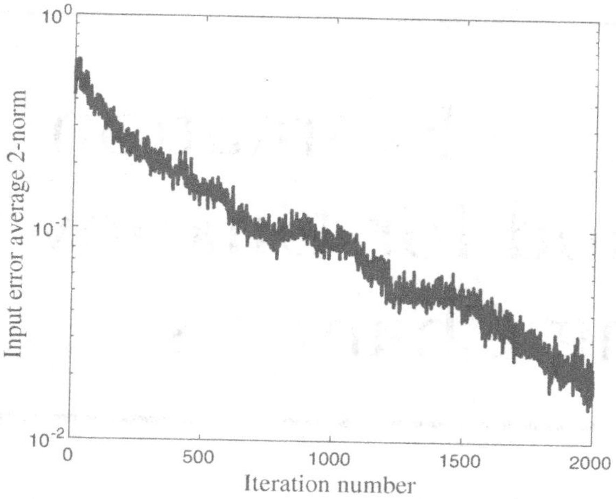

Figure 5.9 Averaged input error profile along the iteration axis: Fixed a_k case.

5.5 SUMMARY

In this chapter, we have proposed a stochastic approximation-based framework to address the learning tracking problem for unknown systems with unknown fading channels. In the proposed framework, measurements are transmitted through the random fading channel, which is modeled by a combination of multiplicative and additive randomness. To generate an effective estimate of the gradient in the presence of various unknowns, the desired reference is sent to the plant to calculate the actual tracking error, which is transmitted back to the controller. In addition, a random difference is introduced to estimate the control update direction, and algorithms with both decreasing gains and constant gains have been designed and discussed. Strict convergence analysis and illustrative simulations have verified the effectiveness of the proposed scheme. Note that we address the fading sensor channel to highlight the idea of the proposed scheme. We should point out that the scheme is also applicable to the fading input case.

CHAPTER 6

Iterative Estimation Method for Unknown Fading Channels

WITH fast developments of communication technologies, a large number of practical systems adopt the networked control structure. For this structure, the fading problem is an emerging issue among other network problems. It has not been extensively investigated how to guarantee superior control performance in the presence of unknown fading channels. This chapter presents a learning strategy for gradually improving the tracking performance. To this end, an iterative estimation mechanism is first introduced to provide necessary statistical information such that the biased signals after transmission can be corrected before being utilized. Then, learning control algorithms incorporating with a decreasing step size sequence are designed for both output and input fading cases respectively. The convergence in both mean-square and almost-sure senses of the proposed schemes are strictly proved under mild conditions.

6.1 INTRODUCTION

In Chapters 2, 3, and 4, the learning control for systems with fading channels are studied depending on a prior knowledge of communication channels and the system. Our objective in this chapter is to investigate the learning tracking ability over unknown fading channels, where the fading effect is modeled by a random variable that is independent of time instants and iterations. In each iteration, before sending the generated signals, we send a

DOI: 10.1201/9781032646404-6

unit signal for test first, and then, we define an empirical iterative estimation based on the received signals. Such estimation is simple but sufficient to provide an unbiased estimation for the learning scheme. Moreover, we revise the conventional learning control algorithms by introducing a decreasing sequence to tackle fading-induced randomness. Further, we rigorously prove the asymptotic convergence of the proposed algorithms in both mean-square and almost-sure senses. We discuss the output and input fading cases separately to clarify the inherent influence of fading channels and provide an integrated formulation. In short, we conduct an intensive analysis of the learning tracking ability and control performance of the proposed scheme based on estimation of fading randomness.

Compared with the previous chapters, results in this chapter have the following novelties. First of all, the learning tracking framework over unknown fading channels is studied using the iterative estimation. Moreover, the essential effect caused by random fading and iterative estimation is carefully analyzed and compared. Further, effective approaches for dealing with various types of randomness are presented for both output and input fading scenarios. Last but not least, precise convergence analysis, as well as general guidelines for practical design, is demonstrated. In short, this chapter presents a systematic framework of the learning tracking problem over unknown fading channels. The significance of this chapter can be understood from three aspects: First, it paves a promising way for complex fading circumstances; second, it reveals the distinctive tracking ability of ILC with a simple iteration-based estimation mechanism for unknown randomness; and third, it provides design and analysis techniques for other networked structure issues.

6.2 PROBLEM FORMULATION

6.2.1 System Formulation

Consider the following discrete-time linear system

$$\begin{aligned} x_k(t+1) =& Ax_k(t) + Bu_k(t) \\ y_k(t) =& Cx_k(t), \end{aligned} \tag{6.1}$$

where k is the iteration index, $k = 1, 2, \dots$, t is the time label, $t = 0, 1, \dots, N$, and N is the iteration length. In other words, the operation of each iteration consists of $N+1$ discrete time instants. The variables $x_k(t) \in \mathbf{R}^n$, $u_k(t) \in \mathbf{R}^p$, and $y_k(t) \in \mathbf{R}^q$ are the system state, input, and output, respectively, with n, p, and q denoting vector dimensions. The system matrices $A \in \mathbf{R}^{n\times n}$, $B \in \mathbf{R}^{n\times p}$, and $C \in \mathbf{R}^{q\times n}$ are compatible with all involved variables. Note that the time-invariant formulation of the plant is mainly to save notations in what follows and the extension to the time-varying case is trivial. In addition, we assume that the input/output coupling matrix CB is of full-column rank. This condition guarantees the existence of a unique input solution to the given output trajectory. Moreover, the system relative degree is one by this condition; extensions to high-order relative degree is straightforward [51].

Let $y_d(t)$ be the desired tracking reference, $t = 0, 1, \dots, N$. Without loss of generality, the tracking reference is assumed realizable as stated in the following assumption.

Assumption 6.1 *There exists a unique input $u_d(t)$ and suitable initial state $x_d(0)$ satisfying the following equation:*

$$\begin{aligned} x_d(t+1) =& Ax_d(t) + Bu_d(t), \\ y_d(t) =& Cx_d(t). \end{aligned} \tag{6.2}$$

As a consequence of Assumption 6.1, to ensure an asymptotical tracking performance as the iteration number increases, it suffices to make the actual input $u_k(t)$ converge to $u_d(t)$ given in Assumption 6.1. Indeed, our analysis targets this in subsequent sections. In addition, Assumption 6.1 is feasible in most applications. Otherwise, no such input $u_d(t)$ exists to generate the given reference and thus, it is impossible to achieve perfect tracking by any control algorithm. For the latter case, the tracking issue can be regarded as an optimization problem in which we track the best possible trajectory closest to the given reference under a certain index. It is beyond the scope of this chapter and thus omitted.

The following initial state resetting condition is assumed.

Assumption 6.2 *The initial state of each iteration $x_k(0)$ is identical to the desired one $x_d(0)$, i.e., $x_k(0) = x_d(0)$.*

Assumption 6.2 is widely accepted as the identical initialization condition in ILC literature [72]. It depicts an essential characteristic of ILC that the operation should start from the same position and ensure a complete repetition such that a learning mechanism can enable a controller to learn the inherent dynamics without knowing system information. The relaxations of this assumption to bounded and random deviation cases have been reported in the literature (e.g., [51]); however, such a discussion is beyond the scope of this chapter, and thus we use Assumption 6.2 for simplicity.

We can state the control objective now. The conventional control objective of ILC is to establish learning algorithms such that the generated input sequence can drive the output $y_k(t)$ to precisely track a given reference

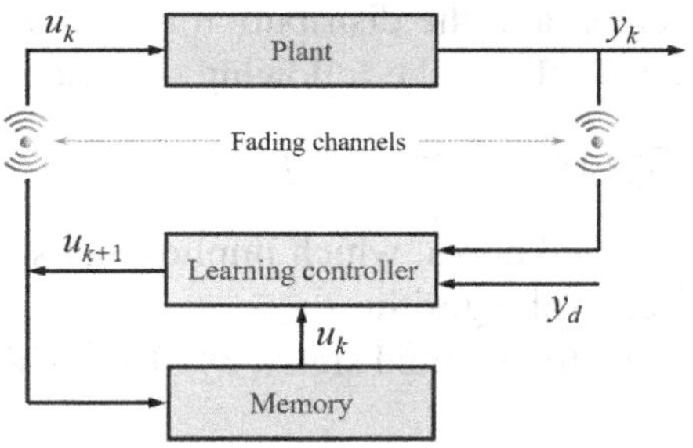

Figure 6.1 Block diagram of learning systems over fading channels.

$y_d(t)$ as the iteration number increases. That is, $y_k(t) \to y_d(t), \forall t$, as $k \to \infty$. From (6.1) and (6.2), this objective can be realized if one can ensure that $u_k(t) \to u_d(t), \forall t$, as $k \to \infty$, where $u_d(t)$ is defined in Assumption 6.1.

6.2.2 Fading Channel Formulation

Fig. 6.1 illustrates the learning system setup, where the plant and the controller are located at different sites and transmit signals over fading channels. To clarify the fundamental effect of fading channels, we consider the following two scenarios in turn: The fading channel at the output side and that at the input side. The general scenario that both sides suffer fading phenomenon is an effortless combination of the above two scenarios. Details will be elaborated in Section 6.4.4.

The fading channel is modeled by a random variable that is multiplied to the transmitted signals as the fading gain. In other words, fading gain introduces multiplicative randomness to involved quantities, which constitutes the major concern of this chapter. Assume that the channels undergo stationary fading such that the statistical information of the fading gain can be estimated and compensated for at the receiver before employed for updating. We consider the case that a scalar fading gain is assigned for each transmitted signal (i.e., the input and output vector) rather than the multiple fading case (where each dimension of the input and output is transmitted and faded separately) to save notations. For the independent multiple fading case, the scalar fading gain hereinbelow can be replaced by a diagonal matrix and all conclusions are still valid. Further, for the case that coupling effect arises between different channels, it requires more exploitation and will be reported in the future.

Let the random fading gain with respect to the time instant t and iteration k be denoted by $\mu_k(t)$. Assume that $\mu_k(t)$ is independent and identically distributed for all t and k, and the distribution function $f(\mu)$ is continuous. Moreover, $\mathbb{P}(\mu_k(t) > 0) = 1$ and the following statistics holds

$$\mu = \mathbb{E}[\mu_k(t)], \quad \sigma^2 = \mathbb{E}[(\mu_k(t) - \mu)^2], \quad \forall t, k \tag{6.3}$$

where both μ and σ are unknown, which implies that such information cannot be utilized in the control algorithms.

Further, denoting the transmitted signal by $m_k(t) \in \mathbf{R}^m$, the received signal is thus given by:

$$m_k^\circ(t) = \mu_k(t) m_k(t). \tag{6.4}$$

Clearly, the received signal has deviated from its original value randomly. This signal should be corrected before being applied in the subsequent steps. An intuitive correction is to multiply the mean inverse of the fading gain by the received signal: $m_k'(t) = \mu^{-1} m_k^\circ(t)$, which yields an unbiased estimate of the original signal. In this chapter, we consider the unknown fading channel, where μ is unknown. Thus, an experimental estimation of the fading channel has to be conducted. We must point out that the additive noise introduced by the fading channel is omitted in (6.4) to clarify our main idea; the results in the following are valid for the channel with additive noise (see Remark 6.2). In addition, the practical fading is generally modeled by a complex number indicating both magnitude variation and phase drift. Here, we assume the phase drift can be well compensated for by the decoder. This general case will be investigated in the future.

In contrast to Chapters 2–4, where the statistics of fading channels is assumed to be known, the fading channel is unknown in this chapter. Moreover, since the physical environments and network devices generally determine the fading channel, it is reasonable to consider the fading phenomenon stationary along the iteration axis. Consequently, an iterative estimation mechanism can be established by sending certain signals; the details will be given in Section 6.2.4.

6.2.3 Control Objective

In consideration of the main objective of ILC and the fading environments, the control objective of this chapter is to provide learning algorithms over unknown fading channels such that the given reference can be tracked as the number of iteration increases, where an iterative estimation of the fading gain is employed. In particular, the design and analysis aim to provide an iterative estimation of the fading gain, design suitable learning algorithms, and analyze the effects of the estimation mechanism and the faded transmission in detail. Additionally, the given reference $y_d(t)$ should be precisely tracked by the entire control framework.

6.2.4 Iterative Estimation of the Fading Gain

Considering the practical implementation of the system setup in Fig. 6.1, we employ an empirical estimation of the unknown mean μ defined in (6.3) by sending a unit signal at the beginning of each iteration; that is, we send the signal $\theta_k \equiv 1$ separately. This unit signal can be regarded as a test signal for probing the random fading. Accordingly, the receiver would receive a faded signal defined by:

$$\theta_k^{\circ} = \mu_k(\star)\theta_k = \mu_k(\star), \tag{6.5}$$

where $\mu_k(\star)$ is the fading variable for the unit signal and it is distributed identically with $\mu_k(t)$. In other words, the random fading gain itself is received. However, this gain cannot be applied for correcting the output $y_k(t)$, $1 \le t \le N$, because $\mu_k(\star)$ is not necessarily equal to $\mu_k(t)$, $\forall\, 1 \le t \le N$.

A natural estimate of μ is given by

$$\widehat{\mu}_k = \frac{1}{k}\sum_{i=1}^{k}\theta_i^{\circ}. \tag{6.6}$$

To be more precise, after sending a unit signal at the beginning of each iteration, we collected the received signals to derive an empirical estimation. Then, we employe the estimation $\widehat{\mu}_k$ to correct the faded signals of the kth iteration.

We first clarify the properties of this estimation:

$$\mathbb{E}[\widehat{\mu}_k] = \frac{1}{k}\sum_{i=1}^{k}\mathbb{E}[\theta_i^{\circ}] = \frac{1}{k}\sum_{i=1}^{k}\mathbb{E}[\mu_i(\star)] = \mu$$

and

$$\begin{aligned}\operatorname{var}(\widehat{\mu}_k) = \mathbb{E}[\widehat{\mu}_k - \mu]^2 &= \mathbb{E}\left[\frac{1}{k}\sum_{i=1}^{k}\mu_i(\star) - \mu\right]^2 \\ &= \frac{1}{k^2}\mathbb{E}\left[\sum_{i=1}^{k}(\mu_i(\star) - \mu)^2\right]\end{aligned}$$

$$+\frac{2}{k^2}\mathbb{E}\left[\sum_{1\le i<j\le k}(\mu_i(\star)-\mu)(\mu_j(\star)-\mu)\right]$$

$$=\frac{1}{k}\sigma^2.$$

Thus, the estimate is unbiased and strongly consistent with respect to k. However, it should be noted that $\widehat{\mu}_k$ is dependent on the iteration axis; this dependency may require additional efforts in the convergence analysis.

Remark 6.1 (Recursive Estimation) *The estimation* (6.6) *requires all historical information, which may occupy much storage in practical application as the iteration number increases. In order to reduce memory burden, an alternative scheme is to transform the estimation* (6.6) *into the recursive form:*

$$\widehat{\mu}_k=\frac{k-1}{k}\widehat{\mu}_{k-1}+\frac{1}{k}\theta_k^\circ. \tag{6.7}$$

Moreover, the estimation $\widehat{\mu}_k$ given by (6.6) *might deviate much from the actual value μ at the first few iterations. Indeed, it is reasonable to acquire relatively precise information about the mean value μ, say $\overline{\mu}$, based on the communication environments and network devices. Thus, a balance between the prior knowledge and online estimation can be achieved by the following sharper estimation,*

$$\widehat{\mu}_k=\left(1-\alpha^k\right)\left(\frac{1}{k}\sum_{i=1}^{k}\theta_k^\circ\right)+\alpha^k\overline{\mu}, \tag{6.8}$$

where $0<\alpha<1$ denotes a forgetting factor. In addition, we can obtain more fading values in one iteration, for example measuring fading value at each time instant, which can further improve the estimation performance.

6.3 LEARNING CONTROL FOR OUTPUT FADING CASE

In this section, we consider learning control for the output fading case. In particular, we assume that the channel from the plant to the controller suffers random fading while the other channel works well. Then, the received output is faded while the control signal for the plant is precise. Under this situation, the iterative estimation in the previous section is employed to correct the received output. We perform effect analysis, algorithm design, and convergence analysis in turn.

6.3.1 Fading Correction and Effect Analysis

Recall that the actual output of the plant is $y_k(t)$ while the received signal by the controller is $y_k^\circ(t)$. We have that $y_k^\circ(t) = \mu_k(t)y_k(t)$. It should be noted that the received output has deviated from its original value and thus it is unsuitable for control update. At this point, a correction must be carried out to generate unbiased information for establishing the learning control algorithm. Precisely, for the correction we utilize the estimated mean $\widehat{\mu}_k$ as follows: $y_k'(t) = \widehat{\mu}_k^{-1} y_k^\circ(t) = \widehat{\mu}_k^{-1}\mu_k(t)y_k(t)$. In particular, we have

$$\begin{aligned} y_k'(t) = y_k(t) &+ \left(\frac{\mu_k(t)}{\mu} - 1\right) y_k(t) \\ &+ \left(\frac{1}{\widehat{\mu}_k} - \frac{1}{\mu}\right) \mu_k(t)y_k(t). \end{aligned} \tag{6.9}$$

A closer observation shows that the estimation-based correction $y_k'(t)$ consists of three parts: The original output $y_k(t)$, an output-dependent error $(\frac{\mu_k(t)}{\mu} - 1)y_k(t)$ caused by the fading gain, and another output-dependent error $(\frac{1}{\widehat{\mu}_k} - \frac{1}{\mu})\mu_k(t)y_k(t)$ caused by the estimation. Both output-dependent errors have the following properties:

1) Due to the independence that exists among the output $y_k(t)$, fading gain $\mu_k(t)$, and estimation $\widehat{\mu}_k$, the expectation of $\mu_k(t)\mu^{-1} - 1$ is equal to zero, while the other error $\widehat{\mu}_k^{-1} - \mu^{-1}$ converges to zero. Thus, the expectation of the corrected signal $y_k'(t)$ approaches to its counterpart $y_k(t)$ as the iteration number increases. Therefore, it is feasible to compute a virtual tracking error for input updating.

2) Although $\mu_k(t)$ and $\widehat{\mu}_k$ have bounded variances, the variance of the newly introduced errors in (6.9) is not generally bounded; instead, it is dependent on its original value $y_k(t)$. This observation implies that the second-moments of the involved quantities are not generally bounded, but dependent on the specific operating values. Accordingly, the asymptotic convergence analysis must be carefully derived (see Subsection 6.3.3).

In a nutshell, these properties enable us to determine specific learning control algorithms. Moreover, since the random deviation of $y_k'(t)$ from $y_k(t)$ is ever-present and unpredictable, it is crucial to introduce a decreasing mechanism such that the effect of this random deviation can be asymptotically eliminated as the number of iteration increases. Details on this will be elaborated in the next subsection.

Remark 6.2 (Additive Noise) *To highlight our main idea, we consider the deterministic system* (6.1) *and the channel* (6.4) *without additive noise. Indeed, the stochastic systems and noisy channels are accommodated in this framework. In particular, if we consider a stochastic system in which system noise and measurement noise are respectively added to the state equation and output equation, both noise terms can be expressed as an additive noise term to* (6.9). *If the communication channel introduces additive noise* $\nu_k(t)$ *in* (6.4), *i.e.,* $m_k^\circ(t) = \mu_k(t)m_k(t) + \nu_k(t)$, *the essential effect is that an additional noise term is added to* (6.9) *by simple calculations. As long as these noise terms are independent of other quantities and with zero-mean and bounded variances, all the results are still valid.*

6.3.2 Learning Algorithm Design

Due to the fading channel from the plant to the controller, the actual output $y_k(t)$ is unknown to compute a tracking error. Instead, the corrected output $y_k'(t)$ is employed to compute a virtual tracking error as $\varepsilon_k(t) \triangleq y_d(t) - y_k'(t)$. Let us denote the actual tracking error by $e_k(t) \triangleq y_d(t) - y_k(t)$. Then, a relation exists between the virtual and actual tracking errors:

$$\varepsilon_k(t) = e_k(t) - \left(\frac{\mu_k(t)}{\mu} - 1\right) y_k(t) - \left(\frac{1}{\widehat{\mu}_k} - \frac{1}{\mu}\right) \mu_k(t) y_k(t). \tag{6.10}$$

We apply the P-type learning control algorithm with variable learning gains:

$$u_{k+1}(t) = u_k(t) + a_k L \varepsilon_k(t+1), \tag{6.11}$$

where $L \in \mathbf{R}^{p\times q}$ denotes the learning gain matrix and $\{a_k\}$ is a decreasing sequence which will be specified in the theorems.

The specific procedure is given as follows:

Algorithm 6.1 Learning control algorithm with output fading

---

step 1: Initialize $k := 1, t := 0$, $u_1(t) = 0$;
step 2: For k, run system (6.1) using $u_k(t)$ and return outputs;
step 3: Generate the fading estimation $\widehat{\mu}_k$ using (6.7);
step 4: Generate the input $u_{k+1}(t)$ using (6.11) and $\widehat{\mu}_k$;
step 5: Check the stopping criterion. If it is not satisfied, let $k := k+1$ and go to *step 2*; otherwise, end the algorithm.

Remark 6.3 (Parameters Selection) *The matrix L is used to regulate the control direction reflected by the input-output coupling matrix CB such that $-LCB$ is a stable matrix. That is, all eigenvalues of LCB have positive real parts. A direct selection of L is $(CB)^T$. If we consider the single-input-single-output case ($p = q = 1$), L can be removed from the learning control algorithm. The decreasing sequence $\{a_k\}$ is the learning step size, where $a_k \downarrow 0$ implies that the influence of additional errors in* (6.9) *is asymptotically eliminated as k approaches infinity. In other words, after sufficiently many learning iterations, the newly arrived tracking information might be dominated by the fading-induced errors and should be greatly suppressed; otherwise, it will be difficult to achieve a stable convergence of the input sequence in the iteration domain. If $\{a_k\}$ is replaced by a constant step size that is sufficiently small, only a bounded convergence of the input sequence can be obtained (see Remark 6.4).*

6.3.3 Convergence Analysis

To simplify notations, we move all variables of each iteration into a supervector. In particular, we define $\boldsymbol{u}_* = [u_*(0)^T, u_*(1)^T, \ldots, u_*(N-1)^T]^T \in \mathbf{R}^{Np}$ and $\boldsymbol{y}_* = [y_*(1)^T, y_*(2)^T, \ldots, y_*(N)^T]^T \in \mathbf{R}^{Nq}$, where the subscript "$*$" denotes "$k$" and "$d$" regarding the actual operation (6.1) and reference model (6.2). Then, we have $\boldsymbol{y}_d = \mathcal{H}\boldsymbol{u}_d + \mathcal{M}x_d(0)$ and $\boldsymbol{y}_k = \mathcal{H}\boldsymbol{u}_k + \mathcal{M}x_k(0)$, where

$$\mathcal{H} = \begin{bmatrix} CB & 0 & 0 & 0 \\ CAB & CB & 0 & 0 \\ \vdots & \vdots & \ddots & \vdots \\ CA^{N-1}B & CA^{N-2}B & \cdots & CB \end{bmatrix} \in \mathbf{R}^{Nq \times Np},$$

$$\mathcal{M} = \left[(CA)^T, \ldots, (CA^N)^T\right]^T \in \mathbf{R}^{Nq \times n}.$$

Let $\boldsymbol{e}_k$ be the lifted supervector of the tracking error $e_k(t)$ from $t = 1$ to $t = N$. Then, we have

$$\boldsymbol{e}_k \triangleq \boldsymbol{y}_d - \boldsymbol{y}_k = \mathcal{H}(\boldsymbol{u}_d - \boldsymbol{u}_k), \tag{6.12}$$

where $x_k(0) = x_d(0)$ in Assumption 6.2 is applied. Moreover, we can define $\boldsymbol{\varepsilon}_k$ similarly to $\boldsymbol{e}_k$. In addition, denote $\phi_k(t) = \frac{\mu_k(t)}{\mu} - 1$ and $\psi_k = \frac{1}{\bar{\mu}_k} - \frac{1}{\mu}$. Note that ψ_k is iteration-dependent but time-independent. Clearly, $\mathbb{E}[\phi_k(t)] = 0$, $\sup_{k,t} \mathbb{E}[\phi_k^2(t)] < \infty$, $\mathbb{E}[\psi_k] \to 0$ and $\beta_k = \mathbb{E}[\psi_k^2] \to 0$. Further, we denote $\Phi_k = \mathrm{diag}\{\phi_k(1), \phi_k(2), \ldots, \phi_k(N)\}$ and $\Psi_k = \psi_k \mathrm{diag}\{\mu_k(1), \mu_k(2), \ldots, \mu_k(N)\}$;

and obtain that $\mathbb{E}[\Phi_k] = 0$. Then, from (6.10) we have

$$\boldsymbol{\varepsilon}_k = \boldsymbol{e}_k - (\Phi_k \otimes I_q)\boldsymbol{y}_k - (\Psi_k \otimes I_q)\boldsymbol{y}_k, \tag{6.13}$$

where $\otimes$ denotes the Kronecker product.

The first theorem is given below for the mean-square convergence.

Theorem 6.1 *Consider system* (6.1) *with output fading channel and Assumptions 6.1–6.2 hold. Then, the input sequence* $\{u_k(t)\}$ *generated by the proposed learning control algorithm* (6.11) *converges to the desired value* $u_d(t)$ *asymptotically in the mean-square sense as iteration number increases, i.e.,* $\mathbb{E}[\|\boldsymbol{u}_k - \boldsymbol{u}_d\|^2] \to 0$, *if the learning gain matrix L is designed such that all eigenvalues of LCB have positive real parts and the decreasing sequence* $\{a_k\}$ *satisfies* $a_k > 0$, $\sum_{k=1}^{\infty} a_k = \infty$, *and* $\lim_{k\to\infty} a_k = 0$. *Hence, the tracking error converges to zero in the mean-square sense, i.e.,* $\mathbb{E}[\|\boldsymbol{e}_k\|^2] \to 0$.

Proof: Denote $\mathcal{L} = \text{diag}\{L, L, \ldots, L\}$. From (6.11) and (6.13), we have

$$\boldsymbol{u}_{k+1} = \boldsymbol{u}_k + a_k\mathcal{L}[\boldsymbol{e}_k - \widehat{\Phi}_k\boldsymbol{y}_k - \widehat{\Psi}_k\boldsymbol{y}_k], \tag{6.14}$$

where $\widehat{\Phi}_k \triangleq \Phi_k \otimes I_q$ and $\widehat{\Psi}_k \triangleq \Psi_k \otimes I_q$.

Further, denote $\Delta\boldsymbol{u}_k = \boldsymbol{u}_d - \boldsymbol{u}_k$. Then, subtracting both sides of (6.14) from $\boldsymbol{u}_d$ leads to

$$\Delta\boldsymbol{u}_{k+1} = \Delta\boldsymbol{u}_k - a_k\mathcal{L}[\boldsymbol{e}_k - \widehat{\Phi}_k\boldsymbol{y}_k - \widehat{\Psi}_k\boldsymbol{y}_k]. \tag{6.15}$$

It should be noted that both $\widehat{\Phi}_k\boldsymbol{y}_k$ and $\widehat{\Psi}_k\boldsymbol{y}_k$ are output-dependent; thus, they are input-dependent. However, this observation creates some boundedness challenge in analyzing the convergence of (6.15). We rewrite (6.15) as follows:

$$\begin{aligned}\Delta\boldsymbol{u}_{k+1} = \Delta\boldsymbol{u}_k &- a_k\mathcal{L}\mathcal{H}\Delta\boldsymbol{u}_k - a_k\mathcal{L}\widehat{\Phi}_k\mathcal{H}\Delta\boldsymbol{u}_k \\ &- a_k\mathcal{L}\widehat{\Psi}_k\mathcal{H}\Delta\boldsymbol{u}_k + a_k\mathcal{L}\widehat{\Phi}_k\boldsymbol{y}_d + a_k\mathcal{L}\widehat{\Psi}_k\boldsymbol{y}_d,\end{aligned} \tag{6.16}$$

where $\boldsymbol{y}_k = \boldsymbol{y}_d - \boldsymbol{e}_k = \boldsymbol{y}_d - \mathcal{H}\Delta\boldsymbol{u}_k$ is applied.

Note that $\mathcal{L}$ is a block diagonal matrix with diagonal elements L, and $\mathcal{H}$ is a block lower-triangular matrix with diagonal elements CB; thus, $\mathcal{L}\mathcal{H}$ is still a block lower-triangular matrix with diagonal blocks LCB. Since L is designed such that all eigenvalues of LCB have positive real parts, all eigenvalues of $\mathcal{L}\mathcal{H}$ also have positive real parts. In other words, $-\mathcal{L}\mathcal{H}$ is stable; moreover, by the Lyapunov stability theory, there exists a positive-definite matrix $\mathcal{Q}$ such that $(\mathcal{L}\mathcal{H})^T\mathcal{Q} + \mathcal{Q}(\mathcal{L}\mathcal{H}) = I_{Np}$.

Further, we employ the following Lyapunov function to demonstrate the convergence analysis,

$$V_k = (\Delta \boldsymbol{u}_k)^T \mathcal{Q}(\Delta \boldsymbol{u}_k). \tag{6.17}$$

Substituting (6.16) into the expression of V_{k+1}, we have

$$\begin{aligned}
V_{k+1} = &(\Delta \boldsymbol{u}_k)^T \mathcal{Q}(\Delta \boldsymbol{u}_k) + a_k^2 (\Delta \boldsymbol{u}_k)^T (\mathcal{L}\mathcal{H})^T \mathcal{Q}\mathcal{L}\mathcal{H}(\Delta \boldsymbol{u}_k)\\
&+ a_k^2 (\Delta \boldsymbol{u}_k)^T (\mathcal{L}\widehat{\Phi}_k \mathcal{H})^T \mathcal{Q}\mathcal{L}\widehat{\Phi}_k \mathcal{H}(\Delta \boldsymbol{u}_k)\\
&+ a_k^2 (\Delta \boldsymbol{u}_k)^T (\mathcal{L}\widehat{\Psi}_k \mathcal{H})^T \mathcal{Q}\mathcal{L}\widehat{\Psi}_k \mathcal{H}(\Delta \boldsymbol{u}_k)\\
&+ a_k^2 \boldsymbol{y}_d^T \left[(\mathcal{L}\widehat{\Phi}_k)^T \mathcal{Q}\mathcal{L}\widehat{\Phi}_k + (\mathcal{L}\widehat{\Psi}_k)^T \mathcal{Q}\mathcal{L}\widehat{\Psi}_k\right] \boldsymbol{y}_d\\
&- a_k (\Delta \boldsymbol{u}_k)^T \left[(\mathcal{L}\mathcal{H})^T \mathcal{Q} + \mathcal{Q}(\mathcal{L}\mathcal{H})\right] (\Delta \boldsymbol{u}_k)\\
&+ 2a_k (\Delta \boldsymbol{u}_k)^T \mathcal{Q}\mathcal{L}[\widehat{\Phi}_k + \widehat{\Psi}_k](\boldsymbol{y}_d - \mathcal{H}(\Delta \boldsymbol{u}_k))\\
&+ 2a_k^2 (\Delta \boldsymbol{u}_k)^T (\mathcal{L}\mathcal{H})^T \mathcal{Q}\mathcal{L}[\widehat{\Phi}_k + \widehat{\Psi}_k](\mathcal{H}(\Delta \boldsymbol{u}_k) - \boldsymbol{y}_d)\\
&+ 2a_k^2 (\Delta \boldsymbol{u}_k)^T (\mathcal{L}\widehat{\Phi}_k \mathcal{H})^T \mathcal{Q}\mathcal{L}\widehat{\Psi}_k \mathcal{H}(\Delta \boldsymbol{u}_k)\\
&+ 2a_k^2 \boldsymbol{y}_d^T (\mathcal{L}\widehat{\Phi}_k)^T \mathcal{Q}\mathcal{L}\widehat{\Psi}_k \boldsymbol{y}_d\\
&- 2a_k^2 (\mathcal{H}\Delta \boldsymbol{u}_k)^T (\widehat{\Phi}_k + \widehat{\Psi}_k)^T \mathcal{L}^T \mathcal{Q}\mathcal{L}(\widehat{\Phi}_k + \widehat{\Psi}_k)\boldsymbol{y}_d.
\end{aligned} \tag{6.18}$$

It is observed that here, most quantities are iteration-dependent, thus we prove the convergence by conditional probability. Now, denote an increasing σ-algebra $\mathcal{F}_k \triangleq \sigma\{u_1(t), x_i(0), \mu_k(t), 0 \le t \le N, 1 \le i \le k\}$ to be the set of all events induced by the random variables up to the kth iteration. Because the fading gain $\mu_k(t)$ occurs independently along the iteration axis, the matrices Φ_k and Ψ_k are independent of $\mathcal{F}_{k-1}$. Following the learning update law, we have that $\boldsymbol{u}_k \in \mathcal{F}_{k-1}$.

Note that since $\mathcal{Q}$ is a positive-definite matrix, there exists a constant c_1 such that $I_{Np} \ge c_1 \mathcal{Q}$ and therefore,

$$\begin{aligned}
&(\Delta \boldsymbol{u}_k)^T \left[(\mathcal{L}\mathcal{H})^T \mathcal{Q} + \mathcal{Q}(\mathcal{L}\mathcal{H})\right] (\Delta \boldsymbol{u}_k)\\
&= (\Delta \boldsymbol{u}_k)^T (\Delta \boldsymbol{u}_k) \ge c_1 (\Delta \boldsymbol{u}_k)^T \mathcal{Q}(\Delta \boldsymbol{u}_k),
\end{aligned} \tag{6.19}$$

where $(\mathcal{L}\mathcal{H})^T \mathcal{Q} + \mathcal{Q}(\mathcal{L}\mathcal{H}) = I_{Np}$ is applied.

Similarly, suitable positive constants c_2, c_3, and c_4 exist such that

$$\begin{aligned}
&(\mathcal{L}\mathcal{H})^T \mathcal{Q}\mathcal{L}\mathcal{H} \le c_2 \mathcal{Q},\\
&\mathbb{E}[(\mathcal{L}\widehat{\Phi}_k \mathcal{H})^T \mathcal{Q}\mathcal{L}\widehat{\Phi}_k \mathcal{H} \mid \mathcal{F}_{k-1}] \le c_3 \mathcal{Q},\\
&\mathbb{E}[(\mathcal{L}\widehat{\Psi}_k \mathcal{H})^T \mathcal{Q}\mathcal{L}\widehat{\Psi}_k \mathcal{H} | \mathcal{F}_{k-1}] \le c_4 \beta_k \mathcal{Q},
\end{aligned}$$

where the boundedness of second-order moments of $\phi_k(t)$ and $\psi_k(t)$ are applied. Moreover, still applying this property, we have

$$\mathbb{E}[\boldsymbol{y}_d^T(\mathcal{L}\widehat{\Phi}_k)^T\mathcal{Q}\mathcal{L}\widehat{\Phi}_k\boldsymbol{y}_d|\mathcal{F}_{k-1}] \le c_5,$$
$$\mathbb{E}[\boldsymbol{y}_d^T(\mathcal{L}\widehat{\Psi}_k)^T\mathcal{Q}\mathcal{L}\widehat{\Psi}_k\boldsymbol{y}_d \mid \mathcal{F}_{k-1}] \le c_6\beta_k,$$

where c_5 and c_6 are suitable positive constants.

Based on the zero-mean property of $\widehat{\Phi}_k$, we obtain

$$\mathbb{E}[(\Delta\boldsymbol{u}_k)^T\mathcal{Q}\mathcal{L}\widehat{\Phi}_k\mathcal{H}(\Delta\boldsymbol{u}_k) \mid \mathcal{F}_{k-1}] = 0,$$
$$\mathbb{E}[(\Delta\boldsymbol{u}_k)^T(\mathcal{L}\mathcal{H})^T\mathcal{Q}\mathcal{L}\widehat{\Phi}_k\mathcal{H}(\Delta\boldsymbol{u}_k) \mid \mathcal{F}_{k-1}] = 0,$$
$$\mathbb{E}[(\Delta\boldsymbol{u}_k)^T\mathcal{Q}\mathcal{L}\widehat{\Phi}_k\boldsymbol{y}_d \mid \mathcal{F}_{k-1}] = 0,$$
$$\mathbb{E}[(\Delta\boldsymbol{u}_k)^T(\mathcal{L}\mathcal{H})^T\mathcal{Q}\mathcal{L}\widehat{\Phi}_k\boldsymbol{y}_d \mid \mathcal{F}_{k-1}] = 0.$$

By the basic inequality, we have

$$\begin{aligned}&2(\Delta\boldsymbol{u}_k)^T\mathcal{Q}\mathcal{L}\widehat{\Psi}_k\mathcal{H}(\Delta\boldsymbol{u}_k)\\&\le \omega^{-1}(\Delta\boldsymbol{u}_k)^T(\mathcal{L}\widehat{\Psi}_k\mathcal{H})^T\mathcal{Q}\mathcal{L}\widehat{\Psi}_k\mathcal{H}(\Delta\boldsymbol{u}_k)\\&\quad + \omega(\Delta\boldsymbol{u}_k)^T\mathcal{Q}(\Delta\boldsymbol{u}_k),\end{aligned}$$

where $\omega > 0$ is a constant to be specified later. This yields

$$\begin{aligned}&\mathbb{E}[2(\Delta\boldsymbol{u}_k)^T\mathcal{Q}\mathcal{L}\widehat{\Psi}_k\mathcal{H}(\Delta\boldsymbol{u}_k) \mid \mathcal{F}_{k-1}]\\&\quad \le (\omega + \omega^{-1}c_4\beta_k)(\Delta\boldsymbol{u}_k)^T\mathcal{Q}(\Delta\boldsymbol{u}_k).\end{aligned}$$

Similarly, we obtain

$$\begin{aligned}&\mathbb{E}[2(\Delta\boldsymbol{u}_k)^T\mathcal{Q}\mathcal{L}\widehat{\Psi}_k\boldsymbol{y}_d \mid \mathcal{F}_{k-1}]\\&\quad \le \omega(\Delta\boldsymbol{u}_k)^T\mathcal{Q}(\Delta\boldsymbol{u}_k) + \omega^{-1}c_6\beta_k.\end{aligned}$$

Using the same scaling technique but removing ω, we have

$$\begin{aligned}&\mathbb{E}[2(\Delta\boldsymbol{u}_k)^T(\mathcal{L}\mathcal{H})^T\mathcal{Q}\mathcal{L}\widehat{\Psi}_k\mathcal{H}(\Delta\boldsymbol{u}_k) \mid \mathcal{F}_{k-1}]\\&\quad \le (c_2 + c_4\beta_k)(\Delta\boldsymbol{u}_k)^T\mathcal{Q}(\Delta\boldsymbol{u}_k),\\&\mathbb{E}[2(\Delta\boldsymbol{u}_k)^T(\mathcal{L}\mathcal{H})^T\mathcal{Q}\mathcal{L}\widehat{\Psi}_k\boldsymbol{y}_d \mid \mathcal{F}_{k-1}]\\&\quad \le c_2(\Delta\boldsymbol{u}_k)^T\mathcal{Q}(\Delta\boldsymbol{u}_k) + c_6\beta_k,\\&\mathbb{E}[2(\Delta\boldsymbol{u}_k)^T[\mathcal{L}\widehat{\Phi}_k\mathcal{H}]^T\mathcal{Q}\mathcal{L}\widehat{\Psi}_k\mathcal{H}(\Delta\boldsymbol{u}_k) \mid \mathcal{F}_{k-1}]\\&\quad \le (c_3 + c_4\beta_k)(\Delta\boldsymbol{u}_k)^T\mathcal{Q}(\Delta\boldsymbol{u}_k),\end{aligned}$$

$$\begin{aligned}
&\mathbb{E}[2\boldsymbol{y}_d^T[\mathcal{L}\widehat{\Phi}_k]^T \mathcal{Q}\mathcal{L}\widehat{\Psi}_k\boldsymbol{y}_d \mid \mathcal{F}_{k-1}] \le c_5 + c_6\beta_k, \\
&\mathbb{E}[2(\Delta\boldsymbol{u}_k)^T\mathcal{H}^T\widehat{\Phi}_k\mathcal{L}^T\mathcal{Q}\mathcal{L}\widehat{\Phi}_k\boldsymbol{y}_d \mid \mathcal{F}_{k-1}] \\
&\quad \le c_3(\Delta\boldsymbol{u}_k)^T\mathcal{Q}(\Delta\boldsymbol{u}_k) + c_5, \\
&\mathbb{E}[2(\Delta\boldsymbol{u}_k)^T\mathcal{H}^T\widehat{\Psi}_k\mathcal{L}^T\mathcal{Q}\mathcal{L}\widehat{\Phi}_k\boldsymbol{y}_d \mid \mathcal{F}_{k-1}] \\
&\quad \le c_4\beta_k(\Delta\boldsymbol{u}_k)^T\mathcal{Q}(\Delta\boldsymbol{u}_k) + c_5, \\
&\mathbb{E}[2(\Delta\boldsymbol{u}_k)^T\mathcal{H}^T\widehat{\Phi}_k\mathcal{L}^T\mathcal{Q}\mathcal{L}\widehat{\Psi}_k\boldsymbol{y}_d \mid \mathcal{F}_{k-1}] \\
&\quad \le c_3(\Delta\boldsymbol{u}_k)^T\mathcal{Q}(\Delta\boldsymbol{u}_k) + c_6\beta_k, \\
&\mathbb{E}[2(\Delta\boldsymbol{u}_k)^T\mathcal{H}^T\widehat{\Psi}_k\mathcal{L}^T\mathcal{Q}\mathcal{L}\widehat{\Psi}_k\boldsymbol{y}_d \mid \mathcal{F}_{k-1}] \\
&\quad \le c_4\beta_k(\Delta\boldsymbol{u}_k)^T\mathcal{Q}(\Delta\boldsymbol{u}_k) + c_6\beta_k.
\end{aligned}$$

Taking conditional expectation of both sides of (6.18) with respect to $\mathcal{F}_{k-1}$ and substituting the above estimates yield

$$\begin{aligned}
\mathbb{E}[V_{k+1} \mid \mathcal{F}_{k-1}] \le\; & V_k - a_k(c_1 - 2\omega)V_k + a_k\beta_k\omega^{-1}c_4V_k \\
& + a_k^2(3c_2 + 4c_3 + 5c_4\beta_k)V_k \\
& + \omega^{-1}c_6a_k\beta_k + a_k^2(4c_5 + 5c_6\beta_k). \qquad (6.20)
\end{aligned}$$

Let $\omega < \frac{c_1}{4}$. Taking the mathematical expectation to both sides of the above equation yields

$$\mathbb{E}[V_{k+1}] \le \left(1 - \frac{c_1}{2}a_k + a_k\gamma_k\right)\mathbb{E}[V_k] + a_k\delta_k, \qquad (6.21)$$

where

$$\gamma_k = \beta_k\omega^{-1}c_4 + a_k(3c_2 + 4c_3 + 5c_4\beta_k), \qquad (6.22)$$

$$\delta_k = \beta_k\omega^{-1}c_6 + a_k(4c_5 + 5c_6\beta_k). \qquad (6.23)$$

It is evident $\gamma_k \to 0$ and $\delta_k \to 0$ as $k \to \infty$.

Regarding Lemma A.3, we correspond ξ_k, τ_k, and χ_k to $\mathbb{E}[V_k]$, $(\frac{c_1}{2} - \gamma_k)a_k$, and $a_k\delta_k$, respectively. Clearly, we have

$$0 \le 1 - \frac{c_1}{2}a_k + a_k\gamma_k < 1, \quad k \ge k_0, \qquad (6.24)$$

$$\sum_{k=1}^{\infty}\left(\frac{c_1}{2} - \gamma_k\right)a_k = \infty, \qquad (6.25)$$

$$\frac{a_k\delta_k}{(\frac{c_1}{2} - \gamma_k)a_k} = \frac{2\delta_k}{1 - 2\gamma_k} \to 0, \quad \text{as } k \to \infty. \qquad (6.26)$$

Thus, by Lemma A.3, we conclude that $\lim_{k\to}\mathbb{E}[V_k] = 0$. In addition, $\mathcal{Q}$ is a positive-definite matrix, which leads to $\mathbb{E}\left[\|\Delta \boldsymbol{u}_k\|^2\right] \leq \lambda_{\min}^{-1}(\mathcal{Q})\mathbb{E}[V_k]$. This inequality results in that $\mathbb{E}\left[\|\Delta \boldsymbol{u}_k\|^2\right] \to 0$ as $k \to \infty$. Then, by Assumption 6.1, we have that $\mathbb{E}[\|\boldsymbol{e}_k\|^2] \to 0$. The proof is completed. □

Theorem 6.1 reveals that the learning control algorithm (6.11) with an output correction using the estimated mean of the fading gain is effective in handling the randomness caused by fading channels. The zero-error asymptotic convergence is guaranteed by a decreasing sequence that is not diminishing too fast, disclosed by the condition $\sum_{k=1}^{\infty} a_k = \infty$. In addition, we emphasize that the output-dependent deviation is addressed by separating its terms into the following two terms: An input-dependent term and an output-independent deviation term. The former can be analyzed similarly to the original input error while the latter can be tackled as a noise.

Remark 6.4 (Constant Step-size Case) *To achieve the zero-error tracking performance, we introduce a decreasing sequence $\{a_k\}$ in (6.11). We replace a_k by a constant step size a^*, i.e., $a_k \equiv a^*$, where a^* satisfies $0 \leq \frac{c_1}{2}a^* - a^*\gamma_k^* <$ 1 and γ_k^* is similar to γ_k in (6.22) with a_k replaced by a^*. Then, (6.21) becomes*

$$\mathbb{E}\left[V_{k+1}\right] \leq \left(1 - \frac{c_1}{2}a^* + a^*\gamma_k^*\right)\mathbb{E}\left[V_k\right] + a^*\delta_k^*, \tag{6.27}$$

where δ_k^* is similar to δ_k in (6.23) with a_k replaced by a^*. For a sufficiently large integer k_0, we can guarantee $\beta_k \leq a^*$, $\forall k \geq k_0$. Then, we can deduce that $\gamma_k^* \leq a^*\gamma_0$ and $\delta_k^* \leq a^*\delta_0$, where γ_0 and δ_0 are constants defined according to the formulation of γ_k^* and δ_k^*. Let $\eta = 1 - \frac{c_1}{2}a^* + (a^*)^2\gamma_0$, one can easily deduce that, $\forall k \geq k_0$,

$$\mathbb{E}\left[V_k\right] \leq \mathbb{E}\left[V_{k_0}\right]\eta^{k-k_0} + \frac{2a^*\delta_0}{c_1 - 2a^*\gamma_0}\left(1 - \eta^{k-k_0}\right). \tag{6.28}$$

This inequality brings us to the discussion of the convergence rate estimate for the constant step size case. Meanwhile, letting k approach infinity, one observes that $\limsup \mathbb{E}[V_k] \leq \frac{2a^*\delta_0}{c_1 - 2a^*\gamma_0}$, where the upper bound is strongly related to the desired reference $y_d(t)$ and fading variance σ^2. Thus, we can only obtain bounded convergence rather than convergence to zero by using a constant step size, which in turn demonstrates the necessity of introducing the decreasing sequence $\{a_k\}$.

Remark 6.5 (Guidelines on Step-size Selections) *From (6.27) and (6.28), we notice that the convergence rate and the upper bound of the convergent range depend on the selection of the constant step size a^*. In particular, as*

a^* decreases, both the convergence rate and upper bound decrease, where the former indicates a slow convergence speed and the latter indicates good tracking performance. A trade-off exists between the convergence speed and tracking precision. This trade-off also exists when determining a constant or a decreasing step size. Based on these facts, we can conclude guidelines of the step size selection for practical applications. If a faster convergence speed is preferred, one can choose an appropriately large constant step size for the scheme; if a better tracking performance is a priority, one can choose a decreasing step size sequence or a sufficiently small constant step size for the scheme. An effective balancing alternative is to conduct the scheme by two stages: In the early stage, a constant step size is used to accelerate the convergence while in the later stage, it is replaced by a decreasing sequence to improve the tracking performance.

The following theorem describes the almost-sure convergence, which is another important notion of convergence.

Theorem 6.2 *Consider system* (6.1) *with output fading channel and Assumptions 6.1–6.2 hold. Then, the input sequence $\{u_k(t)\}$ generated by the proposed learning control algorithm* (6.11) *converges to the desired value $u_d(t)$ asymptotically in the almost-sure sense as the iteration number increases, i.e., $\boldsymbol{u}_k - \boldsymbol{u}_d \to 0$ almost surely, if the learning gain matrix L is designed such that all eigenvalues of LCB have positive real parts and the decreasing sequence $\{a_k\}$ satisfies $a_k > 0$, $\sum_{k=1}^{\infty} a_k = \infty$, and $\sum_{k=1}^{\infty} a_k^2 < \infty$. Hence, the tracking error converges to zero, i.e., $\boldsymbol{e}_k \to 0$ almost surely.*

Proof: Following (6.20), we have that

$$\mathbb{E}\left[V_{k+1} \mid \mathcal{F}_{k-1}\right] \leq \left(1 - \frac{c_1}{2} a_k + a_k \gamma_k\right) \mathbb{E}\left[V_k\right] + a_k \delta_k. \tag{6.29}$$

Further, we respectively correspond V_k, $(\frac{c_1}{2} - \gamma_k)a_k$, and $a_k\delta_k$ to ξ_k, τ_k, and χ_k in Lemma A.4 in the Appendix. By the conditions $\sum_{k=1}^{\infty} a_k^2 < \infty$ and β_k converges to zero of order k^{-1}, we have $\sum_{k=1}^{\infty} \chi_k = \sum_{k=1}^{\infty} a_k \delta_k < \infty$. The other conditions of Lemma A.4 have been verified by (6.24)–(6.26). Therefore, V_k converges to zero almost surely as $k \to \infty$. Consequently, $\Delta \boldsymbol{u}_k$ and $\boldsymbol{e}_k$ converge asymptotically to zero. Moreover, by Lemma A.4 for any $\varepsilon > 0$ and $k \geq k_0$, we have

$$\mathbb{P}\left(V_j \leq \varepsilon \text{ for all } j \geq k\right) \geq 1 - \varepsilon^{-1} \left(\mathbb{E}[V_k] + \sum_{i=k}^{\infty} a_i \delta_i \right).$$

Furthermore, since $\mathbb{E}[V_k] \to 0$ and $\sum_{i=k}^{\infty} a_i \delta_i \to 0$ as $k \to \infty$, we have that $\mathbb{P}(V_j \le \varepsilon \text{ for all } j \ge k)$ converges to one as $k \to \infty$ for any given ε. Hence, the proof is completed. □

Theorem 6.2 presents the almost-sure convergence of the proposed algorithm (6.11). Generally, mean-square convergence and almost-sure convergence cannot imply each other directly. The gap between the two convergence senses is bridged by the principle of uniform integrability and certain moment conditions. Hence, we slightly strengthened the condition of decreasing sequence $\{a_k\}$ by additionally requiring that it decreases sufficiently fast in the sense that $\sum_{k=1}^{\infty} a_k^2 < \infty$.

6.4 LEARNING CONTROL FOR INPUT FADING CASE

In this section, we consider the input fading case. In this case, we assume that the channel from the controller to the plant, which transmits the computed input signals, suffers random fading, whereas the other channel works well. Then, the control signals for the plant are faded during transmission. Similar to the previous section, we send a unit test signal for each iteration to estimate fading statistics and then correct the received control signals. At the end, we combine output and input fading cases into the general framework.

6.4.1 Fading Estimation and Correction

The computed input is denoted by $u_k(t)$ while the received input by the plant, which is faded during the transmission, is denoted by $u_k^{\circ}(t)$, i.e., $u_k^{\circ}(t) = \mu_k(t)u_k(t)$. Clearly, the received input may differ much from its actual value. Thus, it should be corrected before applied to the plant. However, the statistics of the fading gain is unknown and has to be estimated. Identically to the output fading case, we employ the empirical estimation mechanism to compute the mean of fading gains. That is, the estimate in (6.6) is employed that is independent of other involved signals.

The corrected input $u_k'(t) = \widehat{\mu}_k^{-1} u_k^{\circ}(t)$ is given by:

$$\begin{aligned} u_k'(t) &= u_k(t) + \left(\frac{\mu_k(t)}{\mu} - 1\right) u_k(t) \\ &\quad + \left(\frac{1}{\widehat{\mu}_k} - \frac{1}{\mu}\right) \mu_k(t) u_k(t). \end{aligned} \tag{6.30}$$

Therefore, the estimation-based correction of the input signal $u_k'(t)$ consists of two deviation terms: A fading-induced error $(\frac{\mu_k(t)}{\mu} - 1)u_k(t)$ and an estimation-based error $(\frac{1}{\widehat{\mu}_k} - \frac{1}{\mu})\mu_k(t)u_k(t)$. Both errors are input-dependent, which, therefore, affects the convergence analysis in what follows. In a nutshell, it is observed that the deviations for the input fading case are similar to those of the output fading case. This fact motivates us to conduct a similar analysis to the previous section; however, modifications should be made because the position of fading variables in derivations differs.

Specifically, considering the system dynamics, we have

$$\begin{aligned} x_k(t+1) = & Ax_k(t) + Bu_k(t) + B\left(\frac{\mu_k(t)}{\mu} - 1\right)u_k(t) \\ & + B\left(\frac{1}{\widehat{\mu}_k} - \frac{1}{\mu}\right)\mu_k(t)u_k(t). \end{aligned} \tag{6.31}$$

From this formula, one can easily observe that the output is significantly influenced by the fading error, which may result in a large deviation.

Remark 6.6 (Averaging Mechanism) *In order to reduce the deviation effect of faded inputs in* (6.31)*, a possible approach is to introduce the averaging mechanism to smoothen the input signals along the iteration axis. By averaging the historic input signals in a certain sense, the random deviations caused by random fading channels can be effectively suppressed, and then the transient tracking performance is improved. Details can refer to Chapters 3 and 4.*

6.4.2 Learning Algorithm Design

As in the output fading case, the learning control algorithm, in this case, is still of P-type with a decreasing sequence:

$$u_{k+1}(t) = u_k(t) + a_k L e_k(t+1), \tag{6.32}$$

where $e_k(t) = y_d(t) - y_k(t)$ is the tracking error and $L \in \mathbf{R}^{q\times p}$ is the learning gain matrix. Further, $\{a_k\}$ is the decreasing sequence identical to the one in the output fading case.

The specific procedure is given as follows:

Algorithm 6.2 Learning control algorithm with input fading

step 1: Initialize $k := 1, t := 0, u_1(t) = 0$;

step 2: For k, send a unit signal at the input side and generate the fading estimation $\widehat{\mu}_k$ using (6.7);

step 3: Correct the received input $u_k^\circ(t)$, run system (6.1) using $u_k'(t)$, and return outputs;

step 4: Generate the input $u_{k+1}(t)$ using (6.32) and $\widehat{\mu}_k$;

step 5: Check the stopping criterion. If it is not satisfied, let $k := k+1$ and go to *step 2*; otherwise, end the algorithm.

6.4.3 Convergence Analysis

We consider the formulation of the system by noticing that $x_k(t+1) = A^{t+1}x_k(0)+\sum_{i=0}^{t} A^{t-i}Bu'_k(i)$; thus, we have $\boldsymbol{y}_k = \mathcal{H}\boldsymbol{u}'_k + \mathcal{M}x_k(0)$, where $\boldsymbol{u}'_k$ is defined similarly to $\boldsymbol{u}_k$ with the element $u_k(i)$ replaced by $u'_k(i), 0 \le i \le N-1$. Then, $\boldsymbol{y}_k = \widehat{\mu}_k^{-1}\mathcal{H}(\Omega_k \otimes I_p)\boldsymbol{u}_k + \mathcal{M}x_k(0)$, where $\Omega_k \triangleq \text{diag}\{\mu_k(0),\ldots,\mu_k(N-1)\}$. Consequently,

$$\begin{aligned}\boldsymbol{e}_k &= \boldsymbol{y}_d - \boldsymbol{y}_k = \mathcal{H}\left(\boldsymbol{u}_d - \widehat{\mu}_k^{-1}(\Omega_k \otimes I_p)\boldsymbol{u}_k\right)\\ &= \mathcal{H}\Delta\boldsymbol{u}_k - \mathcal{H}\left(\Phi_k \otimes I_p\right)\boldsymbol{u}_k - \mathcal{H}\left(\Psi_k \otimes I_p\right)\boldsymbol{u}_k. \end{aligned} \tag{6.33}$$

Now, we present the main theorem of this section. The proof of this theorem follows the same pattern as the proof of Theorems 6.1 and 6.2; thus it is omitted to save space.

Theorem 6.3 *Consider system* (6.1) *with input fading channel and Assumptions 6.1–6.2 hold. Then, the input sequence $\{u_k(t)\}$ generated by the proposed learning control algorithm* (6.32) *converges to the desired value $u_d(t)$ asymptotically in the mean-square sense as the iteration number increases, i.e., $\mathbb{E}[\|\boldsymbol{u}_k - \boldsymbol{u}_d\|^2] \to 0$, if the learning gain matrix L is designed such that all eigenvalues of LCB have positive real parts and the decreasing sequence $\{a_k\}$ satisfies $a_k > 0$, $\sum_{k=1}^{\infty} a_k = \infty$, and $\lim_{k\to\infty} a_k = 0$. In addition, if we further have $\sum_{k=1}^{\infty} a_k^2 < \infty$, then the convergence holds in the almost-sure sense as the iteration number increases, i.e., $\boldsymbol{u}_k - \boldsymbol{u}_d \to 0$ almost surely.*

Remark 6.7 (Decreasing Sequence) *Although system* (6.1) *is free of random noise, the fading channel introduces randomness to the transmitted signals, and thus, to the algorithm. To guarantee a stable convergence of the learning algorithms* (6.11) *and* (6.32), *we employed the decreasing sequence $\{a_k\}$. The main conditions of $\{a_k\}$ consist of $a_k > 0$, $a_k \to 0$, $\sum_{k=1}^{\infty} a_k = \infty$, and $\sum_{k=1}^{\infty} a_k^2 < \infty$. Clearly, $a_k = a/k^b$ with $a > 0$ and $1/2 < b \le 1$ satisfies these conditions.*

Remark 6.8 (Event-triggered Mechanism) *In practical applications, the decreasing sequence $\{a_k\}$ is usually defined before the operation process; in other words, $\{a_k\}$ is independent of the practical implementation performance of the proposed algorithm. One can consider an event-triggered design of this sequence to obtain additional performance such as increasing convergence rate. That is, we can conduct the renewal of a_k according to some additional even-trigger mechanisms rather than for all iterations. Then, the decreasing speed of a_k is slowed down and determined by operation process itself. Even in that case, our theorems are still valid as long as the newly designed sequence satisfies the above-specified conditions.*

6.4.4 A General Formulation

In this section, we consider a general formulation where fading channels exist at both output and input sides simultaneously. The random fading variable at the output side occurs independently of the one at the input side. The statistics of both fading channels can be different and are unknown prior. Then, we must design two independent estimation processes: One for output fading and the other for input fading.

To distinguish output and input fading channels, we added superscripts "out" and "in" to the corresponding fading variables. At each iteration, say the kth iteration, we run the system using the corrected input $u_k'(t) = (\widehat{\mu}_k^{\mathtt{in}})^{-1}u_k^{\circ}(t)$, which is corrected from the received input $u_k^{\circ}(t) = \mu_k^{\mathtt{in}}(t)u_k(t)$. Then, we have the following dynamics:

$$\begin{aligned} x_k(t+1) =& Ax_k(t) + B(\widehat{\mu}_k^{\mathtt{in}})^{-1}\mu_k^{\mathtt{in}}(t)u_k(t), \\ y_k(t) =& Cx_k(t). \end{aligned}$$

Before transmitting all the outputs back to the controller, we first send a unit signal to obtain a test signal given as $\theta_k^{\circ,\mathtt{out}} = \mu_k^{\mathtt{out}}(\star)$. The fading gain mean at the output side is recursively estimated by $\widehat{\mu}_k^{\mathtt{out}} = \frac{1}{k}\sum_{i=1}^{k}\theta_i^{\circ,\mathtt{out}}$. While the received output is $y_k^{\circ}(t) = \mu_k^{\mathtt{out}}(t)y_k(t)$, the learning control algorithm is given by $u_{k+1}(t) = u_k(t) + a_kL\varepsilon_k(t+1)$, where $\varepsilon_k(t) = y_d(t) - (\widehat{\mu}_k^{\mathtt{out}})^{-1}\mu_k^{\mathtt{out}}(t)y_k(t)$.

Before transmitting all the computed inputs $u_{k+1}(t)$ to the plant, we first send a unit signal to get a test signal given by $\theta_{k+1}^{\circ,\mathtt{in}} = \mu_{k+1}^{\mathtt{in}}(\star)$, which yields the following estimation $\widehat{\mu}_{k+1}^{\mathtt{in}} = \frac{1}{k+1}\sum_{i=1}^{k+1}\theta_i^{\circ,\mathtt{in}}$. By using this estimation, the received input can be corrected and used to drive the system.

Observe that the input fading $\mu_k^{\mathtt{in}}(t)$ is independent of the output fading $\mu_k^{\mathtt{out}}(t)$. The convergence of this general formulation can be analyzed completely as in the previous theorems. Therefore, we omit these steps to avoid repetition.

6.5 ILLUSTRATIVE SIMULATIONS

In this section, we first present a numerical simulation to verify the proposed algorithms for the formulated problem in a multi-input-multi-output (MIMO) model and then consider a permanent magnet linear motor (PMLM) originated from practice to demonstrate the effectiveness in applications.

6.5.1 MIMO System

Consider the following time-varying MIMO systems:

$$x_k(t+1) = \begin{bmatrix} 0.05\sin 0.2t & -0.2 & 0.02t \\ 0.1 & -0.01t & -0.02\cos 0.5t \\ 0.1 & 0.1 & 0.2+0.05\cos 0.2t \end{bmatrix} x_k(t)$$
$$+ \begin{bmatrix} 1-0.2\sin^2(0.5\pi t) & 0 \\ 0.01t & 0.01t \\ 0 & 1+0.1\sin(0.5\pi t) \end{bmatrix} u_k(t),$$
$$y_k(t) = \begin{bmatrix} 0.2+0.1\sin^2(0.5\pi t) & 0.1 & -0.1 \\ 0 & 0.1 & 0.2-0.1\sin(0.5\pi t) \end{bmatrix} x_k(t).$$

We set the iteration length to $N = 50$ and the initial state to $x_k(0) = 0$. Further, the desired reference is set to $y_d(t) = \frac{9}{10}\sin(\frac{t}{3}) - \frac{1}{2}\cos(\frac{t}{4}) + \frac{1}{2}$ for both dimensions. Moreover, the fading gain satisfies a normal distribution $\mu_k(t) \sim N(\mu, \sigma^2)$, where values outside of the interval $[0, 2\mu]$ is deleted to satisfy the positivity assumption of the fading channel. The learning gain matrix is set to

$$L_t = \begin{bmatrix} 9.1632-0.2\sin(0.5\pi t) & 2.6493 \\ -0.5297 & 2.87-0.1\sin(0.5\pi t) \end{bmatrix}.$$

Clearly, all eigenvalues of $LC_{t+1}B_t$ have positive real parts. Furthermore, the decreasing sequence is set to $a_k = \alpha/k^\beta$. For all cases, we run the proposed algorithms for 50 iterations.

We first check the effectiveness of the proposed algorithms with iterative estimation. In this case, we set parameters in the fading gain and decreasing sequence to $\mu = 0.95$, $\sigma = 0.1$, $\alpha = 1$, and $\beta = 0.55$. Fig. 6.2 demonstrate the performance. Fig. 6.2(a) and (b) shows outputs of the first dimension at the 5th and 50th iterations and the desired trajectory (the second dimension behaves the same and is omitted to avoid repetition). It is observed that the tracking performance for the 5th iteration is rather poor, while that for the 50th iteration is relatively acceptable. This fact verifies the effectiveness of the proposed scheme. Moreover, the output at the 50th iteration for the output fading case tracks the desired reference more closely than that for the input fading case. This is because the actual output for the input fading case still suffers random fading effect although the computed input has already been close to the desired one.

To see the fundamental learning ability, we refer to Fig. 6.3(a) and (b) for the input error profiles of the second dimension in output and input fading cases, respectively. The averaged mean-square input error is defined as

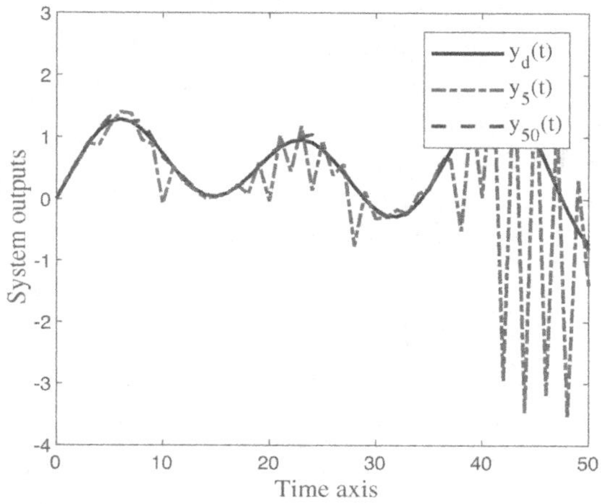

(a) Output fading case

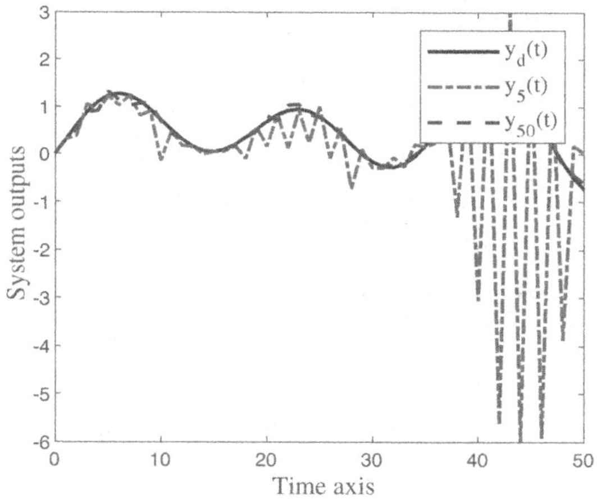

(b) Input fading case

Figure 6.2 Output profiles at the 5th and 50th iterations, and the desired reference for the first dimension: (a) Output fading case and (b) input fading case.

$||\Delta \boldsymbol{u}_k||^2/N$ for the kth iteration in these figures. It is seen that both input error profiles decrease rapidly, indicating that the proposed schemes can provide acceptable convergence rate for applications. In addition, the proposed scheme behaves similarly for both output and input cases. These observations demonstrate that the fading position leads to little difference in convergence

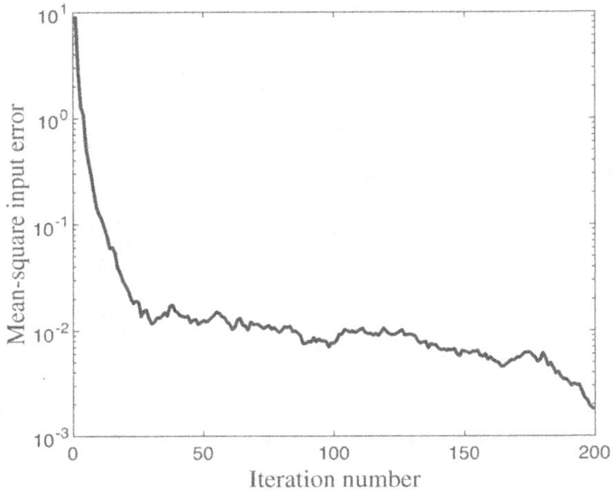

(a) Output fading case

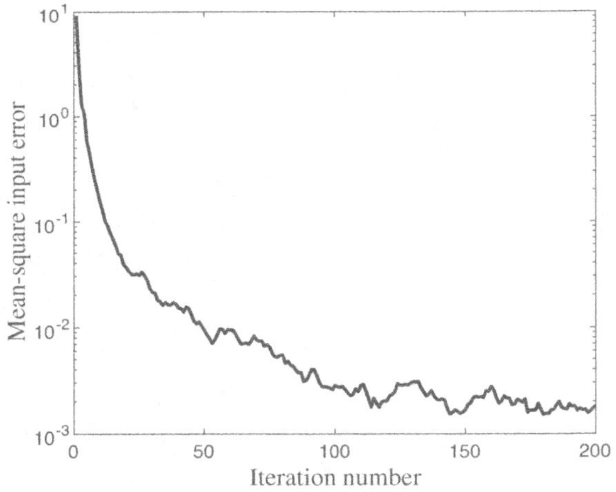

(b) Input fading case

Figure 6.3 Averaged mean square input error profiles: (a) Output fading case and (b) input fading case.

properties of the proposed learning scheme, but significant difference in output tracking performance.

Next, we are interested in the possible influence of fading randomness over the convergence property. To see this point, we consider the following three scenarios of the fading models: $\mu = 0.95$, $\sigma = 0.1$; $\mu = 0.85$, $\sigma = 0.1$;

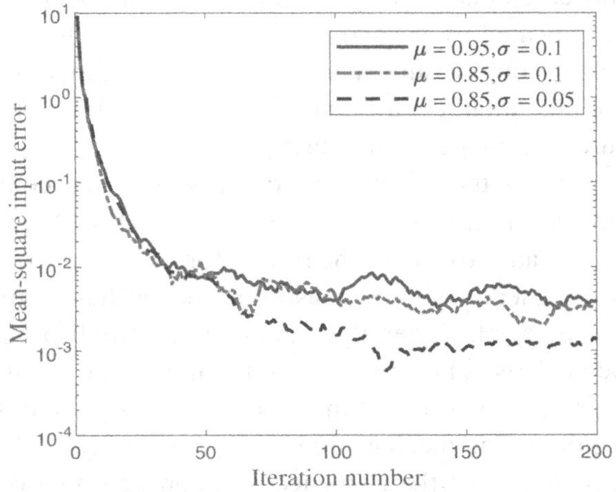

(a) Output fading case

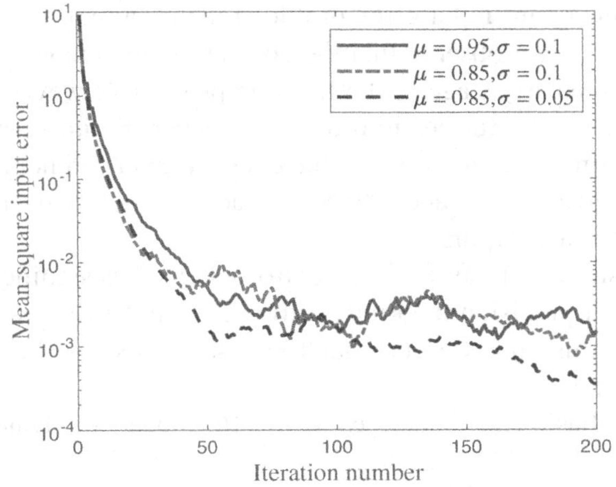

(b) Input fading case

Figure 6.4 Input error profiles for different fading distributions: (a) Output fading case and (b) input fading case.

and $\mu = 0.85$, $\sigma = 0.05$ for an intuitive comparison. Fig. 6.4(a) and (b) shows the mean-square input error profiles along the iteration axis for the output and input fading cases, respectively. One can observe that all the scenarios demonstrate a fast convergence. This reflects that the fading distribution effect can be well compensated for by the estimated statistics. Among the three scenarios, it is observed that a small variation may lead to a fast convergence speed, which is indicated by dashed lines in Fig. 6.4(a) and (b). This is because a smaller variation σ results in a more accurate estimation of the fading gain mean. Generally, a large variation of the fading variable implies higher volatility, which will damage the learning process.

Moreover, we check the effect of the decreasing sequence by simulating the following three scenarios: $\alpha = 1, \beta = 0.55$; $\alpha = 1, \beta = 0.75$; and $\alpha = 0.5$, $\beta = 0.55$. Fig. 6.5(a) and (b) shows the results for the output and input fading cases, respectively. Clearly, the decreasing sequence has distinct influence on the convergence speed. Generally, a large α and small β can lead to the convergence speed. This is because a large learning gain within the feasible range leads to a great contraction of the input error. One can thus consider an event-triggered gain tuning mechanism in the future study.

Further, we demonstrate the influence of a constant gain on the convergence. We consider three scenarios: $a^* = 0.5$, $a^* = 0.3$, and $a^* = 0.15$, all of which satisfy the validation of convergence conditions. Fig. 6.6(a) and (b) shows the mean-square input error profiles for the output and input fading cases, respectively. We observe that the constant gains render a fast convergence speed at the early stage of the learning process; however, the tracking performance cannot be further improved whenever the input error enters a bounded range. In addition, reducing the constant gain can help improve the final tracking performance; accordingly, it sacrifices the convergence speed as more iterations are required.

Lastly, we show that the learning control scheme has significant potential in achieving high-precision tracking performance under different estimation approaches. To this end, we consider four estimators for the mean of the fading randomness:

EST-1: The basic least-square estimator (6.6) or its equivalent recursive formulation (6.7);

EST-2: A variant of (6.7) with a primary guess of the mean, i.e., (6.8), where the forgetting factor is set to $\alpha = 0.8$;

EST-3: A recursive gradient estimator $\widehat{\mu}_k = \widehat{\mu}_{k-1} + \rho(\theta_k^\circ - \widehat{\mu}_{k-1})$, where $\rho > 0$ is a constant steplength (it is set $\rho = 0.05$ in this simulation);

EST-4: A noncumulative estimator that we send the test signal for ten times independently within each iteration and compute the average as an estimate.

The estimate profiles of these estimators are shown in Fig. 6.7(a), where the solid straight line denotes the actual mean of the fading randomness. It can be seen that the estimation profiles of EST-1 and EST-2 converges to the actual mean, the estimation profile of EST-3 converges to a neighborhood of

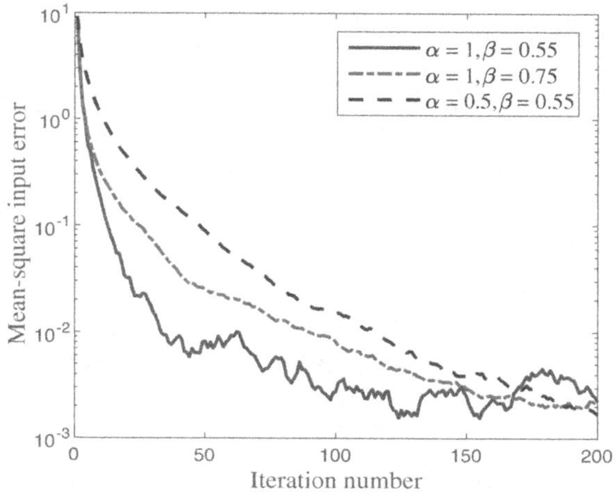

(a) Output fading case

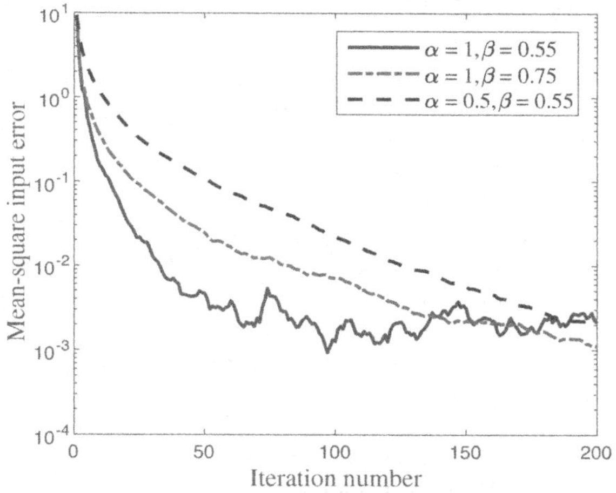

(b) Input fading case

Figure 6.5 Input error profiles for different decreasing gain sequences: (a) Output fading case and (b) input fading case.

the actual mean, and that of EST-4 mainly fluctuates around the actual mean. This observation illustrates the effectiveness of the estimation approach. Besides, using the above four estimators of the fading statistics, we simulate the learning and tracking process for the proposed algorithms under the primary setting of parameters ($\mu = 0.95$, $\sigma = 0.1$, $\alpha = 1$, and $\beta = 0.55$). The

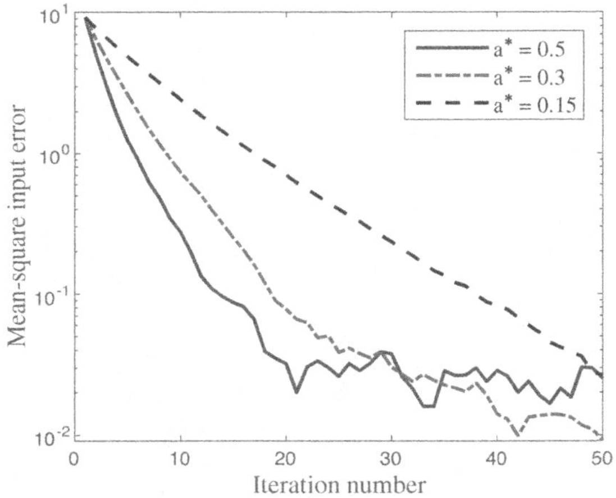

(a) Output fading case

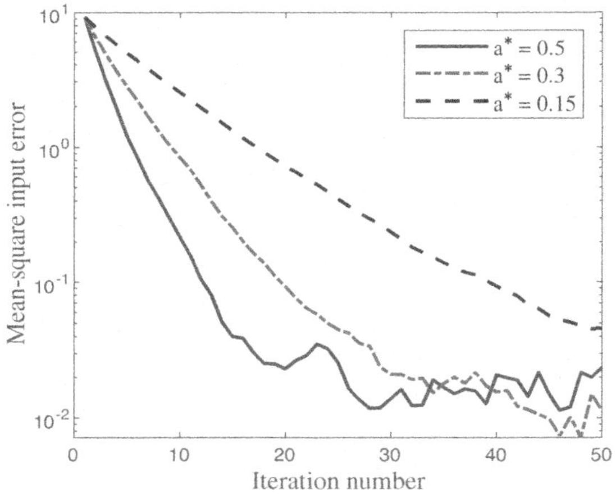

(b) Input fading case

Figure 6.6 Input error profiles for different constant gain: (a) Output fading case and (b) input fading case.

averaged mean-square input error profiles are shown in Fig. 6.7(b) for four cases. It is observed that all profiles retain a continuously decreasing trend in the iteration domain. This observation indicates that the proposed learning framework can achieve good tracking performance even if the fading estimation is rough.

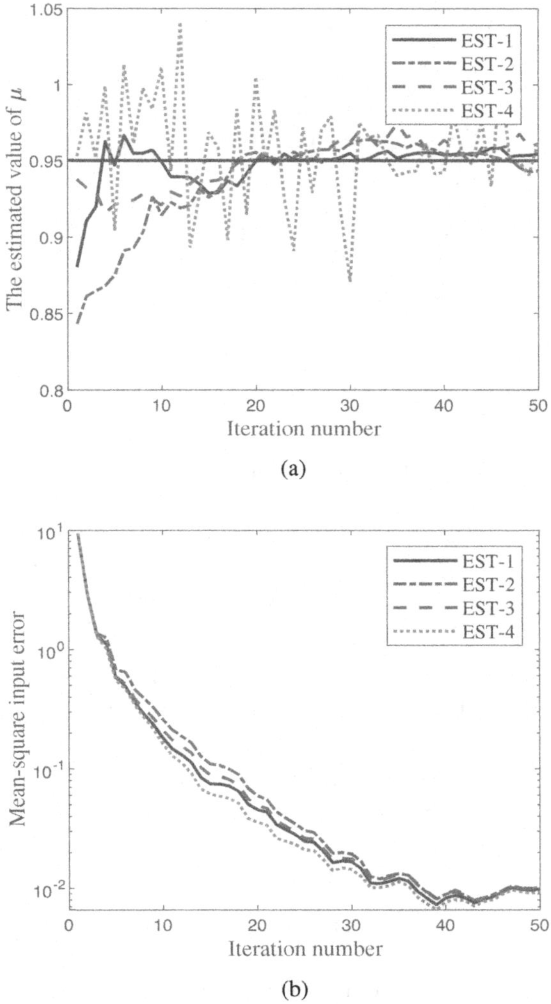

Figure 6.7 (a) Estimation profiles for the proposed four estimators; (b) input error profiles for the proposed learning control scheme with four estimators.

6.5.2 PMLM System

We adopt the following PMLM model:

$$
\begin{aligned}
x(t+1) &= x(t) + v(t)\Delta, \\
v(t+1) &= v(t) - \Delta\frac{k_1 k_2 \Psi_f^2}{Rm}v(t) + \Delta\frac{k_2\Psi_f}{Rm}u(t), \\
y(t) &= v(t),
\end{aligned}
$$

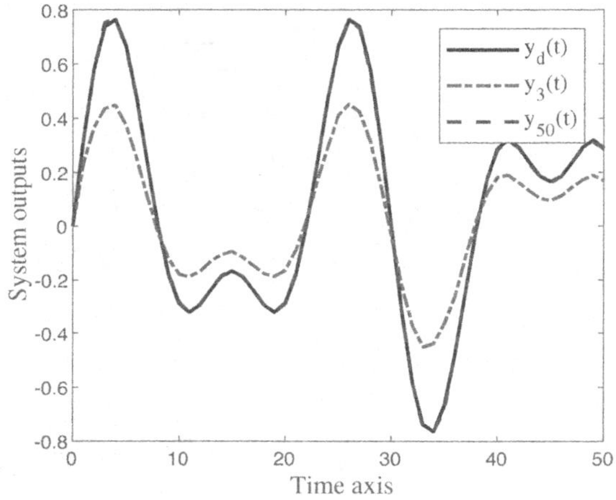

(a) Output fading case

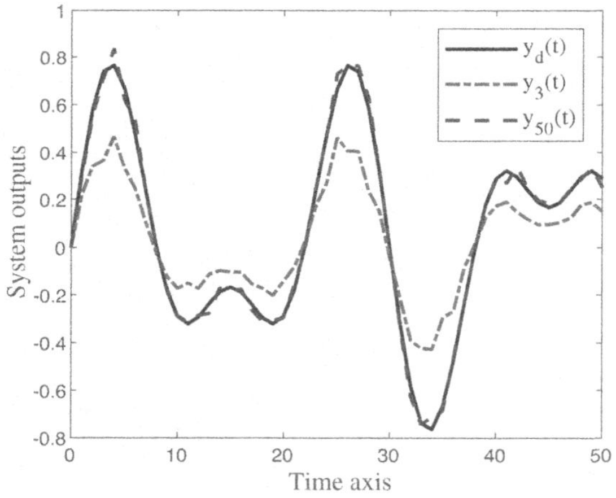

(b) Input fading case

Figure 6.8 Output tracking performance for selected iterations: (a) Output fading case and (b) input fading case.

where $\Delta = 0.01$ s is the sampling time interval, x and v denote motor position and rotor velocity, $R = 8.6\,\Omega$ the resistance of the stator, $m = 1.635$ kg the rotor mass, and $\psi_f = 0.35$ Wb the flux linkage, $k_1 = \pi/\tau$ and $k_2 = 1.5\pi/\tau$, with $\tau = 0.031$ m being the pole pitch. The whole iteration length is $T = 0.5$ s, i.e., $N = 50$.

The desired reference is $y_d(t) = \frac{1}{2}\sin(\frac{\pi t}{10}) + \frac{1}{3}\sin(\frac{\pi t}{6})$, $0 \leq t \leq 50$. Further, the fading gain is described by a normal distribution $N(0.95, 0.05^2)$, while

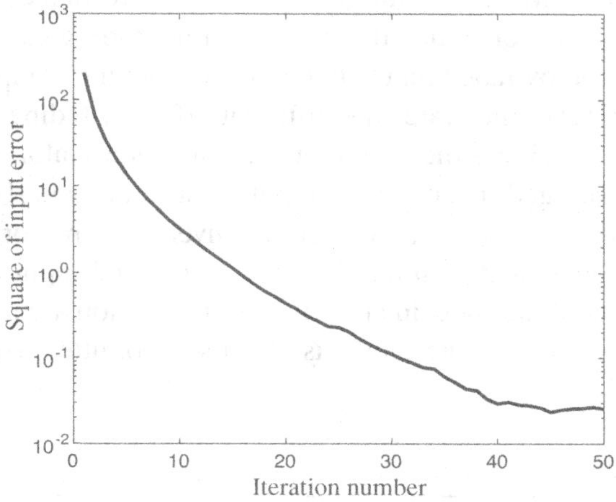

(a) Output fading case

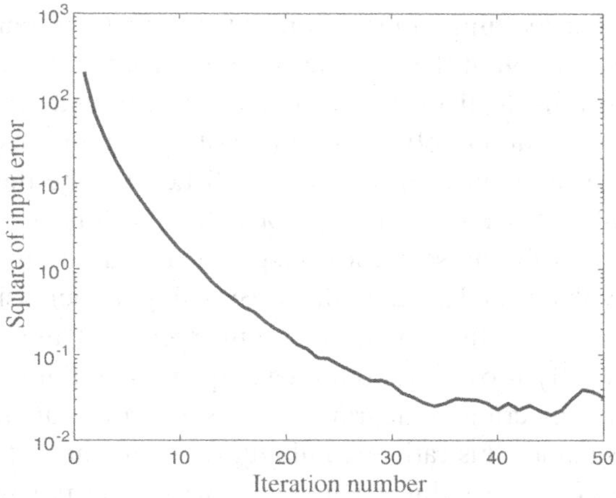

(b) Input fading case

Figure 6.9 Input error profiles along the iteration axis: (a) Output fading case and (b) input fading case.

the learning gain is set to $L = 15$. As for the decreasing sequence, we choose $a_k = 1/k^{0.55}$. Besides, we run learning control algorithms for 50 iterations for both output and input fading cases.

Fig. 6.8 demonstrates the output tracking performance of the 3rd and 50th iterations for both cases. It is seen that the tracking performance has already been acceptable at the 50th iteration, which illustrates the effectiveness of the proposed algorithms. Moreover, the final tracking performance for the input fading case is slightly worse than that for the output fading case because the former case is driven by faded inputs that deviate from the computed input at the controller. This fact illustrates the different effect of fading transmission in both cases. Fig. 6.9 shows the asymptotical convergence along the iteration axis, where the averaged mean-square input error is defined the same as in the previous subsection. Clearly, the overall convergence performance of the proposed scheme is actually similar for both output and input fading cases. Besides, the effects of fading gain and parameter selection are parallel to that obtained in the previous subsection; thus, details are omitted to avoid simple repetition.

6.6 SUMMARY

This chapter addresses the learning tracking problem for a system with unknown fading channels, where we concentrate on the tracking performance improvement by the learning control concept. we first present an intuitive iteration-based estimation of the statistics of unknown fading gains by introducing a simple test mechanism. A unit signal is transmitted separately at the beginning of each iteration to obtain a sample of the random fading variable and then an empirical estimation can be established for the mean of fading variables. With this estimation, learning control algorithms are designed for both output and input fading scenarios, respectively, based on careful effect analysis of all involved random quantities. By using a decreasing sequence as the learning step size, the asymptotic convergence of the generated input sequence is strictly proved in both mean-square and almost-sure senses. Guidelines on the selection of learning step sizes are elaborated in both theoretical analysis and illustrative simulations. As an early study, we consider a basic model of the fading channel; however, the practical fading is generally modeled by a complex number with a gain and a phase. It is of practical significance to investigate the estimation of both gain and phase as well as the learning tracking issues.

CHAPTER 7

Learning-Tracking Framework under Unknown Nonrepetitive Channel Randomness

THIS chapter considers the learning-tracking problem for stochastic systems through unreliable communication channels. The channels suffer from both multiplicative and additive randomness subject to unknown probability distributions. The statistics of this randomness, such as mean and covariance, are nonrepetitive in the iteration domain. This nonrepetitive randomness introduces nonstationary contamination and drifts to the actual signals, yielding essential challenges in signal processing and learning control. Therefore, a practical framework constituted by an unbiased estimator of the mean inverse, a signal correction mechanism, and learning control schemes is proposed. The convergence and tracking performance are strictly established for both constant and decreasing step-lengths. If the statistics satisfy asymptotic repetitiveness in the iteration domain, a consistent estimator applies to the framework while retaining the framework's asymptotic properties.

7.1 INTRODUCTION

In a practical implementation of learning control, an increasing number of systems adopt the networked structure that the plant and controller are separated in different sites. This networked control structure introduces

DOI: 10.1201/9781032646404-7

additional communication randomness to original control issues; for example, data dropouts, communication delays, quantization errors, and channel noise are common in networked control systems. This channel randomness brings challenges in control using imprecise data.

In [6], the data dropout issue was addressed using a binary-valued random variable that was multiplied to signals to denote whether the data are dropped. The random variable is subject to a Bernoulli distribution. It can also be used for the nonuniform trial length problem [40], where the binary-valued variable indicates the available and untrodden parts. Fading is another common phenomenon caused by reflection and refraction during long-distance propagation [54]. A random variable subject to a continuous probability distribution can describe the fading effect. All the above can be classified as multiplicative channel randomness, while additive channel randomness, such as additive white Gaussian noise (AWGN), is common in practice [31]. While transmitting through channels with limited bandwidth, quantization is a promising approach to reduce the communication burden [33]. The quantization error can be regarded as a type of additive randomness to the received signal. This additive randomness can also be applied to describe stochastic noise.

Taking these scenarios as special cases, we address a general formulation of channel randomness. Specifically, we model the channel randomness by multiplicative and additive random variables subject to unknown distributions. The multiplicative randomness introduces signal-dependent drifts because it is multiplied by the transmitted signals. This dependence causes challenges in signal processing and convergence analysis. The additive randomness introduces fluctuations and drifts to the transmitted signals if it is not white. The literature has seldom considered drift led by colored randomness. Although the existing results have involved various types of system and channel randomness, they assume the randomness to be of identical statistics. That is, the randomness is stationary in time and iteration domains. However, in practice, the randomness statistics can vary along the iteration axis because of factors, such as environmental changes and implementation drifts. Here, the conventional asymptotic estimation mechanism for unknowns no longer applies. A natural problem arises whether an effective learning process can be realized if the statistics of the involved randomness are nonidentical in the iteration domain. Therefore, we introduce the concept of nonrepetitive randomness referring to the case that the statistics vary from iteration to iteration.

Some publications address nonrepetitive system uncertainty, but no result has been reported on nonrepetitive randomness. Two distinctions exist between nonrepetitive system uncertainty and randomness. First, the former considers the uncertainty varying in a small range, whereas the latter is random with variable statistics. Second, the former merely yields bounded convergence, whereas the latter should achieve precise tracking performance in the sense that the input sequence converges to the desired input for any given reference. Moreover, it has been investigated when the statistics of the channel randomness are invariant for all iterations, such as stationary fading communication. In Chapter 2, the fading mean is assumed available for direct correction of the received signals. If the fading mean is unknown, an iterative estimation mechanism was introduced in Chapter 6 using historical data, which is asymptotically unbiased as the iteration number increases. However, these techniques are inapplicable to nonrepetitive randomness.

Since the unknown statistics vary in the iteration domain, its estimation can merely be realized using finite data, which is called the nonasymptotic estimation method. It differs from various asymptotic estimation methods in system identification and parameter estimation [42], where data are incessantly generated to improve the estimation performance.

The contributions of this chapter are as follows.

(1) For the first time, we investigate the learning-tracking problem over unreliable channels subject to both multiplicative and additive randomness, where the randomness statistics are unknown and varying from iteration to iteration. This general iteration-dependent exchange environment covers the common channel conditions as special cases.

(2) Using simple pilot signals, we introduce practical nonasymptotic estimates for iteration-dependent mean inverse of the channel randomness, which differs from the widely applied asymptotic estimation method. If the iteration-dependent statistics converge to a constant, a consistent estimator is presented as an alternative.

(3) With these estimates, we propose a learning-tracking control framework to achieve the best tracking performance using biased and contaminated signals. Two learning control schemes with constant and decreasing step-lengths are presented separately.

(4) The effectiveness of the proposed schemes is strictly proved by analyzing channel effect and estimation evaluation via stochastic Lyapunov method.

In short, a systematic and substantial design and analysis framework is established. We emphasize that the novel estimates of statistics pave a promising and necessary way for the learning-tracking framework.

7.2 PROBLEM FORMULATION

7.2.1 Plant Model

Consider a linear time-varying stochastic system described as follows:

$$\begin{aligned} x_k(t+1) &= A_t x_k(t) + B_t u_k(t) + w_k(t+1), \\ y_k(t) &= C_t x_k(t) + v_k(t), \end{aligned} \tag{7.1}$$

where k denotes the iteration number, $k = 1, 2, \ldots$, and t denotes the time instant in an iteration, $t = 0, 1, \ldots, n$ with n being the iteration length. $x_k(t) \in \mathbf{R}^o$, $u_k(t) \in \mathbf{R}^p$, and $y_k(t) \in \mathbf{R}^q$ are the system state, input, and output, respectively. A_t, B_t, and C_t are system matrices with suitable dimensions. $w_k(t)$ and $v_k(t)$ are disturbances and noise, respectively.

Assumption 7.1 *The input/output coupling matrix* $M_t \triangleq C_{t+1}B_t$ *is of full column rank,* $\forall t$.

The desired reference is denoted by $y_d(t)$, $t = 0, 1, \ldots, n$. Assumption 7.1 provides an existence condition of the desired input $u_d(t)$ for a reference $y_d(t)$. In particular, for any given reference $y_d(t)$, the desired input can be calculated recursively by $u_d(t) = [M_t^T M_t]^{-1} M_t^T [y_d(t+1) - C_{t+1}A_t x_d(t)]$ with an initial state $x_d(0)$. However, this solution is unavailable for applications because the system matrices are unknown. If the reference $y_d(t)$ realizable, i.e., the system can generate it precisely in the absence of any randomness and uncertainty, then the desired input satisfies that

$$\begin{aligned} x_d(t+1) &= A_t x_d(t) + B_t u_d(t), \\ y_d(t) &= C_t x_d(t), \end{aligned} \tag{7.2}$$

where the initial state $x_d(0)$ satisfies $y_d(0) = C_0 x_d(0)$. Otherwise, if the reference $y_d(t)$ is unattainable, the desired input $u_d(t)$ still provides the best achievable tracking performance in the least-square sense. Without loss of any generality, we consider the realizable reference $y_d(t)$ to make the derivations clear to follow while highlighting the main contributions.

The operation process runs in a repetitive mode. That is, the system completes a given tracking task within a finite time length n and repeats the process continuously. Therefore, it is a primary requirement that the operation can return to the desired initial state. However, this requirement is challenging to achieve in practical applications. We impose the following condition on the initial state.

Assumption 7.2 *The initial state* $x_k(0)$ *is a random variable such that* $\mathbb{E}[x_k(0)] = x_d(0)$ *and* $\sup_k \mathbb{E}[\|x_k(0) - x_d(0)\|^2] < \infty$*, where* $x_d(0)$ *satisfies* $y_d(0) = C_0 x_d(0)$.

We denote $\pi_k \triangleq \mathbb{E}[\|x_k(0) - x_d(0)\|^2]$ and $\pi = \sup_k \pi_k$. Assumption 7.2 relaxes the identical initialization condition, i.e., $x_k(0) = x_d(0)$, which is widely accepted in the literature [72]. By removing the probability assumption, we can use the assumption that the initialization error is bounded, i.e., $\|x_k(0) - x_d(0)\| < \kappa$ for a certain constant $\kappa > 0$. Moreover, if we introduce a learning or rectifying mechanism for the initial state [61], we can obtain an asymptotically identical initialization property that $x_k(0) - x_d(0) \to 0$ as the iteration number increases to infinity. The proposed scheme is still effective under these conditions.

For system disturbances and measurement noise, we employ the following general conditions.

Assumption 7.3 *The random disturbance* $w_k(t)$ *and noise* $v_k(t)$ *are assumed to be independent for different iterations. Besides,* $\mathbb{E}[w_k(t)] = 0$, $\mathbb{E}[v_k(t)] = 0$, $\sup_k \mathbb{E}[\|w_k(t)\|^2] < \infty$, *and* $\sup_k \mathbb{E}[\|v_k(t)\|^2] < \infty$, $\forall k, t$.

Because the system runs batch by batch, iteration-wise independence is reasonable for applications. Therefore, the standard Gaussian noise satisfies Assumption 7.3. For further analysis, we denote $\phi_k \triangleq \mathbb{E}[\|w_k(t)\|^2]$, $\phi = \sup_k \phi_k$, $\psi_k \triangleq \mathbb{E}[\|v_k(t)\|^2]$, and $\psi = \sup_k \psi_k$.

Remark 7.1 *If the system is unstable, the state can be driven to deviate from the desired value and grow very large even by a slight noise. Here, feedback control can be introduced first to stabilize the system, and the closed-loop system becomes the new nominal plant, i.e.,* (7.1), *for the following learning control design [69].*

7.2.2 Channel-Induced Randomness

Fig. 7.1 shows the control configuration of the learning-tracking process, where the plant's output is transmitted back to the controller through a communication channel. During the transmission, both multiplicative and additive randomness are involved [52]. Therefore, the received signal is contaminated and biased. To simplify the derivations, we consider the case that only

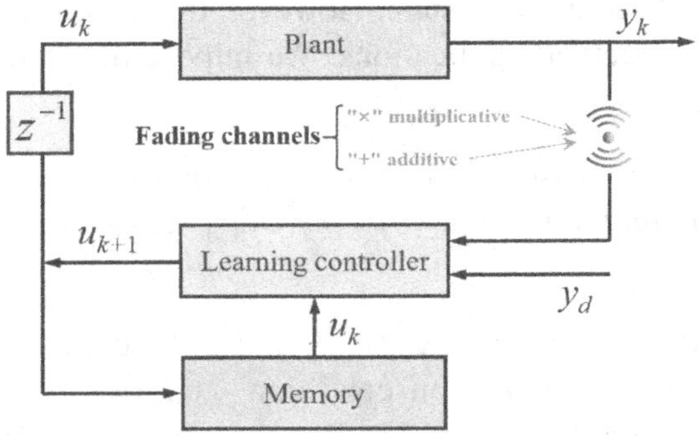

Figure 7.1 Configuration of learning control with channel randomness.

the output suffers channel-induced randomness, whereas the input signal can be fed to the plant precisely. The extension to the general formulation where both output and input are transmitted through unreliable channels can be conducted similarly but with more derivations.

We now depict two types of channel randomness, namely, multiplicative and additive types. Take $m_k(t) \in \mathbf{R}^m$ as the signal that is transmitted at time instant t of the kth iteration. The received signal corresponding to $m_k(t)$ is denoted by $m_k^\circ(t)$. Then, channel randomness is described using

$$m_k^\circ(t) = r_k(t)m_k(t) + s_k(t), \tag{7.3}$$

where $r_k(t)$ and $s_k(t)$ denote the multiplicative and additive randomness, respectively. In the following, we separately explain the details of both randomness.

First, we consider the multiplicative randomness $r_k(t)$, which is usually involved because of unreliable communication environments, such as data dropout and signal random scaling. The existing literature has extensively discussed the issue of data dropout [52], where a binary random variable is introduced to denote the event whether the corresponding data packet is dropped. Fading is a different typical scaling phenomenon during transmission but less addressed in the literature. It is modeled by a random variable, which is multiplied by the signals. In this chapter, we use a general formulation for multiplicative randomness $r_k(t)$.

Assume that $r_k(t)$ is independent for k and t. It is reasonable because the randomness is generated according to the data packet individually. Extensions to the time-dependent case would require some modifications of estimation and design procedures in the subsequence, which are considered future work. Besides, we assume $r_k(t)$ is identically distributed for different time instants within the same iteration, which is necessary to provide an estimate of its statistics for an iteration. In other words, little information can be obtained for multiplicative randomness if it is of nonidentical distribution within an iteration. We note that the statistics of this randomness can vary in the iteration domain, denoting the nonrepetitive characteristic. While the transmitted signal $m_k(t)$ is of high dimension, we consider $r_k(t)$ to be a random variable, i.e., $r_k(t) \in \mathbf{R}$, for derivation simplicity. This form indicates that all dimensions of the vector $m_k(t)$ suffer the same scaling effect because they are usually packed and transmitted together. The extension to a high-dimensional case is straightforward.

Summarizing the above considerations, we model the multiplicative randomness $r_k(t)$ using an iteration-dependent distribution $f_k(s)$, where the function $f_k(s)$ is continuous and satisfies $\mathbb{P}[r_k(t) \geq 0] = 1$. Besides, the following statistics hold

$$r_k = \mathbb{E}[r_k(t)], \quad \tau_k = \mathbb{E}[(r_k(t) - r_k)^2], \tag{7.4}$$

where both r_k and τ_k are unknown and varying regarding k. Thus, such information cannot be used in the algorithm design. We assume $\tau_k \leq \tau$ for a certain constant $\tau > 0$. r_k are assumed upper- and lower-bounded, $0 < a \leq r_k \leq b$ to simplify the derivations, where a and b are unknown.

Next, we consider the additive randomness $s_k(t)$, characterizing the effect of random processes occurring in nature [31]. To simplify the subsequent discussions, we assume the additive randomness $s_k(t)$ is independent along the iteration axis and has the same dimensions as the transmitted signal. Besides, it is independently and identically distributed in the time domain for each dimension using the following statistics:

$$s_k = \mathbb{E}[s_k^{(i)}(t)], \quad \delta_k = \mathbb{E}[(s_k^{(i)}(t) - s_k)^2], \quad \forall t, \tag{7.5}$$

where both s_k and δ_k are unknown and could vary from iteration to iteration. Furthermore, $\delta_k \leq \delta$ for a certain constant $\delta > 0$. The statistics of additive randomness are nonrepetitive.

Remark 7.2 *In the existing literature, it is widely assumed that $s_k = 0$, indicating that the additive noise is of zero mean and can be treated similarly to system disturbances and noise in stochastic control. In this chapter, we allow the mean s_k to be nonzero and iteration-varying. This is significantly extended from the common setting. Note that the iteration-varying channel characteristic introduces new challenges to control design and analysis because the* *iteration-wise estimate/learning methods cannot be applied. Therefore, we introduce a nonasymptotic estimator for these unknowns. The novel estimate and correction mechanisms are necessary to establish an effective learning control framework.*

7.2.3 Control Objective

After the system formulation and communication setting, we now present our control objective. Because of various randomness and uncertainties, it is challenging to require the output $y_k(t)$ to track the desired trajectory $y_d(t)$ without any error. By noticing the system (7.1) and reference model (7.2), it is reasonable to transform the output tracking into the convergence of $u_k(t)$ to the desired input $u_d(t)$ in the iteration domain. Of note, ILC follows a batch-wise learning mode that the input is generated using information of the previous iterations, which differs from the conventional feedback control structure. In other words, in each iteration, ILC operates as an open-loop control that the input has been generated without knowing any real-time measurements.

Control objective: We propose a practical learning-tracking framework, including an iterative-estimator to obtain the necessary knowledge of channel randomness, such that the convergence of the input sequence $\{u_k(t)\}$ to the desired input $u_d(t)$ is established as the iteration number increases. The following two scenarios of convergence will be elaborated on:

1) we prove that $u_k(t) \to u_d(t)$ (asymptotic convergence) and specify the corresponding conditions;

2) otherwise, we prove that $\mathbb{E}[\|u_k(t) - u_d(t)\|^2]$ converges to a bounded zone around zero (bounded convergence) and specify its upper bound.

The proposed learning-tracking framework consists of a nonasymptotic unbiased estimator for the mean inverse of various randomness and a learning control scheme with a constant/decreasing gain. Theoretical analysis reveals that the unbiased estimate using limit information is critical to ensure the tracking performance under the general channel condition subject to iteration-varying statistics. Furthermore, we present an explicit formulation for evaluating the tracking performance under various randomness and uncertainty, where the learning ability will be defined and elaborated. This evaluation can help us understand the essential improvement that we can conduct using learning control schemes and the associated factors that we should suitably tune in practical applications. Note that the conventional stability issue is unspecified in our control objective because the system operates over a finite time interval. Moreover, the learning control scheme presented later is an open-loop control in the time domain but follows the feedback principle in the iteration domain. Thus, it should achieve favorable tracking performance for stochastic systems.

7.3 LEARNING CONTROL SCHEME FOR ZERO-MEAN ADDITIVE RANDOMNESS CASE

In Section 7.2.2, the statistics of the additive randomness are allowed to be iteration-varying. To make our main idea easy to follow, we first consider the case $s_k \equiv 0$ in this section. That is, the additive randomness is of zero mean. The extension to the nonzero-mean case will be discussed in Section 7.4. In Section 7.3.1, we first provide an estimate of the iteration-varying mean of multiplicative randomness and specify its nonasymptotic properties. With this estimate, the received signals can be corrected to provide the necessary information for the learning control scheme. Section 7.3.2 analyzes the effect of all randomness and uncertainties. To facilitate the convergence analysis, Section 7.3.3 provides a transformation to the lifting form, where the signals are preliminarily analyzed. Section 7.3.4 details the main results of the convergence property and tracking performance for both constant and decreasing step-lengths.

7.3.1 Estimation of Multiplicative Randomness

From (7.4), the mathematical expectation of this randomness varies from iteration to iteration; thus, it is challenging to derive an asymptotic estimator for the multiplicative randomness statistics. In this chapter, we can merely provide a nonasymptotic estimate for each iteration separately.

Considering the system setup in Fig. 7.1, we can obtain a direct estimate of the unknown mean r_k defined in (7.4) by sending an individual unit signal along with the actual output and computing the average value of the received signals. That is, we send the signal $\theta_k(t) \equiv 1$ for each time instant individually. The unit signal evaluates random fading. Accordingly, the received signal is

$$\theta_k^\circ(t) = r_k'(t)\theta_k(t) + s_k'(t) = r_k'(t) + s_k'(t), \tag{7.6}$$

where $r_k'(t)$ and $s_k'(t)$ denote the multiplicative and additive randomness imposed on the testing signals, which are independent of $r_k(t)$ and $s_k(t)$ imposed on the output signals. However, $r_k'(t)$ and $s_k'(t)$ are distributed identically to $r_k(t)$ and $s_k(t)$, respectively, due to the same physical environments.

The estimate for r_k is given by

$$\widehat{r}_k = \frac{1}{n}\sum_{t=1}^{n}\theta_k^{\circ}(t), \tag{7.7}$$

where n is the iteration length. Because the operation process for an iteration is finite, the above estimate is nonasymptotic. Therefore,

$$\mathbb{E}[\widehat{r}_k] = \mathbb{E}\left[\frac{1}{n}\sum_{t=1}^{n}\theta_k^{\circ}(t)\right] = \frac{1}{n}\sum_{t=1}^{n}\mathbb{E}[r'_k(t)+s'_k(t)] = r_k.$$

In other words, although the estimate cannot converge asymptotically as n is finite, it is unbiased.

In applications, because of multiplicative randomness, we must multiply the inverse of r_k to the received signal to correct it to be an unbiased random variable of the original signal (Section 7.3.2). Although (7.7) is unbiased for estimating the mean of multiplicative randomness, its inverse $\widehat{r_k^{-1}}$ is a biased estimate of r_k^{-1}. In other words, we cannot use $\widehat{r_k^{-1}}$ to correct the received signals. Therefore, we must introduce an unbiased estimator, defined by $\widehat{\gamma}_k$, for the mean inverse r_k^{-1} using the available data $\theta_k^{\circ}(t)$.

Here, we adopt the *Mean Inverse Estimator* (MIE) is given in [46]. The specific procedure is summarized as follows. First, $\theta_k^{\circ}(t)$ has the same mean as the randomness $r_k(t)$. Without loss of generality, we assume that $\theta_k^{\circ}(t)$ are positive random variables. Otherwise, we can enlarge the value of $\theta_k(t)$ to ensure this requirement. We select a small positive constant ε, such that $0 \le \varepsilon \le r_k^{-1}$, which is feasible because we can understand r_k by the estimate $\widehat{r}_k$ in (7.7). Define two sample moments: $M_{1,h} = \frac{1}{h}\sum_{t=1}^{h}\theta_k^{\circ}(t)$ and $M_{2,h} = \frac{1}{h}\sum_{t=1}^{h}(\theta_k^{\circ}(t))^2$. If $M_{1,h} > 0$, define

$$P_h = 1 - \sqrt{\frac{1}{h}\sum_{t=1}^{h}(1-\omega_h\theta_k^{\circ}(t))}$$
$$\text{with} \quad \omega_h = \min\left(\frac{1}{hM_{1,h}}, \frac{M_{1,h}}{M_{2,h}}, \varepsilon\right).$$

Otherwise, take $P_h = 1/h$ and $\omega_h = \varepsilon/h$. Then, the following MIE is used

$$\widehat{\gamma}_k = \frac{\omega_h}{q_N}\prod_{t=1}^{N}(1-\omega_h\theta_k^{\circ}(t)), \tag{7.8}$$

where N denotes a non-negative integer-valued random variable and $q_i = P_h(1-P_h)^i$ denotes the probability $\mathbb{P}(N=i)$. $\widehat{\gamma}_k$ is an unbiased estimator for r_k^{-1} [46], of which the variance is bounded. That is, χ exists, such that $\mathbb{E}(\widehat{\gamma}_k - r_k^{-1})^2 \le \chi < \infty$.

Remark 7.3 *For specific distributions of the channel randomness, one can provide alternative unbiased estimates for the reciprocal of the mean [43,65]. However, we do not want to establish a novel estimate; instead, our purpose is to reveal the effective approach to address nonrepetitive channel randomness and establish a general framework for learning control. It is sufficient to guarantee the asymptotic convergence of the learning schemes proposed later if we use an unbiased estimate of the reciprocal of the mean of the multiplicative randomness. This fact is demonstrated in Section 7.3.4, where the convergence and performance analyses depend on the unbiasedness and variance-boundedness of the estimate.*

7.3.2 Channel Effect Analysis

From the control configuration in Fig. 7.1, the output is transmitted through the channel. The multiplicative randomness will introduce deviation to the received output. We clarify this effect in this subsection.

The actual and received outputs are denoted by $y_k(t)$ and $y_k^\circ(t)$, respectively. From the channel model (7.3), we have

$$y_k^\circ(t) = r_k(t)y_k(t) + s_k(t), \tag{7.9}$$

where $s_k(t)$ has dimension q, similar to the dimension of $y_k(t)$.

The received output has deviated from its original value because $\mathbb{E}[y_k^\circ(t)] = r_k\mathbb{E}[y_k(t)]$ with $r_k \neq 1$. Thus, this information cannot drive an effective learning process to generate an input sequence converging to the desired input. Therefore, a correction should be made to the received output before updating the control. Note that the estimate of r_k^{-1} applies to the following correction:

$$\begin{aligned}\widehat{y}_k(t) &= \widehat{\gamma}_k y_k^\circ(t)\\ &= y_k(t) + \left(\frac{r_k(t)}{r_k} - 1\right) y_k(t)\\ &\quad + \left(\widehat{\gamma}_k - r_k^{-1}\right) r_k(t)y_k(t) + \widehat{\gamma}_k s_k(t).\end{aligned} \tag{7.10}$$

From this equation, the estimation-based correction approach introduces three additional terms. They are an output-dependent error $(\frac{r_k(t)}{r_k} - 1)y_k(t)$

caused by multiplicative randomness, another output-dependent error $(\widehat{\gamma}_k - r_k^{-1})r_k(t)y_k(t)$ caused by imprecise estimation, and an output-independent error $\widehat{\gamma}_k s_k(t)$ caused by additive randomness. These terms characterize the channel effects to the learning control scheme.

1) All three additional terms are of zero mean by the independence existing among the output $y_k(t)$, multiplicative randomness $r_k(t)$, estimate $\widehat{\gamma}_k$, and additive randomness $s_k(t)$. This property guarantees that the corrected output $\widehat{y}_k(t)$ functions as an unbiased estimate of the actual output $y_k(t)$. Thus, this signal is sufficient to drive the learning process.

2) Because the statistics of channel randomness is nonrepetitive, the estimation error will no longer converge to zero by a nonasymptotic estimation approach. Meanwhile, all other terms will not vanish either. Besides, the output itself contains random disturbances and noise. All these perturbations will continuously destroy the learning process unless a certain mechanism is imposed.

3) The multiplicative randomness-involved terms are output-dependent. Consequently, even though channel randomness and its estimate are with finite variance, the variances for the second and third terms on the right-hand side (RHS) of (7.10) are not naturally bounded. This point requires more efforts in convergence analysis.

In short, the correction paves a way to establish the learning control scheme. However, the essential characteristics should be carefully considered to obtain satisfactory tracking performance. The details will be given in Section 7.3.4.

7.3.3 Lifting Transformation

To simplify notations, we present a lifting transformation of the original system in this subsection. Particularly, we stack all inputs and outputs of each iteration into large vectors: $\boldsymbol{u}_k = [u_k^T(0), u_k^T(1), \ldots, u_k^T(n-1)]^T \in \mathbf{R}^{np}$, $\boldsymbol{y}_k = [y_k^T(1), y_k^T(2), \ldots, y_k^T(n)]^T \in \mathbf{R}^{nq}$. We define the corresponding vectors $\boldsymbol{w}_k$, $\boldsymbol{v}_k$, and $\boldsymbol{s}_k$ similarly to $\boldsymbol{y}_k$, respectively.

From the system model (7.1), we have

$$\begin{aligned} x_k(t+1) &= A_t A_{t-1} x_k(t-1) + A_t B_{t-1} u_k(t-1) + A_t w_k(t) \\ &\quad + B_t u_k(t) + w_k(t+1) \\ &= A_0^t x_k(0) + \sum_{i=0}^{t} A_{i+1}^t B_i u_k(i) + \sum_{i=1}^{t+1} A_i^t w_k(i), \end{aligned}$$

where $A_i^j \triangleq A_j A_{j-1} \cdots A_i$ for $j \geq i$ and $A_{i+1}^i = I$. Then, we have the following relationship between the output and input:

$$\boldsymbol{y}_k = \mathbf{H}\boldsymbol{u}_k + \mathbf{N}x_k(0) + \mathbf{M}\boldsymbol{w}_k + \boldsymbol{v}_k, \tag{7.11}$$

where

$$\mathbf{H} = \begin{bmatrix} C_1 B_0 & 0 & \cdots & 0 \\ C_2 A_1 B_0 & C_2 B_1 & \cdots & 0 \\ \vdots & \vdots & \ddots & \vdots \\ C_n A_1^{n-1} B_0 & C_n A_2^{n-1} B_1 & \cdots & C_n B_{n-1} \end{bmatrix}, \tag{7.12}$$

$$\mathbf{N} = \left[(C_1 A_0)^T \quad (C_2 A_1 A_0)^T \quad \cdots \quad (C_n A_0^{n-1})^T \right]^T, \tag{7.13}$$

$$\mathbf{M} = \begin{bmatrix} C_1 & 0 & \cdots & 0 \\ C_2 A_1 & C_2 & \cdots & 0 \\ \vdots & \vdots & \ddots & \vdots \\ C_n A_1^{n-1} & C_n A_2^{n-1} & \cdots & C_n \end{bmatrix}. \tag{7.14}$$

For the desired trajectory, we have

$$\boldsymbol{y}_d = \mathbf{H}\boldsymbol{u}_d + \mathbf{N}x_d(0), \tag{7.15}$$

where $\boldsymbol{u}_d = [u_d^T(0), u_d^T(1), \ldots, u_d^T(n-1)]^T$ and $\boldsymbol{y}_d = [y_d^T(1), y_d^T(2), \ldots, y_d^T(n)]^T$.

Denote the actual tracking error by $e_k(t) \triangleq y_k(t) - y_d(t)$ and its lifting vector by $\boldsymbol{e}_k$. Then, we have

$$\boldsymbol{e}_k = \boldsymbol{y}_k - \boldsymbol{y}_d = \mathbf{H}\widetilde{\boldsymbol{u}}_k + \mathbf{N}\widetilde{x}_k(0) + \mathbf{M}\boldsymbol{w}_k + \boldsymbol{v}_k, \tag{7.16}$$

where $\widetilde{\boldsymbol{u}}_k \triangleq \boldsymbol{u}_k - \boldsymbol{u}_d$ and $\widetilde{x}_k(0) = x_k(0) - x_d(0)$.

However, the actual tracking error $e_k(t)$ is unavailable to the learning controller. We define an auxiliary tracking error by $\varepsilon_k(t) \triangleq \widehat{y}_k(t) - y_d(t)$. Its lifting form $\boldsymbol{\varepsilon}_k$ is expressed by:

$$\boldsymbol{\varepsilon}_k = \widehat{\boldsymbol{y}}_k - \boldsymbol{y}_d = \mathbf{H}\widetilde{\boldsymbol{u}}_k + \Delta_k, \tag{7.17}$$

where $\Delta_k = \mathbf{N}\widetilde{x}_k(0) + \mathbf{M}\boldsymbol{w}_k + \boldsymbol{v}_k + \left(r_k^{-1}\boldsymbol{\Phi}_k - I_{nq}\right)\boldsymbol{y}_k + (\widehat{\gamma}_k - r_k^{-1})\boldsymbol{\Phi}_k\boldsymbol{y}_k + \widehat{\gamma}_k\boldsymbol{s}_k$ with $\boldsymbol{\Phi}_k = \mathrm{diag}\{r_k(1), r_k(2), \ldots, r_k(n)\} \otimes I_q$. Clearly, Δ_k represents all the randomness and uncertainties that we should consider while designing and analyzing the learning control scheme. Particularly, the term Δ_k comprises the initial state error, process disturbance, measurement noise, the deviation caused by channel multiplicative randomness, imprecise estimation error, and channel additive randomness. The influence of randomness will be detailed in the following.

7.3.4 Algorithm Design and Analysis

In this section, we present two learning control schemes with constant and decreasing step-lengths separately. We begin with a constant step-length case.

The learning control scheme is as follows:

$$u_{k+1}(t) = u_k(t) + \rho G_t \varepsilon_k(t+1), \tag{7.18}$$

where ρ is the step-length, G_t is a learning gain matrix to regulate the control direction for multidimensional systems, and $\varepsilon_k(t)$ is the auxiliary tracking error.

The above learning control scheme leads to the lifting form:

$$\boldsymbol{u}_{k+1} = \boldsymbol{u}_k(t) + \rho \mathbf{G} \boldsymbol{\varepsilon}_k, \tag{7.19}$$

where $\mathbf{G} = \text{diag}\{G_0, G_1, \dots, G_{n-1}\}$ is a block diagonal matrix. Subtracting $\boldsymbol{u}_d$ from both sides of (7.19) and then substituting (7.17) into the derived equation yields

$$\widetilde{\boldsymbol{u}}_{k+1} = (I + \rho \mathbf{GH}) \widetilde{\boldsymbol{u}}_k + \rho \mathbf{G} \Delta_k. \tag{7.20}$$

To establish the convergence property of the recursion (7.20), we first present a characterization of the term Δ_k.

Lemma 7.1 *For the term Δ_k, we have*

$$\begin{aligned}\mathbb{E}\left[\|\Delta_k\|^2\right] \leq\, & \lambda_{\max}(\boldsymbol{N}^T\boldsymbol{N})\pi_k + \lambda_{\max}(\boldsymbol{M}^T\boldsymbol{M})n\phi_k + n\psi_k \\ & + nq(\chi + r_k^{-2})\delta_k + [r_k^{-2}\tau_k + \chi(\tau_k + r_k^2)]\mathbb{E}[\|\boldsymbol{y}_k\|^2],\end{aligned} \tag{7.21}$$

where $\lambda_{\max}(\cdot)$ denotes the maximum eigenvalue.

Proof: Recalling the formulation of Δ_k, we have

$$\begin{aligned}\mathbb{E}\left[\|\Delta_k\|^2\right] =\, & \mathbb{E}\left[\|\mathbf{N}\widetilde{x}_k(0)\|^2\right] + \mathbb{E}\left[\|\mathbf{M}\boldsymbol{w}_k\|^2\right] + \mathbb{E}\left[\|\boldsymbol{v}_k\|^2\right] \\ & + \mathbb{E}\left[\|\left(r_k^{-1}\boldsymbol{\Phi}_k - I_{nq}\right)\boldsymbol{y}_k\|^2\right] \\ & + \mathbb{E}\left[\|(\widehat{\gamma}_k - r_k^{-1})\boldsymbol{\Phi}_k\boldsymbol{y}_k\|^2\right] + \mathbb{E}\left[\|\widehat{\gamma}_k\boldsymbol{s}_k\|^2\right] \\ & + \text{crossing terms},\end{aligned} \tag{7.22}$$

where "crossing terms" indicate the expectation of the crossing products of the six terms in the expansion of Δ_k.

By the independence between the terms of initial state error $\widetilde{x}_k(0)$, system disturbance $\boldsymbol{w}_k$, measurement noise $\boldsymbol{v}_k$, multiplicative randomness $r_k(t)$, estimation $\widehat{\gamma}_k$, and additive randomness $s_k(t)$, and the zero-mean property of all involved terms, we can verify that all crossing terms are equal to zero.

For the square terms, we have

$$\mathbb{E}\left[\|\mathbf{N}\widetilde{x}_k(0)\|^2\right] \leq \lambda_{\max}(\mathbf{N}^T\mathbf{N})\pi_k, \tag{7.23}$$

$$\mathbb{E}\left[\|\mathbf{M}\boldsymbol{w}_k\|^2\right] \leq \lambda_{\max}(\mathbf{M}^T\mathbf{M})n\phi_k, \tag{7.24}$$

$$\mathbb{E}\left[\|\boldsymbol{v}_k\|^2\right] \leq n\psi_k, \tag{7.25}$$

$$\mathbb{E}\left[\|\left(r_k^{-1}\boldsymbol{\Phi}_k - I_{nq}\right)\boldsymbol{y}_k\|^2\right] \leq r_k^{-2}\tau_k\mathbb{E}[\|\boldsymbol{y}_k\|^2], \tag{7.26}$$

$$\mathbb{E}\left[\|(\widehat{\gamma}_k - r_k^{-1})\boldsymbol{\Phi}_k\boldsymbol{y}_k\|^2\right] \leq \chi(\tau_k + r_k^2)\mathbb{E}[\|\boldsymbol{y}_k\|^2], \tag{7.27}$$

$$\mathbb{E}\left[\|\widehat{\gamma}_k\boldsymbol{s}_k\|^2\right] \leq nq(\chi + r_k^{-2})\delta_k. \tag{7.28}$$

Substituting these estimates into (7.22) completes the proof. □

Lemma 7.1 describes the influence of various randomness on tracking performance. The upper bound can be exceptionally large if the system is unstable. As mentioned in Remark 7.1, feedback control can be introduced to first stabilize the dynamics and reduce the upper bounds. Especially, note that output-dependent bounds are involved with (7.21), which, therefore, are input-dependent. These terms introduce additional challenges in convergence analysis. Furthermore, we can compress the estimate (7.21) as follows:

$$\mathbb{E}\left[\|\Delta_k\|^2\right] \leq \eta_1 + \eta_2\mathbb{E}[\|\boldsymbol{y}_k\|^2], \tag{7.29}$$

where $\eta_1 \triangleq \lambda_{\max}(\mathbf{N}^T\mathbf{N})\pi + \lambda_{\max}(\mathbf{M}^T\mathbf{M})n\phi + n\psi + nq(\chi + a^{-2})\delta$ and $\eta_2 = a^{-2}\tau + \chi(\tau + b^2)$. From this estimate, we can obtain the boundedness of the sequence $\{\widetilde{\boldsymbol{u}}_k\}$ generated by (7.20) for sufficiently small ρ.

Lemma 7.2 *For sufficiently small step-length $\rho > 0$, we have $\sup_k \mathbb{E}[\|\widetilde{\boldsymbol{u}}_k\|^2] < \infty$, if the learning gain matrix is designed such that* **GH** *is Hurwitz.*

Proof: We prove this lemma using [4, Chapter 9, Theorem 6]. This theorem establishes the boundedness of z_n generated by the following recursion

$$z_{k+1} = z_k + \rho[h(z_k) + \xi_{k+1}] \tag{7.30}$$

under the following conditions:

(C1) The map h is Lipschitz: $\|h(x) - h(y)\| \leq l_0\|x - y\|$ for some $0 < l_0 < \infty$.

(C2) The functions $h_c(z) \triangleq h(cz)/c$, $c \geq 1$, satisfy $h_c(z) \to h_\infty(z)$ as $c \to \infty$, uniformly. Furthermore, the o.d.e. $\dot{z}(t) = h_\infty(z(t))$ has the origin as its unique globally asymptotically stable equilibrium.

(C3) ξ_k is a martingale difference sequence with respect to an increasing σ-algebra $\mathcal{F}_k \triangleq \sigma\{z_m, \xi_m, m \le k\}$, i.e., $\mathbb{E}[\xi_{k+1}|\mathcal{F}_k] = 0$. Furthermore, $\{\xi_k\}$ is square-integrable with $\mathbb{E}[\|\xi_{k+1}\|^2|\mathcal{F}_k] \le K(1+\|z_k\|^2)$ for some $K > 0$.

First, comparing (7.30) with (7.20), we notice that z_k and ξ_{k+1} correspond to $\widetilde{\boldsymbol{u}}_k$ and $\mathbf{G}\Delta_k$, respectively, and the regression function is $h(z) = \rho\mathbf{GH}z$. Because $\mathbf{G}$ is such that $\mathbf{GH}$ is Hurwitz, (C1) and (C2) hold naturally.

Next, we check (C3). Define an increasing σ-algebra $\mathcal{G}_k = \sigma\{x_i(0), u_1(t), w_i(t), v_i(t), r_i(t), r_i'(t), s_i(t), s_i'(t), 1 \le i \le k, 0 \le t \le n\}$. By the input recursion (7.20) and the definition of Δ_k below (7.17), the σ-algebra $\mathcal{G}_k$ is well defined [14] and we have $\mathbb{E}[\Delta_k|\mathcal{G}_{k-1}] = 0$. From (7.18), we obtain that $\boldsymbol{u}_{k+1} \in \mathcal{G}_k$. Similar to (7.29), we obtain

$$\mathbb{E}\left[\|\Delta_k\|^2 \mid \mathcal{G}_{k-1}\right] \le \eta_1 + \eta_2\mathbb{E}[\|\boldsymbol{y}_k\|^2 \mid \mathcal{G}_{k-1}]. \tag{7.31}$$

By (7.16), we have

$$\begin{aligned}
&\mathbb{E}[\|\boldsymbol{y}_k\|^2 \mid \mathcal{G}_{k-1}] \\
&= \mathbb{E}[\|\mathbf{H}\widetilde{\boldsymbol{u}}_k + \boldsymbol{y}_d + \mathbf{N}\widetilde{x}_k(0) + \mathbf{M}\boldsymbol{w}_k + \boldsymbol{v}_k\|^2|\mathcal{G}_{k-1}] \\
&= \|\boldsymbol{y}_d + \mathbf{H}\widetilde{\boldsymbol{u}}_k\|^2 + \mathbb{E}[\|\mathbf{N}\widetilde{x}_k(0) + \mathbf{M}\boldsymbol{w}_k + \boldsymbol{v}_k\|^2] \\
&\le 2\|\boldsymbol{y}_d\|^2 + 2\|\mathbf{H}\widetilde{\boldsymbol{u}}_k\|^2 + \eta_3,
\end{aligned} \tag{7.32}$$

where the second equality holds because of the fact $\boldsymbol{u}_k \in \mathcal{G}_{k-1}$ and the independence between $\mathbf{N}\widetilde{x}_k(0) + \mathbf{M}\boldsymbol{w}_k + \boldsymbol{v}_k$ and $\mathcal{G}_{k-1}$. Besides, $\eta_3 \triangleq \lambda_{\max}(\mathbf{N}^T\mathbf{N})\pi + \lambda_{\max}(\mathbf{M}^T\mathbf{M})n\phi + n\psi$. Substituting this inequality into (7.31) verifies the validity of (C3). The proof is thus completed. □

Lemma 7.2 proves the boundedness of the sequence $\{\widetilde{\boldsymbol{u}}_k\}$ generated by (7.20), which, equivalently, guarantees the boundedness of $\{\boldsymbol{u}_k\}$. Therefore, the proposed scheme (7.18) will not diverge if the step-length ρ is sufficiently small. This boundedness will help analyze the convergence property in the presence of output-dependent random derivations. Nevertheless, the feasible range of ρ is unspecified in Lemma 7.2, which will be clarified in the following theorem.

Theorem 7.1 *Consider system* (7.1) *under Assumptions 7.1–7.3. The non-asymptotic statistics estimation* (7.8) *of channel randomness and the learning control scheme* (7.18) *with a constant step-length are applied. If the learning gain matrix G_t is designed such that $G_tC_{t+1}B_t$ is Hurwitz and the step-length ρ satisfies $0 < \rho < \rho^\star$, where $\rho^\star$ is given by* (7.42) *in the proof, then the input* *error $\widetilde{\boldsymbol{u}}_k$ converges into a small zone around zero in the mean-square sense, i.e.,*

$$\limsup_{k\to\infty} \mathbb{E}[\|\widetilde{\boldsymbol{u}}_k\|^2] \leq \rho \frac{d_2\left(\eta_1+\eta_2(2\|\boldsymbol{y}_d\|^2+\eta_3)\right)}{1-\rho\eta_4\lambda_{\max}(\boldsymbol{\Omega})}\frac{\lambda_{\max}(\boldsymbol{\Omega})}{\lambda_{\min}(\boldsymbol{\Omega})}, \tag{7.33}$$

where $\boldsymbol{\Omega}$ is a positive-definite matrix solving a Lyapunov function related to the system and learning gain matrix, $d_2=\lambda_{\max}(\boldsymbol{G}^T\boldsymbol{\Omega}\boldsymbol{G})$, $\eta_3=\lambda_{\max}(\boldsymbol{N}^T\boldsymbol{N})\pi+\lambda_{\max}(\boldsymbol{M}^T\boldsymbol{M})n\phi+n\psi$, $\eta_4=d_1+2d_2\eta_2\frac{\lambda_{\max}(\boldsymbol{H}^T\boldsymbol{H})}{\lambda_{\min}(\boldsymbol{\Omega})}$ with d_1 defined by $(\boldsymbol{G}\boldsymbol{H})^T\boldsymbol{\Omega}(\boldsymbol{G}\boldsymbol{H})\leq d_1\boldsymbol{\Omega}$.

Proof: Recall the recursion of the input error (7.20). Note that the matrix $\mathbf{GH}$ is a block lower-triangular matrix, where its diagonal blocks are $G_tC_{t+1}B_t$. Because G_t is designed such that $G_tC_{t+1}B_t$ is Hurwitz, all eigenvalues of $G_tC_{t+1}B_t$ have negative real parts. Thus, all eigenvalues of the lifting matrix $\mathbf{GH}$ have negative real parts. According to the Lyapunov stability theory, for any negative-definite matrix $\mathbf{S}$, there exists a positive-definite matrix $\boldsymbol{\Omega}$ such that $(\mathbf{GH})^T\boldsymbol{\Omega}+\boldsymbol{\Omega}(\mathbf{GH})=\mathbf{S}$. Throughout this chapter, we let $\mathbf{S}=-I_{nq}$, and then, $\boldsymbol{\Omega}=\int_0^\infty \exp((\mathbf{GH})^Tt)\exp((\mathbf{GH})t)dt$.

Define the Lyapunov function

$$L_k=\widetilde{\boldsymbol{u}}_k^T\boldsymbol{\Omega}\widetilde{\boldsymbol{u}}_k. \tag{7.34}$$

Using (7.20) we obtain

$$\begin{aligned} L_{k+1} &= \widetilde{\boldsymbol{u}}_k^T(I+\rho\mathbf{GH})^T\boldsymbol{\Omega}(I+\rho\mathbf{GH})\widetilde{\boldsymbol{u}}_k+\rho^2\Delta_k^T\mathbf{G}^T\boldsymbol{\Omega}\mathbf{G}\Delta_k \\ &\quad +2\widetilde{\boldsymbol{u}}_k^T(I+\rho\mathbf{GH})^T\boldsymbol{\Omega}\mathbf{G}\Delta_k. \end{aligned} \tag{7.35}$$

Let $d_1>0$ be the constant such that $(\mathbf{GH})^T\boldsymbol{\Omega}(\mathbf{GH})\leq d_1\boldsymbol{\Omega}$. Then, we have

$$\begin{aligned} (I+\rho\mathbf{GH})^T\boldsymbol{\Omega}(I+\rho\mathbf{GH}) &= \boldsymbol{\Omega}-\rho I+\rho^2(\mathbf{GH})^T\boldsymbol{\Omega}(\mathbf{GH}) \\ &\leq (1-\rho\lambda_{\max}^{-1}(\boldsymbol{\Omega})+\rho^2 d_1)\boldsymbol{\Omega}. \end{aligned} \tag{7.36}$$

Recalling $\mathcal{G}_k$ in the proof of Lemma 7.2, we note that

$$\begin{aligned} \mathbb{E}[\Delta_k^T\mathbf{G}^T\boldsymbol{\Omega}\mathbf{G}\Delta_k|\mathcal{G}_{k-1}] &\leq \lambda_{\max}(\mathbf{G}^T\boldsymbol{\Omega}\mathbf{G})\mathbb{E}[\|\Delta_k\|^2|\mathcal{G}_{k-1}] \\ &\leq d_2(\eta_1+\eta_2\mathbb{E}[\|\boldsymbol{y}_k\|^2|\mathcal{G}_{k-1}]), \end{aligned} \tag{7.37}$$

where $d_2=\lambda_{\max}(\mathbf{G}^T\boldsymbol{\Omega}\mathbf{G})$.

Noting that $\boldsymbol{y}_k=\boldsymbol{y}_d+\mathbf{H}\widetilde{\boldsymbol{u}}_k+\mathbf{N}\widetilde{x}_k(0)+\mathbf{M}\boldsymbol{w}_k+\boldsymbol{v}_k$, the estimation (7.32) holds. Therefore,

$$\begin{aligned} \mathbb{E}[\Delta_k^T\mathbf{G}^T\boldsymbol{\Omega}\mathbf{G}\Delta_k|\mathcal{G}_{k-1}] &\leq d_2(\eta_1+\eta_2(2\|\boldsymbol{y}_d\|^2+\eta_3)) \\ &\quad +2d_2\eta_2\|\mathbf{H}\widetilde{\boldsymbol{u}}_k\|^2. \end{aligned} \tag{7.38}$$

Note that the initial state error $\widetilde{x}_k(0)$, noise terms $\boldsymbol{w}_k$ and $\boldsymbol{v}_k$, correction error $r_k^{-1}\boldsymbol{\Phi}_k - I$, estimation error $\widehat{\gamma}_k - r_k^{-1}$, and channel additive randomness $\boldsymbol{s}_k$ are all independent of $\mathcal{G}_{k-1}$ and are all of zero mean, yielding that $\mathbb{E}[\Delta_k|\mathcal{G}_{k-1}] = 0$.

Taking conditional expectation of both sides of (7.35) with respect to $\mathcal{G}_{k-1}$ and substituting the above estimates lead to

$$\mathbb{E}[L_{k+1} \mid \mathcal{G}_{k-1}] \leq \left(1 - \rho\lambda_{\max}^{-1}(\boldsymbol{\Omega}) + \rho^2\eta_4\right) L_k + \rho^2\eta_5, \tag{7.39}$$

where

$$\eta_4 \triangleq d_1 + 2d_2\eta_2\frac{\lambda_{\max}(\mathbf{H}^T\mathbf{H})}{\lambda_{\min}(\boldsymbol{\Omega})}, \tag{7.40}$$

$$\eta_5 \triangleq d_2(\eta_1 + \eta_2(2\|\boldsymbol{y}_d\|^2 + \eta_3)). \tag{7.41}$$

To ensure a contraction of the Lyapunov function, we let $0 < \rho\lambda_{\max}^{-1}(\boldsymbol{\Omega}) - \rho^2\eta_4 < 1$. This condition holds if $\lambda_{\max}^{-1}(\boldsymbol{\Omega}) - \rho\eta_4 > 0$ and $\rho\lambda_{\max}^{-1}(\boldsymbol{\Omega}) < 1$, leading to

$$\rho < \rho^\star \triangleq \min\left\{\frac{1}{\eta_4\lambda_{\max}(\boldsymbol{\Omega})}, \lambda_{\max}(\boldsymbol{\Omega})\right\}. \tag{7.42}$$

Taking mathematical expectation of both sides of (7.39) yields

$$\mathbb{E}[L_{k+1}] \leq \left(1 - \rho\lambda_{\max}^{-1}(\boldsymbol{\Omega}) + \rho^2\eta_4\right)\mathbb{E}[L_k] + \rho^2\eta_5, \tag{7.43}$$

which further leads to

$$\begin{aligned}\mathbb{E}[L_k] \leq & \left(1 - \rho\lambda_{\max}^{-1}(\boldsymbol{\Omega}) + \rho^2\eta_4\right)^k\mathbb{E}[L_0] \\ & + \frac{1 - \left(1 - \rho\lambda_{\max}^{-1}(\boldsymbol{\Omega}) + \rho^2\eta_4\right)^k}{\lambda_{\max}^{-1}(\boldsymbol{\Omega}) - \rho\eta_4}\rho\eta_5\end{aligned} \tag{7.44}$$

and

$$\begin{aligned}\limsup_{k\to\infty}\mathbb{E}[L_k] \leq & \frac{\rho\eta_5}{\lambda_{\max}^{-1}(\boldsymbol{\Omega}) - \rho\eta_4} \\ = & \frac{\rho d_2\left(\eta_1 + \eta_2(2\|\boldsymbol{y}_d\|^2 + \eta_3)\right)}{\lambda_{\max}^{-1}(\boldsymbol{\Omega}) - \rho\eta_4}.\end{aligned} \tag{7.45}$$

The mean-square of the input error is thus bounded and the proof is completed. □

Theorem 7.1 establishes the convergence property for the proposed learning control scheme with a constant step-length (7.18). From the performance evaluation (7.33), the plant information, randomness, and reference trajectory $y_d(t)$ determine the upper bound of the final input errors. This is revealed by calculating parameters η_i, $i = 1,2,3,4$, where the variances of randomness are all included. Meanwhile, we note that the upper bound depends linearly on the step-length ρ, that is, the smaller the step-length, the smaller the bound of the input errors. Besides, the design of G_t merely depends on the coupling matrix $C_{t+1}B_t$ rather than exact system information. If it is unavailable, an estimate of this matrix is still sufficient to ensure the validity of the condition due to the continuity of eigenvalues with respect to the matrix entries [30].

However, we must point out that the step-length is not the smaller the better in applications because the step-length meantime affects the convergence speed. Specifically, the convergence rate is determined by the contraction factor $1-\rho\lambda_{\max}^{-1}(\mathbf{\Omega})+\rho^2\eta_4$, which approaches to one as the step-length ρ decreases to zero. Therefore, a trade-off exists between learning performance and convergence speed. To understand this trade-off, we present the following evaluation on the tracking error $\boldsymbol{e}_k$.

Corollary 7.1 *Under the same conditions of Theorem 7.1, the tracking error is estimated by*

$$\begin{aligned}\mathbb{E}[\|\boldsymbol{e}_k\|^2] \le & \left(1-\rho\lambda_{\max}^{-1}(\mathbf{\Omega})+\rho^2\eta_4\right)^k d_3\mathbb{E}[L_0] \\ & + \frac{1-\left(1-\rho\lambda_{\max}^{-1}(\mathbf{\Omega})+\rho^2\eta_4\right)^k}{\lambda_{\max}^{-1}(\mathbf{\Omega})-\rho\eta_4}\rho d_3\eta_5+\eta_3,\end{aligned} \tag{7.46}$$

where $d_3 = \frac{\lambda_{\max}(\boldsymbol{H}^T\boldsymbol{H})}{\lambda_{\min}(\mathbf{\Omega})}$.

Proof: We rewrite the definition of $\boldsymbol{e}_k$ as follows:

$$\boldsymbol{e}_k = \mathbf{H}\widetilde{\boldsymbol{u}}_k + \mathbf{N}\widetilde{x}_k(0) + \mathbf{M}\boldsymbol{w}_k + \boldsymbol{v}_k. \tag{7.47}$$

Then, we have

$$\begin{aligned}\mathbb{E}[\|\boldsymbol{e}_k\|^2] &= \mathbb{E}\left[\mathbb{E}[\|\boldsymbol{e}_k\|^2|\mathcal{G}_{k-1}]\right] \\ &= \mathbb{E}[\|\mathbf{H}\widetilde{\boldsymbol{u}}_k\|^2] + \mathbb{E}[\|\mathbf{N}\widetilde{x}_k(0)+\mathbf{M}\boldsymbol{w}_k+\boldsymbol{v}_k\|^2] \\ &\le \frac{\lambda_{\max}(\mathbf{H}^T\mathbf{H})}{\lambda_{\min}(\mathbf{\Omega})}\mathbb{E}[L_k]+\eta_3.\end{aligned} \tag{7.48}$$

Substituting (7.44) into the RHS of (7.48) completes the proof. □

From Corollary 7.1, the input error determines the major tunable part of the tracking error, as the first item on the RHS of (7.46) converges to zero and the last term is no longer improvable. Thus, a smaller step-length ρ will lead to a better tracking performance but a slower convergence speed. It is still open how to quantitatively describe this issue and determine an optimal step-length according to some index.

Theorem 7.1 has successfully demonstrated the effectiveness of the proposed scheme (7.18) in the presence of various types of randomness. The step-length significantly influences the convergence speed and final tracking performance. If the tracking performance is preferred with the necessary sacrifice of convergence speed, one can consider replacing the constant step-length ρ with a decreasing step-length sequence $\{\rho_k\}$. The results are briefed as follows. Note that these results are parallel to the constant step-length case.

The learning control scheme is as follows:

$$u_{k+1}(t) = u_k(t) + \rho_k G_t \varepsilon_k(t+1), \tag{7.49}$$

where the step-length sequence $\{\rho_k\}$ satisfies $\rho_k > 0$ and $\rho_k \to 0$. Similar to the constant step-length case, the recursion of the input error can be formulated as

$$\widetilde{\boldsymbol{u}}_{k+1} = (I + \rho_k \mathbf{GH})\widetilde{\boldsymbol{u}}_k + \rho_k \mathbf{G}\Delta_k. \tag{7.50}$$

Lemma 7.1 still holds for this learning control scheme because it mainly considers the randomness within an iteration. We must reestablish the boundedness of the sequence $\{\widetilde{\boldsymbol{u}}_k\}$ generated by (7.50), where the decreasing sequence ρ_k is used. This result is revealed in the following lemma.

Lemma 7.3 *For the step-length sequence $\{\rho_k\}$ satisfying $\rho_k > 0$, $\sum_{k=1}^{\infty} \rho_k = \infty$, and $\sum_{k=1}^{\infty} \rho_k^2 < \infty$, we have $\sup_k \|\widetilde{\boldsymbol{u}}_k\| < \infty$, if the learning gain matrix is designed such that* ***GH*** *is Hurwitz.*

Proof: This lemma can be proved using [4, Chapter 3, Theorem 7]. In addition to checking conditions (C1)−(C3) in the proof of Lemma 7.2, a condition of the decreasing step-length sequence, as specified in the lemma, is required. Because conditions (C1)−(C3) are irrelevant with the decreasing step-length, they hold naturally. The proof is completed. □

With such boundedness, we present the main convergence result in the following theorem.

Theorem 7.2 *Consider system* (7.1) *under Assumptions 7.1−7.3. The non-asymptotic statistics estimation* (7.8) *of the channel randomness and the learning control scheme* (7.49) *with a decreasing step-length sequence are applied. If the learning gain matrix G_t is designed such that $G_t C_{t+1} B_t$ is*

Hurwitz and the step-length sequence $\{\rho_k\}$ *satisfies* $\rho_k > 0$, $\rho_k \to 0$, *and* $\sum_{k=1}^{\infty} \rho_k = \infty$, *the input error* $\widetilde{\boldsymbol{u}}_k$ *converges to zero in the mean-square sense, i.e.,* $\lim_{k\to\infty} \mathbb{E}[\|\widetilde{\boldsymbol{u}}_k\|^2] = 0$.

Proof: Following similar steps of the proof of Theorem 7.1, we can obtain a counterpart of (7.39):

$$\mathbb{E}[L_{k+1} \mid \mathcal{G}_{k-1}] \leq \left(1 - \rho_k \lambda_{\max}^{-1}(\boldsymbol{\Omega}) + \rho_k^2 \eta_4\right) L_k + \rho_k^2 \eta_5, \tag{7.51}$$

which implies that

$$\mathbb{E}[L_{k+1}] \leq \left(1 - \rho_k \lambda_{\max}^{-1}(\boldsymbol{\Omega}) + \rho_k^2 \eta_4\right) \mathbb{E}[L_k] + \rho_k^2 \eta_5. \tag{7.52}$$

Comparing with the notations in Lemma A.3, we let $\xi_k \triangleq \mathbb{E}[L_k]$, $\tau_k \triangleq \rho_k \lambda_{\max}^{-1}(\boldsymbol{\Omega}) - \rho_k^2 \eta_4$, and $\chi_k \triangleq \rho_k^2 \eta_5$. The rest of this proof is devoted to verify the conditions of Lemma A.3.

Because $\rho_k \to 0$, it is evident that $0 < \tau_k < 1$, $\tau_k \to 0$, and $\rho_k \eta_4 \leq \frac{1}{2} \lambda_{\max}^{-1}(\boldsymbol{\Omega})$, $\forall k \geq k_0$, where k_0 is a sufficiently large integer. Then, $\forall k \geq k_0$, $\tau_k \geq \frac{1}{2} \rho_k \lambda_{\max}^{-1}(\boldsymbol{\Omega})$, and thus, $\sum_{k=k_0}^{\infty} \tau_k \geq \frac{1}{2} \lambda_{\max}^{-1}(\boldsymbol{\Omega}) \sum_{k=k_0}^{\infty} \rho_k = \infty$. Therefore, $\sum_{k=1}^{\infty} \tau_k = \infty$.

Furthermore,

$$\begin{aligned} \lim_{k\to\infty} \frac{\chi_k}{\tau_k} = 0 &= \lim_{k\to\infty} \frac{\rho_k^2 \eta_5}{\rho_k \lambda_{\max}^{-1}(\boldsymbol{\Omega}) - \rho_k^2 \eta_4} \\ &= \lim_{k\to\infty} \frac{\rho_k \eta_5}{\lambda_{\max}^{-1}(\boldsymbol{\Omega}) - \rho_k \eta_4} = 0. \end{aligned} \tag{7.53}$$

Because $\xi_k = \mathbb{E}[L_k]$ is naturally nonnegative, the proof can be completed by applying Lemma A.3 directly. □

The almost-sure convergence of the proposed scheme is demonstrated in the following proposition.

Proposition 7.1 *Under the same conditions of Theorem 7.2 and additionally requiring that* $\sum_{k=1}^{\infty} \rho_k^2 < \infty$, *the input error* $\widetilde{\boldsymbol{u}}_k$ *converges to zero in the almost-sure sense, i.e.,* $\mathbb{P}(\lim_{k\to\infty} \|\widetilde{\boldsymbol{u}}_k\| = 0) = 1$.

Proof: The proof can be completed by applying the Robbins-Siegmund Theorem [49, pp. 50, Lemma 11] to the inequality (7.51), which is rewritten as follows:

$$\mathbb{E}[L_{k+1} \mid \mathcal{G}_{k-1}] \leq (1+\rho_k^2\eta_4)\, L_k + \rho_k^2\eta_5 \\ - \rho_k\lambda_{\max}^{-1}(\mathbf{\Omega})L_k. \tag{7.54}$$

Therefore, it is sufficient to verify that $\sum_{k=1}^{\infty}\rho_k^2\eta_4 < \infty$ and $\sum_{k=1}^{\infty}\rho_k^2\eta_5 < \infty$, which are valid because of $\sum_{k=1}^{\infty}\rho_k^2 < \infty$. The proof is completed. □

Before ending this section, we remark on the convergence speed of the learning control schemes (7.20) and (7.50). The constant step-length causes an exponential convergence rate, where the rate depends heavily on the step-length ρ, whereas the decreasing step-length case would be more complex depending on the specific selection of $\{\rho_k\}$. By noting the requirements of ρ_k: $\sum_{k=1}^{\infty}\rho_k = \infty$ and $\sum_{k=1}^{\infty}\rho_k^2 < \infty$, a natural selection would be $\rho_k = c/k^d$ with $c > 0$ and $1/2 < d \leq 1$. For this selection, the convergence rate would be a negative power of the iteration number k.

7.4 EXTENSIONS TO THE NON-ZERO-MEAN ADDITIVE RANDOMNESS CASE

In Section 7.3, we assume the additive channel randomness to be of zero mean so that it only affects the learning control scheme as a random fluctuation. In this section, we extend to the general nonrepetitive case (7.5), where the mean of additive randomness is nonzero and varies from iteration to iteration. For this case, we must provide an additional nonasymptotic estimate of the iteration-based mean to separate the additive randomness from the received signals. The estimation method is given in Section 7.4.1. Then, the learning control schemes and their convergence analyses in Section 7.3 are proven still valid. Details are given in Section 7.4.2. When no confusion arises, we use the same notation as the previous section for conciseness.

7.4.1 Estimation of Channel Randomness

To estimate the statistics of both multiplicative and additive randomness, the constant testing signal is insufficient because the essential excitation condition is not satisfied. With a single signal, we can only estimate the sum of two means, i.e., $r_k + s_k$, rather than obtain each of them. To obtain means separately, we must revise the design of testing signals.

We will send an even number of testing signals, half of which are opposite numbers of the other half. Without loss of generality, we assume n is even for notation simplicity. We still use the unit signal assigned as follows: If the time instant label is odd, we send $\theta_k(t) = -1$; otherwise, we send $\theta_k(t) = 1$. Therefore, we send $+1$ and -1 for $n/2$ times in turn. Accordingly, the received signal is given by

$$\begin{aligned}\theta_k^\circ(2i-1) &= -r_k'(2i-1)+s_k'(2i-1),\\ \theta_k^\circ(2i) &= r_k'(2i)+s_k'(2i),\end{aligned} \tag{7.55}$$

for $i=1,\ldots,n/2$. Summarizing all received signals yields

$$\begin{aligned}\sum_{t=1}^{n}\theta_k^\circ(t) &= \sum_{i=1}^{n/2}[\theta_k^\circ(2i-1)+\theta_k^\circ(2i)]\\ &= \sum_{i=1}^{n/2}\left[-r_k'(2i-1)+s_k'(2i-1)+r_k'(2i)+s_k'(2i)\right]\\ &= \sum_{i=1}^{n/2}\left[(r_k'(2i)-r_k)-(r_k'(2i-1)-r_k)\right]\\ &\quad+\sum_{i=1}^{n/2}\left[s_k'(2i-1)+s_k'(2i)-2s_k\right]+ns_k.\end{aligned} \tag{7.56}$$

Thus, we obtain

$$\mathbb{E}\left[\sum_{t=1}^{n}\theta_k^\circ(t)\right] = ns_k. \tag{7.57}$$

An unbiased estimator for the mean of the additive randomness is given by

$$\widehat{s}_k = \frac{1}{n}\sum_{t=1}^{n}\theta_k^\circ(t). \tag{7.58}$$

This estimate is of bounded variance as proven by

$$\begin{aligned}\mathbb{E}[(\widehat{s}_k-s_k)^2] &= \mathbb{E}\left[\left(\frac{1}{n}\sum_{t=1}^{n}\theta_k^\circ(t)-s_k\right)^2\right]\\ &= \frac{1}{n^2}\mathbb{E}\left[\left(\sum_{i=1}^{n/2}(r_k'(2i)-r_k'(2i-1))+\sum_{t=1}^{n}(s_k'(t)-s_k)\right)^2\right]\end{aligned}$$

$$= \frac{1}{n^2}\mathbb{E}\left[\sum_{i=1}^{n/2}\left(r_k'(2i) - r_k'(2i-1)\right)^2 + \sum_{t=1}^{n}(s_k'(t) - s_k)^2\right]$$
$$= \frac{\tau_k + \delta_k}{n} \leq \frac{\tau + \delta}{n}, \tag{7.59}$$

where the expectation of all crossing terms is equal to zero.

With the estimate $\widehat{s}_k$, we revise the received signals as

$$\begin{aligned}\theta_k^*(t) &= (-1)^t\left[\theta_k^\circ(t) - \widehat{s}_k\right] \\ &= r_k'(t) + (-1)^t(s_k'(t) - \widehat{s}_k).\end{aligned} \tag{7.60}$$

It is evident that $\mathbb{E}[\theta_k^*(t)] = r_k$ because of the unbiasedness of $\widehat{s}_k$. Besides, $\mathbb{E}[(\theta_k^*(t) - r_k)^2]$ is bounded because of the conditions of multiplicative randomness and variance boundedness of $\widehat{s}_k$. Therefore, $\theta_k^*(t)$ can be regarded as samples around its expectation r_k. Without loss of generality, we assume that all revised signals $\theta_k^*(t)$ are nonnegative random variables; otherwise, we can enlarge the magnitude of testing signals to ensure this requirement. The treatment would increase the variance of the estimate $\widehat{s}_k$ but the unbiasedness is retained. Then, the MIE introduced in Section 7.3.1 still applies to estimate the inverse of the mean of $r_k(t)$. Specifically, MIE is formulated by

$$\widehat{\gamma}_k = \frac{\omega_h}{q_N}\prod_{t=1}^{N}(1 - \omega_h\theta_k^*(t)), \tag{7.61}$$

where N is a nonnegative integer-valued random variable and q_i is the probability $\mathbb{P}(N = i)$ defined in Section 7.3.1. According to [46], the estimate is unbiased, and its variance is bounded, i.e., $\mathbb{E}(\widehat{\gamma}_k - r_k^{-1})^2 \leq \chi < \infty$.

7.4.2 Channel Effect and Main Results

The actual output is $y_k(t)$ and the received output is $y_k^\circ(t)$. We have

$$y_k^\circ(t) = r_k(t)y_k(t) + s_k(t), \tag{7.62}$$

where s_k has the dimension q, same to the dimension of $y_k(t)$. Because of the non-zero-mean multiplicative and additive randomness, we have

$$\mathbb{E}[y_k^\circ(t)] = r_k\mathbb{E}[y_k(t)] + s_k. \tag{7.63}$$

That is, the received signal deviates from its original value because of both multiplicative and additive randomness. It is not applicable to drive the learning process. The correction of the received signal is defined as follows:

$$\widehat{y}_k(t) = \widehat{\gamma}_k[y_k^\circ(t) - \widehat{s}_k\mathbf{1}_q]$$

$$
\begin{aligned}
&= y_k(t) + \left(\frac{r_k(t)}{r_k} - 1\right) y_k(t) \\
&+ \left(\widehat{\gamma}_k - r_k^{-1}\right) r_k(t) y_k(t) \\
&+ \widehat{\gamma}_k (s_k(t) - \widehat{s}_k \mathbf{1}_q), \qquad (7.64)
\end{aligned}
$$

where $\mathbf{1}_q$ is a vector of dimension q with entries being one.

By comparing (7.64) with (7.10), the main difference lies in the last terms, where the additive randomness $s_k(t)$ is replaced by $s_k(t) - \widehat{s}_k \mathbf{1}_q$. It is evident that $\mathbb{E}[s_k(t) - \widehat{s}_k \mathbf{1}_q] = 0$. Therefore, the learning control schemes (7.18) and (7.49) can be applied, where the auxiliary tracking error $\varepsilon_k(t)$ is defined similarly to the previous section. The results are summarized in the following proposition, whereas the proof is omitted to avoid repetition.

Theorem 7.3 *Consider system* (7.1) *under Assumptions 7.1–7.3. Apply the nonasymptotic statistics estimation* (7.58) *and* (7.61) *for additive and multiplicative randomness, respectively. The learning gain matrix G_t satisfies that $G_t C_{t+1} B_t$ is Hurwitz.*

(1) If the learning control scheme (7.18) *is applied, where the constant step-length ρ satisfies $0 < \rho < \rho^\star$, where $\rho^\star$ is specified as before, the input error $\widetilde{\boldsymbol{u}}_k$ converges into a small zone around zero in the mean-square sense, i.e.,*

$$
\limsup_{k\to\infty} \mathbb{E}[\|\widetilde{\boldsymbol{u}}_k\|^2] \le \rho \frac{d_2\left(\eta_1^* + \eta_2^*(2\|\boldsymbol{y}_d\|^2 + \eta_3^*)\right)}{1 - \rho\eta_4^*\lambda_{\max}(\boldsymbol{\Omega})} \frac{\lambda_{\max}(\boldsymbol{\Omega})}{\lambda_{\min}(\boldsymbol{\Omega})},
$$

where η_i^* is revised from η_i by replacing variance calculations of s_k with those of $s_k(t) - \widehat{s}_k \mathbf{1}_q$, $i = 1,2,3,4$ and replacing χ with χ_0.

(2) If the learning control scheme (7.49) *is applied, where the decreasing step-length sequence $\{\rho_k\}$ satisfies $\rho_k > 0$, $\rho_k \to 0$, and $\sum_{k=1}^{\infty} \rho_k = \infty$, the input error $\widetilde{\boldsymbol{u}}_k$ converges to zero in the mean-square sense, i.e., $\lim_{k\to\infty} \mathbb{E}[\|\widetilde{\boldsymbol{u}}_k\|^2] = 0$.*

7.5 THE CASE OF CONSISTENT ESTIMATION

Because of the nonrepetitive characteristic of channel randomness, we can merely apply a nonasymptotic estimation method to establish unbiased estimators. If a certain statistical repetitiveness is satisfied for the involved randomness, an alternative can be provided. This case will be elaborated in this section. Section 7.5.1 defines asymptotic repetitiveness and an asymptotic estimator. The channel effect and convergence analysis are given in Section 7.5.2.

7.5.1 Asymptotic Repetitiveness and Estimator

We first define the asymptotic repetitiveness of channel randomness.

Definition 7.1 *The statistics of the multiplicative and additive channel randomness are called asymptotically repetitive in the iteration domain if they satisfy that*

$$\lim_{k\to\infty} r_k = \overline{r}, \quad \lim_{k\to\infty} s_k = \overline{s}. \tag{7.65}$$

The asymptotic repetitiveness of channel randomness describes the case that although the statistics of each iteration are still different, they converge to a limit along the iteration axis, corresponding to the case that channel randomness gradually becomes identically distributed as the learning process proceeds. Here, the estimates in the previous iterations can be used to generate an asymptotic estimator of the limit as they contain certain information for understanding channel randomness. Specifically, we can establish the following estimation mechanism for the case where s_k varies in the iteration domain.

Similar to Section 7.4.1, we send the testing signals $\theta_k(t) = \pm 1$ in turn and collect the received signal $\theta_k^\circ(t)$: $\theta_k^\circ(2i-1) = -r_k'(2i-1) + s_k'(2i-1)$ and $\theta_k^\circ(2i) = r_k'(2i) + s_k'(2i)$. The estimate for additive randomness is

$$\widehat{s}_k = \frac{1}{n}\sum_{t=1}^{n} \theta_k^\circ(t). \tag{7.66}$$

The received signals are then corrected as $\theta_k^*(t) = (-1)^t \theta_k^\circ(t)$. An estimator for the mean of multiplicative randomness r_k is

$$\widehat{r}_k = \frac{1}{n}\sum_{t=1}^{n} \theta_k^*(t). \tag{7.67}$$

Note that $\widehat{r}_k$ is an unbiased estimate of r_k; however, $\widehat{r}_k^{-1}$ is a biased estimate of r_k^{-1}. Therefore, we did not use this estimate for correcting the received output in the previous sections. Fortunately, $\widehat{r}_k^{-1}$ is an asymptotically unbiased estimate of r_k^{-1} as the sample amount n increases to infinity. Under the asymptotic repetitiveness of channel randomness, we can establish a consistent estimator.

Before providing the estimator, we first evaluate the variance of $\widehat{s}_k$ and $\widehat{r}_k$. By (7.59), we have $\mathrm{Var}(\widehat{s}_k) \triangleq \mathbb{E}[(\widehat{s}_k - s_k)^2] = \frac{\tau_k+\delta_k}{n}$. Similarly, we obtain

$$\mathrm{Var}(\widehat{r}_k) = \mathbb{E}[(\widehat{r}_k - r_k)^2] = \mathbb{E}\left[\left(\frac{1}{n}\sum_{t=1}^{n} \theta_k^*(t) - r_k\right)^2\right]$$

$$= \frac{1}{n^2}\sum_{t=1}^{n}\mathbb{E}[(r_k'(t)-r_k)^2] + \frac{1}{n^2}\sum_{t=1}^{n}\mathbb{E}[(s_k'(t)-s_k)^2]$$
$$= \frac{\tau_k+\delta_k}{n}, \tag{7.68}$$

where the independence between $r_k'(t)$ and $s_k'(t)$ for all time instants is applied. Note that s_k enters the second line of (7.68) technically because the terms $s_k'(t)$ in the expansion of $\theta_k^*(t)$ are with opposite signs. Therefore, the estimates $\widehat{r}_k$ and $\widehat{s}_k$ have the same variances determined by channel randomness.

When r_k and s_k satisfy the asymptotic repetitiveness property, we present the estimator of $\overline{r}$ as

$$\widehat{r}_k^* = \frac{1}{k}\sum_{j=1}^{k}\widehat{r}_j. \tag{7.69}$$

Therefore, $\mathbb{E}[\widehat{r}_k^*] = \frac{1}{k}\sum_{j=1}^{k}\mathbb{E}[\widehat{r}_j] = \frac{1}{k}\sum_{j=1}^{k} r_j \xrightarrow[k\to\infty]{} \overline{r}$. We evaluate the second moment for this estimate:

$$\mathbb{E}[(\widehat{r}_k^* - \overline{r})^2] = \frac{1}{k^2}\mathbb{E}\left[\left(\sum_{j=1}^{k}(\widehat{r}_j - \overline{r})\right)^2\right]$$
$$= \frac{1}{k^2}\mathbb{E}\left[\sum_{j=1}^{k}(\widehat{r}_j-\overline{r})^2 + 2\sum_{1\le i<j\le k}(\widehat{r}_i-\overline{r})(\widehat{r}_j-\overline{r})\right]. \tag{7.70}$$

For the first term on the RHS of (7.70), we have

$$\mathbb{E}\left[\sum_{j=1}^{k}(\widehat{r}_j-\overline{r})^2\right] = \mathbb{E}\left[\sum_{j=1}^{k}(\widehat{r}_j - r_j + r_j - \overline{r})^2\right]$$
$$= \mathbb{E}\left[\sum_{j=1}^{k}(\widehat{r}_j - r_j)^2 + \sum_{j=1}^{k}(r_j-\overline{r})^2\right]$$
$$\le \sum_{j=1}^{k}(\tau_j+\delta_j)/n + \sum_{j=1}^{k}(r_j-\overline{r})^2, \tag{7.71}$$

where $\mathbb{E}[\widehat{r}_j - r_j] = 0$ is applied, $\forall j$, to the second equality. For the second term on the RHS of (7.70), we have

$$\begin{aligned}
&\mathbb{E}\left[2\sum_{1\le i<j\le k}(\widehat{r}_i-\overline{r})(\widehat{r}_j-\overline{r})\right]\\
&=\mathbb{E}\left[2\sum_{1\le i<j\le k}(\widehat{r}_i-r_i+r_i-\overline{r})(\widehat{r}_j-r_j+r_j-\overline{r})\right]\\
&=\mathbb{E}\left[\sum_{1\le i<j\le k}(r_i-\overline{r})(r_j-\overline{r})\right]\\
&\le (k-1)\sum_{j=1}^{k}(r_i-\overline{r})^2,
\end{aligned} \tag{7.72}$$

where $\mathbb{E}[\widehat{r}_j - r_j] = 0$ and the iteration-wise dependence of the involved random variables are applied to the second equality.

Denote $\alpha_k = |r_k - \overline{r}|$. By Definition 7.1, $\alpha_k \to 0$. Substituting (7.71) and (7.72) into (7.70) yields

$$\mathbb{E}[(\widehat{r}_k^* - \overline{r})^2] \le \frac{\tau+\delta}{kn} + \frac{1}{k}\sum_{j=1}^{k}\alpha_j \xrightarrow[k\to\infty]{} 0. \tag{7.73}$$

The estimator in (7.69) is consistent in the iteration domain. Compared with the unbiased estimator for nonrepetitive randomness, the asymptotic estimator (7.69) provides low-cost computation resources and has a vanishing fluctuation.

Remark 7.4 *The estimator defined by* (7.69) *averages the estimates of all available iterations. It can be formulated recursively to save computation memory:* $\widehat{r}_k^* = \frac{k-1}{k}\widehat{r}_{k-1}^* + \frac{1}{k}\widehat{r}_k$. *Besides this estimate, one can use some alternatives. For example, a weighted average* $\widehat{r}_k^* = \frac{1-\varphi}{1-\varphi^k}\sum_{j=1}^{k}\varphi^{k-j}\widehat{r}_j$, *where* $0 < \varphi < 1$ *is a constant, indicating that more weights are imposed on the latest estimates. If a relatively precise initial estimate of* $\overline{r}$ *is available, say* r°, *one can apply the estimate:* $\widehat{r}_k^* = (1-\varphi^k)\left(\frac{1}{k}\sum_{j=1}^{k}\widehat{r}_j\right) + \varphi^k r^\circ$, *where* $0 < \varphi < 1$ *is a factor indicating the forgetting speed of the initial estimate.*

7.5.2 Channel Effect and Main Results

With the estimates (7.66), (7.67), and (7.69), the correction of the received output $y_k^\circ(t)$ is provided by

$$\begin{aligned}\widehat{y}_k(t) &= (\widehat{r}_k^*)^{-1}(y_k^\circ(t) - \widehat{s}_k \mathbf{1}_q) \\ &= y_k(t) + \left(\frac{r_k(t)}{r_k} - 1\right) y_k(t) + \left(\frac{1}{\widehat{r}_k^*} - \frac{1}{r_k}\right) r_k(t) y_k(t) \\ &\quad + (\widehat{r}_k^*)^{-1}(s_k(t) - \widehat{s}_k \mathbf{1}_q). \end{aligned} \tag{7.74}$$

It is similar to (7.64) except for the last two terms on the RHS of (7.74). Besides, the zero-mean and independence properties of the error $(\widehat{r}_k^*)^{-1} - r_k^{-1}$ are invalid. Consequently, the convergence analysis should be revised accordingly.

Using the lifting formulation given in Section 7.2.3, we obtain the auxiliary tracking error using

$$\boldsymbol{\varepsilon}_k = \mathbf{H}\widetilde{\boldsymbol{u}}_k + \overline{\Delta}_k, \tag{7.75}$$

where

$$\begin{aligned}\overline{\Delta}_k &= \mathbf{N}\widetilde{x}_k(0) + \mathbf{M}\boldsymbol{w}_k + \boldsymbol{v}_k + (r_k^{-1}\boldsymbol{\Phi}_k - I_{nq})\boldsymbol{y}_k \\ &\quad + ((\widehat{r}_k^*)^{-1} - r_k^{-1})\boldsymbol{\Phi}_k \boldsymbol{y}_k + (\widehat{r}_k^*)^{-1}(\boldsymbol{s}_k - \widehat{s}_k \mathbf{1}_{nq}). \end{aligned} \tag{7.76}$$

Similar to Lemma 7.1, a calculation of the second moment of $\overline{\Delta}_k$ can be given.

Lemma 7.4 *For the term $\overline{\Delta}_k$, we have*

$$\mathbb{E}[\|\overline{\Delta}_k\|^2] \leq m_1 + m_2 \mathbb{E}[\|\boldsymbol{y}_k\|^2], \tag{7.77}$$

where m_1 and m_2 are suitable positive constants.

Proof: Noting (7.76), we have

$$\mathbb{E}[\|\overline{\Delta}_k\|^2] = \eta_6 + \mathbb{E}[\|\overline{\Delta}_k^{\texttt{left}}\|^2], \tag{7.78}$$

where

$$\eta_6 = \mathbb{E}[\|\mathbf{N}\widetilde{x}_k(0)\|^2] + \mathbb{E}[\|\mathbf{M}\boldsymbol{w}_k\|^2] + \mathbb{E}[\|\boldsymbol{v}_k\|^2] \leq \eta_3$$

and

$$\overline{\Delta}_k^{\texttt{left}} \triangleq (r_k^{-1}\boldsymbol{\Phi}_k - I_{nq})\boldsymbol{y}_k + ((\widehat{r}_k^*)^{-1} - r_k^{-1})\boldsymbol{\Phi}_k \boldsymbol{y}_k + (\widehat{r}_k^*)^{-1}(\boldsymbol{s}_k - \widehat{s}_k \mathbf{1}_{nq}).$$

Therefore,

$$\begin{aligned}\mathbb{E}[\|\overline{\Delta}_k^{\texttt{left}}\|^2] \leq 3\big(&\mathbb{E}[\|(r_k^{-1}\boldsymbol{\Phi}_k - I_{nq})\boldsymbol{y}_k\|^2] \\ &+\mathbb{E}[\|((\widehat{r}_k^*)^{-1} - r_k^{-1})\boldsymbol{\Phi}_k\boldsymbol{y}_k\|^2] \\ &+\mathbb{E}[\|(\widehat{r}_k^*)^{-1}(\boldsymbol{s}_k - \widehat{s}_k\mathbf{1}_{nq})\|^2]\big). \qquad (7.79)\end{aligned}$$

Denote $g_k = \mathbb{E}[\|(\widehat{r}_k^*)^{-1} - r_k^{-1}\|^2]$. Note that

$$g_k \leq 2\mathbb{E}[\|(\widehat{r}_k^*)^{-1} - \overline{r}^{-1}\|^2] + 2\|r_k^{-1} - \overline{r}^{-1}\|^2 \xrightarrow[k\to\infty]{} 0.$$

Then,

$$\mathbb{E}[\|((\widehat{r}_k^*)^{-1} - r_k^{-1})\boldsymbol{\Phi}_k\boldsymbol{y}_k\|^2] \leq g_k(\tau_k + r_k^2)\mathbb{E}[\|\boldsymbol{y}_k\|^2]. \qquad (7.80)$$

A constant $d_4 > 0$ exists, such that $|(\widehat{r}_k^*)^{-1}| < d_4$. Then,

$$\begin{aligned}&\mathbb{E}[\|(\widehat{r}_k^*)^{-1}(\boldsymbol{s}_k - \widehat{s}_k\mathbf{1}_{nq})\|^2] \leq d_4^2\mathbb{E}[\|\boldsymbol{s}_k - \widehat{s}_k\mathbf{1}_{nq}\|^2] \\ &\leq 2d_4^2(\mathbb{E}[\|\boldsymbol{s}_k - s_k\mathbf{1}_{nq}\|^2] + nq\mathbb{E}[(\widehat{s}_k - s_k)^2]) \\ &\leq 2d_4^2 nq\left(\delta_k + \frac{\tau_k + \delta_k}{n}\right). \qquad (7.81)\end{aligned}$$

Summarizing the above estimates completes the proof by noting that $m_1 = \eta_3 + 6d_4^2 q((n+1)\delta + \tau)$ and $m_2 = 3[r_k^{-2}\tau + (\tau + r_k^2)\sup_k g_k]$. □

Now, we consider the learning control scheme (7.18) with a constant step-length ρ, where the auxiliary tracking error $\varepsilon_k(t)$ is calculated using the new correction of the received signal (7.74). By direct verification, we can confirm that Lemma 7.2 is still valid for this case. We have the following bounded convergence for this scheme.

Theorem 7.4 *Consider system* (7.1) *under Assumptions 7.1–7.3. The unbiased estimator* (7.66) *for additive randomness, the consistent estimator* (7.69) *for multiplicative randomness, and the learning control scheme* (7.18) *with a constant step-length are applied. If the learning gain matrix G_t is designed such that $G_tC_{t+1}B_t$ is Hurwitz and the step-length ρ is sufficiently small, the input error $\widetilde{\boldsymbol{u}}_k$ converges into a small zone around zero in the mean-square sense, i.e.,*

$$\limsup_{k\to\infty} \mathbb{E}[\|\widetilde{\boldsymbol{u}}_k\|^2] \leq \rho\frac{d_2(m_1 + 2m_2\|\boldsymbol{y}_d\|^2 + m_2\eta_3)}{\lambda_{\min}(\boldsymbol{\Omega})\underline{\mu}}, \qquad (7.82)$$

where $\underline{\mu}$ is a positive constant specified in the proof.

Proof: Recall the recursion of the input error

$$\widetilde{\boldsymbol{u}}_{k+1} = (I+\rho\mathbf{GH})\widetilde{\boldsymbol{u}}_k + \rho\mathbf{G}\overline{\Delta}_k, \tag{7.83}$$

where $\overline{\Delta}_k$ is defined by (7.76). We use the Lyapunov function $L_k = \widetilde{\boldsymbol{u}}_k^T\boldsymbol{\Omega}\widetilde{\boldsymbol{u}}_k$ and follow the same proof steps as in Theorem 7.1. The major difference lies in the treatment of the term $2\rho\widetilde{\boldsymbol{u}}_k^T(I+\rho\mathbf{GH})^T\boldsymbol{\Omega}\mathbf{G}\overline{\Delta}_k$. Its counterpart in Theorem 7.1 is eliminated by taking conditional expectation to $\mathcal{G}_{k-1}$. It is invalid when the consistent estimate is employed. In the following, we utilize the vanishing property of g_k to establish the evaluations of $2\rho\widetilde{\boldsymbol{u}}_k^T(I+\rho\mathbf{GH})^T\boldsymbol{\Omega}\mathbf{G}\overline{\Delta}_k$ and the contraction of L_k.

By noticing the zero-mean property of the involved randomness and conditional independence between the randomness and input, we have

$$\begin{aligned}
&\mathbb{E}[2\rho\widetilde{\boldsymbol{u}}_k^T(I+\rho\mathbf{GH})^T\boldsymbol{\Omega}\mathbf{G}\overline{\Delta}_k \mid \mathcal{G}_{k-1}]\\
&\quad= 2\rho\widetilde{\boldsymbol{u}}_k^T(I+\rho\mathbf{GH})^T\boldsymbol{\Omega}\mathbf{G}\\
&\qquad\times\mathbb{E}[((\widehat{r}_k^*)^{-1}-r_k^{-1})\boldsymbol{\Phi}_k\boldsymbol{y}_k \mid \mathcal{G}_{k-1}].
\end{aligned}\tag{7.84}$$

Moreover, $\boldsymbol{y}_k = \boldsymbol{y}_d + \mathbf{H}\widetilde{\boldsymbol{u}}_k + \mathbf{N}\widetilde{x}_k(0) + \mathbf{M}\boldsymbol{w}_k + \boldsymbol{v}_k$. Thus,

$$\begin{aligned}
&\mathbb{E}[2\rho\widetilde{\boldsymbol{u}}_k^T(I+\rho\mathbf{GH})^T\boldsymbol{\Omega}\mathbf{G}\overline{\Delta}_k \mid \mathcal{G}_{k-1}]\\
&\quad= 2\rho\widetilde{\boldsymbol{u}}_k^T(I+\rho\mathbf{GH})^T\boldsymbol{\Omega}\mathbf{G}\\
&\qquad\times\mathbb{E}[((\widehat{r}_k^*)^{-1}-r_k^{-1})\boldsymbol{\Phi}_k(\boldsymbol{y}_d+\mathbf{H}\widetilde{\boldsymbol{u}}_k) \mid \mathcal{G}_{k-1}]\\
&\quad= 2\rho\widetilde{\boldsymbol{u}}_k^T(I+\rho\mathbf{GH})^T\boldsymbol{\Omega}\mathbf{G}\\
&\qquad\times\mathbb{E}[((\widehat{r}_k^*)^{-1}-r_k^{-1})\boldsymbol{\Phi}_k \mid \mathcal{G}_{k-1}](\boldsymbol{y}_d+\mathbf{H}\widetilde{\boldsymbol{u}}_k)\\
&\quad= 2\rho\widetilde{\boldsymbol{u}}_k^T(I+\rho\mathbf{GH})^T\boldsymbol{\Omega}\mathbf{G}\mathbb{E}[(\widehat{r}_k^*)^{-1}r_k-1]\\
&\qquad\times(\boldsymbol{y}_d+\mathbf{H}\widetilde{\boldsymbol{u}}_k).
\end{aligned}\tag{7.85}$$

By the Young's inequality $2\boldsymbol{a}^T\boldsymbol{b} \le \vartheta\boldsymbol{a}^T\boldsymbol{a} + \frac{1}{\vartheta}\boldsymbol{b}^T\boldsymbol{b}$, $\forall\vartheta > 0$, we can obtain

$$\begin{aligned}
&2\widetilde{\boldsymbol{u}}_k^T\boldsymbol{\Omega}\mathbf{G}\mathbb{E}[(\widehat{r}_k^*)^{-1}r_k-1]\boldsymbol{y}_d\\
&\qquad\le \vartheta\widetilde{\boldsymbol{u}}_k^T\boldsymbol{\Omega}\widetilde{\boldsymbol{u}}_k + \frac{g_k r_k^2}{\vartheta}d_2\|\boldsymbol{y}_d\|^2,
\end{aligned}\tag{7.86}$$

$$\begin{aligned}
&2\widetilde{\boldsymbol{u}}_k^T\boldsymbol{\Omega}\mathbf{G}\mathbb{E}[(\widehat{r}_k^*)^{-1}r_k-1]\mathbf{H}\widetilde{\boldsymbol{u}}_k\\
&\qquad\le \vartheta\widetilde{\boldsymbol{u}}_k^T\boldsymbol{\Omega}\widetilde{\boldsymbol{u}}_k + \frac{g_k r_k^2}{\vartheta}d_1\widetilde{\boldsymbol{u}}_k^T\boldsymbol{\Omega}\widetilde{\boldsymbol{u}}_k,
\end{aligned}\tag{7.87}$$

$$2\widetilde{\boldsymbol{u}}_k^T(\mathbf{GH})^T\boldsymbol{\Omega}\mathbf{G}\mathbb{E}[(\widehat{r}_k^*)^{-1}r_k-1]\boldsymbol{y}_d$$

$$\leq d_1 \widetilde{\boldsymbol{u}}_k^T \boldsymbol{\Omega} \widetilde{\boldsymbol{u}}_k + g_k r_k^2 d_2 \|\boldsymbol{y}_d\|^2, \tag{7.88}$$

$$2\widetilde{\boldsymbol{u}}_k^T (\mathbf{GH})^T \boldsymbol{\Omega} \mathbf{G} \mathbb{E}[(\widehat{r}_k^*)^{-1} r_k - 1] \mathbf{H} \widetilde{\boldsymbol{u}}_k$$

$$\leq d_1 (1 + g_k r_k^2) \widetilde{\boldsymbol{u}}_k^T \boldsymbol{\Omega} \widetilde{\boldsymbol{u}}_k, \tag{7.89}$$

where $d_2 = \lambda_{\max}(\mathbf{G}^T \boldsymbol{\Omega} \mathbf{G})$ and d_1 satisfy $(\mathbf{GH})^T \boldsymbol{\Omega} (\mathbf{GH}) \leq d_1 \boldsymbol{\Omega}$. Besides, $\vartheta > 0$ is a suitable constant to be defined later.

By substituting (7.86)–(7.89) into (7.85) and combining the proof of Theorem 7.1, meanwhile considering (7.77), we obtain

$$\mathbb{E}[L_{k+1} \mid \mathcal{G}_{k-1}] \leq (1 - \mu_k) L_k + \nu_k, \tag{7.90}$$

where μ_k and ν_k indicates the iteration-varying contraction,

$$\begin{aligned}\mu_k = & \rho \left(\lambda_{\max}^{-1}(\boldsymbol{\Omega}) - 2\vartheta - g_k r_k^2 \vartheta^{-1} d_1\right) \\ & - \rho^2 \left(d_1 (3 + g_k r_k^2) + d_2 m_2 \frac{\lambda_{\max}(\mathbf{H}^T \mathbf{H})}{\lambda_{\min}(\boldsymbol{\Omega})} \right),\end{aligned} \tag{7.91}$$

$$\begin{aligned}\nu_k = & \rho^2 d_2 (m_1 + (2m_2 + g_k r_k^2) \|\boldsymbol{y}_d\|^2 + m_2 \eta_3) \\ & + \rho g_k r_k^2 d_2 \vartheta^{-1} \|\boldsymbol{y}_d\|^2.\end{aligned} \tag{7.92}$$

Recalling $g_k \to 0$, all terms involved with g_k in (7.91) and (7.92) would converge to zero. Then, after sufficiently many iterations, say $k \geq k_0$, $g_k r_k^2 \vartheta^{-1} d_1 < \lambda_{\max}^{-1}(\boldsymbol{\Omega})/4$. Let the constant ϑ be sufficiently small: $\vartheta < \lambda_{\max}^{-1}(\boldsymbol{\Omega})/4$. Then, $\lambda_{\max}^{-1}(\boldsymbol{\Omega}) - 2\vartheta - g_k r_k^2 \vartheta^{-1} d_1 \geq \lambda_{\max}^{-1}(\boldsymbol{\Omega})/4$. Selecting sufficiently small ρ (similar to the calculation for $\rho^\star$) leads to $0 < \rho \underline{\mu} \leq \mu_k < 1$, resulting in a continuous contraction of L_k along the iteration axis, where $\underline{\mu}$ is a positive constant. Moreover, $\nu_k > 0$, $\forall k$. Taking mathematical expectation to (7.90) yields

$$\begin{aligned}\mathbb{E}[L_{k+1}] & \leq (1 - \mu_k) \mathbb{E}[L_k] + \nu_k \\ & \leq (1 - \rho \underline{\mu})^{k - k_0} \mathbb{E}[L_{k_0}] \\ & \quad + \frac{1 - (1 - \rho \underline{\mu})^{k - k_0}}{\rho \underline{\mu}} \nu_{k_0},\end{aligned} \tag{7.93}$$

We let k approach to infinity first and then let k_0 increase to infinity,

$$\limsup_{k \to \infty} \mathbb{E}[L_k] \leq \rho d_2 (m_1 + 2m_2 \|\boldsymbol{y}_d\|^2 + m_2 \eta_3) \underline{\mu}^{-1}. \tag{7.94}$$

The bounded convergence of the input error is completed. □

Theorem 7.4 characterizes the asymptotic property of the input error along the iteration axis. From the proof, replacing the unbiased estimator (of the mean inverse in Section 7.3) with a consistent estimator (of the mean limitation in this section) introduces a diminishing term rather than a zero-mean random variable into the recursion of the input error. Therefore, the crossing terms in derivations of the Lyapunov function are no longer of zero mean but should be estimated differently. This point constitutes the main difference between these two cases. Following a similar procedure, the results in Section 7.3 are still valid.

Now, we present the convergence for the learning control scheme (7.49) with a decreasing step-length sequence $\{\rho_k\}$.

Theorem 7.5 *Consider system* (7.1) *under Assumptions 7.1–7.3. The unbiased estimator* (7.66) *for additive randomness, the consistent estimator* (7.69) *for multiplicative randomness, and the learning control scheme* (7.49) *with a decreasing step-length are applied. If the learning gain matrix G_t is designed such that $G_tC_{t+1}B_t$ is Hurwitz and the step-length sequence ρ_k satisfies $\rho_k > 0$, $\rho_k \to 0$, and $\sum_{k=1}^{\infty}\rho_k = \infty$, the input error $\widetilde{\boldsymbol{u}}_k$ converges to zero in the mean-square sense, i.e.,* $\lim_{k\to\infty}\mathbb{E}[\|\widetilde{\boldsymbol{u}}_k\|^2] = 0$.

Proof: Following the same steps as in the proof of Theorem 7.4 but replacing the constant step-length ρ with ρ_k, we obtain a counterpart of (7.90):

$$\mathbb{E}[L_{k+1} \mid \mathcal{G}_{k-1}] \leq (1-\mu_k^*)L_k + \nu_k^*, \tag{7.95}$$

where

$$\begin{aligned}\mu_k^* &= \rho_k\left(\lambda_{\max}^{-1}(\boldsymbol{\Omega}) - 2\vartheta - g_k r_k^2 \vartheta^{-1} d_1\right)\\ &\quad - \rho_k^2\left(d_1(3+g_k r_k^2) + d_2 m_2 \frac{\lambda_{\max}(\mathbf{H}^T\mathbf{H})}{\lambda_{\min}(\boldsymbol{\Omega})}\right),\end{aligned} \tag{7.96}$$

$$\begin{aligned}\nu_k^* &= \rho_k^2 d_2(m_1 + (2m_2 + g_k r_k^2)\|\boldsymbol{y}_d\|^2 + m_2\eta_3)\\ &\quad + \rho_k g_k r_k^2 d_2 \vartheta^{-1}\|\boldsymbol{y}_d\|^2.\end{aligned} \tag{7.97}$$

We still select $\vartheta < \lambda_{\max}^{-1}(\boldsymbol{\Omega})/4$ and let k be sufficiently large, then $0 < \mu_k^* < 1$, $\mu_k^* \to 0$, and $\sum_{k=1}^{\infty}\mu_k^* = \infty$. Furthermore,

$$\frac{\nu_k^*}{\mu_k^*} = \frac{O(\rho_k) + O(g_k)}{\lambda_{\max}^{-1}(\boldsymbol{\Omega})/2 - O(g_k) - O(\rho_k)} \xrightarrow[k\to\infty]{} 0, \tag{7.98}$$

where $a_k = O(b_k)$ means that there exists a constant $d > 0$ such that $a_k \leq d b_k$. From Lemma A.3, we have $\lim_{k\to\infty}\mathbb{E}[L_k] = 0$. The proof is completed. □

Remark 7.5 *Similar to the asymptotic estimator of $\widehat{r}_k^*$, we can define an asymptotic estimator $\widehat{s}_k^* = \frac{1}{k}\sum_{j=1}^{k}\widehat{s}_j$. Similarly, we have $\mathbb{E}[\widehat{s}_k^*] \xrightarrow[k\to\infty]{} \bar{s}$. Denote $\beta_k = |s_k - \bar{s}|$. Therefore, $\beta_k \to 0$. Following the same procedure, we obtain*

$$\mathbb{E}[(\widehat{s}_k^* - \bar{s})^2] \le \frac{\tau+\delta}{kn} + \frac{1}{k}\sum_{j=1}^{k}\beta_j \xrightarrow[k\to\infty]{} 0. \tag{7.99}$$

This estimate can be used to correct the received output similar to (7.74); however, it introduces no distinct advantage but rather an additional uncertainty in the evaluation. Thus, we use the unbiased estimate for additive randomness directly.

7.6 ILLUSTRATIVE SIMULATIONS

In this section, we present a numerical simulation to demonstrate the effectiveness of the proposed framework. Consider the following MIMO system:

$$\begin{aligned} x_k(t+1) &= \begin{bmatrix} 0.05\sin 0.2t & -0.2 & 0.02t \\ 0.2 & -0.01t & -0.02\cos 0.5t \\ 0.2 & 0.2 & 0.2-0.05\cos 0.2t \end{bmatrix} x_k(t) \\ &+ \begin{bmatrix} 1-0.2\sin^2(0.5\pi t) & 0 \\ 0.01t & 0.01t \\ 0 & 1+0.1\sin(0.5\pi t) \end{bmatrix} u_k(t), \\ y_k(t) &= \begin{bmatrix} 0.2+0.1\sin^2(0.5\pi t) & 0.1 & -0.1 \\ 0 & 0.1 & 0.2-0.1\sin(0.5\pi t) \end{bmatrix} x_k(t). \end{aligned}$$

Set the iteration length $n = 100$ and the initial state $x_k(0) = 0$. The reference is $y_d(t) = 0.9\sin\left(\frac{t}{3}\right) + 0.5\left(1-\cos\left(\frac{t}{4}\right)\right)$ for both dimensions. The noise $w_k(t)$ and $v_k(t)$ are subject to normal distribution, $w_k(t) \sim N(0,\phi_k)$ and $v_k(t) \sim N(0,\psi_k)$, where both $\sqrt{\phi_k}$ and $\sqrt{\psi_k}$ are generated according to uniform distribution $U[0.01, 0.05]$.

Because Section 7.3 demonstrates a special case of Section 7.4, we conduct simulations for the general case directly. Both the mean and variance for multiplicative and additive randomness are generated randomly in the iteration domain. Therefore, both multiplicative and additive randomness are nonrepetitive along the iteration axis. Particularly, for multiplicative randomness, the mean r_k is randomly generated according to a uniform distribution over the interval $[0.5, 1.1]$ and the variance square-root $\sqrt{\tau_k}$ is randomly generated according to a uniform distribution over $[0.01, 0.1]$. The multiplicative random variable $r_k(t)$ is subject to a normal distribution $N(r_k, \tau_k)$. Similarly,

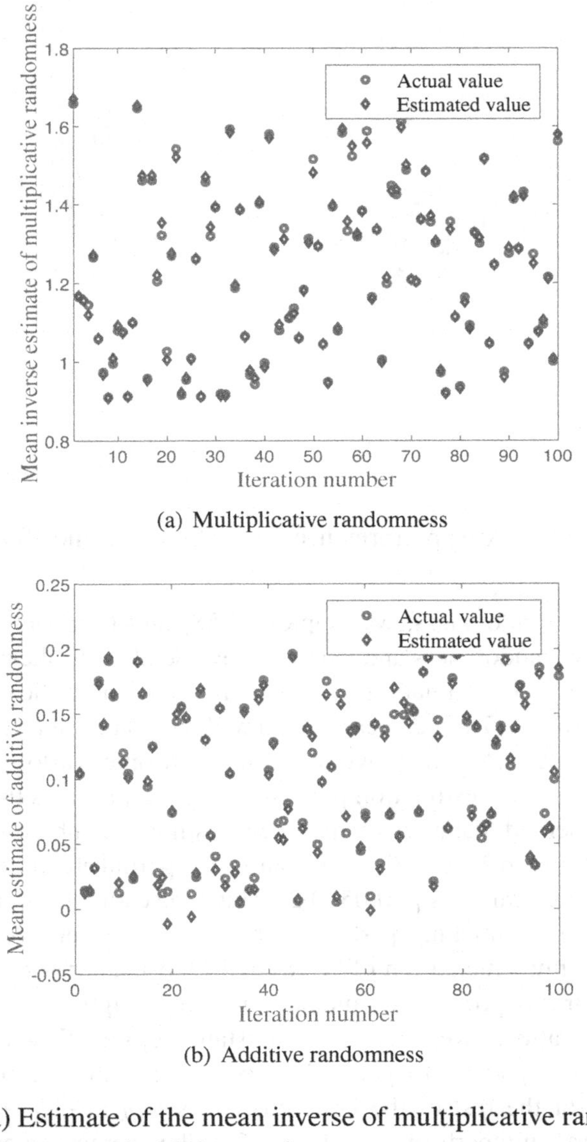

(a) Multiplicative randomness

(b) Additive randomness

Figure 7.2 (a) Estimate of the mean inverse of multiplicative randomness; (b) estimate of the mean of additive randomness.

the mean s_k and variance square-root $\sqrt{\delta_k}$ of additive randomness is generated according to uniform distributions $U[0.01, 0.2]$ and $U[0.01, 0.1]$, respectively. The additive random variable $s_k^{(i)}(t)$ is then generated subject to a normal distribution $N(s_k, \delta_k)$.

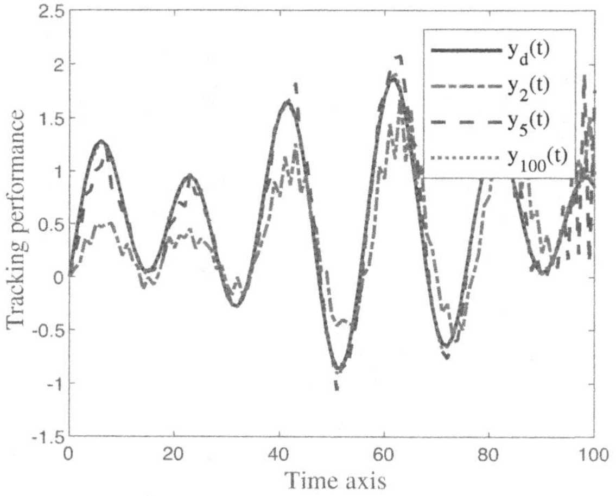

Figure 7.3 Output tracking performance for the 2nd, 5th, and 100th iterations.

For channel randomness, we employ (7.58) and (7.61) to estimate the mean of additive randomness and the mean inverse of multiplicative randomness, respectively. For estimating the mean inverse of multiplicative randomness, a single trial of (7.61) can cause a large deviation even if it is unbiased. With the available test signals, we can conduct Monte Carlo trials and use the average to improve estimation precision. Fig. 7.2 provides the estimation results. It is observed that a relatively precise estimate can be achieved. Note that the deviations in Fig. 7.2(b) seem large for partial iterations; however, note that the y-axis range is $[-0.05, 0.2]$. Thus, the estimate is precise.

To achieve high tracking performance and fast convergence speed, we use a cascaded implementation of (7.18) and (7.49). Therefore, in the early stage of the learning process, we maintain the step-length constant, whereas after certain iterations, we replace the constant step-length with a decreasing step-length sequence. In particular, for the first 30 iterations, we set $\rho = 0.2$, and for the rest of the iterations, we set $\rho_k = \frac{0.2}{k^{0.45}}$. Figs. 7.3 and 7.4 show the tracking performance. In Fig. 7.4, the averaged input error profile is defined by $\|\widetilde{\boldsymbol{u}}_k\|^2/n$. From the solid line, the proposed framework can achieve outstanding tracking performance. As a comparison, the dashed line denotes the case where the unbiased estimate is replaced by an asymptotic estimate $\widehat{r}_k = \frac{1}{nk}\sum_{j=1}^{k}\sum_{t=1}^{n}\theta_j^*(t)$ for the multiplicative randomness mean, where $\theta_j^*(t)$ is the corrected testing signals defined in Section 7.4.

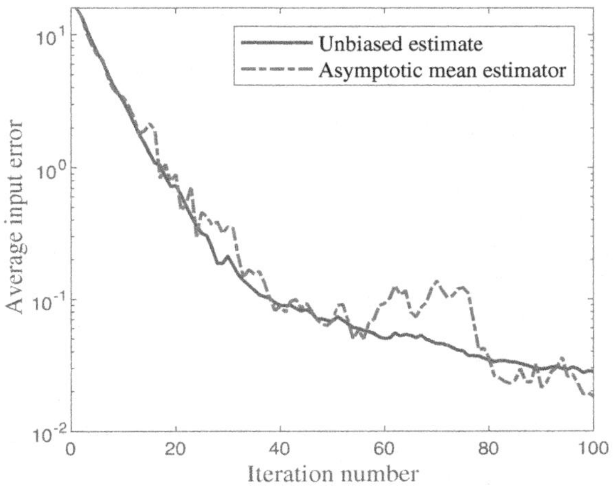

Figure 7.4 Averaged input error profiles in the iteration domain.

If the nonrepetitive channel randomness satisfies the asymptotic repetitiveness specified in Section 7.5, we can replace the mean inverse estimate (7.61) with an asymptotic mean estimate (7.69) and apply the proposed framework, but with a new auxiliary tracking error given by (7.75). The obtained results are similar to Figs. 7.2–7.4. We omit the figures to save space.

7.7 SUMMARY

In this chapter, we proposed a practical learning-tracking framework for stochastic systems with nonrepetitive randomness. We characterize the nonrepetitive property based on channel multiplicative and additive randomness rather than all involved random variables to highlight the main idea. The statistics, including the mean and variance, are assumed to be variable with respect to the iteration index without satisfying any specific distribution. Therefore, this statistical information cannot be predicted iteration by iteration. We propose a practical framework constituted by an unbiased estimator of the mean inverse for multiplicative randomness and the mean for additive randomness, a signal correction mechanism before the learning process, and a learning control scheme with constant or decreasing step-lengths. It is proven that the proposed framework is effective in estimating the necessary information and achieving high-precision tracking performance. Furthermore, a consistent mean estimate for multiplicative randomness is also proposed if the statistics satisfy asymptotic repetitiveness along the iteration axis. The proposed framework still applies using this estimate.

III

Extensions of Systems and Problems

CHAPTER 8

Learning Consensus with Faded Neighborhood Information

THIS chapter addresses the batch-based learning consensus for linear and nonlinear multi-agent systems (MAS) with faded neighborhood information. The motivation comes from the observation that agents exchange information via wireless networks, which inevitably introduces random fading effect and channel additive noise to the transmitted signals. It is therefore of great significance to investigate how to ensure the precise consensus tracking to a given reference leader using heavily contaminated information. To this end, a novel distributed learning consensus scheme is proposed, which consists of a classic distributed control structure, a preliminary correction mechanism, and a separated design of learning gain and regulation matrix. The influence of biased and unbiased randomness is discussed in detail according to the convergence rate and consensus performance. The iteration-wise asymptotic consensus tracking is strictly established for linear MAS first to demonstrate the inherent principles for the effectiveness of the proposed scheme. Then, the results are extended to nonlinear systems with nonidentical initialization condition and diverse gain design. The obtained results show that the distributed learning consensus scheme can achieve high precision tracking performance for a MAS under reliable communications. The theoretical results are verified by two illustrative simulations.

DOI: 10.1201/9781032646404-8

8.1 INTRODUCTION

A multi-agent system (MAS) refers to a network system composed of a group of agents, where each agent has adaptive and autonomous capabilities in a specific environment. MAS transforms the traditional centralized control strategy into a more convenient distributed control approach. It completes the system coordination in an effective and flexible way via cooperation among the agents. Scholars have conducted a large number of researches regarding the consensus problem of a MAS from various aspects. Specifically, the communication topology among agents includes the leader-follower model and leaderless model. The topology conditions for ensuring the consensus have been examined in [34, 50]. The agent dynamics covers various types such as second-order dynamics, higher order dynamics, linear systems, and nonlinear systems.

In the literature, the consensus tracking problem of MAS was discussed in the time domain; in other words, the consensus objective is gradually achieved as the time index approaches to infinity. A large number of practical systems and processes execute the operation over a finite time interval repeatedly. For these systems, it is a significant issue to realize the complete consensus tracking performance over the whole time interval. This observation motives the proposal of learning consensus tracking problem, which refers to the output consensus of all agents in a MAS to a given reference [45, 56]. In [45], a distributed ILC algorithm using adjacent agent information was introduced to solve the robustness problems under state shifts, disturbances, and topological switching. In [56], the heterogeneous high-order nonlinear MAS with output constraints was investigated. The consensus tracking problem was solved by the proposed scheme by introducing a barrier Lyapunov function. These works provide both control schemes and performance analysis. However, when the exchanging data are not fully available, the proposed control schemes may be not applicable.

In MAS, the communication between agents makes the whole system a networked structure, where the potential channel effect cannot be ignored. In particular, the signals received by the other ends are often randomly damaged by fading, data loss, and communication constraints because of unreliable networks. This fact promotes a significant direction of control over networks with randomness and uncertainty. For the traditional networked systems with fading channels, the previous chapters have been made to solve the tracking problem, where the fading phenomena introduced by wireless channels are carefully analyzed. However, all the results are derived for single linear systems, where a single plant and a controller are connected by fading channels.

While considering MAS, the fading channel introduces multiplicative and additive randomness to the neighborhood information independently for different connections. Thus, merely the faded neighborhood information (FNI) is available for learning consensus. The channel randomness affects the consensus performance in MAS significantly, which has not been investigated in the literature. This observation motivates the research in this chapter.

In this chapter, the learning concept is applied to study the batch-based consensus tracking problem of MAS with FNI. Particularly, signals transmitted between agents are affected by channel randomness, where channel randomness consists of random fading and additive noise. To solve the learning consensus problem, a preliminary correction to the received measurements is presented with the help of the statistics of the fading phenomenon. Then, a distributed learning scheme is proposed to realize the batch-wise convergence to the given reference while achieving consensus for all agents. The agent dynamics is considered to be linear type first to highlight the design and analysis of the distributed scheme and then is extended to nonlinear type together with relaxed initialization condition and gain selection. The expected performance is strictly established by introducing a variable gain. Theoretical results are verified by two illustrative simulations and extensive discussions are presented regarding the practical design.

Graph Theory: The directed graph $\mathcal{G} = (\mathcal{V}, \mathcal{E})$ is utilized to explain the topology of communication between n agents. The vertex set $\mathcal{V} = (v_1, v_2, \cdots, v_n)$ and the edge set $\mathcal{E} \subseteq \mathcal{V} \times \mathcal{V}$, where each vertex in $\mathcal{V}$ represents an agent. The edge formed between vertex v_i and vertex v_j is (v_i, v_j), indicating that vertex v_i can receive the information of vertex v_j, and $j \in \mathcal{N}_i$, $\mathcal{N}_i = \{v_j \in \mathcal{V}, (v_i, v_j) \in \mathcal{E}\}$ is the adjacent vertex set of vertex v_i. The adjacency matrix is denoted by $\mathcal{A}$, where the diagonal elements $a_{i,i} = 0$ and $a_{i,j} = 1$ represent $(v_i, v_j) \in \mathcal{E}$. A directed spanning tree in graph $\mathcal{G}$ refers to that there is a vertex that has a directed path along the direction of an edge in the graph to any other vertex. The Laplacian matrix is denoted by $\mathcal{L} = \mathcal{O} - \mathcal{A}$, where $\mathcal{O} = \text{diag}\{o_1, o_2, \cdots, o_n\}$ and $o_i = \sum_{j \in \mathcal{N}} a_{i,j}$ is the in-degree matrix of graph $\mathcal{G}$.

8.2 PROBLEM FORMULATION

For the jth agent in MAS, we consider the following linear time-variant dynamics:

$$\begin{aligned} x_{k,j}(t+1) &= A_t x_{k,j}(t) + B_t u_{k,j}(t), \\ y_{k,j}(t) &= C_t x_{k,j}(t), \end{aligned} \tag{8.1}$$

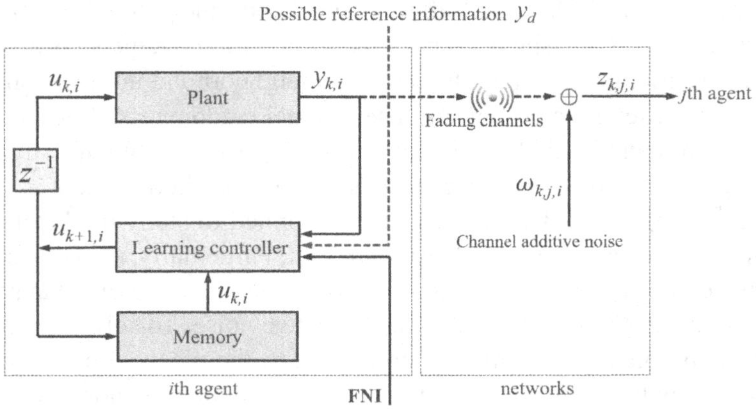

Figure 8.1 Communication network of agents with faded neighborhood information (FNI).

where the subscript $k \in \mathbf{Z}_+$ is the iteration index. The agent index and the time index are represented by $j = 1, 2, \cdots, n$ and $t = 0, 1, \cdots, N$, respectively. n and N are positive integers and refer to the amount of agents and the iteration length, respectively. $x_{k,j}(t) \in \mathbf{R}^s$ is the jth agent's state, $u_{k,j}(t) \in \mathbf{R}^p$ is the jth agent's input, and $y_{k,j}(t) \in \mathbf{R}^q$ is the jth agent's output. A_t, B_t and C_t are system matrices with appropriate dimensions. In addition, we assume that $C_{t+1}B_t$ is of full-column rank for all t without loss of generality.

As presented in Fig. 8.1, the communication between agent v_i and v_j is completed through unreliable networks, where both random fading phenomenon and channel additive noise exist. The fading is model by a random multiplicative variable $\theta_{k,j,i}(t)$. In particular, the FNI of the ith agent received by the jth agent $z_{k,j,i}(t)$ is expressed as follows:

$$z_{k,j,i}(t) = \theta_{k,j,i}(t)y_{k,i}(t) + \omega_{k,j,i}(t), \tag{8.2}$$

where $\theta_{k,j,i}(t)$ is the corresponding fading gain and $\omega_{k,j,i}(t)$ is channel additive randomness (CAN).

In this chapter, the statistics of fading gain is determined because most wireless channels undergo slow fading and then, the received signals can be corrected. Moreover, the following assumptions on random fading and CAN is imposed for further analysis.

Assumption 8.1 *The fading gain $\theta_{k,j,i}(t)$ subject to a continuous distribution $\mathbb{P}(\theta_{k,j,i}(t) > 0) = 1$, which is independent and identically distributed with* *respect to all index. In addition,* $\mathbb{E}[\theta_{k,j,i}(t)] = \mu$ *and* $\mathbb{E}[(\theta_{k,j,i}(t) - \mu)^2] = \sigma^2$*, where* μ *is known in advance to perform preliminary correction on the received signals.*

Assumption 8.2 *The CAN* $\omega_{k,j,i}(t)$ *is assumed to be independent with respect to k, t, and j, i. In addition,* $\omega_{k,j,i}(t)$ *is of zero mean and bounded second moment.*

Assumption 8.3 *The desired trajectory* $y_d(t)$ *is realizable, i.e., there exist an initial state* $x_d(0)$ *and input* $u_d(t)$ *such that*

$$\begin{aligned} x_d(t+1) &= A_t x_d(t) + B_t u_d(t), \\ y_d(t) &= C_t x_d(t). \end{aligned} \tag{8.3}$$

Assumption 8.4 *The system state* $x_{k,j}(t)$ *is equal to the desired state* $x_d(t)$ *when* $t = 0$*, i.e.,* $x_{k,j}(0) = x_d(0)$*,* $\forall k, j$*.*

The most common initial state condition in the field of ILC is the identical initialization condition (i.i.c.). Considering that i.i.c. may be difficult to achieve in some practical applications, multiple relaxations for i.i.c. have been researched in the literature [72]. The relaxation condition of asymptotically identical initialization condition is presented in Section 8.4.

The MAS under consideration has a distributed structure and desired trajectory $y_d(t)$ information is not directly available to every agent except for part of the agents. It is assumed that the reference information is stored on the virtual leader v_0. The reference information can be accessed by partial agents precisely, i.e., without fading and channel noise. Then, the information relationships among all agents including virtual leaders are represented by a new edge set $\overline{\mathcal{E}}$ and a new graph $\overline{\mathcal{G}}$, $\overline{\mathcal{G}} = \{\mathcal{V} \cup 0, \overline{\mathcal{E}}\}$. Additionally, the matrix $\mathcal{D} \triangleq \text{diag}\{d_1, d_2, \ldots, d_n\}$ is employed to represent the connections between virtual agent and other agents in the graph $\overline{\mathcal{G}}$, where $d_i = 1$ indicates that agent v_i has communication with v_0; otherwise, $d_i = 0$. In particular, each agent can only get information from its neighbor agent and/or virtual leader.

Assumption 8.5 *A spanning tree is contained in the graph* $\overline{\mathcal{G}} = \{\mathcal{V} \cup 0, \overline{\mathcal{E}}\}$*. The root of spanning tree is the virtual leader agent.*

The spanning tree condition is an adequate condition to accomplish the consensus tracking objective in the MAS, which ensures that the desired trajectory information are globally accessible. We provide the following lemma for further analysis.

Lemma 8.1 ([32]) *The eigenvalues of $\mathcal{L}+\mathcal{D}$ have positive real parts when the virtual agent is the root of the spanning tree of the graph $\overline{\mathcal{G}}$.*

For the MAS (8.1) that performs repetitive tasks, our control objective is to obtain learning consensus scheme for each agent through iterative operation. This helps to ensure that the trajectory of each agent is identical to the desired trajectory $y_d(t)$ within the time interval. The above objective is equivalent to the consensus problem of the distributed MAS within a finite time interval by finding the appropriate control input $u_{k,j}(t)$ that satisfies

$$\lim_{k\to\infty} \mathbb{E}[\|y_d(t)-y_{k,j}(t)\|]^2=0, \quad \forall t\in\{0,1,\cdots,N\}. \tag{8.4}$$

In other words, each agent in the MAS converges to the desired trajectory as the batch number increases goes to infinity.

8.3 DISTRIBUTED LEARNING CONSENSUS SCHEME AND ITS ANALYSIS

In this section, the impacts of channel randomness on the transmitted signals is first analyzed. Then, the corresponding learning consensus scheme is introduced. Finally, we prove the consensus convergence of the learning scheme in detail.

8.3.1 Distributed Learning Consensus Scheme

Due to the existence of the FNI, the received signal (as can be seen from (8.2)) is not precise. According to the statistics of $\theta_{k,j,i}(t)$, the received signal is corrected as follows:

$$\begin{aligned}\bar{z}_{k,j,i}(t)=&\mu^{-1}z_{k,j,i}(t)\\ =&\mu^{-1}\theta_{k,j,i}(t)y_{k,i}(t)+\mu^{-1}\omega_{k,j,i}(t)\\ =&y_{k,i}(t)-(1-\mu^{-1}\theta_{k,j,i}(t))y_{k,i}(t)\\ &+\mu^{-1}\omega_{k,j,i}(t),\end{aligned} \tag{8.5}$$

where $\bar{z}_{k,j,i}(t)$ presents corrected output signal.

Remark 8.1 *The correction is conducted by multiplying the mean inverse to the received signals provided that the mean μ is available. If it is unknown, an alternative is to employ its iteration-wise estimate such as the one proposed in Chapter 6. With the correction, it is seen that the corrected signal is unbiased with respect to its original value. In other words, the error term*

$(1-\mu^{-1}\theta_{k,j,i}(t))y_{k,i}(t)$ in (8.5) is of zero mean. Thus, the corrected signal can be applied in the learning consensus scheme. This explains the feasibility of the proposed scheme. In addition, it is assumed that channels between all agents follow the same distribution in this chapter. When the fading distributions in various channels are different, we can also adopt the correction method such as (8.5) because the various fading gains are independent from each other. In this case, (8.5) can be written as $\bar{z}_{k,j,i}(t) = y_{k,i}(t) - (1-\mu_{j,i}^{-1}\theta_{k,j,i}(t))y_{k,i}(t) + \mu_{j,i}^{-1}\omega_{k,j,i}(t)$, where $\mu_{j,i}$ is the fading mean in the channel from agent v_i to agent v_j.

The collected and corrected FNI of the jth agent is presented by $\xi_{k,j}(t)$:

$$\begin{aligned}
\xi_{k,j}(t) &= \sum_{i\in\mathcal{N}_j} a_{j,i}(\bar{z}_{k,j,i}(t) - y_{k,j}(t)) + d_j(y_d(t) - y_{k,j}(t)) \\
&= \sum_{i\in\mathcal{N}_j} a_{j,i}(y_{k,i}(t) - y_{k,j}(t)) + d_j(y_d(t) - y_{k,j}(t)) \\
&\quad - \sum_{i\in\mathcal{N}_j} a_{j,i}(1-\mu^{-1}\theta_{k,j,i}(t))y_{k,i}(t) \\
&\quad + \sum_{i\in\mathcal{N}_j} a_{j,i}\mu^{-1}\omega_{k,j,i}(t) \\
&= \sum_{i\in\mathcal{N}_j} a_{j,i}(y_{k,i}(t) - y_{k,j}(t)) + d_j e_{k,j}(t) \\
&\quad + \sum_{i\in\mathcal{N}_j} a_{j,i}(1-\mu^{-1}\theta_{k,j,i}(t))e_{k,i}(t) \\
&\quad - \sum_{i\in\mathcal{N}_j} a_{j,i}(1-\mu^{-1}\theta_{k,j,i}(t))y_d(t) \\
&\quad + \sum_{i\in\mathcal{N}_j} a_{j,i}\mu^{-1}\omega_{k,j,i}(t),
\end{aligned} \tag{8.6}$$

where $e_{k,i}(t) \triangleq y_d(t) - y_{k,i}(t)$ is the actual tracking error of the ith agent.

For the MAS (8.1) with FNI, the distributed learning control scheme is formulated as follows:

$$u_{k+1,j}(t) = u_{k,j}(t) + \lambda_k \Gamma_t \xi_{k,j}(t+1), \tag{8.7}$$

where Γ_t is the regulation matrix and $\{\lambda_k\}$ is a decreasing gain sequence such that $\lambda_k > 0$, $\lambda_k \xrightarrow[k\to\infty]{} 0$, $\sum_{k=1}^{\infty}\lambda_k = \infty$.

Substituting (8.6) into the scheme (8.7), we have

$$\begin{aligned}
& u_{k+1,j}(t) \\
&= u_{k,j}(t) + \lambda_k \Gamma_t \sum_{i\in\mathcal{N}_j} a_{j,i}(e_{k,j}(t+1) - e_{k,i}(t+1)) \\
&\quad + \lambda_k \Gamma_t d_j e_{k,j}(t+1) \\
&\quad + \lambda_k \sum_{i\in\mathcal{N}_j} (1-\mu^{-1}\theta_{k,j,i}(t+1)) a_{j,i}\Gamma_t e_{k,i}(t+1) \\
&\quad - \lambda_k \sum_{i\in\mathcal{N}_j} (1-\mu^{-1}\theta_{k,j,i}(t+1)) a_{j,i}\Gamma_t y_d(t+1) \\
&\quad + \lambda_k \Gamma_t \sum_{i\in\mathcal{N}_j} a_{j,i}\mu^{-1}\omega_{k,j,i}(t+1). \qquad (8.8)
\end{aligned}$$

Without loss of generality, we consider homogeneous agents for notation simplicity, i.e., each agent has identical dynamics. Then, (8.8) can be reformulate as below:

$$\begin{aligned}
u_{k+1}(t) = u_k(t) &+ \lambda_k[(\mathcal{L}+\mathcal{D})\otimes\Gamma_t]e_k(t+1) \\
&+ \lambda_k \Upsilon_k(t+1)[\mathcal{A}_c\otimes\Gamma_t]e_k(t+1) \\
&- \lambda_k \Upsilon_k(t+1)[\mathcal{A}_c\otimes\Gamma_t]\times[1_n\otimes y_d(t+1)] \\
&+ \lambda_k[\mathcal{A}_r\otimes\Gamma_t]\Omega_k(t+1), \qquad (8.9)
\end{aligned}$$

where

$$\begin{aligned}
e_k(t) &= [e_{k,1}^T(t), e_{k,2}^T(t), \cdots, e_{k,n}^T(t)]^T \in \mathbf{R}^{qn}, \\
u_k(t) &= [u_{k,1}^T(t), u_{k,2}^T(t), \cdots, u_{k,n}^T(t)]^T \in \mathbf{R}^{pn}, \\
\omega_{k,j}(t) &= [\omega_{k,j,1}^T(t), \omega_{k,j,2}^T(t), \cdots, \omega_{k,j,n}^T(t)]^T, \\
\Omega_k(t) &= [\mu^{-1}\omega_{k,1}^T(t), \mu^{-1}\omega_{k,2}^T(t), \cdots, \mu^{-1}\omega_{k,n}^T(t)]^T, \\
\mathcal{A}_c &= \mathrm{diag}\{\mathcal{A}_{c,1}, \mathcal{A}_{c,2}, \cdots, \mathcal{A}_{c,n}\} \in \mathbf{R}^{n^2\times n}, \\
\mathcal{A}_r &= \mathrm{diag}\{\mathcal{A}_{r,1}, \mathcal{A}_{r,2}, \cdots, \mathcal{A}_{r,n}\} \in \mathbf{R}^{n\times n^2}, \\
\Upsilon_{k,i}(t) &= \mathrm{diag}\left\{1-\frac{\theta_{k,1,i}(t)}{\mu}, 1-\frac{\theta_{k,2,i}(t)}{\mu}, \cdots, 1-\frac{\theta_{k,n,i}(t)}{\mu}\right\}, \\
\Upsilon_k(t) &= \left[\Upsilon_{k,1}(t), \Upsilon_{k,2}(t), \cdots, \Upsilon_{k,n}(t)\right]\otimes I_p \in \mathbf{R}^{pn\times pn^2}.
\end{aligned}$$

Here, $\mathcal{A}_{c,i}$ and $\mathcal{A}_{r,i}$ denote the ith column and the ith row of the adjacency matrix $\mathcal{A}$, respectively.

To facilitate the design and analysis procedures, a lifting technique is used to transform the state-space model into the lifted-system framework along the time axis. Specifically, we rewrite the system equation (8.1) into a compact form as follows:

$$\begin{aligned} x_k(t+1) &= (I_n \otimes A_t)x_k(t) + (I_n \otimes B_t)u_k(t), \\ y_k(t) &= (I_n \otimes C_t)x_k(t), \end{aligned} \tag{8.10}$$

where

$$\begin{aligned} x_k(t) &= [x_{k,1}^T(t), x_{k,2}^T(t), \cdots, x_{k,n}^T(t)]^T \in \mathbf{R}^{sn}, \\ y_k(t) &= [y_{k,1}^T(t), y_{k,2}^T(t), \cdots, y_{k,n}^T(t)]^T \in \mathbf{R}^{qn}. \end{aligned}$$

Let

$$G = \begin{bmatrix} I_n \otimes C_1 B_0 & 0 & \dots & 0 \\ I_n \otimes \Lambda_{2,1}^{(1)} & I_n \otimes C_2 B_1 & \dots & 0 \\ \vdots & \vdots & \ddots & \vdots \\ I_n \otimes \Lambda_{N,1}^{(1)} & I_n \otimes \Lambda_{N,2}^{(1)} & \dots & I_n \otimes C_N B_{N-1} \end{bmatrix},$$

$$H = [(I_n \otimes \Lambda_1^{(2)})^T, (I_n \otimes \Lambda_2^{(2)})^T, \cdots, (I_n \otimes \Lambda_N^{(2)})^T]^T,$$

where $\Lambda_{N,i}^{(1)} = C_N \left(\prod_{j=i}^{N-1} A_j\right) B_{i-1}$, $i \le N-1$ and $\Lambda_i^{(2)} = C_i \left(\prod_{j=0}^{i-1} A_j\right)$.

Then, we have the following relationship between the output and the input:

$$y_k = Gu_k + Hx_k(0), \tag{8.11}$$

where

$$\begin{aligned} y_k &= [y_k^T(1), y_k^T(2), \cdots, y_k^T(N)]^T \in \mathbf{R}^{qnN}, \\ u_k &= [u_k^T(0), u_k^T(1), \cdots, u_k^T(N-1)]^T \in \mathbf{R}^{pnN}. \end{aligned}$$

The reference trajectory y_d is

$$y_d = Gu_d + Hx_d(0). \tag{8.12}$$

Define $\Delta u_k \triangleq u_d - u_k$. Combining (8.9), (8.11), and (8.12), we have

$$\begin{aligned} u_{k+1} &= u_k + \lambda_k \Psi_1 e_k + \lambda_k \Upsilon_k \Psi_2 e_k - \lambda_k \Upsilon_k \Psi_2 Y_d + \lambda_k \Psi_3 \Omega_k \\ &= u_k + \lambda_k \Psi_1 G \Delta u_k + \lambda_k \Upsilon_k \Psi_2 G \Delta u_k \\ &\quad - \lambda_k \Upsilon_k \Psi_2 Y_d + \lambda_k \Psi_3 \Omega_k, \end{aligned} \tag{8.13}$$

where

$$
\begin{aligned}
e_k &= [e_k^T(1), e_k^T(2), \cdots, e_k^T(N)]^T \in \mathbf{R}^{qnN},\\
Y_d &= [(1_n \otimes y_d(1))^T, (1_n \otimes y_d(2))^T, \cdots, (1_n \otimes y_d(N))^T]^T,\\
\Omega_k &= [\Omega_k^T(1), \Omega_k^T(2), \cdots, \Omega_k^T(N)]^T \in \mathbf{R}^{qn^2N},\\
\Upsilon_k &= \operatorname{diag}\{\Upsilon_k(1), \Upsilon_k(2), \cdots, \Upsilon_k(N)\} \in \mathbf{R}^{pnN\times pn^2N},\\
\Psi_1 &= \operatorname{diag}\{(\mathcal{L}+\mathcal{D})\otimes\Gamma_0, (\mathcal{L}+\mathcal{D})\otimes\Gamma_1, \cdots\\
&\qquad \cdots, (\mathcal{L}+\mathcal{D})\otimes\Gamma_{N-1}\} \in \mathbf{R}^{pnN\times qnN},\\
\Psi_2 &= \operatorname{diag}\{\mathcal{A}_c\otimes\Gamma(0), \mathcal{A}_c\otimes\Gamma(1), \cdots, \mathcal{A}_c\otimes\Gamma(N-1)\},\\
\Psi_3 &= \operatorname{diag}\{\mathcal{A}_r\otimes\Gamma(0), \mathcal{A}_r\otimes\Gamma(1), \cdots, \mathcal{A}_r\otimes\Gamma(N-1)\}.
\end{aligned}
$$

8.3.2 Performance Analysis

For the convergence analysis, we introduce the following technical lemma:

Lemma 8.2 *If the regulation matrix Γ_t satisfies that the eigenvalues of matrix $\Gamma_t C_{t+1} B_t$ are all positive real numbers, then $-(\mathcal{L}+\mathcal{D})\otimes(\Gamma_t C_{t+1} B_t)$ is stable for all time instants.*

Proof: Suppose that ϕ_i, x_i $(i = 1, 2, \cdots, n)$ represents the eigenvalues and the eigenvectors of $\mathcal{L}+\mathcal{D}$, respectively. Moreover, φ_j, y_j $(j = 1, 2, \cdots, p)$ represents the eigenvalues and the eigenvectors of $\Gamma_t C_{t+1} B_t$, respectively. By the properties of the Kronecker product, we have the following equation:

$$
\begin{aligned}
&[(\mathcal{L}+\mathcal{D})\otimes(\Gamma_t C_{t+1} B_t)](x_i \otimes y_j)\\
&= (\mathcal{L}+\mathcal{D})x_i \otimes (\Gamma_t C_{t+1} B_t) y_j\\
&= \phi_i x_i \otimes \varphi_j y_j\\
&= \phi_i \varphi_j (x_i \otimes y_j),
\end{aligned}
$$

which implies that the eigenvalues of $(\mathcal{L}+\mathcal{D})\otimes(\Gamma_t C_{t+1} B_t)$ are $\phi_i\varphi_j$, and the corresponding eigenvectors are $x_i y_j$. Moreover, we have that the real part of ϕ_i is positive by Lemma 8.1. Consequently, the eigenvalues of $(\mathcal{L}+\mathcal{D})\otimes(\Gamma_t C_{t+1} B_t)$ have positive real part; that is, $-(\mathcal{L}+\mathcal{D})\otimes(\Gamma_t C_{t+1} B_t)$ is stable. The proof is completed. □

The major results for the MAS with FNI are summarized as follows:

Theorem 8.1 *Consider the linear system* (8.1) *under Assumptions 8.1–8.5. If we design Γ_t such that the eigenvalues of $\Gamma_t C_{t+1} B_t$ are positive real number for all time instants, then the learning consensus scheme would guarantee* *that the input error of all agents converge to zero in the mean-square sense, i.e.,* $\lim_{k\to\infty}\mathbb{E}[\|u_d - u_k\|^2] = 0$. *Thus, the mean-square of tracking error of all agents* $\mathbb{E}[\|y_d(t) - y_k(t)\|]^2$ *converges to zero.*

Proof: The input error expression is derived form (8.13)

$$\begin{aligned}\Delta u_{k+1} &= \Delta u_k - \lambda_k \Psi_1 G \Delta u_k - \lambda_k \Upsilon_k \Psi_2 G \Delta u_k \\ &\quad + \lambda_k \Upsilon_k \Psi_2 Y_d - \lambda_k \Psi_3 \Omega_k. \end{aligned} \tag{8.14}$$

The regulation matrix Γ_t is selected such that the eigenvalues of $\Gamma_t C_{t+1} B_t$ are positive real number. According to the Lemma 8.2, we have the conclusion that $-(\mathcal{L}+\mathcal{D}) \otimes (\Gamma_t C_{t+1} B_t)$ is stable. Considering that $(\mathcal{L}+\mathcal{D}) \otimes (\Gamma_t C_{t+1} B_t)$ is the diagonal blocks of block lower-triangular matrix $\Psi_1 G$, we can obtain that the real part of all eigenvalues of $\Psi_1 G$ is positive. Define $\Xi \triangleq \Psi_1 G$. Then, the following equation holds:

$$\Xi^T \mathcal{P} + \Xi \mathcal{P} = I,$$

where the positive-definite matrix $\mathcal{P}$ satisfies that $\mathcal{P} = \int_0^\infty e^{-[\Xi^T + \Xi]t} dt$.

Define a Lyapunov function $V_k = (\Delta u_k^T)\mathcal{P}(\Delta u_k)$. Substituting the input error expression (8.14) into the Lyapunov function, we obtain:

$$\begin{aligned} V_{k+1} &= \Delta u_{k+1}^T \mathcal{P} \Delta u_{k+1} \\ &= (\Delta u_k)^T \mathcal{P}(\Delta u_k) + \lambda_k^2 (\Delta u_k)^T \Xi^T \mathcal{P} \Xi (\Delta u_k) \\ &\quad + \lambda_k^2 (\Delta u_k)^T [\Upsilon_k \Psi_2 G]^T \mathcal{P} [\Upsilon_k \Psi_2 G](\Delta u_k) \\ &\quad + \lambda_k^2 Y_d^T [\Upsilon_k \Psi_2]^T \mathcal{P} [\Upsilon_k \Psi_2] Y_d + \lambda_k^2 \Omega_k^T \Psi_3^T \mathcal{P} \Psi_3 \Omega_k \\ &\quad - \lambda_k (\Delta u_k)^T [\Xi^T \mathcal{P} + \mathcal{P} \Xi](\Delta u_k) \\ &\quad - \lambda_k (\Delta u_k)^T \{[\Upsilon_k \Psi_2 G]^T \mathcal{P} + \mathcal{P}[\Upsilon_k \Psi_2 G]\}(\Delta u_k) \\ &\quad + 2\lambda_k (\Delta u_k)^T \mathcal{P} [\Upsilon_k \Psi_2] Y_d - 2\lambda_k (\Delta u_k)^T \mathcal{P} \Psi_3 \Omega_k \\ &\quad + 2\lambda_k^2 (\Delta u_k)^T \Xi^T \mathcal{P} [\Upsilon_k \Psi_2 G](\Delta u_k) \\ &\quad - 2\lambda_k^2 (\Delta u_k)^T \Xi^T \mathcal{P} [\Upsilon_k \Psi_2] Y_d \\ &\quad + 2\lambda_k^2 (\Delta u_k)^T \Xi^T \mathcal{P} \Psi_3 \Omega_k \\ &\quad - 2\lambda_k^2 (\Delta u_k)^T [\Upsilon_k \Psi_2 G]^T \mathcal{P} [\Upsilon_k \Psi_2] Y_d \\ &\quad + 2\lambda_k^2 (\Delta u_k)^T [\Upsilon_k \Psi_2 G]^T \mathcal{P} \Psi_3 \Omega_k \\ &\quad - 2\lambda_k^2 Y_d^T [\Upsilon_k \Psi_2]^T \mathcal{P} \Psi_3 \Omega_k. \end{aligned} \tag{8.15}$$

We define an increasing σ-algebra $\mathcal{F}_k \triangleq \sigma\{x_{l,j},\ u_{l,j}(t),\ y_{l,j}(t),\ \theta_{l,j,i}(t),\ \omega_{l,j,i}(t),\ 0 \le t \le N, 1 \le l \le k, 1 \le j,i \le n\}$. Obviously, $\Delta u_k \in \mathcal{F}_{k-1}$, while Υ_k and Ω_k are independent from $\mathcal{F}_{k-1}$. Therefore, by the definition of Υ_k and Ω_k, we know that $\mathbb{E}[\Upsilon_k] = 0$ and $\mathbb{E}[\Omega_k] = 0$. Therefore, we have:

$$\mathbb{E}[(\Delta u_k)^T\{[\Upsilon_k\Psi_2 G]^T\mathcal{P} + \mathcal{P}[\Upsilon_k\Psi_2 G]\}(\Delta u_k)|\mathcal{F}_{k-1}] = 0, \tag{8.16}$$

$$\mathbb{E}[(\Delta u_k)^T\mathcal{P}[\Upsilon_k\Psi_2]Y_d|\mathcal{F}_{k-1}] = 0, \tag{8.17}$$

$$\mathbb{E}[(\Delta u_k)^T\Xi^T\mathcal{P}[\Upsilon_k\Psi_2 G](\Delta u_k)|\mathcal{F}_{k-1}] = 0, \tag{8.18}$$

$$\mathbb{E}[(\Delta u_k)^T\Xi^T\mathcal{P}[\Upsilon_k\Psi_2]Y_d|\mathcal{F}_{k-1}] = 0, \tag{8.19}$$

$$\mathbb{E}[(\Delta u_k)^T\mathcal{P}\Psi_3\Omega_k|\mathcal{F}_{k-1}] = 0, \tag{8.20}$$

$$\mathbb{E}[(\Delta u_k)^T\Xi^T\mathcal{P}\Psi_3\Omega_k|\mathcal{F}_{k-1}] = 0, \tag{8.21}$$

$$\mathbb{E}[(\Delta u_k)^T[\Upsilon_k\Psi_2 G]^T\mathcal{P}\Psi_3\Omega_k|\mathcal{F}_{k-1}] = 0, \tag{8.22}$$

$$\mathbb{E}[Y_d^T[\Upsilon_k\Psi_2]^T\mathcal{P}\Psi_3\Omega_k|\mathcal{F}_{k-1}] = 0. \tag{8.23}$$

Moreover,

$$\begin{aligned}
&\mathbb{E}[(\Delta u_k)^T\Xi^T\mathcal{P}\Xi(\Delta u_k)|\mathcal{F}_{k-1}] \\
&\quad \le (\Delta u_k)^T\mathbb{E}[\Xi^T\mathcal{P}\Xi|\mathcal{F}_{k-1}](\Delta u_k) \\
&\quad \le \rho_1(\Delta u_k)^T\mathcal{P}(\Delta u_k) = \rho_1 V_k, \qquad (8.24)\\
&\mathbb{E}[(\Delta u_k)^T[\Upsilon_k\Psi_2 G]^T\mathcal{P}[\Upsilon_k\Psi_2 G](\Delta u_k)|\mathcal{F}_{k-1}] \\
&\quad \le (\Delta u_k)^T\mathbb{E}\{[\Upsilon_k\Psi_2 G]^T\mathcal{P}[\Upsilon_k\Psi_2 G]|\mathcal{F}_{k-1}\}(\Delta u_k) \\
&\quad \le \rho_2(\Delta u_k)^T\mathcal{P}(\Delta u_k) = \rho_2 V_k, \qquad (8.25)\\
&\mathbb{E}[Y_d^T[\Upsilon_k\Psi_2]^T\mathcal{P}[\Upsilon_k\Psi_2]Y_d|\mathcal{F}_{k-1}] \le \rho_3, \qquad (8.26)\\
&\mathbb{E}[\Omega_k^T\Psi_3^T\mathcal{P}\Psi_3\Omega_k|\mathcal{F}_{k-1}] \le \rho_4, \qquad (8.27)
\end{aligned}$$

where $\rho_* \ge 0, * = 1,2,3,4$ are the appropriate constants.

$$\begin{aligned}
&\mathbb{E}[(\Delta u_k)^T[\Xi^T\mathcal{P} + \mathcal{P}\Xi](\Delta u_k)|\mathcal{F}_{k-1}] \\
&= \mathbb{E}[(\Delta u_k)^T(\Delta u_k)|\mathcal{F}_{k-1}] \\
&\quad \ge \rho_5(\Delta u_k)^T\mathcal{P}(\Delta u_k) = \rho_5 V_k,
\end{aligned} \tag{8.28}$$

where ρ_5 is selected such that $I \ge \rho_5\mathcal{P}$.

Using the basic inequality $2ab \le a^2 + b^2$, we have:

$$\mathbb{E}[-2(\Delta u_k)^T[\Upsilon_k\Psi_2 G]^T\mathcal{P}[\Upsilon_k\Psi_2]Y_d|\mathcal{F}_{k-1}] \le \rho_2 V_k + \rho_3. \tag{8.29}$$

Combining (8.15)–(8.29) results in

$$\mathbb{E}[V_{k+1}|\mathcal{F}_{k-1}] \leq V_k - \lambda_k \rho_5 V_k + \lambda_k^2(\rho_1 + 2\rho_2)V_k + \lambda_k^2(2\rho_3 + \rho_4). \tag{8.30}$$

Taking the mathematical expectation to (8.30), we have

$$\mathbb{E}[V_{k+1}] \leq (1 - p_k)\mathbb{E}[V_k] + q_k, \tag{8.31}$$

where $p_k = \lambda_k[\rho_5 - \lambda_k(\rho_1 + 2\rho_3)]$ and $q_k = \lambda_k^2(2\rho_3 + \rho_4)$. We correspond $\mathbb{E}[V_k], p_k$, and q_k to ξ_k, τ_k, χ_k in Lemma A.3, respectively. Note that $\lambda_k \to 0$, thus for adequately large integer k, we can obtain $\lambda_k(\rho_1 + 2\rho_3) \leq \frac{1}{2}\rho_5$. Then, we have $p_k \geq \frac{\rho_5}{2}\lambda_k$. Therefore, it is evident that $0 < p_k \leq 1$ for sufficiently large k, $p_k \to 0$, and $\sum_{k=1}^{\infty} p_k = \infty$.

For q_k, it is clear that $q_k \geq 0$. In addition:

$$\begin{aligned}\frac{q_k}{p_k} &= \frac{\lambda_k^2(2\rho_3 + \rho_4)}{\lambda_k[\rho_5 - \lambda_k(\rho_1 + 2\rho_3)]} \leq \frac{\lambda_k^2(2\rho_3 + \rho_4)}{\lambda_k \rho_5} \\ &\leq \frac{(2\rho_3 + \rho_4)}{\rho_5}\lambda_k \xrightarrow[k\to\infty]{} 0.\end{aligned}$$

By Lemma A.3, we can conclude that $\mathbb{E}[V_k] \to 0$ as k goes to infinity. Moreover, since $\mathcal{P}$ is positive definite, one can conclude that $\mathbb{E}[\|u_d - u_k\|^2] \leq \lambda_{min}^{-1}(\mathcal{P})\mathbb{E}[V_k]$. It implies that $\lim_{k\to\infty}\mathbb{E}[\|u_d - u_k\|^2] = 0$. The agent dynamics is without random noise, thus $\lim_{k\to\infty}\mathbb{E}[\|y_d - y_k\|^2] = 0$ is straightforward. □

Theorem 8.1 reveals that the proposed learning consensus tracking scheme can achieve consensus convergence of the MAS with FNI. From the proof, we observe that the unbiased correction of the received signals is realized by using a preliminary correction mechanism. In addition, the effect of channel randomness on the convergence of the system is successfully suppressed by decreasing the learning gain. The effectiveness of the learning consensus scheme will be further verified through simulations in Section 8.5.

Remark 8.2 *The eigenvalue requirement of $\Gamma_t C_{t+1} B_t$ in the Theorem 8.1 is to guarantee the consensus convergence of MAS. Based on the Lemma 8.2, it can be found that the network structure information $\mathcal{L} + \mathcal{D}$ is not necessary for establishing the design conditions of the regulation matrix to ensure the consensus tracking. In other words, the precise consensus tracking can be achieved without network structure information, which relaxes the restriction of convergence condition. The matrix Γ_t can be obtained by solving a linear matrix inequality $\Gamma_t C_{t+1} B_t > 0$ if matrices B_t and C_{t+1} are available.*

Otherwise, these matrices B_t and C_t can be estimated and used to derive the calculation of Γ_t. It has been shown that the estimated model has certain tolerance of model uncertainty [7], which guarantees the feasibility of the selection of Γ_t.

To demonstrate the convergence performance of learning control schemes, we present a rough estimate of the convergence rate for $\mathbb{E}[V_k]$. Taking the sum of (8.31) from $k = 1$ to an arbitrary integer m, we have

$$\sum_{k=1}^{m} \mathbb{E}[V_{k+1}] \leq \sum_{k=1}^{m} \mathbb{E}[V_k] - \sum_{k=1}^{m} p_k \mathbb{E}[V_k] + \sum_{k=1}^{m} q_k.$$

By Theorem 8.1, we obtain that $\mathbb{E}[V_k]$ is bounded and then $\sum_{k=1}^{\infty} \lambda_k^2 \mathbb{E}[V_k] < \infty$. Substituting $p_k = \lambda_k[\rho_5 - \lambda_k(\rho_1 + 2\rho_3)]$ into the above equation, we have

$$\begin{aligned}\sum_{k=1}^{m} \lambda_k \mathbb{E}[V_k] &\leq \rho_5^{-1}(\mathbb{E}[V_1] + (\rho_1 + 2\rho_3)\sum_{k=1}^{m} \lambda_k^2 \mathbb{E}[V_k]) + \sum_{k=1}^{m} q_k \\ &< \rho_5^{-1}(\mathbb{E}[V_1] + (\rho_1 + 2\rho_3)\sum_{k=1}^{\infty} \lambda_k^2 \mathbb{E}[V_k]) + \sum_{k=1}^{\infty} q_k \\ &< \infty.\end{aligned}$$

Letting $m \to \infty$, we have $\sum_{k=1}^{\infty} \lambda_k \mathbb{E}[V_k] < \infty$. Moreover, by the Kronecker Lemma, it can be further deduced that $\lim_{k\to\infty} \lambda_k \sum_{i=1}^{k} \mathbb{E}[V_i] = 0$. Therefore, an estimate of the convergence rate is given by

$$\frac{1}{k}\sum_{i=1}^{k} \sqrt{\mathbb{E}[V_i]} \leq \frac{1}{\sqrt{k\lambda_k}} \left(\lambda_k \sum_{i=1}^{k} \mathbb{E}[V_i]\right)^{1/2} = o\left(\frac{1}{\sqrt{k\lambda_k}}\right).$$

To reveal the effect of random fading and channel noise on the convergence, we remove the correction mechanism from the proposed scheme. In other words, we remove the term μ^{-1} from (8.5), i.e., $\overline{z}_{k,j,i}(t) = z_{k,j,i}(t)$. Therefore, we remove μ^{-1} from Υ_k and Ω_k leading to $\overline{\Upsilon}_k$ and $\overline{\Omega}_k$, whose component blocks are $\overline{\Upsilon}_k(t) = \text{diag}\{1 - \theta_{k,1,i}(t), 1 - \theta_{k,2,i}(t), \cdots, 1 - \theta_{k,n,i}(t)\} \otimes I_p$ and $\overline{\Omega}_k(t) = [\omega_{k,1}^T(t), \omega_{k,2}^T(t), \cdots, \omega_{k,n}^T(t)]^T$. Then, differing from the case with a correction mechanism, we have $\mathbb{E}[\Upsilon_k] \neq 0$ and bounded second-order moment. Then, inequalities (8.25)-(8.27) and (8.29) become

$$\begin{aligned}&\mathbb{E}[(\Delta u_k)^T [\overline{\Upsilon}_k \Psi_2 G]^T \mathcal{P} [\overline{\Upsilon}_k \Psi_2 G](\Delta u_k) | \mathcal{F}_{k-1}] \\ &\leq (\Delta u_k)^T \mathbb{E}\{[\Psi_2 G]^T \overline{\Upsilon}_k^T \mathcal{P} \overline{\Upsilon}_k [\Psi_2 G] | \mathcal{F}_{k-1}\}(\Delta u_k) \leq \rho_6 V_k,\end{aligned}$$

$$\mathbb{E}[Y_d^T[\overline{\Upsilon}_k\Psi_2]^T\mathcal{P}[\overline{\Upsilon}_k\Psi_2]Y_d|\mathcal{F}_{k-1}] \triangleq \rho_7,$$
$$\mathbb{E}[\overline{\Omega}_k^T\Psi_3^T\mathcal{P}\Psi_3\overline{\Omega}_k|\mathcal{F}_{k-1}] \leq \lambda_{\max}(\mathcal{P})\sigma_\omega^2\|\Psi_3\|^2 \triangleq \rho_8,$$
$$\mathbb{E}[-2(\Delta u_k)^T[\overline{\Upsilon}_k\Psi_2 G]^T\mathcal{P}[\overline{\Upsilon}_k\Psi_2]Y_d|\mathcal{F}_{k-1}] \leq \rho_6 V_k + \rho_7,$$

where ρ_i, $6 \leq i \leq 8$ are the appropriate constants and σ_ω^2 denotes the variance of channel additive noise $\omega_{k,j,i}(t)$. Accordingly, inequalities (8.16)-(8.19) become

$$\mathbb{E}[(\Delta u_k)^T\{[\overline{\Upsilon}_k\Psi_2 G]^T\mathcal{P}+\mathcal{P}[\overline{\Upsilon}_k\Psi_2 G]\}(\Delta u_k)|\mathcal{F}_{k-1}] \leq V_k + \rho_6 V_k,$$
$$\mathbb{E}[(\Delta u_k)^T\mathcal{P}[\overline{\Upsilon}_k\Psi_2]Y_d|\mathcal{F}_{k-1}] \leq V_k + \rho_7,$$
$$\mathbb{E}[(\Delta u_k)^T\Xi^T\mathcal{P}[\overline{\Upsilon}_k\Psi_2 G](\Delta u_k)|\mathcal{F}_{k-1}] \leq \rho_1 V_k + \rho_6 V_k,$$
$$\mathbb{E}[(\Delta u_k)^T\Xi^T\mathcal{P}[\overline{\Upsilon}_k\Psi_2]Y_d|\mathcal{F}_{k-1}] \leq \rho_1 V_k + \rho_7.$$

Then

$$\mathbb{E}[V_{k+1}|\mathcal{F}_{k-1}] \leq V_k - \lambda_k(\rho_5+\rho_6+2)V_k + 3\lambda_k^2(\rho_1 + \rho_6)V_k + \lambda_k^2[3\rho_7+\rho_8] + \lambda_k\rho_7.$$

Define $p_k \triangleq \lambda_k(\rho_5+\rho_6+2) - 3\lambda_k^2(\rho_1+\rho_6)$ and $q_k \triangleq \lambda_k^2[3\rho_7+\rho_8] + \lambda_k\rho_7$. Then, we have

$$\mathbb{E}[V_{k+1}] \leq (1-p_k)\mathbb{E}[V_k] + q_k.$$

Notice that

$$\lim_{k\to\infty}\frac{q_k}{p_k} = \frac{\lambda_k(3\rho_7+\rho_8)+\rho_7}{(\rho_5+\rho_6+2)-3\lambda_k(\rho_1+\rho_6)} \neq 0.$$

Therefore, the zero-error convergence of the input error of all agents in the mean square sense cannot be ensured without a correction mechanism.

Define $\tilde{\lambda} \triangleq \lim_{k\to\infty}\lambda_k$. We have

$$\lim_{k\to\infty}\mathbb{E}[\Delta u_k^T\Delta u_k] \leq \frac{q_{\max}}{\lambda_{\min}(\mathcal{P})p_{\min}},$$

where $q_{\max} \triangleq \tilde{\lambda}(3\rho_7+\rho_8)+\rho_7$ and $p_{\min} \triangleq (\rho_5+\rho_6+2) - 3\tilde{\lambda}(\rho_1+\rho_6)$. If we consider the constant learning gain $\lambda_k \equiv \lambda$, the upper bound in the above estimate is not zero, indicating that a constant learning gain cannot guarantee the perfect consensus. If we consider a decreasing gain $\lambda_k \to 0$, i.e., $\tilde{\lambda} = 0$, the limit upper bound of $\mathbb{E}[\Delta u_k^T\Delta u_k]$ is $\rho_7/(2+\rho_5+\rho_6)$. Note that ρ_7 is determined by $\mathbb{E}[(1-\theta_{k,j,i}(t))^2]$, which is certainly nonzero when $\mu \neq 1$. Thus, the input error sequence cannot converge to zero if the correction mechanism is absent. This observation indicates the necessity of introducing a correction mechanism.

8.4 EXTENSION TO NONLINEAR SYSTEMS

In this section, the results for linear agent dynamics are comprehensively extended to nonlinear dynamics. In particular, three aspects of the problem have been significantly improved. First, the agent dynamics is extended to affine nonlinear type. Moreover, the identical initialization condition is replaced with an asymptotically identical initialization condition. This condition offers a freedom of practical design that an initial state learning mechanism can be introduced to realize this requirement. Last, the scalar learning gain γ_k in Section 8.3 is relaxed to be diverse for different agents. This relaxation offers the freedom for individual agent-related gain selection.

8.4.1 Problem Extensions and Learning Consensus Scheme

In particular, an affine nonlinear agent dynamics is considered as follows:

$$\begin{aligned} x_{k,j}(t+1) &= f(t,x_{k,j}(t)) + B_t u_{k,j}(t), \\ y_{k,j}(t) &= C_t x_{k,j}(t). \end{aligned} \tag{8.32}$$

The following assumptions on the nonlinear system and initial condition is imposed for further analysis.

Assumption 8.6 *The desired trajectory $y_d(t)$ is realizable, i.e., there exist an initial state $x_d(0)$ and input $u_d(t)$ such that*

$$\begin{aligned} x_d(t+1) &= f(t,x_d(t)) + B_t u_d(t), \\ y_d(t) &= C_t x_d(t). \end{aligned} \tag{8.33}$$

Assumption 8.7 *For any time instant t, the nonlinear function $f(t,x)$ is continuous with respect to x.*

Assumption 8.8 *For the jth agent, the initial state $x_{k,j}(0)$ converges to the desired state $x_d(0)$ as $k \to \infty$.*

In addition to the extension of systems, it could be readily found that the initial state condition is extended and the variable initial state is allowable. This condition relaxes i.i.c. from the aspect of repetition, where $x_{k,j}(0)$ does not coincide with $x_d(0)$ for any given iteration number k.

Therefore, we can obtain the tracking error expression:

$$e_k(t+1) = \Delta f_k(t) + E(t)\Delta u_k(t), \tag{8.34}$$

where

$$\begin{aligned}\Delta f_k(t) &= [(C_{t+1}\Delta f_{k,1}(t))^T, (C_{t+1}\Delta f_{k,2}(t))^T, \cdots, (C_{t+1}\Delta f_{k,n}(t))^T]^T,\\ \Delta f_{k,j}(t) &= f(t, x_d(t)) - f(t, x_{k,j}(t)),\\ E(t) &= I_n \otimes (C_{t+1}B_t).\end{aligned}$$

Combining (8.9) and (8.34), we have

$$\begin{aligned}u_{k+1}(t) = u_k(t) &+ \Lambda_k[(\mathcal{L}+\mathcal{D})\otimes\Gamma_t]E(t)\Delta u_k(t)\\ &+ \Lambda_k[(\mathcal{L}+\mathcal{D})\otimes\Gamma_t]\Delta f_k(t)\\ &+ \Lambda_k\Upsilon_k(t+1)[\mathcal{A}_c\otimes\Gamma_t]E(t)\Delta u_k(t)\\ &+ \Lambda_k\Upsilon_k(t+1)[\mathcal{A}_c\otimes\Gamma_t]\Delta f_k(t)\\ &- \Lambda_k\Upsilon_k(t+1)[\mathcal{A}_c\otimes\Gamma_t]\times[1_n\otimes y_d(t+1)]\\ &+ \Lambda_k[\mathcal{A}_r\otimes\Gamma_t]\Omega_k(t+1),\end{aligned} \tag{8.35}$$

where $\Lambda_k = \text{diag}\{\lambda_{k,1}, \lambda_{k,2}, \cdots, \lambda_{k,np}\}$ is a decreasing gain matrix that the diagonal elements satisfy the condition of λ_k in the linear case. In particular, for any $1 \leq i, j \leq nq$, $\lambda_{k,i}$ and $\lambda_{k,j}$ are infinitesimals of the same order, i.e., $\lim_{k\to\infty}\lambda_{k,i}/\lambda_{k,j} = h$ (h is a positive constant).

Remark 8.3 *The decreasing gain matrix Λ_k is the general formulation of decreasing gain sequence $\{\lambda_k\}$ used in update law* (8.7). *In particular, $\{\lambda_k\}$ is considered to be a scale variable that exerts the same influence on each dimension of tracking errors in each agent. This general formulation means that the learning gains used in different dimensions of different agents can be adjusted according to the practical application, respectively. Thus, the algorithm efficiency will be improved by selecting each learning gain reasonably.*

For the sake of simplicity, we define $\Phi_1(t) = [(\mathcal{L}+\mathcal{D})\otimes\Gamma_t]$, $\Phi_2(t) = [\mathcal{A}_c\otimes\Gamma_t]$, $\Phi_3(t) = [\mathcal{A}_r\otimes\Gamma_t]$ and $Y_d(t) = [1_n\otimes y_d(t+1)]$. Then, (8.35) can be rewritten as follows:

$$\begin{aligned}u_{k+1}(t) =& u_k(t) + \Lambda_k\Phi_1(t)E(t)\Delta u_k(t) + \Lambda_k\Phi_1(t)\Delta f_k(t)\\ &- \Lambda_k\Upsilon_k(t+1)\Phi_2(t)Y_d(t+1) + \Lambda_k\Phi_3(t)\Omega_k(t+1)\\ &+ \Lambda_k\Upsilon_k(t+1)\Phi_2(t)\Delta f_k(t)\\ &+ \Lambda_k\Upsilon_k(t+1)\Phi_2(t)E(t)\Delta u_k(t).\end{aligned} \tag{8.36}$$

Remark 8.4 *The major difference between linear case* (8.13) *and nonlinear case* (8.36) *lies in the nonlinear terms $\Lambda_k\Phi_1(t)\Delta f_k(t)$ and $\Lambda_k\Upsilon_k(t+1)\Phi_2(t)\Delta f_k(t)$. Furthermore, the lifting technique is no longer applicable in* (8.36) *because of the inherent nonlinearity. In this case, the impacts of the state at the previous time instants should be thoroughly dealt with.*

Remark 8.5 *We should emphasize that the channel additive noise is assumed to be white to simplify the technical derivations. If colored stationary noise is involved in the communication channels, introducing an estimation mechanism can help guarantee the effectiveness of the proposed scheme. In particular, we may establish an online or offline estimation method, possibly with pilot signals, to obtain the estimate of the mean of the colored noise, which should be asymptotically consistent to the actual value. Then, the colored noise can be transformed into white noise and the proposed scheme is applicable.*

8.4.2 Performance Analysis

Before the convergence analysis, the following lemma is provided:

Lemma 8.3 *For the nonlinear system* (8.32), *Assumptions 8.6–8.8 are maintained. Assume that* $\lim_{k\to\infty}\Delta u_k(m) = 0$ *when* $0 \le m \le t$. *Then, for* $m = t+1$, $\|\Delta x_k(t+1)\|$ *and* $\|\Delta f_k(t+1)\|$ *converge to 0 as* $k \to 0$ *for all* j, $1 \le j \le n$.

The proof is straightforward. Then, the extended result for the nonlinear system is summarized in the following theorem:

Theorem 8.2 *Consider the nonlinear system* (8.32) *under Assumption 8.1–8.3 and 8.6–8.8. If we design* Γ_t *such that the eigenvalues of* $\Gamma_t C_{t+1} B_t$ *are positive real number for all time instants, then the learning consensus scheme would guarantee that the input error of all agents converges to zero in the mean-square sense, i.e.,* $\lim_{k\to\infty}\mathbb{E}[\|u_d(t)-u_k(t)\|^2] = 0$. *Thus, the mean-square of tracking error of all agents* $\mathbb{E}[\|y_d(t)-y_k(t)\|]^2$ *converges to zero.*

Proof: For a nonlinear system, the lifting method used in Theorem 8.1 to prove the convergence of all time dimensions is no longer applicable. Instead, the consistent convergence for nonlinear systems is proved by induction. In particular, we first prove the convergence of the input error for $t = 0$. Then, we need to prove that it holds for time $t = s$ under the assumption that the convergence has been proved at the previous time instants.

Initial Step: Since $\lambda_{k,i}$ and $\lambda_{k,1}$ are infinitesimals of the same order, $\forall 1 \le i \le pn$, we have

$$
\begin{aligned}
\Lambda_k &= \text{diag}\{\lambda_{k,1}, \lambda_{k,2}, \cdots, \lambda_{k,pn}\} \\
&= \lambda_{k,1}\text{diag}\{1, \frac{\lambda_{k,2}}{\lambda_{k,1}}, \cdots, \frac{\lambda_{k,qn}}{\lambda_{k,1}}\} \\
&\le \lambda_{k,1}\text{diag}\{1, h_{k,2}, \cdots, h_{k,pn}\} = \lambda_{k,1} H_k,
\end{aligned}
$$

where $h_{k,i} \triangleq \sup_{1\le j\le k}\{\lambda_{k,i}/\lambda_{k,1}\}$ represents the upper bound of the ratio of decreasing gain $\lambda_{k,i}$ to $\lambda_{k,1}$. Moreover, $H_k = \text{diag}\{1, h_{k,2}, \cdots, h_{k,pn}\}$ is a positive-definite matrix. Then, (8.36) can be rewritten as follows:

$$
\begin{aligned}
&\Delta u_{k+1}(0)\\
&\le \Delta u_k(0) - \lambda_{k,1}\underbrace{[H_k\Phi_1(0)E(0) - H_k\Upsilon_k(1)\Phi_2(0)E(0)]}_{M_{u,0}}\Delta u_k(0)\\
&\quad - \lambda_{k,1}\underbrace{[H_k\Phi_1(0) - H_k\Upsilon_k(1)\Phi_2(0)]}_{M_{f,0}}\Delta f_k(0)\\
&\quad + \lambda_{k,1}\underbrace{[H_k\Upsilon_k(1)\Phi_2(0)Y_d(1) - H_k\Phi_3(0)\Omega_k(1)]}_{M_{\omega,0}}\\
&\le \Delta u_k(0) - \lambda_{k,1}M_{u,0}\Delta u_k(0) - \lambda_{k,1}M_{f,0}\Delta f_k(0) + \lambda_{k,1}M_{\omega,0}.
\end{aligned}
\tag{8.37}
$$

Comparing (8.15) and (8.37), we can realize that the major difference lies in the expressions containing the nonlinear term $\Delta f_k(0)$. Define $\Xi(t) \triangleq H_k\Phi_1(t)E(t)$. There exists a positive definite matrix $\mathcal{P}(0)$ that satisfies $\Xi(0)^T\mathcal{P}(0) + \Xi(0)\mathcal{P}(0) = I$. Construct a Lyapunov function $V_k(0) = \Delta u_k^T(0)\mathcal{P}(0)\Delta u_k(0)$. Then, we have:

$$
\begin{aligned}
V_{k+1}(0) &= \Delta u_{k+1}^T(0)\mathcal{P}(0)\Delta u_{k+1}(0)\\
&\le \Delta u_k^T(0)\mathcal{P}(0)\Delta u_k(0) + \lambda_k^2\Delta u_k^T(0)M_{u,0}^T\mathcal{P}(0)M_{u,0}\Delta u_k(0)\\
&\quad + \lambda_{k,1}^2\Delta f_k^T(0)M_{f,0}^T\mathcal{P}(0)M_{f,0}\Delta f_k(0) + \lambda_k^2 M_{\omega,0}^T\mathcal{P}(0)M_{\omega,0}\\
&\quad - \lambda_{k,1}\Delta u_k^T(0)[M_{u,0}^T\mathcal{P}(0) + \mathcal{P}(0)M_{u,0}]\Delta u_k(0)\\
&\quad - 2\lambda_{k,1}\Delta u_k^T(0)\mathcal{P}(0)M_{f,0}\Delta f_k(0) + 2\lambda_k\Delta u_k^T(0)\mathcal{P}(0)M_{\omega,0}\\
&\quad + 2\lambda_{k,1}^2\Delta u_k^T(0)M_{u,0}^T\mathcal{P}(0)M_{f,0}\Delta f_k(0)\\
&\quad - 2\lambda_{k,1}^2[\Delta u_k^T(0)M_{u,0}^T - \Delta f_k(0)^T M_{f,0}^T]\mathcal{P}(0)M_{\omega,0}.
\end{aligned}
\tag{8.38}
$$

Similar to the linear case, we still utilize an increasing σ-algebra $\mathcal{F}_k$. Obviously, $\Delta u_k(0) \in \mathcal{F}_{k-1}$, while $\Upsilon_k(1)$ and $\Omega_k(1)$ are independent with $\mathcal{F}_{k-1}$. Then, we can obtain:

$$\mathbb{E}[\Delta u_k^T(0)M_{u,0}^T\mathcal{P}(0)M_{u,0}\Delta u_k(0)|\mathcal{F}_{k-1}] \le \rho_1 V_k(0), \tag{8.39}$$

$$\mathbb{E}[M_{\omega,0}^T\mathcal{P}(0)M_{\omega,0}|\mathcal{F}_{k-1}] \le \rho_2, \tag{8.40}$$

$$\mathbb{E}[\Delta u_k^T(0)\mathcal{P}(0)M_{\omega,0}|\mathcal{F}_{k-1}] = 0, \tag{8.41}$$

$$
\begin{aligned}
&\mathbb{E}[\Delta u_k^T(0)[M_{u,0}^T\mathcal{P}(0) + \mathcal{P}(0)M_{u,0}]\Delta u_k(0)|\mathcal{F}_{k-1}]\\
&= \mathbb{E}[\Delta u_k^T(0)[\Xi(0)^T\mathcal{P}(0) + \mathcal{P}(0)\Xi(0)]\Delta u_k(0)|\mathcal{F}_{k-1}]
\end{aligned}
$$

$$\geq \rho_3 V_k(0), \tag{8.42}$$

$$\mathbb{E}[2\Delta u_k^T(0)M_{u,0}\mathcal{P}(0)M_{\omega,0}|\mathcal{F}_{k-1}] \leq \rho_1 V_k(0) + \rho_2. \tag{8.43}$$

Define $m_k \triangleq \|\Delta f_k(0)\| \to 0$. We have:

$$\mathbb{E}[\Delta f_k^T(0)M_{f,0}^T\mathcal{P}(0)M_{f,0}\Delta f_k(0)] \leq \rho_4 m_k^2, \tag{8.44}$$

$$\mathbb{E}[2\Delta f_k(0)^T M_{f,0}^T\mathcal{P}(0)M_{\omega,0}|\mathcal{F}_{k-1}] \leq \rho_2 + \rho_4 m_k^2, \tag{8.45}$$

$$\mathbb{E}[2\Delta u_k^T(0)M_{u,0}^T\mathcal{P}(0)M_{f,0}\Delta f_k(0)|\mathcal{F}_{k-1}]$$
$$\leq \rho_1 V_k(0) + \rho_4 m_k^2, \tag{8.46}$$

where $\rho_* \geq 0$, $1 \leq * \leq 4$ are suitable constants.

Moreover, by the inequality $2ab \leq \varsigma a^2 + \frac{1}{\varsigma}b^2$ we have

$$\mathbb{E}[-2\Delta u_k^T(0)\mathcal{P}(0)M_{f,0}\Delta f_k(0)|\mathcal{F}_{k-1}] \leq \varsigma V_k(0) + \frac{1}{\varsigma}\rho_4 m_k^2, \tag{8.47}$$

where $\varsigma > 0$ is a constant that will be discussed later.

Similar to the linear case, we have:

$$\mathbb{E}[V_{k+1}(0)] \leq (1 - p_k)\mathbb{E}[V_k(0)] + q_k, \tag{8.48}$$

where $p_k = \lambda_{k,1}[\rho_3 - \varsigma - \lambda_{k,1}(3\rho_1 + 2\rho_2)]$ and $q_k = \lambda_{k,1}^2(2\rho_2 + 3\rho_4 m_k^2) + \lambda_{k,1}\frac{1}{\varsigma}\rho_4 m_k^2$. We correspond $\mathbb{E}[V_k(0)], p_k$, and q_k to ξ_k, τ_k, χ_k in Lemma A.3, respectively. Therefore, by the analysis given in Theorem 8.1, we obtain $\lim_{k\to\infty}\mathbb{E}[\|u_d(0) - u_k(0)\|^2] = 0$.

Inductive Step: For $t = 0, 1, \cdots, s-1$, the convergence results that $\lim_{k\to\infty}\mathbb{E}[\|u_d(t) - u_k(t)\|^2] = 0$ are assumed to be proved. Then, we continue to prove the convergence of $\Delta u_k(t)$ for $t = s$. For $t = s$, according to Lemma 8.3, we have $\lim_{k\to\infty}\Delta x_k(m) = 0$ and $\lim_{k\to\infty}\Delta f_k(m) = 0$. Referring to the case of $t = 0$, it can be concluded that $\lim_{k\to\infty}\mathbb{E}[\|u_d(s) - u_k(s)\|^2] = 0$. Since the agent dynamics is without random noise, it can be further deduced that $\lim_{k\to\infty}\mathbb{E}[\|y_d(s) - y_k(s)\|^2] = 0$. This completes the proof. □

Remark 8.6 *We make some clarifications of fading effect between the linear and nonlinear system cases. First of all, the inherent principle for establishing the convergence is the same for both cases. That is, the random disturbances generated by fading channels is suppressed by the decreasing gain, which is essential to guarantee the iteration-wise convergence. The primary difference lies in the fact that nonlinear terms of the input/state error is introduced to the nonlinear agent case, which cannot be treated as a random*

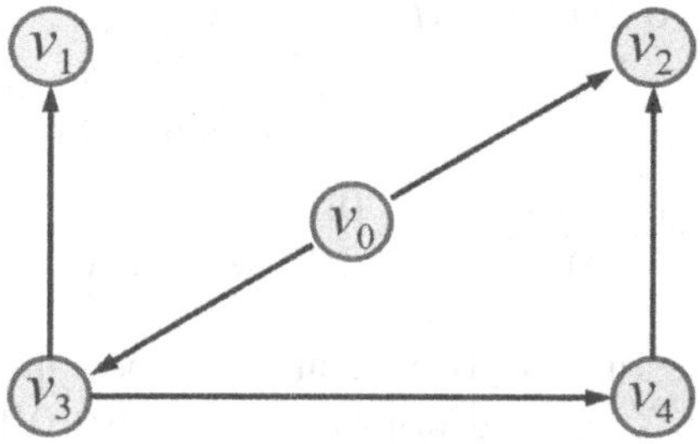

Figure 8.2 Topology diagram of the multi-agent system.

variable similarly to the linear agent case. Due to the existence of these nonlinear terms, the induction principle is applied with respect to the time axis and the coupling effect of nonlinear dynamics and randomness is carefully examined.

8.5 SIMULATIONS

We first present a numerical simulation on an MIMO time-varying system, where the influences of various factors are carefully analyzed. Then, we present the simulation on a nonlinear system. In particular, we consider a MAS with a topology as shown in Fig. 8.2, where v_0 represents the virtual leader and v_i denotes the ith agent. Fig. 8.2 shows that v_2 and v_3 have a direct connection with v_0 and can directly receive the reference information. On the other hand, v_1 and v_4 cannot directly obtain the desired trajectory information, but they can exchange information with v_2 and v_3, respectively. Therefore, from the graph theory, we have

$$\mathcal{L}=\begin{bmatrix} 1 & 0 & -1 & 0 \\ 0 & 1 & 0 & -1 \\ 0 & 0 & 0 & 0 \\ 0 & 0 & -1 & 1 \end{bmatrix}, \quad \mathcal{D}=\begin{bmatrix} 0 & 0 & 0 & 0 \\ 0 & 1 & 0 & 0 \\ 0 & 0 & 1 & 0 \\ 0 & 0 & 0 & 0 \end{bmatrix}.$$

8.5.1 Linear Agent Dynamics

Consider a linear system as follows:

$$A_t=\begin{bmatrix} 0.04\sin 0.01t & -0.1 & 0.01t \\ 0.2 & -0.02t & -0.01\sin 0.5t \\ 0.1 & 0.1 & 0.2+0.05\cos 0.2t \end{bmatrix},$$

$$B_t = \begin{bmatrix} 1-0.2\sin^2 0.5\pi t & 0 \\ 0.01t & 0.01t \\ 0 & 1+0.1\sin 0.5\pi t \end{bmatrix},$$

$$C_t = \begin{bmatrix} 0.2+0.1\sin^2 0.5t & 0.1 & -0.1 \\ 0 & 0.1 & 0.4-0.1\sin 0.4\pi t \end{bmatrix}.$$

Let the algorithms run for 100 iterations. The random fading variable $\theta_{k,j,i}(t) \sim N(0.95, 0.1^2)$ and the noise $\omega_k(t) \sim N(0, 0.1^2)$. The decreasing learning gain sequence is set to be $\lambda_k = 0.4/k^{0.8}$. The reference trajectory and the regulation matrix are given as follows:

$$y_d(t) = \begin{bmatrix} 0.9\sin\frac{t}{3} + 0.5(1-\cos\frac{t}{4}) \\ -0.2\sin\frac{\pi}{12}t - 0.45\sin\pi 8t \end{bmatrix}, \quad t \in [0, 30],$$

$$L = \begin{bmatrix} 8.8-0.2\sin 0.5\pi t & 3 \\ -0.6 & 3-0.1\sin 0.5\pi t \end{bmatrix}.$$

Figs. 8.3 and 8.4 show the output of the two dimensions of the four agents in the system in different iteration batches. Fig. 8.3(a) and (b) shows the actual output and desired trajectory of all four agents in the second iteration. It can be viewed that in the early iterations of simulation, the output of the agents differs greatly from the desired trajectory. With the increase of iteration number, the output approaches to the desired trajectory. Fig. 8.4(a) and (b) shows the output of all agents in the 100th iteration. Compared with Fig. 8.3, it can be viewed that the outputs of the four agents in MAS have basically coincided with the expected trajectories and completed the consistency task.

Fig. 8.5 shows the Euclidean norm profiles of input error for all four agents along the iteration axis. The convergence results demonstrate that the consistent convergence goal of the system has been achieved. Note that the convergence performance of agent v_3 is better than the other three agents because agent v_3 only receives information from the virtual leader without any influence of the channel randomness. This observation implies that channel randomness may slow down the convergence rate. Moreover, the profiles of agents v_1, v_2, and v_4 are similar to each other. In addition, all the input error profiles keep a decreasing trend along the iteration axis, indicating the asymptotic convergence of the proposed scheme.

To illustrate the impacts of the channel fading on the tracking performance, we simulate three cases of the fading distributions, where the CAN

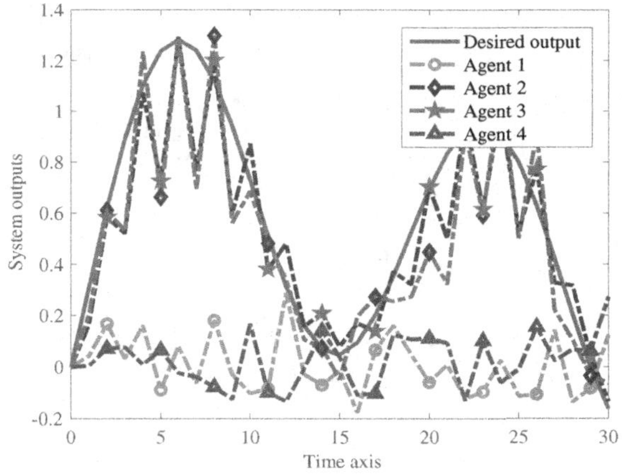

(a) 1st Dimension

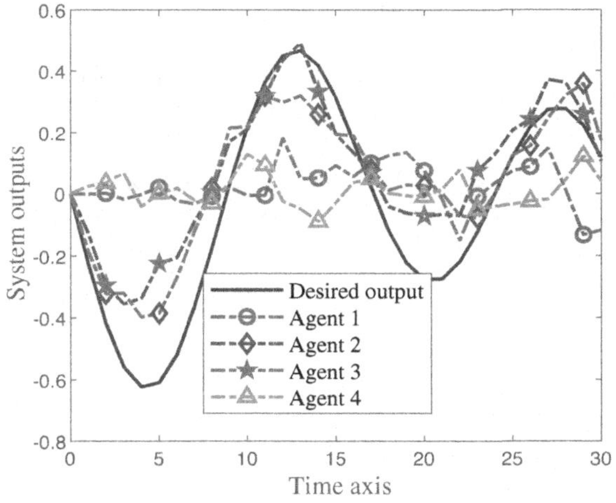

(b) 2nd Dimension

Figure 8.3 Output profiles of all four agents at the 2nd iteration: (a) 1st Dimension and (b) 2nd dimension.

$\omega_k(t)$ is removed to highlight the fading impact. First, three fading distributions with different mean μ and variance σ are considered: $N(0.95, 0.1^2)$, $N(0.95, 0.4^2)$, and $N(0.8, 0.1^2)$. Then, three types of fading distribution are considered: $\theta_{k,j,i} \sim N(0.95, 0.1^2)$, $\theta_{k,j,i} \sim Laplace(0.95, 0.1^2)$, and $\ln \theta_{k,j,i} \sim N(0.95, 0.1^2)$. Fig. 8.6 shows the Euclidean norm profiles of

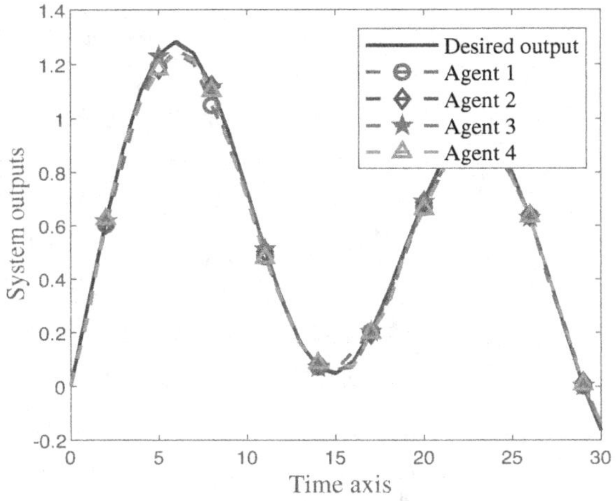

(a) 1st Dimension

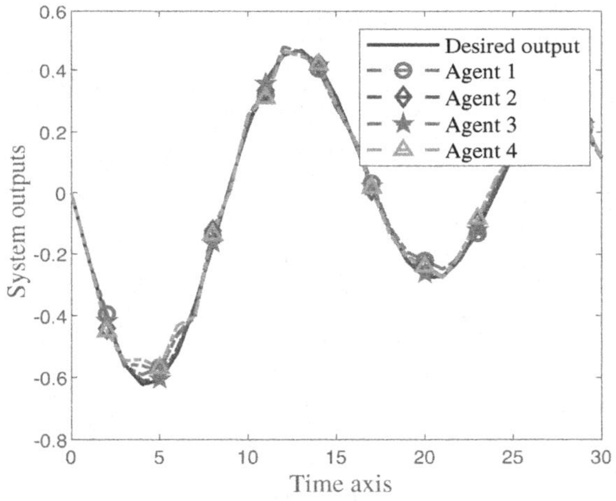

(b) 2nd Dimension

Figure 8.4 Output profiles of all four agents at the 100th iteration: (a) 1st Dimension and (b) 2nd dimension.

input errors. The convergence performance is generally similar to that of each other's, indicating the effectiveness of the proposed learning scheme. Moreover, the variance σ has a significant impact on the tracking performance. Specifically, the smaller fading gain variance corresponds to better tracking performance within finite learning iterations.

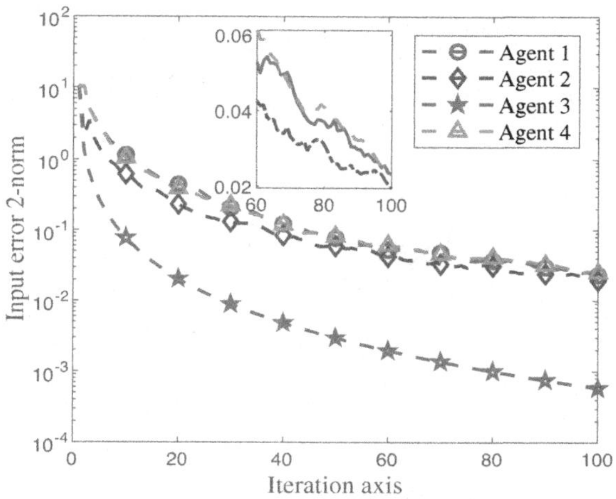

Figure 8.5 Norm profiles of the input error ($\|u_d - u_k\|^2/N$).

Finally, three different learning gain sequences are simulated to check the effect of the decreasing gain $\lambda_k = \alpha/k^{\beta}$. The following three cases are considered: $0.4/k^{0.6}$, $0.4/k^{0.9}$, and $0.2/k^{0.6}$. The Euclidean norm profiles of input errors are demonstrated in Fig. 8.7. Apparently, the input error converges slowly when α decreases or β increases. One of the reasons behind this might be the ability of the learning gain to correct the input becomes weaker after the change. This is just a group of experiments to explain the impact of different choices of learning gain, and the best choice for learning gain is worth further research.

8.5.2 Nonlinear Agent Dynamics

In this subsection, we consider a nonlinear DC-motor system from [66] to formulate the agent dynamics in a MAS, whose topology is described by Fig. 8.2. The state-space model of the DC-motor system is given by

$$f(x,t) = \begin{bmatrix} x_1(t) + \Delta x_2(t) \\ x_2(t) + \frac{\Delta}{J_m + J_l/n^2}\left[-\left(B_m + \frac{B_l}{n^2}\right)x_2(t) \right. \\ \left. -\frac{\text{Mgl}}{n}\sin\left(\frac{x_1(t)}{n}\right)\right] \end{bmatrix},$$

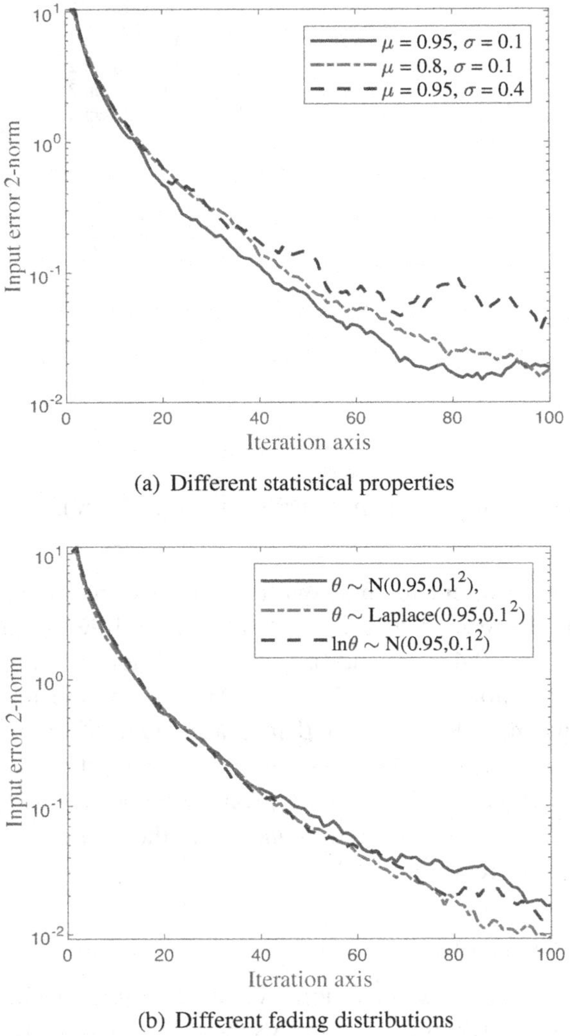

Figure 8.6 Input error profiles for different distributions (agent 1): (a) Different statistical properties and (b) different fading distributions.

$$B = \begin{bmatrix} 0 \\ \dfrac{\Delta}{J_m + J_l/n^2} \end{bmatrix}, \quad C = \left[0, \frac{1}{n}\right]. \tag{8.49}$$

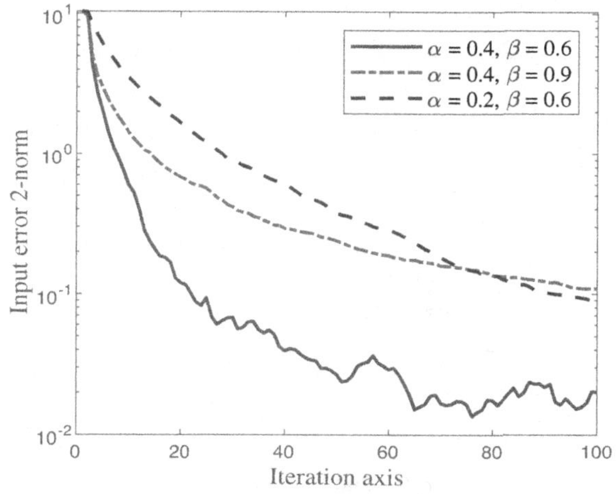

Figure 8.7 Input error profiles for different decreasing gains ($\lambda_k = \alpha/\beta^k$).

Here, the parameter are as follows: the discrete time interval $\Delta = 50$ ms, motor inertia $J_m = 0.3$, the motor damping coefficient $B_m = 0.3$, the link inertia $J_l = 0.44$, the link damping coefficient $B_l = 0.25$, the gear ratio $n = 1.6$, the lumped mass $M = 0.5$, the gravitational acceleration $g = 9.8$, and the center of mass from the axis of motion $l = 0.15$.

Let the algorithms run for 200 iterations. The operation period is 3 s, and the iteration length be $N = 60$. The distributions of fading variable and CAN are $\theta_{k,j,i}(t) \sim N(0.8, 0.1^2)$ and $\omega_k(t) \sim N(0, 0.05^2)$. The desired trajectory is set to $y_d(t) = 0.4\pi/6t^2 - \pi/27t^3, 0 \leq t \leq 3$, and the regulation matrix $\Lambda_k = 1/k^{0.7}$. Fig. 8.8 presents the tracking performance for the 2nd and 200th iterations, respectively. It is seen that high-precision tracking performance is realized.

To demonstrate the necessity of correction mechanism, we consider the learning consensus scheme without fading correction for two scenarios using the fixed gain and the decreasing gain, respectively. Fig. 8.9 provides the Euclidean norm profiles of input error in the iteration domain, taking agent v_1 as an example. From the dotted and dashed lines corresponding to the fixed and decreasing gains, the scheme without correction mechanism cannot ensure a continuous improvement of the input after a few iterations. Furthermore, the simulations for parameter variations are similar to those of Subsection 8.5.1. We omit the details to avoid repetition.

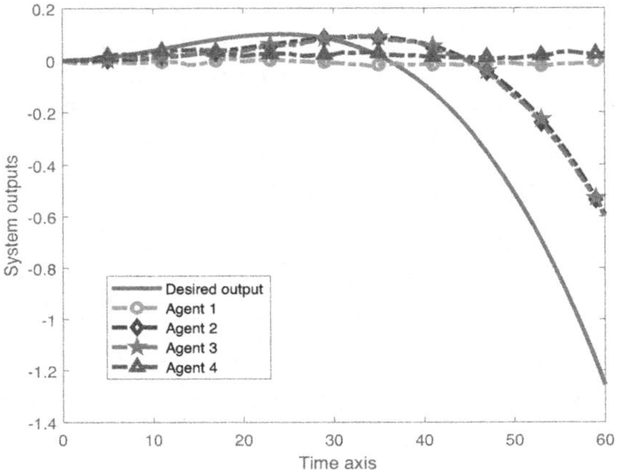

(a) 2nd Iteration

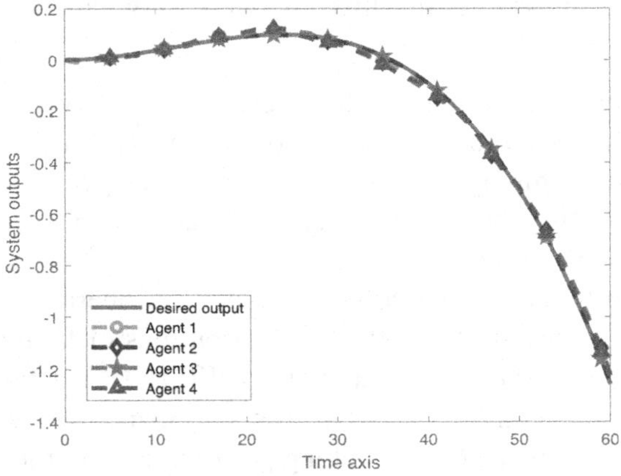

(b) 200th Iteration

Figure 8.8 Output profiles of all four agents: (a) 2nd Iteration and (b) 200th iteration.

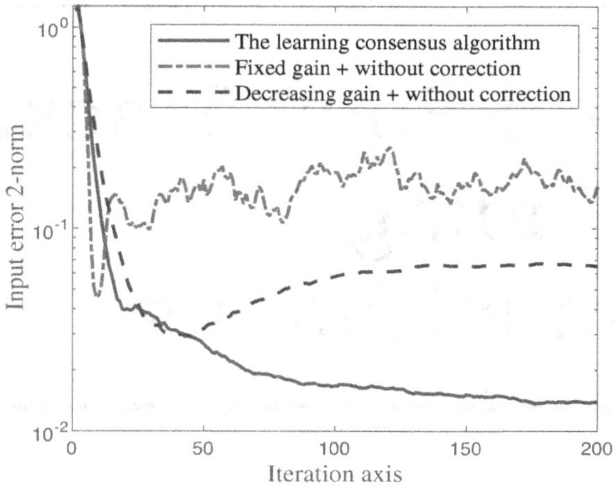

Figure 8.9 Input error profiles for different learning algorithms.

8.6 SUMMARY

In this chapter, the batch-based learning consensus tracking problem of MAS with FNI is investigated. The FNI is considered because of the existence of channel randomness, which is described by multiplicative and additive random variables subject to certain distributions. Because of the biased communication networks, the agent cannot obtain any precise neighbors' information. The traditional learning consensus scheme fails to apply this scenario to achieve batch-wise asymptotical consensus tracking performance for the MAS. This chapter has proposed a new distributed learning consensus scheme for the MAS with FNI. By using a direct correction mechanism, the proposed scheme is proved effective to realize precise consensus tracking based on the biased exchanging data. The input and output of each agent are shown convergent to the desired counterparts of the given leader agent or desired objective in the mean-square sense. Both linear and nonlinear dynamics are considered for the agents in detail.

CHAPTER 9

Point-to-Point Tracking with Fading Communications

THIS chapter studies the point-to-point learning and tracking problem for networked stochastic systems with fading communications by iterative learning control. The point-to-point tracking problem indicates that only partial positions rather than the whole reference are required to achieve high tracking precision. An auxiliary matrix is introduced to connect the entire reference and the required tracking targets. The fading communication introduces multiplicative randomness to the transmitted signals, which leads to the biased available information. A direct correction mechanism is employed using statistics of the communication channel. A learning control scheme is then proposed with a decreasing gain sequence to ensure steady convergence in the presence of various types of randomness. Two scenarios of varying initial states are considered. The convergence of the proposed scheme is strictly established.

9.1 INTRODUCTION

In the previous chapters, attempts have been made on the possible learning strategy for tracking problem under fading communications. In these results, the fading effect at both input and output sides was carefully analyzed. An initial attempt of ILC with faded data was discussed in Chapter 2, where the fundamental convergence was establish for the conventional learning control scheme. In Chapter 3, an iteration moving average operator was employed

DOI: 10.1201/9781032646404-9

to smooth the fluctuation owing to the input fading randomness. Extensive explorations on the function of various iteration-wise average operators were compared and analyzed in Chapter 4. In Chapter 7, the case of unknown nonrepetitive channel randomness has been investigated using a novel mean inverse estimation method. These results have paved a promising way to improve the tracking performance using lossy data.

In these works, the target is to track an entire trajectory; that is, all points of the reference are required to be tracked. However, in many applications, only a few points of the entire trajectory must be seriously considered while the rest of the trajectory allows a large degree of freedom. For example, in a "pick and place" robotic task, it is only required that the robot can accurately pick and place the object at the designated positions whereas the moving process is not strictly restricted. This problem is called point-to-point (P2P) tracking problem. The motivation of this work includes a wide range of applications such as stroke rehabilitation [25], where stroke patients are expected to complete a series of point-to-point movements such as pressing buttons, and satellite antenna pointing control [1], where an antenna is steered to direct towards the desired azimuth and elevation angles at the designated positions.

ILC has been applied to deal with the P2P tracking problem [12, 13, 23, 24, 26, 47, 58]. A reference update scheme was proposed and investigated in [24,58] instead of the conventional input update scheme used in other publications. Additional constraints and objectives were discussed in [23,26,58] by formulating diverse optimization indices. A comprehensive norm-optimal ILC solution was proposed and experimentally verified in [47]. In the above papers, critical tracking time points are fixed and known to establish the performance cost function. An extension to the case of variable tracking time allocations was proposed in [12], where an optimal allocation solution was provided. Recently, a data-driven framework was established to achieve P2P tracking for a class of unknown nonlinear systems via the so-called dynamic linearization technique [13]. In a recent work [35], an extension to stochastic systems was reported, where accelerated learning control schemes were designed using the gain adaptation mechanism triggered by practical tracking errors.

Although the P2P tracking problem can be transformed into the traditional ILC problem by assigning arbitrary values to free reference points, such a disposal would waste the inherent freedom and opportunity to further improve the other related control indices such as saving control energy. Meanwhile, it is unclear how to determine the optimal supplementation for those free points; indeed, inappropriate supplementation can lead to bad tracking performance. Thus, it is important to know whether the designed scheme can automatically determine suitable values for those free points. These distinctions introduce difficulties in design and analysis.

While the P2P tracking system is implemented with wired/wireless communication channels, the fading issue should be carefully studied. A critical problem is that the fading channel surely introduces randomness to the limited available tracking data and then affects the overall tracking performance. This problem has not been resolved in the existing literature, which motivates this research. We study the P2P tracking problem for networked stochastic systems with fading communications by using the learning scheme. In particular, a random multiplicative variable is applied to model the fading. We first provide a performance index for the P2P learning and tracking problem. Then, we present a direct correction to the received measurements using the statistics of the fading phenomenon. Following that, a learning scheme with varying gain sequences is established to accomplish the control objective, where two cases of varying initial states are addressed in turn. The strict convergence analysis is conducted in both almost sure and mean square senses. Illustrative simulations are given to verify the effectiveness and demonstrate the influence of the involved parameters.

9.2 PROBLEM FORMULATION

Consider the following linear discrete-time system:

$$\begin{aligned} x_k(t+1) &= A_t x_k(t) + B_t u_k(t) + \omega_k(t) \\ y_k(t) &= C_t x_k(t) + \upsilon_k(t) \end{aligned} \tag{9.1}$$

where the subscript $k \in \mathbf{Z}_+$ is the iteration index and t denotes the time index, $t = 0, 1, \ldots, N$. N is a positive integer and refers to the iteration length. $x_k(t) \in \mathbf{R}^n$ is the system state, $u_k(t) \in \mathbf{R}^p$ is the system input, and $y_k(t) \in \mathbf{R}^q$ is system output. A_t, B_t, and C_t are system matrices with appropriate dimensions. $\omega_k(t)$ and $\upsilon_k(t)$ are the process disturbances and measurements noise, respectively.

The following assumptions are needed for system (9.1).

Assumption 9.1 *The system relative degree is one and the input-output coupling matrix $C_{t+1}B_t$ is of full-row rank.*

This assumption is common in ILC literature that ensure the precise tracking performance for an arbitrary reference in absence of additional randomness. It implies that the number of the output dimension is less than that of the input dimension. In this chapter, we employ this assumption to ensure the validity of a technical lemma, i.e., Lemma 9.1.

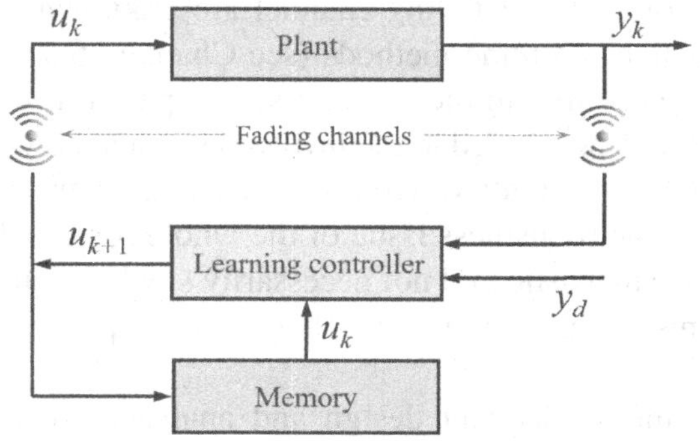

Figure 9.1 Diagram of ILC over fading networks.

Assumption 9.2 *Both of the process disturbance $\omega_k(t)$ and measurements noise $\upsilon_k(t)$ are assumed to be independent with respect to iteration index k and $\omega_k(t)$ is independent of $\upsilon_k(t)$. Both terms are with zero mean and bounded second moment.*

This assumption is mild for practical applications because the system operates in a batch mode. That is, the randomness from different batches are generated independently. Thus, it is reasonable to assume them to be independent. Besides, all signals are with finite energy and therefore, the second moments of these disturbance and noise are bounded.

In this study, the block diagram with fading networks is illustrated in Fig. 9.1. The random fading may occur in the exchange channels between plant and controller. The fading effect behaves similarly for the actuator side and measurement side. Thus, we consider the output fading only to save derivations. The extension to fading communication at both sides can be conducted following a similar procedure. We employ a random variable $\gamma_k(t)$ multiplied to the transmitted signals to model a fading channel. The statistics of fading gain is determined because most wireless channels undergo slow fading. Then, the received signals can be corrected using this statistics.

Assumption 9.3 *The fading gain $\gamma_k(t)$ is independently and identically distributed with respect to t and k and subject to a continuous distribution $\mathbb{P}(\gamma_k(t) > 0) = 1$. Besides, $\mathbb{E}[\gamma_k(t)] = \rho$ and $\mathbb{E}[(\gamma_k(t) - \rho)^2] = \sigma^2$, where ρ is known to perform preliminary correction on the received signals.*

The availability of the fading mean is reasonable because this statistics information is generally determined by physical environments and devices.

If the statistical property of fading channel are unknown, we can conduct estimates by off-line or online methods (see Chapters 5-7). The fading formulation of note is similar to the actuator/sensor partial loss fault, where an additional variable is multiplied to the involved signals; however, several distinctions exist. The loss fault variable is usually invariant and smaller than one, which raises the robustness issue of the whole system. By contrast, the fading variable is stochastic and not necessarily smaller than one. The focus of fading transmission is a suitable mechanism to acquire the implicit information.

To simplify the subsequent design and analysis, we employ a lifting form of system signals. To this end, we put the input and output into super-vectors as follows: $u_k = [u_k^T(0), u_k^T(1), \ldots, u_k^T(N-1)]^T \in \mathbf{R}^{pN}$ and $y_k = [y_k^T(1), y_k^T(2), \ldots, y_k^T(N)]^T \in \mathbf{R}^{qN}$.

The lifted vectors of desired output y_d is defined similarly by replacing k with d. Let

$$G = \begin{bmatrix} C_1B_0 & 0 & \cdots & 0 \\ C_2A_1B_0 & C_2B_1 & \cdots & 0 \\ \vdots & \vdots & \ddots & \vdots \\ C_N\prod_{j=1}^{N-1}A_jB_0 & C_N\prod_{j=2}^{N-1}A_jB_1 & \cdots & C_NB_{N-1} \end{bmatrix}.$$

Then, system (9.1) can be rewritten as

$$y_k = Gu_k + y_k^0 + \varepsilon_k \tag{9.2}$$

where $y_k^0 = [(C_1A_0)^T, (C_2A_1A_0)^T, \ldots, (C_N\prod_{m=0}^{N-1}A_m)^T]^T\ x_k(0)$ is the initial state response and the stochastic noise ε_k is given as follows:

$$\varepsilon_k = \begin{bmatrix} \upsilon_k(1) + C_1\omega_k(1) \\ \upsilon_k(2) + C_2\omega_k(2) + C_2A_1\omega_k(1) \\ \vdots \\ \upsilon_k(N) + C_N\sum_{i=1}^{N}(\prod_{j=i}^{N-1}A_j)\omega_k(i) \end{bmatrix}.$$

Clearly, ε_k is with zero-mean and bounded variance.

The reference for the entire time interval is denoted by $y_d = [y_d^T(1), y_d^T(2), \ldots, y_d^T(N)]^T \in \mathbf{R}^{qN}$.

In some practical applications, only part of y_d needs to be tracked rather than the whole reference y_d. Here, we assume that only f dimensions of y_d need to be tracked, $1 \le f \le qN$. It means that $qN - f$ dimensions of y_d can be completely disregarded. After removing the entries of y_d that do not need to be tracked, a new tracking reference y_r with dimension f is obtained. To transform the original y_d to the shortened reference y_r, we employ a row vector T with the dimension qN, where $T(i) = 1$ if the ith dimension of y_d needs to be tracked and $T(i) = 0$ otherwise. Then, we can construct a matrix $\Phi \in \mathbf{R}^{f \times qN}$ as follows:

$$\Phi_{i,j} = \begin{cases} 1, & \text{if } T(j) = 1 \text{ and } \sum_{k=1}^{j} T(k) = i \\ 0, & \text{otherwise} \end{cases} \tag{9.3}$$

In the following, we call Φ the extracting matrix that extracts the required entries of the whole reference. Consequently, y_r and y_d satisfy the following relationship:

$$y_r = \Phi y_d. \tag{9.4}$$

If the ith trace point of y_r is located in the jth dimension of the original reference y_d, then $\Phi_{i,j} = 1$ and otherwise, $\Phi_{i,j} = 0$. The following lemma states a property of the matrix ΦG.

Lemma 9.1 ([74]) *Under Assumption 9.1, the matrix ΦG is of full-row rank.*

Notice that the properties of y_k^0 are mainly determined by $x_k(0)$. In the existing ILC literature, the identical initial condition (i.i.c) is widely accepted: $x_k(0) = x_d(0)$, where $x_d(0)$ is the desired initial state corresponding to y_d^0. However, in P2P control, the solution of the desired initial state $x_d(0)$ may not be determined since we only have partial reference trajectory information rather than the entire trajectory information. Without loss of generality, we assume the desired initial state to be $x_d(0) = 0$. The varying initial state issue will be elaborated in this chapter for the P2P control problem.

Two cases of varying initial state are formulated as follows:

Case I: random initialization condition:

$$\mathbb{E}[x_k(0)] = 0 \text{ and } \sup_k \mathbb{E}[\|x_k(0)\|^2] < \infty.$$

Case II: asymptotically precise initialization condition:

$$x_k(0) \xrightarrow[k\to\infty]{} 0.$$

Remark 9.1 *Case I indicates that the initial state varies around the desired initial state randomly. This is common when the initialization process is governed by multiple factors. Case II indicates that the initial state can converge to the desired one. This condition is usually valid if we impose additional learning mechanism for the initial state. The design of initial state learning has been studied in [72]. This issue differs from our idea to achieve high tracking performance without any initial state learning mechanism.*

Control Objective: For the P2P tracking problem, the objective is to drive the system process to produce output that can accurately track the desired reference points. However, due to the existence of random noise in (9.1), it is difficult to guarantee the conventional tracking error $y_r - \Phi y_k$ to converge to zero. Instead, we define an auxiliary tracking error $\Phi\hat{e}_k \triangleq y_r - \Phi G u_k$, which implies the best inherent tracking performance of the input signal excluding noise influence. The practical objective is to design a learning scheme such that the auxiliary tracking error $\Phi\hat{e}_k$ can converge to zero.

9.3 LEARNING CONTROL SCHEME AND ITS ANALYSIS

9.3.1 Algorithm Design

To highlight the main novelty, we consider the fading communication of the outputs only. That is, the communication channel from the system output to the controller suffers random fading, while the channel from the controller back to the plant works normally. It is clear that the received output at the controller is biased from the original signals. Denote the received output as y_k^F. By Assumption 9.3, we have

$$y_k^F = (\Gamma_k \otimes I_q) y_k, \tag{9.5}$$

where $\Gamma_k \triangleq \text{diag}\{\gamma_k(1), \gamma_k(2), \ldots, \gamma_k(N)\}$, $\otimes$ denotes Kronecker product, and I_q denotes identity matrix with dimension q. This equation indicates that the received output signal y_k^F has been deviated from the actual output. Based on the statistics of γ_k, the received signal is corrected as follows:

$$y_k^c = \rho^{-1}(\Gamma_k \otimes I_q) y_k, \tag{9.6}$$

where $y_k^c(t)$ denoted the corrected output signal.

Remark 9.2 *The term $\rho^{-1}(\Gamma_k \otimes I_q) y_k$ can be rewritten as $y_k - (I - \rho^{-1}(\Gamma_k \otimes I_q)) y_k$, where y_k is the original output and $(I - \rho^{-1}(\Gamma_k \otimes I_q)) y_k$ is an output-dependent error caused by the random fading. Given that the fading variable Γ_k and the output y_k are independent, the mathematical expectation of $-(I - \rho^{-1}(\Gamma_k \otimes I_q)) y_k$ is zero. In other words, the corrected signal has become an unbiased estimate of the original output. If ρ is unknown, one can conduct an rough estimate before the following derivations.*

Remark 9.3 *The fading variable is assumed to follow the same distribution in each dimension for brevity. That is, the fading variable is considered to be a scale variable that exerts the same influence on each dimension of the* *transmitted signal. The extension to the multi-dimensional but decoupled fading effect is straightforward. For the latter case, one can replace the scalar* ρ *in (9.6) with a diagonal matrix, whose diagonal entries are the corresponding fading mean for each dimension. The following results are still valid. For those multi-dimensional fading channels with strong coupling, much effort should be devoted to future investigation.*

The learning control scheme is defined as follows:

$$u_{k+1} = u_k + d_k L(y_r - \Phi y_k^c), \tag{9.7}$$

where L is the control direction matrix and $\{d_k\}$ is the learning gain sequence such that

$$d_k > 0, \quad d_k \xrightarrow[k\to\infty]{} 0, \quad \sum_{k=1}^{\infty} d_k = \infty, \quad \sum_{k=1}^{\infty} d_k^2 < \infty,$$
$$\frac{d_k - d_{k+1}}{d_k d_{k+1}} \xrightarrow[k\to\infty]{} \phi \geq 0. \tag{9.8}$$

Remark 9.4 *The decreasing sequence* $\{d_k\}$ *is widely used in the processing of stochastic systems. If a fixed gain is applied, it is difficult to guarantee steady convergence of the input sequence due to the influence of random disturbances. Indeed, the decreasing sequence* $\{d_k\}$ *helps suppress or eliminate the essential effect of random disturbances. In practice, it is difficult to present an optimal selection of the gain sequence because it is independent of actual operation procedure. A promising candidate is* $d_k = \alpha/k^\beta$, $\alpha > 0$, $1/2 < \beta < 1$.

The control flowchart is shown in Fig. 9.2. Denote $\Upsilon_k \triangleq (\Gamma_k \otimes I_q)$. Then, we can rewrite (9.7) as

$$u_{k+1} = u_k + d_k L[y_r - \rho^{-1}\Phi\Upsilon_k y_k]. \tag{9.9}$$

For the convergence analysis below, we introduce a technical lemma. This lemma establishes a relationship between the extracting matrix Φ and fading matrix Υ_k.

Lemma 9.2 *There exists a diagonal matrix* Ψ_k *such that* $\Phi\Upsilon_k = \Psi_k\Phi$, *where* Ψ_k *is of dimension* f *and its diagonal entries are from the diagonal entries of* Υ_k.

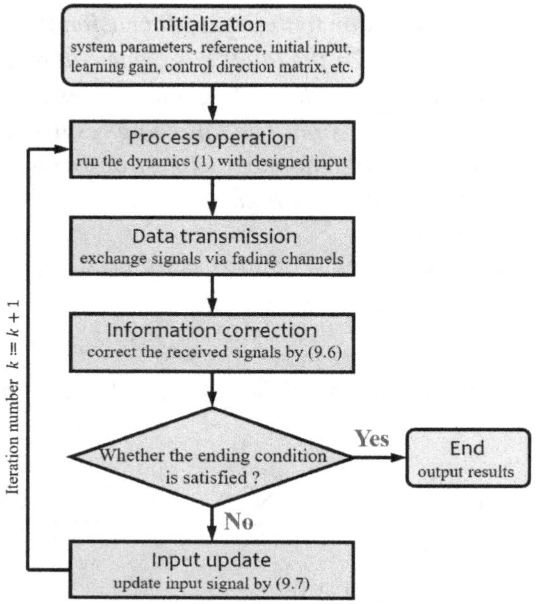

Figure 9.2 Flowchart of the P2P learning control via fading channels.

Proof: By (9.3), there is only one entry in each row of the matrix Φ that is equal to one, while the rest entries are equal to zero. That is, $\sum_{j=1}^{qN} \Phi_{i,j} = 1$, $\forall 1 \leq i \leq f$. Besides, each column of the matrix Φ has at most one entry that is equal to one while all of the rest entries are equal to zero. That is, $\sum_{i=1}^{f} \Phi_{i,j} = 1$ or 0, $\forall 1 \leq j \leq qN$. We denote the dimension of the reference to be tracked by t_i, $1 \leq t_i \leq qN$, $1 \leq i \leq f$. Then, the extracting matrix Φ is given as follows:

$$\Phi = \begin{array}{c} \begin{matrix} 1 & \dots & t_1 & \dots & t_2 & \dots & t_f & \dots & qN \end{matrix} \\ \begin{pmatrix} 0 & \dots & 1 & \dots & 0 & \dots & 0 & \dots & 0 \\ 0 & \dots & 0 & \dots & 1 & \dots & 0 & \dots & 0 \\ 0 & \dots & 0 & \dots & 0 & \dots & 0 & \dots & 0 \\ \vdots & & \vdots & & \vdots & & \vdots & & \vdots \\ 0 & \dots & 0 & \dots & 0 & \dots & 1 & \dots & 0 \end{pmatrix} \end{array}.$$

Define $t_i^* \triangleq \lceil t_i/q \rceil$, where $\lceil \cdot \rceil$ represents the round up function. Since Υ_k is a diagonal matrix with dimension qN, we have the specific formulation of

$\Phi\Upsilon_k$ as follows:

$$\begin{array}{c} \begin{matrix} 1 & \dots & t_1 & \dots & t_2 & \dots & t_f & \dots & qN \end{matrix} \\ \begin{pmatrix} 0 & \dots & \gamma_k(t_1^*) & \dots & 0 & \dots & 0 & \dots & 0 \\ 0 & \dots & 0 & \dots & \gamma_k(t_2^*) & \dots & 0 & \dots & 0 \\ 0 & \dots & 0 & \dots & 0 & \dots & 0 & \dots & 0 \\ \vdots & & \vdots & & \vdots & & \vdots & & \vdots \\ 0 & \dots & 0 & \dots & 0 & \dots & \gamma_k(t_f^*) & \dots & 0 \end{pmatrix} \end{array}.$$

Clearly, the presentation of $\Phi\Upsilon_k$ can be regarded as a matrix that replaces the entry Φ_{i,t_i} of the matrix Φ with the fading variable at time instant t_i^*. Then, we can collect these fading variables and establish the following diagonal matrix Ψ_k:

$$\begin{array}{cc} & \begin{matrix} 1 & 2 & \dots & f \end{matrix} \\ \Psi_k = & \begin{pmatrix} \gamma_k(t_1^*) & & & \\ & \gamma_k(t_2^*) & & \\ & & \ddots & \\ & & & \gamma_k(t_f^*) \end{pmatrix} \end{array}$$

By direct calculations, we have $\Psi_k\Phi = \Phi\Upsilon_k$. This completes the proof. □

Remark 9.5 *For P2P control, we concentrate on tracking performance of the specified points: Φy_k. Then, it is reasonable to treat Φy_k as a whole in the proof. However, it is not straightforward to do so according to (9.9), where Υ_k exists between Φ and y_k. In Lemma 9.2, an equivalent transformation of $\Phi\Upsilon_k$ is obtained by analyzing the structure of Φ and Υ_k. This fact can be interpreted from the physical angle. For the term $\Phi\Upsilon_k y_k$, it indicates that we first obtain the received outputs, which has been perturbed by the fading channels, and then select the entries that correspond to the required tracking reference points. For the term $\Psi_k\Phi y_k$, it can be understood as that we only transmit the outputs corresponding to the practical tracking reference y_r. These two cases are identical, which reveals the inherent principle for the identity $\Phi\Upsilon_k = \Psi_k\Phi$.*

Denote $\Lambda_k \triangleq \rho^{-1}\Psi_k$. Then, we can rewrite (9.9) as

$$u_{k+1} = u_k + d_k L[\Phi y_d - \Lambda_k \Phi y_k]. \tag{9.10}$$

9.3.2 Convergence Analysis for Case I

In this subsection, we address the convergence for the random initialization condition, i.e., Case I. For this case, the initial state can be regarded as a part of the system noise. In other words, the statistical properties can help establish the convergence analysis. The following theorem describes the mean-square convergence of the proposed scheme for Case I.

Theorem 9.1 *Consider system* (9.1) *under Assumptions 9.1-9.3. The initial state* $x_k(0)$ *satisfies the condition* $\mathbb{E}[x_k(0)] = 0$ *and* $\sup_k \mathbb{E}[\|x_k(0)\|^2] < \infty$. *If we design L such that* $-\Phi GL$ *is stable, then the proposed scheme* (9.7) *guarantees that the auxiliary tracking error* $\Phi\hat{e}_k$ *converges to zero in the mean-square sense.*

Proof: Recall the definition of auxiliary tracking error $\Phi\hat{e}_k = y_r - \Phi G u_k$. Combining (9.2) and (9.10), we have

$$\begin{aligned}\Phi\hat{e}_{k+1} =& y_r - \Phi G u_{k+1}\\ =& y_r - \Phi G[u_k + d_k L(y_r - \Lambda_k\Phi(Gu_k + y_k^0 + \varepsilon_k))]\\ =& \Phi\hat{e}_k - d_k\Phi GL\Phi\hat{e}_k + d_k\Phi GL(I-\Lambda_k)\Phi\hat{e}_k\\ & - d_k\Phi GL(I-\Lambda_k)y_r + d_k\Phi GL\Lambda_k\Phi\varepsilon_k\\ & + d_k\Phi GL\Lambda_k\Phi y_k^0.\end{aligned} \tag{9.11}$$

Note that L is designed to ensure that $-\Phi GL$ is stable. Define $\Xi \triangleq \Phi GL$. Then, the identity $\Xi^T\Omega + \Omega\Xi = I_f$ holds, where Ω is positive definite. With Ω, we can define a Lyapunov function $Y_{k+1} = (\Phi\hat{e}_{k+1})^T\Omega(\Phi\hat{e}_{k+1})$.

Substituting (9.11) into this function leads to

$$\begin{aligned}Y_{k+1} =& (\Phi\hat{e}_{k+1})^T\Omega(\Phi\hat{e}_{k+1})\\ =& (\Phi\hat{e}_k)^T\Omega(\Phi\hat{e}_k) + d_k^2(\Phi\hat{e}_k)^T\Xi^T\Omega\Xi(\Phi\hat{e}_k)\\ & + d_k^2(\Phi\hat{e}_k)^T[\Xi(I-\Lambda_k)]^T\Omega[\Xi(I-\Lambda_k)](\Phi\hat{e}_k)\\ & + d_k^2 y_r^T[\Xi(I-\Lambda_k)]^T\Omega[\Xi(I-\Lambda_k)]y_r\\ & + d_k^2(\Phi\varepsilon_k)^T(\Xi\Lambda_k)^T\Omega(\Xi\Lambda_k)(\Phi\varepsilon_k)\\ & + d_k^2(\Phi y_k^0)^T(\Xi\Lambda_k)^T\Omega(\Xi\Lambda_k)(\Phi y_k^0)\\ & - d_k(\Phi\hat{e}_k)^T[\Xi^T\Omega + \Omega\Xi](\Phi\hat{e}_k)\\ & + d_k(\Phi\hat{e}_k)^T\{[\Xi(I-\Lambda_k)]^T\Omega + \Omega[\Xi(I-\Lambda_k)]\}(\Phi\hat{e}_k)\\ & - 2d_k(\Phi\hat{e}_k)^T\Omega[\Xi(I-\Lambda_k)y_r - \Xi\Lambda_k\Phi\varepsilon_k]\\ & - 2d_k(\Phi\hat{e}_k)^T\Omega\Xi\Lambda_k\Phi y_k^0\\ & - 2d_k^2(\Phi\hat{e}_k)^T\Xi^T\Omega[\Xi(I-\Lambda_k)](\Phi\hat{e}_k)\\ & + 2d_k^2(\Phi\hat{e}_k)^T\Xi^T\Omega[\Xi(I-\Lambda_k)]y_r\\ & - 2d_k^2(\Phi\hat{e}_k)^T\Xi^T\Omega(\Xi\Lambda_k)(\Phi\varepsilon_k)\end{aligned}$$

$$
\begin{aligned}
& -2d_k^2(\Phi\hat{e}_k)^T\Xi^T\Omega(\Xi\Lambda_k)(\Phi y_k^0) \\
& -2d_k^2(\Phi\hat{e}_k)^T[\Xi(I-\Lambda_k)]^T\Omega[\Xi(I-\Lambda_k)]y_r \\
& +2d_k^2(\Phi\hat{e}_k)^T[\Xi(I-\Lambda_k)]^T\Omega(\Xi\Lambda_k)(\Phi\varepsilon_k) \\
& -2d_k^2 y_r^T[\Xi(I-\Lambda_k)]^T\Omega(\Xi\Lambda_k)(\Phi\varepsilon_k) \\
& +2d_k^2(\Phi\hat{e}_k)^T[\Xi(I-\Lambda_k)]^T\Omega(\Xi\Lambda_k)(\Phi y_k^0) \\
& -2d_k^2 y_r^T[\Xi(I-\Lambda_k)]^T\Omega(\Xi\Lambda_k)(\Phi y_k^0) \\
& +2d_k^2(\Phi\varepsilon_k)^T(\Xi\Lambda_k)^T\Omega(\Xi\Lambda_k)(\Phi y_k^0).
\end{aligned} \tag{9.12}
$$

For further analysis, we define an increasing σ-algebra $\mathcal{F}_k \triangleq \sigma\{x_j(0), u_j(t), y_j(t), \omega_j(t), \upsilon_j(t), \gamma_j(t), 0 \le t \le N, 1 \le j \le k\}$. By the update law (9.7), it is evident that $\Phi\hat{e}_k \in \mathcal{F}_{k-1}$. Moreover, Λ_k and ε_k are independent of $\mathcal{F}_{k-1}$. According to the definition of Λ_k, we have $\mathbb{E}[I-\Lambda_k]=0$. Thus,

$$\mathbb{E}[(\Phi\hat{e}_k)^T([I-\Lambda_k]^T\Xi^T\Omega+\Omega\Xi[I-\Lambda_k])(\Phi\hat{e}_k)|\mathcal{F}_{k-1}]=0, \tag{9.13}$$

$$\mathbb{E}[(\Phi\hat{e}_k)^T\Omega\Xi\Lambda_k\Phi\varepsilon_k|\mathcal{F}_{k-1}]=0, \tag{9.14}$$

$$\mathbb{E}[(\Phi\hat{e}_k)^T\Omega\Xi\Lambda_k\Phi y_k^0|\mathcal{F}_{k-1}]=0, \tag{9.15}$$

$$\mathbb{E}[(\Phi\hat{e}_k)^T\Omega[\Xi(I-\Lambda_k)y_r]|\mathcal{F}_{k-1}]=0, \tag{9.16}$$

$$\mathbb{E}[(\Phi\hat{e}_k)^T\Xi^T\Omega[\Xi(I-\Lambda_k)](\Phi\hat{e}_k)|\mathcal{F}_{k-1}]=0, \tag{9.17}$$

$$\mathbb{E}[(\Phi\hat{e}_k)^T\Xi^T\Omega[\Xi(I-\Lambda_k)]y_r|\mathcal{F}_{k-1}]=0, \tag{9.18}$$

$$\mathbb{E}[(\Phi\hat{e}_k)^T\Xi^T\Omega(\Xi\Lambda_k)(\Phi\varepsilon_k)|\mathcal{F}_{k-1}]=0, \tag{9.19}$$

$$\mathbb{E}[(\Phi\hat{e}_k)^T[\Xi(I-\Lambda_k)]^T\Omega(\Xi\Lambda_k)(\Phi\varepsilon_k)|\mathcal{F}_{k-1}]=0, \tag{9.20}$$

$$\mathbb{E}[(\Phi\hat{e}_k)^T[\Xi(I-\Lambda_k)]^T\Omega(\Xi\Lambda_k)(\Phi y_k^0)|\mathcal{F}_{k-1}]=0, \tag{9.21}$$

$$\mathbb{E}[y_r^T[\Xi(I-\Lambda_k)]^T\Omega(\Xi\Lambda_k)(\Phi\varepsilon_k)|\mathcal{F}_{k-1}]=0, \tag{9.22}$$

$$\mathbb{E}[y_r^T[\Xi(I-\Lambda_k)]^T\Omega(\Xi\Lambda_k)(\Phi y_k^0)|\mathcal{F}_{k-1}]=0, \tag{9.23}$$

$$\mathbb{E}[(\Phi\varepsilon_k)^T(\Xi\Lambda_k)^T\Omega(\Xi\Lambda_k)(\Phi y_k^0)|\mathcal{F}_{k-1}]=0. \tag{9.24}$$

Moreover, there exist $\rho_1 > 0$ and $\rho_2 > 0$ such that

$$
\begin{aligned}
& \mathbb{E}[(\Phi\hat{e}_k)^T\Xi^T\Omega\Xi(\Phi\hat{e}_k)|\mathcal{F}_{k-1}] \\
& \quad \le (\Phi\hat{e}_k)^T\mathbb{E}[\Xi^T\Omega\Xi|\mathcal{F}_{k-1}](\Phi\hat{e}_k) \\
& \quad \le \rho_1(\Phi\hat{e}_k)^T\Omega(\Phi\hat{e}_k)=\rho_1 Y_k,
\end{aligned} \tag{9.25}
$$

$$
\begin{aligned}
& \mathbb{E}[(\Phi\hat{e}_k)^T[\Xi(I-\Lambda_k)]^T\Omega[\Xi(I-\Lambda_k)](\Phi\hat{e}_k)|\mathcal{F}_{k-1}] \\
& \quad \le (\Phi\hat{e}_k)^T\mathbb{E}[[\Xi(I-\Lambda_k)]^T\Omega[\Xi(I-\Lambda_k)]|\mathcal{F}_{k-1}](\Phi\hat{e}_k) \\
& \quad \le \rho_2(\Phi\hat{e}_k)^T\Omega(\Phi\hat{e}_k)=\rho_2 Y_k.
\end{aligned} \tag{9.26}
$$

Furthermore, we have

$$\mathbb{E}[y_r^T[\Xi(I-\Lambda_k)]^T\Omega[\Xi(I-\Lambda_k)]y_r|\mathcal{F}_{k-1}] \le \rho_3, \tag{9.27}$$

$$\mathbb{E}[(\Phi\varepsilon_k)^T(\Xi\Lambda_k)^T\Omega(\Xi\Lambda_k)(\Phi\varepsilon_k)|\mathcal{F}_{k-1}] \le \rho_4, \tag{9.28}$$

$$\mathbb{E}[(\Phi y_k^0)^T(\Xi\Lambda_k)^T\Omega(\Xi\Lambda_k)(\Phi y_k^0)|\mathcal{F}_{k-1}] \le \rho_5, \tag{9.29}$$

where ρ_3, ρ_4 and ρ_5 are suitable constants. Consequently,

$$\begin{aligned}
&\mathbb{E}[-2(\Phi\hat{e}_k)^T[\Xi(I-\Lambda_k)]^T\Omega[\Xi(I-\Lambda_k)]y_r|\mathcal{F}_{k-1}]\\
\le&\mathbb{E}[2\left|(\Phi\hat{e}_k)^T[\Xi(I-\Lambda_k)]^T\Omega^{\frac{1}{2}}\Omega^{\frac{1}{2}}[\Xi(I-\Lambda_k)]y_r\right||\mathcal{F}_{k-1}]\\
\le&\mathbb{E}[(\Phi\hat{e}_k)^T[\Xi(I-\Lambda_k)]^T\Omega[\Xi(I-\Lambda_k)](\Phi\hat{e}_k)|\mathcal{F}_{k-1}]\\
&+\mathbb{E}[y_r^T[\Xi(I-\Lambda_k)]^T\Omega[\Xi(I-\Lambda_k)]y_r|\mathcal{F}_{k-1}]\\
\le&\rho_2 Y_k+\rho_3.
\end{aligned} \tag{9.30}$$

Moreover,

$$\begin{aligned}
&\mathbb{E}[(\Phi\hat{e}_k)^T[\Xi^T\Omega+\Omega\Xi](\Phi\hat{e}_k)|\mathcal{F}_{k-1}]\\
=&\mathbb{E}[(\Phi\hat{e}_k)^T(\Phi\hat{e}_k)|\mathcal{F}_{k-1}]\\
\ge&\rho_6(\Phi\hat{e}_k)^T\Omega(\Phi\hat{e}_k)=\rho_6 Y_k,
\end{aligned} \tag{9.31}$$

where ρ_6 is selected such that $I_{Nf} \ge \rho_6\Omega$.

Combining (9.13)-(9.31) yields

$$\begin{aligned}
\mathbb{E}[Y_{k+1}|\mathcal{F}_{k-1}] \le& Y_k - d_k\rho_6 Y_k + d_k^2(\rho_1+2\rho_2)Y_k\\
&+d_k^2(2\rho_3+\rho_4+\rho_5).
\end{aligned} \tag{9.32}$$

Taking expectation to the inequality (9.32), we have

$$\begin{aligned}
\mathbb{E}[Y_{k+1}] \le&(1-\rho_6 d_k)\mathbb{E}[Y_k]\\
&+(\rho_1+2\rho_2)d_k^2\left\{\frac{2\rho_3+\rho_4+\rho_5}{\rho_1+2\rho_2}+\mathbb{E}[Y_k]\right\}.
\end{aligned}$$

Therefore, by Lemma A.1, $\mathbb{E}[Y_k] \to 0$ as $k \to \infty$. Since the matrix Ω is positive definite, it can be deduced that $\mathbb{E}[\|y_r - \Phi G u_k\|^2] \le \lambda_{min}^{-1}(\Omega)\mathbb{E}[Y_k]$. This implies $\lim_{k\to\infty}\mathbb{E}[\|\Phi\hat{e}_k\|^2] = \lim_{k\to\infty}\mathbb{E}[\|y_r - \Phi G u_k\|^2] = 0$. The proof is thus completed. □

Theorem 9.1 proves the mean-square convergence of the algorithm for the random initial condition case. It can be seen from the proof that the fading channel introduces multiplicative randomness to the received output, which is biased comparing with its original value. A preliminary correction mechanism is necessary to provide an unbiased estimate for the received signals. However, this correction introduces output-dependent perturbations to the signals, which cause nontrivial difficulties in the convergence analysis. To deal with various types of randomness, a decreasing learning gain sequence is introduced to suppress and eliminate the influence. The effectiveness of the proposed scheme is shown in this theorem.

We now establish the almost sure convergence of the proposed scheme.

Theorem 9.2 *Consider system* (9.1) *under Assumptions 9.1-9.3. The initial state $x_k(0)$ satisfies the condition $\mathbb{E}[x_k(0)] = 0$ and $\sup_k \mathbb{E}[\|x_k(0)\|^2] < \infty$. If we design L such that $-\Phi GL$ is stable, then the proposed scheme* (9.7) *guarantees that the auxiliary tracking error $\Phi\hat{e}_k$ converges to zero in the almost sure sense.*

Proof: From (9.32), we have

$$\mathbb{E}[Y_{k+1}|\mathcal{F}_{k-1}] \leq Y_k + d_k^2(\rho_7 Y_k + \rho_8),$$

where $\rho_7 = \rho_1 + 2\rho_2$ and $\rho_8 = 2\rho_3 + \rho_4 + \rho_5$. We correspond Y_k and $d_k^2(\rho_7 Y_k + \rho_8)$ to $\mathcal{O}_k$ and $\mathcal{D}_k$ in Lemma A.2, respectively. By Theorem 9.1, we have proved $\mathbb{E}[Y_k] \to 0$. Thus, it is evident that the condition (A.3) holds. Therefore, we conclude that Y_k converges almost surely. The limitation of Y_k has been proved to be zero in the mean-square sense by Theorem 9.1. Therefore, the auxiliary tracking error $\Phi\hat{e}_k$ converges to zero in the almost sure sense. □

Remark 9.6 *From* (9.11), *one can observe that the effect of random fading after the correction mechanism has been implemented. The effect is described by two terms: $\Phi GL(I - \Lambda_k)\Phi\hat{e}_k$ and $\Phi GL(I - \Lambda_k)y_r$. The first term is an auxiliary-tracking-error-dependent perturbation. This term will vanish as the auxiliary tracking error converges to zero. In other words, this effect will not significantly destroy the tracking performance. The second term is a tracking-reference-dependent perturbation. The variance of this term increases as the value of tracking reference increases. In other words, the received signal would be greatly perturbed. Besides, both terms are with zero mean, implying that the correction mechanism is effective.*

Remark 9.7 *Because ΦG is of full-row rank, we can obtain L by solving a linear matrix inequality (LMI): $\Phi GL \succeq 0$. A simple solution for the inequality is $L = (\Phi G)^T$. However, it requires precise system information, which is unattractive for applications. Moreover, calculating L from the LMI may lead* *to a large computational burden when the process length N is large. To address these disadvantages, alternative selections are given as follows. Considering that $C_{t+1}B_t$ are diagonal blocks of the block lower-triangular matrix G, we construct a matrix $G_1 = \mathrm{diag}\{C_1B_0,\ldots,C_NB_{N-1}\}$, which merely requires the coupling matrices. A generalization of G_1 is to select L_t satisfying that $C_{t+1}B_tL_t$ is positive definite for all time instants and construct $G_2 = \mathrm{diag}\{L_0,\ldots,L_{N-1}\}$. Then, L is given by $(\Phi G_1)^T$ or $(\Phi G_2)^T$.*

Remark 9.8 *In this chapter, the output fading case is addressed to highlight the main novelty and simplify the derivations. The input fading case can be analyzed following the same procedure. Assume that the output can be well transmitted while the generated input signals are transmitted through fading channel. In this case, the received input signal deviates from the generated values in the form $u_k^F(t) = \gamma_k(t)u_k(t)$, where $u_k^F(t)$ denotes the received signal. The corrected input signal $u_k^c(t)$ is given by*

$$\begin{aligned} u_k^c(t) &= \rho^{-1}u_k^F(t) = \rho^{-1}\gamma_k(t)u_k(t) \\ &= u_k(t) - (1-\rho^{-1}\gamma_k(t))u_k(t). \end{aligned}$$

As discussed in Remark 9.2, the input-dependent term $(1-\rho^{-1}\gamma_k(t))u_k(t)$ is of zero mean, laying a foundation for the convergence analysis. In addition, a linear growth issue of the newly involved error term may arise similarly to output case. The system dynamics becomes

$$\begin{aligned} x_k(t+1) &= Ax_k(t) + B_t\rho^{-1}\gamma_k(t)u_k(t) + \omega_k(t), \\ y_k(t) &= C_tx_k(t) + \upsilon_k(t). \end{aligned}$$

The scheme is revised to $u_{k+1}(t) = u_k(t) + d_kL(y_r - \Phi y_k)$. Then, the auxiliary tracking error $\Phi\hat{e}_k$ becomes

$$\begin{aligned} \Phi\hat{e}_{k+1} = \Phi\hat{e}_k - d_k\Phi GL\Phi\hat{e}_k - d_k\Phi GL\Phi G[I-\rho^{-1}(\Gamma_k \otimes I_p)]u_k \\ + d_k\Phi GL\Phi y_k^0 + d_k\Phi GL\Phi\varepsilon_k. \end{aligned} \quad (9.33)$$

It is evident that this recursion can be disposed similarly to the output fading case. We should point out that the actual input received by plant is deviated from the generated input and this deviation can lead to bad practical performance. To address this issue, a promising mechanism is to iteratively average the input signals (see Chapter 3).

9.3.3 Convergence Analysis for Case II

In this subsection, we proceed to consider the convergence analysis for the asymptotically precise initialization condition, i.e., Case II. For this case, the statistics of the initial state error is removed and therefore, the procedures in the previous subsection cannot be applied directly. We have the following mean-square convergence result.

Theorem 9.3 *Consider system* (9.1) *under Assumptions 9.1-9.3. The initial state* $x_k(0)$ *satisfies* $x_k(0) \longrightarrow 0$ *as* k *increases. If we design* L *such that* $-\Phi GL$ *is stable, the proposed scheme* (9.7) *guarantees that the auxiliary tracking error* $\Phi\hat{e}_k$ *converges to zero in the mean-square sense.*

Proof: The proof for this theorem is similar to Theorem 9.1 except the analysis on initial response-related terms. Thus, in this proof, we follow the steps of Theorem 9.1 and clarify the necessary modifications. In particular, the major difference lies in the treatment of the initialization condition. In other words, the derivations from (9.11) to (9.12) are valid. On the right-hand side of (9.12), the following terms should be reanalyzed:

$$
\begin{aligned}
\varphi_1 &= d_k^2(\Phi y_k^0)^T(\Xi\Lambda_k)^T\Omega(\Xi\Lambda_k)(\Phi y_k^0),\\
\varphi_2 &= -2d_k(\Phi\hat{e}_k)^T\Omega\Xi\Lambda_k\Phi y_k^0,\\
\varphi_3 &= -2d_k^2(\Phi\hat{e}_k)^T\Xi^T\Omega(\Xi\Lambda_k)(\Phi y_k^0),\\
\varphi_4 &= 2d_k^2(\Phi\hat{e}_k)^T[\Xi(I-\Lambda_k)]^T\Omega(\Xi\Lambda_k)(\Phi y_k^0),\\
\varphi_5 &= -2d_k^2y_r^T[\Xi(I-\Lambda_k)]^T\Omega(\Xi\Lambda_k)(\Phi y_k^0),\\
\varphi_6 &= 2d_k^2(\Phi\varepsilon_k)^T(\Xi\Lambda_k)^T\Omega(\Xi\Lambda_k)(\Phi y_k^0).
\end{aligned}
$$

Owing to the random noise ε_k, $\mathbb{E}[\varphi_6|\mathcal{F}_{k-1}]=0$. Moreover, $\mathbb{E}[\varphi_1|\mathcal{F}_{k-1}] = \mathbb{E}[d_k^2(\Phi y_k^0)^T(\Xi\Lambda_k)^T\Omega(\Xi\Lambda_k)(\Phi y_k^0)|\mathcal{F}_{k-1}] \le \varepsilon d_k^2 m_k^2$, where $m_k \triangleq \|y_k^0\| \to 0$ and $\varepsilon > 0$ is a suitable constant. By the basic inequality $2ab \le a^2+b^2$, we have

$$
\begin{aligned}
&-2(\Phi\hat{e}_k)^T\Xi^T\Omega(\Xi\Lambda_k)(\Phi y_k^0)\\
&\quad\le(\Phi\hat{e}_k)^T\Xi^T\Omega\Xi(\Phi\hat{e}_k)\\
&\qquad+(\Phi y_k^0)^T(\Xi\Lambda_k)^T\Omega(\Xi\Lambda_k)(\Phi y_k^0), \qquad (9.34)\\
&2(\Phi\hat{e}_k)^T[\Xi(I-\Lambda_k)]^T\Omega(\Xi\Lambda_k)(\Phi y_k^0)\\
&\quad\le(\Phi\hat{e}_k)^T[\Xi(I-\Lambda_k)]^T\Omega[\Xi(I-\Lambda_k)](\Phi\hat{e}_k)\\
&\qquad+(\Phi y_k^0)^T(\Xi\Lambda_k)^T\Omega(\Xi\Lambda_k)(\Phi y_k^0), \qquad (9.35)\\
&-2y_r^T[\Xi(I-\Lambda_k)]^T\Omega(\Xi\Lambda_k)(\Phi y_k^0)
\end{aligned}
$$

$$\leq y_r^T[\Xi(I-\Lambda_k)]^T\Omega[\Xi(I-\Lambda_k)]y_r \\ +(\Phi y_k^0)^T(\Xi\Lambda_k)^T\Omega(\Xi\Lambda_k)(\Phi y_k^0). \tag{9.36}$$

Thus, $\mathbb{E}[\varphi_3|\mathcal{F}_{k-1}] \leq \rho_1 d_k^2 Y_k + \varepsilon d_k^2 m_k^2$, $\mathbb{E}[\varphi_4|\mathcal{F}_{k-1}] \leq \rho_2 d_k^2 Y_k + \varepsilon d_k^2 m_k^2$, and $\mathbb{E}[\varphi_5|\mathcal{F}_{k-1}] \leq \rho_3 d_k^2 + \varepsilon d_k^2 m_k^2$.

For the remaining term φ_2, we notice that

$$-2(\Phi\hat{e}_k)^T\Omega\Xi\Lambda_k\Phi y_k^0 \\ \leq \zeta(\Phi\hat{e}_k)^T\Omega(\Phi\hat{e}_k)+\frac{1}{\zeta}(\Xi\Lambda_k\Phi y_k^0)^T\Omega\Xi\Lambda_k\Phi y_k^0, \tag{9.37}$$

where $\zeta > 0$ is a constant to be specified later.

Substituting these estimates in $\mathbb{E}[Y_{k+1}|\mathcal{F}_{k-1}]$ of (9.12) yields

$$\mathbb{E}[Y_{k+1}|\mathcal{F}_{k-1}] \leq Y_k - \rho_6 d_k Y_k + \zeta d_k Y_k \\ + d_k^2(2\rho_1+3\rho_2)Y_k + d_k^2(3\rho_3+\rho_4) \\ + 4\varepsilon d_k^2 m_k^2 + \frac{\varepsilon}{\zeta}d_k m_k^2. \tag{9.38}$$

Taking expectation to the inequality (9.38) leads to $\mathbb{E}[Y_{k+1}] \leq (1-p_k)\mathbb{E}[Y_k]+q_k$. where $p_k = d_k[\rho_6-\zeta-d_k(2\rho_1+3\rho_2)]$ and $q_k = d_k^2(3\rho_3+\rho_4)+4\varepsilon d_k^2 m_k^2+\frac{\varepsilon}{\zeta}d_k m_k^2$. We correspond $\mathbb{E}[Y_k]$, p_k, and q_k to ξ_k, τ_k, and χ_k in Lemma A.3, respectively. Thus, to show $\mathbb{E}[Y_k] \to 0$, we check conditions of Lemma A.3.

Noticing $d_k \to 0$, for sufficiently large integer k, we obtain $d_k(2\rho_1+3\rho_2) \leq \frac{1}{4}\rho_6$. Moreover, ζ is an arbitrary number, we can set $\zeta < \frac{1}{4}\rho_6$. Then, we have $p_k \geq \frac{\rho_6}{2}d_k$. Therefore, $0 < p_k \leq 1$ for sufficiently large k, $p_k \to 0$, and $\sum_{k=1}^{\infty} p_k = \infty$.

For q_k, it is clear that $q_k \geq 0$. Besides,

$$\frac{q_k}{p_k} = \frac{d_k^2(3\rho_3+\rho_4)+4\varepsilon d_k^2 m_k^2+\frac{\varepsilon}{\zeta}d_k m_k^2}{d_k[\rho_6-\zeta-d_k(2\rho_1+3\rho_2)]} \\ \leq \frac{2\left[d_k^2(3\rho_3+\rho_4)+4\varepsilon d_k^2 m_k^2+\frac{\varepsilon}{\zeta}d_k m_k^2\right]}{d_k\rho_6} \\ = \frac{2(3\rho_3+\rho_4)}{\rho_6}d_k+\frac{8\varepsilon}{\rho_6}d_k m_k^2+\frac{2\varepsilon}{\zeta\rho_6}m_k^2 \\ \xrightarrow[k\to\infty]{} 0. \tag{9.39}$$

By Lemma A.3, we obtain $\mathbb{E}[Y_k] \to 0$ as $k \to \infty$. Similarly to the proof of Theorem 9.1, we can complete the proof. □

To prove the almost sure convergence of the proposed scheme under the asymptotically precise initialization condition, the technical Lemma A.3 is no longer applicable. In this case, we adopt Lemma A.5 from the stochastic approximation theory for further analysis.

Theorem 9.4 *Consider system* (9.1) *under Assumptions 9.1-9.3. The initial state* $x_k(0)$ *satisfies* $x_k(0) \longrightarrow 0$ *as* k *increases. If we design* L *such that* $-\Phi GL$ *is stable, then the proposed scheme* (9.7) *guarantees that the auxiliary tracking error* $\Phi\hat{e}_k$ *converges to zero in the almost sure sense.*

Proof: We copy the recursion (9.11) as follows:

$$\begin{aligned}\Phi\hat{e}_{k+1} =& y_r - \Phi G u_{k+1} \\ =& \Phi\hat{e}_k - d_k\Phi GL\Phi\hat{e}_k + d_k\Phi GL(I-\Lambda_k)\Phi\hat{e}_k \\ & - d_k\Phi GL(I-\Lambda_k)y_r + d_k\Phi GL\Lambda_k\Phi\varepsilon_k \\ & + d_k\Phi GL\Lambda_k\Phi y_k^0.\end{aligned} \tag{9.40}$$

The learning matrix L is selected such that $-\Phi GL$ is stable. Then, the term $-\Phi GL$ in (9.40) corresponds to the matrix H_k of Lemma A.5. We employ the increasing σ-algebra $\mathcal{F}_k \triangleq \sigma\{x_j(0), u_j(t), y_j(t), \omega_j(t), \upsilon_j(t), \gamma_j(t), 0 \le t \le N, 1 \le j \le k\}$. Similar to Theorem 9.1, we have $\mathbb{E}[d_k\Phi GL(I-\Lambda_k)\Phi\hat{e}_k|\mathcal{F}_{k-1}] = 0$. That is, $\{\Phi GL(I-\Lambda_k)\Phi\hat{e}_k, \mathcal{F}_{k-1}\}$ is a martingale difference sequence. By Theorem 9.2, we have $\mathbb{E}[Y_k] \to 0$. Besides, (9.40) is a linear recursion of $\Phi\hat{e}_k$, thus $\Phi\hat{e}_k$ is bounded a.s. [4].

We have

$$\begin{aligned}&\sum_{k=1}^{\infty}\mathbb{E}[\|d_k^2\Phi GL(I-\Lambda_k)\Phi\hat{e}_k\|^2|\mathcal{F}_{k-1}] \\ &\le \text{trace}(\Xi\Xi^T)\sup\|\Phi\hat{e}_k\|^2\sum_{k=1}^{\infty}d_k^2\mathbb{E}[\|I-\Lambda_k\|^2|\mathcal{F}_{k-1}] \\ &\le \kappa_1\sum_{k=1}^{\infty}d_k^2 < \infty,\end{aligned}$$

where $\kappa_1 > 0$ is a constant. By Chow convergence theorem of martingale difference sequence [14], we have $\sum_{k=1}^{\infty}[d_k\Phi GL(I-\Lambda_k)\Phi\hat{e}_k] < \infty$, a.s. That is, condition (A.5) is satisfied for $d_k\Phi GL(I-\Lambda_k)\Phi\hat{e}_k$.

For the fourth and fifth terms on the right-hand side of (9.40), the iteration-independence of Λ_k and ε_k can be applied. We have $\mathbb{E}[\Phi GL(I-\Lambda_k)y_r] = 0$ and

$$\begin{aligned}
&\sum_{k=1}^{\infty} \mathbb{E}[\|d_k \Phi GL(I-\Lambda_k)y_r\|^2] \\
&\le \operatorname{trace}(\Xi\Xi^T)\|y_r\|^2 \sum_{k=1}^{\infty} d_k^2 \mathbb{E}[\|I-\Lambda_k\|^2 | \mathcal{F}_{k-1}] \\
&\le \kappa_2 \sum_{k=1}^{\infty} d_k^2 < \infty.
\end{aligned}$$

Thus, by Khintchine-Kolmogorov convergence theorem [14], we obtain $\sum_{k=1}^{\infty}[d_k \Phi GL(I-\Lambda_k)y_r] < \infty$. That is, the condition (A.5) is satisfied by the term $d_k \Phi GL(I-\Lambda_k)y_r$. The same conclusion goes to the term $d_k \Phi GL\Lambda_k \Phi \varepsilon_k$ following a completely same step.

Next, we proceed to check the last term $d_k \Phi GL\Lambda_k \Phi y_k^0$. Under the asymptotically precise initialization condition, no statistics of the initial response y_k^0 is available. However, $y_k^0 \to 0$ as $k \to \infty$ and all the other involved matrices are bounded, thus condition in (A.5) that $N_k \to 0$ can be satisfied.

Thus, by Lemma A.5, $\Phi \hat{e}_k \to 0$ as $k \to \infty$ almost surely. □

Theorems 9.3 and 9.4 establish the mean-square and almost sure convergence properties of the proposed scheme under the asymptotically precise initialization condition. In this case, the statistics of the initial response is removed and thus the proof should be revised accordingly. We should emphasize that the almost sure and mean-square convergence cannot imply each other in the probability theory generally. In this chapter, we establish these convergence properties using different techniques. Two initialization cases are the most common relaxations of the identical initialization condition. Therefore, the results in this chapter can be applied to other problems with these initialization conditions.

9.4 ILLUSTRATIVE SIMULATIONS

9.4.1 Numerical Example

Consider a linear system with the state-space matrices:

$$A(t) = \begin{bmatrix} 0.5+0.1\sin(0.2t) & -0.06 & -0.28 \\ -0.03 & 0.36 & -0.3 \\ -0.1 & -0.12 & 0.36 \end{bmatrix},$$

TABLE 9.1 Simulation parameters

Parameter	Value
Maximum iteration numbers	100
the condensed reference y_r	$[1.2, 1.5, 0.9, 1.6, 1.4, 0.9]^T$
System noise $\omega_k(t)$	$\omega_k(t) \sim N(0, 0.1^2)$
Measurement noise $\upsilon_k(t)$	$\upsilon_k(t) \sim N(0, 0.1^2)$
Fading gain $\gamma_k(t)$	$\gamma_k(t) \sim N(0.95, 0.1^2)$ and $\gamma_k(t) > 0$
Decreasing gain sequence d_k	$0.2/k^{0.9}$
The initial input $u_1(t)$	0

$$B(t) = \begin{bmatrix} -1 & 0.1 - 0.1\cos((t-2)\pi/8) & 0 \\ 0 & -1 & 0.36 \\ 0.2 & 0 & -1 \end{bmatrix},$$

$$C(t) = \begin{bmatrix} 1.7 & 0.45 & 0.3 \\ 0.35 & 1.57 & 1.15 - 0.2\sin(0.5\pi t) \end{bmatrix}.$$

Let the trial length N be 15. Noticing that the output is two-dimensional, the dimension of the lifting output supervector y_k and y_d is 30. However, not all dimensions of this supervector are required to track some given values; instead, we only track a part of these dimensions. The selected reference points are $y_d^{(2)}(1), y_d^{(1)}(3), y_d^{(2)}(5), y_d^{(2)}(7), y_d^{(2)}(9), y_d^{(2)}(13)$, where the superscript denotes the dimension of the corresponding output vector. As discussed in Remark 9.7, we set the learning matrix $L = (\Phi G)^T$. Then, we can calculate the eigenvalues of ΦGL as $\{2.4959, 2.8072, 2.9300, 3.1125, 3.4471, 4.7000\}$, which satisfies the design condition. Other parameters are listed in Table 9.1 for an intuitive understanding.

The results for both initialization conditions are similar and therefore, we will elaborate one case as an illustration to save space. Note that the initial response under the random initialization condition can be regarded as a part of the measurement noise, thus its effect on the convergence can be reflected by the measurement noise. In consideration of this point, we first consider the asymptotically precise initialization condition and then provide a comparison result of both cases at the end of this subsection. In particular, we set the initial state to be $x_k(0) = 1/k$.

Fig. 9.3 shows the tracking performance at the 100th iteration. The horizonal axis denotes the dimension of the lifting output supervector and the vertical axis denotes the specific values. The red circles represent the desired reference values of the specified tracking dimensions while the black rhombuses represent the actual output for all dimensions. Clearly, the actual output

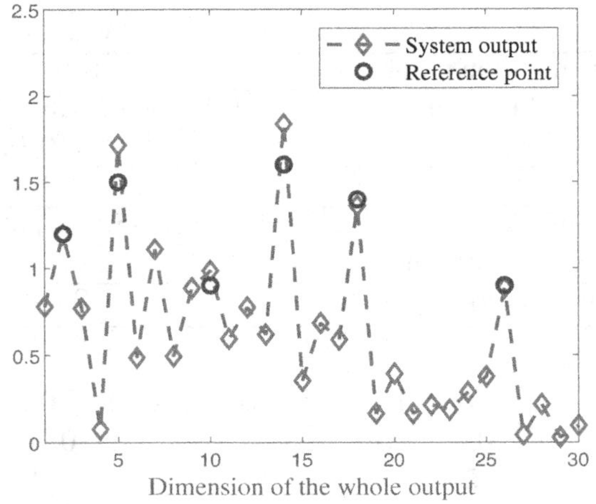

Figure 9.3 System output at the 100th iterations and the reference point.

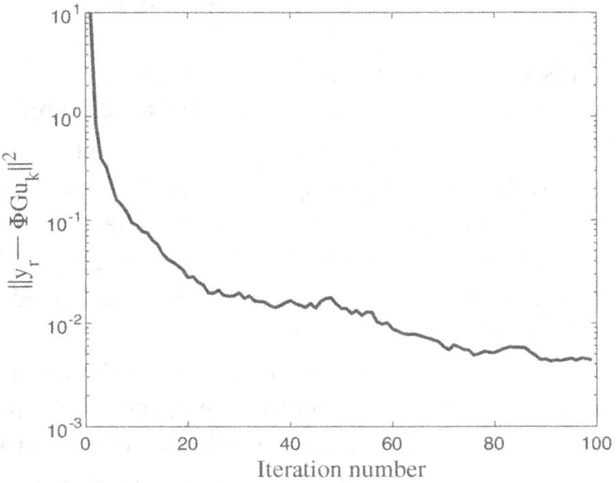

Figure 9.4 Norm of tracking error $||y_r - \Phi Gu_k||^2$.

of the system matches with the desired reference with high precision at the specified dimensions, where the minor deviations are mainly due to irremovable various types of randomness in the system and fading channel.

To deeply understand the learning performance of the proposed scheme, we plot the profile of 2-norm of the auxiliary tracking error in Fig. 9.4. Here, the auxiliary denote the essential tracking performance of the generated input

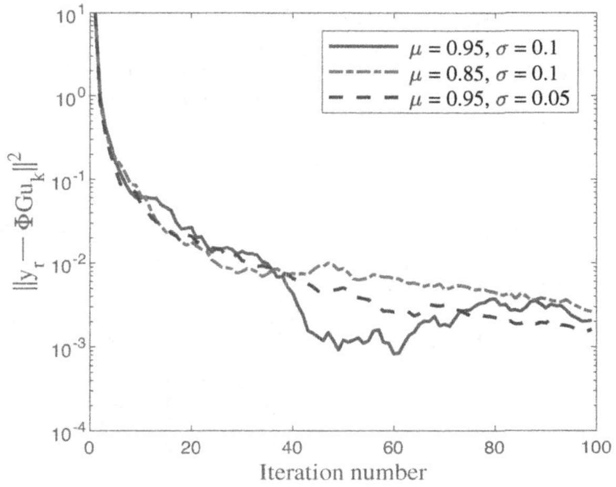

Figure 9.5 Tracking error for different distributions.

signal to the desired reference by excluding all other randomness within each iteration and its 2-norm is defined by $\|y_r - \Phi G u_k\|^2$ for the kth iteration. From Fig. 9.4, the profile decreases rapidly as the iteration number increase. The proposed scheme is witnessed to achieve zero-error tracking performance effectively.

To illustrate the influence of the fading channel on the tracking performance, we simulate three cases of the fading distributions. In particular, we select the fading mean ρ and variance σ as follows: $(\rho = 0.95, \sigma = 0.1)$, $(\rho = 0.85, \sigma = 0.1)$ and $(\rho = 0.95, \sigma = 0.05)$. Fig. 9.5 presents the 2-norm of the auxiliary tracking error for these three cases. Compared with the mean ρ, the variance σ^2 has more impact on the tracking performance. A smaller fading gain variance corresponds to better tracking performance within finite learning iterations. This observation is consistent with our intuition.

The decreasing gain sequence d_k is introduced to suppress the influence of random noise and fading and to ensure the steady convergence of the input sequence along the iteration axis. To reveal the role of the sequence d_k, we conduct two comparative simulations in turn: different choices of d_k and the proposed scheme with a fixed gain. First, we run the algorithm for three different selections of the decreasing gain: $(\alpha = 0.2,\ \beta = 0.9)$, $(\alpha = 0.2,\ \beta = 0.55)$ and $(\alpha = 0.15,\ \beta = 0.9)$. The corresponding profiles of the auxiliary tracking error are provided in Fig. 9.6. It is observed that both α and β has significant influence on the convergence process, where α mainly

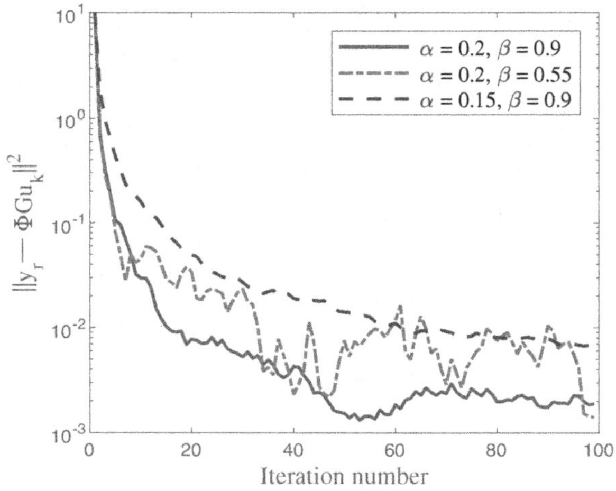

Figure 9.6 Tracking error for different decreasing gains($d_k = \alpha/k^{\beta}$).

affects the convergence speed while β affects the smoothness of iteration-wise curve. However, both parameters are surely not the larger the better. It is open how to generate an optimal selection of the decreasing gain sequence.

Then, we proceed to conduct the proposed scheme with a fixed gain so as to illustrate the necessity of the decreasing gain sequence. In particular, the fixed gain is set to $d_k \equiv 0.2$. The profile of the 2-norm of the auxiliary tracking error for this case is shown by the dotted line in Fig. 9.7, where the solid line corresponds to the case of the decreasing gain sequence $d_k = 0.2/k^{0.9}$. It can be seen from the figure that the fixed gain leads to a faster convergence speed at the early stage; however, the learning process will cease after a few iterations because the fixed gain fails to suppress the influence of various randomness. Consequently, the generated input sequence cannot achieve steady convergence. This reveals the necessity of a decreasing gain for stochastic systems.

At the end of this subsection, we conduct the simulation under the random initialization condition to demonstrate the effectiveness of the proposed scheme and provide an intuitive comparison for both cases of the reinitialization. For the random initialization condition, the initial state follows a normal distribution $x_k(0) \sim N(0, 0.1^2)$. Moreover, two initial conditions are provided for comparison: bounded initialization ($\|x_k(0) - x_d(0)\| \leq C$) and fixed drift condition ($x_k(0) = C \neq x_d(0)$). In particular, they are given by $x_k(0) \sim U(0,1)$ and $x_k(0) = 2$. All other parameters remain the same to that of the

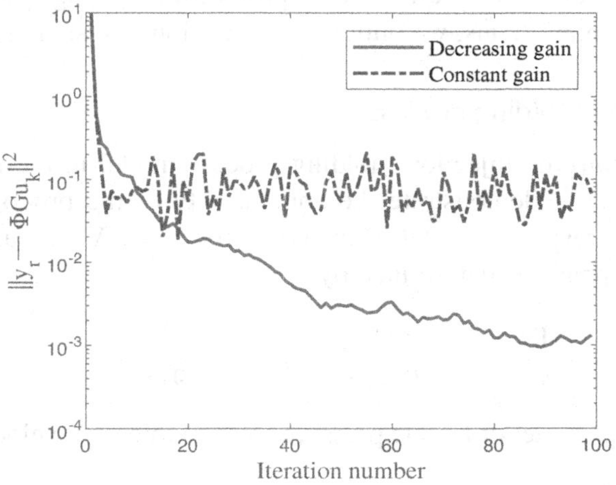

Figure 9.7 Tracking error for different learning algorithms.

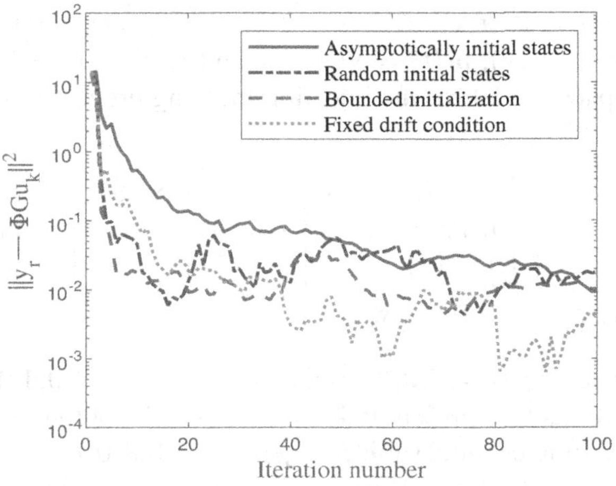

Figure 9.8 Tracking error for different initial state conditions.

asymptotically precise initialization condition. The profiles of the auxiliary tracking error in the iteration domain are plotted in Fig. 9.8. We observe that the profiles are close to each other, which implies that the proposed scheme can realize effective convergence under various initialization conditions. By the lifted dynamics in (9.2), the variants of other disturbances and uncertainties can be reflected by the initial state error. Moreover, the proposed scheme has been numerically shown effectiveness for various fading distributions in the previous chapters. Thus, we omit these extensions for saving space.

9.4.2 Injection Molding Process

In this subsection, the injection molding process model in the filling stage [68] is employed to demonstrate the applicability of the proposed scheme in practice. The response model of injection velocity (IV) to valve opening (VO), in filling phase, is determined by

$$\frac{\mathrm{IV}}{\mathrm{VO}} = \frac{8.687z^{-1} - 5.617z^{-2}}{1 - 0.9291z^{-1} - 0.03191z^{-2}}, \tag{9.41}$$

and the response model of nozzle pressure (NP) to injection velocity is given by

$$\frac{\mathrm{NP}}{\mathrm{IV}} = \frac{0.1054}{1 - z^{-1}}. \tag{9.42}$$

Define $x_k^{(1)}(t) = \mathrm{IV}(t,k)$, $x_k^{(2)}(t) = \mathrm{NP}(t,k)$, $x_k^{(3)}(t) = 0.03191\mathrm{IV}(t-1,k) - 5.617\mathrm{VO}(t-1,k)$, $u_k(t) = \mathrm{VO}(t,k)$, and $y_k(t) = \mathrm{IV}(t,k)$. Then, we have the state space model for the injection molding process in filling phase as follows:

$$\begin{aligned} x_k(t+1) &= \begin{bmatrix} 0.9291 & 1 & 0 \\ 0.1054 & 0 & 1 \\ 0.03191 & 0 & 0 \end{bmatrix} x_k(t) + \begin{bmatrix} 8.687 \\ 0 \\ -5.617 \end{bmatrix} u_k(t), \\ y_k(t) &= \begin{bmatrix} 1 & 0 & 0 \end{bmatrix} x_k(t). \end{aligned}$$

We add disturbance $\omega_k(t) \sim N(0, 0.1^2)$ and noise $\upsilon_k(t) \sim N(0, 1^2)$ to the state and output equations to represent unknown noise. The output is transmitted back through a fading channel subject to $\gamma_k(t) \sim N(0.8, 0.1^2)$.

The required tracking positions are $y_d(3), y_d(7), y_d(10)$ and the condensed reference is $y_r = [2,1,3]^T$. The initialization condition is set to $x_k(0) = 1/k$. The decreasing learning gain sequence is set to be $d_k = 0.01/k$. The gain matrix is set to $L = (\Phi G)^T$. The eigenvalues of ΦGL are $\{0.0435, 0.0469, 0.0488\}$, which satisfy the design condition. The maximum number of iterations is set to 100.

Fig. 9.9 presents the tracking performance for the 100th iteration, where read circles and black rhombuses denotes the reference values and the actual output, respectively. It can be seen that a perfect tracking performance is realized. Fig. 9.10 demonstrates the Euclidean norm profiles of input errors along

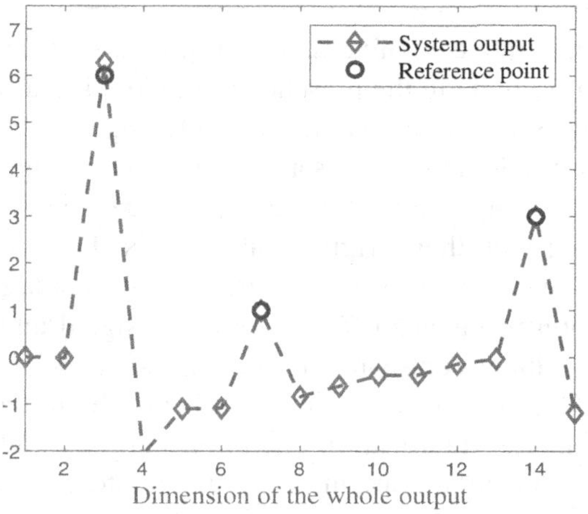

Figure 9.9 System output at the 100th iterations and the reference point.

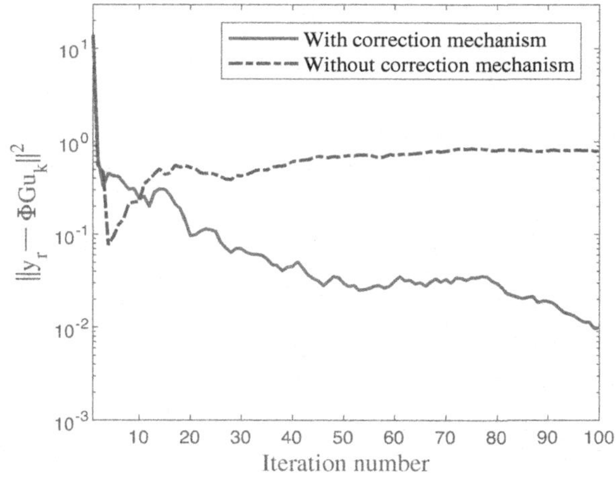

Figure 9.10 Norm of tracking error $||y_r - \Phi G u_k||^2$.

the iteration axis for both cases: with and without correction mechanism. It is observed that the algorithm without correction mechanism can diverge after certain iterations. This observation reflects that the influence of the biased fading randomness is inherent distinct from the traditional measurement noise. The simulations for various variations are similar to the previous example and we omit them for brevity.

9.5 SUMMARY

In this chapter, an iterative learning scheme is proposed to deal with the point-to-point tracking problem in the presence of random initialization condition, system disturbances, measurement noise, and fading randomness. The point-to-point tracking problem introduces a lack of reference signals to correct the input signals. The fading channel introduces biased deviations of the received outputs comparing with their original values. It is shown that the proposed scheme is effective to achieve perfect learning and tracking performance by a simple correction mechanism for the received signal and an iterative update mode for the input command. Two common cases of the initialization condition are addressed in this chapter, both of which evidently relax the conventional identical initialization condition that is widely applied in the literature. Various techniques are introduced and integrated to establish both mean-square and almost sure convergence of the proposed scheme. This has provided the strongest convergence results for a randomized scheme. The approach can be utilized to solve engineering issues such as sensor networks and power systems provided that the required conditions can be satisfied.

CHAPTER 10

Point-to-Point Tracking Using Reference Update Strategy

THIS chapter concentrates on the point-to-point tracking problem via fading communications by proposing a reference update strategy. Using this strategy, the tracking performance is continuously improved even with faded information as the number of iterations increases. A learning control scheme is established and proved to be convergent in both mean-square and almost sure senses under mild conditions. The convergence rate is accelerated by introducing the virtual reference compared with the traditional update approach.

10.1 INTRODUCTION

Iterative learning control (ILC) has been a considerable control direction in process control. Its learning capability offers superior control performance without specific knowledge of the system model. The targeted trajectory typically assigns values for all sampling time points. However, it is unnecessary to track targets at every time point but merely for a subset of whole trajectory for some systems. For example, considering the mechanical arm's pick and place operation, only the start and end points are of concern while no restriction is desired for its route. This is referred to as the point-to-point (P2P) tracking problem, in which the system must track certain values at the specified time points. For a P2P tracking problem, the total number of target points is generally fewer than that of sampling points.

DOI: 10.1201/9781032646404-10

Some methods were proposed to solve the P2P tracking problem. The first method is to construct a complete reference trajectory passing the target values and use a typical learning control algorithm for learning. In [19], authors used T-curve and S-curve to design a complete reference trajectory and applied the P-type learning controller. In [24,58], the reference trajectory was updated such that the tracking performance can be improved by refining the references. The second method updates the input using the tracking errors at the specified points without reconstructing a complete reference trajectory. In this method, optimization techniques are usually used to evaluate the improvement performance. Several typical representatives include the norm optimal ILC [47], gradient descent method [22], and Newton algorithm [26]. A recent study [35] established an accelerated gradient algorithm by introducing a performance-dependent gain sequence using the tracking errors and proved for the first time that the input sequence converged to a certain limit related to the initial input.

Further, the existing ILC algorithms for the P2P tracking problem usually depend on reliable communication networks. In practice, the system often adopts the network structure to improve flexibility and robustness. In this structure, the controller and plant are separated in different sites connected to each other by wire/wireless networks. This structure introduces randomness to the transmitted signals and brings challenges to algorithm design and affecting the control performance. Among various channel randomness, fading communication is an important issue. However, fading has received less attenuation in the literature than other communication limitations. A fading channel is often encountered in wireless networked control systems, which would lead to signal distortion and interference. In this chapter, we keep addressing the P2P tracking problem via fading channels, where the fading randomness is modeled by a random variable multiplied by the signals.

In Chapter 9, the P2P tracking problem is studied for networked stochastic systems with fading communications by directly updating the input signal. In this chapter, we propose a reference update strategy that both the reference trajectory and input signal are updated for each iteration. A decreasing gain sequence is used to reduce the impact of randomness in the learning process. The asymptotic convergence of the proposed scheme is established in both mean-square and almost sure senses. To highlight the fundamental effect of fading channels, the output and input fading cases are examined individually. In addition, we provide a framework for the general case that both output and input channels suffer from fading and demonstrate the effectiveness of the proposed algorithm on a robot system. The learning performance and tracking ability are disclosed using the reference update strategy. In short, we provide a systematic framework for the P2P learning tracking control via fading communications by a reference update strategy.

10.2 PROBLEM FORMULATION

Consider a linear time-varying stochastic system:

$$\begin{aligned} x_k(t+1) &= A_t x_k(t) + B_t u_k(t) + \omega_k(t), \\ y_k(t) &= C_t x_k(t) + \upsilon_k(t), \end{aligned} \tag{10.1}$$

where k denotes the iteration index, $k \in \mathbf{Z}_+$, i.e., $k = 1, 2, \ldots$ and t denotes the time index, $t = 0, 1, \ldots, n$ with n being a proper integer as the iteration length. $x_k(t) \in \mathbf{R}^n$, $u_k(t) \in \mathbf{R}^p$, $y_k(t) \in \mathbf{R}^q$ represent the system state, input and output, respectively. A_t, B_t, C_t denote the system matrices with appropriate dimensions. Furthermore, $w_k(t)$ and $v_k(t)$ are system disturbances and measurement noise, respectively.

The following assumptions are required for analysis.

Assumption 10.1 *The input/output coupling matrix $C_{t+1}B_t$ is of full-row rank, $t \in 0, 1, \ldots, n-1$.*

This assumption means that the input dimension is greater than the output dimension and guarantees the existence of the input for any reference trajectory. Further, the system relative degree is one as $C_{t+1}B_t \neq 0$, $\forall t$. The extension to high-order relative degrees is straightforward and thus omitted to make the main idea clear.

Assumption 10.2 *The noise terms $w_k(t)$ and $v_k(t)$ are independent with respect to the iteration index k and time index t. Additionally, $\mathbb{E}[w_k(t)] = 0$, $\mathbb{E}[v_k(t)] = 0$, and $\sup_{k,t} \mathbb{E}[\|w_k(t)\|^2] < \infty$, $\sup_{k,t} \mathbb{E}[\|v_k(t)\|^2] < \infty$.*

In practice, this assumption is valid because the system operates batch by batch. Thus, the noise terms are uncorrelated for different batches. We denote $\phi_k \triangleq \mathbb{E}[\|w_k(t)\|^2]$ and $\psi_k \triangleq \mathbb{E}[\|v_k(t)\|^2]$.

Assumption 10.3 *The initial state $x_k(0)$ is a random variable satisfying $\mathbb{E}[x_k(0)] = x_d(0)$, where $x_d(0)$ is the desired initial state defined by the reference trajectory. Moreover, $\sup_k \mathbb{E}[x_k(0)] = \mathbb{E}[\|x_k(0) - x_d(0)\|^2] < \infty$.*

The initialization condition $x_k(0) = x_d(0)$ has been widely applied in the literature such that the repetition starts from the same position. Assumption

10.3 relaxes the condition. It can be removed by introducing an additional rectifying mechanism if the initial position is unnecessary to track. We denote $\pi_k \triangleq \mathbb{E}[\|x_k(0) - x_d(0)\|^2]$ for analysis.

The input/output can be rewritten in a lifted form:

$$u_k = [u_k^T(0), u_k^T(1), \ldots, u_k^T(n-1)]^T \in \mathbf{R}^{pn},$$
$$y_k = [y_k^T(1), y_k^T(2), \ldots, y_k^T(n)]^T \in \mathbf{R}^{qn}.$$

In addition, let

$$G = \begin{bmatrix} C_1B_0 & 0 & \cdots & 0 \\ C_2A_1B_0 & C_2B_1 & \cdots & 0 \\ \vdots & \vdots & \ddots & \vdots \\ C_nA_1^{n-1}B_0 & C_nA_2^{n-1}B_1 & \cdots & C_nB_{n-1} \end{bmatrix},$$

where $A_i^j \triangleq A_jA_{j-1}\cdots A_i$ for $j \geq i$ and $A_{i+1}^i = I$. Clearly, $G \in \mathbf{R}^{qn\times pn}$. Subsequently, the system dynamics becomes

$$y_k = Gu_k + Nx_k(0) + Mw_k + v_k, \tag{10.2}$$

where

$$N = [(C_1A_0)^T \ (C_2A_1A_0)^T \ \cdots (C_nA_0^{n-1})]^T, \tag{10.3}$$

$$M = \begin{bmatrix} C_1 & 0 & \cdots & 0 \\ C_2A_1 & C_2 & \cdots & 0 \\ \vdots & \vdots & \ddots & \vdots \\ C_nA_1^{n-1} & C_nA_2^{n-1} & \cdots & C_n \end{bmatrix}. \tag{10.4}$$

We denote the complete reference trajectory by y_d:

$$y_d = [y_d^T(1), y_d^T(2), \ldots, y_d^T(n)]^T \in \mathbf{R}^{qn}.$$

In a P2P tracking problem, it is unnecessary to follow y_d completely. Instead, we only need to track several specific points of y_d. Here, we assume that only l dimensions of y_d is required to track, $0 < l \leq qn$. In other words, $qn - l$ dimensions of y_d are neglected. Disregarding all points in y_d that are not necessary to track, we obtain a subreference $y_r \in \mathbf{R}^l$, connected with y_d by

$$y_r = \Phi y_d, \tag{10.5}$$

where $\Phi \in \mathbf{R}^{l\times qn}$ is a transformation matrix whose elements are either 0 or 1. The entry of Φ is defined as follows: $\Phi_{i,j} = 1$ if the jth element of y_d constitutes the ith target to be tracked (i.e., the ith element of y_r); otherwise $\Phi_{i,j} = 0$. It is worth emphasizing that the matrix Φ has only one entry of 1 in each row and the rest entries of the row are 0.

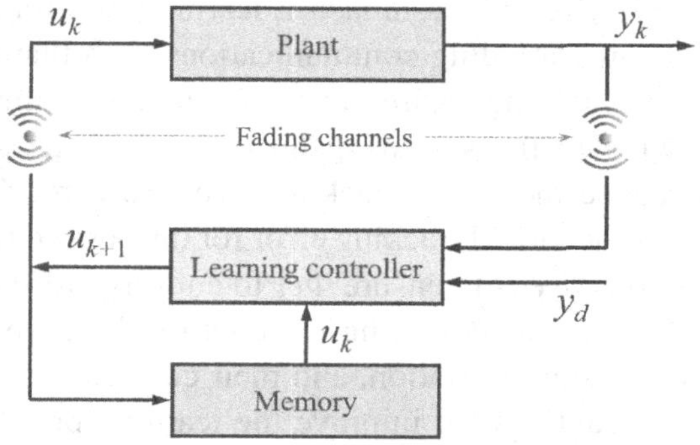

Figure 10.1 Diagram of control systems over fading channels.

Remark 10.1 *The matrix Φ is critical to connect the complete reference y_d and the subreference y_r. This matrix can be determined by comparing the complete reference and selected tracking points. In other words, no additional estimation or computation is required. Introducing the term Φ ensures the update of the input signals unaffected by irrelevant points of y_d. Therefore, only the selected tracking points of y_d rather than the complete trajectory are used in the learning control algorithm, while the unselected points are replaced by artificial reference values generated by the reference update strategy.*

Fig. 10.1 shows how the fading channel affects the system performance. We will check the effects of output fading and input fading separately. In this chapter, the fading channel effect is modeled by a random variable that is multiplied to the transmitted signals. Thus, each dimension of the input/output is communicated and faded irrespective of time and iteration labels. The dimension coupled fading impact is left for future investigation.

Assumption 10.4 *Denote the fading gain by $\mu_k(t)$, which identically and independently distributed with respect to t and k. The distribution function $f(\mu)$ is continuous and $\mathbb{P}(\mu_k(t) > 0) = 1$. Moreover, $\mathbb{E}[\mu_k(t)] = \mu$ and $\mathbb{E}[(\mu_k(t) - \mu)^2] = \tau^2$, where μ is assumed known.*

Assumption 10.4 is reasonable because the statistics of fading channels are usually determined by the hardware conditions. If the statistics are unknown, we can transmit test signals and use the received signals to estimate the fading statistics.

The control objective is to establish a learning control scheme for the P2P tracking problem via fading communications such that the system outputs asymptotically track the desired reference points as the iteration number increases. Owing to the system disturbances and measurement noise, it is difficult to reduce the actual tracking errors to zero. Thus, we define $\Phi\hat{e}_k \triangleq y_r - \Phi G u_k$ as the virtual tracking error for the desired reference points. The convergence objective is to ensure $\Phi\hat{e}_k$ to converge to zero as $k \to \infty$.

The technical issues in addressing the control objective come from the P2P tracking, fading communication, and their coupling effect. For the P2P tracking, it is significant how to improve the learning process by using the unspecified tracking points of the complete reference. This motivates us to propose a reference update strategy. For the fading communication, a major difficulty lies in treating the output-dependent uncertainties. For the coupling effect, a two-step update mechanism including a reference update and an input update is proposed.

10.3 LEARNING CONTROL SCHEME AND ITS ANALYSIS FOR OUTPUT FADING

10.3.1 Fading Correction and Algorithm Design

In this section, we address the case when the output communication channel experiences random fading. By Assumption 10.4, we have

$$y_k^r = \Gamma_k y_k, \tag{10.6}$$

where $\Gamma_k \triangleq \text{diag}\{\mu_k(1), \mu_k(2), \ldots, \mu_k(n)\} \otimes I_q$. Because the biased signal is unsuitable for the control, a correction mechanism should be implemented to acquire unbiased information. The corrected signal is defined by

$$y_k^c = \mu^{-1}\Gamma_k y_k, \tag{10.7}$$

where y_k^c represents the corrected output signals.

Remark 10.2 *It is clear that y_k^c is an unbiased estimate of y_k. Indeed, the right-hand side of* (10.7) *can be rewritten as $y_k - (I - \mu^{-1}\Gamma_k)y_k = y_k - \Upsilon_k y_k$, whose mathematical expectation is y_k because the mean of Υ_k is zero.*

We present a learning control scheme that updates not only the control signal but also the reference trajectory. The purpose is to improve the learning process and convergence speed by producing a new reference trajectory.

We denote the points need to track by a set $T^s \triangleq \{t_i^s\}$, $0 \leq i \leq qn$ and $\sharp T^s = l$, where $\sharp T^s$ denotes the number of points of T^s. The desired outputs at these specific points are denoted by $y_d(t_i^s)$. Therefore, the goal is to create an input update rule such that the system outputs converge to the specified values: $y_k(t_i^s) \to y_d(t_i^s)$, $t_i^s \in T^s$. To this end, we generate virtual reference trajectories while keeping the specified tracking points constant. The virtual reference is denoted by $r_k(t)$ for the kth iteration, $t \in [0,n]$, which must satisfy the following condition:

$$r_k(t_i^s) = y_d(t_i^s), \quad t_i^s \in T^s. \tag{10.8}$$

Given an arbitrary initial reference $r_0(t)$ satisfying $r_0(t_i^s) = y_d(t_i^s)$, the learning control scheme is given as follows:

$$R_{k+1} = R_k + \Lambda_k(R_k - y_k^c), \tag{10.9}$$

$$u_{k+1} = u_k + a_k L(R_{k+1} - y_k^c), \tag{10.10}$$

where $R_k = [r_k^T(1), r_k^T(2), \ldots, r_k^T(n)]^T \in \mathbf{R}^{qn}$ and L is a learning gain matrix, $L \in \mathbf{R}^{pn \times qn}$. Λ_k is a matrix to update the trajectory defined by

$$\Lambda_k = a_k \Theta_k H, \tag{10.11}$$

where $\{a_k\}$ is a decreasing sequence satisfying

$$a_k > 0, a_k \xrightarrow[k\to\infty]{} 0, \sum_{k=1}^{\infty} a_k = \infty, \sum_{k=1}^{\infty} a_k^2 < \infty. \tag{10.12}$$

Besides, $h(t) = \prod_i (t - t_i^s)$, $t_i^s \in T^s$, $H = \mathrm{diag}\{h(1), h(2), \ldots, h(qn)\}$, $\Theta_k = \mathrm{diag}[\theta_k(1), \theta_k(2), \ldots, \theta_k(n)] \otimes I_q$, where $\theta_k(t)$ is an arbitrary function ensuring $\Theta_k H < 0$.

Remark 10.3 *According to the update law of $\{R_k\}$, we have $h(t) = 0$ at $t \in T^s$ in each batch; therefore, the trajectory $r_k(t)$ guarantees* (10.8). *In the following, we shall focus on $R_k - y_k$ for convenience of analysis because the specified target points are unchanged while updating the reference trajectory. The convergence speed is hopefully enhanced by the anticipation learning* (10.9) *of the unspecified points in the virtual reference, i.e., the complementary set of T^s.*

The specific procedure is given in Algorithm 10.1.

Algorithm 10.1 The learning algorithm to output fading networks

---

Without loss of generality, the initial condition is set as $u_0(t) = 0$ and $x_k(0) = 0$. The initial trajectory R_0 can be fitted by any smooth method such as a cubic spline regression curve.

Step 1:

a) Using Equation (10.2), generate output y_k;
b) Using Equation (10.7), compute the corrected output y_k^c;
c) Compute the tracking error the control $R_k - y_k^c$;
d) Using Equation (10.9), update input R_{k+1};
e) Using Equation (10.10), update input u_{k+1};

Step 2:

$k = k+1$, repeat whole process until the stopping criteria is satisfied.

10.3.2 Convergence Analysis for Output Fading Case

To develop convergence for the scheme (10.9) and (10.10), we check the boundedness of u_k first. We have

$$\begin{bmatrix} R_{k+1} \\ u_{k+1} \end{bmatrix} = \begin{bmatrix} I + a_k\Theta_k H & -a_k\Theta_k H(I-\Upsilon_k)G \\ a_k L(I+a_k\Theta_k H) & I - a_k L(I+a_k\Theta_k H)(I-\Upsilon_k)G \end{bmatrix} \begin{bmatrix} R_k \\ u_k \end{bmatrix} + a_k \begin{bmatrix} -\Theta_k H(I-\Upsilon_k) \\ -L(I+a_k\Theta_k H)(I-\Upsilon_k) \end{bmatrix} \delta_k, \tag{10.13}$$

where $\delta_k = Nx_k(0) + Mw_k + v_k$. For the term

$$\begin{bmatrix} I + a_k\Theta_k H & -a_k\Theta_k H(I-\Upsilon_k)G \\ a_k L(I+a_k\Theta_k H) & I - a_k L(I+a_k\Theta_k H)(I-\Upsilon_k)G \end{bmatrix},$$

because $I + a_k\Theta_k H$ is invertible, it can be transformed into

$$\begin{bmatrix} I + a_k\Theta_k H & -a_k\Theta_k H(I-\Upsilon_k)G \\ 0 & I - a_k L(I-\Upsilon_k)G \end{bmatrix}.$$

By designing Θ_k and L, it becomes a stable matrix. The term

$$a_k \begin{bmatrix} -\Theta_k H(I-\Upsilon_k) \\ -L(I+a_k\Theta_k H)(I-\Upsilon_k) \end{bmatrix} \delta_k$$

is independent in the iteration domain and of zero mean. By the convergence theorem of independent random variables [14], a finite limit is ensured for

(10.13). Thus, $\{R_k\}$ and $\{u_k\}$ are bounded along the iteration axis. This fact is useful for understanding the learning scheme's convergence feature.

We continue to solve work on the proposed scheme's convergence. The first theorem is given on convergence in the mean-square sense.

Theorem 10.1 *Consider system* (10.1) *with an output fading channel and Assumptions 10.1-10.4 hold. Apply the learning control scheme* (10.9) *and* (10.10) *for the reference and input, respectively. If the learning matrix L is designed such that $-GL$ is Hurwitz and the decreasing gain sequence $\{a_k\}$ satisfies* (10.12)*, then the virtual tracking error $\hat{e}_k \triangleq R_k - Gu_k$ converges to zero in the mean-square sense, i.e., $\lim_{k\to\infty}\mathbb{E}[\|\hat{e}_k\|^2] = 0$.*

Proof: Note that $\hat{e}_{k+1} = R_{k+1} - Gu_{k+1}$. Substituting R_{k+1} and u_{k+1} into (10.9) and (10.10), we have

$$\begin{aligned}
\hat{e}_{k+1} &= R_{k+1} - Gu_{k+1} \\
&= R_k + \Lambda_k(R_k - y_k^c) - G[u_k + a_k L(R_{k+1} - y_k^c)] \\
&= \hat{e}_k + \Lambda_k(R_k - y_k^c) - a_k GL(I + \Lambda_k)(R_k - y_k^c) \\
&= \hat{e}_k + (\Lambda_k - a_k GL - a_k GL\Lambda_k)(R_k - y_k + \Upsilon_k y_k) \\
&= \hat{e}_k + a_k(\Theta_k H - GL - a_k GL\Theta_k H)[\hat{e}_k - Nx_k(0) - \\
&\quad Mw_k - v_k] + \Upsilon_k(Gu_k + Nx_k(0) + Mw_k + v_k)] \\
&= \hat{e}_k + a_k(\Theta_k H - GL)\hat{e}_k - a_k^2 GL\Theta_k H\hat{e}_k \\
&\quad + a_k(\Theta_k H - GL - a_k GL\Theta_k H)(\Upsilon_k(Gu_k + \delta_k) - \delta_k) \\
&= \hat{e}_k - a_k(\Xi - \Psi_k)\hat{e}_k + a_k(\Xi - \Psi_k)\delta_k \\
&\quad - a_k(\Xi - \Psi_k)\Upsilon_k(Gu_k + \delta_k),
\end{aligned} \tag{10.14}$$

where $\Xi \triangleq GL$, $\Psi_k \triangleq \Theta_k H - a_k GL\Theta_k H$, and $\delta_k \triangleq Nx_k(0) + Mw_k + v_k$.

Note that L is designed to ensure that $-GL$ is Hurwitz, i.e., all eigenvalues of GL have positive real parts. Referring to the Lyapunov stability theory that there exists a positive-definite matrix $\mathcal{Q}$ that satisfies $\Xi^T\mathcal{Q} + \mathcal{Q}\Xi = I_{nq}$, we can define a Lyapunov function

$$Y_{k+1} = (\Phi\hat{e}_{k+1})^T\mathcal{Q}(\Phi\hat{e}_{k+1}). \tag{10.15}$$

Then, we have

$$\begin{aligned}
Y_{k+1} &= \hat{e}_{k+1}^T\mathcal{Q}\hat{e}_{k+1} \\
&= \hat{e}_k^T\mathcal{Q}\hat{e}_k - a_k\hat{e}_k^T(\Xi^T\mathcal{Q} + \mathcal{Q}\Xi)\hat{e}_k \\
&\quad + a_k^2(\Xi\hat{e}_k)^T\mathcal{Q}\Xi\hat{e}_k + a_k^2(\Psi_k\hat{e}_k)^T\mathcal{Q}\Psi_k\hat{e}_k
\end{aligned}$$

$$
\begin{aligned}
&+a_k\hat{e}_k^T(\Psi_k^T\mathcal{Q}+\mathcal{Q}\Psi_k)\hat{e}_k\\
&+2a_k\hat{e}_k^T\mathcal{Q}(\Xi-\Psi_k)\delta_k\\
&+2a_k^2\hat{e}_k^T\Xi^T\mathcal{Q}(\Xi-\Psi_k)\delta_k\\
&-2a_k^2(\Psi_k\hat{e}_k)^T\mathcal{Q}(\Xi-\Psi_k)\delta_k\\
&+a_k^2[(\Xi-\Psi_k)\delta_k]^T\mathcal{Q}(\Xi-\Psi_k)\delta_k\\
&-2a_k^2[(\Xi-\Psi_k)\delta_k]^T\mathcal{Q}(\Xi-\Psi_k)\Upsilon_k(Gu_k+\delta_k)\\
&-2a_k\hat{e}_k^T\mathcal{Q}(\Xi-\Psi_k)\Upsilon_k(Gu_k+\delta_k)\\
&-2a_k^2\hat{e}_k^T\Xi^T\mathcal{Q}\Psi_k\hat{e}_k\\
&+2a_k^2\hat{e}_k^T\Xi^T\mathcal{Q}(\Xi-\Psi_k)\Upsilon_k(Gu_k+\delta_k)\\
&-2a_k^2\hat{e}_k^T\Psi_k^T\mathcal{Q}(\Xi-\Psi_k)\Upsilon_k(Gu_k+\delta_k)\\
&+a_k^2[(\Xi-\Psi_k)\Upsilon_k(Gu_k+\delta_k)]^T\mathcal{Q}\\
&\quad\times(\Xi-\Psi_k)\Upsilon_k(Gu_k+\delta_k)\\
&-2a_k\hat{e}_k^T\mathcal{Q}(\Xi-\Psi_k)\Upsilon_k(Gu_k+\delta_k).
\end{aligned}
\tag{10.16}
$$

Now, we define an increasing σ−algebra: $\mathcal{F}_k \triangleq \sigma\{x_j(0),\ u_1(t),\ y_j(t),\ w_j(t),\ v_j(t),\ \mu_j(t),\ 0\le t\le n,\ 1\le j\le k\}$, which is a set of all events up to the kth iteration by all these variables. Thus, $\hat{e}_k\in\mathcal{F}_{k-1}$. Meanwhile, due to the independence property of $\mu_k(t)$ between iterations, Υ_k is independent of the σ-algebra $\mathcal{F}_{k-1}$. Furthermore, $\mathbb{E}[\mu_k(t)|\mathcal{F}_{k-1}]=\mu$, $\mathbb{E}[\Upsilon_k(t)|\mathcal{F}_{k-1}]=0$, $\mathbb{E}[w_k(t)|\mathcal{F}_{k-1}]=0$, and $\mathbb{E}[v_k(t)|\mathcal{F}_{k-1}]=0$. By the updating law, $u_k\in\mathcal{F}_{k-1}$. Based on above properties, we have the following equalities:

$$\mathbb{E}[a_k^2(\Psi_k\hat{e}_k)^T\mathcal{Q}(\Xi-\Psi_k)\delta_k|\mathcal{F}_{k-1}]=0, \tag{10.17}$$

$$\mathbb{E}[a_k\hat{e}_k^T\mathcal{Q}(\Xi-\Psi_k)\delta_k|\mathcal{F}_{k-1}]=0, \tag{10.18}$$

$$\mathbb{E}[a_k^2\hat{e}_k^T\Xi^T\mathcal{Q}(\Xi-\Psi_k)\delta_k|\mathcal{F}_{k-1}]=0, \tag{10.19}$$

$$
\begin{aligned}
&\mathbb{E}\{a_k^2[(\Xi-\Psi_k)\delta_k]^T\mathcal{Q}(\Xi-\Psi_k)\\
&\quad\times\Upsilon_k(Gu_k+\delta_k)|\mathcal{F}_{k-1}\}=0,
\end{aligned}
\tag{10.20}
$$

$$\mathbb{E}[a_k\hat{e}_k^T\mathcal{Q}(\Xi-\Psi_k)\Upsilon_k(Gu_k+\delta_k)|\mathcal{F}_{k-1}]=0, \tag{10.21}$$

$$\mathbb{E}[a_k^2\hat{e}_k^T\Xi^T\mathcal{Q}(\Xi-\Psi_k)\Upsilon_k(Gu_k+\delta_k)|\mathcal{F}_{k-1}]=0, \tag{10.22}$$

$$\mathbb{E}[a_k^2\hat{e}_k^T\Psi_k^T\mathcal{Q}(\Xi-\Psi_k)\Upsilon_k(Gu_k+\delta_k)|\mathcal{F}_{k-1}]=0, \tag{10.23}$$

$$\mathbb{E}[a_k\hat{e}_k\mathcal{Q}(\Xi-\Psi_k)\Upsilon_k(Gu_k+\delta_k)|\mathcal{F}_{k-1}]=0. \tag{10.24}$$

Next, let us deal with the left terms on the right-hand side of (10.16) as follows:

$$\mathbb{E}[(\Xi\hat{e}_k)\mathcal{Q}(\Xi\hat{e}_k)|\mathcal{F}_{k-1}]=\hat{e}_k^T\mathbb{E}[\Xi^T\mathcal{Q}\Xi|\mathcal{F}_{k-1}]\hat{e}_k$$

$$\leq \rho_1 \hat{e}_k^T \mathcal{Q} \hat{e}_k = \rho_1 Y_k, \tag{10.25}$$

$$\mathbb{E}[(\Psi_k \hat{e}_k)^T \mathcal{Q} \Psi_k \hat{e}_k | \mathcal{F}_{k-1}] = \hat{e}_k^T \mathbb{E}[(\Psi_k)^T \mathcal{Q} \Psi_k | \mathcal{F}_{k-1}] \hat{e}_k$$

$$\leq \rho_2 \hat{e}_k^T \mathcal{Q} \hat{e}_k = \rho_2 Y_k, \tag{10.26}$$

$$\mathbb{E}[\hat{e}_k^T (\Xi^T \mathcal{Q} + \mathcal{Q} \Xi) \hat{e}_k | \mathcal{F}_{k-1}] = \mathbb{E}[\hat{e}_k^T \hat{e}_k | \mathcal{F}_{k-1}]$$

$$\geq \rho_3 \hat{e}_k^T \mathcal{Q} \hat{e}_k = \rho_3 Y_k. \tag{10.27}$$

Notice that $\mathcal{Q}$ is a positive-definite matrix. Then, we have

$$\begin{aligned}
\mathbb{E}[\hat{e}_k^T \Psi_k^T \mathcal{Q} \hat{e}_k | \mathcal{F}_{k-1}] &\leq \frac{1}{2} \mathbb{E}[2 \hat{e}_k^T \Psi_k^T \mathcal{Q}^{\frac{1}{2}} \mathcal{Q}^{\frac{1}{2}} \hat{e}_k | \mathcal{F}_{k-1}] \\
&\leq \mathbb{E}[\hat{e}_k^T \Psi_k^T \mathcal{Q} \Psi_k \hat{e}_k | \mathcal{F}_{k-1}] + \mathbb{E}[\hat{e}_k^T \mathcal{Q} \hat{e}_k | \mathcal{F}_{k-1}] \\
&\leq \rho_4 Y_k.
\end{aligned} \tag{10.28}$$

Similarly, we have

$$\mathbb{E}[\hat{e}_k^T \mathcal{Q} \Psi_k \hat{e}_k | \mathcal{F}_{k-1}] \leq \rho_5 Y_k, \tag{10.29}$$

$$\mathbb{E}[\hat{e}_k^T \Xi^T \mathcal{Q} \Psi_k \hat{e}_k | \mathcal{F}_{k-1}] \leq \rho_6 Y_k. \tag{10.30}$$

By the second-order moment boundedness of w_k, v_k, and u_k,

$$\mathbb{E}\{[(\Xi - \Psi_k)\delta_k]^T \mathcal{Q} (\Xi - \Psi_k)\delta_k | \mathcal{F}_{k-1}\} \leq \rho_7, \tag{10.31}$$

$$\begin{aligned}
&\mathbb{E}\{[(\Xi - \Psi_k)\Upsilon_k (G u_k + \delta_k)]^T \mathcal{Q} (\Xi - \Psi_k)\Upsilon_k \\
&\quad \times (G u_k + \delta_k) | \mathcal{F}_{k-1}\} \leq \rho_8.
\end{aligned} \tag{10.32}$$

Combining (10.18)-(10.32), we have

$$\begin{aligned}
\mathbb{E}[Y_{k+1} | \mathcal{F}_{k-1}] =& Y_k + a_k^2 \rho_1 Y_k - a_k^2 \rho_2 Y_k + a_k \rho_3 Y_k \\
&+ a_k (\rho_4 + \rho_5 + 2\rho_6) Y_k \\
&+ a_k^2 \rho_7 + a_k^2 \rho_8.
\end{aligned} \tag{10.33}$$

Taking mathematical expectation to (10.33) leads to

$$\begin{aligned}
\mathbb{E}[Y_{k+1}] \leq& [1 - (\rho_3 + \rho_4 + \rho_5 + 2\rho_6) a_k] \mathbb{E}[Y_k] \\
&+ (\rho_1 + \rho_2) a_k^2 (\mathbb{E}[Y_k] + \frac{\rho_7 + \rho_8}{\rho_1 + \rho_2}).
\end{aligned} \tag{10.34}$$

Comparing (10.34) and (A.1) in the Appendix, the terms m_k, α_1, α_2 and α_3 correspond to $\mathbb{E}[Y_k]$, $(\rho_3 + \rho_4 + \rho_5 + 2\rho_6)$, $(\rho_1 + \rho_2)$ and $\frac{\rho_7 + \rho_8}{\rho_1 + \rho_2}$, respectively. Further, by Lemma A.1, we have $\lim_{k \to \infty} \mathbb{E}[\|\hat{e}_k\|^2] = \lim_{k \to \infty} \mathbb{E}[\|R_k -$

$Gu_k\|^2] = 0$. Moreover, Q is a positive-definite matrix, thus $\mathbb{E}[\|R_k - Gu_k\|^2] \leq \lambda_{\min}^{-1}(\Omega)\mathbb{E}[Y_k]$. The proof is completed. □

Theorem 10.1 demonstrates the learning control scheme's mean-square convergence for the output fading case. A fading channel introduces multiplicative randomness to the outputs, thus we need to correct the received signals to drive the learning process. The correction of the biased signals additionally complicates convergence study as it introduces the output-dependent uncertainty. A decreasing sequence is used to update the reference trajectory and system input to suppress the influence and improve the learning performance. The following theorem proves the almost sure convergence, which is another crucial concept for a randomized algorithm. To finish the proof, we employe Lemma A.2 in the Appendix.

Theorem 10.2 *Consider system* (10.1) *with an output fading channel and Assumptions 10.1-10.4 hold. Apply the learning control scheme* (10.9) *and* (10.10). *If the learning gain matrix L is designed such that $-GL$ is Hurwitz and the decreasing sequence $\{a_k\}$ satisfies* (10.12), *then the virtual tracking error $R_k - Gu_k$ converges to zero in the almost sure sense as the iteration number increases, i.e., $\mathbb{P}(R_k - Gu_k \to 0) = 1$.*

Proof: From (10.33), we have

$$\mathbb{E}[Y_{k+1}|\mathcal{F}_{k-1}] \leq Y_k + d_k^2(\rho_9 Y_k + \rho_{10}), \tag{10.35}$$

where $\rho_9 = \rho_1 + \rho_2$ and $\rho_{10} = \rho_7 + \rho_8$.

We correspond Y_k and $a_k^2(\rho_9 Y_k + \rho_{10})$ to $\mathcal{O}_k$ and $\mathcal{D}_k$ in Lemma A.2 in the Appendix, respectively. It is clear that the condition (A.3) holds by the result $\mathbb{E}[Y_k] \to 0$ in Theorem 10.1. Thus, we conclude that Y_k converges almost surely. Moreover, Theorem 10.1 shows that the auxiliary tracking error $\hat{e}_k$ converges to zero. The proof is completed. □

Theorem 10.2 shows the almost sure convergence of the proposed scheme (10.9) and (10.10). The uniform integrality principle of the involved quantity helps us to establish mean-square and almost sure convergence simultaneously. If the decreasing sequence $\{a_k\}$ is replaced by a suitable constant, the above theorems still hold except that the limit of $R_k - Gu_k$ is no longer zero but within a bounded zone.

10.4 LEARNING CONTROL SCHEME AND ITS ANALYSIS FOR INPUT FADING

This section addresses the input fading case that the channel from the controller to the plant suffers random fading. In this case, the received control is biased. We establish the learning control scheme and its convergence analysis.

10.4.1 Fading Correction and Analysis

The input signal received by the plant is faded during the transmission, which is denoted by u_k^r:

$$u_k^r = \Gamma_k u_k, \tag{10.36}$$

where $\Gamma_k \triangleq \mathrm{diag}\{\mu_k(1), \mu_k(2), \ldots, \mu_k(n)\} \otimes I_q$. Thus, the plant's control signal deviates from the initial control signal and must be rectified before being applied to the plant. The corrected control signal is given below:

$$\begin{aligned} u_k^c &= \mu^{-1} u_k^r = \mu^{-1}\Gamma_k u_k \\ &= u_k - (1 - \mu^{-1}\Gamma_k) u_k \\ &= u_k - \Upsilon_k u_k. \end{aligned} \tag{10.37}$$

Because of the independence of the input $u_k(t)$ and fading parameter $\mu_k(t)$, the expectation of $(1-\mu^{-1}\mu_k(t))u_k(t)$ is equal to zero. Therefore, the corrected input signal u_k^c is an unbiased estimation for its counterpart.

10.4.2 Learning Control Scheme

The learning control scheme follows the strategy of simultaneously updating reference trajectory and input signal. Particularly, we have

$$R_{k+1} = R_k + \Lambda_k (R_k - y_k), \tag{10.38}$$

$$u_{k+1} = u_k + a_k L (R_{k+1} - y_k), \tag{10.39}$$

where Λ_k, $L \in \mathbf{R}^{qn\times pn}$, and $\{a_k\}$ are the same to the output fading case. Note that the input signal fed to the system should be corrected after its receiving; that is, u_k^c rather than u_k is applied. The specific procedure is given in Algorithm 10.2.

10.4.3 Convergence Analysis

Theorem 10.3 *Consider system* (10.1) *with input fading channel and Assumptions 10.1-10.4 hold. Apply the learning control scheme* (10.38) *and* (10.39)*. If the learning gain matrix L is designed such that* $-GL$ *is Hurwitz and the decreasing sequence* $\{a_k\}$ *satisfies* (10.12)*, then the auxiliary tracking error* $\hat{e}_k$ *converges to zero in the mean-square sense, i.e.,* $\mathbb{E}[\|\hat{e}_k\|^2] \to 0$,.

Algorithm 10.2 The learning algorithm to input fading networks

Without loss of generality, the initial condition is set as $u_0(t) = 0$ and $x_k(0) = 0$. The initial trajectory R_0 can be fitted by any smooth method such as a cubic spline regression curve.

Step 1:

b) Using Equation (10.37), compute the corrected input u_k^c;

a) Using Equation (10.2), generate output y_k;

c) Compute the tracking error the control $R_k - y_k$;

d) Using Equation (10.9), update input R_{k+1};

e) Using Equation (10.10), update input u_{k+1};

Step 2:

$k = k+1$, repeat whole process until the stopping criteria is satisfied.

Proof: We write the auxiliary tracking error $\hat{e}_{k+1} = R_{k+1} - Gu_{k+1}$ and substitute (10.38) and (10.39) into it:

$$\begin{aligned}\hat{e}_{k+1} &= R_{k+1} - Gu_{k+1}\\ &= R_k + \Lambda_k(R_k - y_k) - Gu_k - a_k GL(R_{k+1} - y_k)\\ &= \hat{e}_k + \Lambda_k(R_k - y_k) - a_k GL(\Lambda_k + I)(R_k - y_k)\\ &= \hat{e}_k - a_k(\Xi - \Psi_k)(\hat{e}_k + \Upsilon_k u_k - \delta_k),\end{aligned} \tag{10.40}$$

where $\Xi \triangleq GL$, $\Psi_k \triangleq \Theta_k H - a_k GL\Theta_k H$ and $\delta_k \triangleq Nx_k(0) + Mw_k + v_k$.

Observing that (10.40) is similar to (10.14), we still use the positive-definite matrix $\mathcal{Q}$ satisfying $\Xi^T\mathcal{Q} + \mathcal{Q}\Xi = I_{nq}$ and the Lyapunov function $Y_{k+1} = (\Phi\hat{e}_{k+1})^T\mathcal{Q}(\Phi\hat{e}_{k+1})$.

Substituting (10.40) into the expression of Y_{k+1}, we have

$$\begin{aligned}Y_{k+1} =& \hat{e}_{k+1}\mathcal{Q}\hat{e}_{k+1}\\ =& \hat{e}_k^T\mathcal{Q}\hat{e}_k + a_k^2(\Xi\hat{e}_k)^T\mathcal{Q}(\Xi\hat{e}_k) + a_k^2(\Psi_k\hat{e}_k)^T\mathcal{Q}(\Xi\hat{e}_k)\\ &+ a_k^2[(\Xi - \Psi_k)(\Upsilon_k u_k - \delta_k)]^T\mathcal{Q}(\Xi - \Psi_k)(\Upsilon_k u_k - \delta_k)\\ &- a_k\hat{e}_k^T(\Xi^T\mathcal{Q} + \mathcal{Q}\Xi)\hat{e}_k + a_k\hat{e}_k^T(\Psi_k^T\mathcal{Q} + \mathcal{Q}\Psi_k)\hat{e}_k\\ &- 2a_k^2(\Xi\hat{e}_k)^T\mathcal{Q}\Psi_k\hat{e}_k + 2a_k^2(\Xi\hat{e}_k)^T\mathcal{Q}(\Xi - \Psi_k)\Upsilon_k u_k\\ &- 2a_k^2(\Xi\hat{e}_k)^T\mathcal{Q}(\Xi - \Psi_k)\delta_k - 2a_k^2(\Psi_k\hat{e}_k)^T\mathcal{Q}(\Xi - \Psi_k)\Upsilon_k u_k\\ &+ 2a_k^2(\Psi_k\hat{e}_k)^T\mathcal{Q}(\Xi - \Psi_k)\delta_k.\end{aligned} \tag{10.41}$$

Similar to the proof of the output fading case, we define an increasing σ-algebra $\mathcal{F}_k \triangleq \sigma\{x_j(0), u_1(t), y_j(t), \omega_j(t), \upsilon_j(t), \mu_j(t), 0 \le t \le n, 1 \le j \le k\}$. The proof of the convergence of Y_k is similar to that of Theorem 10.1. □

The almost sure convergence is as follows.

Theorem 10.4 *Consider system* (10.1) *with input fading channel and Assumptions 10.1-10.4 hold. Apply the learning control scheme* (10.38) *and* (10.39). *If the learning gain matrix L satisfies that $-GL$ is Hurwitz and the decreasing sequence $\{a_k\}$ satisfies* (10.12) *then the auxiliary tracking error $\hat{e}_k$ converges to zero in the almost sure sense, i.e.,* $\mathbb{P}(\hat{e}_k \to 0) = 1$.

The proof of Theorem 10.4 is the same as that of Theorem 10.2. It is omitted for brevity. We have now established convergence of the reference update strategy for both the input and output fading cases. To reduce the effect of various randomness, a decreasing gain sequence is employed. However, the optimal selection of the decreasing sequence based on tracking performance is yet open. The proposed scheme serves to generate complete reference trajectories for increasing the system's capability. More efforts can be contributed on optimizing the candidate virtual reference according to a certain index.

10.4.4 General Formulation

In this subsection, we outline the general formulation that both input and output are affected by fading channels simultaneously. Assume that the fading variable in the output channel is independent of that in the input channel; then, the correction processes for input and output are independent.

We use the superscripts "`in`" and "`out`" to distinguish the input and output channels, respectively. During each iteration, we have:

$$u_k^c = (\mu^{\mathtt{in}})^{-1}\Gamma_k^{\mathtt{in}} u_k, \tag{10.42}$$

$$y_k^c = (\mu^{\mathtt{out}})^{-1}\Gamma_k^{\mathtt{out}} y_k. \tag{10.43}$$

This yields the following dynamics:

$$y_k = Gu_k^c + \upsilon_k, \tag{10.44}$$

$$R_{k+1} = R_k + \Lambda_k(R_k - y_k^c), \tag{10.45}$$

$$u_{k+1} = u_k + a_k L(R_{k+1} - y_k^c). \tag{10.46}$$

Because of the independence of $\mu^{\mathtt{in}}$ and $\mu^{\mathtt{out}}$, convergence of the general formulation can be analyzed similarly to Theorems 10.1-10.4. Thus, we omit the derivations to avoid repetition.

Remark 10.4 *According to conditions in Theorems 10.1-10.4, an intuitive selection of L is $L = G^T$ yielding a positive-definite matrix GL. This selection requires precise system information, which is difficult to satisfy in applications. An alternative selection is given by* $L = diag\{C_1B_0, \ldots, C_nB_{n-1}\}^T$, *where merely the input/output coupling matrix is necessary. All eigenvalues of GL are positive constants for this selection. Due to the continuity of the eigenvalues with respect to the matrix entry, an estimate of the system is sufficient to ensure the feasibility of the proposed scheme.*

10.5 ILLUSTRATIVE SIMULATIONS

10.5.1 Numerical Example

Consider the following linear state-space model:

$$A_t = \begin{bmatrix} 0.5+0.1\sin(0.2t) & -0.06 & -0.28 \\ -0.03 & 0.36 & -0.3 \\ -0.1 & -0.12 & 0.36 \end{bmatrix},$$

$$B_t = \begin{bmatrix} -1 & 0.1-0.1\cos((t-2)\pi/8) & 0 \\ 0 & -1 & 0.36 \\ 0.2 & 0 & -1 \end{bmatrix},$$

$$C_t = \begin{bmatrix} 1.7 & 0.45 & 0.3 \\ 0.35 & 1.57 & 1.15-0.2\sin(0.5\pi t) \end{bmatrix}.$$

The number of iterations is set to 100 and the trial length is $n = 50$. The output is of two dimensions. The selected reference points are $y_d^{(2)}(1), y_d^{(1)}(3), y_d^{(2)}(5), y_d^{(2)}(7), y_d^{(2)}(9), y_d^{(2)}(13), y_d^{(2)}(17), y_d^{(2)}(21), y_d^{(2)}(26)$, $y_d^{(2)}(33)$, $y_d^{(2)}(37)$, $y_d^{(2)}(41)$, and $y_d^{(2)}(48)$, where y_d denotes the full reference trajectory and the superscript represents the dimension of the corresponding output vector. The tracking target vector is given by $y_r = [1.2, 1.5, 1, 1.6, 1.4, 0.9, 0.8, 1.7, 1.3, 1.8, 1.1, 0.7, 1.2]^T$. The random fading is modeled by $\mu_k(t) \sim \mathcal{N}(0.95, 0.1^2)$. The disturbance and noise are denoted by $\omega_k(t) \sim \mathcal{N}(0, 0.1^2)$ and $\upsilon_k(t) \sim \mathcal{N}(0, 0.1^2)$, respectively.

We set the learning gain matrix $L = G^T$, which is computed by A_t, B_t and C_t. All eigenvalues of LG are positive constants satisfying the design conditions. We use cubic spline interpolation to fit a curve and ensure that it will pass all the points in y_r. This curve is set as R_0. To simplify the calculation, the random matrix $\Theta_k H$ in (10.11) is realized by a negative random diagonal matrix $S \in \mathbf{R}^{96\times 96}$ satisfying that $S(i,i) = 0$, for $i = 2, 3, 10, 14, 18, 26, 34, 42, 52, 66, 74, 82, 96$. The decreasing sequence is set to $a_k = 0.1/k^{0.9}$. The first batch's input is set to zero. The algorithm is performed for 100 iterations.

Fig. 10.2(a) and (b) shows the target tracking performance at the 100th iteration for output and input fading cases, respectively. The abscissa axis

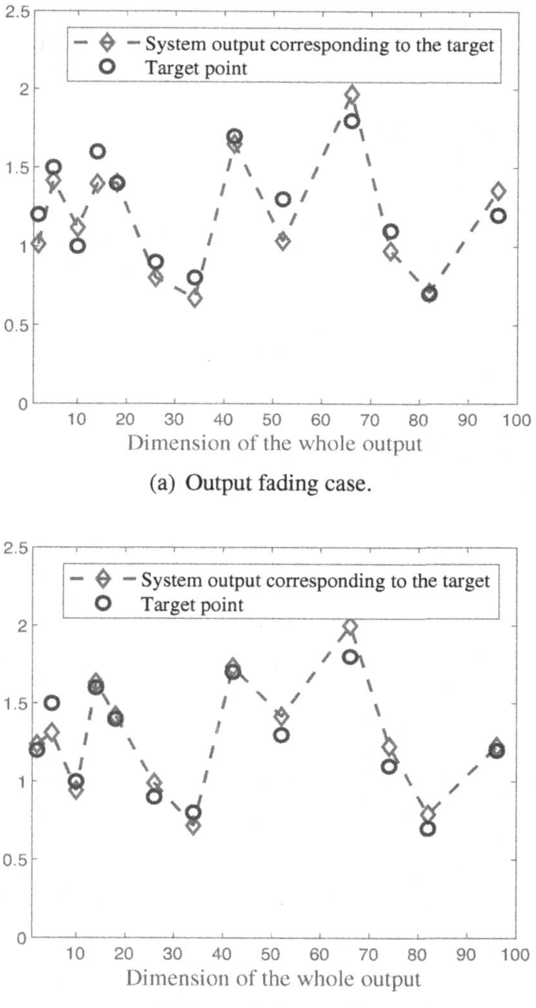

(a) Output fading case.

(b) Input fading case.

Figure 10.2 System output at the 100th iterations and the reference points: (a) Output fading case and (b) input fading case.

denotes the dimension of the lifted output super-vector and the vertical axis denotes the specific values. The red circles are the specified target points and the black diamonds denote the actual system outputs. It is seen that the tracking performance is acceptable. The deviations of the outputs from the target values are due to random fading and system noise.

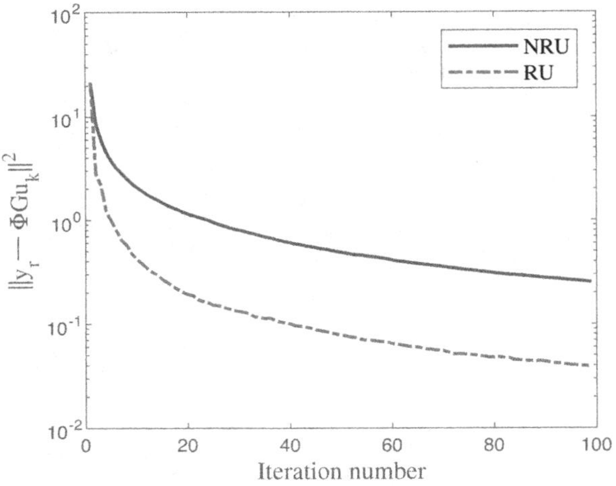

(a) Output fading case.

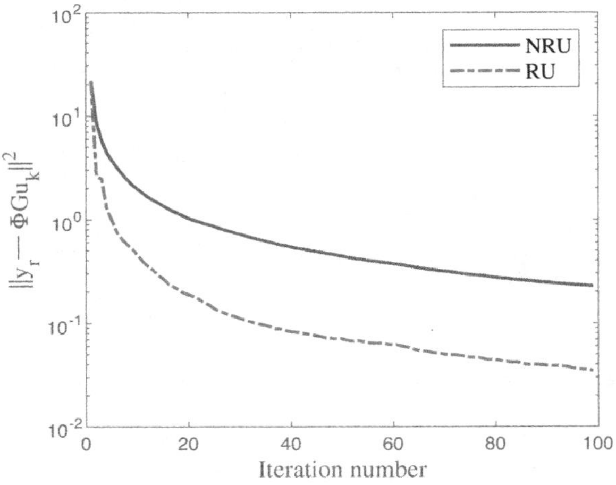

(b) Input fading case.

Figure 10.3 Norm profiles of the virtual tracking error $\|y_r - \Phi Gu_k\|^2$ of NRU and RU: (a) Output fading case and (b) input fading case.

To demonstrate asymptotic convergence, Euclidean-norm profiles of the virtual tracking errors with respect to the iteration number, defined by $\|y_r - Gu_k\|^2$, are shown in Fig. 10.3(a) and (b) for output and input fading cases, respectively. As the iteration number increases, the virtual tracking error decreases rapidly. In other words, the proposed algorithm can asymptotically achieve perfect tracking performance.

The conventional ILC strategy for the P2P tracking problem is to update the input using the tracking information at the target points merely instead of turning it to a complete trajectory. The learning control algorithm is formulated by:

$$u_{k+1} = u_k + d_k L[y_r - \mu^{-1}\Phi\Gamma_k y_k]. \tag{10.47}$$

This algorithm is referred to as the non-reference update (NRU) strategy and our proposed scheme is referred to as reference update (RU) strategy. It is seen from Fig. 10.3 that the RU strategy, denoted by the dashed lines, achieves a faster convergence speed than that of the NRU strategy, denoted by the solid lines. This observation demonstrates the advantage of the RU strategy, where a suitable anticipation is introduced for free points of the original entire trajectory. Meanwhile, such a design sacrifices certain algorithm complexity and computation resources in applications.

To study the potential impact of fading channel, we consider three scenarios of the fading distributions: $\mu = 0.95, \sigma = 0.1$; $\mu = 0.85, \sigma = 0.1$; and $\mu = 0.85, \sigma = 0.05$. The Euclidean-norm profiles of virtual tracking errors are shown in Fig. 10.4(a) and (b) for the output and input fading cases, respectively. It is seen that fast convergence is achieved for all scenarios. In other words, the proposed scheme has considerable robustness against fading distributions. Furthermore, a smaller variation may lead to a faster convergence speed.

Moreover, we focus on the decreasing gain sequence for the scheme (10.9) and (10.10). We check three scenarios of the gain sequence α/k^{β}: $\alpha = 0.1, \beta = 0.55$; $\alpha = 0.1, \beta = 0.75$; and $\alpha = 0.2, \beta = 0.8$. From Fig. 10.5, we observe that a large α and a small β can cause a fast convergence speed. However, it is yet open how to find an optimal decreasing sequence to improve the learning and tracking performance.

Finally, we replace the decreasing gain sequence $\{a_k\}$ with a sufficiently small constant to demonstrate its necessity in addressing various randomness. The constant gain is set to $a_k \equiv 0.08$. The Euclidean-norm profiles of virtual tracking errors are shown in Fig. 10.6. It is seen that the constant gain ensures a fast convergence speed in the early stage; however, the decreasing trend ceases after a few iterations. In other words, a constant gain cannot guarantee the learning control scheme to be steadily convergent. In contrast, the decreasing gain sequence can ensure continuous improvement even under various randomness. Unlike Figs. 10.2 and 10.4, we set the total number of iterations to 200 in Fig. 10.6 to clearly demonstrate the nondecreasing and fluctuating trend for the constant gain case. This shows the necessity of the decreasing gain for the learning process under random noise.

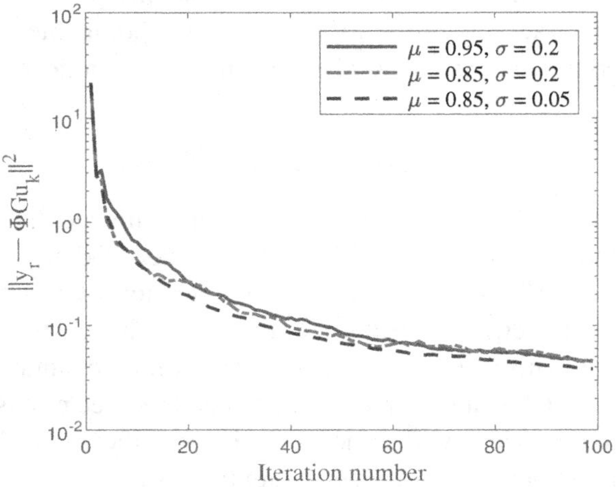

(a) Output fading case.

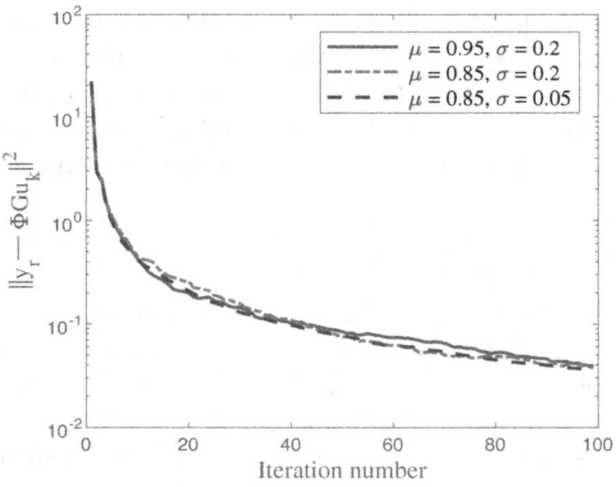

(b) Input fading case.

Figure 10.4 Norm profiles of the virtual tracking error for different fading distributions: (a) Output fading case and (b) input fading case.

10.5.2 Industrial SCARA Robot

In this subsection, we present simulations on an industrial SCARA robot borrowed from [77] to show the applicability of the proposed technique.

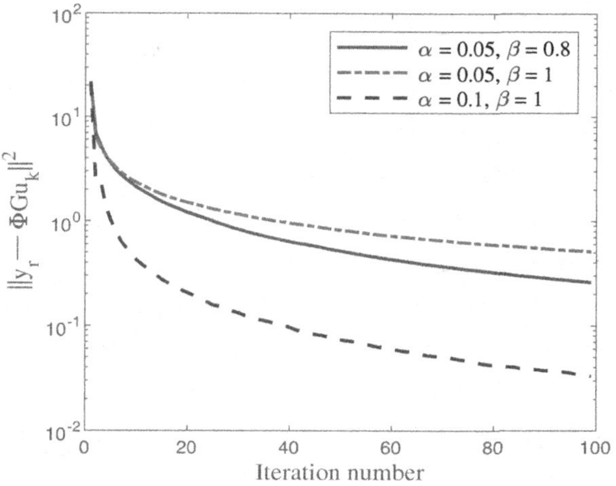

(a) Output fading case.

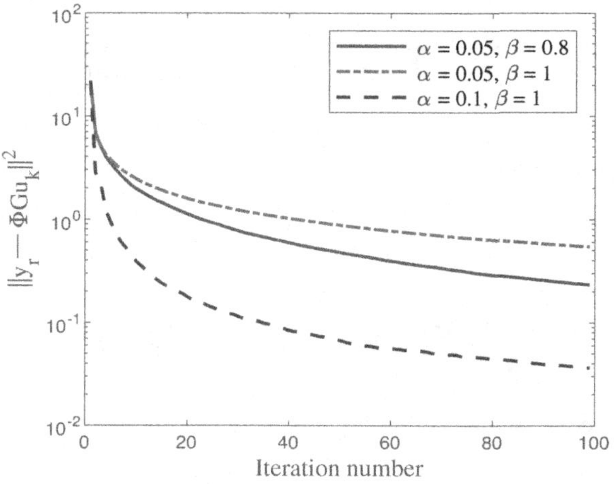

(b) Input fading case.

Figure 10.5 Norm profiles of the virtual tracking error for difference decreasing gain sequences: (a) Output fading case and (b) input fading case.

The nominal model of the closed-loop robot joint is given by the following transfer function

$$G = \frac{948}{s^2 + 42s + 948}, \tag{10.48}$$

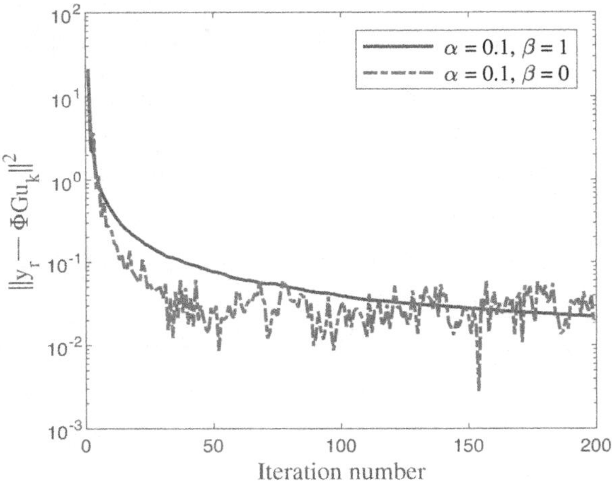

(a) Output fading case.

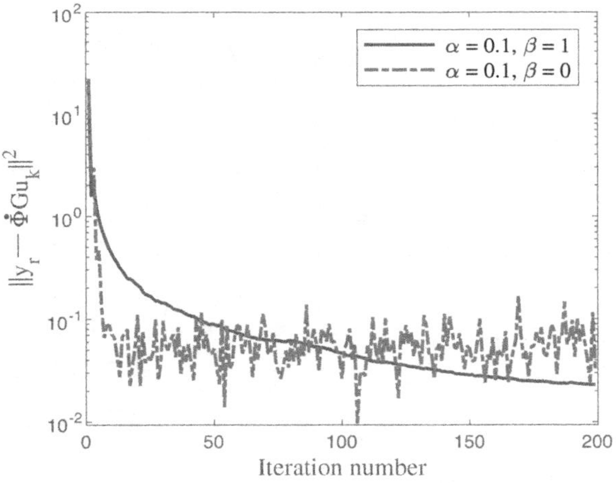

(b) Input fading case.

Figure 10.6 Norm profiles of the virtual tracking error for constant and decreasing gains: (a) Output fading case and (b) input fading case.

which is converted into a discrete-time state-space model

$$\begin{aligned} x_k(t+1) =& \begin{bmatrix} 0.6213 & -7.6196 \\ 0.008 & 0.9589 \end{bmatrix} x_k(t) + \begin{bmatrix} 0.008 \\ 0 \end{bmatrix} u_k(t), \\ y_k(t) =& [948 \quad 0] x_k(t). \end{aligned}$$

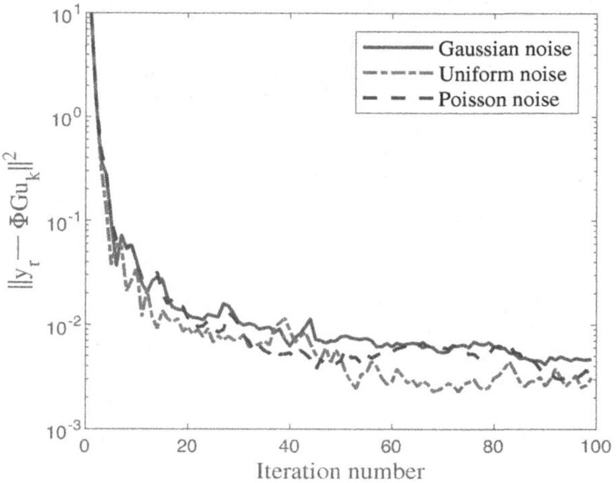

Figure 10.7 Norm profiles of the virtual tracking errors under three types of noises for the robot system.

The output and input signals are transmitted through fading channels described by $\mu_k^{\mathtt{out}}(t) \sim \mathcal{N}(0.95, 0.05^2)$ and $\mu_k^{\mathtt{in}}(t) \sim \mathcal{N}(0.8, 0.01^2)$. Besides, we add both input disturbances and measurement noise to simulate the stochastic operating environments. Three distributions are considered for the additional noises: Gaussian distribution $\omega_{1k}(t) \sim \mathcal{N}(0, 0.1^2)$ and $\upsilon_{1k}(t) \sim \mathcal{N}(0, 0.1^2)$, uniform distribution $\omega_{2k}(t) \sim \mathcal{U}(0, 0.05)$ and $\upsilon_{2k}(t) \sim \mathcal{U}(0, 0.05)$, and Poisson distribution $\omega_{3k}(t) \sim \mathcal{P}(1)$ and $\upsilon_{3k}(t) \sim \mathcal{P}(1)$.

The target tracking points are $y_d(1)$, $y_d(3)$, $y_d(5)$, $y_d(7)$, $y_d(9)$, and $y_d(13)$. The corresponding subreference is $y_r = [1.2, 1.5, 1, 1.6, 1.4, 0.9]^T$. We set the initial state $x(0) = 0$, the decreasing learning gain $a_k = 0.01/k^{0.9}$, the learning matrix $L = G^T$, and the number of iterations 100.

Fig. 10.7 provides Euclidean-norm profiles of virtual tracking errors for the robot system along the iteration axis under three types of noise. It is seen that perfect tracking performance is realized as the tracking errors decrease significantly. To demonstrate effectiveness of the proposed scheme, Fig. 10.8 provides Euclidean-norm profiles of virtual tracking errors for schemes with and without a correction mechanism. Without a fading correction, the virtual tracking error profile would not decrease continuously, but keep a considerably large value after a few iterations. In other words, the fading correction is necessary to realize perfect tracking performance. In addition, the

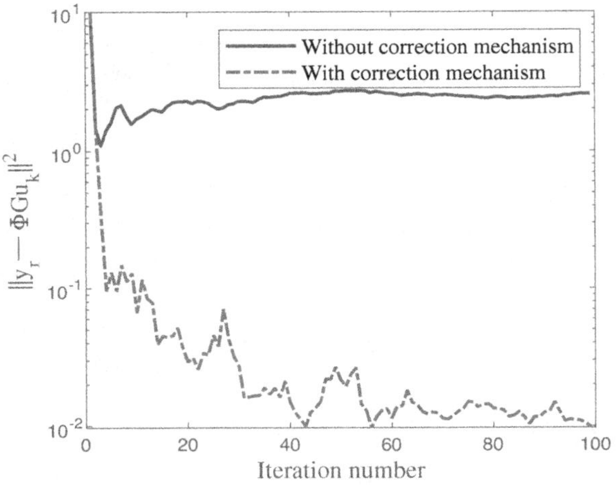

Figure 10.8 Norm profiles of the virtual tracking errors for the robot system.

simulations of various parameter changes are similar to the previous subsection; thus, we omit them to save space.

10.6 SUMMARY

In this chapter, a reference update strategy is proposed to address the P2P tracking problem via fading communication. The random fading is described by a random variable multiplied by the signal, which causes multiplicative deviations to the transmitted signal. A signal correction mechanism is introduced and a novel learning control scheme is designed by simultaneously updating the virtual reference and input signal for each iteration, where a decreasing gain sequence is employed. The asymptotic convergence to zero is established for the virtual tracking error in both mean-square and almost sure senses. Two numerical simulations are conducted to verify the theoretical results and demonstrate effect of the involved parameters. These results pave a novel way for the P2P tracking problem under the fading environments.

CHAPTER 11

Multi-Objective Learning Tracking with Faded Measurements

THIS chapter studies the multi-objective tracking problem with faded measurements by a learning control scheme. A discrete-time linear multi-sensor system is considered, where the output of each sensor is required to track an individual trajectory. These reference trajectories are not consistent in the sense that improving the tracking precision of one sensor can worsen the tracking performance of another sensor. A weighted performance index is presented to balance the overall tracking performance of all the involved sensors. Based on this weighted index, the group of the best achievable references and their corresponding desired input are explicitly defined. In addition, all outputs are transmitted back to the controller via random fading channels, where the fading randomness is described by both multiplicative and additive random variables. A learning control scheme is proposed to resolve the multi-objective tracking problem in the presence of fading communication. Both constant and decreasing gains are examined and the generated input sequence is proved convergent to the desired input which optimizes the weighted performance index in the mean-square and almost-sure senses.

11.1 INTRODUCTION

Multi-sensor systems have attracted attention in a wide range of applications, such as fault detection, habitat monitoring, and integrated navigation [37].

DOI: 10.1201/9781032646404-11

In contrast to a single-sensor system, the multi-sensor system features several individual sensors/outputs that have access to more information [20]. Rich information can help improve the control performance. The mainstream research for multi-sensor systems is state estimation and information fusion [41, 75, 81]. For example, an optimal linear estimation was established for a multiple-channel system with sensor measurement losses in [41]. The stability theory on Kalman filtering with intermittent measurements was studied for multi-sensor systems in [75].

While considering the tracking problem for a multi-sensor system, each sensor is required to track an individual reference trajectory. These references are usually independent; however, we consider a general case where the references may be conflicting in the sense that improving the tracking performance of one sensor might reduce the performance of other sensors. In this case, a multi-objective tracking problem arises where no single input exists such that all reference trajectories can be generated simultaneously. The trade-off among diverse sensors should be explicitly expressed and carefully examined. However, very limited results have been witnessed. For example, communication conditions for stability were derived in [36] for a partially observable multi-sensor system. This observation motivates us to investigate the inconsistent tracking of a multi-sensor system with multiple references. It is a novel problem related to practical complex sensing systems.

A lot of processes operate in a batch mode in which they complete the given task over a finite time interval repeatedly. The input for the next batch can be generated using the input and tracking errors from the previous batch. This control structure constitutes the primary characteristic of the learning control strategy. A primary attempt to resolve the multi-objective tracking problem was studied in [53] using a weighted optimization index of the involved tracking errors. However, the confliction among the diverse references was not rigorously formulated. The input/output coupling matrix is assumed to be of full rank there. In this chapter, we completely refine the formulation of the multi-objective tracking problem. A rigorous mathematical formulation is presented, where a group of the best achievable references and their corresponding input are explicitly defined. The full rank assumption of the coupling matrix is removed.

This chapter comprises two major contributions. The first part defines and formulates the multi-objective tracking problem for a multi-sensor system. We can obtain multiple sensor outputs that are required to track multiple trajectories. However, these tracking trajectories are possibly inconsistent in the sense that optimizing the tracking performance of one sensor can reduce the tracking performance of other sensors. We apply a weighted optimization index to balance the tracking performance over the whole iteration among multiple sensors. This topic was first considered in [53]; however, the conflicts among multiple sensors are generally explained rather than rigorously defined. In contrast, the multi-objective tracking problem is substantially refined and rigorously formulated in this chapter. A new concept of best achievable reference group and the desired input are mathematically defined and explicitly expressed. The second part is concerned with designing suitable learning schemes and analyzing the convergence properties. We analyze the effects of fading channels on data transmission and reveal that fading channels introduce a signal-dependent bias error and independent noise to the actual tracking error. Then, we propose a learning control scheme with constant and decreasing gains. Both the mean-square and almost-sure convergence criteria for the proposed scheme are established.

11.2 PROBLEM FORMULATION

11.2.1 Multi-Sensor Systems

Consider the following linear discrete-time system

$$\begin{aligned} x_k(t+1) =& Ax_k(t) + Bu_k(t), \\ y_{k,i}(t) =& C_i x_k(t), \end{aligned} \tag{11.1}$$

where k denotes the iteration number, $k = 0, 1, \ldots$, and t denotes the time instant over an time interval, $t = 0, 1, \ldots, N$. Here, N is the interval length. Variables $u_k(t) \in \mathbf{R}^p$ and $x_k(t) \in \mathbf{R}^n$ denote the input and state, respectively. $y_{k,i}(t) \in \mathbf{R}^{q_i}$ is the output of the ith sensor, $i = 1, 2, \ldots, m$, where m is the number of sensors in the multi-sensor system. Matrices A, B, and C_i denote the system matrices. For each sensor/output, (11.1) is a multi-input-multi-output (MIMO) model. The results can be extended to the time-varying case.

Because a batch-wise learning mechanism is considered, we use the following conditions for the system.

Assumption 11.1 *The initial state $x_k(0)$ is set to 0 for all iterations.*

Assumption 11.2 *For an arbitrary sensor i, the relative input-output degree is 1; i.e., the coupling matrix $C_iB \neq 0$.*

The control diagram is shown in Fig. 11.1, where $\mathbf{S}_i$ denotes the sensor and $\mathbf{Z}^{-1}$ denotes the iteration-wise backward shift operator. As illustrated in Fig. 11.1, the plant has m individual sensors/outputs. Each output $y_{k,i}(t)$ is

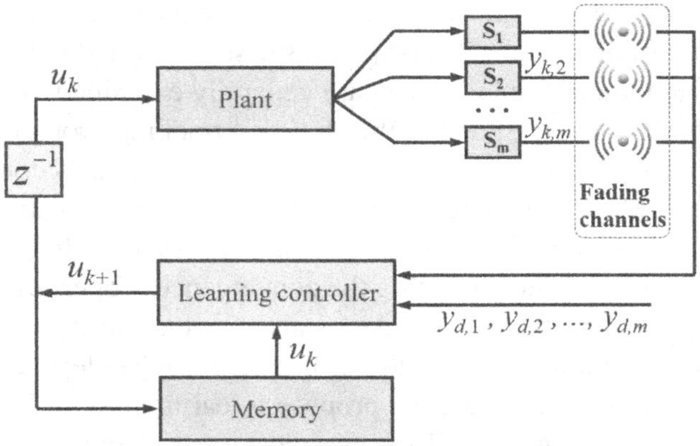

Figure 11.1 Block diagram of a multi-sensor system.

required to track a given reference, denoted by $y_{d,i}(t)$, $0 \leq t \leq N$, $\forall i$. Consequently, we have m individual tracking objectives. Generally, these tracking references might conflict in the sense that all of the desired references cannot be precisely tracked simultaneously. Therefore, a trade-off should be considered among these objectives. This issue will be elaborated in Section 11.3.

11.2.2 Fading Communication

We consider fading channels from the plant to controller. As is shown in Fig. 11.1, the outputs $y_{k,i}(t)$ cannot be perfectly transmitted to the controllers, but suffer from random fading during propagation. This scenario is commonly encountered owing to the application of low-cost devices and remote data exchange. In this chapter, fading is modeled by a multiplicative random variable as the fading gain. Assume that the channels undergo slow fading such that the statistical information of the fading gain can be obtained. For arbitrary t and k, a scalar variable $\theta_{k,i}(t)$ is introduced for the ith output $y_{k,i}(t)$. We assume the random variable $\theta_{k,i}(t)$ to be independently and identically distributed with respect to k, t, and i, and follow a continuous fading distribution $g(\theta)$ such that $\mathbb{P}(\theta_{k,i}(t) > 0) = 1$. The statistics of $\theta_{k,i}(t)$ are as follows:

$$\mathbb{E}[\theta_{k,i}(t)] = \theta, \quad \mathbb{E}[(\theta_{k,i}(t) - \theta)^2] = \sigma_\theta^2. \tag{11.2}$$

In addition, random noise is inevitable in data transmission such as additive white Gaussian noise, which is independent of the multiplicative randomness. It cannot be predicted but unrelated to other quantities. For the ith output $y_{k,i}(t)$, a random vector $\xi_{k,i}(t) \in \mathbf{R}^{q_i}$ with zero mean and bounded covariance is employed to denote the noise, i.e.,

$$\mathbb{E}[\xi_{k,i}(t)] = 0, \quad \mathbb{E}[\xi_{k,i}(t)\xi_{k,i}^T(t)] = R_{t,i}. \tag{11.3}$$

The noise is assumed independent of the iteration number k, time instant t, and sensor number i. In short, we make the following assumption for the fading channels.

Assumption 11.3 *For the ith output $y_{k,i}(t)$, the received signal, denoted by $y_{k,i}^{\circ}(t)$, is described as follows:*

$$y_{k,i}^{\circ}(t) = \theta_{k,i}(t)y_{k,i}(t) + \xi_{k,i}(t), \tag{11.4}$$

where $\theta_{k,i}(t)$ and $\xi_{k,i}(t)$ satisfy the statistical properties (11.2) *and* (11.3), *respectively. $\theta_{k,i}(t)$ is independent of $\xi_{k,i}(t)$, $\forall k,t,i$.*

Assumption 11.3 provides a specific model of the fading channel satisfying certain statistical conditions. The conditions of (11.2) and (11.3) are mild because they are mainly determined by the physical environments and devices and thus stationary for different iterations and time instants. Moreover, the statistical information such as θ can be acquired to a correction for the algorithm. Although we consider output fading communication, the results are also valid for the input fading case. We omit the extensions to focus on novel points.

11.2.3 Control Objective

We present the control objective. For a multi-sensor system, each sensor/output is required to track an individual trajectory. Taking the ith sensor as an example, the reference is denoted by $y_{d,i}(t)$. Here, we do not assume any realizability of the desired reference $y_{d,i}(t)$; that is, an input $u_d(t)$ does not necessarily exist such that $y_{d,i}(t)$ can be precisely generated. Removing the realizability requirement of the desired reference makes this chapter distinct from the literature. The best tracking performance for the ith sensor is defined by minimizing the following index of the entire iteration:

$$V_i \triangleq \limsup_{k\to\infty} \frac{1}{k} \sum_{l=1}^{k} \sum_{t=1}^{N} \|y_{d,i}(t) - y_{l,i}(t)\|^2. \tag{11.5}$$

Its solution will be elaborated in Section 11.3.1.

Considering a multi-sensor system, we need to minimize a group of indices $V_1, V_2, \ldots, V_m$ simultaneously. Yet, these indices may conflict with one another while trying to achieving the minimization; that is, there may not exist an input such that all indices V_i can be minimized simultaneously, even if there exists a corresponding input for each index. We need to introduce a suitable overall tracking performance index to balance all the individual indices. We introduce weights $\lambda_1, \ldots, \lambda_m$ such that $\sum_{i=1}^m \lambda_i = 1$ and $\lambda_i > 0$, and the overall index is defined by $V \triangleq \sum_{i=1}^m \lambda_i V_i$, i.e.,

$$V = \limsup_{k \to \infty} \frac{1}{k} \sum_{i=1}^{m} \lambda_i \left(\sum_{l=1}^{k} \sum_{t=1}^{N} \|y_{d,i}(t) - y_{l,i}(t)\|^2 \right). \tag{11.6}$$

The elaboration of this index is given in Section 11.3.2. If we lift all outputs in sequence as an integrated output, a regular MIMO model is obtained. This transformation can be regarded as a special case of the proposed formulation in the sense that the tracking performance index (11.5) for the new transformation corresponds to a special case of (11.6) where all λ_i are equal.

The control objective of this chapter is to investigate the best tracking performance for a multi-sensor system (11.1) according to a weighted index (11.6) and propose learning control algorithms such that the generated input sequence can drive the system to achieve its best tracking performance. In particular, we will elaborate the following items:

1) clarifying the solution to the multi-objective optimization index (11.6) rigorously subject to the system constraints that each output is generated by the dynamics of (11.1);

2) designing learning control algorithms such that the generated input sequence can achieve the minimum of index (11.6) using faded measurements rather than actual outputs; and

3) providing an in-depth effect analysis of fading channels on the tracking performance and rigorous convergence proofs of the proposed algorithms.

11.3 SOLUTION TO MULTI-OBJECTIVE TRACKING PROBLEM

11.3.1 Solution to Single-Sensor Tracking Problem

We first lift the quantities over the whole operation interval. Define $\boldsymbol{y}_{k,i} = [y_{k,i}^T(1), y_{k,i}^T(2), \ldots, y_{k,i}^T(N)]^T$ and $\boldsymbol{u}_k = [u_k^T(0), u_k^T(1), \ldots, u_k^T(N-1)]^T$. Then, we obtain a lifted form $\boldsymbol{y}_{k,i} = G_i \boldsymbol{u}_k$, where matrix G_i is defined as follows:

$$G_i = \begin{bmatrix} C_iB & 0 & \cdots & 0 \\ C_iAB & C_iB & \cdots & 0 \\ \vdots & \vdots & \ddots & \vdots \\ C_iA^{N-1}B & C_iA^{N-2}B & \cdots & C_iB \end{bmatrix}. \tag{11.7}$$

Now, the tracking index for (11.5) can be written as

$$V_i = \limsup_{k\to\infty} \frac{1}{k} \sum_{l=1}^{k} \|\boldsymbol{y}_{d,i} - \boldsymbol{y}_{l,i}\|^2, \tag{11.8}$$

where $\boldsymbol{y}_{d,i} = [y_{d,i}^T(1), y_{d,i}^T(2), \ldots, y_{d,i}^T(N)]^T$.

To find the minimum of (11.8), we introduce a concept of the *best achievable reference* $\widehat{\boldsymbol{y}}_{r,i}$ as follows.

Definition 11.1 *For the ith sensor, the best achievable reference $\widehat{\boldsymbol{y}}_{r,i}$ is defined as the solution to the optimization problem:*

$$\begin{aligned} &\min \|\boldsymbol{y}_{d,i} - \boldsymbol{y}_{r,i}\|^2 \\ &\text{such that} \quad \boldsymbol{y}_{r,i} = G_i \boldsymbol{u}, \end{aligned} \tag{11.9}$$

where $\boldsymbol{u}$ is an arbitrary vector, $\boldsymbol{u} \in \boldsymbol{R}^{pN}$.

Clearly, $\widehat{\boldsymbol{y}}_{r,i}$ is generated by the given dynamics of (11.1) with a suitable input $\boldsymbol{u}$ specified by the solution to (11.9). In other words, there must exist at least one input such that $\widehat{\boldsymbol{y}}_{r,i}$ is realized. Moreover, $\widehat{\boldsymbol{y}}_{r,i}$ is the reference that is closest to the desired trajectory $\boldsymbol{y}_{d,i}$ in the Euclidean norm sense, which we refer to as the best achievable reference.

Denote the space spanned by all columns of G_i by $\mathcal{S}_i$, i.e., $\mathcal{S}_i = \text{span}\{G_i\}$. Then, we have $\widehat{\boldsymbol{y}}_{r,i} \in \mathcal{S}_i$. A geometric interpretation of $\widehat{\boldsymbol{y}}_{r,i}$ is the projection of $\boldsymbol{y}_{d,i}$ onto the space $\mathcal{S}_i$. That is, we have the solution to (11.9): $\widehat{\boldsymbol{y}}_{r,i} = \mathcal{P}_{\mathcal{S}_i}[\boldsymbol{y}_{d,i}]$, where $\mathcal{P}_{\mathcal{S}_i}[\cdot]$ is the projection operator with respect to the space $\mathcal{S}_i$.

Denote the residual of the desired trajectory $\boldsymbol{y}_{d,i}$ by $\widetilde{\boldsymbol{y}}_{r,i} \triangleq \boldsymbol{y}_{d,i} - \widehat{\boldsymbol{y}}_{r,i}$. According to Definition 11.1, $\widetilde{\boldsymbol{y}}_{r,i}$ is orthogonal to the best achievable reference $\widehat{\boldsymbol{y}}_{r,i}$; that is, $\widetilde{\boldsymbol{y}}_{r,i}^T \widehat{\boldsymbol{y}}_{r,i} = 0$. In fact, $\widetilde{\boldsymbol{y}}_{r,i}$ is perpendicular to the space $\mathcal{S}_i$; thus, $\widetilde{\boldsymbol{y}}_{r,i}$ is orthogonal to all columns of matrix G_i, i.e., $\widetilde{\boldsymbol{y}}_{r,i}^T G_i = 0$.

Remark 11.1 *We consider a special case of G_i being of full column rank, which is ensured if C_iB is so. In this case, the least square solution to the problem* $\min \|\boldsymbol{y}_{d,i} - G_i \boldsymbol{u}\|^2$ *yields a unique form $\boldsymbol{u}_{\text{LS}} = (G_i^T G_i)^{-1} G_i^T \boldsymbol{y}_{d,i}$. Then, the projection matrix P_i for $\mathcal{P}_{\mathcal{S}_i}[\cdot]$ is formulated as $P_i = G_i(G_i^T G_i)^{-1} G_i^T$. That is,*

$$\mathcal{P}_{\mathcal{S}_i}[\boldsymbol{y}_{d,i}] = P_i \boldsymbol{y}_{d,i} = G_i(G_i^T G_i)^{-1} G_i^T \boldsymbol{y}_{d,i}.$$

Once the best achievable reference is determined, we can compute the desired input $\widehat{\boldsymbol{u}}_{r,i}$ accordingly as follows:

$$\widehat{\boldsymbol{u}}_{r,i} = G_i^{\dagger}\widehat{\boldsymbol{y}}_{r,i}, \tag{11.10}$$

where $G_i^{\dagger}$ is the Moore-Penrose pseudoinverse of G_i. This inverse is the least-norm least-square solution of the optimization problem. For this solution, we have the following lemmas.

Lemma 11.1 *For arbitrary vector* $\boldsymbol{u}$*,*

$$\|G_i\widehat{\boldsymbol{u}}_{r,i} - \boldsymbol{y}_{d,i}\|^2 \leq \|G_i\boldsymbol{u} - \boldsymbol{y}_{d,i}\|^2, \tag{11.11}$$

where $\widehat{\boldsymbol{u}}_{r,i}$ *is defined by* (11.10). *The equality holds if and only if* $\boldsymbol{u} - \widehat{\boldsymbol{u}}_{r,i}$ *lies in the null space of* G_i.

Lemma 11.1 indicates that $\widehat{\boldsymbol{u}}_{r,i}$ defined by (11.10) is an optimal input candidate to track the given trajectory $\boldsymbol{y}_{d,i}$. The optimality of index in (11.8) is characterized in the following lemma.

Lemma 11.2 *The desired input* $\widehat{\boldsymbol{u}}_{r,i}$ *defined by* (11.10) *is an optimal solution to index* (11.8) *in the sense that index* (11.8) *achieves its minimum for an arbitrary input sequence* $\{\boldsymbol{u}_k\}$ *satisfying the condition* $\boldsymbol{u}_k \to \widehat{\boldsymbol{u}}_{r,i}$ *as* $k \to \infty$. *The minimum of index* (11.8) *is* $\|\widetilde{\boldsymbol{y}}_{r,i}\|^2$.

Proof: We start by writing (11.8) as

$$\begin{aligned} V_i &= \limsup_{k\to\infty} \frac{1}{k}\sum_{l=1}^{k} \|\boldsymbol{y}_{d,i} - \boldsymbol{y}_{l,i}\|^2 \\ &= \limsup_{k\to\infty} \frac{1}{k}\sum_{l=1}^{k} \|\boldsymbol{y}_{d,i} - \widehat{\boldsymbol{y}}_{r,i} + \widehat{\boldsymbol{y}}_{r,i} - \boldsymbol{y}_{l,i}\|^2 \\ &= \limsup_{k\to\infty} \frac{1}{k}\sum_{l=1}^{k} \left(\|\boldsymbol{y}_{d,i} - \widehat{\boldsymbol{y}}_{r,i}\|^2 + \|\widehat{\boldsymbol{y}}_{r,i} - \boldsymbol{y}_{l,i}\|^2\right) \\ &\quad \text{[by orthogonality between } \widetilde{\boldsymbol{y}}_{r,i} \text{ and } \boldsymbol{y}_{l,i}] \\ &\geq \|\boldsymbol{y}_{d,i} - \widehat{\boldsymbol{y}}_{r,i}\|^2, \end{aligned}$$

where the equality holds if $\|\widehat{\boldsymbol{y}}_{r,i} - \boldsymbol{y}_{l,i}\|^2 \to 0$ as $k \to \infty$. Clearly, if $\boldsymbol{u}_k \to \widehat{\boldsymbol{u}}_{r,i}$, the equality condition is satisfied. The proof is completed. □

Although $\widehat{\boldsymbol{u}}_{r,i}$ has been defined by (11.10), it cannot be applied in applications because precise information of G_i is generally unavailable. By Lemma 11.2, our target is to design learning control algorithms such that the generated input sequence $\{\boldsymbol{u}_k\}$ converges to $\widehat{\boldsymbol{u}}_{r,i}$. Note that the convergence to $\widehat{\boldsymbol{u}}_{r,i}$ is a sufficient rather than necessary condition for minimizing the index (11.8); however, $\widehat{\boldsymbol{u}}_{r,i}$ is the least-square solution.

11.3.2 Solution to Multi-Sensor Tracking Problem

We consider the overall index (11.6). The index can be written as follows:

$$V = \limsup_{k\to\infty} \frac{1}{k} \sum_{l=1}^{k} \left(\sum_{i=1}^{m} \lambda_i \|\boldsymbol{y}_{d,i} - \boldsymbol{y}_{l,i}\|^2 \right) \tag{11.12}$$

with weights λ_i satisfying $\sum_{i=1}^{m} \lambda_i = 1$, $\lambda_i > 0$.

Remark 11.2 *The weights λ_i play a critical role in determining the minimum of* (11.12) *as the weights reflect our evaluation of the individual indices* (11.8) *when they are conflicting with one another. Loosely speaking, a larger weight implies more concern to the corresponding index. Further, scaling all of the weights by any positive number does not change the minimizer of the index. Thus, we impose a constraint $\sum_{i=1}^{m} \lambda_i = 1$. For a set of weights satisfying this constraint, we can compute a minimum of the overall index. As the weights vary over all possible combinations, we obtain a surface that characterizes an optimal trade-off among all individual indices.*

We introduce the concept of the *best achievable reference group* for the multi-objective tracking problem.

Definition 11.2 *For a given set of weights $\{\lambda_1, \ldots, \lambda_m\}$ such that $\sum_{i=1}^{m} \lambda_i = 1$ and $\lambda_i > 0$, the best achievable reference group is a set of references $\{\boldsymbol{y}_{r,1}, \ldots, \boldsymbol{y}_{r,m}\}$ which is the solution to the following optimization problem*

$$\begin{aligned} &\min \sum_{i=1}^{m} \lambda_i \|\boldsymbol{y}_{d,i} - \boldsymbol{y}_{r,i}\|^2 \\ &\text{such that} \quad \boldsymbol{y}_{r,1} = G_1 \boldsymbol{u}, \ldots, \boldsymbol{y}_{r,m} = G_m \boldsymbol{u} \end{aligned} \tag{11.13}$$

where $\boldsymbol{u}$ is an arbitrary vector, $\boldsymbol{u} \in \boldsymbol{R}^{pN}$.

Let

$$\boldsymbol{y}_r = \begin{bmatrix} \boldsymbol{y}_{r,1} \\ \vdots \\ \boldsymbol{y}_{r,m} \end{bmatrix}, \boldsymbol{y}_d = \begin{bmatrix} \boldsymbol{y}_{d,1} \\ \vdots \\ \boldsymbol{y}_{d,m} \end{bmatrix}, \mathbf{G} = \begin{bmatrix} G_1 \\ \vdots \\ G_m \end{bmatrix},$$

and Λ be a diagonal matrix

$$\Lambda = \begin{bmatrix} \lambda_1 I_{q_1 N} & & & \\ & \lambda_2 I_{q_2 N} & & \\ & & \ddots & \\ & & & \lambda_m I_{q_m N} \end{bmatrix}.$$

Then (11.13) is rewritten as

$$\begin{aligned} &\min \|\sqrt{\Lambda}(\boldsymbol{y}_d - \boldsymbol{y}_r)\|^2 \\ &\text{such that} \quad \boldsymbol{y}_r = \mathbf{G}\boldsymbol{u}. \end{aligned} \tag{11.14}$$

According to (11.14), $\boldsymbol{y}_r$ must lie in the space spanned by all columns of $\mathbf{G}$. Then, $\sqrt{\Lambda}\boldsymbol{y}_r$ must lie in the space spanned by all columns of $\sqrt{\Lambda}\mathbf{G}$. Denote $\mathcal{S} = \text{span}\{\sqrt{\Lambda}\mathbf{G}\}$. Assuming $\sqrt{\Lambda}\boldsymbol{y}_r$ as a free vector in $\mathcal{S}$, $q = q_1 + \cdots + q_m$, we obtain that the minimizer of the optimization function $\|\sqrt{\Lambda}\boldsymbol{y}_d - \sqrt{\Lambda}\boldsymbol{y}_r\|^2$ is the projection of $\sqrt{\Lambda}\boldsymbol{y}_d$ onto the space $\mathcal{S}$:

$$\widehat{\sqrt{\Lambda}\boldsymbol{y}_r} = \mathcal{P}_{\mathcal{S}}[\boldsymbol{y}_d], \tag{11.15}$$

where $\mathcal{P}_{\mathcal{S}}$ is the projection operator. Then, the best achievable reference group is given by

$$\widehat{\boldsymbol{y}}_r = \sqrt{\Lambda}^{-1}\mathcal{P}_{\mathcal{S}}[\boldsymbol{y}_d]. \tag{11.16}$$

Further, the residual $\sqrt{\Lambda}\boldsymbol{y}_d - \sqrt{\Lambda}\boldsymbol{y}_r$ must be orthogonal to the space $\mathcal{S}$. That is, $\sqrt{\Lambda}\boldsymbol{y}_d - \sqrt{\Lambda}\boldsymbol{y}_r$ is orthogonal to each column of $\sqrt{\Lambda}\mathbf{G}$, i.e.,

$$\left(\sqrt{\Lambda}\boldsymbol{y}_d - \sqrt{\Lambda}\boldsymbol{y}_r\right)^T \sqrt{\Lambda}\mathbf{G} = 0. \tag{11.17}$$

Denote $\widetilde{\boldsymbol{y}}_r \triangleq \boldsymbol{y}_d - \widehat{\boldsymbol{y}}_r$. From the above equation, we have

$$\widetilde{\boldsymbol{y}}_r^T \sqrt{\Lambda}^T \sqrt{\Lambda}\mathbf{G} = \widetilde{\boldsymbol{y}}_r^T \Lambda\mathbf{G} = 0. \tag{11.18}$$

This relationship will be used to clarify optimality of the overall index and prove convergence of the proposed learning control algorithms.

For any given set of weights $\{\lambda_1, \dots, \lambda_m\}$, the best achievable reference group is denoted by $\widehat{\boldsymbol{y}}_r$; then, the corresponding desired input $\widehat{\boldsymbol{u}}_r$ can be calculated as follows:

$$\widehat{\boldsymbol{u}}_r = \mathbf{G}^{\dagger}\widehat{\boldsymbol{y}}_r, \tag{11.19}$$

where $\mathbf{G}^{\dagger}$ stands for the Moore-Penrose pseudoinverse of $\mathbf{G}$. We emphasize that all of the solutions derived above depends on the set of weights. In other words, different selections of the weight set can lead to different solutions to $\widehat{\boldsymbol{y}}_r$ and $\widehat{\boldsymbol{u}}_r$.

We now present the following lemmas, of which the proofs are omitted as they are similar to Lemmas 11.1 and 11.2.

Lemma 11.3 *For any given set of weights* $\{\lambda_1, \dots, \lambda_m\}$,

$$\begin{aligned}&(\mathbf{G}\widehat{\boldsymbol{u}}_r - \boldsymbol{y}_d)^T \Lambda (\mathbf{G}\widehat{\boldsymbol{u}}_r - \boldsymbol{y}_d)\\ &\leq (\mathbf{G}\boldsymbol{u} - \boldsymbol{y}_d)^T \Lambda (\mathbf{G}\boldsymbol{u} - \boldsymbol{y}_d),\end{aligned} \tag{11.20}$$

where $\widehat{\boldsymbol{u}}_r$ *is given by* (11.19) *and* $\boldsymbol{u}$ *is an arbitrary vector. The equality holds if and only if* $\boldsymbol{u} - \widehat{\boldsymbol{u}}_r$ *lies in the null space of* $\sqrt{\Lambda}\mathbf{G}$*. Specially, the optimal solution for* (11.13) *is unique if and only if* $\mathbf{G}$ *is of full column rank.*

Note that $\sqrt{\Lambda}$ is a diagonal matrix, therefore each row of $\sqrt{\Lambda}\mathbf{G}$ is parallel to its corresponding row of $\mathbf{G}$. That is, $\forall j$, the jth row of $\sqrt{\Lambda}\mathbf{G}$ is equal to the product of the jth row of $\mathbf{G}$ and a positive constant. As a consequence, the null space of $\sqrt{\Lambda}\mathbf{G}$ is identical to the null space of $\mathbf{G}$, which is the intersection of the null spaces of all G_i, $1 \leq i \leq m$. Thus, the validity of (11.20) in Lemma 11.3 requires that $\boldsymbol{u} - \widehat{\boldsymbol{u}}_r$ lie in the intersection of the null spaces of all G_i. This observation connects the single-sensor and multi-sensor tracking problems. Consequently, the more sensors, the smaller intersection; the intersection is often null in practice.

Lemma 11.4 *For any given set of weights* $\{\lambda_1, \dots, \lambda_m\}$*, the desired input* $\widehat{\boldsymbol{u}}_r$ *defined by* (11.19) *is an optimal solution to index* (11.12) *in the sense that index* (11.12) *achieves its minimum for an arbitrary input sequence* $\{\boldsymbol{u}_k\}$ *satisfying the condition* $\boldsymbol{u}_k \to \widehat{\boldsymbol{u}}_r$ *as* $k \to \infty$*. The minimum of index* (11.12) *is* $\|\sqrt{\Lambda}\widetilde{\boldsymbol{y}}_r\|^2$.

From Lemma 11.4, we note that the minimum of index (11.12) depends strongly on the set of weights $\{\lambda_1, \dots, \lambda_m\}$. Clearly, by varying weights $\{\lambda_1, \dots, \lambda_m\}$ over the space $[0,1]^m$, we can obtain an infimum

$\inf_{0<\lambda_1,\ldots,\lambda_m<1,\sum\lambda_i=1}\|\sqrt{\Lambda}\widetilde{y}_r\|^2$. We should emphasize that finding this infimum is not our objective, because it only holds for a specific set of weights. It is a user-defined selection of weights for applications, which should reflect our consideration on the practical requirements of various sensors.

11.4 LEARNING CONTROL SCHEME USING FADED MEASUREMENTS

In this section, we provide specific learning control algorithms to generate the input sequence solving the previous optimization problem with faded measurements. The effect of faded measurements is elaborated and compensated for. We adopt the classical P-type update scheme with constant and decreasing gains in turn. Lastly, we present the best performance evaluation.

11.4.1 Effect of Faded Measurements

For the ith sensor, the actual output is $\boldsymbol{y}_{k,i}$, and the signal received by the controller is denoted by $\boldsymbol{y}^{\circ}_{k,i}$. According to the fading channel setting, we have

$$\boldsymbol{y}^{\circ}_{k,i}=\Theta_{k,i}\boldsymbol{y}_{k,i}+\boldsymbol{\xi}_{k,i}, \tag{11.21}$$

where $\Theta_{k,i}=\text{diag}\{\theta_{k,i}(1)I_{q_i},\ \ldots,\ \theta_{k,i}(N)I_{q_i}\}$ and $\boldsymbol{\xi}_{k,i}=[\xi^T_{k,i}(1),\ \xi^T_{k,i}(2),\ \ldots,\ \xi^T_{k,i}(N)]^T$.

The main effect of fading measurements is that the received signals are generally biased in the probability sense compared with its original signals. Therefore, the received signal cannot be applied to update the input directly. A correction is necessary for the learning control scheme. In this chapter, we assume to know the mean of $\theta_{k,i}(t)$ to correct the received signal by $\boldsymbol{y}^{\star}_{k,i}=\theta^{-1}\boldsymbol{y}^{\circ}_{k,i}$. By direct calculation, we obtain

$$\begin{aligned}\boldsymbol{y}^{\star}_{k,i}&=\theta^{-1}\Theta_{k,i}\boldsymbol{y}_{k,i}+\theta^{-1}\boldsymbol{\xi}_{k,i}\\&=\boldsymbol{y}_{k,i}-\left(I-\theta^{-1}\Theta_{k,i}\right)\boldsymbol{y}_{k,i}+\theta^{-1}\boldsymbol{\xi}_{k,i}.\end{aligned} \tag{11.22}$$

By comparing $\boldsymbol{y}^{\star}_{k,i}$ with $\boldsymbol{y}_{k,i}$, we note additional effects of fading randomness, reflected by the second term on the right-hand side (RHS) of (11.22), i.e., $\left(I-\theta^{-1}\Theta_{k,i}\right)\boldsymbol{y}_{k,i}$. This term denotes the bias error, which is of zero-mean and bounded-variance provided that the output signal is bounded. It should be emphasized that the output-dependence introduces additional difficulty to the analysis. In addition, $\theta^{-1}\boldsymbol{\xi}_{k,i}$ denotes the independent noise. By Assumption 11.3, this term is of zero-mean and bounded-variance.

Other than these effects, a multi-sensor system provides multiple outputs to update the input signal. The combination of these outputs can provide a degree of offset among the randomness generated by different channels to a certain extent.

11.4.2 Learning Algorithm with Constant Gain

In this subsection, we consider a learning control algorithm with a constant gain. The input update is given by:

$$\boldsymbol{u}_{k+1} = \boldsymbol{u}_k + \gamma \sum_{i=1}^{m} \lambda_i L_i \boldsymbol{\varepsilon}_{k,i}, \tag{11.23}$$

where $\boldsymbol{\varepsilon}_{k,i} = \boldsymbol{y}_{d,i} - \boldsymbol{y}^{\star}_{k,i}$ is the modified tracking error, $\gamma > 0$ is a constant learning gain, $L_i \in \mathbf{R}^{pN \times q_i N}$ is the direction regulation matrix, and $\{\lambda_i, 1 \leq i \leq m\}$ are weights defined in (11.12). Let L_i be $L_i = I_N \otimes L_i'$ with $L_i' \in \mathbf{R}^{p \times q_i}$.

The direction regulation matrix L_i plays a role of adjusting the dimension mismatch between $\boldsymbol{u}_k$ and $\boldsymbol{\varepsilon}_{k,i}$. Moreover, the algorithm (11.23) can be implemented in a time-wise manner, i.e., $u_{k+1}(t) = u_k(t) + \gamma \sum_{i=1}^{m} \lambda_i L_i' \varepsilon_{k,i}(t+1)$, where $\varepsilon_{k,i}(t) = y_{d,i}(t) - \theta^{-1} \theta_{k,i}(t) y_{k,i}(t)$. From this formulation, the high-dimension of (11.23) will not hinder practical applications.

The following theorem summarizes the mean-square convergence of the learning control algorithm (11.23).

Theorem 11.1 *Consider Assumptions 11.1-11.3 for system* (11.1) *and apply the learning control algorithm* (11.23). *Then, the generated input sequence* $\{\boldsymbol{u}_k\}$ *guarantees that the input error* $\widehat{\boldsymbol{u}}_r - \boldsymbol{u}_k$ *converges to a bounded sphere of zero in the mean-square sense, i.e.,* $\lim_{k\to\infty} \mathbb{E}[\|\widehat{\boldsymbol{u}}_r - \boldsymbol{u}_k\|^2] \leq \tau$, *where* $\tau > 0$ *is defined later, if the constant gain* γ *is sufficiently small, the direction regulation matrices* L_i *satisfy that all eigenvalues of* $\sum_{i=1}^{m} \lambda_i L_i' C_i B$ *have positive real parts, and all of the columns of* $\mathbf{L}^T$ *belong to the space spanned by* $\mathbf{G}$, *where* $\mathbf{L} = [L_1, L_2, \ldots, L_m]$.

Proof: Denote

$$\boldsymbol{\varepsilon}_k = [\boldsymbol{\varepsilon}_{k,1}^T, \boldsymbol{\varepsilon}_{k,2}^T, \ldots, \boldsymbol{\varepsilon}_{k,m}^T]^T \in \mathbf{R}^{qN},$$
$$\boldsymbol{\Theta}_k = \mathrm{diag}\{\Theta_{k,1}, \Theta_{k,2}, \ldots, \Theta_{k,m}\} \in \mathbf{R}^{qN \times qN}.$$

Then, (11.23) can be written as

$$\begin{aligned}\boldsymbol{u}_{k+1} &= \boldsymbol{u}_k + \gamma\mathbf{L}\Lambda\boldsymbol{\varepsilon}_k \\ &= \boldsymbol{u}_k + \gamma\mathbf{L}\Lambda(\boldsymbol{y}_d - \boldsymbol{y}_k^\star) \\ &= \boldsymbol{u}_k + \gamma\mathbf{L}\Lambda\left(\boldsymbol{y}_d - \theta^{-1}\boldsymbol{\Theta}_k\boldsymbol{y}_k - \theta^{-1}\boldsymbol{\xi}_k\right),\end{aligned} \tag{11.24}$$

where $\boldsymbol{y}_k$, $\boldsymbol{y}_k^\star$, and $\boldsymbol{\xi}_k$ are defined similar to $\boldsymbol{y}_d$. Clearly, $\boldsymbol{y}_k = \mathbf{G}\boldsymbol{u}_k$. By the definition of $\widehat{\boldsymbol{y}}_r$ and $\widehat{\boldsymbol{u}}_r$, we have $\widehat{\boldsymbol{y}}_r = \mathbf{G}\widehat{\boldsymbol{u}}_r$.

Denote $\Delta\boldsymbol{u}_k \triangleq \widehat{\boldsymbol{u}}_r - \boldsymbol{u}_k$. Subtracting both sides of (11.24) from $\widehat{\boldsymbol{u}}_r$ yields

$$\begin{aligned}\Delta\boldsymbol{u}_{k+1} &= \Delta\boldsymbol{u}_k - \gamma\mathbf{L}\Lambda\left(\boldsymbol{y}_d - \theta^{-1}\boldsymbol{\Theta}_k\boldsymbol{y}_k - \theta^{-1}\boldsymbol{\xi}_k\right) \\ &= \Delta\boldsymbol{u}_k - \gamma\mathbf{L}\Lambda\left(\boldsymbol{y}_d - \boldsymbol{y}_r\right) \\ &\quad - \gamma\mathbf{L}\Lambda\left(\boldsymbol{y}_r - \theta^{-1}\boldsymbol{\Theta}_k\boldsymbol{y}_k\right) + \gamma\theta^{-1}\mathbf{L}\Lambda\boldsymbol{\xi}_k \\ &= \Delta\boldsymbol{u}_k - \gamma\mathbf{L}\Lambda\widetilde{\boldsymbol{y}}_r - \gamma\mathbf{L}\Lambda\mathbf{G}\Delta\boldsymbol{u}_k \\ &\quad - \gamma\mathbf{L}\Lambda(I - \theta^{-1}\boldsymbol{\Theta}_k)\boldsymbol{y}_k + \gamma\theta^{-1}\mathbf{L}\Lambda\boldsymbol{\xi}_k.\end{aligned} \tag{11.25}$$

We examine the term $\mathbf{L}\Lambda\widetilde{\boldsymbol{y}}_r$. Note that all columns of $\mathbf{L}^T$ belong to the space spanned by $\mathbf{G}$; thus, each column of $\mathbf{L}^T$ can be expressed as a linear combination of the columns of $\mathbf{G}$. Consequently, there exists a matrix M such that $\mathbf{L}^T = \mathbf{G}M$. Applying the weighted orthogonal property of the best achievable reference group leads to $\mathbf{L}\Lambda\widetilde{\boldsymbol{y}}_r = M^T\mathbf{G}^T\Lambda\widetilde{\boldsymbol{y}}_r = 0$.

Now, (11.25) becomes

$$\begin{aligned}\Delta\boldsymbol{u}_{k+1} &= \Delta\boldsymbol{u}_k - \gamma\mathbf{L}\Lambda\mathbf{G}\Delta\boldsymbol{u}_k + \gamma\mathbf{L}\Lambda\Phi_k\mathbf{G}\Delta\boldsymbol{u}_k \\ &\quad - \gamma\mathbf{L}\Lambda\boldsymbol{\omega}_k + \gamma\theta^{-1}\mathbf{L}\Lambda\boldsymbol{\xi}_k,\end{aligned} \tag{11.26}$$

where $\Phi_k \triangleq I - \theta^{-1}\boldsymbol{\Theta}_k$ and $\boldsymbol{\omega}_k \triangleq \Phi_k\widehat{\boldsymbol{y}}_r$.

Consider

$$\mathbf{L}\Lambda\mathbf{G} = \sum_{i=1}^{m}\lambda_i L_i G_i, \tag{11.27}$$

where L_i is a block diagonal matrix and G_i is a block lower-triangular matrix. Thus, the product L_iG_i is block lower-triangular and its diagonal blocks are $L_i'C_iB$. Then, the sum $\sum_{i=1}^m \lambda_i L_i G_i$ is also block lower-triangular, where the diagonal blocks are $\sum_{i=1}^m \lambda_i L_i' C_i B$. Because all eigenvalues of $\sum_{i=1}^m \lambda_i L_i' C_i B$ have positive real parts, all eigenvalues of $\mathbf{L}\Lambda\mathbf{G}$ have positive real parts and then, by the Lyapunov theory, there exists a positive-definite matrix $\mathbf{P} \in \mathbf{R}^{pN\times pN}$ such that

$$\mathbf{P}(\mathbf{L}\Lambda\mathbf{G}) + (\mathbf{L}\Lambda\mathbf{G})^T\mathbf{P} = I_{pN}. \tag{11.28}$$

Define a Lyapunov function of the input error

$$\mathcal{L}_k \triangleq \|\Delta \boldsymbol{u}_k\|_{\mathbf{P}}^2 = (\Delta \boldsymbol{u}_k)^T \mathbf{P} (\Delta \boldsymbol{u}_k). \tag{11.29}$$

Then, we have

$$\begin{aligned}
\mathcal{L}_{k+1} &= (\Delta \boldsymbol{u}_{k+1})^T \mathbf{P} (\Delta \boldsymbol{u}_{k+1}) \\
&= \|\Delta \boldsymbol{u}_{k+1}\|_{\mathbf{P}}^2 + \gamma^2 \|\mathbf{L}\Lambda\mathbf{G}\Delta \boldsymbol{u}_k\|_{\mathbf{P}}^2 \\
&\quad + \gamma^2 \|\mathbf{L}\Lambda\Phi_k\mathbf{G}\Delta \boldsymbol{u}_k\|_{\mathbf{P}}^2 \\
&\quad + \gamma^2 \|\mathbf{L}\Lambda\boldsymbol{\omega}_k\|_{\mathbf{P}}^2 + \gamma^2\theta^{-2} \|\mathbf{L}\Lambda\boldsymbol{\xi}_k\|_{\mathbf{P}}^2 \\
&\quad - \gamma(\Delta \boldsymbol{u}_k)^T \left[\mathbf{P}(\mathbf{L}\Lambda\mathbf{G}) + (\mathbf{L}\Lambda\mathbf{G})^T \mathbf{P}\right] (\Delta \boldsymbol{u}_k) \\
&\quad + 2\gamma(\Delta \boldsymbol{u}_k)^T \mathbf{P}\mathbf{L}\Lambda\Phi_k\mathbf{G}(\Delta \boldsymbol{u}_k) \\
&\quad - 2\gamma(\Delta \boldsymbol{u}_k)^T \mathbf{P}\mathbf{L}\Lambda(\boldsymbol{\omega}_k - \theta^{-1}\boldsymbol{\xi}_k) \\
&\quad - 2\gamma^2(\Delta \boldsymbol{u}_k)^T (\mathbf{L}\Lambda\mathbf{G})^T \mathbf{P}\mathbf{L}\Lambda\Phi_k\mathbf{G}(\Delta \boldsymbol{u}_k) \\
&\quad + 2\gamma^2(\Delta \boldsymbol{u}_k)^T (\mathbf{L}\Lambda\mathbf{G})^T \mathbf{P}\mathbf{L}\Lambda(\boldsymbol{\omega}_k - \theta^{-1}\boldsymbol{\xi}_k) \\
&\quad - 2\gamma^2(\Delta \boldsymbol{u}_k)^T (\mathbf{L}\Lambda\Phi_k\mathbf{G})^T \mathbf{P}\mathbf{L}\Lambda(\boldsymbol{\omega}_k - \theta^{-1}\boldsymbol{\xi}_k) \\
&\quad - 2\gamma^2\theta^{-1}\boldsymbol{\omega}_k^T\Lambda^T\mathbf{L}^T\mathbf{L}\Lambda\boldsymbol{\xi}_k.
\end{aligned} \tag{11.30}$$

To deal with the terms in (11.30), we define a σ-algebra $\mathcal{F}_k \triangleq \sigma\{u_0(t), x_j(0), \theta_{j,i}(t), \xi_{j,i}(t), 0 \le t \le N, 1 \le i \le m, 0 \le j \le k\}$ indicating the set of all events induced by the random variables up to the kth iteration. By (11.23), we obtain $\boldsymbol{u}_{k+1} \in \mathcal{F}_k$; we recall that $\boldsymbol{u}_k$ is adapted to the σ-algebra $\mathcal{F}_k$. Furthermore, by Assumption 11.3, the multiplicative and additive randomness $\theta_{k,i}(t)$ and $\xi_{k,i}(t)$ are independent in the iteration domain; therefore, both $\theta_{k,i}(t)$ and $\xi_{k,i}(t)$ are independent of $\mathcal{F}_{k-1}$. As a consequence, we have $\mathbb{E}[\theta_{k,i}(t)|\mathcal{F}_{k-1}] = 0$ and $\mathbb{E}[(1-\theta^{-1}\theta_{k,i}(t))|\mathcal{F}_{k-1}] = 0$. Moreover, $\boldsymbol{\omega}_k$ and $\boldsymbol{\xi}_k$ are conditionally independent with respect to $\mathcal{F}_{k-1}$. Then, except for the first six terms and $2\gamma^2(\Delta \boldsymbol{u}_k)^T (\mathbf{L}\Lambda\Phi_k\mathbf{G})^T \mathbf{P}\mathbf{L}\Lambda\boldsymbol{\omega}_k$, the conditional expectations of the terms on the RHS of (11.30) with respect to $\mathcal{F}_{k-1}$ are zero, i.e.,

$$\begin{aligned}
&\mathbb{E}\left[\gamma(\Delta \boldsymbol{u}_k)^T \mathbf{P}\mathbf{L}\Lambda\Phi_k\mathbf{G}(\Delta \boldsymbol{u}_k) \mid \mathcal{F}_{k-1}\right] \\
&\quad = \gamma(\Delta \boldsymbol{u}_k)^T \mathbf{P}\mathbf{L}\Lambda\mathbb{E}\left[\Phi_k \mid \mathcal{F}_{k-1}\right]\mathbf{G}(\Delta \boldsymbol{u}_k) = 0,
\end{aligned} \tag{11.31}$$

$$\begin{aligned}
&\mathbb{E}\left[\gamma(\Delta \boldsymbol{u}_k)^T \mathbf{P}\mathbf{L}\Lambda(\boldsymbol{\omega}_k - \theta^{-1}\boldsymbol{\xi}_k) \mid \mathcal{F}_{k-1}\right] \\
&\quad = \gamma(\Delta \boldsymbol{u}_k)^T \mathbf{P}\mathbf{L}\Lambda\mathbb{E}\left[(\boldsymbol{\omega}_k - \theta^{-1}\boldsymbol{\xi}_k) \mid \mathcal{F}_{k-1}\right] = 0,
\end{aligned} \tag{11.32}$$

$$\begin{aligned}
&\mathbb{E}\left[\gamma^2(\Delta \boldsymbol{u}_k)^T (\mathbf{L}\Lambda\mathbf{G})^T \mathbf{P}\mathbf{L}\Lambda\Phi_k\mathbf{G}(\Delta \boldsymbol{u}_k) \mid \mathcal{F}_{k-1}\right] \\
&\quad = \gamma^2 (\mathbf{L}\Lambda\mathbf{G}\Delta \boldsymbol{u}_k)^T \mathbf{P}\mathbf{L}\Lambda\mathbb{E}\left[\Phi_k \mid \mathcal{F}_{k-1}\right]\mathbf{G}\Delta \boldsymbol{u}_k = 0,
\end{aligned} \tag{11.33}$$

$$\mathbb{E}\left[\gamma^2(\Delta \boldsymbol{u}_k)^T(\mathbf{L}\Lambda\mathbf{G})^T\mathbf{P}\mathbf{L}\Lambda\boldsymbol{\omega}_k \mid \mathcal{F}_{k-1}\right]$$
$$= \gamma^2(\mathbf{L}\Lambda\mathbf{G}\Delta \boldsymbol{u}_k)^T\mathbf{P}\mathbf{L}\Lambda\mathbb{E}\left[\boldsymbol{\omega}_k \mid \mathcal{F}_{k-1}\right] = 0, \tag{11.34}$$
$$\mathbb{E}\left[\gamma^2(\Delta \boldsymbol{u}_k)^T(\mathbf{L}\Lambda\mathbf{G})^T\mathbf{P}\mathbf{L}\Lambda\theta^{-1}\boldsymbol{\xi}_k \mid \mathcal{F}_{k-1}\right]$$
$$= \gamma^2\theta^{-1}(\mathbf{L}\Lambda\mathbf{G}\Delta \boldsymbol{u}_k)^T\mathbf{P}\mathbf{L}\Lambda\mathbb{E}\left[\boldsymbol{\xi}_k \mid \mathcal{F}_{k-1}\right] = 0, \tag{11.35}$$
$$\mathbb{E}\left[\gamma^2\theta^{-1}(\Delta \boldsymbol{u}_k)^T(\mathbf{L}\Lambda\Phi_k\mathbf{G})^T\mathbf{P}\mathbf{L}\Lambda\boldsymbol{\xi}_k \mid \mathcal{F}_{k-1}\right]$$
$$= \gamma^2\theta^{-1}(\mathbf{G}\Delta \boldsymbol{u}_k)^T\mathbb{E}[\Phi_k \mid \mathcal{F}_{k-1}]^T(\mathbf{L}\Lambda)^T$$
$$\times \mathbf{P}\mathbf{L}\Lambda\mathbb{E}\left[\boldsymbol{\xi}_k \mid \mathcal{F}_{k-1}\right] = 0, \tag{11.36}$$
$$\mathbb{E}\left[\gamma^2\theta^{-1}\boldsymbol{\omega}_k^T\Lambda^T\mathbf{L}^T\mathbf{L}\Lambda\boldsymbol{\xi}_k \mid \mathcal{F}_{k-1}\right]$$
$$= \gamma^2\theta^{-1}\mathbb{E}\left[\boldsymbol{\omega}_k|\mathcal{F}_{k-1}\right]^T\Lambda^T\mathbf{L}^T\mathbf{L}\Lambda\mathbb{E}\left[\boldsymbol{\xi}_k|\mathcal{F}_{k-1}\right] = 0, \tag{11.37}$$

where $\mathbb{E}[\Delta \boldsymbol{u}_k|\mathcal{F}_{k-1}] = \Delta \boldsymbol{u}_k$ is applied. We now check the left terms on the RHS of (11.30).

There exist positive constants c_1 and c_2 such that

$$\mathbb{E}\left[\|\mathbf{L}\Lambda\mathbf{G}\Delta \boldsymbol{u}_k\|_{\mathbf{P}}^2|\mathcal{F}_{k-1}\right] \le c_1(\Delta \boldsymbol{u}_k)^T\mathbf{P}\Delta \boldsymbol{u}_k = c_1\mathcal{L}_k, \tag{11.38}$$
$$\mathbb{E}\left[\|\mathbf{L}\Lambda\Phi_k\mathbf{G}\Delta \boldsymbol{u}_k\|_{\mathbf{P}}^2|\mathcal{F}_{k-1}\right] \le c_2\mathcal{L}_k, \tag{11.39}$$

where the boundedness of the second-moment of Φ_k is used.

Further, by Assumption 11.3, the second-moments of both $\boldsymbol{\omega}_k$ and $\boldsymbol{\xi}_k$ are conditionally bounded with respect to $\mathcal{F}_{k-1}$. That is, there exist $c_3 > 0$ and $c_4 > 0$ such that

$$\mathbb{E}\left[\|\mathbf{L}\Lambda\boldsymbol{\omega}_k\|_{\mathbf{P}}^2 \mid \mathcal{F}_{k-1}\right] \le c_3, \tag{11.40}$$
$$\mathbb{E}\left[\|\mathbf{L}\Lambda\boldsymbol{\xi}_k\|_{\mathbf{P}}^2 \mid \mathcal{F}_{k-1}\right] \le c_4. \tag{11.41}$$

Note that $\boldsymbol{\omega}_k$ depends on Φ_k. A specific estimation of the term $(\Delta \boldsymbol{u}_k)^T(\mathbf{L}\Lambda\Phi_k\mathbf{G})^T\mathbf{P}\mathbf{L}\Lambda\boldsymbol{\omega}_k$ is given as follows:

$$\begin{aligned}
&2(\Delta \boldsymbol{u}_k)^T(\mathbf{L}\Lambda\Phi_k\mathbf{G})^T\mathbf{P}\mathbf{L}\Lambda\boldsymbol{\omega}_k \\
&\quad \le 2|\underbrace{(\Delta \boldsymbol{u}_k)^T(\mathbf{L}\Lambda\Phi_k\mathbf{G})^T\mathbf{P}^{\frac{1}{2}}}_{\boldsymbol{\varphi}^T}\underbrace{\mathbf{P}^{\frac{1}{2}}\mathbf{L}\Lambda\boldsymbol{\omega}_k}_{\boldsymbol{\psi}}| \\
&\quad \le \underbrace{(\Delta \boldsymbol{u}_k)^T(\mathbf{L}\Lambda\Phi_k\mathbf{G})^T\mathbf{P}(\mathbf{L}\Lambda\Phi_k\mathbf{G})\Delta \boldsymbol{u}_k}_{\boldsymbol{\varphi}^T\boldsymbol{\varphi}} \\
&\qquad + \underbrace{\boldsymbol{\omega}_k^T(\mathbf{L}\Lambda)^T\mathbf{P}(\mathbf{L}\Lambda)\boldsymbol{\omega}_k}_{\boldsymbol{\psi}^T\boldsymbol{\psi}},
\end{aligned} \tag{11.42}$$

where $\mathbf{P}^{\frac{1}{2}}$ denotes the principle square root of $\mathbf{P}$. The estimation gives

$$\begin{aligned}
&\mathbb{E}\left[2(\Delta \boldsymbol{u}_k)^T (\mathbf{L}\Lambda\Phi_k\mathbf{G})^T \mathbf{P}\mathbf{L}\Lambda\boldsymbol{\omega}_k \mid \mathcal{F}_{k-1}\right] \\
&\leq \mathbb{E}\left[\|\mathbf{L}\Lambda\Phi_k\mathbf{G}\Delta\boldsymbol{u}_k\|_{\mathbf{P}}^2 \mid \mathcal{F}_{k-1}\right] + \mathbb{E}\left[\|\mathbf{L}\Lambda\boldsymbol{\omega}_k\|_{\mathbf{P}}^2 \mid \mathcal{F}_{k-1}\right] \\
&\leq c_2\mathcal{L}_k + c_3.
\end{aligned} \tag{11.43}$$

Using $\mathbf{P}(\mathbf{L}\Lambda\mathbf{G}) + (\mathbf{L}\Lambda\mathbf{G})^T\mathbf{P} = I_{pN}$ and noting that a constant $c_5 > 0$ exists such that $c_5\mathbf{P} \leq I$, we have

$$\begin{aligned}
&\mathbb{E}\left[(\Delta \boldsymbol{u}_k)^T \left[\mathbf{P}(\mathbf{L}\Lambda\mathbf{G}) + (\mathbf{L}\Lambda\mathbf{G})^T\mathbf{P}\right](\Delta\boldsymbol{u}_k) \mid \mathcal{F}_{k-1}\right] \\
&= (\Delta \boldsymbol{u}_k)^T \left[\mathbf{P}(\mathbf{L}\Lambda\mathbf{G}) + (\mathbf{L}\Lambda\mathbf{G})^T\mathbf{P}\right](\Delta\boldsymbol{u}_k) \\
&= (\Delta \boldsymbol{u}_k)^T(\Delta\boldsymbol{u}_k) \geq c_5(\Delta\boldsymbol{u}_k)^T\mathbf{P}(\Delta\boldsymbol{u}_k) = c_5\mathcal{L}_k.
\end{aligned} \tag{11.44}$$

Taking the conditional expectation of both sides of (11.30) with respect to $\mathcal{F}_{k-1}$ and substituting the above estimations yields

$$\begin{aligned}
\mathbb{E}[\mathcal{L}_{k+1} \mid \mathcal{F}_{k-1}] &\leq \mathcal{L}_k + c_1\gamma^2\mathcal{L}_k + c_2\gamma^2\mathcal{L}_k + c_3\gamma^2 + c_4\gamma^2\theta^{-2} \\
&\quad - c_5\gamma\mathcal{L}_k + \gamma^2(c_2\mathcal{L}_k + c_3) \\
&= \mathcal{L}_k - c_5\gamma\mathcal{L}_k + \gamma^2(c_1 + 2c_2)\mathcal{L}_k \\
&\quad + \gamma^2(2c_3 + c_4\theta^{-2}).
\end{aligned} \tag{11.45}$$

Taking the mathematical expectation of both sides of the above inequality leads to

$$\begin{aligned}
\mathbb{E}[\mathcal{L}_{k+1}] &\leq (1 - \gamma(c_5 - \gamma(c_1 + 2c_2)))\mathbb{E}[\mathcal{L}_k] \\
&\quad + \gamma^2(2c_3 + c_4\theta^{-2}) \\
&= \rho\mathbb{E}[\mathcal{L}_k] + \delta,
\end{aligned} \tag{11.46}$$

where $\rho = 1 - \gamma(c_5 - \gamma(c_1 + 2c_2))$ and $\delta = \gamma^2(2c_3 + c_4\theta^{-2})$. Then, it holds that $\rho < 1$ if γ is sufficiently small to satisfy $c_5 - \gamma(c_1 + 2c_2) > 0$ and $\gamma c_5 < 1$. The latter yields the range of γ as $\gamma < \min\{\frac{c_5}{c_1+2c_2}, \frac{1}{c_5}\}$. Under this condition, $\rho < 1$ is guaranteed and furthermore, $\mathbb{E}[\mathcal{L}_k]$ converges to a sphere of zero, where the upper bound is given as $\frac{\delta}{1-\rho}$. That is,

$$\lim_{k\to\infty} \mathbb{E}[\mathcal{L}_k] \leq \frac{\delta}{1-\rho}. \tag{11.47}$$

Note that δ is proportional to γ^2 and $1-\rho$ is proportional to γ, thus the upper bound of the convergence sphere can be tuned by the learning gain γ.

Since $\mathbf{P}$ is positive definite, we have

$$\lim_{k\to\infty} \mathbb{E}[\|\Delta \boldsymbol{u}_k\|^2] \le \tau \triangleq \frac{\delta}{\lambda_{\min}(\mathbf{P})[1-\rho]}, \tag{11.48}$$

where $\lambda_{\min}(\mathbf{P})$ is the minimum eigenvalue of $\mathbf{P}$. The proof is completed. □

Theorem 11.1 characterizes convergence of the generated input sequence in the mean-square sense. The essential convergence performance depends on two factors: One is the range of learning gain and the other is the selection of suitable direction regulation matrix. They will be elaborated in the remarks.

Remark 11.3 *For the input errors, its convergent upper bound is determined by $\delta/(\lambda_{\min}(\mathbf{P})[1-\rho])$. As $\gamma \to 0$, we have $\rho \to 1$ and $\delta \to 0$. Note that $\delta = O(\lambda^2)$ and $1-\rho = O(\lambda)$; thus, the upper bound is reduced as $\gamma \to 0$. Moreover, by noting that $\delta = \gamma^2(2c_3 + c_4\theta^{-2})$, the upper bound can be reduced if $c_3 \to 0$ and $c_4 \to 0$; the latter conditions imply vanishing of both the random noise and the random fading. The parameter range of γ is given by $(0, \min\{\frac{c_5}{c_1+2c_2}, \frac{1}{c_5}\})$, which depends on the system information and fading communication. In practice, this parameter can be selected by a rough computation of the range bound and choosing a suitably small one.*

Remark 11.4 *We remark on the selection of L_i. Note that $\mathbf{L}$ is a horizontal stack of L_i and $\mathbf{G}$ is a vertical stack of G_i. The requirement that all columns of $\mathbf{L}^T$ lie in the space spanned by $\mathbf{G}$ indicates that each column of L_i^T is a linear combination of the columns of G_i with the same coefficients for all i. In other words, there exists a common matrix M such that $L_i^T = G_i M$ for all i. A special example is $L_i' = C_i^T$ provided that the output is controllable, i.e., $\mathrm{rank}(CB) = \mathrm{rank}(C)$, where $C = [C_1^T, \ldots, C_m^T]^T$ [38]. Thus, the requirement does not need full knowledge of $\mathbf{G}$.*

Remark 11.5 *For a multi-sensor system, the condition that all eigenvalues of $\sum_{i=1}^m \lambda_i L_i' C_i B$ have positive real parts has greatly relaxed the convergence conditions for a single-sensor system. It is the major distinction of learning control for a multi-sensor system. Particularly, for a single-sensor system (taking the ith sensor, for example), the condition turns into that the eigenvalues of $L_i' C_i B$ have positive real parts, which requires the coupling matrix $C_i B$ to be of a full-column rank. However, $C_i B$ is unnecessary to be of a full-column rank for a multi-sensor system. Even if each coupling matrix is not of full-column rank, we can still guarantee that the weighted sum $\sum_{i=1}^m \lambda_i L_i' C_i B$ have eigenvalues with positive real parts. In short, the range of systems have been expanded.*

The almost-sure convergence of the learning control algorithm with a constant gain is given by the following theorem.

Theorem 11.2 *Consider Assumptions 11.1-11.3 for system of* (11.1) *and apply the learning control algorithm of* (11.23)*. Then, the generated input sequence* $\{\boldsymbol{u}_k\}$ *guarantees that the input error* $\widehat{\boldsymbol{u}}_r - \boldsymbol{u}_k$ *converges to a bounded sphere of zero in the almost-sure sense, i.e.,*

$$\mathbb{P}\left(\lim_{k\to\infty} \|\widehat{\boldsymbol{u}}_r - \boldsymbol{u}_k\|^2 \leq \tau\right) = 1, \tag{11.49}$$

provided that the conditions of Theorem 11.1 are ensured.

Proof: To demonstrate the almost-sure convergence, we recall the estimation (11.45):

$$\mathbb{E}[\mathcal{L}_{k+1} \mid \mathcal{F}_{k-1}] \leq \rho\mathcal{L}_k + \delta. \tag{11.50}$$

Then, we have

$$\mathbb{E}\left[\mathcal{L}_{k+1} - \frac{\delta}{1-\rho}\middle|\mathcal{F}_{k-1}\right] \leq \rho\left(\mathcal{L}_k - \frac{\delta}{1-\rho}\right). \tag{11.51}$$

Assume $\lim_{k\to\infty}(\mathcal{L}_k - \frac{\delta}{1-\rho}) > 0$, then the sequence $\{\mathcal{L}_k - \frac{\delta}{1-\rho}\}$ is a nonnegative supermartingale and thus $\{\mathcal{L}_k - \frac{\delta}{1-\rho}\}$ converges in the almost-sure sense. Moreover, $\rho < 1$ if the learning gain γ is sufficiently small, thus $\lim_{k\to\infty}(\mathcal{L}_k - \frac{\delta}{1-\rho}) = 0$. This contradicts the assumption and leads to $\mathbb{P}\left(\lim_{k\to\infty}\mathcal{L}_k \leq \frac{\delta}{1-\rho}\right) = 1$; therefore, $\mathbb{P}\left(\lim_{k\to\infty}\|\widehat{\boldsymbol{u}}_r - \boldsymbol{u}_k\|^2 \leq \tau\right) = 1$. □

Theorem 11.2 presents the convergence in the almost-sure sense, where the primary technique is to apply the convergence principle of a nonnegative supermartingale sequence.

11.4.3 Learning Algorithm with Decreasing Gain

In this subsection, we replace the constant gain in (11.23) with a decreasing gain. The learning control algorithm becomes

$$\boldsymbol{u}_{k+1} = \boldsymbol{u}_k + \gamma_k \sum_{i=1}^{m} \lambda_i L_i \boldsymbol{\varepsilon}_{k,i}, \tag{11.52}$$

where $\gamma_k > 0$, $\gamma_k \to 0$, and $\boldsymbol{\varepsilon}_{k,i} = \boldsymbol{y}_{d,i} - \boldsymbol{y}^{\star}_{k,i}$.

The following theorems summarize the mean-square and almost-sure convergence to the desired input for (11.52).

Theorem 11.3 *Consider Assumptions 11.1-11.3 hold for the system of* (11.1) *and apply the learning control algorithm* (11.52). *Then, the generated input sequence* $\{\boldsymbol{u}_k\}$ *guarantees that the input error* $\widehat{\boldsymbol{u}}_r - \boldsymbol{u}_k$ *converges to zero in the mean-square sense, i.e.,*

$$\lim_{k\to\infty} \mathbb{E}[\|\widehat{\boldsymbol{u}}_r - \boldsymbol{u}_k\|^2] = 0, \tag{11.53}$$

if the decreasing gain γ_k *satisfies* $\sum_{k=1}^{\infty} \gamma_k = \infty$, *the direction regulation matrices* L_i *satisfy the condition that all eigenvalues of* $\sum_{i=1}^{m} \lambda_i L_i' C_i B$ *have positive real parts, and all of the columns of* $\mathbf{L}^T$ *belong to the space spanned by* $\mathbf{G}$, *where* $\mathbf{L} = [L_1, L_2, \ldots, L_m]$.

Proof: The algorithm (11.52) is written as

$$\boldsymbol{u}_{k+1} = \boldsymbol{u}_k + \gamma_k \mathbf{L}\Lambda\boldsymbol{\varepsilon}_k. \tag{11.54}$$

We apply the Lyapunov function as $\mathcal{L}_k = (\Delta\boldsymbol{u}_k)^T \mathbf{P}(\Delta\boldsymbol{u}_k)$. Using the same steps as the proof to Theorem 11.1, we have

$$\begin{aligned}\mathbb{E}[\mathcal{L}_{k+1} \mid \mathcal{F}_{k-1}] \le{}& (1 - c_5\gamma_k)\mathcal{L}_k + \gamma_k^2(c_1 + 2c_2)\mathcal{L}_k \\ &+ \gamma_k^2(2c_3 + c_4\theta^{-2}).\end{aligned} \tag{11.55}$$

Taking mathematical expectation of (11.55) yields

$$\begin{aligned}\mathbb{E}[\mathcal{L}_{k+1}] \le{}& \left(1 - c_5\gamma_k + (c_1 + 2c_2)\gamma_k^2\right)\mathbb{E}[\mathcal{L}_k] \\ &+ (2c_3 + c_4\theta^{-2})\gamma_k^2.\end{aligned} \tag{11.56}$$

Denote $\mu_k = [c_5 - (c_1 + 2c_2)\gamma_k]\gamma_k$ and $\nu_k = (2c_3 + c_4\theta^{-2})\gamma_k^2$. Since $\gamma_k \to 0$ as $k \to \infty$, there exists a sufficiently large k_0 such that $\mu_k < 1$ for all $k \ge k_0$, implying that $1 - \mu_k > 0$ for $k \ge k_0$. Moreover, $\mu_k = O(\gamma_k)$ as $k \to \infty$; therefore, $\sum_{k=1}^{\infty} \mu_k = \infty$. In addition, $\nu_k/\mu_k = O(\gamma_k) \to 0$. Thus, we conclude that $\lim_{k\to\infty} \mathbb{E}[\mathcal{L}_k] = 0$. Again, by the positive-definiteness of $\mathbf{P}$, we have $\lim_{k\to\infty} \mathbb{E}[\|\Delta\boldsymbol{u}_k\|^2] = 0$. The proof is completed. □

Theorem 11.4 *Consider Assumptions 11.1-11.3 hold for the system of* (11.1) *and apply the learning control algorithm* (11.52). *Then, the generated input sequence* $\{\boldsymbol{u}_k\}$ *guarantees that the input error* $\widehat{\boldsymbol{u}}_r - \boldsymbol{u}_k$ *converges to zero in the almost-sure sense, i.e.,*

$$\mathbb{P}\left(\lim_{k\to\infty} \|\widehat{\boldsymbol{u}}_r - \boldsymbol{u}_k\|^2 = 0\right) = 1, \tag{11.57}$$

if the decreasing gain γ_k *satisfies* $\sum_{k=1}^{\infty} \gamma_k = \infty$ *and* $\sum_{k=1}^{\infty} \gamma_k^2 < \infty$, *and the other conditions of Theorem 11.3 are ensured.*

Proof: By (11.55), we have

$$\mathbb{E}[\mathcal{L}_{k+1}|\mathcal{F}_{k-1}] \leq \mathcal{L}_k + \gamma_k^2\left[(c_1+2c_2)\mathcal{L}_k + (2c_3+c_4\theta^{-2})\right]. \tag{11.58}$$

Using the mean-square convergence result given in Theorem 11.3, we can verify that

$$\sum_{k=1}^{\infty}\mathbb{E}\left[\gamma_k^2\left((c_1+2c_2)\mathcal{L}_k + (2c_3+c_4\theta^{-2})\right)\right] < \infty. \tag{11.59}$$

Then, using Lemma A.2, we obtain the almost-sure convergence of $\mathcal{L}_k$. We have shown that $\mathcal{L}_k$ converges to zero in the mean-square sense. Therefore, the almost-sure convergence limit of $\mathcal{L}_k$ should also be zero, completing the proof. □

Theorems 11.3 and 11.4 provide the mean-square and almost-sure convergence for the learning control scheme with a decreasing gain. From these results, although random fading and noise exists in the faded measurements, a stable convergence of the input sequence is still ensured by the decreasing gain. As a consequence, the actual output driven by the input converges to the best achievable reference group.

Remark 11.6 *The mean-square convergence of* (11.52) *only requires the decreasing gain γ_k to satisfy $\sum_{k=1}^{\infty}\gamma_k = \infty$. Loosely speaking, the decreasing gain should not approach zero too quickly. However, the almost-sure convergence requires the decreasing gain to satisfy $\sum_{k=1}^{\infty}\gamma_k = \infty$ and $\sum_{k=1}^{\infty}\gamma_k^2 < \infty$ simultaneously. Loosely speaking, the decreasing gain cannot approach zero too slowly either.*

Remark 11.7 *The original optimization problem* (11.13) *can allow multiple solutions of the input for the best achievable reference, whereas Theorems 11.1-11.4 indicate a specific convergence limit of $\widehat{\mathbf{u}}_r$. The latter is guaranteed by the additional condition of the direction regulation matrices L_i, i.e., all eigenvalues of $\sum_{i=1}^{m}\lambda_i L_i' C_i B$ have positive real parts. This condition implies that the lifted system matrix* **G** *is of full column rank and the uniqueness of the solution to the optimization problem. If this condition is violated, further elaborations are required on the potential convergence of the input sequence to the set of possible solutions of the optimization problem.*

The tracking performance involves two primary indices: Convergence rate and final tracking precision. The learning control algorithm with a decreasing gain achieves the zero-error convergence to the desired input as the iteration number increases, which is more advantageous than the outcome of the algorithm with a constant gain. However, the convergence rate of the former is slower than that of the latter. In particular, with a constant gain, we can obtain an exponential convergence rate by observing (11.46); however, with a decreasing gain, the convergence rate heavily depends on the decreasing gain. In short, there exists a trade-off between the final tracking precision and convergence rate. In practice, the selection of a constant or decreasing gain is determined by whether the convergence rate or the final tracking precision is preferred. A promising integration for applications is to employ a constant gain at the early learning stage such that fast convergence can be ensured and change into the decreasing gain after certain iterations such that the tracking precision can be improved gradually.

11.4.4 Best Tracking Performance Evaluation

We now examine the modified tracking error $\boldsymbol{\varepsilon}_k = \boldsymbol{y}_d - \boldsymbol{y}_k^\star$. This error consists of four parts, listed as follows:

$$\boldsymbol{\varepsilon}_k = \underbrace{\boldsymbol{y}_d - \widehat{\boldsymbol{y}}_r}_{\text{residual}} + \underbrace{\widehat{\boldsymbol{y}}_r - \boldsymbol{y}_k}_{\text{learning}} + \underbrace{(I - \theta^{-1}\boldsymbol{\Theta}_k)\boldsymbol{y}_k}_{\text{fading}} - \underbrace{\theta^{-1}\boldsymbol{\xi}_k}_{\text{noise}}, \tag{11.60}$$

where $\boldsymbol{y}_k = \boldsymbol{G}\boldsymbol{u}_k$. In other words, the innovation information for correcting input is a combination of various uncertainties. The first part $\boldsymbol{y}_d - \widehat{\boldsymbol{y}}_r$ is the residual error, which cannot be tracked by the system. This part is eliminated in the proposed learning control algorithms through selecting suitable direction regulation matrices. The second part $\widehat{\boldsymbol{y}}_r - \boldsymbol{y}_k$ can be regarded as the learning error, which indicates the learning performance of the input signal. It is the primary term for correcting input signals. The third part $(I - \theta^{-1}\boldsymbol{\Theta}_k)\boldsymbol{y}_k$ and the last part $\theta^{-1}\boldsymbol{\xi}_k$ are random errors caused by the multiplicative fading gain and additive noise, respectively. Both parts are of zero means and bounded covariances. For the constant gain case, these parts bring continuous fluctuations into input signals, thus the input sequence cannot converge to a stable limit. For the decreasing gain case, the influence of these parts vanishes as the gain decreases to zero and a steady convergence of the input sequence is obtained.

For the proposed multi-sensor system, one may consider lifting outputs of all sensors into a large vector such that the multi-tracking problem can be transformed into the conventional tracking problem. That is, instead of studying $\boldsymbol{y}_{k,1}, \ldots, \boldsymbol{y}_{k,m}$ to track $\boldsymbol{y}_{d,1}, \ldots, \boldsymbol{y}_{d,m}$ with possibly different weights, we consider the tracking problem of $\boldsymbol{y}_k$ to $\boldsymbol{y}_d$ directly, where $\boldsymbol{y}_k$ and $\boldsymbol{y}_d$ are defined in Subsection 11.3.2. In this case, the performance index is formulated so as to minimize $V' = \limsup_{k\to\infty} \frac{1}{k}\sum_{l=1}^{k} \|\boldsymbol{y}_d - \boldsymbol{y}_k\|^2$, which is a special case of (11.12). That is, V' corresponds to (11.12) with $\lambda_i = 1/m$, $\forall i$. This observation reveals the connection between the proposed multi-objective tracking problem and the conventional tracking problem. It implies that the proposed scheme can be applied to underactuated systems with multiple faded outputs.

11.5 ILLUSTRATIVE SIMULATIONS

To verify the previous results, we will perform numerical simulations for the following dynamics:

$$\begin{aligned} x_k(t+1) &= \begin{bmatrix} 0.1-0.05\sin(0.2t) & 0.01t \\ 0.1 & 0.1\cos(0.2t) \end{bmatrix} x_k(t) \\ &+ \begin{bmatrix} 1-0.1(\sin(0.5\pi t))^2 & 0 \\ 0.2 & 0.5+0.02(\cos(\pi t))^3 \end{bmatrix} u_k(t), \end{aligned}$$

which has three sensors/outputs $y_{k,1}(t) = [-2\ 2]x_k(t)$, $y_{k,2}(t) = [1\ 2]x_k(t)$, and $y_{k,3}(t) = [-0.4\ 3]x_k(t)$. Fading is modeled by two random variables: $\theta_{k,i}(t) \sim N(0.9, 0.1^2)$ and $\xi_{k,i}(t) \sim N(0, 0.1^2)$, $\forall i,k,t$. The trial length is $T = 50$. The number of trials for each experiment is 50.

The desired trajectories for the three sensors are defined by $y_{d,1}(t) = \sin(0.1\pi t)$, $y_{d,2} = \cos(0.1\pi t) - 1/(t+1)$, and $y_{d,3}(t) = \sin(0.1\pi t) + 0.5\cos(0.1\pi t) - 0.5$. The system has only two inputs but three outputs. It can be verified that the desired trajectories for all the three sensors are inconsistent in the sense that none input exists to generate all trajectories simultaneously. Therefore, we need to balance different sensors. The weights are set to $\lambda_1 = 0.4$, $\lambda_2 = 0.3$, and $\lambda_3 = 0.3$ in (11.6). Accordingly, the best achievable reference group is computed by $\widehat{\boldsymbol{y}}_r = \sqrt{\Lambda}^{-1}\mathcal{P}_S[\sqrt{\Lambda}\boldsymbol{y}_d]$ and the residual part $\widetilde{\boldsymbol{y}}_r$ is plotted in Fig. 11.2. It is observed that each desired trajectory contains a untraceable part over the whole iteration.

11.5.1 Constant Gain Case

In this subsection, we consider the learning control algorithm (11.23). The constant learning gain is set to $\gamma = 1/4$. Direction regulation matrices are set to $L_i' = (C_iB)^T$. The tracking performance of the 50th iteration is shown in Fig. 11.3, where the solid line and the dashed line in each subplot indicate the best achievable reference and the actual output, respectively. It can be observed that the outputs track the best achievable references with high precision at the 50th iteration except for small fluctuations around the peaks and valleys.

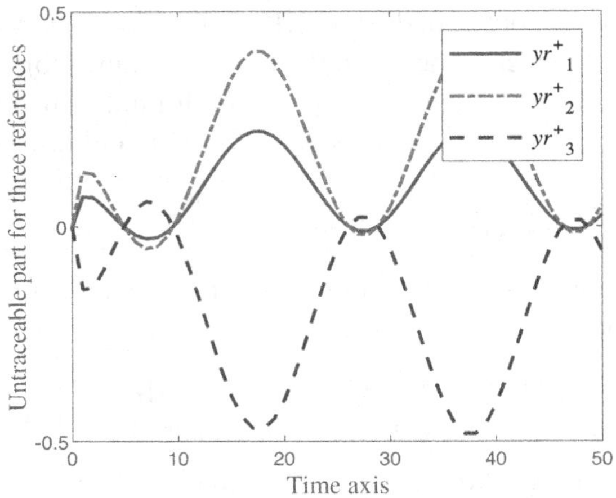

Figure 11.2 Residual part of the desired trajectories for all three sensors (y_r^+ is used to denote the residual part).

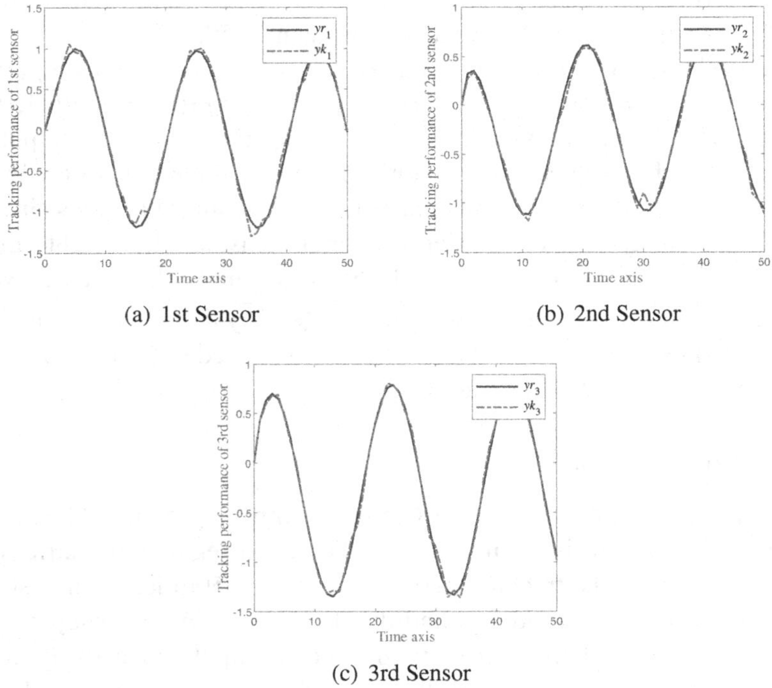

Figure 11.3 Tracking performance at the 50th iteration of three sensors for algorithm (11.23).

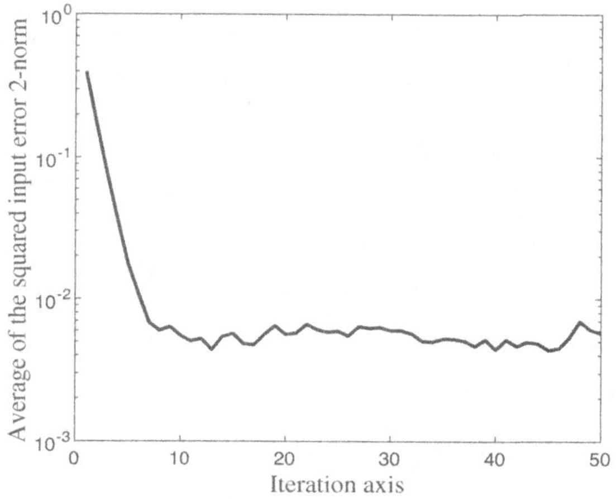

Figure 11.4 Input error profile along the iteration axis for algorithm (11.23).

To demonstrate the iteration-wise convergence of the input, we compute the average value of the squared input errors, which is defined by $\frac{1}{T}\sum_{t=1}^{T}\|u_r(t)-u_k(t)\|^2$ for the kth iteration. The profile of this value changes with iterations is shown in Fig. 11.4. We demonstrate the maximum learning error $\max_{1\le t\le T}|y_r(t)-y_{k,i}(t)|$ for each sensor in Fig. 11.5, $i=1,2,3$. It is seen that both input errors and learning errors converge to a bounded sphere quickly.

To see the iteration-wise improvement of the tracking performance, the index (11.6) is replaced with an alternative $\sum_{i=1}^{m}\lambda_i(\sum_{t=1}^{N}\|y_{d,i}(t)-y_{k,i}(t)\|^2)$, which is calculated merely with the data of the kth iteration and used throughout the simulations. The profiles is shown in Fig. 11.6, where the solid line denotes the index value computed with the practical outputs and the dashed line indicates its minimum (i.e., $\|\sqrt{\Lambda}\tilde{\mathbf{y}}_r\|^2$). It can be seen that a small gap exists between the practical values and the minimum value. This is consistent with the analysis in Section 11.4.2.

To demonstrate the influence of the multiplicative gain $\theta_{k,i}(t)$, we consider the three parametric scenarios of θ and σ_θ: (1) $\theta=0.9$ and $\sigma_\theta=0.1$, (2) $\theta=0.6$ and $\sigma_\theta=0.1$, and (3) $\theta=0.9$ and $\sigma_\theta=0.2$, respectively. The tracking performance indices for three scenarios are shown in Fig. 11.7(a). A subplot is included to zoom into the back-end part for clarity. It can be seen

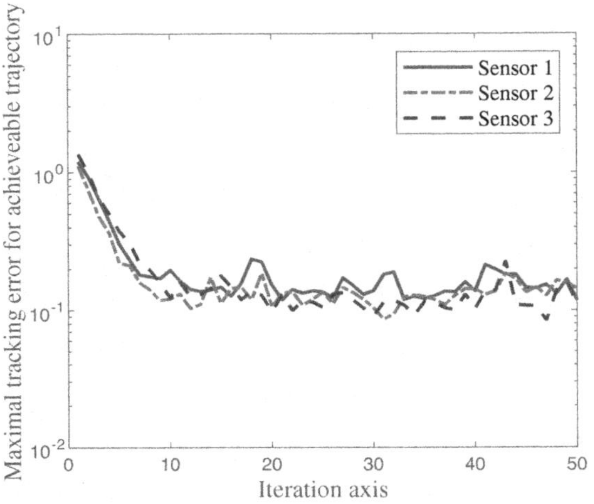

Figure 11.5 Maximum learning error profiles of the three sensors for algorithm (11.23).

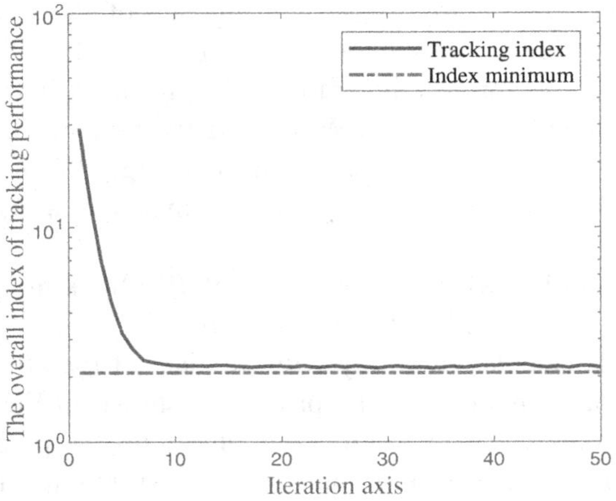

Figure 11.6 Overall tracking performance index for algorithm (11.23) and the minimum of (11.6).

that decreasing the mean θ and increasing the variance σ_θ can worsen the tracking performance.

Further, to demonstrate the influence of the learning gain γ, we consider the following three parametric scenarios: $\gamma = 1/4$, $\gamma = 1/10$ and $\gamma = 1/20$,

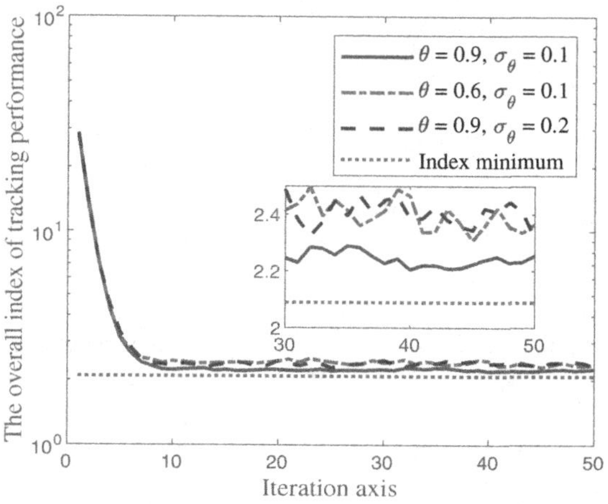

(a)

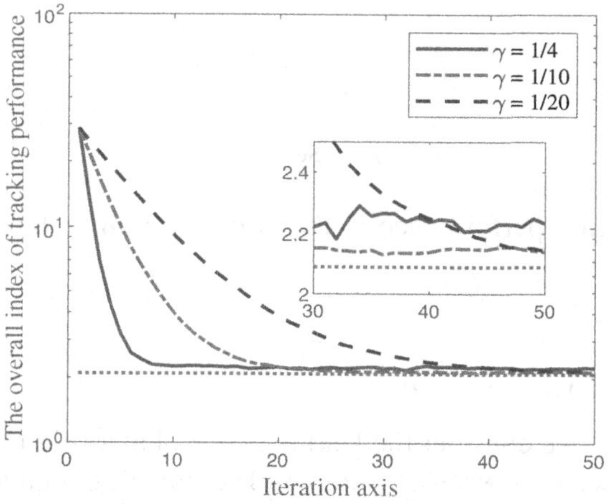

(b)

Figure 11.7 Overall tracking performance index for algorithm (11.23) with (a) different multiplicative gain distributions and (b) different learning gains.

respectively. The tracking performance index profiles are shown in Fig. 11.7(b) for the three scenarios. From this figure, we can observe that as the learning gain decreases, both the convergence rate and the upper bound of the convergent sphere decrease. In other words, there exists a trade-off between the convergence rate and tracking precision.

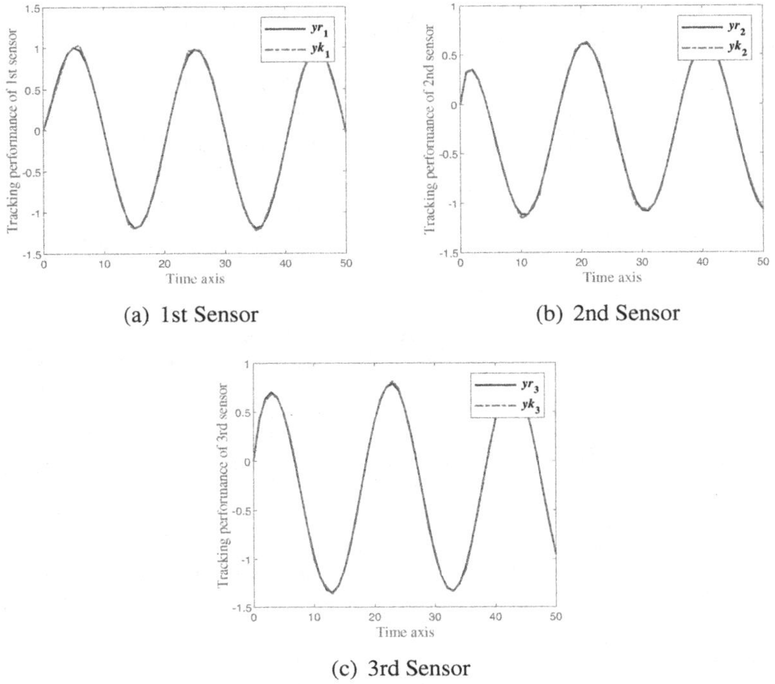

Figure 11.8 Tracking performance at the 50th iteration of three sensors for algorithm (11.52).

11.5.2 Decreasing Gain Case

In this subsection, we consider the learning control algorithm (11.52) with a decreasing gain which we set to $\gamma_k = 1/k$. The direction regulation matrices are still set to $L_i^{\prime} = (C_i B)^T$. The tracking performance of the 50th iteration is shown in Fig. 11.8, where the solid lines and the dashed lines indicate the best achievable references and actual outputs, respectively. It is observed that the tracking performance has been significantly improved compared to Fig. 11.3 that analyzed the constant gain case. Especially, the performance around the peaks and valleys is significantly improved compared to the constant gain case.

The profile of the average value of the squared input errors is shown in Fig. 11.9 along the iteration axis. The input error in this case is generally smaller than that of the constant gain case and a slowly decreasing trend can be observed. The maximum learning errors are plotted in Fig. 11.10 for

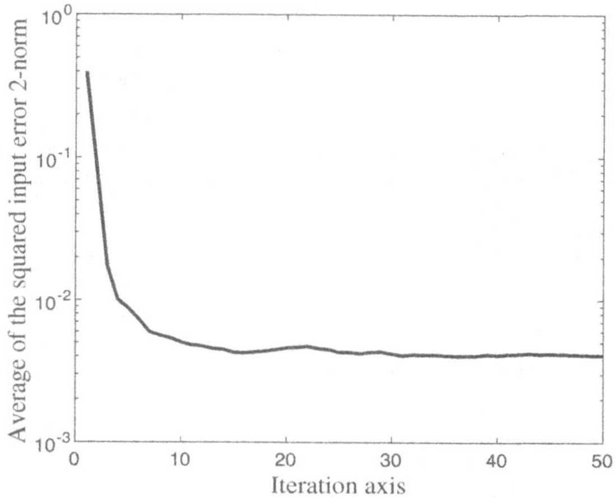

Figure 11.9 Input error profile along the iteration axis for algorithm (11.52).

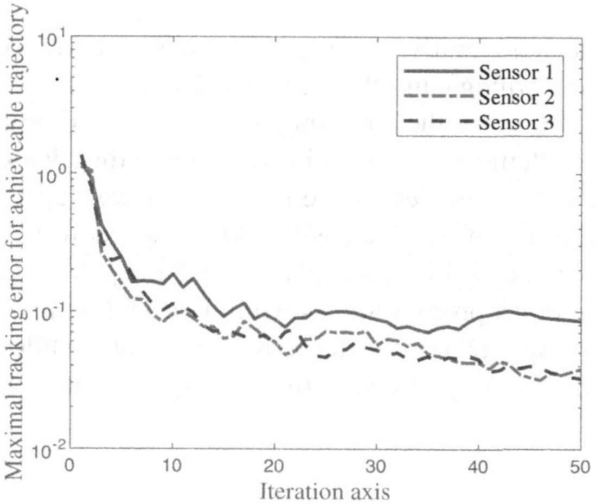

Figure 11.10 Maximal learning error profiles of the three sensors for algorithm (11.52).

the three sensors. Compared with the constant gain case, it is seen that the tracking errors are distinctly reduced and obey a decreasing trend along the iteration axis. Fig. 11.11 shows the comparison between the overall tracking performance index and its minimum, and we can observe that the practical index value converges to the minimum asymptotically.

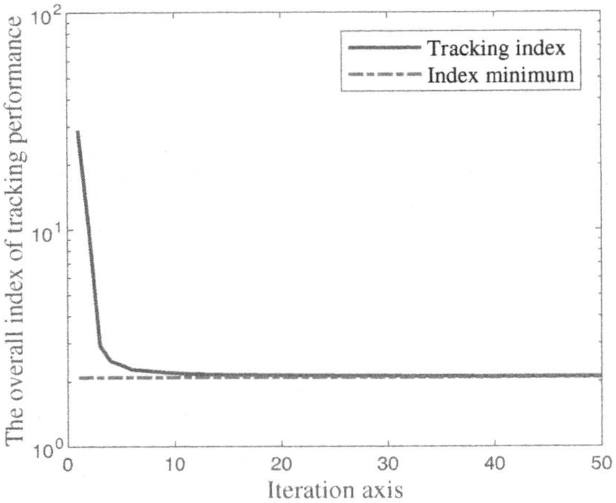

Figure 11.11 Overall tracking performance index for algorithm (11.52) and the minimum of (11.6).

We also conduct comparative experiments to demonstrate the influence of the fading gain and learning gain. We first consider the same three parametric scenarios of θ and σ_θ as for the constant gain. The index profiles are plotted in Fig. 11.12(a), and demonstrate that different fading distributions introduce little difference in term of achieving the minimum index values. Further, we consider three scenarios of the decreasing gain α/k^β as follows: (1) $\alpha = 1$ and $\beta = 1$, (2) $\alpha = 0.3$ and $\beta = 1$, and (3) $\alpha = 0.3$ and $\beta = 2/3$, respectively. The corresponding index profiles are shown in Fig. 11.12(b), where it can be observed that decreasing α reduces the convergence rate, while decreasing β within the specified range can enhance the convergence rate.

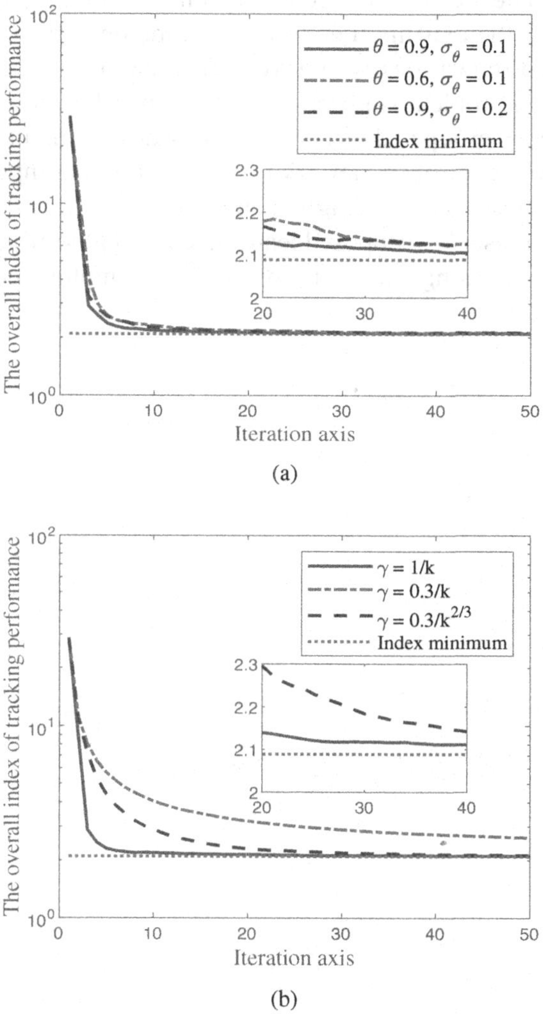

Figure 11.12 Overall tracking performance index for algorithm (11.52) with (a) different multiplicative gain distributions and (b) different learning gain sequences.

11.6 SUMMARY

This chapter contributes to the multi-objective learning tracking problem for a multi-sensor system where the outputs are transmitted through fading channels. First, we introduced a weighted optimization index over the whole iteration to formulate the possibly inconsistent multi-objective tracking problem. In contrast to the existing literature, the common realizability assumption of the desired trajectories is removed. The solution to the newly introduced optimization problem is given explicitly using the concept of the best achievable reference group and its corresponding desired input. Then, we established a learning control framework to find the optimal input in the presence of fading randomness. Fading channels have a random multiplicative gain and additive noise. We proposed learning control algorithms with a constant gain and a decreasing gain and proved their asymptotic convergence in the iteration domain.

APPENDIX A

Technical Lemmas

Lemma A.1 ([55]) *Let $\{m_k\}$ be a sequence of positive real numbers satisfying the regression*

$$m_{k+1} \leq (1 - \alpha_1 a_k)m_k + \alpha_2 a_k^2(\alpha_3 + m_k), \tag{A.1}$$

where $\alpha_i > 0$, $i = 1,2,3$, are constants and a_k satisfies $a_k > 0$, $\sum_{k=1}^{\infty} a_k = \infty$, and $\sum_{k=1}^{\infty} a_k^2 < \infty$, then $\lim_{k\to\infty} m_k = 0$.

Lemma A.2 ([63]) *Let $\mathcal{O}_k$, $\mathcal{D}_k$ be nonnegative stochastic processes with finite expectation satisfying $\mathcal{O}_k \in \mathcal{F}_k$ and $\mathcal{D}_k \in \mathcal{F}_k$, where $\mathcal{F}_k$ is well-defined a σ-algebra. Meanwhile,*

$$\mathbb{E}[\mathcal{O}_{k+1} \mid \mathcal{F}_k] \leq \mathcal{O}_k + \mathcal{D}_k, \tag{A.2}$$

$$\sum_{k=1}^{\infty} \mathbb{E}[\mathcal{D}_k] < \infty. \tag{A.3}$$

Then $\mathcal{O}_k$ converges to a finite limit almost surely.

Lemma A.3 ([49]) *Let $\{\xi_k, k = 1,2,\ldots\}$, $\{\tau_k, k = 1,2,\ldots\}$, and $\{\chi_k, k = 1,2,\ldots\}$ be real sequences, satisfying $0 < \tau_k \leq 1$, $\chi_k \geq 0$, $\tau_k \to 0$, $\sum_{k=1}^{\infty} \tau_k = \infty$, and $\xi_{k+1} \leq (1 - \tau_k)\xi_k + \chi_k$. Then, $\lim_{k\to\infty} \xi_k = \lim_{k\to\infty} \chi_k/\tau_k$, provided that the limit on the right-hand side exists. In addition, if $\chi_k/\tau_k \to 0$ and $\xi_k \geq 0$, then $\lim_{k\to\infty} \xi_k = 0$.*

Lemma A.4 ([49]) *Let $\{\xi_k, k = 1,2,\ldots\}$ be a sequence of random variables, $\xi_k \geq 0$, $\mathbb{E}[\xi_1] < \infty$, and let $\mathbb{E}\left[\xi_{k+1} \mid \xi_1, \ldots, \xi_k\right] \leq (1 - \tau_k)\xi_k + \chi_k$, $0 \leq \tau_k \leq 1$, $\chi_k > 0$, $\sum_{k=1}^{\infty} \tau_k = \infty$, $\sum_{k=1}^{\infty} \chi_k < \infty$, and $\chi_k/\tau_k \to 0$; then, $\xi_k \to 0$ a.s., and for every $\varepsilon > 0$, $k > 0$, $\mathbb{P}(\xi_j \leq \varepsilon$ for all $j \geq k) \geq 1 - \varepsilon^{-1}\left(\mathbb{E}[\xi_k] + \sum_{i=k}^{\infty} \chi_i\right)$.*

DOI: 10.1201/9781032646404-A

Lemma A.5 ([10]) *Let H be a $d \times d$ stable matrix that each eigenvalue of H has negative real part. $\{a_k\}$ is a sequence satisfying*

$$a_k > 0, \sum_{k=1}^{\infty} a_k = \infty, \text{ and } \sum_{k=1}^{\infty} a_k^2 < \infty.$$

The d-dimensional sequence $\{X_k\}$ is generated by the following recursive algorithm:

$$X_{k+1} = X_k + a_k(HX_k + M_{k+1} + N_{k+1}), \tag{A.4}$$

with any initial condition $X_0 \in \boldsymbol{R}^d$. If vectors M_k and N_k in (A.4) *satisfy the following conditions:*

$$\sum_{k=1}^{\infty} a_k M_{k+1} < \infty \quad \text{and} \quad N_k \to 0 \text{ as } k \to \infty, \tag{A.5}$$

then we have $X_k \to 0$ almost surely.

Bibliography

[1] Hyo-Sung Ahn, D. Chung, K. H. Ko, S. Wang, and S. Choi. Satellite antenna control: Design and performance validation under given TPF. In *2010 International Conference on Control, Automation and Systems (ICCAS 2010)*, 2010. 27–30 October 2010, Gyeonggi-do, South Korea.

[2] Suguru Arimoto, Sadao Kawamura, and Fumio Miyazaki. Bettering operation of robots by learning. *Journal of Robotic Systems*, 1(2): 123–140, 1984.

[3] Michel Benaim. A dynamical system approach to stochastic approximations. *SIAM Journal on Control and Optimization*, 34(2):437–472, 1996.

[4] Vivek S Borkar. *Stochastic Approximation: A Dynamical Systems Viewpoint*. Springer, 2009.

[5] Vivek S Borkar and Sean P Meyn. The ode method for convergence of stochastic approximation and reinforcement learning. *SIAM Journal on Control and Optimization*, 38(2):447–469, 2000.

[6] Xuhui Bu, Zhongsheng Hou, Shangtai Jin, and Ronghu Chi. An iterative learning control design approach for networked control systems with data dropouts. *International Journal of Robust and Nonlinear Control*, 26(1):91–109, 2016.

[7] Mark Butcher, Alireza Karimi, and Roland Longchamp. Iterative learning control based on stochastic approximation. *IFAC Proceedings Volumes*, 41(2):1478–1483, 2008.

[8] Zhixing Cao, Hans-Bernd Durr, Christian Ebenbauer, Frank Allgower, and Furong Gao. Iterative learning and extremum seeking for repetitive time-varying mappings. *IEEE Transactions on Automatic Control*, 62(7):3339–3353, 2017.

[9] Giuseppe Casalino and Giorgio Bartolini. A learning procedure for the control of movements of robotic manipulators. In *Proc. IASTED International Symposium on Robotics & Automation*, pages 108–111, 1984. November 12-14, 1984, New Orleans United States.

[10] Han-Fu Chen. *Stochastic Approximation and Its Applications.* Kluwer Academic Publishers, 2002.

[11] Han-Fu Chen and Lei Guo. *Identification and Stochastic Adaptive Control.* Birkhäuser, Boston, 1991.

[12] Yiyang Chen, Bing Chu, and Christopher T. Freeman. Point-to-point iterative learning control with optimal tracking time allocation. *IEEE Transactions on Control Systems Technology*, 26(5):1685–1698, 2018.

[13] Ronghu Chi, Zhongsheng Hou, Shangtai Jin, and Biao Huang. An improved data-driven point-to-point ILC using additional on-line control inputs with experimental verification. *IEEE Transactions on Systems, Man, and Cybernetics: Systems*, 49(4):687–696, 2019.

[14] Yuan Shih Chow and Henry Teicher. *Probability Theory: Independence, Interchangeability, Martingales.* Springer-Verlag, New York, 1997.

[15] John J Craig. Adaptive control of manipulators through repeated trials. In *American Control Conference*, pages 1566–1573, 1984. 6-8 June 1984, San Diego, CA, United States.

[16] Subhrakanti Dey, Alex S Leong, and Jamie S Evans. Kalman filtering with faded measurements. *Automatica*, 45(10):2223–2233, 2009.

[17] Derui Ding, Zidong Wang, James Lam, and Bo Shen. Finite-horizon $\mathcal{H}_\infty$ control for discrete time-varying systems with randomly occurring nonlinearities and fading measurements. *IEEE Transactions on Automatic Control*, 60(9):2488–2493, 2015.

[18] Derui Ding, Zidong Wang, Bo Shen, and Hongli Dong. Envelope-constrained $\mathcal{H}_\infty$ filtering with fading measurements and randomly occurring nonlinearities: the finite horizon case. *Automatica*, 55:37–45, 2015.

[19] Han Ding and Jianhua Wu. Point-to-point motion control for a high-acceleration positioning table via cascaded learning schemes. *IEEE Transactions on Industrial Electronics*, 54(5):2735–2744, 2007.

[20] Hugh F Durrant-Whyte. *Integration, Coordination and Control of Multi-Sensor Robot Systems*. Kluwer Academic Publishers, 1988.

[21] Nicola Elia. Remote stabilization over fading channels. *Systems & Control Letters*, 54(3):237–249, 2005.

[22] Chris Freeman and Ying Tan. Point-to-point iterative learning control with mixed constraints. In *Proceedings of the 2011 American Control Conference*, pages 3657–3662, 2011. 29 June - 1 July 2011, San Francisco, California, United States.

[23] Chris T. Freeman. Constrained point-to-point iterative learning control with experimental verification. *Control Engineering Practice*, 20(5):489–498, 2012.

[24] Chris T. Freeman, Zhonglun Cai, Eric Rogers, and Paul L. Lewin. Iterative learning control for multiple point-to-point tracking application. *IEEE Transactions on Control Systems Technology*, 19(3): 590–600, 2011.

[25] Chris T Freeman, A-M Hughes, Jane H Burridge, PH Chappell, PL Lewin, and Eric Rogers. Iterative learning control of FES applied to the upper extremity for rehabilitation. *Control Engineering Practice*, 17(3):368–381, 2009.

[26] Chris T. Freeman and Ying Tan. Iterative learning control with mixed constraints for point-to-point tracking. *IEEE Transactions on Control Systems Technology*, 21(3):604–616, 2013.

[27] Alvin Fu, Eytan Modiano, and John N. Tsitsiklis. Optimal transmission scheduling over a fading channel with energy and deadline constraints. *IEEE Transactions on Wireless Communications*, 5(3):630–641, 2006.

[28] Hang Geng, Zidong Wang, Yan Liang, Yuhua Cheng, and Fuad E Alsaadi. Tobit kalman filter with fading measurements. *Signal Processing*, 140:60–68, 2017.

[29] Joo P Hespanha, Payam Naghshtabrizi, and Yonggang Xu. A survey of recent results in networked control systems. *Proceedings of the IEEE*, 95(1):138–162, 2007.

[30] Roger A. Horn and Charles R. Johnson. *Matrix Analysis*. Cambridge University Press, 1985.

[31] S Host. *Information and Communication Theory*. Wiley-IEEE Press, 2019.

[32] Jiangping Hu and Yiguang Hong. Leader-following coordination of multi-agent systems with coupling time delays. *Physica A Statistical Mechanics & Its Applications*, 374(2):853–863, 2007.

[33] Niu Huo and Dong Shen. Encoding-decoding mechanism-based finite-level quantized iterative learning control with random data dropouts. *IEEE Transactions on Automation Science and Engineering*, 17(3):1343–1360, 2020.

[34] A. Jadbabaie, Jie Lin, and A.S. Morse. Coordination of groups of mobile autonomous agents using nearest neighbor rules. *IEEE Transactions on Automatic Control*, 48(6):988–1001, 2003.

[35] Hao Jiang, Dong Shen, Shunhao Huang, and Xinghuo Yu. Accelerated learning control for point-to-point tracking systems. *IEEE Transactions on Neural Networks and Learning Systems*, pages 1–13, 2022.

[36] Andrew P Johnston and Serdar Yüksel. Stochastic stabilization of partially observed and multi-sensor systems driven by unbounded noise under fixed-rate information constraints. *IEEE Transactions on Automatic Control*, 59(3):792–798, 2013.

[37] Bahador Khaleghi, Alaa Khamis, Fakhreddine O Karray, and Saiedeh N Razavi. Multisensor data fusion: A review of the state-of-the-art. *Information Fusion*, 14(1):28–44, 2013.

[38] Patrik Leissner, Svante Gunnarsson, and Mikael Norrlöf. Some controllability aspects for iterative learning control. *Asian Journal of Control*, 21(3):1057–1063, 2019.

[39] Alex S. Leong and Daniel E. Quevedo. Kalman filtering with relays over wireless fading channels. *IEEE Transactions on Automatic Control*, 61(6):1643–1648, 2016.

[40] Xuefang Li, Jian-Xin Xu, and Deqing Huang. An iterative learning control approach for linear systems with randomly varying trial lengths. *IEEE Transactions on Automatic Control*, 59(7):1954–1960, 2014.

[41] Hong Lin, Yuman Li, James Lam, and Zheng-Guang Wu. Multi-sensor optimal linear estimation with unobservable measurement losses. *IEEE Transactions on Automatic Control*, 67(1):481–488, 2022.

[42] Lennart Ljung. *System Identification: Theory for the User*. Prentice-Hall, 1999.

[43] Francisco Louzada, Pedro Luiz Ramos, and Diego Nascimento. The inverse Nakagami-m distribution: A novel approach in reliability. *IEEE Transactions on Reliability*, 67(3):1030–1042, 2018.

[44] Magdi S Mahmoud and Mutaz M Hamdan. Fundamental issues in networked control systems. *IEEE/CAA Journal of Automatica Sinica*, 5(5):902–922, 2018.

[45] Deyuan Meng, Yingmin Jia, and Junping Du. Robust consensus tracking control for multiagent systems with initial state shifts, disturbances, and switching topologies. *IEEE Transactions on Neural Networks and Learning Systems*, 26(4):809–824, 2015.

[46] Sarat Babu Moka, Dirk P Kroese, and Sandeep Juneja. Unbiased estimation of the reciprocal mean for non-negative random variables. In *2019 Winter Simulation Conference (WSC)*, pages 404–415. IEEE, 2019. December 8-11, 2019, National Harbor, MD, United States.

[47] David H. Owens, Christopher T. Freeman, and Thanh Van Dinh. Norm-optimal iterative learning control with intermediate point weighting: Theory, algorithms, and experimental evaluation. *IEEE Transactions on Control Systems Technology*, 21(3):999–1007, 2013.

[48] Ali ParandehGheibi, Atilla Eryilmaz, Asuman Ozdaglar, and Muriel Médard. On resource allocation in fading multiple-access channels–an efficient approximate projection approach. *IEEE Transactions on Information Theory*, 56(9):4417–4437, 2010.

[49] Boris T Polyak. *Introduction to Optimization*. Optimization Software Inc., New York, 1987.

[50] Wei Ren and R.W. Beard. Consensus seeking in multiagent systems under dynamically changing interaction topologies. *IEEE Transactions on Automatic Control*, 50(5):655–661, 2005.

[51] Dong Shen. *Iterative Learning Control with Passive Incomplete Information: Algorithms Design and Convergence Analysis*. Springer, Singapore, 2018.

[52] Dong Shen. A technical overview of recent progresses on stochastic iterative learning control. *Unmanned Systems*, 6(03):147–164, 2018.

[53] Dong Shen, Chen Liu, Lanjing Wang, and Xinghuo Yu. Iterative learning tracking for multisensor systems: A weighted optimization approach. *IEEE Transactions on Cybernetics*, 51(3):1286–1299, 2021.

[54] Dong Shen and Ganggui Qu. Performance enhancement of learning tracking systems over fading channels with multiplicative and additive randomness. *IEEE Transactions on Neural Networks and Learning Systems*, 31(4):1196–1210, 2020.

[55] Dong Shen and Jian-Xin Xu. A novel Markov chain based ILC analysis for linear stochastic systems under general data dropouts environments. *IEEE Transactions on Automatic Control*, 62(11):5850–5857, 2017.

[56] Dong Shen and Jian-Xin Xu. Distributed learning consensus for heterogenous high-order nonlinear multi-agent systems with output constraints. *Automatica*, 97:64–72, 2018.

[57] Dong Shen and Jian-Xin Xu. An iterative learning control algorithm with gain adaptation for stochastic systems. *IEEE Transactions on Automatic Control*, 65(3):1280–1287, 2020.

[58] Tong Duy Son, Hyo-Sung Ahn, and Kevin L. Moore. Iterative learning control in optimal tracking problems with specified data points. *Automatica*, 49(5):1465–1472, 2013.

[59] Lanlan Su and Graziano Chesi. Robust stability analysis and synthesis for uncertain discrete-time networked control systems over fading channels. *IEEE Transactions on Automatic Control*, 62(4):1966–1971, 2017.

[60] Mingxuan Sun, Tao Wu, Lejian Chen, and Guofeng Zhang. Neural AILC for error tracking against arbitrary initial shifts. *IEEE Transactions on Neural Networks and Learning Systems*, 29(7):2705–2716, 2018.

[61] Mingxuan Sun, Tao Wu, Lejian Chen, and Guofeng Zhang. Neural AILC for error tracking against arbitrary initial shifts. *IEEE Transactions on Neural Networks and Learning Systems*, 29(7):2705–2716, 2018.

[62] David Tse and Pramod Viswanath. *Fundamentals of Wireless Communication*. Cambridge University Press, 2005.

[63] John Tsitsiklis, Dimitri Bertsekas, and Michael Athans. Distributed asynchronous deterministic and stochastic gradient optimization algorithms. *IEEE Transactions on Automatic Control*, 31(9):803–812, 1986.

[64] Masaru Uchiyama. Formation of high-speed motion pattern of a mechanical arm by trial. *Transactions of the Society of Instrument and Control Engineers*, 14(6):706–712, 1978.

[65] VG Voinov. Unbiased estimation of powers of the inverse of mean and related problems. *Sankhya: The Indian Journal of Statistics, Series B*, 47(3): 354-364, 1985.

[66] Danwei Wang. Convergence and robustness of discrete time nonlinear systems with iterative learning control. *Automatica*, 34(11):1445–1448, 1998.

[67] Xin Wang and Georgios B. Giannakis. Power-efficient resource allocation for time-division multiple access over fading channels. *IEEE Transactions on Information Theory*, 54(3):1225–1240, 2008.

[68] Youqing Wang, Donghua Zhou, and Furong Gao. Iterative learning model predictive control for multi-phase batch processes. *Journal of Process Control*, 18(6):543–557, 2008.

[69] Zi-Bo Wei, Quan Quan, and Kai-Yuan Cai. Output feedback ILC for a class of nonminimum phase nonlinear systems with input saturation: An additive-state-decomposition-based method. *IEEE Transactions on Automatic Control*, 62(1):502–508, 2017.

[70] Nan Xiao, Lihua Xie, and Li Qiu. Feedback stabilization of discrete-time networked systems over fading channels. *IEEE Transactions on Automatic Control*, 57(9):2176–2189, 2012.

[71] Tengfei Xiao and Han-Xiong Li. Eigenspectrum-based iterative learning control for a class of distributed parameter system. *IEEE Transactions on Automatic Control*, 62(2):824–836, 2017.

[72] Jian-Xin Xu and Rui Yan. On initial conditions in iterative learning control. *IEEE Transactions on Automatic Control*, 50(9):1349–1354, 2005.

[73] Liang Xu, Yilin Mo, Lihua Xie, and Nan Xiao. Mean square stabilization of linear discrete-time systems over power-constrained fading channels. *IEEE Transactions on Automatic Control*, 62(12):6505–6512, 2017.

[74] Yun Xu, Dong Shen, and Xiao-Dong Zhang. Stochastic point-to-point iterative learning control based on stochastic approximation. *Asian Journal of Control*, 19(5):1748–1755, 2017.

[75] Chao Yang, Jiangying Zheng, Xiaoqiang Ren, Wen Yang, Hongbo Shi, and Ling Shi. Multi-sensor kalman filtering with intermittent measurements. *IEEE Transactions on Automatic Control*, 63(3):797–804, 2018.

[76] Keyou You and Lihua Xie. Survey of recent progress in networked control systems. *Acta Automatica Sinica*, 39(2):101–117, 2013.

[77] Bin Zhang, Yongqiang Ye, Keliang Zhou, and Danwei Wang. Case studies of filtering techniques in multirate iterative learning control. *Control Engineering Practice*, 26:116–124, 2014.

[78] Dan Zhang, Peng Shi, Qing-Guo Wang, and Li Yu. Analysis and synthesis of networked control systems: A survey of recent advances and challenges. *ISA Transactions*, 66:376–392, 2017.

[79] Lixian Zhang, Zepeng Ning, and Zidong Wang. Distributed filtering for fuzzy time-delay systems with packet dropouts and redundant channels. *IEEE Transactions on Systems, Man, and Cybernetics: Systems*, 46(4):559–572, 2015.

[80] Sunjie Zhang, Zidong Wang, Derui Ding, and Huisheng Shu. $\mathcal{H}_\infty$ output-feedback control with randomly occurring distributed delays and nonlinearities subject to sensor saturations and channel fadings. *Journal of the Franklin Institute*, 351(8):4124–4141, 2014.

[81] Xian-Ming Zhang and Qing-Long Han. A decentralized event-triggered dissipative control scheme for systems with multiple sensors to sample the system outputs. *IEEE Transactions on Cybernetics*, 46(12):2745–2757, 2016.

[82] Xian-Ming Zhang, Qing-Long Han, and Xinghuo Yu. Survey on recent advances in networked control systems. *IEEE Transactions on Industrial Informatics*, 12(5):1740–1752, 2015.

Index